MARVEL MASTERWORKS

PRESENTS

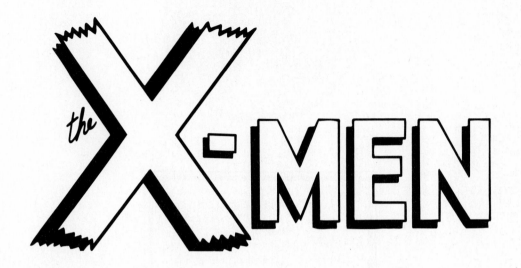

VOLUME **1**

COLLECTING

THE X-MEN Nos. 1-10

STAN LEE • JACK KIRBY

Collection Editor
Cory Sedlmeier

Book Design
Nickel DesignWorks

SVP of Print & Digital Publishing Sales
David Gabriel

Editor in Chief
Axel Alonso

Chief Creative Officer
Joe Quesada

Publisher
Dan Buckley

Executive Producer
Alan Fine

MARVEL MASTERWORKS: THE X-MEN VOL. 1. Contains material originally published in magazine form as X-MEN #1-10. Third printing 2013. ISBN# 978-0-7851-3698-9. Published by MARVEL WORLDWIDE, INC., a subsidiary of MARVEL ENTERTAINMENT, LLC. OFFICE OF PUBLICATION: 135 West 50th Street, New York, NY 10020. Copyright © 1963, 1964, 1965 and 2009 Marvel Characters, Inc. All rights reserved. All characters featured in this issue and the distinctive names and likenesses thereof, and all related indicia are trademarks of Marvel Characters, Inc. No similarity between any of the names, characters, persons, and/or institutions in this magazine with those of any living or dead person or institution is intended, and any such similarity which may exist is purely coincidental. **Printed in the U.S.A.** ALAN FINE, EVP - Office of the President, Marvel Worldwide, Inc. and EVP & CMO Marvel Characters B.V.; DAN BUCKLEY, Publisher & President - Print, Animation & Digital Divisions; JOE QUESADA, Chief Creative Officer; TOM BREVOORT, SVP of Publishing; DAVID BOGART, SVP of Operations & Procurement, Publishing; RUWAN JAYATILLEKE, SVP & Associate Publisher, Publishing; C.B. CEBULSKI, SVP of Creator & Content Development; DAVID GABRIEL, SVP of Print & Digital Publishing Sales; JIM O'KEEFE, VP of Operations & Logistics; DAN CARR, Executive Director of Publishing Technology; SUSAN CRESPI, Editorial Operations Manager; ALEX MORALES, Publishing Operations Manager; STAN LEE, Chairman Emeritus. For information regarding advertising in Marvel Comics or on Marvel.com, please contact Niza Disla, Director of Marvel Partnerships, at ndisla@marvel.com. For Marvel subscription inquiries, please call 800-217-9158. **Manufactured between 2/25/2013 and 3/25/2013 by R.R. DONNELLEY, INC., SALEM, VA, USA.**

10 9 8 7 6 5 4 3

MARVEL MASTERWORKS
CREDITS

THE
X - MEN
NOS. 1-10

Writer: **Stan Lee**

Penciler: **Jack Kirby**

Inkers: Paul Reiman (Nos. 1-5)
Chic Stone (Nos. 6-10)

Letterers: Sam Rosen (Nos. 1, 2, 5, 6, 8-10)
Art Simek (Nos. 3, 4, 7)

Color Reconstruction: Laurie Smith (Interiors)
Michael Kelleher (Covers)

Art Reconstruction: Laurie Smith & Pacific Rim Graphics
Michael Kelleher (Covers)

Collection Cover Art: Jack Kirby & Dean White

Special Thanks: Ralph Macchio

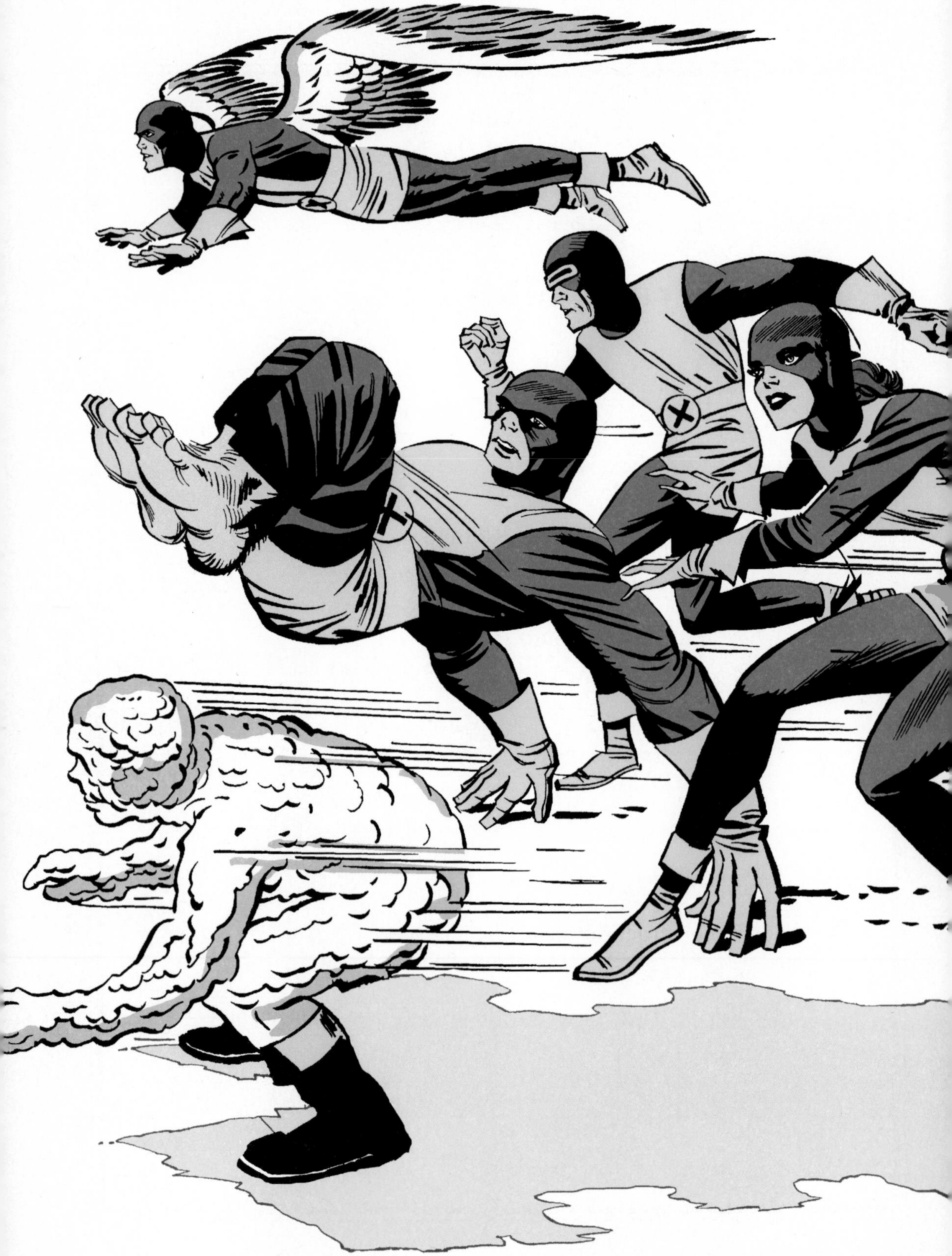

MARVEL MASTERWORKS
CONTENTS

INTRODUCTION
BY STAN LEE

Life is full of surprises. Who'd ever have thought that a bunch of costumed mutants, hated and distrusted by mankind and led by a bald-headed, wheelchair-bound professor, would become—and get this—the biggest-selling comic book series in the world!

Even their name was a problem to us at the beginning. Wanna know why? I hoped you'd ask.

Originally, I proposed naming the chronicle of our merry little misfits *The Mutants*. I thought it would make a great title. But I was outvoted by the powers-that-be in the front office. I was told, with much conviction, that nobody knew what a mutant was, therefore that couldn't be the title of the magazine. I tried, in my stumbling, bumbling way, to say that some people knew the word, and those that didn't would soon learn after the book was published. But, as you can tell by the present title, unlike our sterling super heroes, yours truly didn't always emerge victorious!

However, undaunted and unbowed, I returned with another name—*The X-Men*. I truly expected to be booted out of the office for that one. I mean, if people didn't know what a mutant was, how would they know what an X-Man was? But I guess I'll never make my mark as a logician—everyone okayed the title!

Of course, I'm kind of glad about it now. I've learned to love the name. It was, as you probably know, taken from the first letter of Professor Xavier's name, and also represents the fact that each of our mutants has an X-tra power! The spelling's atrocious, but you get the idea.

Anyway, once everything had been okayed, I bellowed for my favorite super-hero artist, none other than Jolly Jack Kirby, or as I later christened him, Jack "King" Kirby—the one man who I was sure could depict our merry mutants at their colorful best. And how right I was!

After discussing the concept with ol' J.K., he tore into the project with his usual zesty zeal (or is it his zealous zest? You think it's easy writing corny?) I've always half-suspected that Jack was part mutant himself; nobody human could be so talented. And he did nothing to allay my suspicions. His representations of the action in the Danger Room, his costuming of characters like Magneto and the Brotherhood of Evil Mutants were nothing short of inspired. But I don't have to tell you, you're about to see it all for yourself.

As far as the basic concept of the series, the thing I liked the most about *The X-Men* (and I must admit I'm prejudiced since I consider them all my babies!) is the fact that we tried to play against type.

For example, I loved making The Beast, who was the biggest, shaggiest, most bestial-seeming of all, the most literary, cultured and articulate of the group. Cyclops, whom I always thought of as a second-in-command next to Professor X, who should have been somewhat of a swashbuckler, became a brooding, tragic figure, dreading the dangerous impact of his tremendous power. And take Professor X himself. It was quite a challenge to take a guy in a wheelchair, with no physical power, to say nothing of no hair, and make him seem glamorous to millions of young readers—but I don't think we fell too short of that mark. And then there was Iceman. I was really worried about how readers would accept him, but I figured what the hey, if they dug the Human Torch, why not? Once again, the gamble paid off.

Y'know, for those of you who are discovering the X-Men for the first time, I rather envy you. I've been reading them faithfully for years, even though it's been quite a while since I did the scripting myself, and I still get a tremendous charge out of them. But now, you yourself will be experiencing the never-to-be-repeated thrill of discovery, and I sure hope it'll give you the same charge to read them as it gave me to write 'em.

One other thing I should mention about our offbeat little band of heroes. Unlike most other comic book groups, they're always in a state of flux. New X-Men appear and older ones are put on the shelf for a while. In fact, with today's present X-Men series, if you let too many months go by between readings, you'll find that you need a whole new introduction to the proceedings, which somehow seems to be what excites so many readers about our mellow mutants. We like the idea, too, because you know how greedy we are. Soon we'll be selling scorecards with each issue—"Can't tell the heroes without a scorecard?"

But now it's time to see what all the fuss is about. So let me welcome you to the marvelous world of mutancy as we share the wonderment together!

EXCELSIOR!

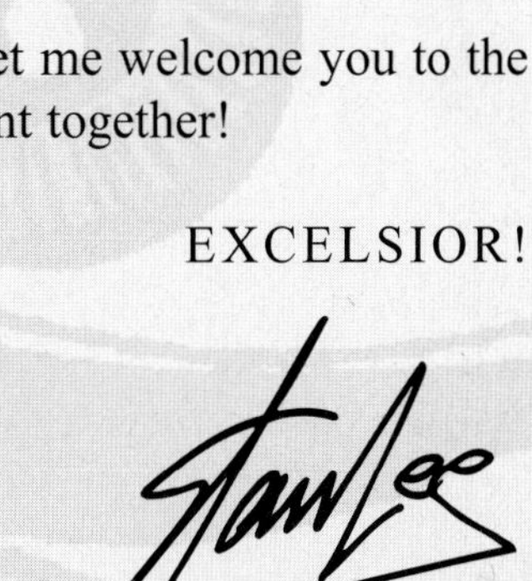

1987

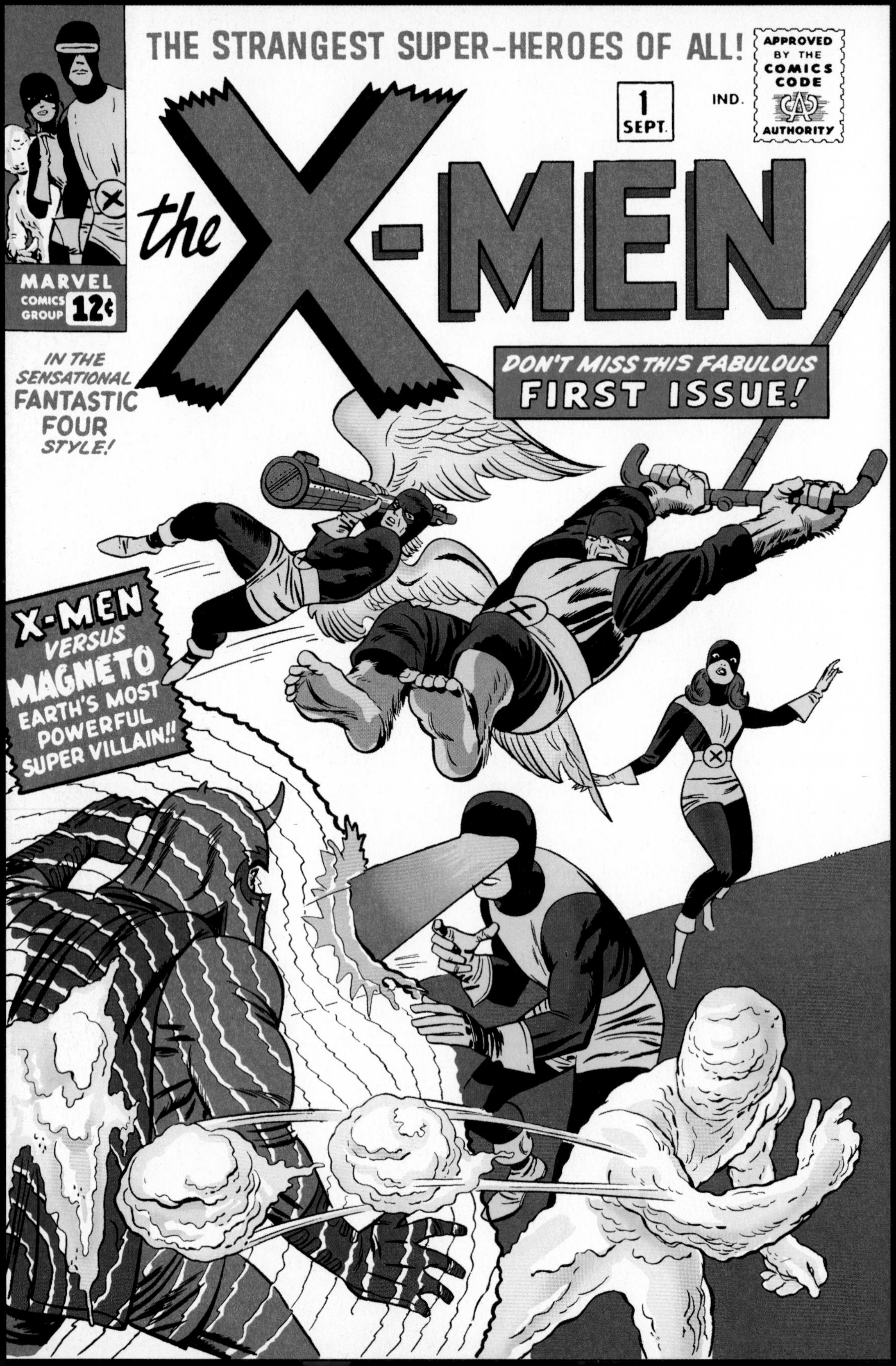

THE STRANGEST SUPER-HEROES OF ALL!
APPROVED BY THE COMICS CODE AUTHORITY
1 SEPT.
IND.
MARVEL COMICS GROUP 12¢
the X-MEN
IN THE SENSATIONAL FANTASTIC FOUR STYLE!
DON'T MISS THIS FABULOUS FIRST ISSUE!
X-MEN VERSUS MAGNETO EARTH'S MOST POWERFUL SUPER VILLAIN!!

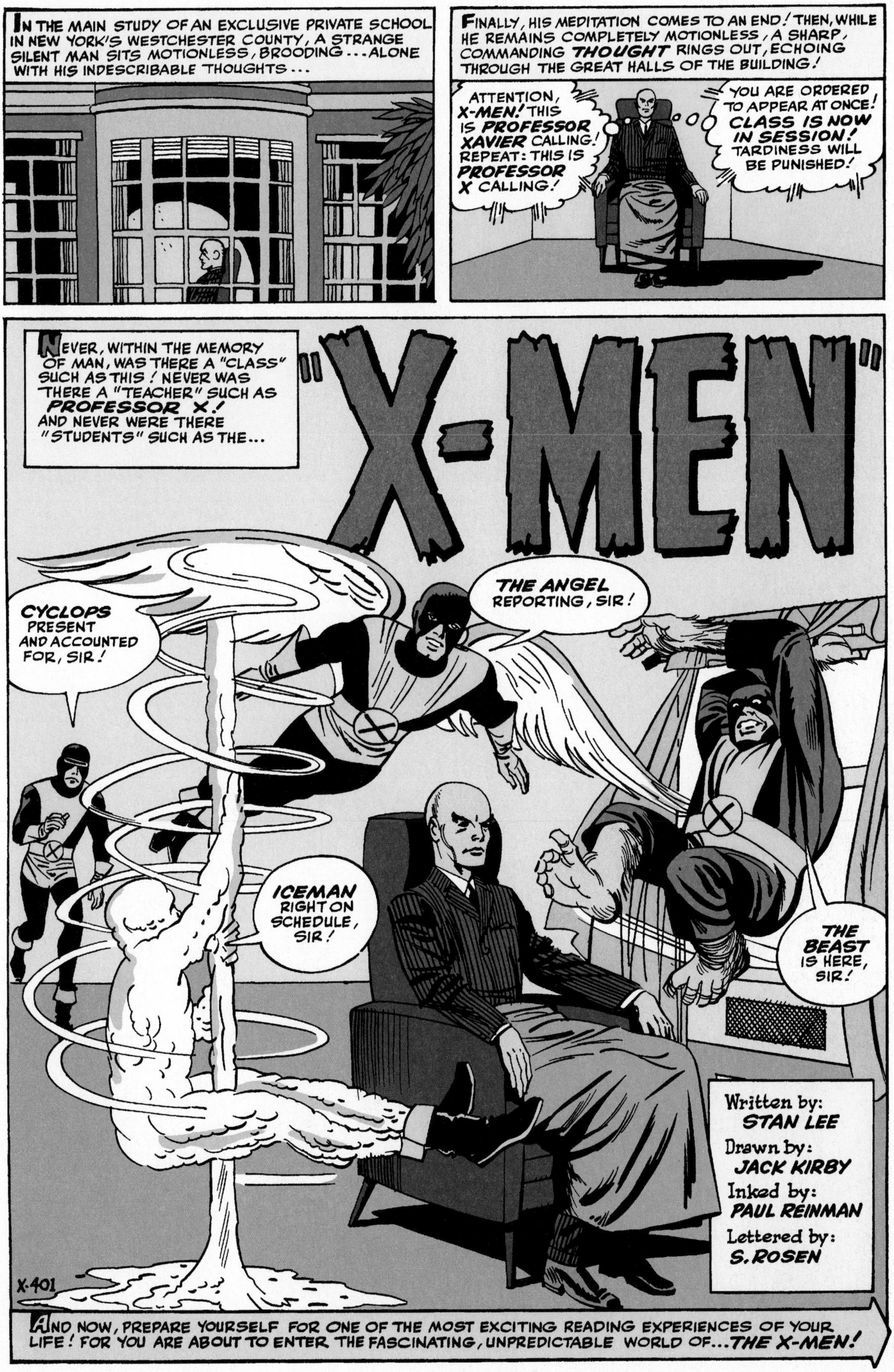
IN THE MAIN STUDY OF AN EXCLUSIVE PRIVATE SCHOOL IN NEW YORK'S WESTCHESTER COUNTY, A STRANGE SILENT MAN SITS MOTIONLESS, BROODING ... ALONE WITH HIS INDESCRIBABLE THOUGHTS ...
FINALLY, HIS MEDITATION COMES TO AN END! THEN, WHILE HE REMAINS COMPLETELY MOTIONLESS, A SHARP, COMMANDING THOUGHT RINGS OUT, ECHOING THROUGH THE GREAT HALLS OF THE BUILDING!
ATTENTION, X-MEN! THIS IS PROFESSOR XAVIER CALLING! REPEAT: THIS IS PROFESSOR X CALLING!
YOU ARE ORDERED TO APPEAR AT ONCE! CLASS IS NOW IN SESSION! TARDINESS WILL BE PUNISHED!
NEVER, WITHIN THE MEMORY OF MAN, WAS THERE A "CLASS" SUCH AS THIS! NEVER WAS THERE A "TEACHER" SUCH AS PROFESSOR X! AND NEVER WERE THERE "STUDENTS" SUCH AS THE...
"X-MEN"
CYCLOPS PRESENT AND ACCOUNTED FOR, SIR!
THE ANGEL REPORTING, SIR!
ICEMAN RIGHT ON SCHEDULE, SIR!
THE BEAST IS HERE, SIR!
Written by: STAN LEE
Drawn by: JACK KIRBY
Inked by: PAUL REINMAN
Lettered by: S. ROSEN
X-401
AND NOW, PREPARE YOURSELF FOR ONE OF THE MOST EXCITING READING EXPERIENCES OF YOUR LIFE! FOR YOU ARE ABOUT TO ENTER THE FASCINATING, UNPREDICTABLE WORLD OF... THE X-MEN!

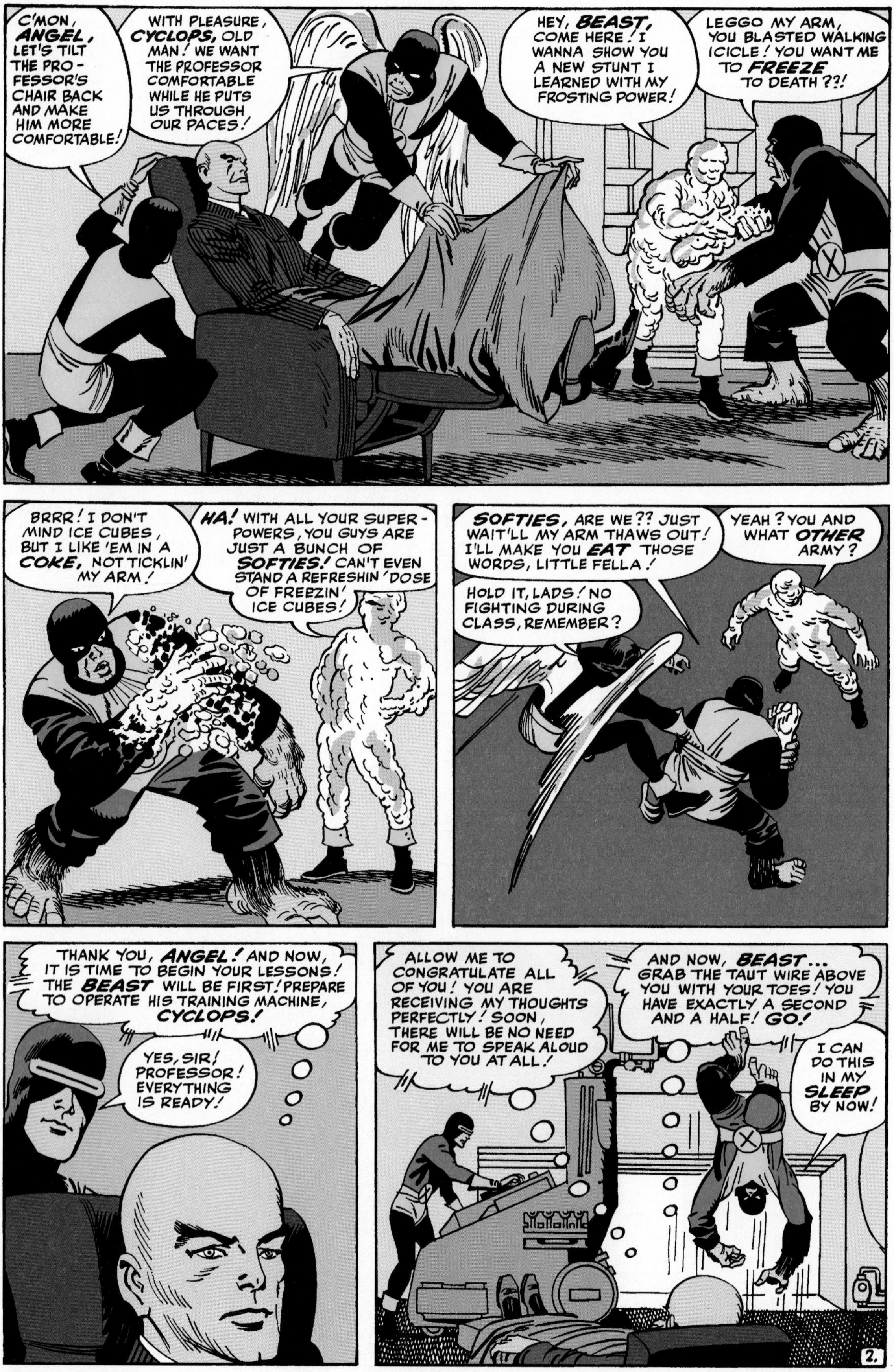

C'MON, ANGEL, LET'S TILT THE PRO-FESSOR'S CHAIR BACK AND MAKE HIM MORE COMFORTABLE!
WITH PLEASURE, CYCLOPS, OLD MAN! WE WANT THE PROFESSOR COMFORTABLE WHILE HE PUTS US THROUGH OUR PACES!
HEY, BEAST, COME HERE! I WANNA SHOW YOU A NEW STUNT I LEARNED WITH MY FROSTING POWER!
LEGGO MY ARM, YOU BLASTED WALKING ICICLE! YOU WANT ME TO FREEZE TO DEATH??!
BRRR! I DON'T MIND ICE CUBES, BUT I LIKE 'EM IN A COKE, NOT TICKLIN' MY ARM!
HA! WITH ALL YOUR SUPER-POWERS, YOU GUYS ARE JUST A BUNCH OF SOFTIES! CAN'T EVEN STAND A REFRESHIN' DOSE OF FREEZIN' ICE CUBES!
SOFTIES, ARE WE?? JUST WAIT'LL MY ARM THAWS OUT! I'LL MAKE YOU EAT THOSE WORDS, LITTLE FELLA!
YEAH? YOU AND WHAT OTHER ARMY?
HOLD IT, LADS! NO FIGHTING DURING CLASS, REMEMBER?
THANK YOU, ANGEL! AND NOW, IT IS TIME TO BEGIN YOUR LESSONS! THE BEAST WILL BE FIRST! PREPARE TO OPERATE HIS TRAINING MACHINE, CYCLOPS!
YES, SIR! PROFESSOR! EVERYTHING IS READY!
ALLOW ME TO CONGRATULATE ALL OF YOU! YOU ARE RECEIVING MY THOUGHTS PERFECTLY! SOON, THERE WILL BE NO NEED FOR ME TO SPEAK ALOUD TO YOU AT ALL!
AND NOW, BEAST... GRAB THE TAUT WIRE ABOVE YOU WITH YOUR TOES! YOU HAVE EXACTLY A SECOND AND A HALF! GO!
I CAN DO THIS IN MY SLEEP BY NOW!
2.

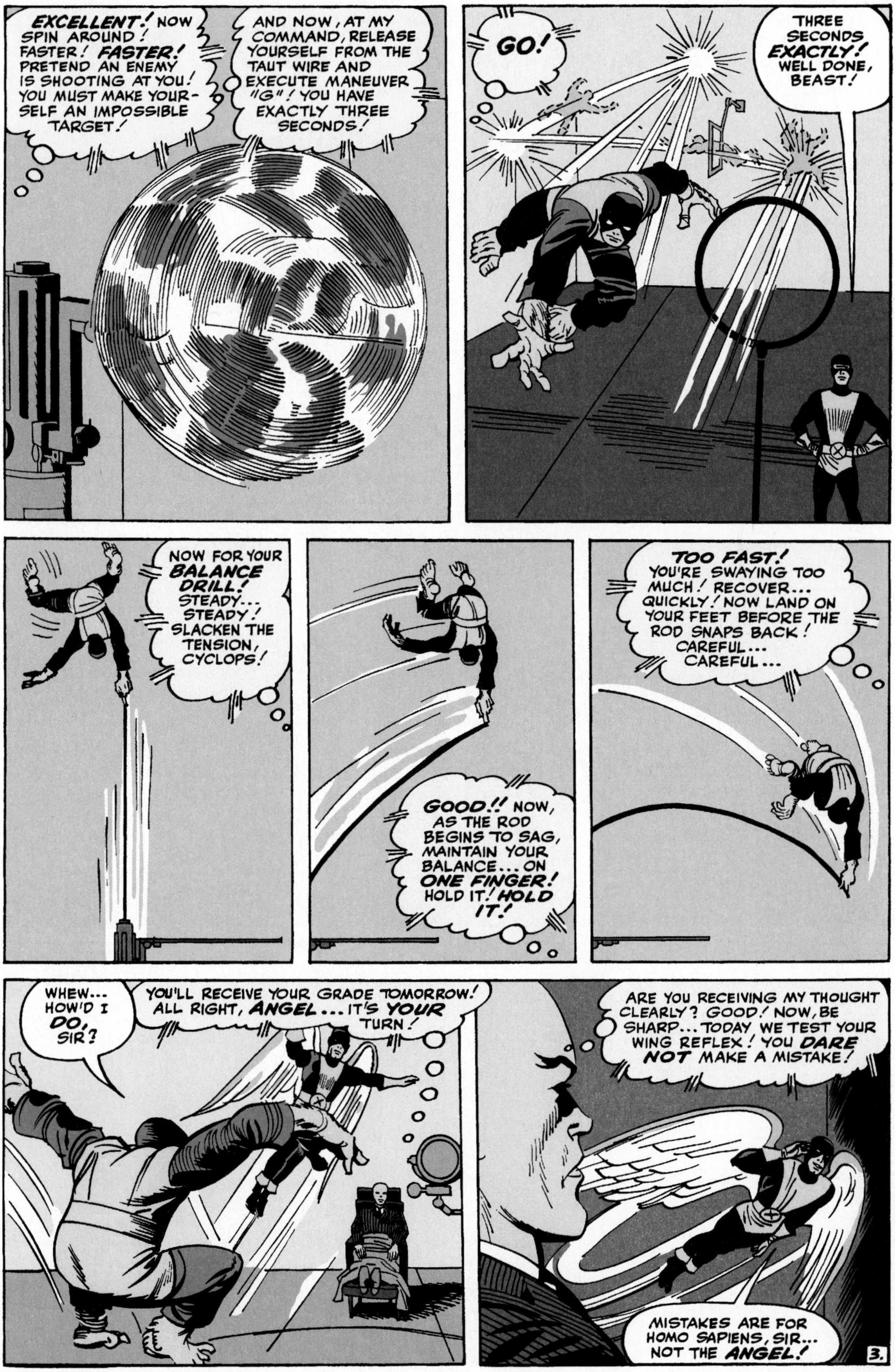
EXCELLENT! NOW SPIN AROUND! FASTER! FASTER! PRETEND AN ENEMY IS SHOOTING AT YOU! YOU MUST MAKE YOURSELF AN IMPOSSIBLE TARGET!
AND NOW, AT MY COMMAND, RELEASE YOURSELF FROM THE TAUT WIRE AND EXECUTE MANEUVER "G"! YOU HAVE EXACTLY THREE SECONDS!
GO!
THREE SECONDS EXACTLY! WELL DONE, BEAST!
NOW FOR YOUR BALANCE DRILL! STEADY... STEADY! SLACKEN THE TENSION, CYCLOPS!
GOOD!! NOW, AS THE ROD BEGINS TO SAG, MAINTAIN YOUR BALANCE... ON ONE FINGER! HOLD IT! HOLD IT!
TOO FAST! YOU'RE SWAYING TOO MUCH! RECOVER... QUICKLY! NOW LAND ON YOUR FEET BEFORE THE ROD SNAPS BACK! CAREFUL... CAREFUL...
WHEW... HOW'D I DO, SIR?
YOU'LL RECEIVE YOUR GRADE TOMORROW! ALL RIGHT, ANGEL... IT'S YOUR TURN!
ARE YOU RECEIVING MY THOUGHT CLEARLY? GOOD! NOW, BE SHARP... TODAY WE TEST YOUR WING REFLEX! YOU DARE NOT MAKE A MISTAKE!
MISTAKES ARE FOR HOMO SAPIENS, SIR... NOT THE ANGEL!
3.

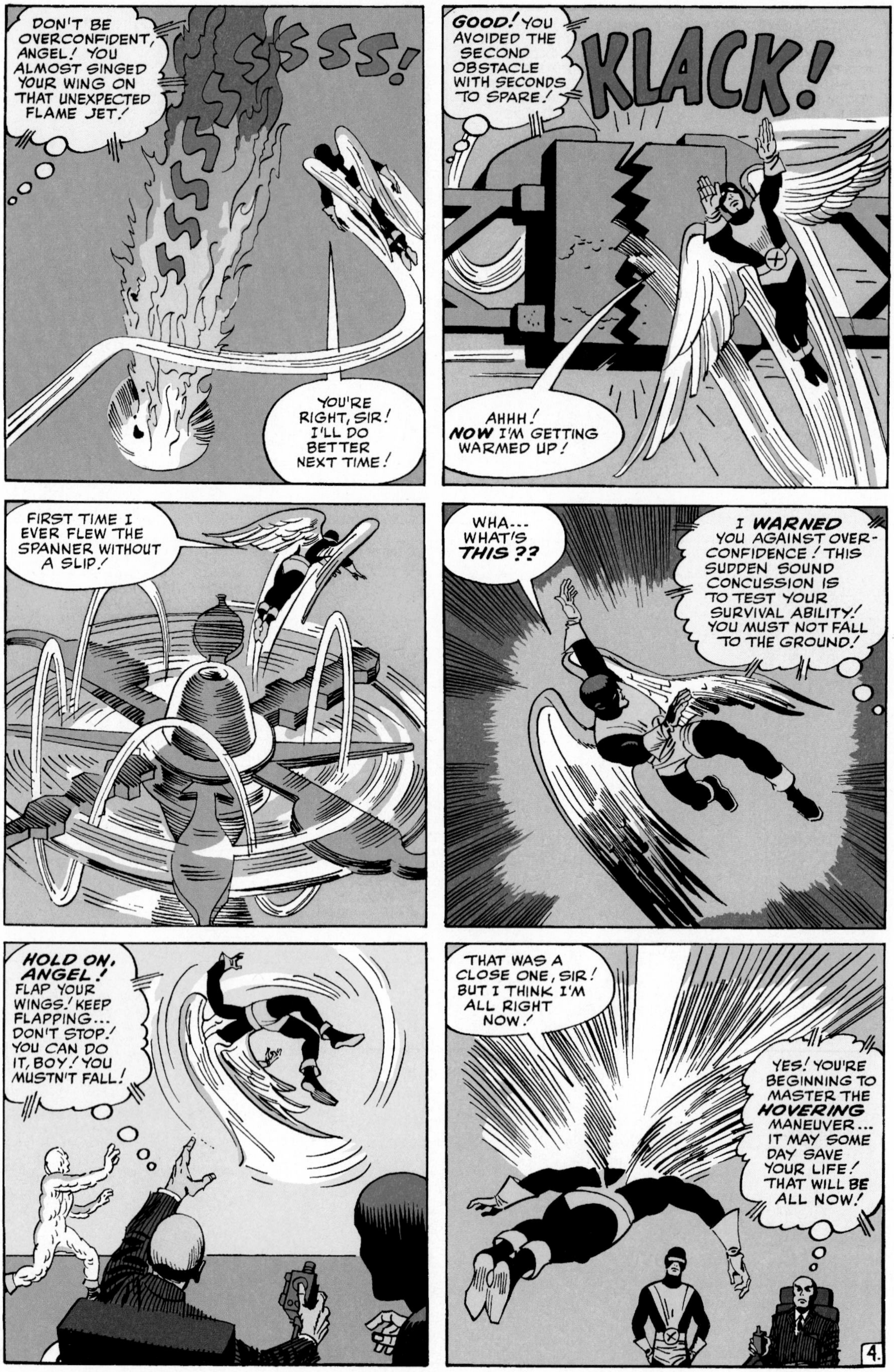
DON'T BE OVERCONFIDENT, ANGEL! YOU ALMOST SINGED YOUR WING ON THAT UNEXPECTED FLAME JET!
SSSSS!
YOU'RE RIGHT, SIR! I'LL DO BETTER NEXT TIME!
GOOD! YOU AVOIDED THE SECOND OBSTACLE WITH SECONDS TO SPARE!
KLACK!
AHHH! NOW I'M GETTING WARMED UP!
FIRST TIME I EVER FLEW THE SPANNER WITHOUT A SLIP!
WHA... WHAT'S THIS??
I WARNED YOU AGAINST OVER-CONFIDENCE! THIS SUDDEN SOUND CONCUSSION IS TO TEST YOUR SURVIVAL ABILITY! YOU MUST NOT FALL TO THE GROUND!
HOLD ON, ANGEL! FLAP YOUR WINGS! KEEP FLAPPING... DON'T STOP! YOU CAN DO IT, BOY! YOU MUSTN'T FALL!
THAT WAS A CLOSE ONE, SIR! BUT I THINK I'M ALL RIGHT NOW!
YES! YOU'RE BEGINNING TO MASTER THE HOVERING MANEUVER... IT MAY SOME DAY SAVE YOUR LIFE! THAT WILL BE ALL NOW!
4.

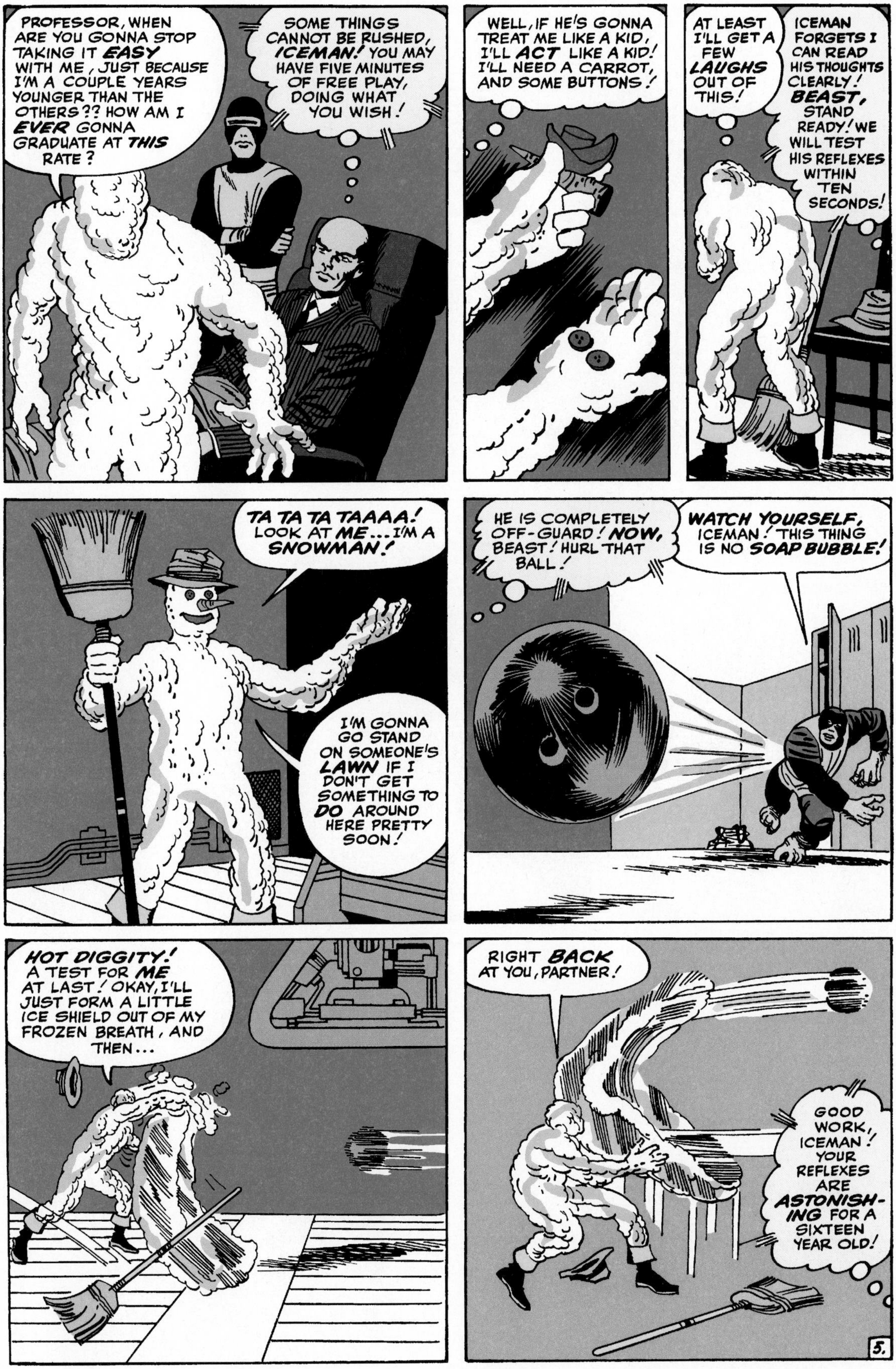
PROFESSOR, WHEN ARE YOU GONNA STOP TAKING IT EASY WITH ME, JUST BECAUSE I'M A COUPLE YEARS YOUNGER THAN THE OTHERS?? HOW AM I EVER GONNA GRADUATE AT THIS RATE?
SOME THINGS CANNOT BE RUSHED, ICEMAN! YOU MAY HAVE FIVE MINUTES OF FREE PLAY, DOING WHAT YOU WISH!
WELL, IF HE'S GONNA TREAT ME LIKE A KID, I'LL ACT LIKE A KID! I'LL NEED A CARROT, AND SOME BUTTONS!
AT LEAST I'LL GET A FEW LAUGHS OUT OF THIS!
ICEMAN FORGETS I CAN READ HIS THOUGHTS CLEARLY! BEAST, STAND READY! WE WILL TEST HIS REFLEXES WITHIN TEN SECONDS!
TA TA TA TAAAA! LOOK AT ME... I'M A SNOWMAN!
I'M GONNA GO STAND ON SOMEONE'S LAWN IF I DON'T GET SOMETHING TO DO AROUND HERE PRETTY SOON!
HE IS COMPLETELY OFF-GUARD! NOW, BEAST! HURL THAT BALL!
WATCH YOURSELF, ICEMAN! THIS THING IS NO SOAP BUBBLE!
HOT DIGGITY! A TEST FOR ME AT LAST! OKAY, I'LL JUST FORM A LITTLE ICE SHIELD OUT OF MY FROZEN BREATH, AND THEN...
RIGHT BACK AT YOU, PARTNER!
GOOD WORK, ICEMAN! YOUR REFLEXES ARE ASTONISHING FOR A SIXTEEN YEAR OLD!
5.

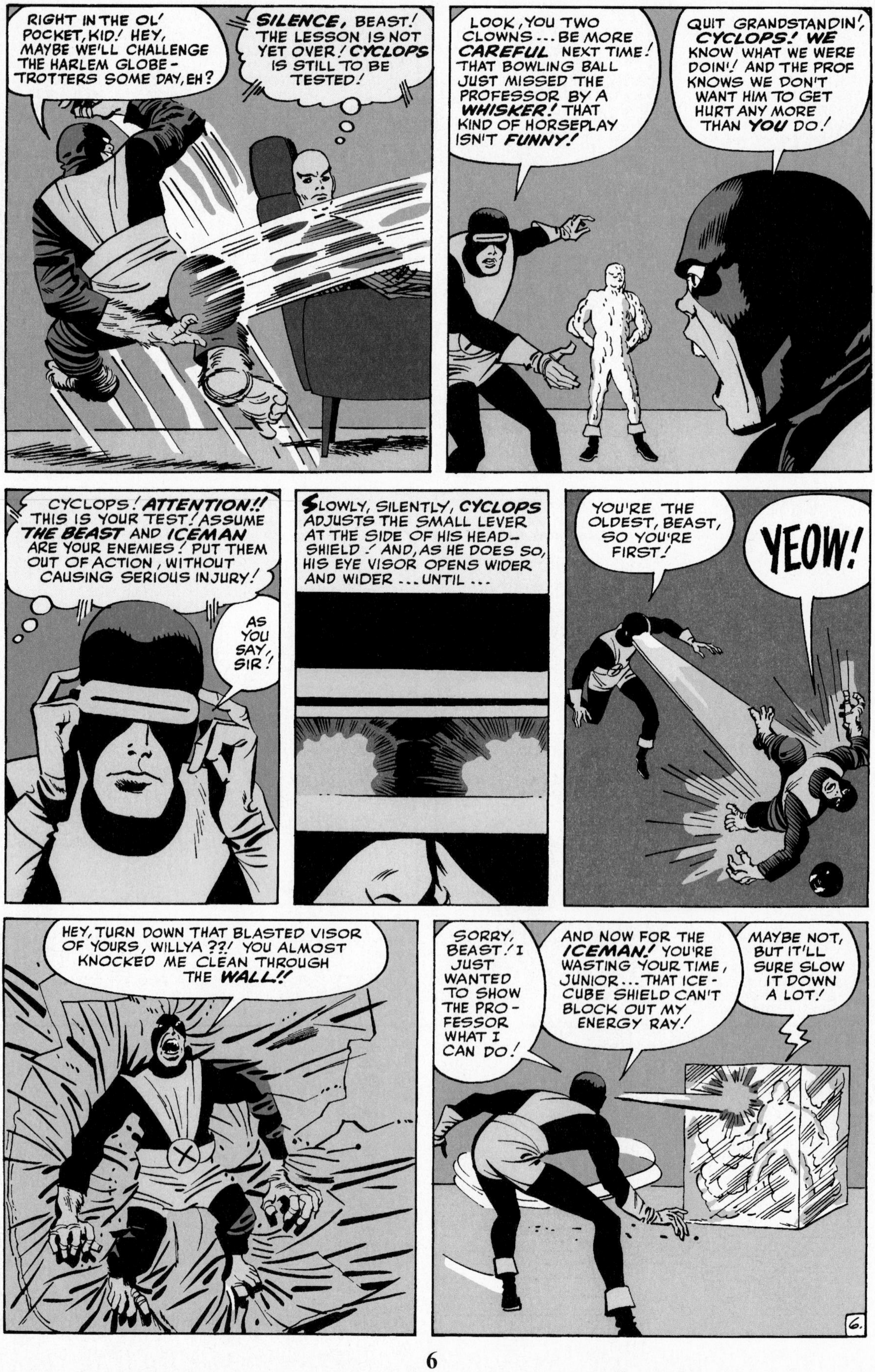
RIGHT IN THE OL' POCKET, KID! HEY, MAYBE WE'LL CHALLENGE THE HARLEM GLOBE-TROTTERS SOME DAY, EH?
SILENCE, BEAST! THE LESSON IS NOT YET OVER! CYCLOPS IS STILL TO BE TESTED!
LOOK, YOU TWO CLOWNS... BE MORE CAREFUL NEXT TIME! THAT BOWLING BALL JUST MISSED THE PROFESSOR BY A WHISKER! THAT KIND OF HORSEPLAY ISN'T FUNNY!
QUIT GRANDSTANDIN', CYCLOPS! WE KNOW WHAT WE WERE DOIN'! AND THE PROF KNOWS WE DON'T WANT HIM TO GET HURT ANY MORE THAN YOU DO!
CYCLOPS! ATTENTION!! THIS IS YOUR TEST! ASSUME THE BEAST AND ICEMAN ARE YOUR ENEMIES! PUT THEM OUT OF ACTION, WITHOUT CAUSING SERIOUS INJURY!
AS YOU SAY, SIR!
SLOWLY, SILENTLY, CYCLOPS ADJUSTS THE SMALL LEVER AT THE SIDE OF HIS HEAD-SHIELD! AND, AS HE DOES SO, HIS EYE VISOR OPENS WIDER AND WIDER... UNTIL...
YOU'RE THE OLDEST, BEAST, SO YOU'RE FIRST!
YEOW!
HEY, TURN DOWN THAT BLASTED VISOR OF YOURS, WILLYA??! YOU ALMOST KNOCKED ME CLEAN THROUGH THE WALL!!
SORRY, BEAST! I JUST WANTED TO SHOW THE PROFESSOR WHAT I CAN DO!
AND NOW FOR THE ICEMAN! YOU'RE WASTING YOUR TIME, JUNIOR... THAT ICE-CUBE SHIELD CAN'T BLOCK OUT MY ENERGY RAY!
MAYBE NOT, BUT IT'LL SURE SLOW IT DOWN A LOT!
6.

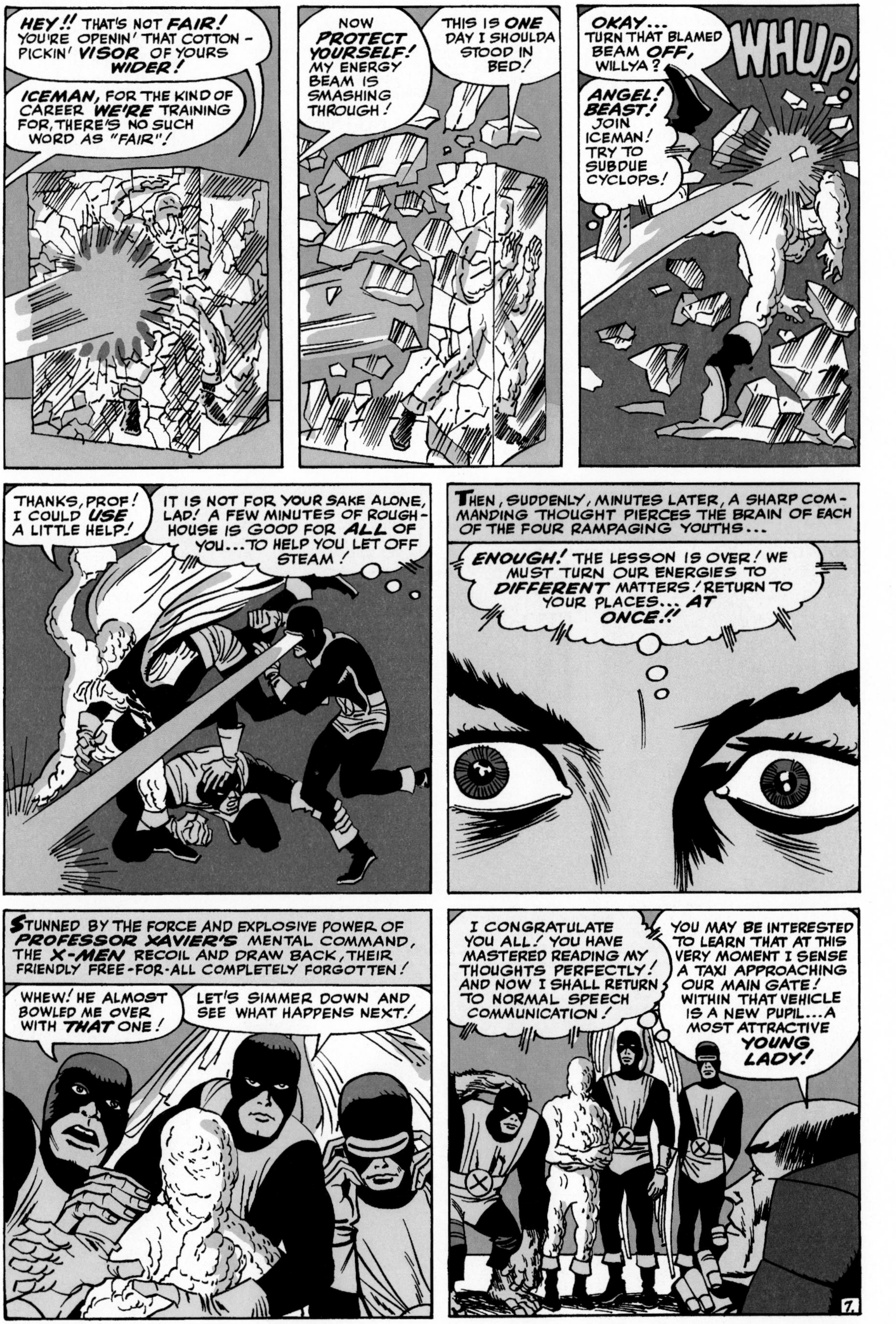
HEY!! THAT'S NOT FAIR! YOU'RE OPENIN' THAT COTTON-PICKIN' VISOR OF YOURS WIDER!
ICEMAN, FOR THE KIND OF CAREER WE'RE TRAINING FOR, THERE'S NO SUCH WORD AS "FAIR"!
NOW PROTECT YOURSELF! MY ENERGY BEAM IS SMASHING THROUGH!
THIS IS ONE DAY I SHOULDA STOOD IN BED!
OKAY... TURN THAT BLAMED BEAM OFF, WILLYA?
WHUP!
ANGEL! BEAST! JOIN ICEMAN! TRY TO SUBDUE CYCLOPS!
THANKS, PROF! I COULD USE A LITTLE HELP!
IT IS NOT FOR YOUR SAKE ALONE, LAD! A FEW MINUTES OF ROUGH-HOUSE IS GOOD FOR ALL OF YOU...TO HELP YOU LET OFF STEAM!
THEN, SUDDENLY, MINUTES LATER, A SHARP COMMANDING THOUGHT PIERCES THE BRAIN OF EACH OF THE FOUR RAMPAGING YOUTHS...
ENOUGH! THE LESSON IS OVER! WE MUST TURN OUR ENERGIES TO DIFFERENT MATTERS! RETURN TO YOUR PLACES... AT ONCE!!
STUNNED BY THE FORCE AND EXPLOSIVE POWER OF PROFESSOR XAVIER'S MENTAL COMMAND, THE X-MEN RECOIL AND DRAW BACK, THEIR FRIENDLY FREE-FOR-ALL COMPLETELY FORGOTTEN!
WHEW! HE ALMOST BOWLED ME OVER WITH THAT ONE!
LET'S SIMMER DOWN AND SEE WHAT HAPPENS NEXT!
I CONGRATULATE YOU ALL! YOU HAVE MASTERED READING MY THOUGHTS PERFECTLY! AND NOW I SHALL RETURN TO NORMAL SPEECH COMMUNICATION!
YOU MAY BE INTERESTED TO LEARN THAT AT THIS VERY MOMENT I SENSE A TAXI APPROACHING OUR MAIN GATE! WITHIN THAT VEHICLE IS A NEW PUPIL...A MOST ATTRACTIVE YOUNG LADY!
7.

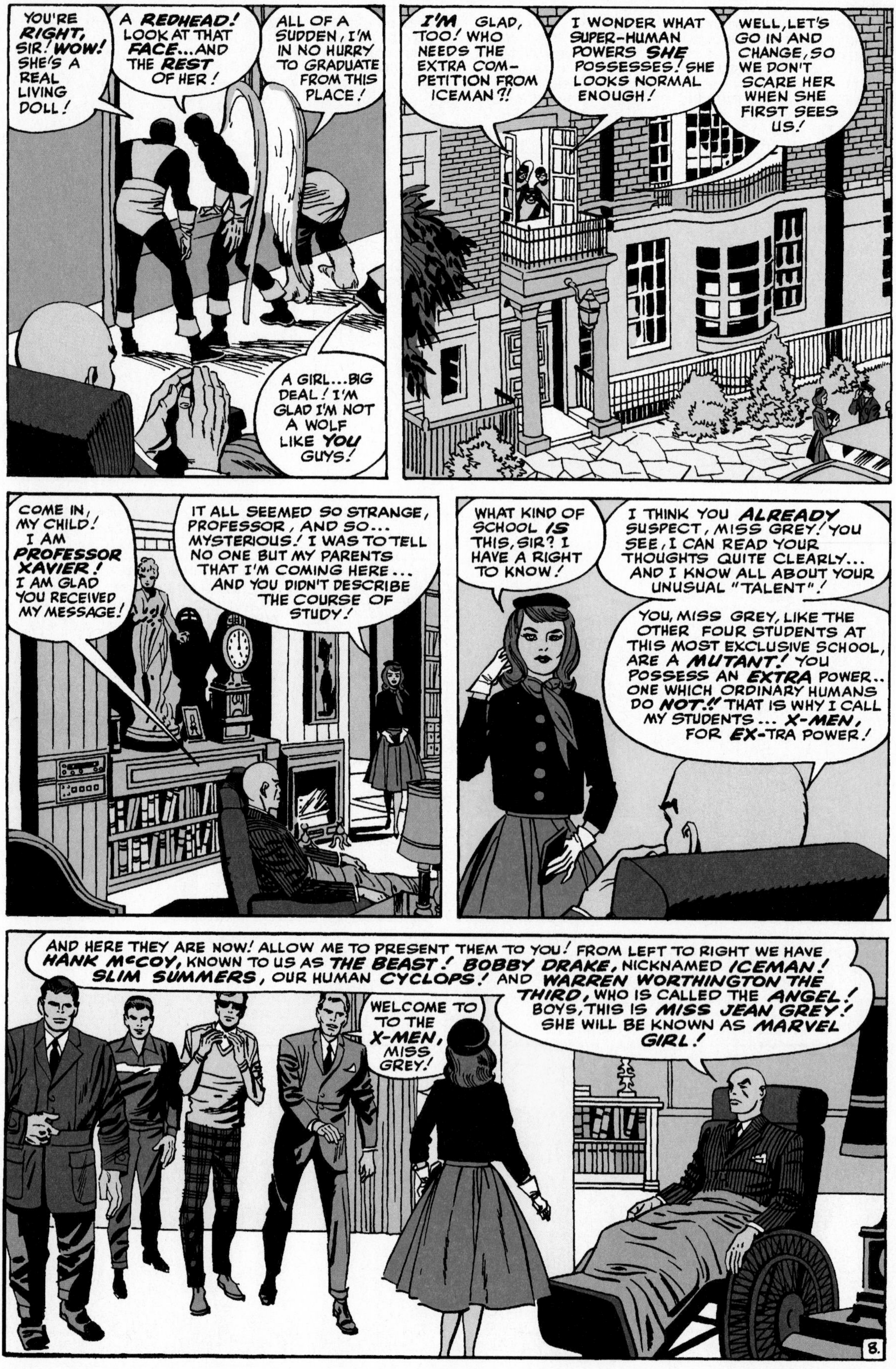
YOU'RE RIGHT, SIR! WOW! SHE'S A REAL LIVING DOLL!
A REDHEAD! LOOK AT THAT FACE...AND THE REST OF HER!
ALL OF A SUDDEN, I'M IN NO HURRY TO GRADUATE FROM THIS PLACE!
A GIRL...BIG DEAL! I'M GLAD I'M NOT A WOLF LIKE YOU GUYS!
I'M GLAD, TOO! WHO NEEDS THE EXTRA COMPETITION FROM ICEMAN?!
I WONDER WHAT SUPER-HUMAN POWERS SHE POSSESSES! SHE LOOKS NORMAL ENOUGH!
WELL, LET'S GO IN AND CHANGE, SO WE DON'T SCARE HER WHEN SHE FIRST SEES US!
COME IN, MY CHILD! I AM PROFESSOR XAVIER! I AM GLAD YOU RECEIVED MY MESSAGE!
IT ALL SEEMED SO STRANGE, PROFESSOR, AND SO... MYSTERIOUS! I WAS TO TELL NO ONE BUT MY PARENTS THAT I'M COMING HERE... AND YOU DIDN'T DESCRIBE THE COURSE OF STUDY!
WHAT KIND OF SCHOOL IS THIS, SIR? I HAVE A RIGHT TO KNOW!
I THINK YOU ALREADY SUSPECT, MISS GREY! YOU SEE, I CAN READ YOUR THOUGHTS QUITE CLEARLY... AND I KNOW ALL ABOUT YOUR UNUSUAL "TALENT"!
YOU, MISS GREY, LIKE THE OTHER FOUR STUDENTS AT THIS MOST EXCLUSIVE SCHOOL, ARE A MUTANT! YOU POSSESS AN EXTRA POWER.. ONE WHICH ORDINARY HUMANS DO NOT!! THAT IS WHY I CALL MY STUDENTS ... X-MEN, FOR EX-TRA POWER!
AND HERE THEY ARE NOW! ALLOW ME TO PRESENT THEM TO YOU! FROM LEFT TO RIGHT WE HAVE HANK McCOY, KNOWN TO US AS THE BEAST! BOBBY DRAKE, NICKNAMED ICEMAN! SLIM SUMMERS, OUR HUMAN CYCLOPS! AND WARREN WORTHINGTON THE THIRD, WHO IS CALLED THE ANGEL! BOYS, THIS IS MISS JEAN GREY! SHE WILL BE KNOWN AS MARVEL GIRL!
WELCOME TO TO THE X-MEN, MISS GREY!
8.

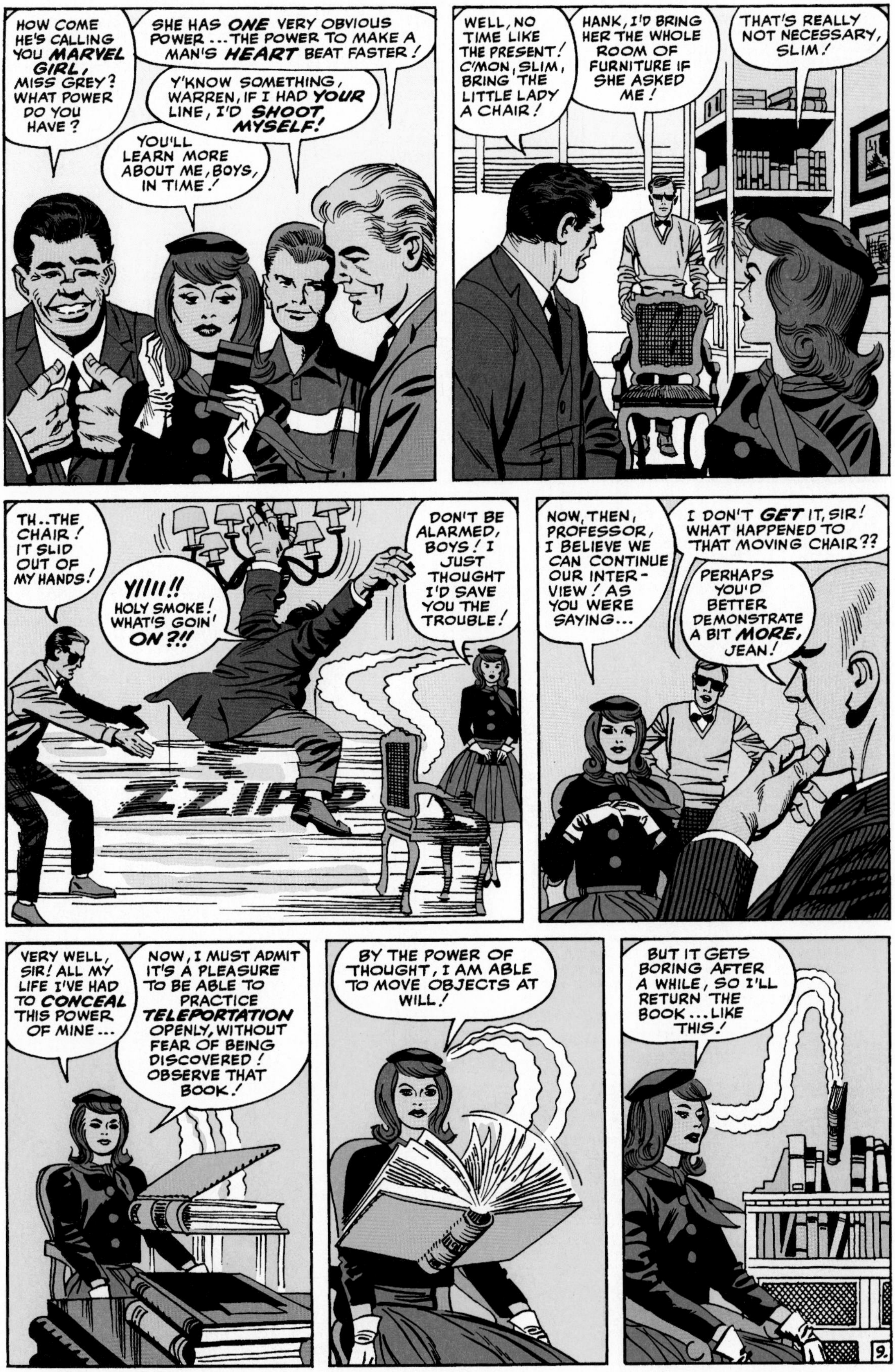
HOW COME HE'S CALLING YOU MARVEL GIRL, MISS GREY? WHAT POWER DO YOU HAVE?
SHE HAS ONE VERY OBVIOUS POWER ... THE POWER TO MAKE A MAN'S HEART BEAT FASTER!
Y'KNOW SOMETHING, WARREN, IF I HAD YOUR LINE, I'D SHOOT MYSELF!
YOU'LL LEARN MORE ABOUT ME, BOYS, IN TIME!
WELL, NO TIME LIKE THE PRESENT! C'MON, SLIM, BRING THE LITTLE LADY A CHAIR!
HANK, I'D BRING HER THE WHOLE ROOM OF FURNITURE IF SHE ASKED ME!
THAT'S REALLY NOT NECESSARY, SLIM!
TH..THE CHAIR! IT SLID OUT OF MY HANDS!
YIIII!! HOLY SMOKE! WHAT'S GOIN' ON?!!
DON'T BE ALARMED, BOYS! I JUST THOUGHT I'D SAVE YOU THE TROUBLE!
ZZIPP
NOW, THEN, PROFESSOR, I BELIEVE WE CAN CONTINUE OUR INTER-VIEW! AS YOU WERE SAYING...
I DON'T GET IT, SIR! WHAT HAPPENED TO THAT MOVING CHAIR??
PERHAPS YOU'D BETTER DEMONSTRATE A BIT MORE, JEAN!
VERY WELL, SIR! ALL MY LIFE I'VE HAD TO CONCEAL THIS POWER OF MINE...
NOW, I MUST ADMIT IT'S A PLEASURE TO BE ABLE TO PRACTICE TELEPORTATION OPENLY, WITHOUT FEAR OF BEING DISCOVERED! OBSERVE THAT BOOK!
BY THE POWER OF THOUGHT, I AM ABLE TO MOVE OBJECTS AT WILL!
BUT IT GETS BORING AFTER A WHILE, SO I'LL RETURN THE BOOK... LIKE THIS!
9.

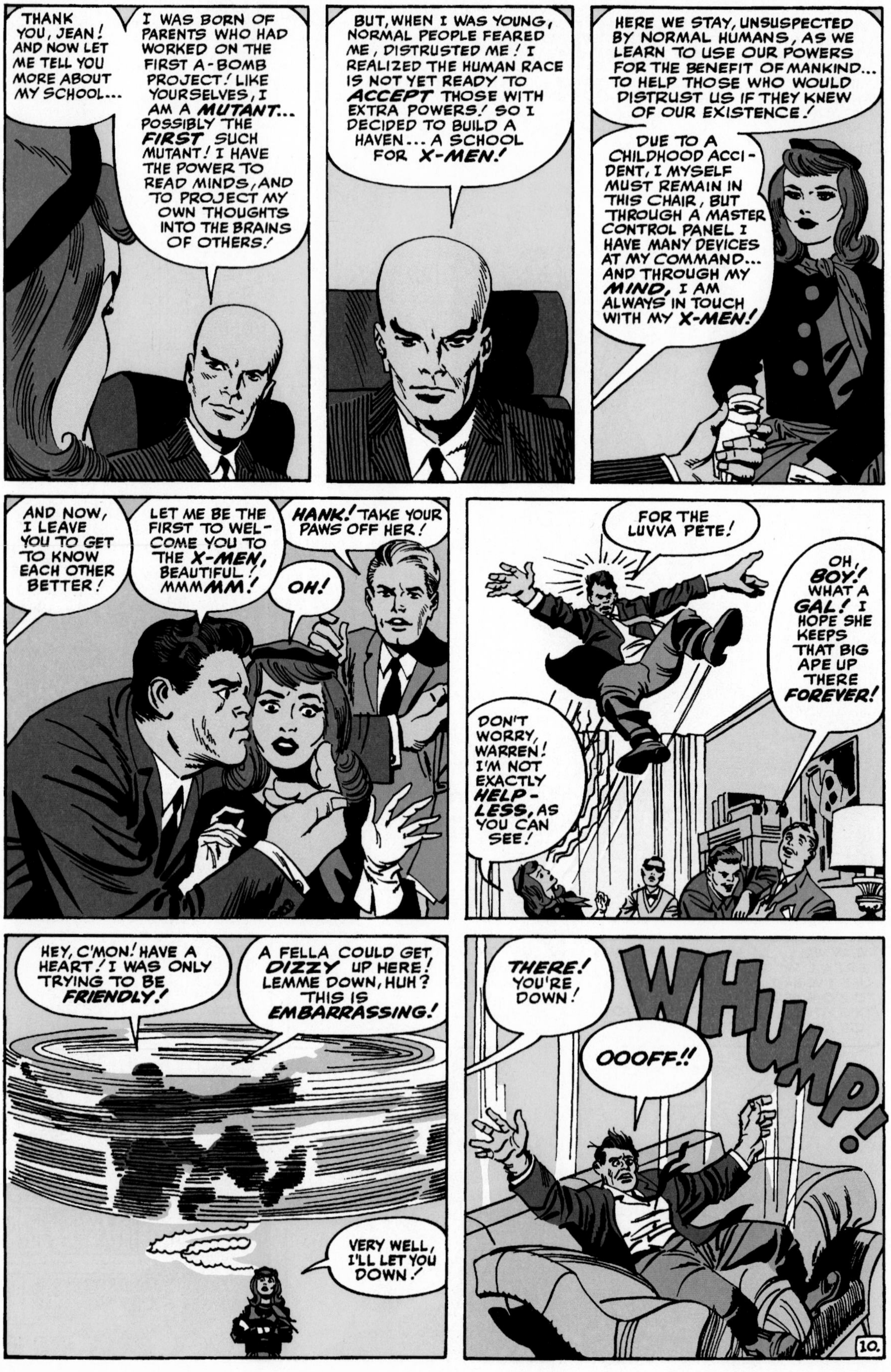
THANK YOU, JEAN! AND NOW LET ME TELL YOU MORE ABOUT MY SCHOOL...
I WAS BORN OF PARENTS WHO HAD WORKED ON THE FIRST A-BOMB PROJECT! LIKE YOURSELVES, I AM A MUTANT... POSSIBLY THE FIRST SUCH MUTANT! I HAVE THE POWER TO READ MINDS, AND TO PROJECT MY OWN THOUGHTS INTO THE BRAINS OF OTHERS!
BUT, WHEN I WAS YOUNG, NORMAL PEOPLE FEARED ME, DISTRUSTED ME! I REALIZED THE HUMAN RACE IS NOT YET READY TO ACCEPT THOSE WITH EXTRA POWERS! SO I DECIDED TO BUILD A HAVEN... A SCHOOL FOR X-MEN!
HERE WE STAY, UNSUSPECTED BY NORMAL HUMANS, AS WE LEARN TO USE OUR POWERS FOR THE BENEFIT OF MANKIND... TO HELP THOSE WHO WOULD DISTRUST US IF THEY KNEW OF OUR EXISTENCE!
DUE TO A CHILDHOOD ACCI-DENT, I MYSELF MUST REMAIN IN THIS CHAIR, BUT THROUGH A MASTER CONTROL PANEL I HAVE MANY DEVICES AT MY COMMAND... AND THROUGH MY MIND, I AM ALWAYS IN TOUCH WITH MY X-MEN!
AND NOW, I LEAVE YOU TO GET TO KNOW EACH OTHER BETTER!
LET ME BE THE FIRST TO WEL-COME YOU TO THE X-MEN, BEAUTIFUL! MMMMM!
HANK! TAKE YOUR PAWS OFF HER!
OH!
FOR THE LUVVA PETE!
OH, BOY! WHAT A GAL! I HOPE SHE KEEPS THAT BIG APE UP THERE FOREVER!
DON'T WORRY, WARREN! I'M NOT EXACTLY HELP-LESS, AS YOU CAN SEE!
HEY, C'MON! HAVE A HEART! I WAS ONLY TRYING TO BE FRIENDLY!
A FELLA COULD GET DIZZY UP HERE! LEMME DOWN, HUH? THIS IS EMBARRASSING!
VERY WELL, I'LL LET YOU DOWN.
THERE! YOU'RE DOWN!
WHUMP!
OOOFF!!
10.

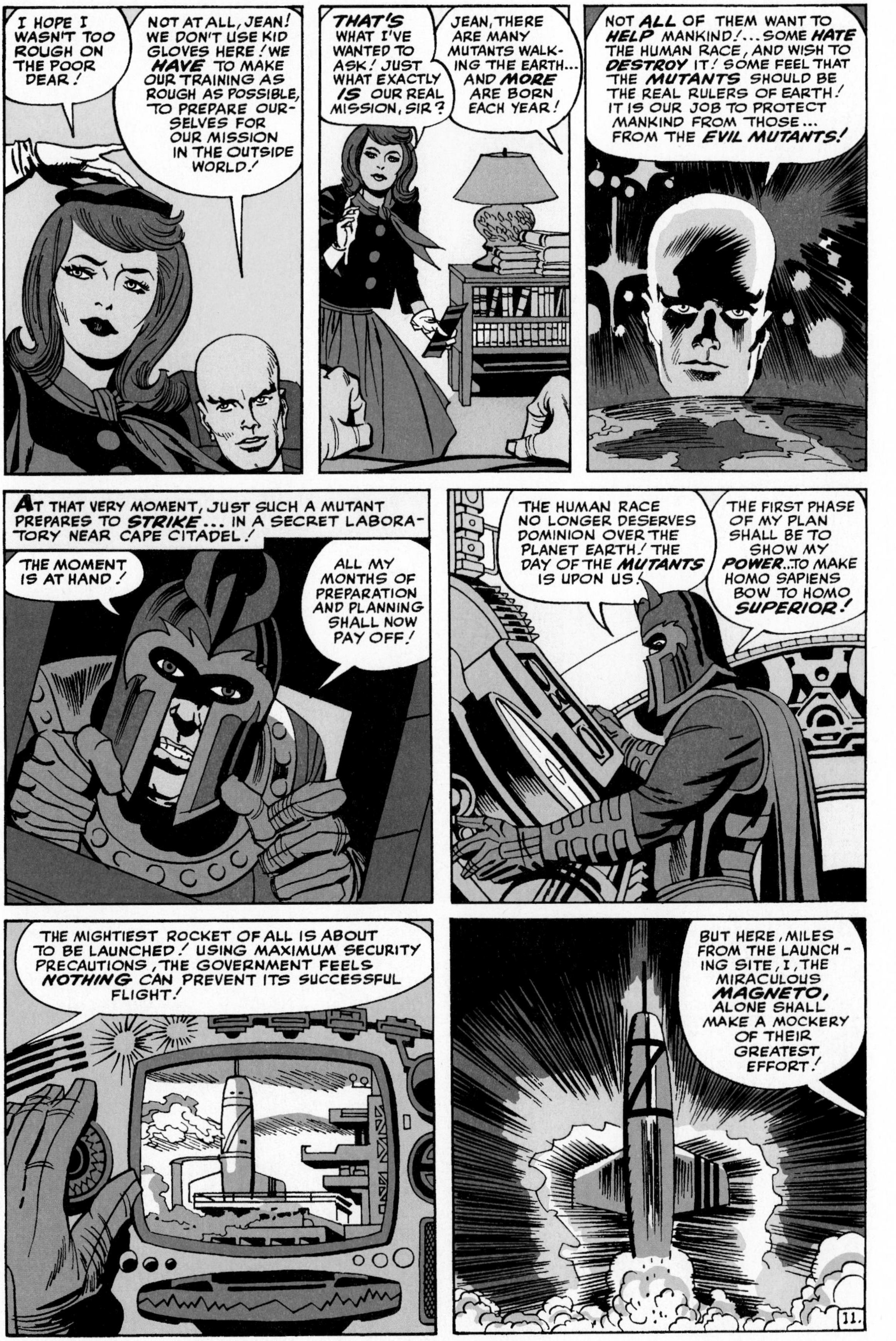
I HOPE I WASN'T TOO ROUGH ON THE POOR DEAR!
NOT AT ALL, JEAN! WE DON'T USE KID GLOVES HERE! WE HAVE TO MAKE OUR TRAINING AS ROUGH AS POSSIBLE, TO PREPARE OURSELVES FOR OUR MISSION IN THE OUTSIDE WORLD!
THAT'S WHAT I'VE WANTED TO ASK! JUST WHAT EXACTLY IS OUR REAL MISSION, SIR?
JEAN, THERE ARE MANY MUTANTS WALKING THE EARTH... AND MORE ARE BORN EACH YEAR!
NOT ALL OF THEM WANT TO HELP MANKIND!... SOME HATE THE HUMAN RACE, AND WISH TO DESTROY IT! SOME FEEL THAT THE MUTANTS SHOULD BE THE REAL RULERS OF EARTH! IT IS OUR JOB TO PROTECT MANKIND FROM THOSE... FROM THE EVIL MUTANTS!
AT THAT VERY MOMENT, JUST SUCH A MUTANT PREPARES TO STRIKE... IN A SECRET LABORATORY NEAR CAPE CITADEL!
THE MOMENT IS AT HAND!
ALL MY MONTHS OF PREPARATION AND PLANNING SHALL NOW PAY OFF!
THE HUMAN RACE NO LONGER DESERVES DOMINION OVER THE PLANET EARTH! THE DAY OF THE MUTANTS IS UPON US!
THE FIRST PHASE OF MY PLAN SHALL BE TO SHOW MY POWER...TO MAKE HOMO SAPIENS BOW TO HOMO SUPERIOR!
THE MIGHTIEST ROCKET OF ALL IS ABOUT TO BE LAUNCHED! USING MAXIMUM SECURITY PRECAUTIONS, THE GOVERNMENT FEELS NOTHING CAN PREVENT ITS SUCCESSFUL FLIGHT!
BUT HERE, MILES FROM THE LAUNCHING SITE, I, THE MIRACULOUS MAGNETO, ALONE SHALL MAKE A MOCKERY OF THEIR GREATEST EFFORT!
11.

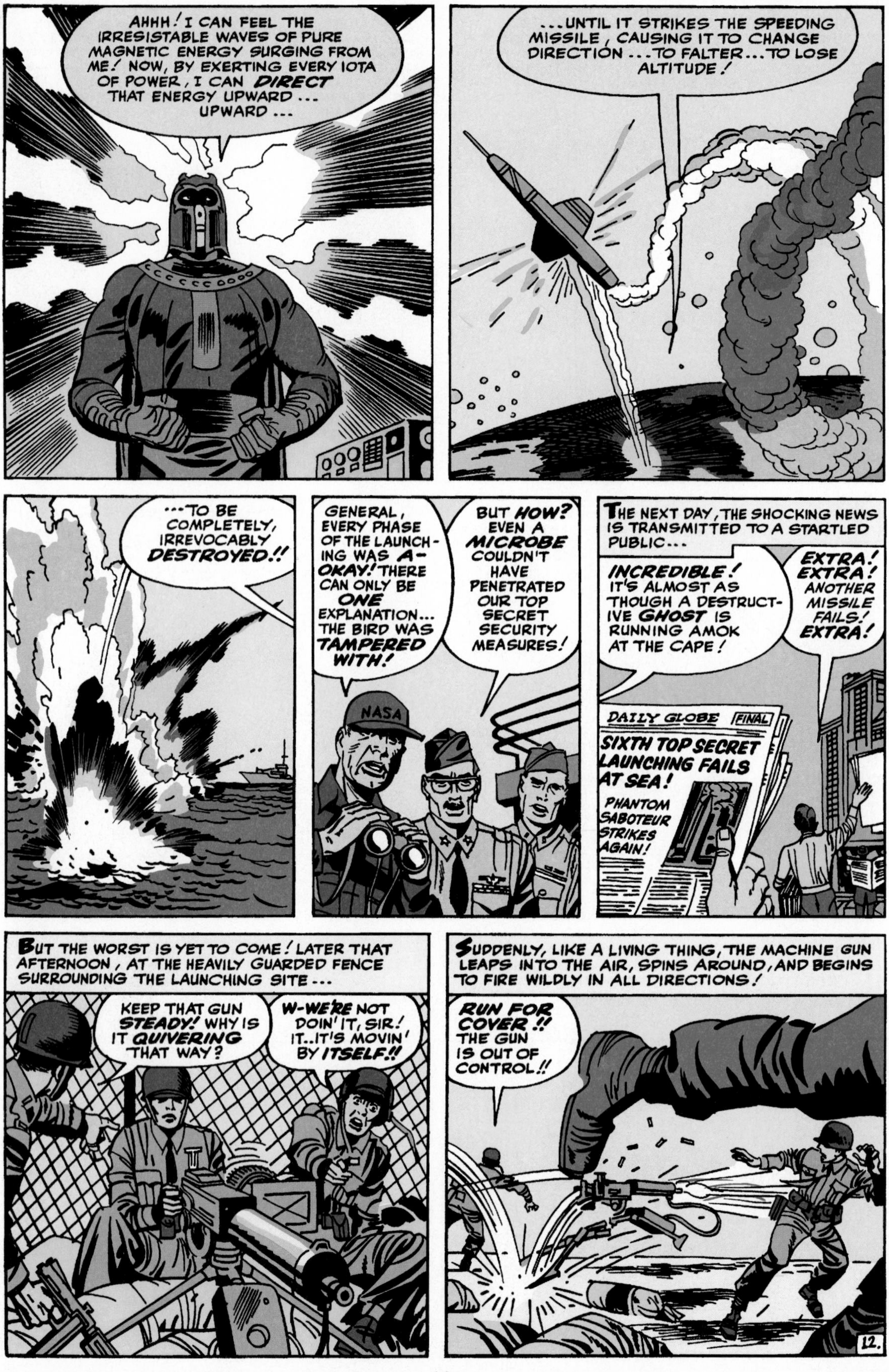
AHHH! I CAN FEEL THE IRRESISTABLE WAVES OF PURE MAGNETIC ENERGY SURGING FROM ME! NOW, BY EXERTING EVERY IOTA OF POWER, I CAN DIRECT THAT ENERGY UPWARD ... UPWARD ...
...UNTIL IT STRIKES THE SPEEDING MISSILE, CAUSING IT TO CHANGE DIRECTION ... TO FALTER ... TO LOSE ALTITUDE!
...TO BE COMPLETELY, IRREVOCABLY DESTROYED.!!
GENERAL, EVERY PHASE OF THE LAUNCHING WAS A-OKAY! THERE CAN ONLY BE ONE EXPLANATION... THE BIRD WAS TAMPERED WITH!
BUT HOW? EVEN A MICROBE COULDN'T HAVE PENETRATED OUR TOP SECRET SECURITY MEASURES!
NASA
THE NEXT DAY, THE SHOCKING NEWS IS TRANSMITTED TO A STARTLED PUBLIC...
INCREDIBLE! IT'S ALMOST AS THOUGH A DESTRUCTIVE GHOST IS RUNNING AMOK AT THE CAPE!
EXTRA! EXTRA! ANOTHER MISSILE FAILS! EXTRA!
DAILY GLOBE FINAL
SIXTH TOP SECRET LAUNCHING FAILS AT SEA!
PHANTOM SABOTEUR STRIKES AGAIN!
BUT THE WORST IS YET TO COME! LATER THAT AFTERNOON, AT THE HEAVILY GUARDED FENCE SURROUNDING THE LAUNCHING SITE ---
KEEP THAT GUN STEADY! WHY IS IT QUIVERING THAT WAY?
W-WE'RE NOT DOIN' IT, SIR! IT..IT'S MOVIN' BY ITSELF.!!
SUDDENLY, LIKE A LIVING THING, THE MACHINE GUN LEAPS INTO THE AIR, SPINS AROUND, AND BEGINS TO FIRE WILDLY IN ALL DIRECTIONS!
RUN FOR COVER!! THE GUN IS OUT OF CONTROL!!
12.

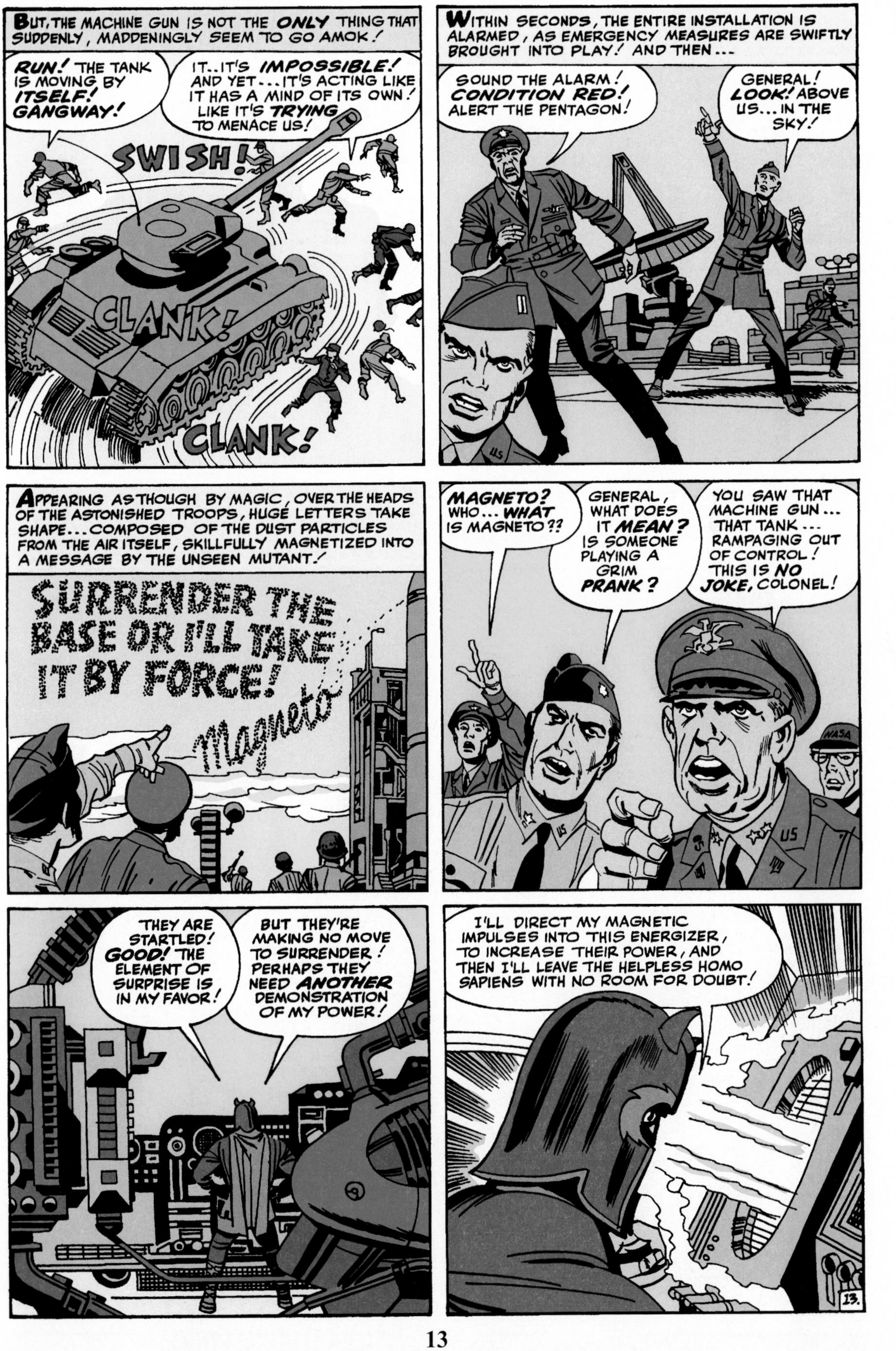

BUT, THE MACHINE GUN IS NOT THE ONLY THING THAT SUDDENLY, MADDENINGLY SEEM TO GO AMOK!
RUN! THE TANK IS MOVING BY ITSELF! GANGWAY!
IT..IT'S IMPOSSIBLE! AND YET...IT'S ACTING LIKE IT HAS A MIND OF ITS OWN! LIKE IT'S TRYING TO MENACE US!
SWISH!
CLANK!
CLANK!
WITHIN SECONDS, THE ENTIRE INSTALLATION IS ALARMED, AS EMERGENCY MEASURES ARE SWIFTLY BROUGHT INTO PLAY! AND THEN...
SOUND THE ALARM! CONDITION RED! ALERT THE PENTAGON!
GENERAL! LOOK! ABOVE US... IN THE SKY!
APPEARING AS THOUGH BY MAGIC, OVER THE HEADS OF THE ASTONISHED TROOPS, HUGE LETTERS TAKE SHAPE...COMPOSED OF THE DUST PARTICLES FROM THE AIR ITSELF, SKILLFULLY MAGNETIZED INTO A MESSAGE BY THE UNSEEN MUTANT!
SURRENDER THE BASE OR I'LL TAKE IT BY FORCE!
Magneto
MAGNETO? WHO... WHAT IS MAGNETO??
GENERAL, WHAT DOES IT MEAN? IS SOMEONE PLAYING A GRIM PRANK?
YOU SAW THAT MACHINE GUN... THAT TANK... RAMPAGING OUT OF CONTROL! THIS IS NO JOKE, COLONEL!
THEY ARE STARTLED! GOOD! THE ELEMENT OF SURPRISE IS IN MY FAVOR!
BUT THEY'RE MAKING NO MOVE TO SURRENDER! PERHAPS THEY NEED ANOTHER DEMONSTRATION OF MY POWER!
I'LL DIRECT MY MAGNETIC IMPULSES INTO THIS ENERGIZER, TO INCREASE THEIR POWER, AND THEN I'LL LEAVE THE HELPLESS HOMO SAPIENS WITH NO ROOM FOR DOUBT!
13.

AN INSTANT LATER, INVISIBLE WAVES OF PURE, POWERFUL MAGNETIC ENERGY FLOW IRRESISTIBLY INTO AN UNDERGROUND SILO WHERE ONE OF DEMOCRACY'S SILENT SENTINELS WAIT, AT THE READY!

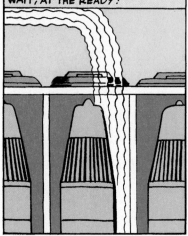

AND THEN, MANIPULATED BY A SINISTER INTELLIGENCE, MANY HUNDREDS OF YARDS AWAY, THE MAGNETIC FORCE LIFTS THE SILO HEAD, ACTIVATING THE MIGHTY MISSILE!!

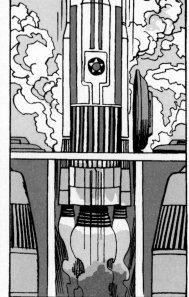

DEMONSTRATING A POWER WHICH THE HUMAN BRAIN IS ALMOST UNABLE TO COMPREHEND, MAGNETO CAUSES THE GRIM ROCKET TO FALL INTO THE SEA MANY MILES FROM SHORE, NEXT TO AN UNMANNED TARGET SHIP!

BUT STILL, THE THOUGHT OF SURRENDER NEVER CROSSES THE MINDS OF THE FIGHTING-MAD BASE PERSONNEL!

SERGEANT! ORDER THE GUARD DOUBLED AT EVERY MISSILE CONTROL CENTER! ANY ROCKET DEEMED A MENACE IS TO BE DESTROYED INSTANTLY!

SOME POWER BEYOND OUR UNDERSTANDING IS AFFECTING OUR WEAPONS! WE MUST FIND THIS MAGNETO!

GENERAL, LOOK! THAT COMMOTION AT THE MAIN GATE! IT SEEMS THAT HE HAS FOUND US FIRST!

HOLD IT, MAC! IF YOU'RE LOOKIN' FOR A MASQUERADE PARTY, YOU'VE COME TO THE WRONG PLACE! BEAT IT!

WELL SAID, GUARD! WHAT A PITY YOU HAVE NO POWER TO BACK UP SUCH IMPRESSIVE WORDS! YOUR PUNY WEAPONS CANNOT STOP ME!

THEY CAN'T, EH? ONE LITTLE BURST OVER YOUR HEAD WILL SURELY CHANGE YOUR MIND!

HEY! WHA— WHAT GIVES? THE GUN WON'T FIRE! THE TRIGGER SEEMS LOCKED IN PLACE!

I CAN'T EVEN LIFT MY GUN! FEELS LIKE IT WEIGHS A TON!

14.

NOW I'LL MERELY ALTER MY MAGNETIC WAVES FROM POSITIVE TO *NEGATIVE*, SO THAT THEY WILL *REPEL* ANYTHING THAT COMES WITHIN RANGE! *NOTHING* CAN TOUCH ME AS I WALK TO MY OBJECTIVE!

WE CAN'T *STOP* HIM! CALL FOR RE-INFORCEMENTS!

I'M 'WAY *AHEAD* OF YA, PAL!

BUT, THE ADDITIONAL REINFORCEMENTS ARE EQUALLY POWERLESS TO STOP THE ONE-MAN INVASION OF THE STRATEGIC BASE!

IT..IT'S LIKE HE'S GOT AN INVISIBLE *BARRIER* 'ROUND HIM, HURLING US AWAY!

THERE! BY SIMPLY NARROWING MY MAGNETIC WAVES ALL AROUND THE LESSER HUMANS, I CAN KEEP THEM CONFINED TO THAT AREA UNTIL I REACH THEIR OFFICER-IN-COMMAND!

AND FINALLY...

HOLD IT, MEN! ALL RIGHT, WHO-EVER YOU ARE...IF YOU'VE SOMETHING TO SAY, YOU'VE GOT SIXTY SECONDS TO SAY IT!

WRONG, GENERAL! I HAVE ALL THE TIME IN THE WORLD! AND NOW, I, THE MIRACULOUS *MAGNETO*, CLAIM THIS ENTIRE INSTAL-LATION...IN THE NAME OF *HOMO SUPERIOR!!*

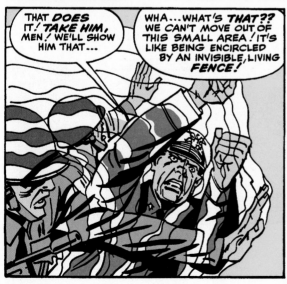

THAT *DOES* IT! *TAKE HIM*, MEN! WE'LL SHOW HIM THAT...

WHA...WHAT'S *THAT??* WE CAN'T MOVE OUT OF THIS SMALL AREA! IT'S LIKE BEING ENCIRCLED BY AN INVISIBLE, LIVING *FENCE!*

THAT "LIVING FENCE" AS YOU CALL IT, IS THE SYMBOL OF MY GREAT POWER! IT IS A MIGHTY SHIELD OF *MAGNETIC ENERGY!*

AND SO I HAVE NOW ACCOMPLISHED MY FIRST OBJECTIVE! GENTLEMEN, CAPE CITADEL IS *MINE!*

15.

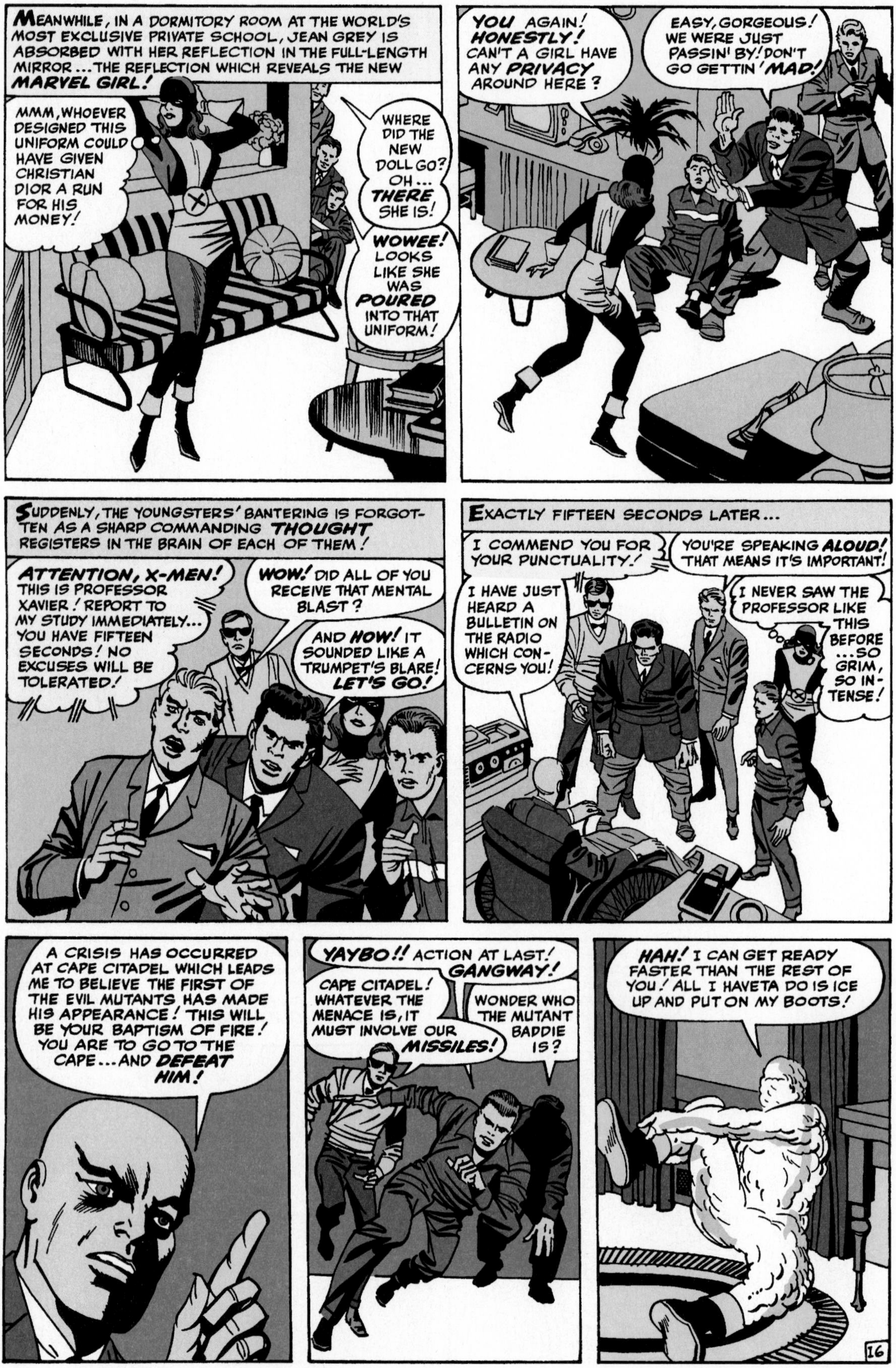
MEANWHILE, IN A DORMITORY ROOM AT THE WORLD'S MOST EXCLUSIVE PRIVATE SCHOOL, JEAN GREY IS ABSORBED WITH HER REFLECTION IN THE FULL-LENGTH MIRROR...THE REFLECTION WHICH REVEALS THE NEW MARVEL GIRL!
MMM, WHOEVER DESIGNED THIS UNIFORM COULD HAVE GIVEN CHRISTIAN DIOR A RUN FOR HIS MONEY!
WHERE DID THE NEW DOLL GO? OH... THERE SHE IS!
WOWEE! LOOKS LIKE SHE WAS POURED INTO THAT UNIFORM!
YOU AGAIN! HONESTLY! CAN'T A GIRL HAVE ANY PRIVACY AROUND HERE?
EASY, GORGEOUS! WE WERE JUST PASSIN' BY! DON'T GO GETTIN' MAD!
SUDDENLY, THE YOUNGSTERS' BANTERING IS FORGOTTEN AS A SHARP COMMANDING THOUGHT REGISTERS IN THE BRAIN OF EACH OF THEM!
ATTENTION, X-MEN! THIS IS PROFESSOR XAVIER! REPORT TO MY STUDY IMMEDIATELY... YOU HAVE FIFTEEN SECONDS! NO EXCUSES WILL BE TOLERATED!
WOW! DID ALL OF YOU RECEIVE THAT MENTAL BLAST?
AND HOW! IT SOUNDED LIKE A TRUMPET'S BLARE! LET'S GO!
EXACTLY FIFTEEN SECONDS LATER...
I COMMEND YOU FOR YOUR PUNCTUALITY!
I HAVE JUST HEARD A BULLETIN ON THE RADIO WHICH CONCERNS YOU!
YOU'RE SPEAKING ALOUD! THAT MEANS IT'S IMPORTANT!
I NEVER SAW THE PROFESSOR LIKE THIS BEFORE ...SO GRIM, SO INTENSE!
A CRISIS HAS OCCURRED AT CAPE CITADEL WHICH LEADS ME TO BELIEVE THE FIRST OF THE EVIL MUTANTS HAS MADE HIS APPEARANCE! THIS WILL BE YOUR BAPTISM OF FIRE! YOU ARE TO GO TO THE CAPE...AND DEFEAT HIM!
YAYBO!! ACTION AT LAST! GANGWAY!
CAPE CITADEL! WHATEVER THE MENACE IS, IT MUST INVOLVE OUR MISSILES!
WONDER WHO THE MUTANT BADDIE IS?
HAH! I CAN GET READY FASTER THAN THE REST OF YOU! ALL I HAVETA DO IS ICE UP AND PUT ON MY BOOTS!
16

AS FOR **ME**, IT'LL BE A PLEASURE TO GET OUT OF THIS HARNESS I HAVE TO WEAR!

HAVING A PAIR OF WINGS CAN BE MORE TROUBLE THAN YOU'D GUESS!

THESE RESTRAINING BELTS OF MINE KEEP MY WINGS FROM BULGING UNDER MY SUIT, BUT AFTER A WHILE THEY FEEL LIKE I'M WEARING A **STRAIT-JACKET!**

AHHH! THAT'S MORE LIKE IT! NOW I FEEL LIKE MYSELF AGAIN! NOW THE **ANGEL** IS READY TO SPREAD HIS WINGS ..AND **FLY!**

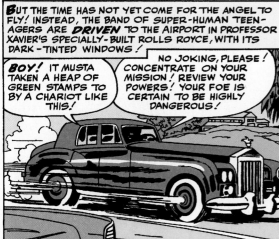

BUT THE TIME HAS NOT YET COME FOR THE ANGEL TO FLY! INSTEAD, THE BAND OF SUPER-HUMAN TEEN-AGERS ARE **DRIVEN** TO THE AIRPORT IN PROFESSOR XAVIER'S SPECIALLY-BUILT ROLLS ROYCE, WITH ITS DARK-TINTED WINDOWS!

BOY! IT MUSTA TAKEN A HEAP OF GREEN STAMPS TO BY A CHARIOT LIKE THIS!

NO JOKING, PLEASE! CONCENTRATE ON YOUR MISSION! REVIEW YOUR POWERS! YOUR FOE IS CERTAIN TO BE HIGHLY DANGEROUS!

MINUTES LATER, IN THE PROFESSOR'S REMOTE-CONTROL PRIVATE JET, THE **X-MEN** AND **MARVEL GIRL** ARE WINGING TOWARDS **CAPE CITADEL** AT NEARLY THE SPEED OF SOUND!

YOU MEAN THE PROFESSOR IS GUIDING THIS PLANE FROM THE GROUND... BY **THOUGHT IMPULSES?!** IT'S UN-BELIEVABLE!

LOOK, DOLL... WHEN YOU JOIN THE **X-MEN**, YOU REALIZE **NOTHING'S** UN-BELIEVABLE!

A SHORT TIME LATER, AT THE CAPE!...

CEASE FIRING! IT'S USELESS! WE HAVEN'T ANYTHING IN OUR ARSENAL THAT'LL PENETRATE **MAGNETO'S** MAGNETIC FORCE FIELD!

TO ALL INTENTS AND PURPOSES, HE'S IN FULL CONTROL OF THE INSTALLATION, WHILE WE'RE ON THE OUTSIDE, LOOKING IN!

WITH DUE RESPECT, GENERAL, I REPRESENT THE **X-MEN!** PERHAPS **WE** CAN HELP!

X-MEN?! WHAT THE..?!

17.

17

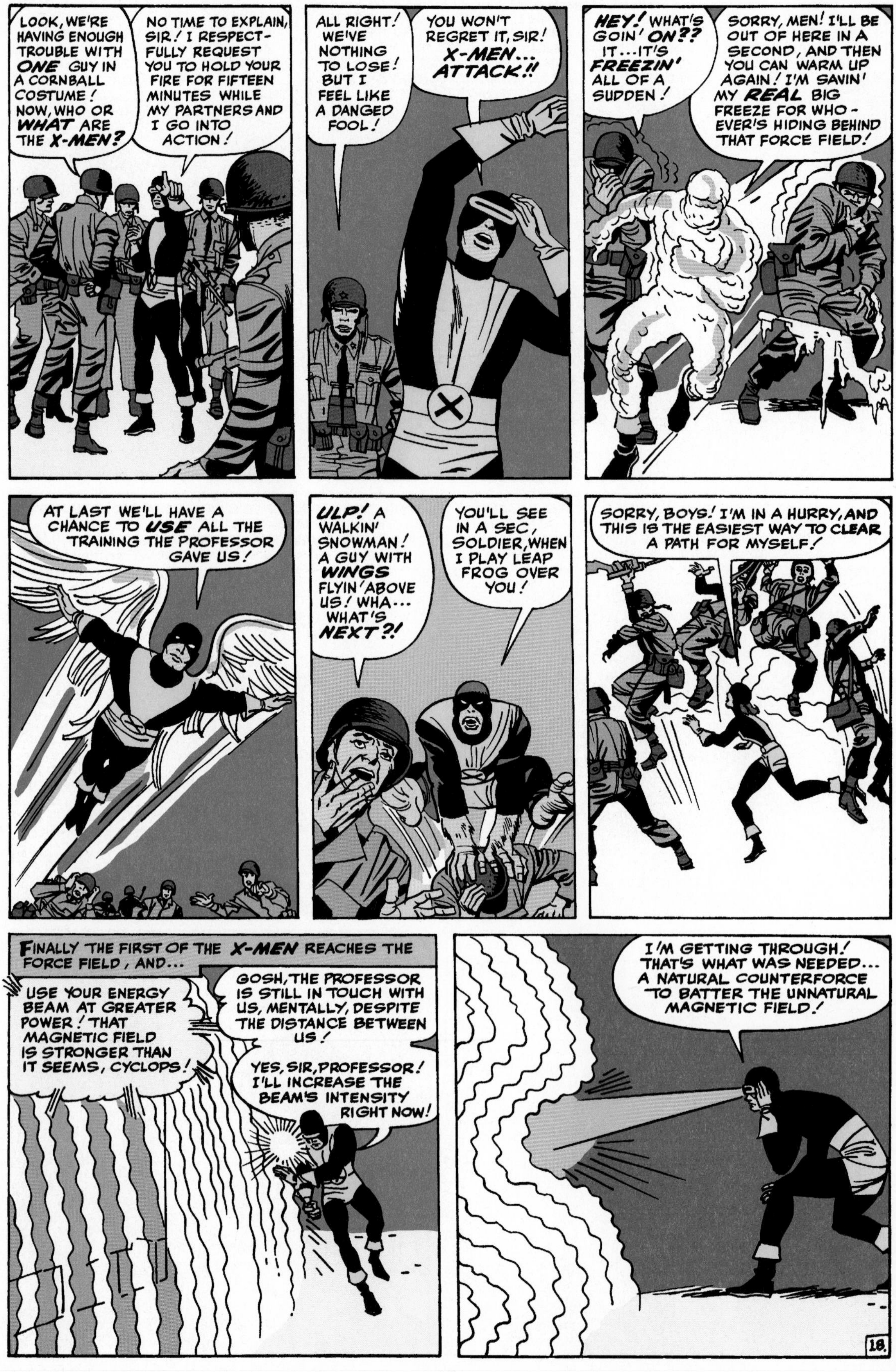

LOOK, WE'RE HAVING ENOUGH TROUBLE WITH ONE GUY IN A CORNBALL COSTUME! NOW, WHO OR WHAT ARE THE X-MEN?
NO TIME TO EXPLAIN, SIR! I RESPECTFULLY REQUEST YOU TO HOLD YOUR FIRE FOR FIFTEEN MINUTES WHILE MY PARTNERS AND I GO INTO ACTION!
ALL RIGHT! WE'VE NOTHING TO LOSE! BUT I FEEL LIKE A DANGED FOOL!
YOU WON'T REGRET IT, SIR! X-MEN... ATTACK!!
HEY! WHAT'S GOIN' ON?? IT...IT'S FREEZIN' ALL OF A SUDDEN!
SORRY, MEN! I'LL BE OUT OF HERE IN A SECOND, AND THEN YOU CAN WARM UP AGAIN! I'M SAVIN' MY REAL BIG FREEZE FOR WHO-EVER'S HIDING BEHIND THAT FORCE FIELD!
AT LAST WE'LL HAVE A CHANCE TO USE ALL THE TRAINING THE PROFESSOR GAVE US!
ULP! A WALKIN' SNOWMAN! A GUY WITH WINGS FLYIN' ABOVE US! WHA... WHAT'S NEXT?!
YOU'LL SEE IN A SEC, SOLDIER, WHEN I PLAY LEAP FROG OVER YOU!
SORRY, BOYS! I'M IN A HURRY, AND THIS IS THE EASIEST WAY TO CLEAR A PATH FOR MYSELF!
FINALLY THE FIRST OF THE X-MEN REACHES THE FORCE FIELD, AND...
USE YOUR ENERGY BEAM AT GREATER POWER! THAT MAGNETIC FIELD IS STRONGER THAN IT SEEMS, CYCLOPS!
GOSH, THE PROFESSOR IS STILL IN TOUCH WITH US, MENTALLY, DESPITE THE DISTANCE BETWEEN US!
YES, SIR, PROFESSOR! I'LL INCREASE THE BEAM'S INTENSITY RIGHT NOW!
I'M GETTING THROUGH! THAT'S WHAT WAS NEEDED... A NATURAL COUNTERFORCE TO BATTER THE UNNATURAL MAGNETIC FIELD!
18.

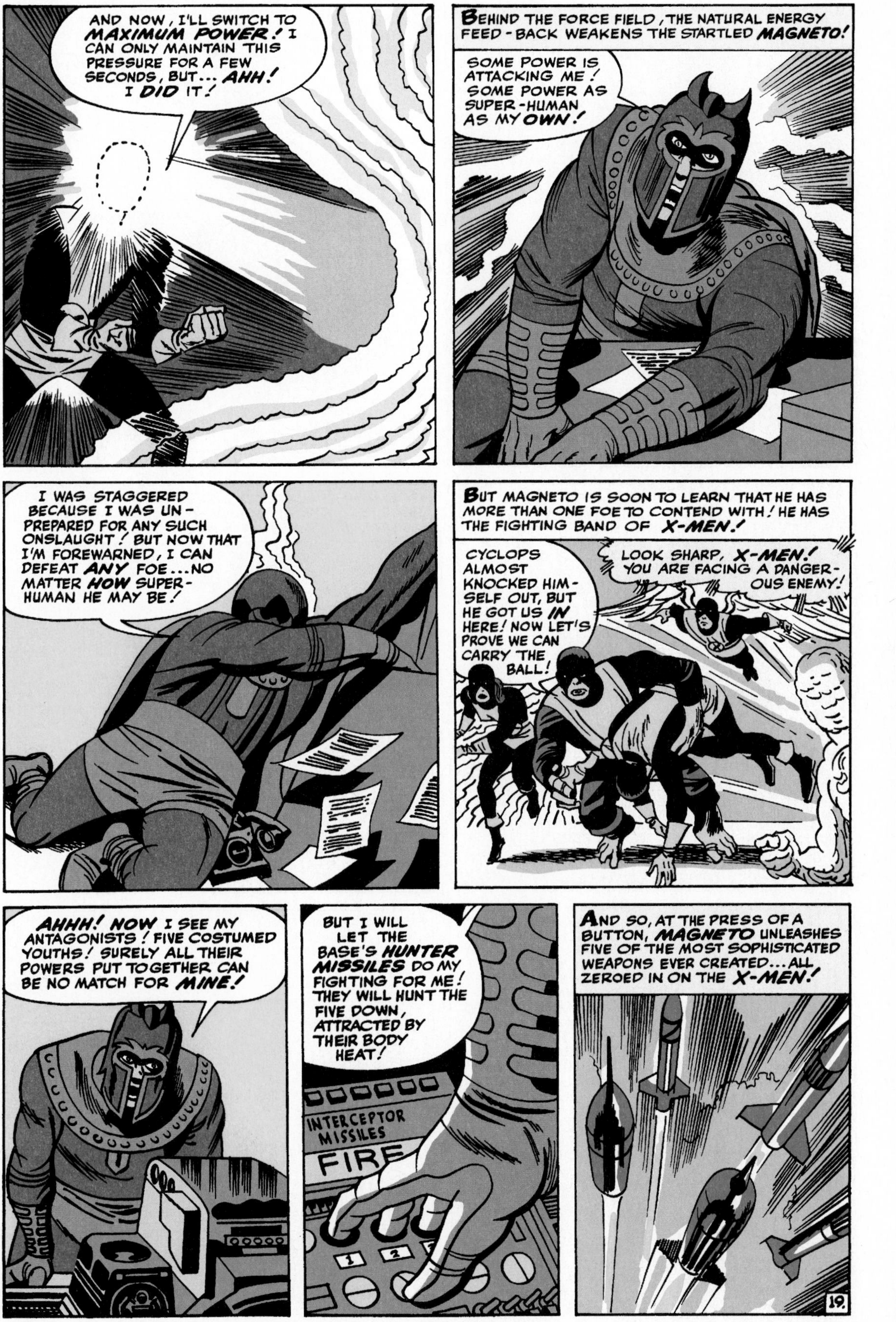

AND NOW, I'LL SWITCH TO MAXIMUM POWER! I CAN ONLY MAINTAIN THIS PRESSURE FOR A FEW SECONDS, BUT... AHH! I DID IT!
BEHIND THE FORCE FIELD, THE NATURAL ENERGY FEED-BACK WEAKENS THE STARTLED MAGNETO!
SOME POWER IS ATTACKING ME! SOME POWER AS SUPER-HUMAN AS MY OWN!
I WAS STAGGERED BECAUSE I WAS UN-PREPARED FOR ANY SUCH ONSLAUGHT! BUT NOW THAT I'M FOREWARNED, I CAN DEFEAT ANY FOE...NO MATTER HOW SUPER-HUMAN HE MAY BE!
BUT MAGNETO IS SOON TO LEARN THAT HE HAS MORE THAN ONE FOE TO CONTEND WITH! HE HAS THE FIGHTING BAND OF X-MEN!
CYCLOPS ALMOST KNOCKED HIM-SELF OUT, BUT HE GOT US IN HERE! NOW LET'S PROVE WE CAN CARRY THE BALL!
LOOK SHARP, X-MEN! YOU ARE FACING A DANGER-OUS ENEMY!
AHHH! NOW I SEE MY ANTAGONISTS! FIVE COSTUMED YOUTHS! SURELY ALL THEIR POWERS PUT TOGETHER CAN BE NO MATCH FOR MINE!
BUT I WILL LET THE BASE'S HUNTER MISSILES DO MY FIGHTING FOR ME! THEY WILL HUNT THE FIVE DOWN, ATTRACTED BY THEIR BODY HEAT!
INTERCEPTOR MISSILES
FIRE
1
2
AND SO, AT THE PRESS OF A BUTTON, MAGNETO UNLEASHES FIVE OF THE MOST SOPHISTICATED WEAPONS EVER CREATED... ALL ZEROED IN ON THE X-MEN!
19.

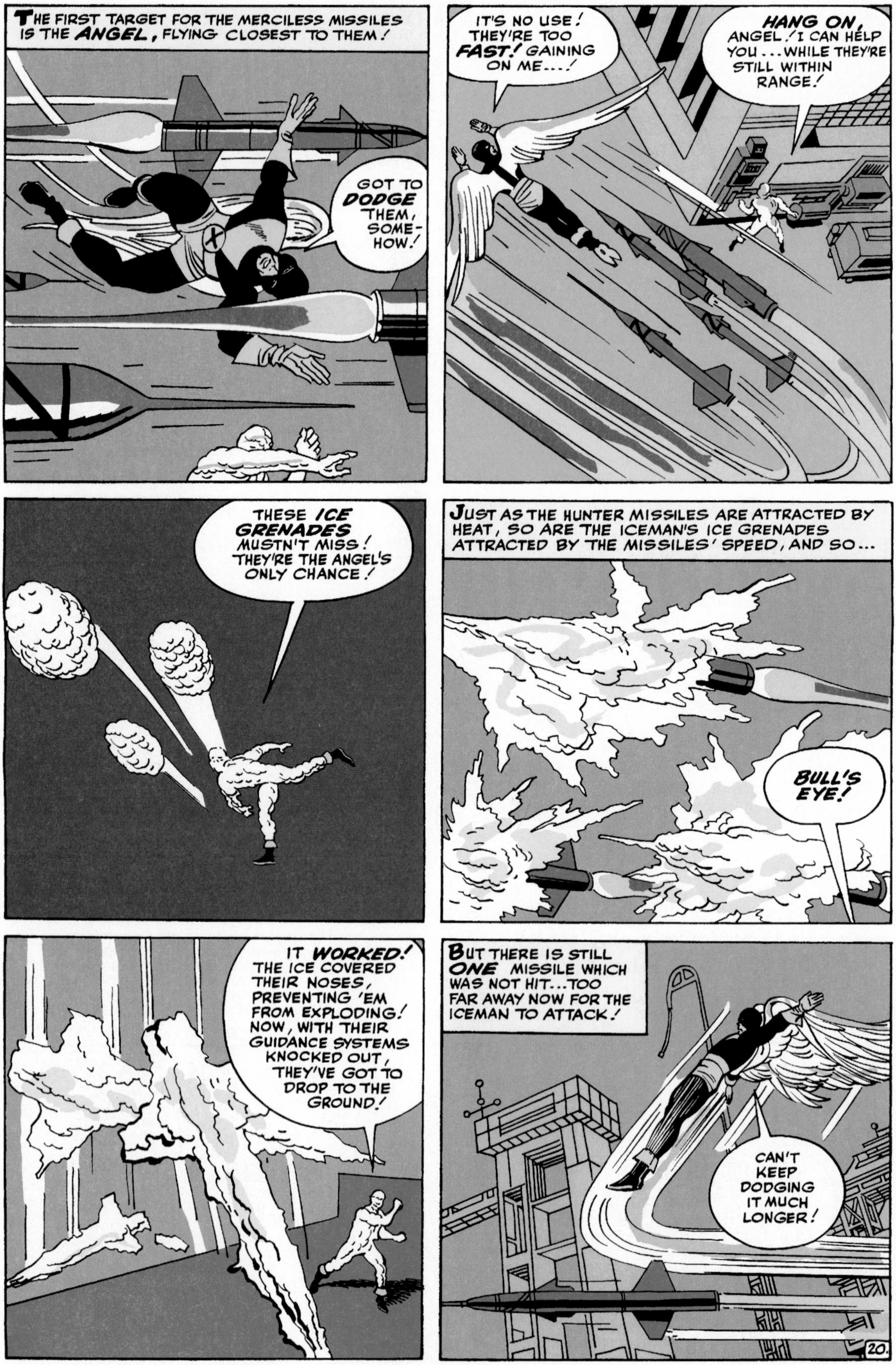
THE FIRST TARGET FOR THE MERCILESS MISSILES IS THE ANGEL, FLYING CLOSEST TO THEM!
GOT TO DODGE THEM, SOME-HOW!
IT'S NO USE! THEY'RE TOO FAST! GAINING ON ME...!
HANG ON, ANGEL! I CAN HELP YOU... WHILE THEY'RE STILL WITHIN RANGE!
THESE ICE GRENADES MUSTN'T MISS! THEY'RE THE ANGEL'S ONLY CHANCE!
JUST AS THE HUNTER MISSILES ARE ATTRACTED BY HEAT, SO ARE THE ICEMAN'S ICE GRENADES ATTRACTED BY THE MISSILES' SPEED, AND SO...
BULL'S EYE!
IT WORKED! THE ICE COVERED THEIR NOSES, PREVENTING 'EM FROM EXPLODING! NOW, WITH THEIR GUIDANCE SYSTEMS KNOCKED OUT, THEY'VE GOT TO DROP TO THE GROUND!
BUT THERE IS STILL ONE MISSILE WHICH WAS NOT HIT... TOO FAR AWAY NOW FOR THE ICEMAN TO ATTACK!
CAN'T KEEP DODGING IT MUCH LONGER!
20.

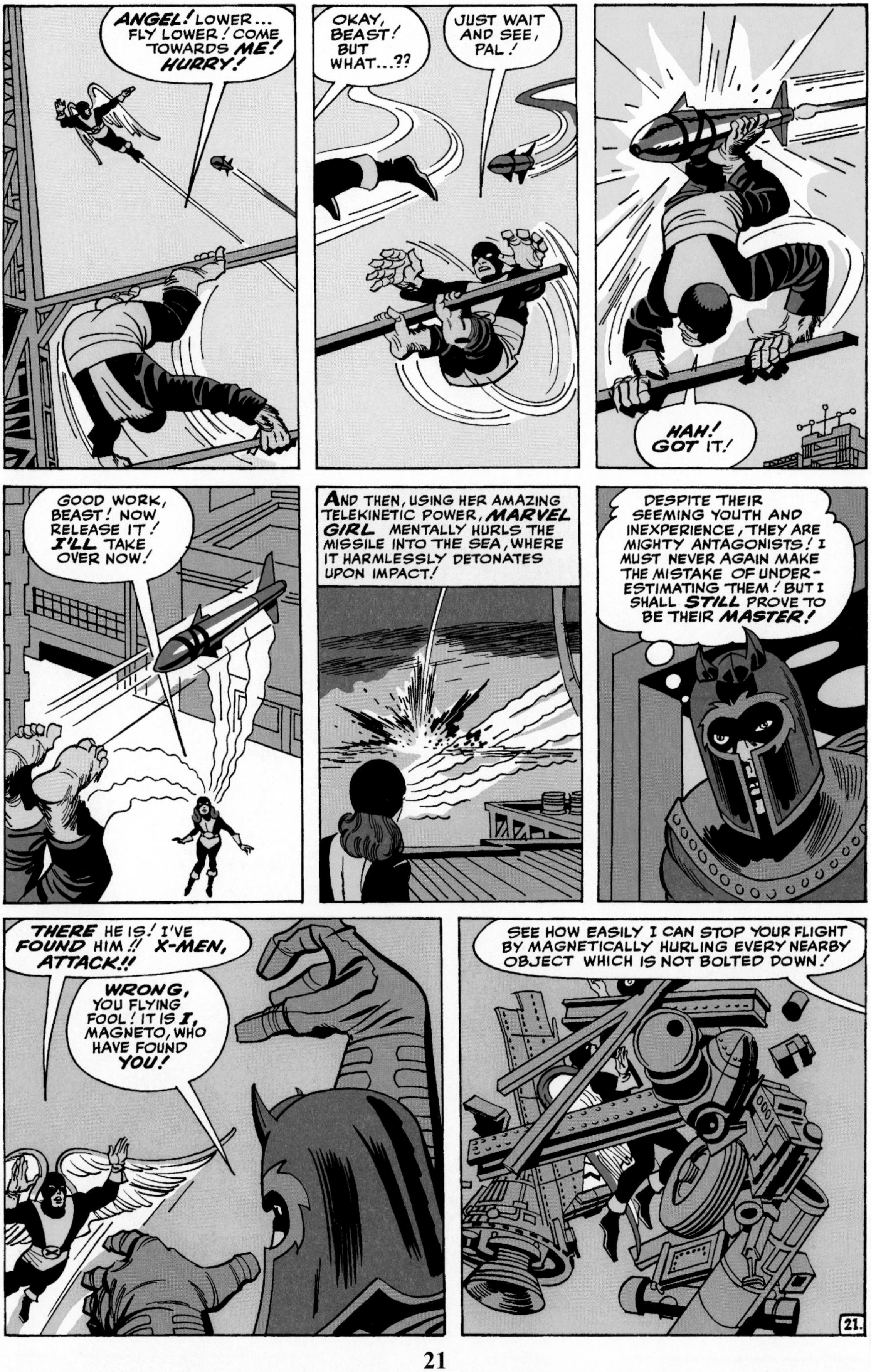
ANGEL! LOWER... FLY LOWER! COME TOWARDS ME! HURRY!
OKAY, BEAST! BUT WHAT...??
JUST WAIT AND SEE, PAL!
HAH! GOT IT!
GOOD WORK, BEAST! NOW RELEASE IT! I'LL TAKE OVER NOW!
AND THEN, USING HER AMAZING TELEKINETIC POWER, MARVEL GIRL MENTALLY HURLS THE MISSILE INTO THE SEA, WHERE IT HARMLESSLY DETONATES UPON IMPACT!
DESPITE THEIR SEEMING YOUTH AND INEXPERIENCE, THEY ARE MIGHTY ANTAGONISTS! I MUST NEVER AGAIN MAKE THE MISTAKE OF UNDER-ESTIMATING THEM! BUT I SHALL STILL PROVE TO BE THEIR MASTER!
THERE HE IS! I'VE FOUND HIM!! X-MEN, ATTACK!!
WRONG, YOU FLYING FOOL! IT IS I, MAGNETO, WHO HAVE FOUND YOU!
SEE HOW EASILY I CAN STOP YOUR FLIGHT BY MAGNETICALLY HURLING EVERY NEARBY OBJECT WHICH IS NOT BOLTED DOWN!
21.

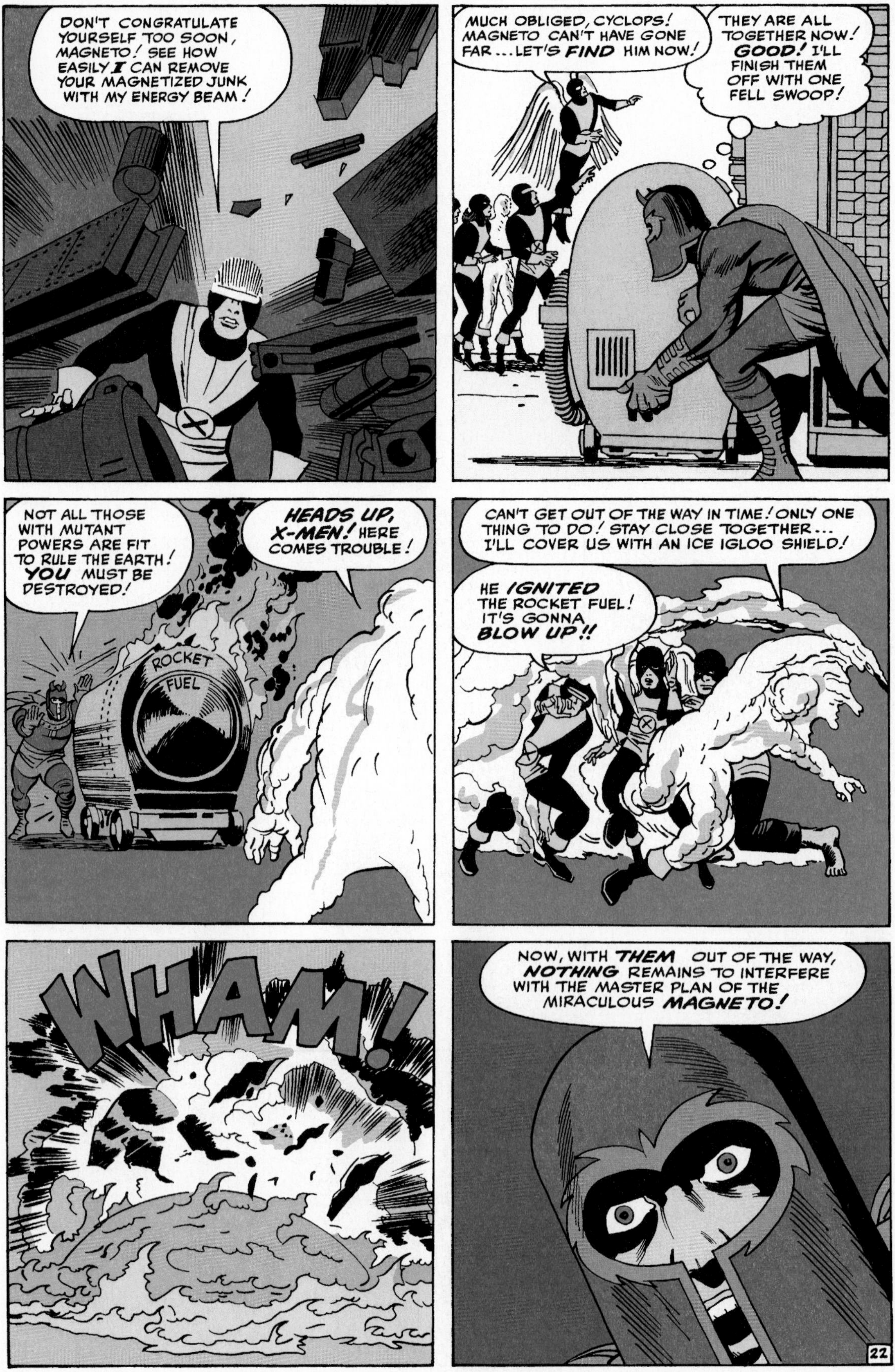
DON'T CONGRATULATE YOURSELF TOO SOON, MAGNETO! SEE HOW EASILY I CAN REMOVE YOUR MAGNETIZED JUNK WITH MY ENERGY BEAM!
MUCH OBLIGED, CYCLOPS! MAGNETO CAN'T HAVE GONE FAR...LET'S FIND HIM NOW!
THEY ARE ALL TOGETHER NOW! GOOD! I'LL FINISH THEM OFF WITH ONE FELL SWOOP!
NOT ALL THOSE WITH MUTANT POWERS ARE FIT TO RULE THE EARTH! YOU MUST BE DESTROYED!
HEADS UP, X-MEN! HERE COMES TROUBLE!
ROCKET FUEL
CAN'T GET OUT OF THE WAY IN TIME! ONLY ONE THING TO DO! STAY CLOSE TOGETHER... I'LL COVER US WITH AN ICE IGLOO SHIELD!
HE IGNITED THE ROCKET FUEL! IT'S GONNA BLOW UP!!
WHAM!
NOW, WITH THEM OUT OF THE WAY, NOTHING REMAINS TO INTERFERE WITH THE MASTER PLAN OF THE MIRACULOUS MAGNETO!
22

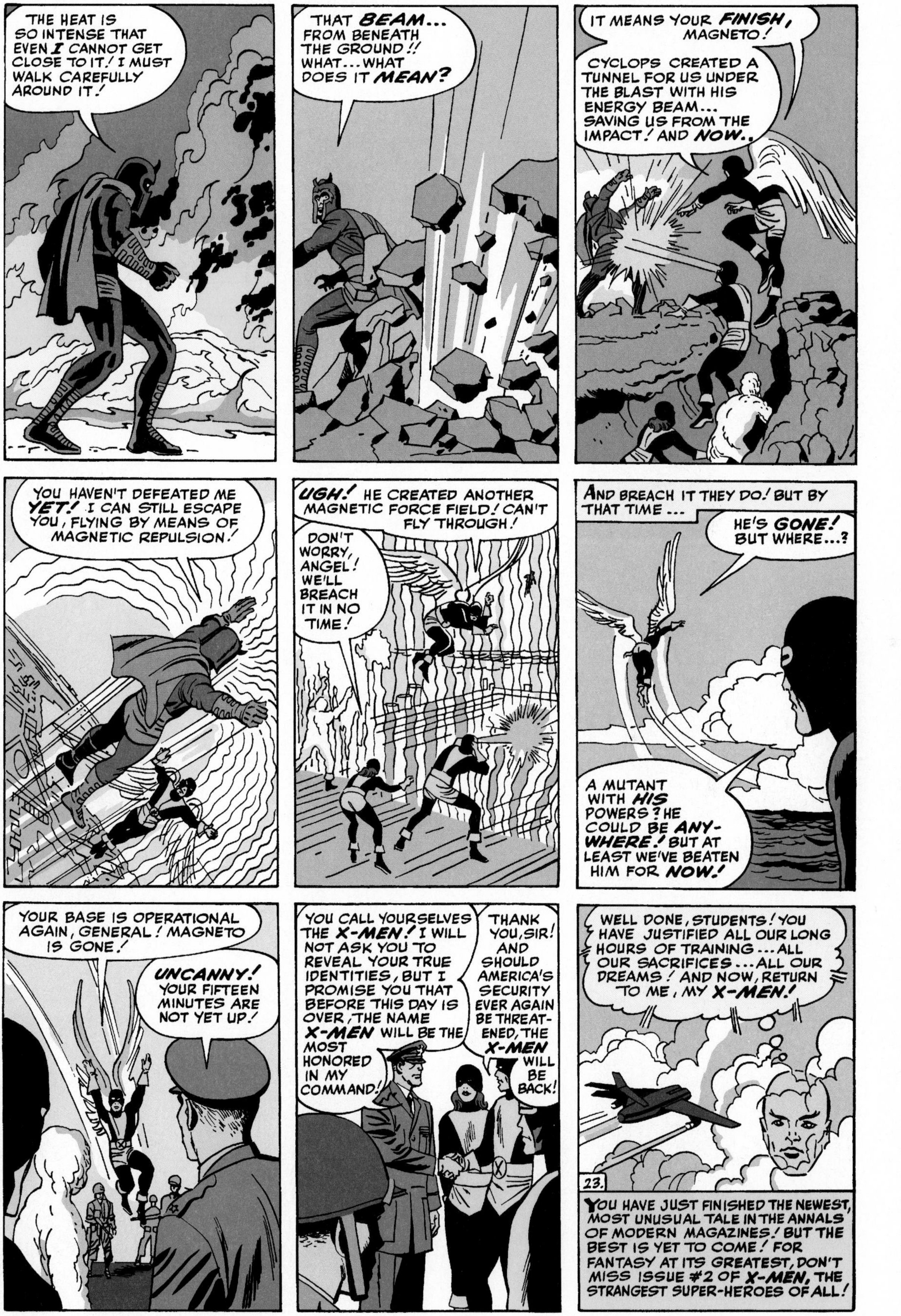
THE HEAT IS SO INTENSE THAT EVEN I CANNOT GET CLOSE TO IT! I MUST WALK CAREFULLY AROUND IT!
THAT BEAM... FROM BENEATH THE GROUND!! WHAT...WHAT DOES IT MEAN?
IT MEANS YOUR FINISH, MAGNETO!
CYCLOPS CREATED A TUNNEL FOR US UNDER THE BLAST WITH HIS ENERGY BEAM... SAVING US FROM THE IMPACT! AND NOW..
YOU HAVEN'T DEFEATED ME YET! I CAN STILL ESCAPE YOU, FLYING BY MEANS OF MAGNETIC REPULSION!
UGH! HE CREATED ANOTHER MAGNETIC FORCE FIELD! CAN'T FLY THROUGH!
DON'T WORRY, ANGEL! WE'LL BREACH IT IN NO TIME!
AND BREACH IT THEY DO! BUT BY THAT TIME ...
HE'S GONE! BUT WHERE...?
A MUTANT WITH HIS POWERS? HE COULD BE ANYWHERE! BUT AT LEAST WE'VE BEATEN HIM FOR NOW!
YOUR BASE IS OPERATIONAL AGAIN, GENERAL! MAGNETO IS GONE!
UNCANNY! YOUR FIFTEEN MINUTES ARE NOT YET UP!
YOU CALL YOURSELVES THE X-MEN! I WILL NOT ASK YOU TO REVEAL YOUR TRUE IDENTITIES, BUT I PROMISE YOU THAT BEFORE THIS DAY IS OVER, THE NAME X-MEN WILL BE THE MOST HONORED IN MY COMMAND!
THANK YOU, SIR! AND SHOULD AMERICA'S SECURITY EVER AGAIN BE THREATENED, THE X-MEN WILL BE BACK!
WELL DONE, STUDENTS! YOU HAVE JUSTIFIED ALL OUR LONG HOURS OF TRAINING ... ALL OUR SACRIFICES ... ALL OUR DREAMS! AND NOW, RETURN TO ME, MY X-MEN!
23.
YOU HAVE JUST FINISHED THE NEWEST, MOST UNUSUAL TALE IN THE ANNALS OF MODERN MAGAZINES! BUT THE BEST IS YET TO COME! FOR FANTASY AT ITS GREATEST, DON'T MISS ISSUE #2 OF X-MEN, THE STRANGEST SUPER-HEROES OF ALL!

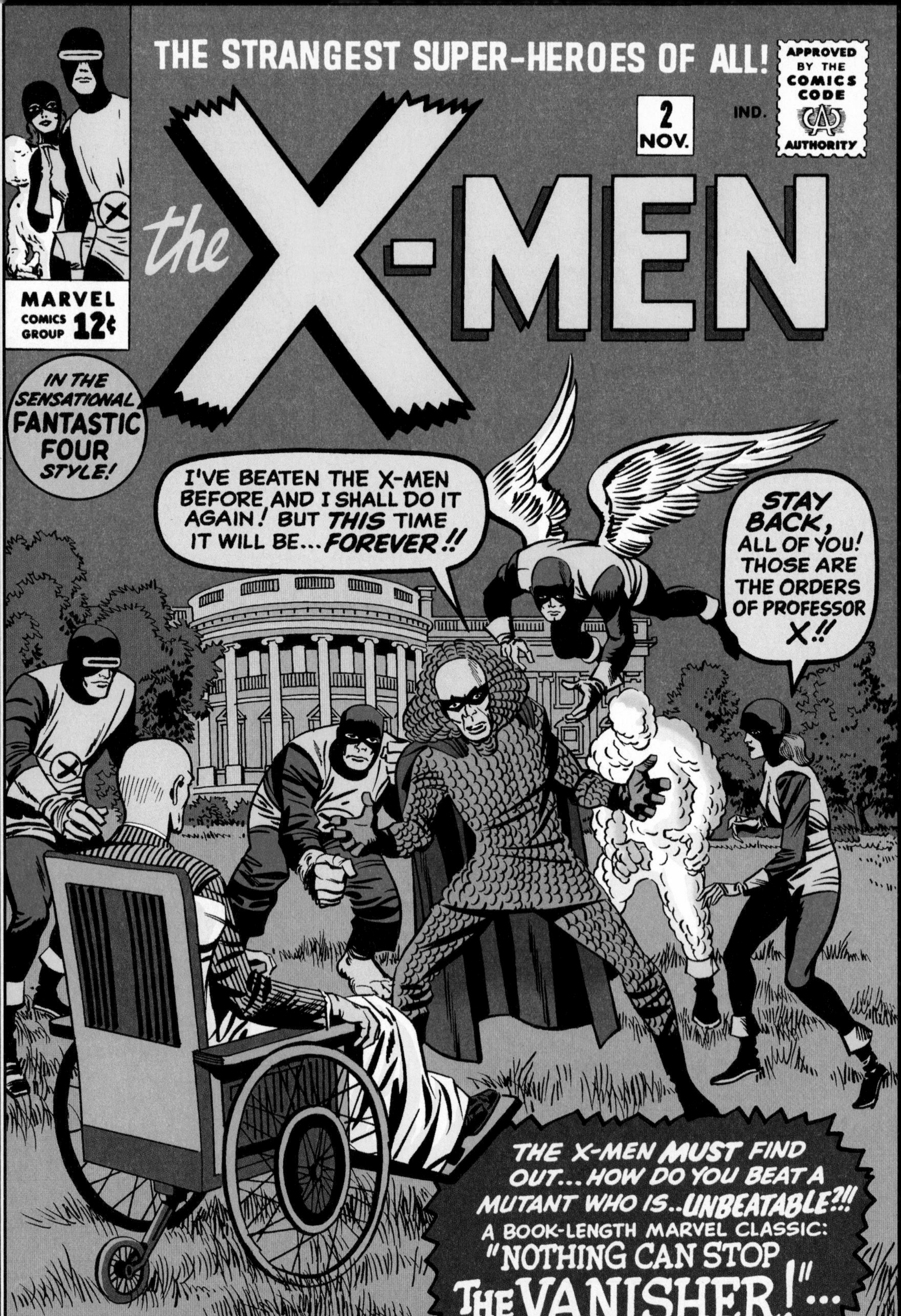
THE STRANGEST SUPER-HEROES OF ALL!
APPROVED BY THE COMICS CODE AUTHORITY
2 NOV.
IND.
the X-MEN
MARVEL COMICS GROUP 12¢
IN THE SENSATIONAL FANTASTIC FOUR STYLE!
I'VE BEATEN THE X-MEN BEFORE AND I SHALL DO IT AGAIN! BUT THIS TIME IT WILL BE... FOREVER!!
STAY BACK, ALL OF YOU! THOSE ARE THE ORDERS OF PROFESSOR X!!
THE X-MEN MUST FIND OUT... HOW DO YOU BEAT A MUTANT WHO IS.. UNBEATABLE?!!
A BOOK-LENGTH MARVEL CLASSIC:
"NOTHING CAN STOP THE VANISHER!"...

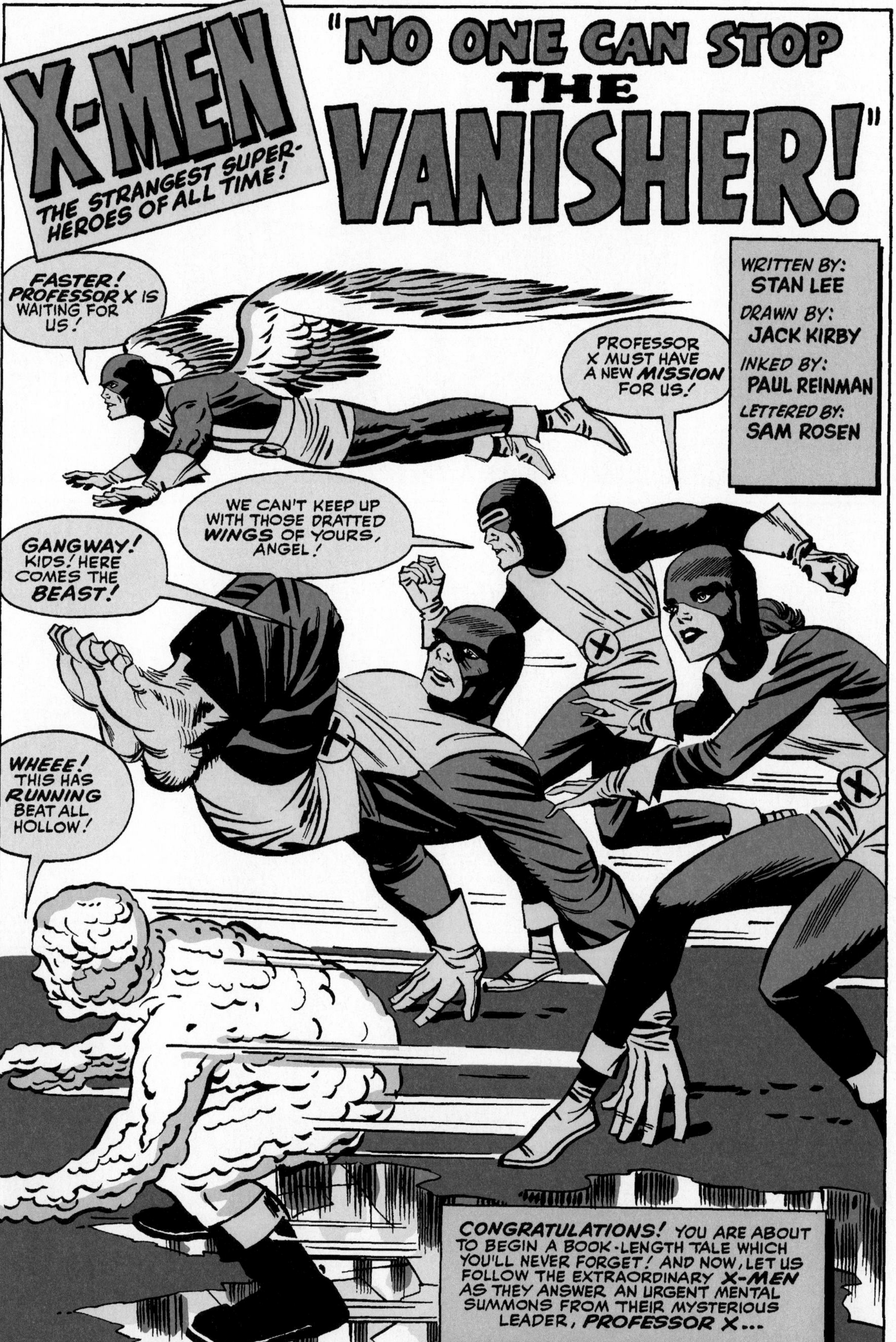
X-MEN
THE STRANGEST SUPER-HEROES OF ALL TIME!
"NO ONE CAN STOP THE VANISHER!"
WRITTEN BY: STAN LEE
DRAWN BY: JACK KIRBY
INKED BY: PAUL REINMAN
LETTERED BY: SAM ROSEN
FASTER! PROFESSOR X IS WAITING FOR US!
PROFESSOR X MUST HAVE A NEW MISSION FOR US!
WE CAN'T KEEP UP WITH THOSE DRATTED WINGS OF YOURS, ANGEL!
GANGWAY! KIDS! HERE COMES THE BEAST!
WHEEE! THIS HAS RUNNING BEAT ALL HOLLOW!
CONGRATULATIONS! YOU ARE ABOUT TO BEGIN A BOOK-LENGTH TALE WHICH YOU'LL NEVER FORGET! AND NOW, LET US FOLLOW THE EXTRAORDINARY X-MEN AS THEY ANSWER AN URGENT MENTAL SUMMONS FROM THEIR MYSTERIOUS LEADER, PROFESSOR X...

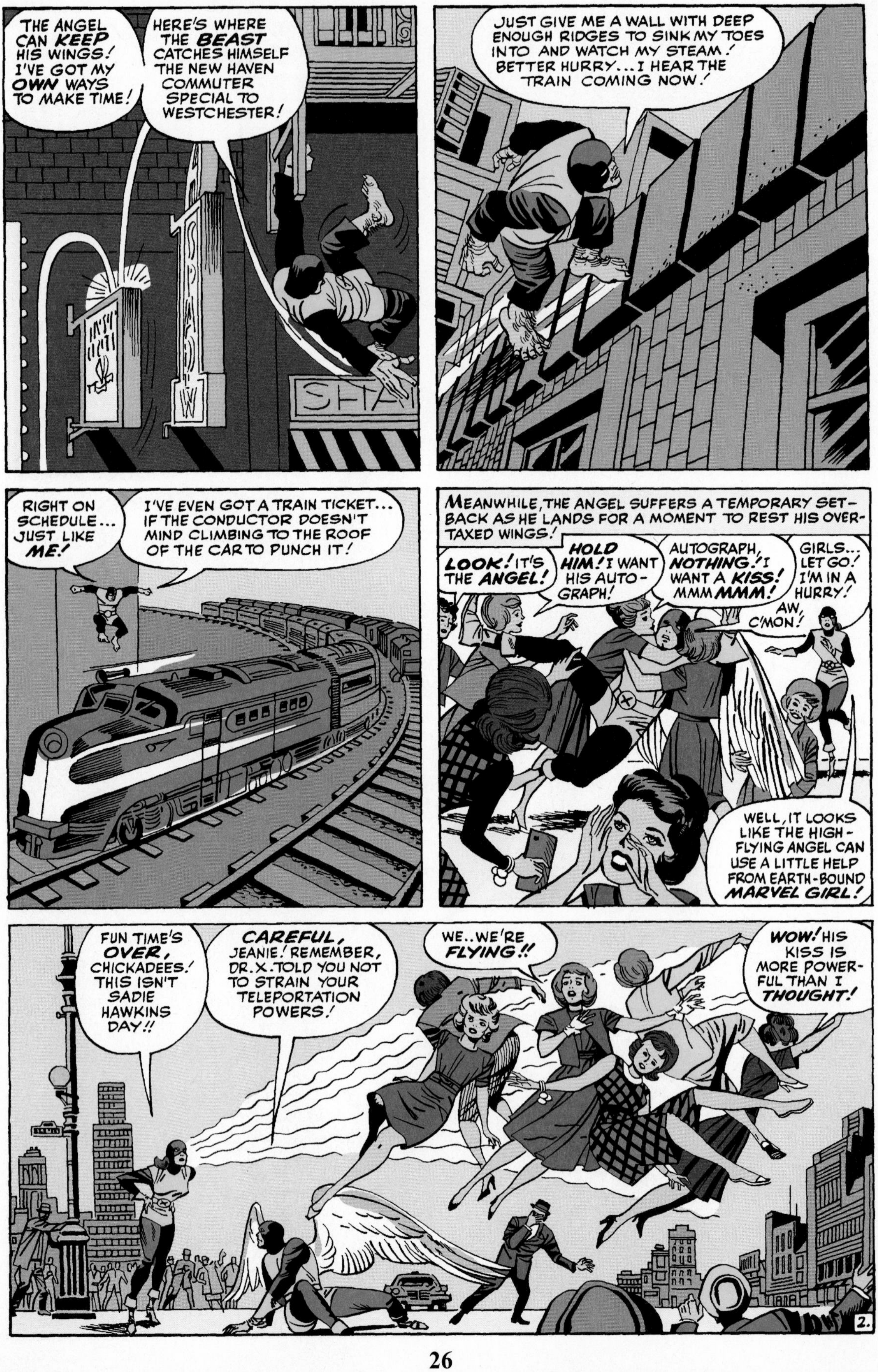
THE ANGEL CAN KEEP HIS WINGS! I'VE GOT MY OWN WAYS TO MAKE TIME!
HERE'S WHERE THE BEAST CATCHES HIMSELF THE NEW HAVEN COMMUTER SPECIAL TO WESTCHESTER!
SHA
JUST GIVE ME A WALL WITH DEEP ENOUGH RIDGES TO SINK MY TOES INTO AND WATCH MY STEAM! BETTER HURRY... I HEAR THE TRAIN COMING NOW!
RIGHT ON SCHEDULE... JUST LIKE ME!
I'VE EVEN GOT A TRAIN TICKET... IF THE CONDUCTOR DOESN'T MIND CLIMBING TO THE ROOF OF THE CAR TO PUNCH IT!
MEANWHILE, THE ANGEL SUFFERS A TEMPORARY SET-BACK AS HE LANDS FOR A MOMENT TO REST HIS OVER-TAXED WINGS!
LOOK! IT'S THE ANGEL!
HOLD HIM! I WANT HIS AUTO-GRAPH!
AUTOGRAPH, NOTHING! I WANT A KISS! MMM MMM!
GIRLS... LET GO! I'M IN A HURRY!
AW, C'MON!
WELL, IT LOOKS LIKE THE HIGH-FLYING ANGEL CAN USE A LITTLE HELP FROM EARTH-BOUND MARVEL GIRL!
FUN TIME'S OVER, CHICKADEES! THIS ISN'T SADIE HAWKINS DAY!!
CAREFUL, JEANIE! REMEMBER, DR. X. TOLD YOU NOT TO STRAIN YOUR TELEPORTATION POWERS!
WE..WE'RE FLYING!!
WOW! HIS KISS IS MORE POWER-FUL THAN I THOUGHT!
2.

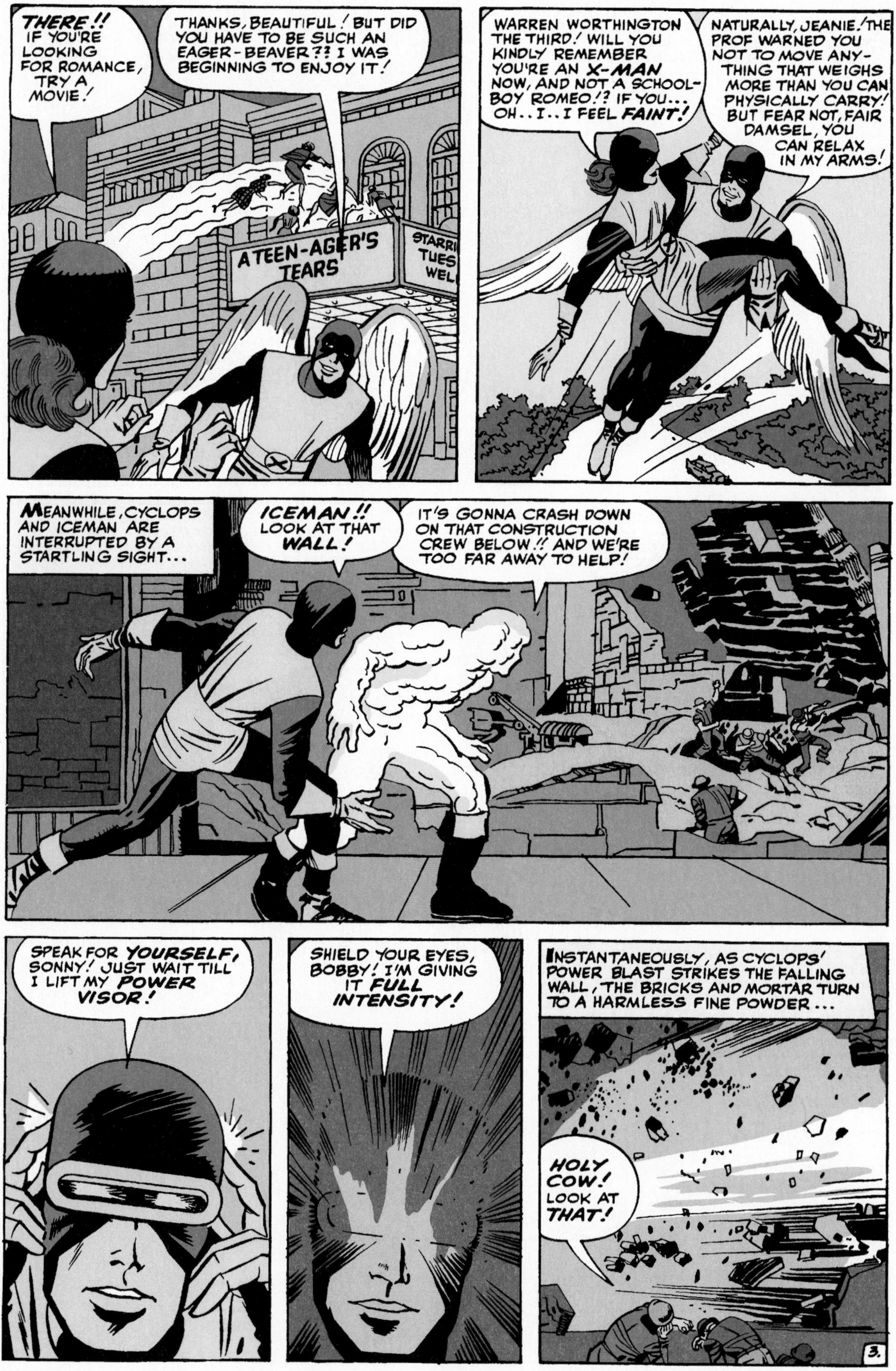
THERE!! IF YOU'RE LOOKING FOR ROMANCE, TRY A MOVIE!
THANKS, BEAUTIFUL! BUT DID YOU HAVE TO BE SUCH AN EAGER-BEAVER?? I WAS BEGINNING TO ENJOY IT!
A TEEN-AGER'S TEARS
WARREN WORTHINGTON THE THIRD! WILL YOU KINDLY REMEMBER YOU'RE AN X-MAN NOW, AND NOT A SCHOOL-BOY ROMEO!? IF YOU... OH.. I.. I FEEL FAINT!
NATURALLY, JEANIE! THE PROF WARNED YOU NOT TO MOVE ANY-THING THAT WEIGHS MORE THAN YOU CAN PHYSICALLY CARRY! BUT FEAR NOT, FAIR DAMSEL, YOU CAN RELAX IN MY ARMS!
MEANWHILE, CYCLOPS AND ICEMAN ARE INTERRUPTED BY A STARTLING SIGHT...
ICEMAN!! LOOK AT THAT WALL!
IT'S GONNA CRASH DOWN ON THAT CONSTRUCTION CREW BELOW!! AND WE'RE TOO FAR AWAY TO HELP!
SPEAK FOR YOURSELF, SONNY! JUST WAIT TILL I LIFT MY POWER VISOR!
SHIELD YOUR EYES, BOBBY! I'M GIVING IT FULL INTENSITY!
INSTANTANEOUSLY, AS CYCLOPS' POWER BLAST STRIKES THE FALLING WALL, THE BRICKS AND MORTAR TURN TO A HARMLESS FINE POWDER...
HOLY COW! LOOK AT THAT!
3.

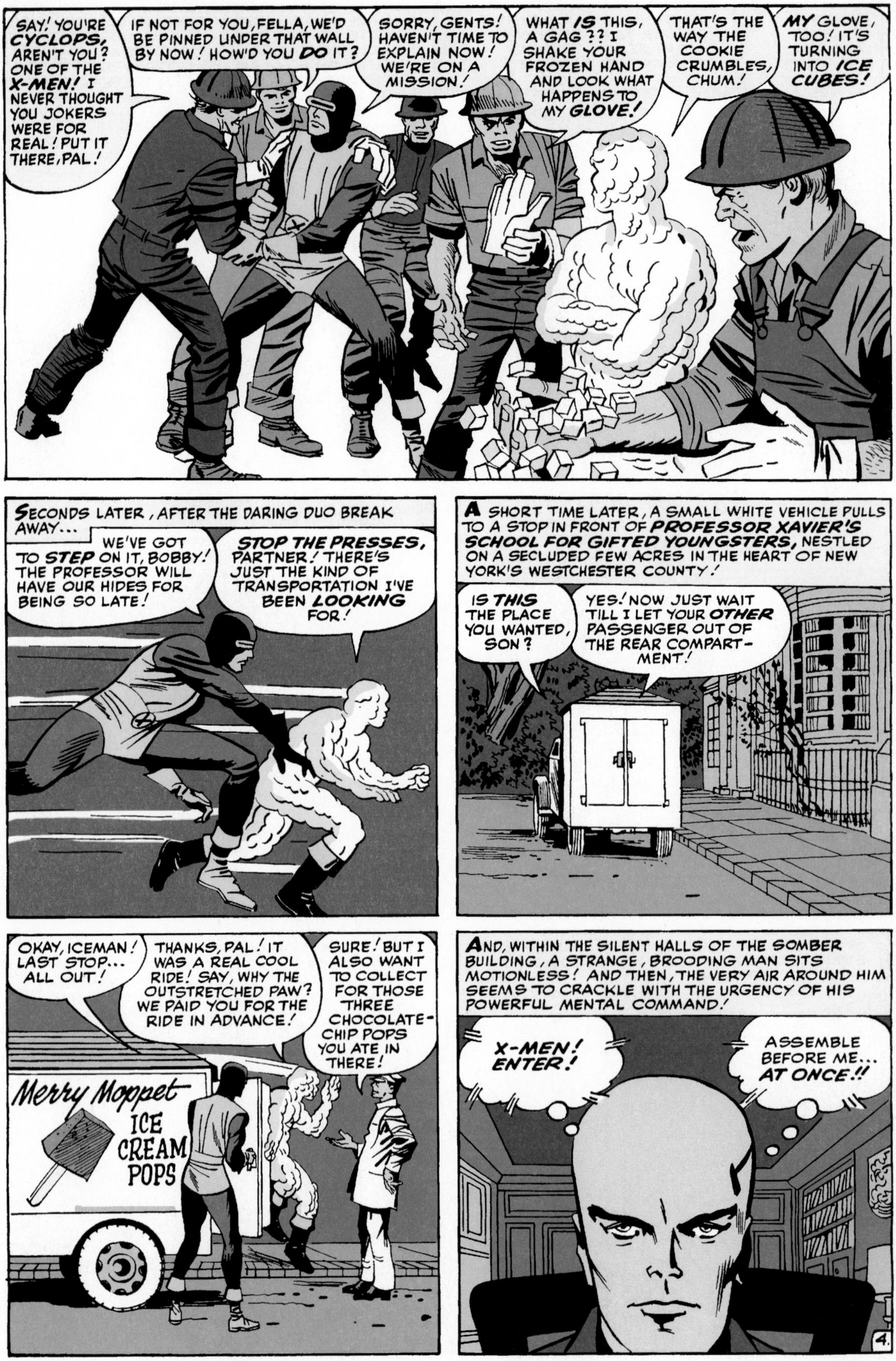
SAY! YOU'RE CYCLOPS, AREN'T YOU? ONE OF THE X-MEN! I NEVER THOUGHT YOU JOKERS WERE FOR REAL! PUT IT THERE, PAL!
IF NOT FOR YOU, FELLA, WE'D BE PINNED UNDER THAT WALL BY NOW! HOW'D YOU DO IT?
SORRY, GENTS! HAVEN'T TIME TO EXPLAIN NOW! WE'RE ON A MISSION!
WHAT IS THIS, A GAG ?? I SHAKE YOUR FROZEN HAND AND LOOK WHAT HAPPENS TO MY GLOVE!
THAT'S THE WAY THE COOKIE CRUMBLES, CHUM!
MY GLOVE, TOO! IT'S TURNING INTO ICE CUBES!
SECONDS LATER, AFTER THE DARING DUO BREAK AWAY...
WE'VE GOT TO STEP ON IT, BOBBY! THE PROFESSOR WILL HAVE OUR HIDES FOR BEING SO LATE!
STOP THE PRESSES, PARTNER! THERE'S JUST THE KIND OF TRANSPORTATION I'VE BEEN LOOKING FOR!
A SHORT TIME LATER, A SMALL WHITE VEHICLE PULLS TO A STOP IN FRONT OF PROFESSOR XAVIER'S SCHOOL FOR GIFTED YOUNGSTERS, NESTLED ON A SECLUDED FEW ACRES IN THE HEART OF NEW YORK'S WESTCHESTER COUNTY!
IS THIS THE PLACE YOU WANTED, SON?
YES! NOW JUST WAIT TILL I LET YOUR OTHER PASSENGER OUT OF THE REAR COMPART-MENT!
OKAY, ICEMAN! LAST STOP... ALL OUT!
THANKS, PAL! IT WAS A REAL COOL RIDE! SAY, WHY THE OUTSTRETCHED PAW? WE PAID YOU FOR THE RIDE IN ADVANCE!
SURE! BUT I ALSO WANT TO COLLECT FOR THOSE THREE CHOCOLATE-CHIP POPS YOU ATE IN THERE!
Merry Moppet
ICE CREAM POPS
AND, WITHIN THE SILENT HALLS OF THE SOMBER BUILDING, A STRANGE, BROODING MAN SITS MOTIONLESS! AND THEN, THE VERY AIR AROUND HIM SEEMS TO CRACKLE WITH THE URGENCY OF HIS POWERFUL MENTAL COMMAND!
X-MEN! ENTER!
ASSEMBLE BEFORE ME... AT ONCE!!
4.

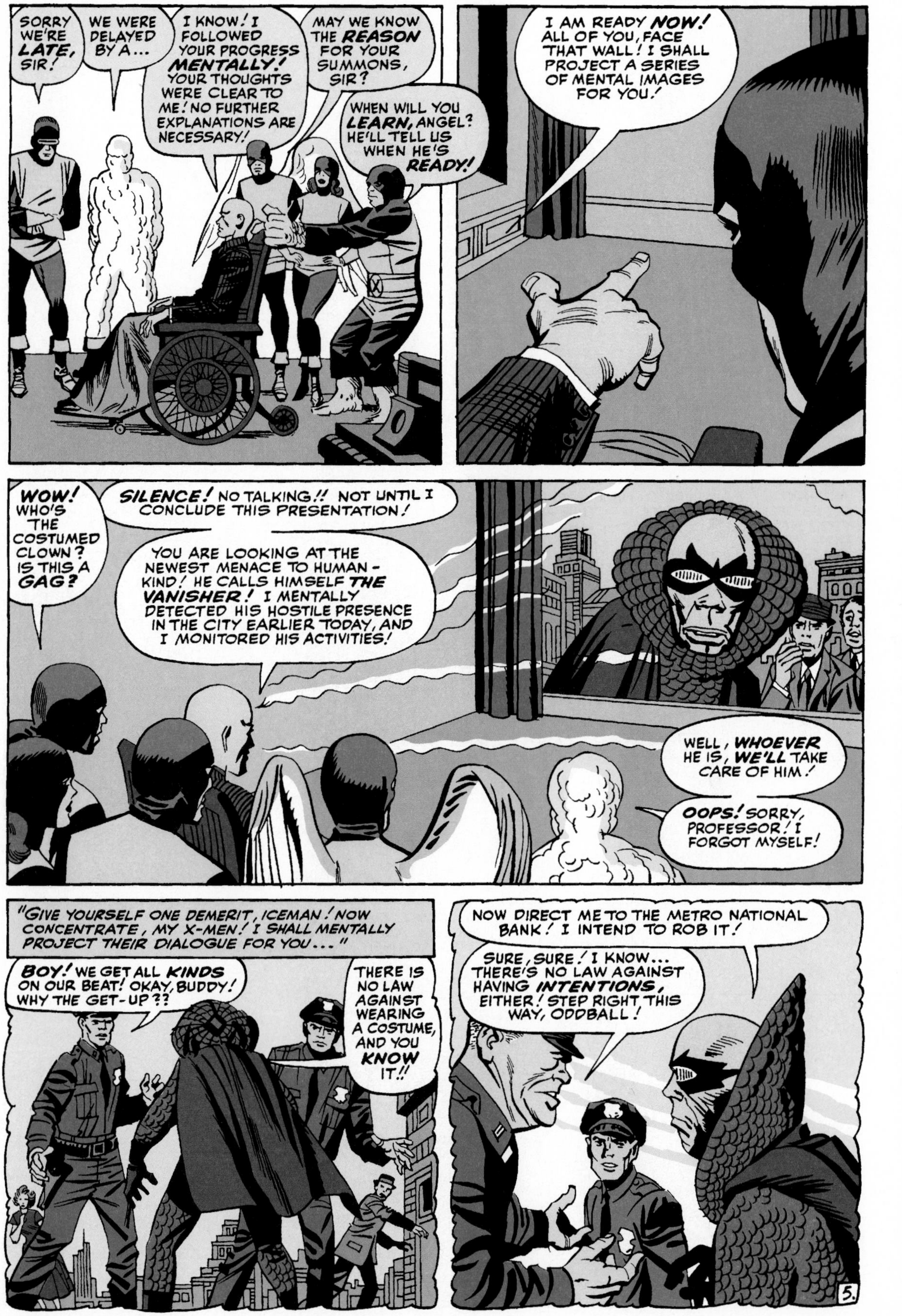
SORRY WE'RE LATE, SIR!
WE WERE DELAYED BY A...
I KNOW! I FOLLOWED YOUR PROGRESS MENTALLY! YOUR THOUGHTS WERE CLEAR TO ME! NO FURTHER EXPLANATIONS ARE NECESSARY!
MAY WE KNOW THE REASON FOR YOUR SUMMONS, SIR?
WHEN WILL YOU LEARN, ANGEL? HE'LL TELL US WHEN HE'S READY!
I AM READY NOW! ALL OF YOU, FACE THAT WALL! I SHALL PROJECT A SERIES OF MENTAL IMAGES FOR YOU!
WOW! WHO'S THE COSTUMED CLOWN? IS THIS A GAG?
SILENCE! NO TALKING!! NOT UNTIL I CONCLUDE THIS PRESENTATION!
YOU ARE LOOKING AT THE NEWEST MENACE TO HUMAN-KIND! HE CALLS HIMSELF THE VANISHER! I MENTALLY DETECTED HIS HOSTILE PRESENCE IN THE CITY EARLIER TODAY, AND I MONITORED HIS ACTIVITIES!
WELL, WHOEVER HE IS, WE'LL TAKE CARE OF HIM!
OOPS! SORRY, PROFESSOR! I FORGOT MYSELF!
"GIVE YOURSELF ONE DEMERIT, ICEMAN! NOW CONCENTRATE, MY X-MEN! I SHALL MENTALLY PROJECT THEIR DIALOGUE FOR YOU..."
BOY! WE GET ALL KINDS ON OUR BEAT! OKAY, BUDDY! WHY THE GET-UP??
THERE IS NO LAW AGAINST WEARING A COSTUME, AND YOU KNOW IT!!
NOW DIRECT ME TO THE METRO NATIONAL BANK! I INTEND TO ROB IT!
SURE, SURE! I KNOW... THERE'S NO LAW AGAINST HAVING INTENTIONS, EITHER! STEP RIGHT THIS WAY, ODDBALL!
5.

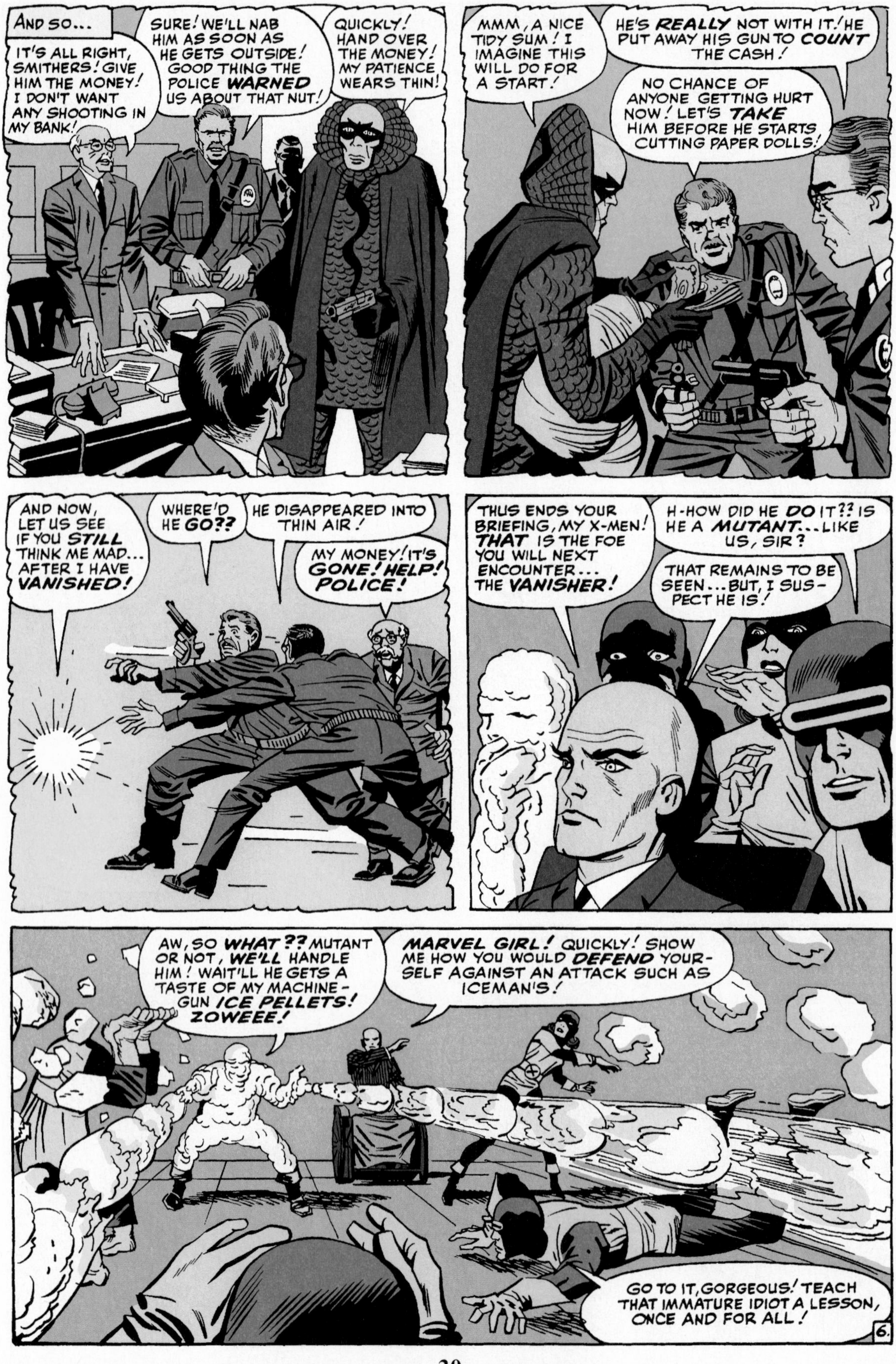

AND SO...
IT'S ALL RIGHT, SMITHERS! GIVE HIM THE MONEY! I DON'T WANT ANY SHOOTING IN MY BANK!
SURE! WE'LL NAB HIM AS SOON AS HE GETS OUTSIDE! GOOD THING THE POLICE WARNED US ABOUT THAT NUT!
QUICKLY! HAND OVER THE MONEY! MY PATIENCE WEARS THIN!
MMM, A NICE TIDY SUM! I IMAGINE THIS WILL DO FOR A START!
HE'S REALLY NOT WITH IT! HE PUT AWAY HIS GUN TO COUNT THE CASH!
NO CHANCE OF ANYONE GETTING HURT NOW! LET'S TAKE HIM BEFORE HE STARTS CUTTING PAPER DOLLS!
AND NOW, LET US SEE IF YOU STILL THINK ME MAD... AFTER I HAVE VANISHED!
WHERE'D HE GO??
HE DISAPPEARED INTO THIN AIR!
MY MONEY! IT'S GONE! HELP! POLICE!
THUS ENDS YOUR BRIEFING, MY X-MEN! THAT IS THE FOE YOU WILL NEXT ENCOUNTER... THE VANISHER!
H-HOW DID HE DO IT?? IS HE A MUTANT... LIKE US, SIR?
THAT REMAINS TO BE SEEN... BUT, I SUSPECT HE IS!
AW, SO WHAT?? MUTANT OR NOT, WE'LL HANDLE HIM! WAIT'LL HE GETS A TASTE OF MY MACHINE-GUN ICE PELLETS! ZOWEEE!
MARVEL GIRL! QUICKLY! SHOW ME HOW YOU WOULD DEFEND YOURSELF AGAINST AN ATTACK SUCH AS ICEMAN'S!
GO TO IT, GORGEOUS! TEACH THAT IMMATURE IDIOT A LESSON, ONCE AND FOR ALL!
6.

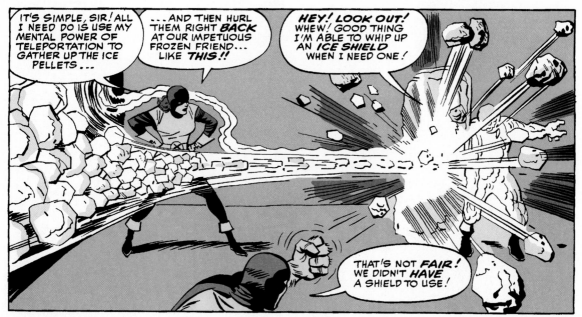

IT'S SIMPLE, SIR! ALL I NEED DO IS USE MY MENTAL POWER OF TELEPORTATION TO GATHER UP THE ICE PELLETS...

...AND THEN HURL THEM RIGHT *BACK* AT OUR IMPETUOUS FROZEN FRIEND... LIKE *THIS!!*

HEY! LOOK OUT! WHEW! GOOD THING I'M ABLE TO WHIP UP AN ICE SHIELD WHEN I NEED ONE!

THAT'S NOT *FAIR!* WE DIDN'T *HAVE* A SHIELD TO USE!

ENOUGH! GIVE ME YOUR ATTENTION NOW! SUCH BATTERING TACTICS WILL DO YOU NO GOOD AGAINST A FOE LIKE THE VANISHER!

WELL, THEN, WHAT...???

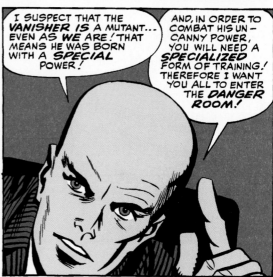

I SUSPECT THAT THE *VANISHER IS* A MUTANT... EVEN AS *WE* ARE! THAT MEANS HE WAS BORN WITH A *SPECIAL* POWER!

AND, IN ORDER TO COMBAT HIS UN-CANNY POWER, YOU WILL NEED A *SPECIALIZED* FORM OF TRAINING! THEREFORE I WANT YOU ALL TO ENTER THE DANGER ROOM!

THE *DANGER ROOM!* A HUGE UNFURNISHED CHAMBER WHICH HOUSES COUNTLESS HIDDEN PERILS!

ANGEL! YOUR TEST SHALL BE THE FIRST! YOU ARE TO FLY TO THE CENTER OF THE CHAMBER, AND CIRCLE THE ROOM AT *TOP SPEED!*

PREPARE YOURSELF FOR MISSILES WHICH SHALL HURTLE TOWARDS YOU UNEXPECTEDLY!

ROGER, SIR!

THERE GO THE FIRST FEW MISSILES! SO FAR, THIS TEST IS A *SNAP!*

7.

31

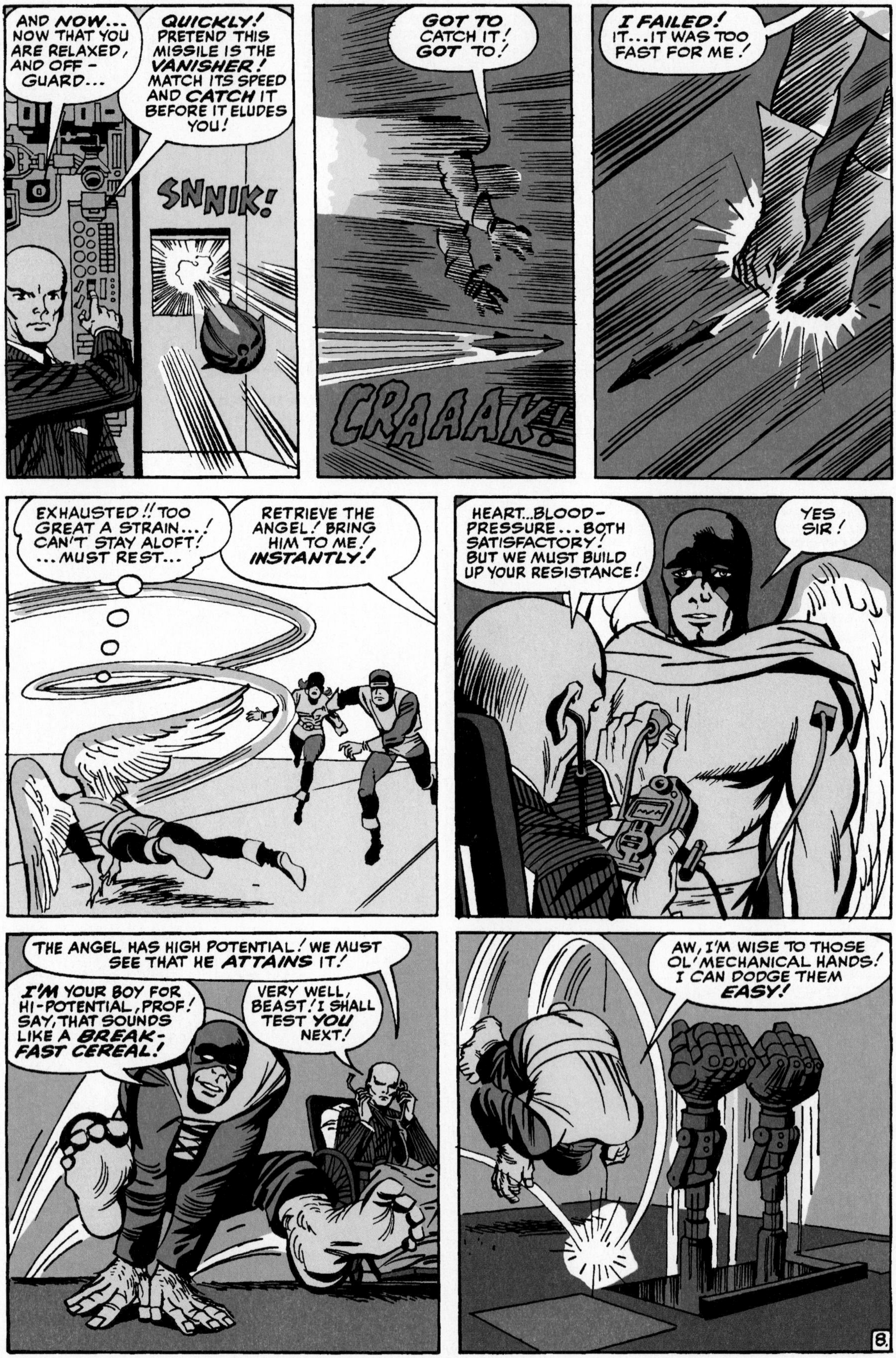
AND NOW... NOW THAT YOU ARE RELAXED, AND OFF-GUARD...
QUICKLY! PRETEND THIS MISSILE IS THE VANISHER! MATCH ITS SPEED AND CATCH IT BEFORE IT ELUDES YOU!
SNNIK!
GOT TO CATCH IT! GOT TO!
CRAAAK!
I FAILED! IT...IT WAS TOO FAST FOR ME!
EXHAUSTED!! TOO GREAT A STRAIN...! CAN'T STAY ALOFT! ...MUST REST...
RETRIEVE THE ANGEL! BRING HIM TO ME! INSTANTLY!
HEART...BLOOD-PRESSURE...BOTH SATISFACTORY! BUT WE MUST BUILD UP YOUR RESISTANCE!
YES SIR!
THE ANGEL HAS HIGH POTENTIAL! WE MUST SEE THAT HE ATTAINS IT!
I'M YOUR BOY FOR HI-POTENTIAL, PROF! SAY, THAT SOUNDS LIKE A BREAK-FAST CEREAL!
VERY WELL, BEAST! I SHALL TEST YOU NEXT!
AW, I'M WISE TO THOSE OL' MECHANICAL HANDS! I CAN DODGE THEM EASY!
8.

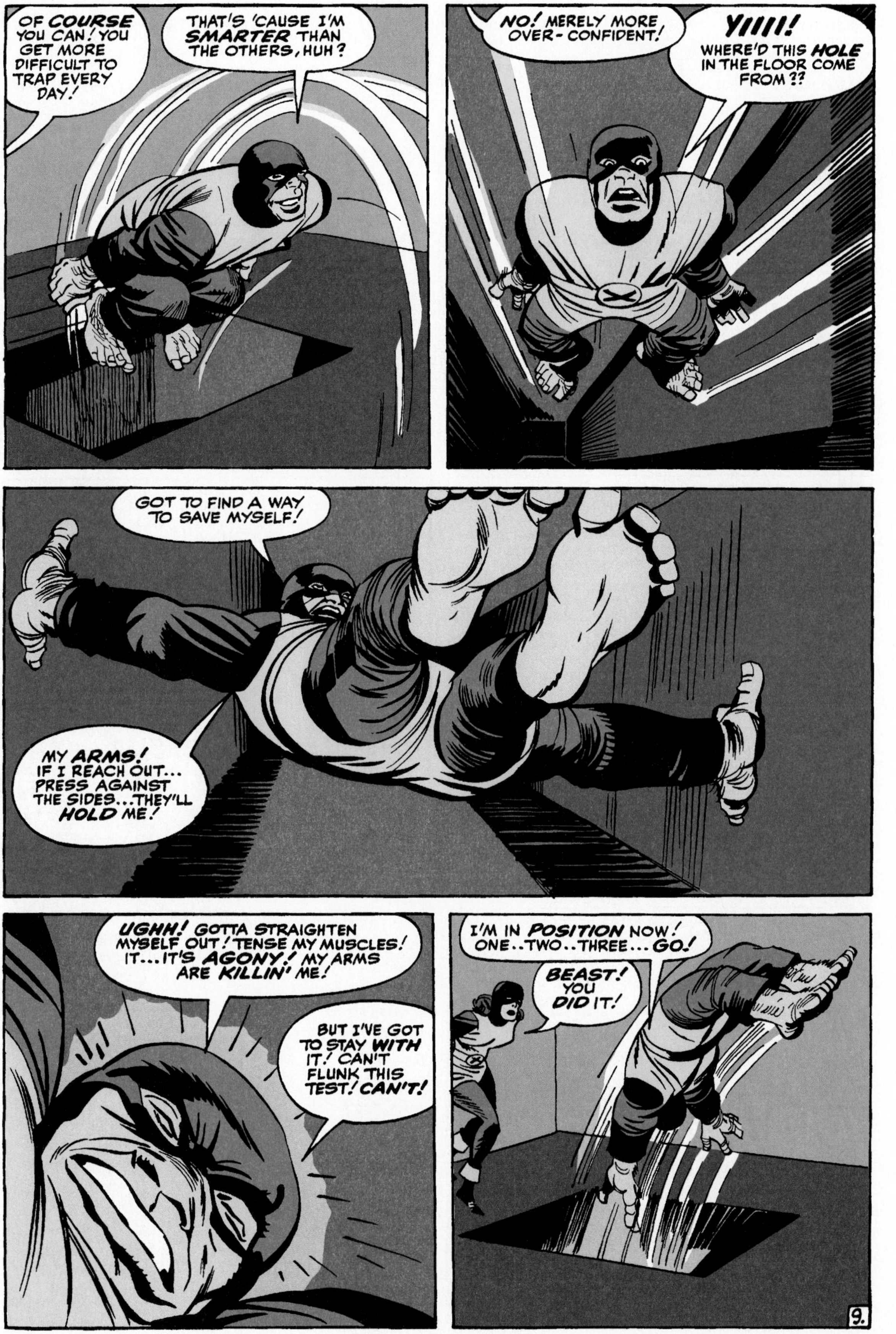
OF COURSE YOU CAN! YOU GET MORE DIFFICULT TO TRAP EVERY DAY!
THAT'S 'CAUSE I'M SMARTER THAN THE OTHERS, HUH?
NO! MERELY MORE OVER-CONFIDENT!
YIIII! WHERE'D THIS HOLE IN THE FLOOR COME FROM??
GOT TO FIND A WAY TO SAVE MYSELF!
MY ARMS! IF I REACH OUT... PRESS AGAINST THE SIDES... THEY'LL HOLD ME!
UGHH! GOTTA STRAIGHTEN MYSELF OUT! TENSE MY MUSCLES! IT... IT'S AGONY! MY ARMS ARE KILLIN' ME!
BUT I'VE GOT TO STAY WITH IT! CAN'T FLUNK THIS TEST! CAN'T!
I'M IN POSITION NOW! ONE.. TWO.. THREE... GO!
BEAST! YOU DID IT!
9.

HEY! NOW WHAT'S GOIN' ON ???

YOU JUST RELAX, HANK! YOU'VE BEEN UNDER ENOUGH STRAIN! I'LL HELP YOU DOWN GENTLY!

I'D LIKE TO HELP THAT BIG GORILLA! WITH A CACTUS PLANT!

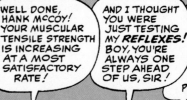

WELL DONE, HANK McCOY! YOUR MUSCULAR TENSILE STRENGTH IS INCREASING AT A MOST SATISFACTORY RATE!

AND I THOUGHT YOU WERE JUST TESTING MY REFLEXES! BOY, YOU'RE ALWAYS ONE STEP AHEAD OF US, SIR!

AND IT'S LUCKY FOR US THAT HE IS, BEAST! CONSIDERING THAT WE HAVE ALL PUT OUR DESTINIES IN THE HANDS OF PROFESSOR X!

MEANWHILE, A FEW HUNDRED MILES TO THE SOUTH, THE VANISHER NEXT APPEARS INSIDE THE MIGHTY PENTAGON BUILDING...

HOLD IT, MISTER! NOBODY GOES PAST HERE WITHOUT A PERMIT!

PERMITS ARE FOR HOMO SAPIENS, FOOL! NOT FOR THE VANISHER!

FOR I AM INDEED A TRUE MUTANT... ONE OF THOSE DESTINED TO REPLACE THE HUMAN RACE! I AM HOMO SUPERIOR!

HE-HE VANISHED!

CHIEF OF STAFF

AND, NEARBY, IN A LOCKED, HEAVILY-GUARDED CONFERENCE ROOM...

LET'S REVIEW THOSE CONTINENTAL DEFENSE PLANS AGAIN, HENDERSHOOT!

YES, SIR, GENERAL! WE CAN'T BE TOO CAREFUL OF OUR PROCEDURES!

BE SURE TO TAKE GOOD CARE OF THOSE PLANS, GENTLEMEN! FOR THEY WILL SOON BE MINE!

I INTEND TO STEAL THEM WITHIN A FEW DAYS!

IT'S THE VANISHER! H-HOW DID YOU GET IN HERE!

10.

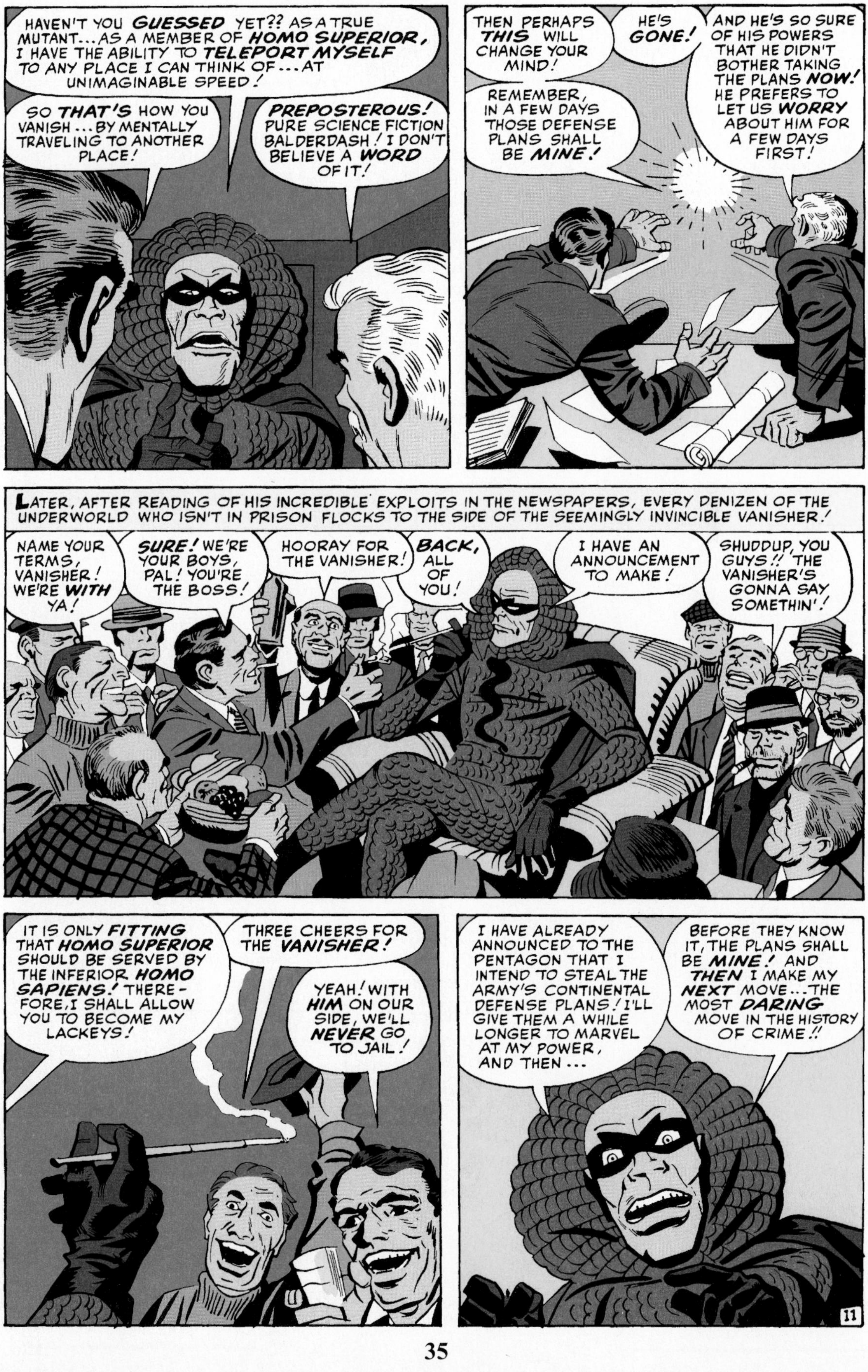
HAVEN'T YOU GUESSED YET?? AS A TRUE MUTANT...AS A MEMBER OF HOMO SUPERIOR, I HAVE THE ABILITY TO TELEPORT MYSELF TO ANY PLACE I CAN THINK OF...AT UNIMAGINABLE SPEED!
SO THAT'S HOW YOU VANISH...BY MENTALLY TRAVELING TO ANOTHER PLACE!
PREPOSTEROUS! PURE SCIENCE FICTION BALDERDASH! I DON'T BELIEVE A WORD OF IT!
THEN PERHAPS THIS WILL CHANGE YOUR MIND!
REMEMBER, IN A FEW DAYS THOSE DEFENSE PLANS SHALL BE MINE!
HE'S GONE!
AND HE'S SO SURE OF HIS POWERS THAT HE DIDN'T BOTHER TAKING THE PLANS NOW! HE PREFERS TO LET US WORRY ABOUT HIM FOR A FEW DAYS FIRST!
LATER, AFTER READING OF HIS INCREDIBLE EXPLOITS IN THE NEWSPAPERS, EVERY DENIZEN OF THE UNDERWORLD WHO ISN'T IN PRISON FLOCKS TO THE SIDE OF THE SEEMINGLY INVINCIBLE VANISHER!
NAME YOUR TERMS, VANISHER! WE'RE WITH YA!
SURE! WE'RE YOUR BOYS, PAL! YOU'RE THE BOSS!
HOORAY FOR THE VANISHER!
BACK, ALL OF YOU!
I HAVE AN ANNOUNCEMENT TO MAKE!
SHUDDUP, YOU GUYS!! THE VANISHER'S GONNA SAY SOMETHIN'!
IT IS ONLY FITTING THAT HOMO SUPERIOR SHOULD BE SERVED BY THE INFERIOR HOMO SAPIENS! THERE-FORE, I SHALL ALLOW YOU TO BECOME MY LACKEYS!
THREE CHEERS FOR THE VANISHER!
YEAH! WITH HIM ON OUR SIDE, WE'LL NEVER GO TO JAIL!
I HAVE ALREADY ANNOUNCED TO THE PENTAGON THAT I INTEND TO STEAL THE ARMY'S CONTINENTAL DEFENSE PLANS! I'LL GIVE THEM A WHILE LONGER TO MARVEL AT MY POWER, AND THEN...
BEFORE THEY KNOW IT, THE PLANS SHALL BE MINE! AND THEN I MAKE MY NEXT MOVE...THE MOST DARING MOVE IN THE HISTORY OF CRIME!!
11

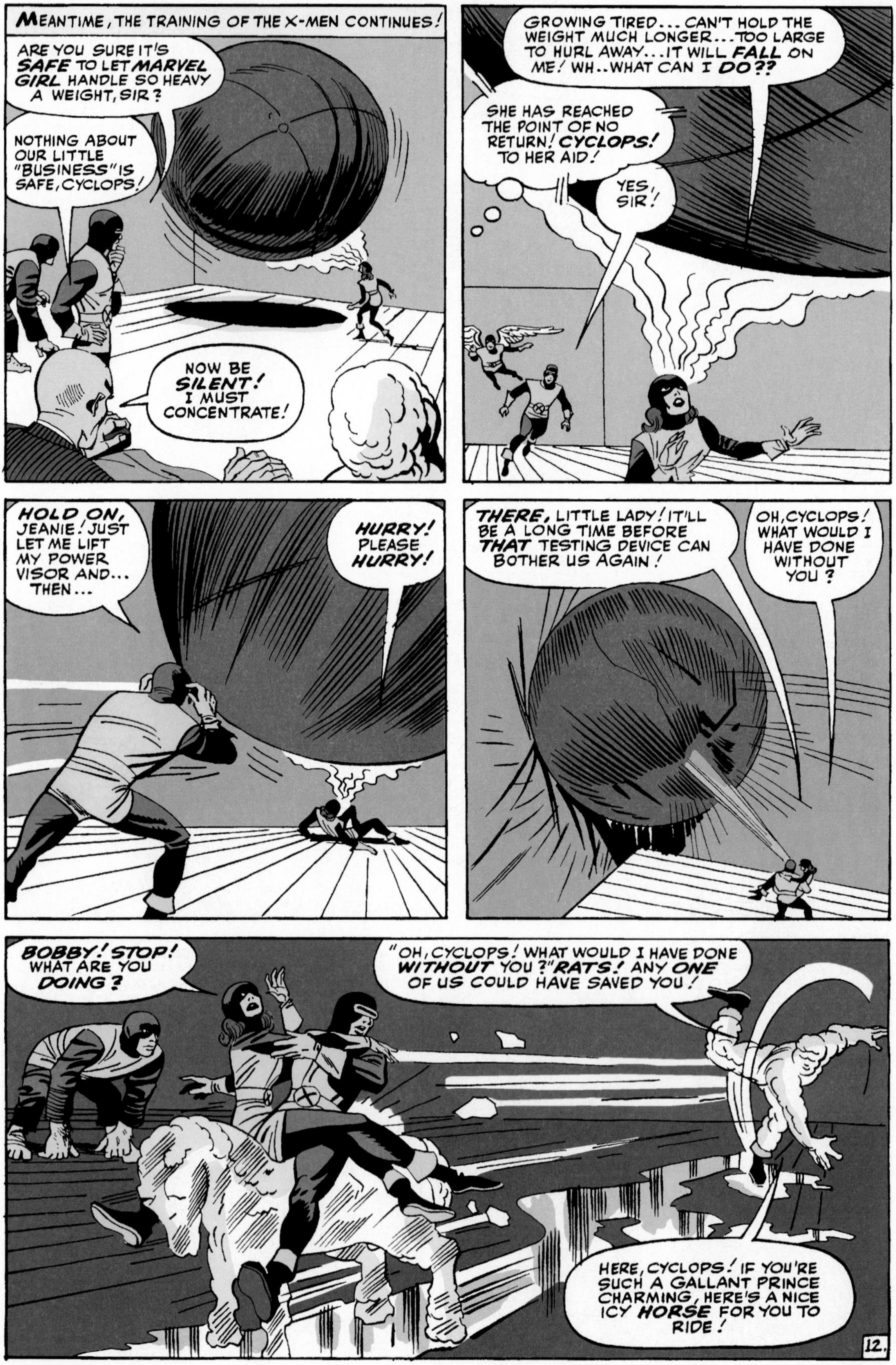
MEANTIME, THE TRAINING OF THE X-MEN CONTINUES!
ARE YOU SURE IT'S SAFE TO LET MARVEL GIRL HANDLE SO HEAVY A WEIGHT, SIR?
NOTHING ABOUT OUR LITTLE "BUSINESS" IS SAFE, CYCLOPS!
NOW BE SILENT! I MUST CONCENTRATE!
GROWING TIRED... CAN'T HOLD THE WEIGHT MUCH LONGER... TOO LARGE TO HURL AWAY... IT WILL FALL ON ME! WH..WHAT CAN I DO??
SHE HAS REACHED THE POINT OF NO RETURN! CYCLOPS! TO HER AID!
YES, SIR!
HOLD ON, JEANIE! JUST LET ME LIFT MY POWER VISOR AND... THEN...
HURRY! PLEASE HURRY!
THERE, LITTLE LADY! IT'LL BE A LONG TIME BEFORE THAT TESTING DEVICE CAN BOTHER US AGAIN!
OH, CYCLOPS! WHAT WOULD I HAVE DONE WITHOUT YOU?
BOBBY! STOP! WHAT ARE YOU DOING?
"OH, CYCLOPS! WHAT WOULD I HAVE DONE WITHOUT YOU?" RATS! ANY ONE OF US COULD HAVE SAVED YOU!
HERE, CYCLOPS! IF YOU'RE SUCH A GALLANT PRINCE CHARMING, HERE'S A NICE ICY HORSE FOR YOU TO RIDE!
12.

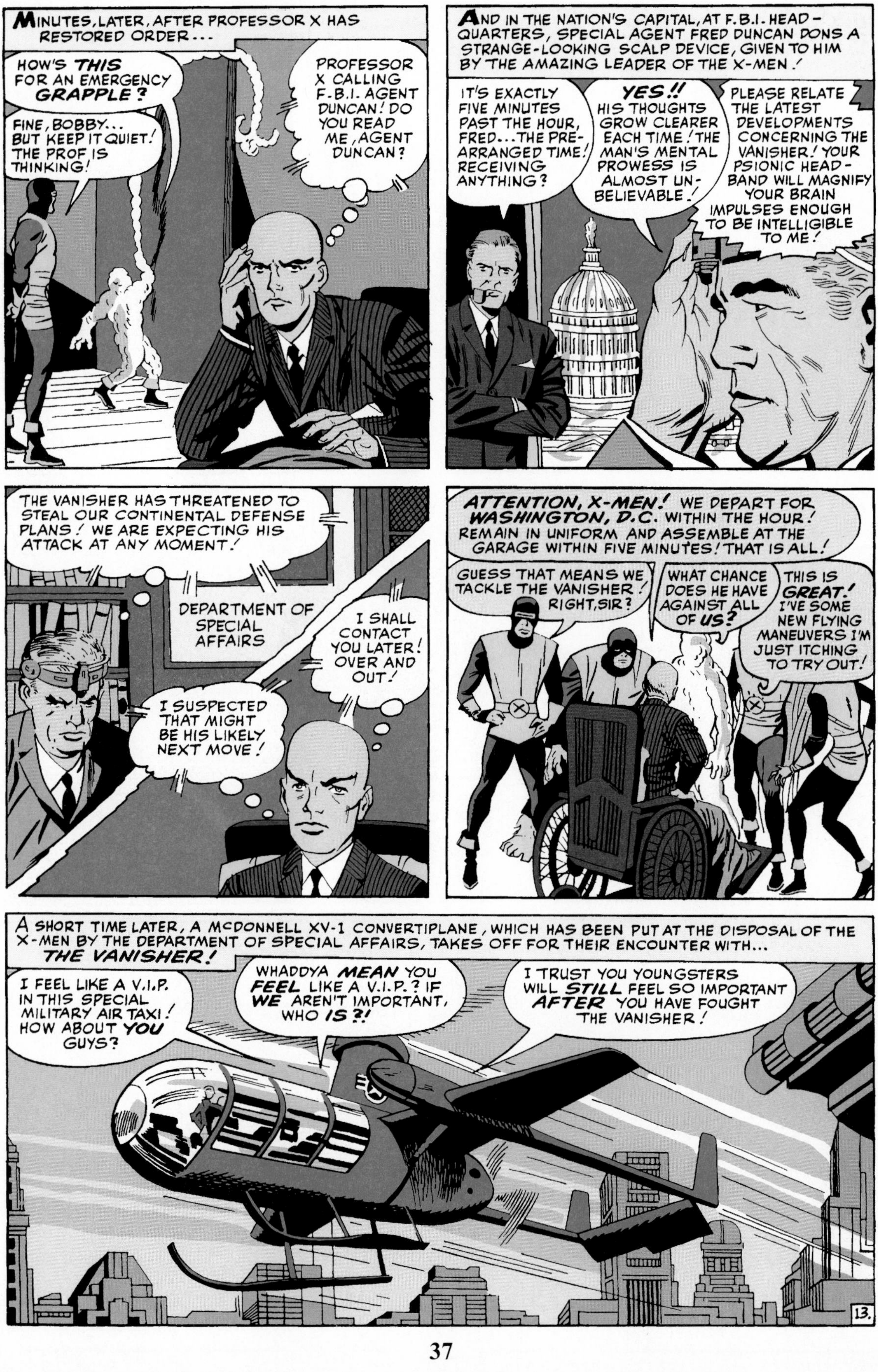
MINUTES, LATER, AFTER PROFESSOR X HAS RESTORED ORDER...
HOW'S THIS FOR AN EMERGENCY GRAPPLE?
FINE, BOBBY... BUT KEEP IT QUIET! THE PROF IS THINKING!
PROFESSOR X CALLING F.B.I. AGENT DUNCAN! DO YOU READ ME, AGENT DUNCAN?
AND IN THE NATION'S CAPITAL, AT F.B.I. HEAD-QUARTERS, SPECIAL AGENT FRED DUNCAN DONS A STRANGE-LOOKING SCALP DEVICE, GIVEN TO HIM BY THE AMAZING LEADER OF THE X-MEN!
IT'S EXACTLY FIVE MINUTES PAST THE HOUR, FRED... THE PRE-ARRANGED TIME! RECEIVING ANYTHING?
YES!! HIS THOUGHTS GROW CLEARER EACH TIME! THE MAN'S MENTAL PROWESS IS ALMOST UN-BELIEVABLE!
PLEASE RELATE THE LATEST DEVELOPMENTS CONCERNING THE VANISHER! YOUR PSIONIC HEAD-BAND WILL MAGNIFY YOUR BRAIN IMPULSES ENOUGH TO BE INTELLIGIBLE TO ME!
THE VANISHER HAS THREATENED TO STEAL OUR CONTINENTAL DEFENSE PLANS! WE ARE EXPECTING HIS ATTACK AT ANY MOMENT!
DEPARTMENT OF SPECIAL AFFAIRS
I SHALL CONTACT YOU LATER! OVER AND OUT!
I SUSPECTED THAT MIGHT BE HIS LIKELY NEXT MOVE!
ATTENTION, X-MEN! WE DEPART FOR WASHINGTON, D.C. WITHIN THE HOUR! REMAIN IN UNIFORM AND ASSEMBLE AT THE GARAGE WITHIN FIVE MINUTES! THAT IS ALL!
GUESS THAT MEANS WE TACKLE THE VANISHER! RIGHT, SIR?
WHAT CHANCE DOES HE HAVE AGAINST ALL OF US?
THIS IS GREAT! I'VE SOME NEW FLYING MANEUVERS I'M JUST ITCHING TO TRY OUT!
A SHORT TIME LATER, A McDONNELL XV-1 CONVERTIPLANE, WHICH HAS BEEN PUT AT THE DISPOSAL OF THE X-MEN BY THE DEPARTMENT OF SPECIAL AFFAIRS, TAKES OFF FOR THEIR ENCOUNTER WITH... THE VANISHER!
I FEEL LIKE A V.I.P. IN THIS SPECIAL MILITARY AIR TAXI! HOW ABOUT YOU GUYS?
WHADDYA MEAN YOU FEEL LIKE A V.I.P.? IF WE AREN'T IMPORTANT, WHO IS?!
I TRUST YOU YOUNGSTERS WILL STILL FEEL SO IMPORTANT AFTER YOU HAVE FOUGHT THE VANISHER!
13.

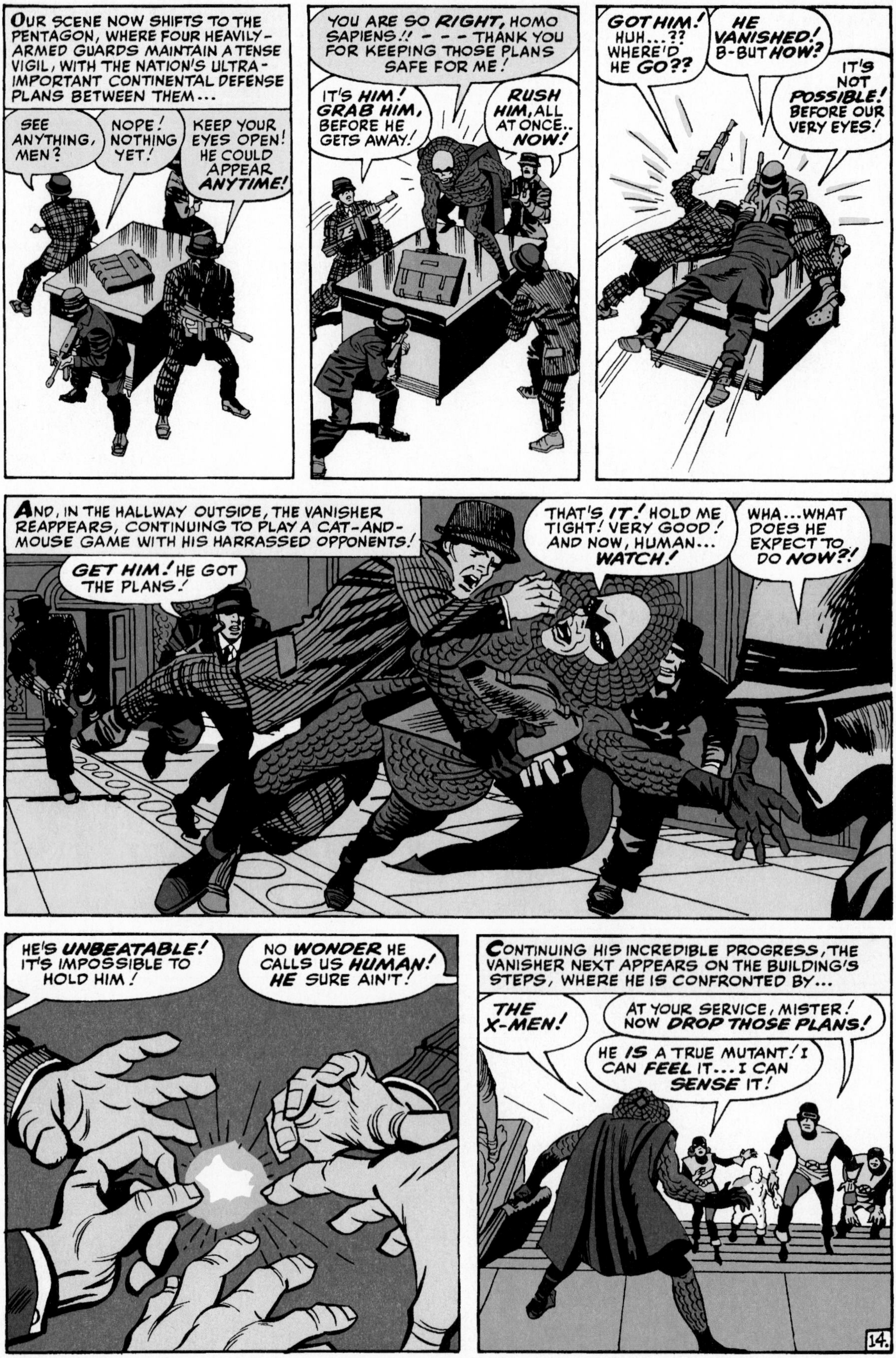

OUR SCENE NOW SHIFTS TO THE PENTAGON, WHERE FOUR HEAVILY-ARMED GUARDS MAINTAIN A TENSE VIGIL, WITH THE NATION'S ULTRA-IMPORTANT CONTINENTAL DEFENSE PLANS BETWEEN THEM...
SEE ANYTHING, MEN?
NOPE! NOTHING YET!
KEEP YOUR EYES OPEN! HE COULD APPEAR ANYTIME!
YOU ARE SO RIGHT, HOMO SAPIENS!! --- THANK YOU FOR KEEPING THOSE PLANS SAFE FOR ME!
IT'S HIM! GRAB HIM, BEFORE HE GETS AWAY!
RUSH HIM, ALL AT ONCE.. NOW!
GOT HIM! HUH...?? WHERE'D HE GO??
HE VANISHED! B-BUT HOW?
IT'S NOT POSSIBLE! BEFORE OUR VERY EYES!
AND, IN THE HALLWAY OUTSIDE, THE VANISHER REAPPEARS, CONTINUING TO PLAY A CAT-AND-MOUSE GAME WITH HIS HARRASSED OPPONENTS!
GET HIM! HE GOT THE PLANS!
THAT'S IT! HOLD ME TIGHT! VERY GOOD! AND NOW, HUMAN... WATCH!
WHA...WHAT DOES HE EXPECT TO DO NOW?!
HE'S UNBEATABLE! IT'S IMPOSSIBLE TO HOLD HIM!
NO WONDER HE CALLS US HUMAN! HE SURE AIN'T!
CONTINUING HIS INCREDIBLE PROGRESS, THE VANISHER NEXT APPEARS ON THE BUILDING'S STEPS, WHERE HE IS CONFRONTED BY...
THE X-MEN!
AT YOUR SERVICE, MISTER! NOW DROP THOSE PLANS!
HE IS A TRUE MUTANT! I CAN FEEL IT... I CAN SENSE IT!
14.

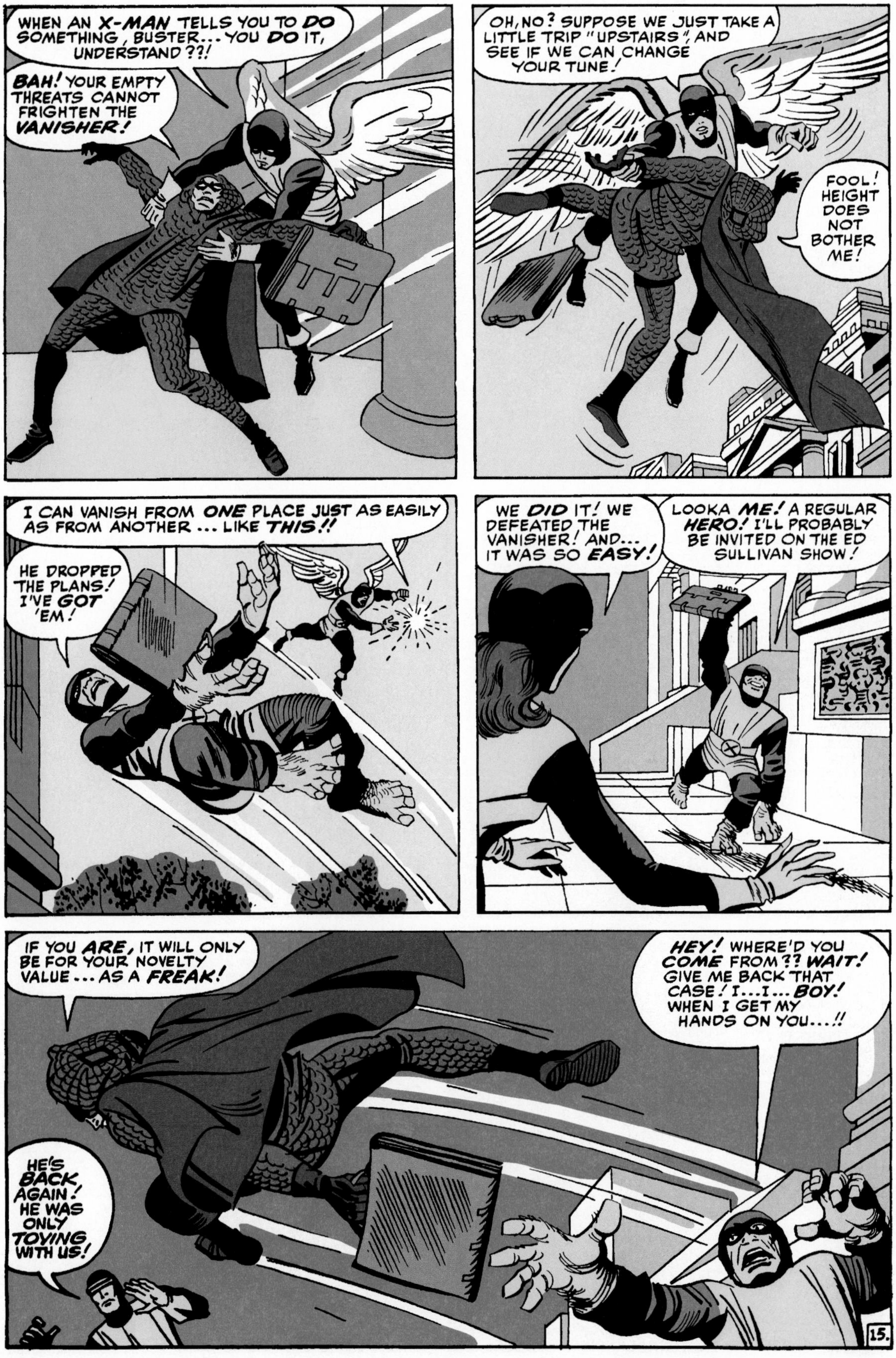
WHEN AN X-MAN TELLS YOU TO DO SOMETHING, BUSTER... YOU DO IT, UNDERSTAND??!
BAH! YOUR EMPTY THREATS CANNOT FRIGHTEN THE VANISHER!
OH, NO? SUPPOSE WE JUST TAKE A LITTLE TRIP "UPSTAIRS", AND SEE IF WE CAN CHANGE YOUR TUNE!
FOOL! HEIGHT DOES NOT BOTHER ME!
I CAN VANISH FROM ONE PLACE JUST AS EASILY AS FROM ANOTHER ... LIKE THIS!!
HE DROPPED THE PLANS! I'VE GOT 'EM!
WE DID IT! WE DEFEATED THE VANISHER! AND... IT WAS SO EASY!
LOOKA ME! A REGULAR HERO! I'LL PROBABLY BE INVITED ON THE ED SULLIVAN SHOW!
IF YOU ARE, IT WILL ONLY BE FOR YOUR NOVELTY VALUE ... AS A FREAK!
HEY! WHERE'D YOU COME FROM?? WAIT! GIVE ME BACK THAT CASE! I...I... BOY! WHEN I GET MY HANDS ON YOU...!!
HE'S BACK AGAIN! HE WAS ONLY TOYING WITH US!
15.

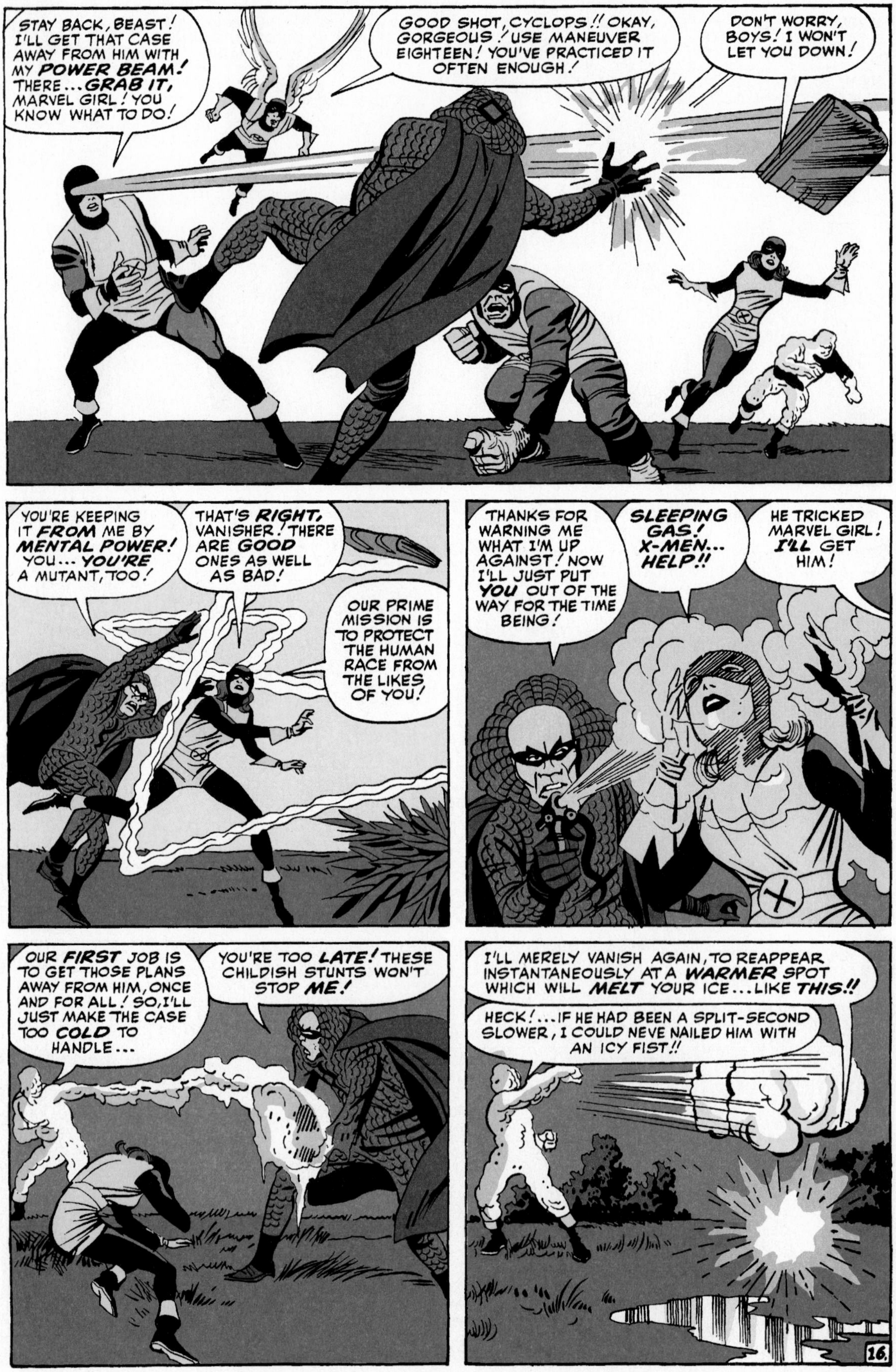
STAY BACK, BEAST! I'LL GET THAT CASE AWAY FROM HIM WITH MY POWER BEAM! THERE... GRAB IT, MARVEL GIRL! YOU KNOW WHAT TO DO!
GOOD SHOT, CYCLOPS!! OKAY, GORGEOUS! USE MANEUVER EIGHTEEN! YOU'VE PRACTICED IT OFTEN ENOUGH!
DON'T WORRY, BOYS! I WON'T LET YOU DOWN!
YOU'RE KEEPING IT FROM ME BY MENTAL POWER! YOU... YOU'RE A MUTANT, TOO!
THAT'S RIGHT, VANISHER! THERE ARE GOOD ONES AS WELL AS BAD!
OUR PRIME MISSION IS TO PROTECT THE HUMAN RACE FROM THE LIKES OF YOU!
THANKS FOR WARNING ME WHAT I'M UP AGAINST! NOW I'LL JUST PUT YOU OUT OF THE WAY FOR THE TIME BEING!
SLEEPING GAS! X-MEN... HELP!!
HE TRICKED MARVEL GIRL! I'LL GET HIM!
OUR FIRST JOB IS TO GET THOSE PLANS AWAY FROM HIM, ONCE AND FOR ALL! SO, I'LL JUST MAKE THE CASE TOO COLD TO HANDLE...
YOU'RE TOO LATE! THESE CHILDISH STUNTS WON'T STOP ME!
I'LL MERELY VANISH AGAIN, TO REAPPEAR INSTANTANEOUSLY AT A WARMER SPOT WHICH WILL MELT YOUR ICE... LIKE THIS!!
HECK!... IF HE HAD BEEN A SPLIT-SECOND SLOWER, I COULD NEVE NAILED HIM WITH AN ICY FIST!!
16.

JEAN! ARE YOU OKAY, KID?

Y-YES! BUT WHAT ABOUT THE VANISHER?

HE GOT AWAY... PLANS AND ALL!

HE TOOK EVERYTHING WE COULD DISH OUT... AND HE BEAT US BUT *GOOD!*

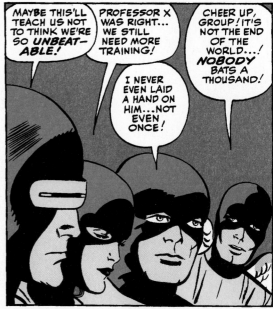

MAYBE THIS'LL TEACH US NOT TO THINK WE'RE SO *UNBEATABLE!*

PROFESSOR X WAS RIGHT... WE STILL NEED MORE TRAINING!

CHEER UP, GROUP! IT'S NOT THE END OF THE WORLD...! *NOBODY* BATS A THOUSAND!

I NEVER EVEN LAID A HAND ON HIM...NOT EVEN ONCE!

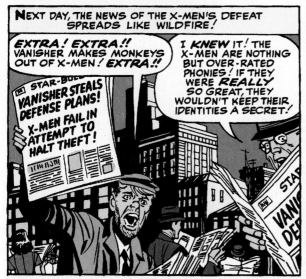

NEXT DAY, THE NEWS OF THE X-MEN'S DEFEAT SPREADS LIKE WILDFIRE!

EXTRA! EXTRA!! VANISHER MAKES MONKEYS OUT OF X-MEN! *EXTRA!!*

STAR-B... VANISHER STEALS DEFENSE PLANS! X-MEN FAIL IN ATTEMPT TO HALT THEFT!

I *KNEW* IT! THE X-MEN ARE NOTHING BUT OVER-RATED PHONIES! IF THEY WERE *REALLY* SO GREAT, THEY WOULDN'T KEEP THEIR IDENTITIES A SECRET!

AND, AS THE HOURS SPEED BY, TEMPERS GET FRAYED...NERVES GET RAW...AS PANIC SEEMS TO MOUNT AMONG THE POPULACE...

IF THERE'S NO WAY TO STOP THAT VANISHER, I'M ALL FOR SKIPPIN' TOWN! NO TELLIN' *WHAT* HE'LL DO NEXT!

WHAT GOOD WILL *RUNNING* DO? HE CAN BE *ANYWHERE!* THERE'S *NO* PLACE THAT'S SAFE!

THEY SAY HE BEAT THE X-MEN WITHOUT EVEN HALF-TRYING! CAN YOU IMAGINE HOW *POWERFUL* HE MUST BE.!?

WHILE, AT PROFESSOR XAVIER'S SCHOOL...

FLASH! THE VANISHER HAS JUST DEMANDED TEN MILLION DOLLARS, TAX-FREE, FROM THE GOVERNMENT, AS HIS PRICE FOR NOT TURNING OUR CONTINENTAL DEFENSE PLANS OVER TO THE COMMUNISTS!

IT'S PURE *BLACKMAIL!* ON THE LARGEST SCALE EVER ATTEMPTED!

I WAS RIGHT *NEXT* TO HIM...AND I COULDN'T LAY A HAND ON HIM!

YOU AND THOSE FLAPPIN' WINGS OF YOURS SURE WEREN'T ANY HELP!

THEY DID AS MUCH GOOD AS THAT CORNY SNOWBALL FIST OF *YOURS!*

17.

41

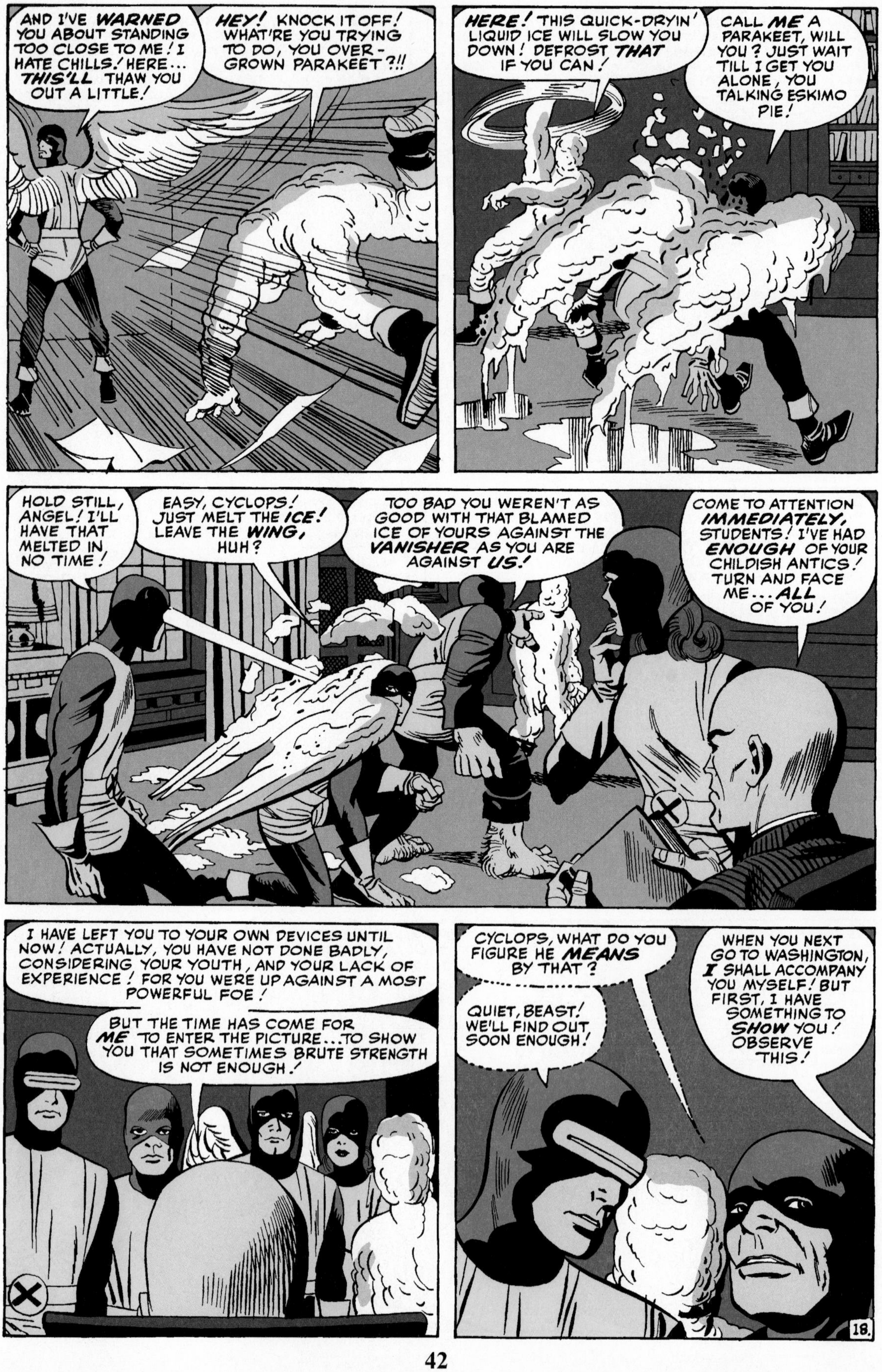
AND I'VE WARNED YOU ABOUT STANDING TOO CLOSE TO ME! I HATE CHILLS! HERE... THIS'LL THAW YOU OUT A LITTLE!
HEY! KNOCK IT OFF! WHAT'RE YOU TRYING TO DO, YOU OVER-GROWN PARAKEET ?!!
HERE! THIS QUICK-DRYIN' LIQUID ICE WILL SLOW YOU DOWN! DEFROST THAT IF YOU CAN!
CALL ME A PARAKEET, WILL YOU? JUST WAIT TILL I GET YOU ALONE, YOU TALKING ESKIMO PIE!
HOLD STILL, ANGEL! I'LL HAVE THAT MELTED IN NO TIME!
EASY, CYCLOPS! JUST MELT THE ICE! LEAVE THE WING, HUH?
TOO BAD YOU WEREN'T AS GOOD WITH THAT BLAMED ICE OF YOURS AGAINST THE VANISHER AS YOU ARE AGAINST US!
COME TO ATTENTION IMMEDIATELY, STUDENTS! I'VE HAD ENOUGH OF YOUR CHILDISH ANTICS! TURN AND FACE ME... ALL OF YOU!
I HAVE LEFT YOU TO YOUR OWN DEVICES UNTIL NOW! ACTUALLY, YOU HAVE NOT DONE BADLY, CONSIDERING YOUR YOUTH, AND YOUR LACK OF EXPERIENCE! FOR YOU WERE UP AGAINST A MOST POWERFUL FOE!
BUT THE TIME HAS COME FOR ME TO ENTER THE PICTURE...TO SHOW YOU THAT SOMETIMES BRUTE STRENGTH IS NOT ENOUGH!
CYCLOPS, WHAT DO YOU FIGURE HE MEANS BY THAT?
QUIET, BEAST! WE'LL FIND OUT SOON ENOUGH!
WHEN YOU NEXT GO TO WASHINGTON, I SHALL ACCOMPANY YOU MYSELF! BUT FIRST, I HAVE SOMETHING TO SHOW YOU! OBSERVE THIS!
18.

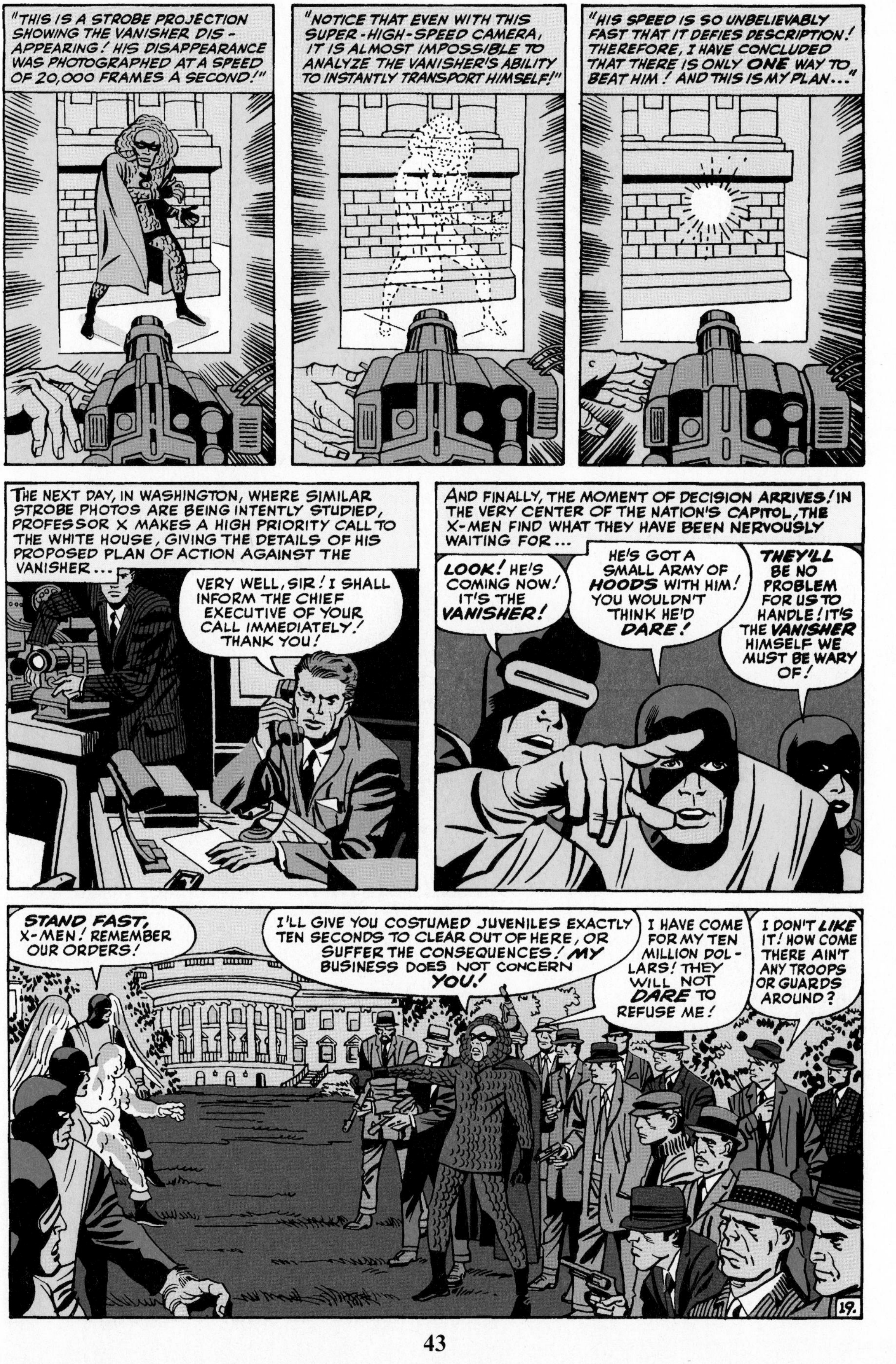
"THIS IS A STROBE PROJECTION SHOWING THE VANISHER DIS-APPEARING! HIS DISAPPEARANCE WAS PHOTOGRAPHED AT A SPEED OF 20,000 FRAMES A SECOND!"
"NOTICE THAT EVEN WITH THIS SUPER-HIGH-SPEED CAMERA, IT IS ALMOST IMPOSSIBLE TO ANALYZE THE VANISHER'S ABILITY TO INSTANTLY TRANSPORT HIMSELF!"
"HIS SPEED IS SO UNBELIEVABLY FAST THAT IT DEFIES DESCRIPTION! THEREFORE, I HAVE CONCLUDED THAT THERE IS ONLY ONE WAY TO BEAT HIM! AND THIS IS MY PLAN..."
THE NEXT DAY, IN WASHINGTON, WHERE SIMILAR STROBE PHOTOS ARE BEING INTENTLY STUDIED, PROFESSOR X MAKES A HIGH PRIORITY CALL TO THE WHITE HOUSE, GIVING THE DETAILS OF HIS PROPOSED PLAN OF ACTION AGAINST THE VANISHER...
VERY WELL, SIR! I SHALL INFORM THE CHIEF EXECUTIVE OF YOUR CALL IMMEDIATELY! THANK YOU!
AND FINALLY, THE MOMENT OF DECISION ARRIVES! IN THE VERY CENTER OF THE NATION'S CAPITOL, THE X-MEN FIND WHAT THEY HAVE BEEN NERVOUSLY WAITING FOR...
LOOK! HE'S COMING NOW! IT'S THE VANISHER!
HE'S GOT A SMALL ARMY OF HOODS WITH HIM! YOU WOULDN'T THINK HE'D DARE!
THEY'LL BE NO PROBLEM FOR US TO HANDLE! IT'S THE VANISHER HIMSELF WE MUST BE WARY OF!
STAND FAST, X-MEN! REMEMBER OUR ORDERS!
I'LL GIVE YOU COSTUMED JUVENILES EXACTLY TEN SECONDS TO CLEAR OUT OF HERE, OR SUFFER THE CONSEQUENCES! MY BUSINESS DOES NOT CONCERN YOU!
I HAVE COME FOR MY TEN MILLION DOL-LARS! THEY WILL NOT DARE TO REFUSE ME!
I DON'T LIKE IT! HOW COME THERE AIN'T ANY TROOPS OR GUARDS AROUND?
19.

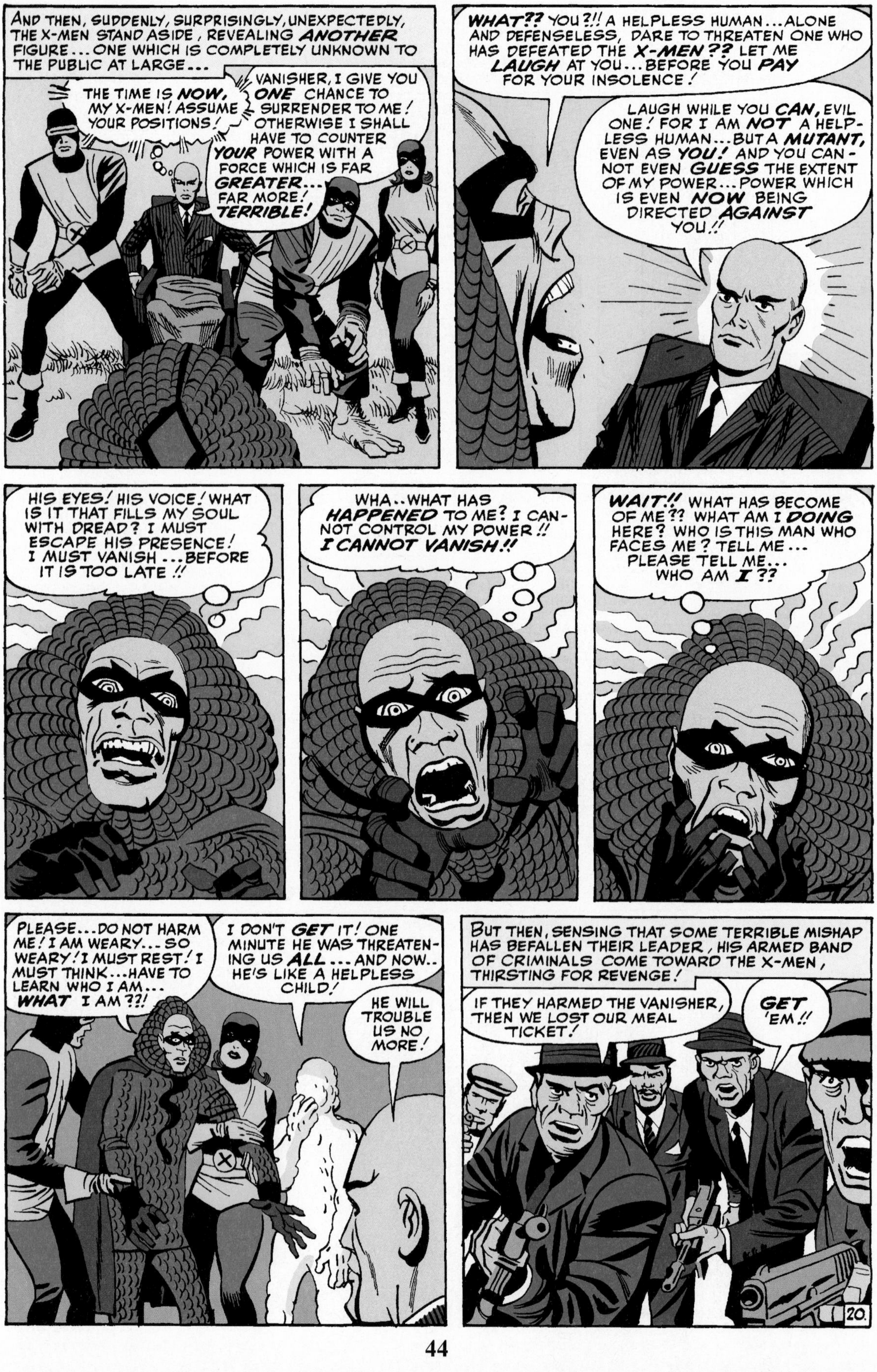
AND THEN, SUDDENLY, SURPRISINGLY, UNEXPECTEDLY, THE X-MEN STAND ASIDE, REVEALING ANOTHER FIGURE... ONE WHICH IS COMPLETELY UNKNOWN TO THE PUBLIC AT LARGE...
THE TIME IS NOW, MY X-MEN! ASSUME YOUR POSITIONS!
VANISHER, I GIVE YOU ONE CHANCE TO SURRENDER TO ME! OTHERWISE I SHALL HAVE TO COUNTER YOUR POWER WITH A FORCE WHICH IS FAR GREATER... FAR MORE! TERRIBLE!
WHAT?? YOU?!! A HELPLESS HUMAN... ALONE AND DEFENSELESS, DARE TO THREATEN ONE WHO HAS DEFEATED THE X-MEN?? LET ME LAUGH AT YOU... BEFORE YOU PAY FOR YOUR INSOLENCE!
LAUGH WHILE YOU CAN, EVIL ONE! FOR I AM NOT A HELPLESS HUMAN... BUT A MUTANT, EVEN AS YOU! AND YOU CANNOT EVEN GUESS THE EXTENT OF MY POWER... POWER WHICH IS EVEN NOW BEING DIRECTED AGAINST YOU!!
HIS EYES! HIS VOICE! WHAT IS IT THAT FILLS MY SOUL WITH DREAD? I MUST ESCAPE HIS PRESENCE! I MUST VANISH ... BEFORE IT IS TOO LATE!!
WHA.. WHAT HAS HAPPENED TO ME? I CANNOT CONTROL MY POWER!! I CANNOT VANISH!!
WAIT!! WHAT HAS BECOME OF ME?? WHAT AM I DOING HERE? WHO IS THIS MAN WHO FACES ME? TELL ME... PLEASE TELL ME... WHO AM I??
PLEASE... DO NOT HARM ME! I AM WEARY... SO WEARY! I MUST REST! I MUST THINK... HAVE TO LEARN WHO I AM... WHAT I AM??!
I DON'T GET IT! ONE MINUTE HE WAS THREATENING US ALL ... AND NOW.. HE'S LIKE A HELPLESS CHILD!
HE WILL TROUBLE US NO MORE!
BUT THEN, SENSING THAT SOME TERRIBLE MISHAP HAS BEFALLEN THEIR LEADER, HIS ARMED BAND OF CRIMINALS COME TOWARD THE X-MEN, THIRSTING FOR REVENGE!
IF THEY HARMED THE VANISHER, THEN WE LOST OUR MEAL TICKET!
GET 'EM!!
20.

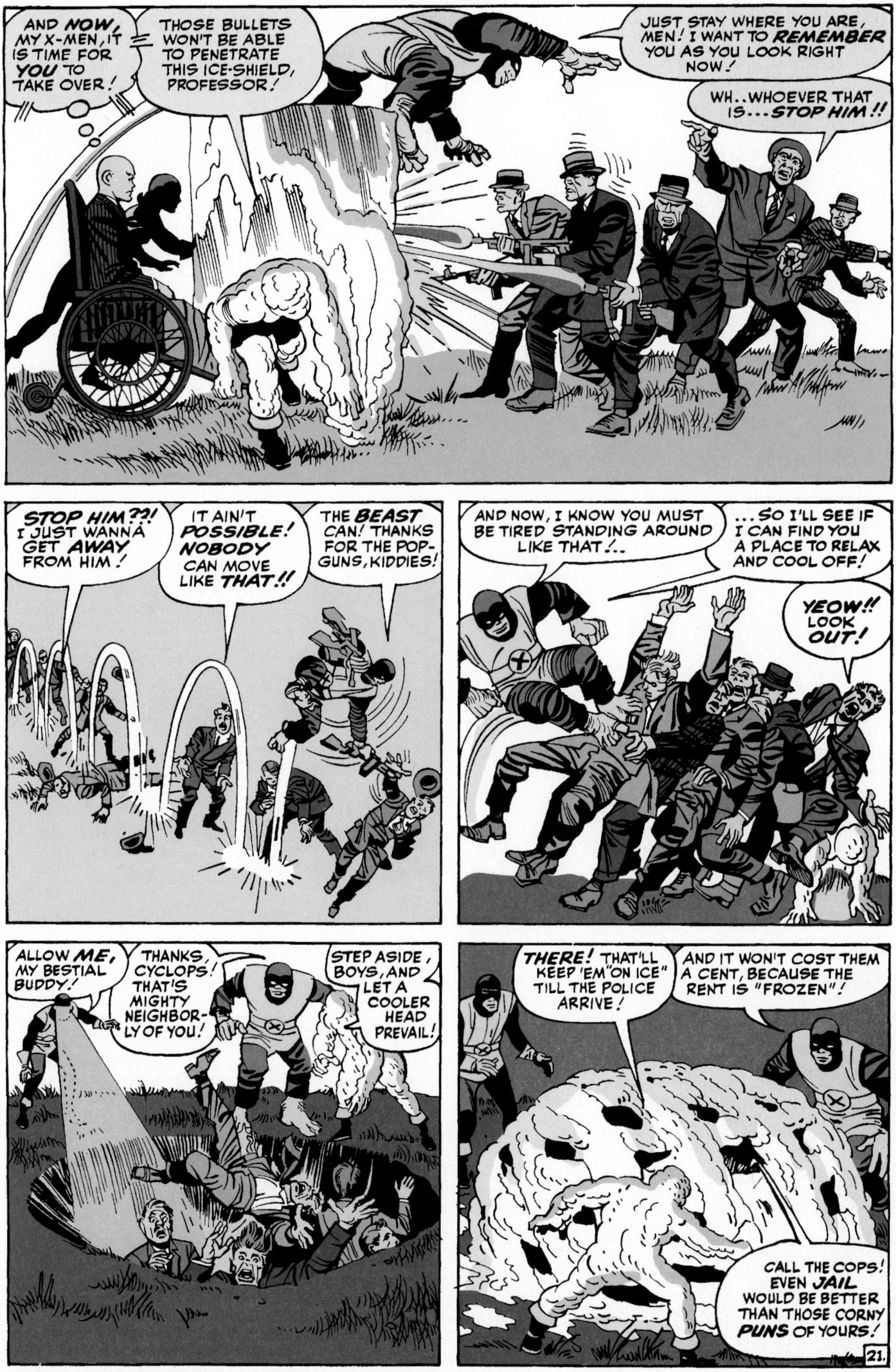
AND NOW, MY X-MEN, IT IS TIME FOR YOU TO TAKE OVER!
THOSE BULLETS WON'T BE ABLE TO PENETRATE THIS ICE-SHIELD, PROFESSOR!
JUST STAY WHERE YOU ARE, MEN! I WANT TO REMEMBER YOU AS YOU LOOK RIGHT NOW!
WH..WHOEVER THAT IS...STOP HIM!!
STOP HIM??! I JUST WANNA GET AWAY FROM HIM!
IT AIN'T POSSIBLE! NOBODY CAN MOVE LIKE THAT!!
THE BEAST CAN! THANKS FOR THE POP-GUNS, KIDDIES!
AND NOW, I KNOW YOU MUST BE TIRED STANDING AROUND LIKE THAT!..
...SO I'LL SEE IF I CAN FIND YOU A PLACE TO RELAX AND COOL OFF!
YEOW!! LOOK OUT!
ALLOW ME, MY BESTIAL BUDDY!
THANKS, CYCLOPS! THAT'S MIGHTY NEIGHBOR-LY OF YOU!
STEP ASIDE, BOYS, AND LET A COOLER HEAD PREVAIL!
THERE! THAT'LL KEEP 'EM "ON ICE" TILL THE POLICE ARRIVE!
AND IT WON'T COST THEM A CENT, BECAUSE THE RENT IS "FROZEN"!
CALL THE COPS! EVEN JAIL WOULD BE BETTER THAN THOSE CORNY PUNS OF YOURS!
21.

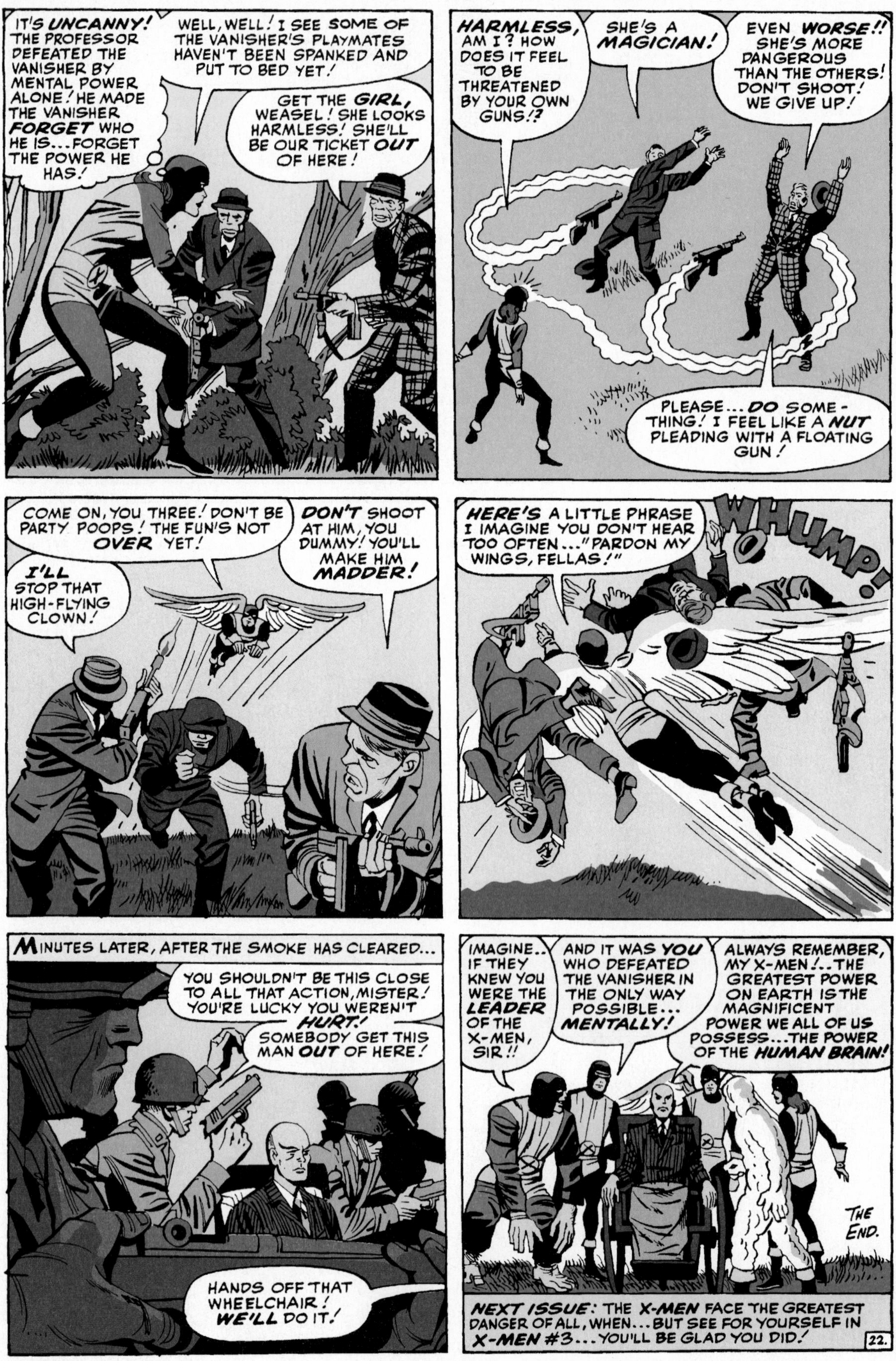
IT'S UNCANNY! THE PROFESSOR DEFEATED THE VANISHER BY MENTAL POWER ALONE! HE MADE THE VANISHER FORGET WHO HE IS...FORGET THE POWER HE HAS!
WELL, WELL! I SEE SOME OF THE VANISHER'S PLAYMATES HAVEN'T BEEN SPANKED AND PUT TO BED YET!
GET THE GIRL, WEASEL! SHE LOOKS HARMLESS! SHE'LL BE OUR TICKET OUT OF HERE!
HARMLESS, AM I? HOW DOES IT FEEL TO BE THREATENED BY YOUR OWN GUNS!?
SHE'S A MAGICIAN!
EVEN WORSE!! SHE'S MORE DANGEROUS THAN THE OTHERS! DON'T SHOOT! WE GIVE UP!
PLEASE... DO SOME-THING! I FEEL LIKE A NUT PLEADING WITH A FLOATING GUN!
COME ON, YOU THREE! DON'T BE PARTY POOPS! THE FUN'S NOT OVER YET!
I'LL STOP THAT HIGH-FLYING CLOWN!
DON'T SHOOT AT HIM, YOU DUMMY! YOU'LL MAKE HIM MADDER!
HERE'S A LITTLE PHRASE I IMAGINE YOU DON'T HEAR TOO OFTEN..."PARDON MY WINGS, FELLAS!"
WHUMP!
MINUTES LATER, AFTER THE SMOKE HAS CLEARED...
YOU SHOULDN'T BE THIS CLOSE TO ALL THAT ACTION, MISTER! YOU'RE LUCKY YOU WEREN'T HURT!
SOMEBODY GET THIS MAN OUT OF HERE!
HANDS OFF THAT WHEELCHAIR! WE'LL DO IT!
IMAGINE.. IF THEY KNEW YOU WERE THE LEADER OF THE X-MEN, SIR!!
AND IT WAS YOU WHO DEFEATED THE VANISHER IN THE ONLY WAY POSSIBLE... MENTALLY!
ALWAYS REMEMBER, MY X-MEN!..THE GREATEST POWER ON EARTH IS THE MAGNIFICENT POWER WE ALL OF US POSSESS...THE POWER OF THE HUMAN BRAIN!
THE END.
NEXT ISSUE: THE X-MEN FACE THE GREATEST DANGER OF ALL, WHEN...BUT SEE FOR YOURSELF IN X-MEN #3... YOU'LL BE GLAD YOU DID!
22.

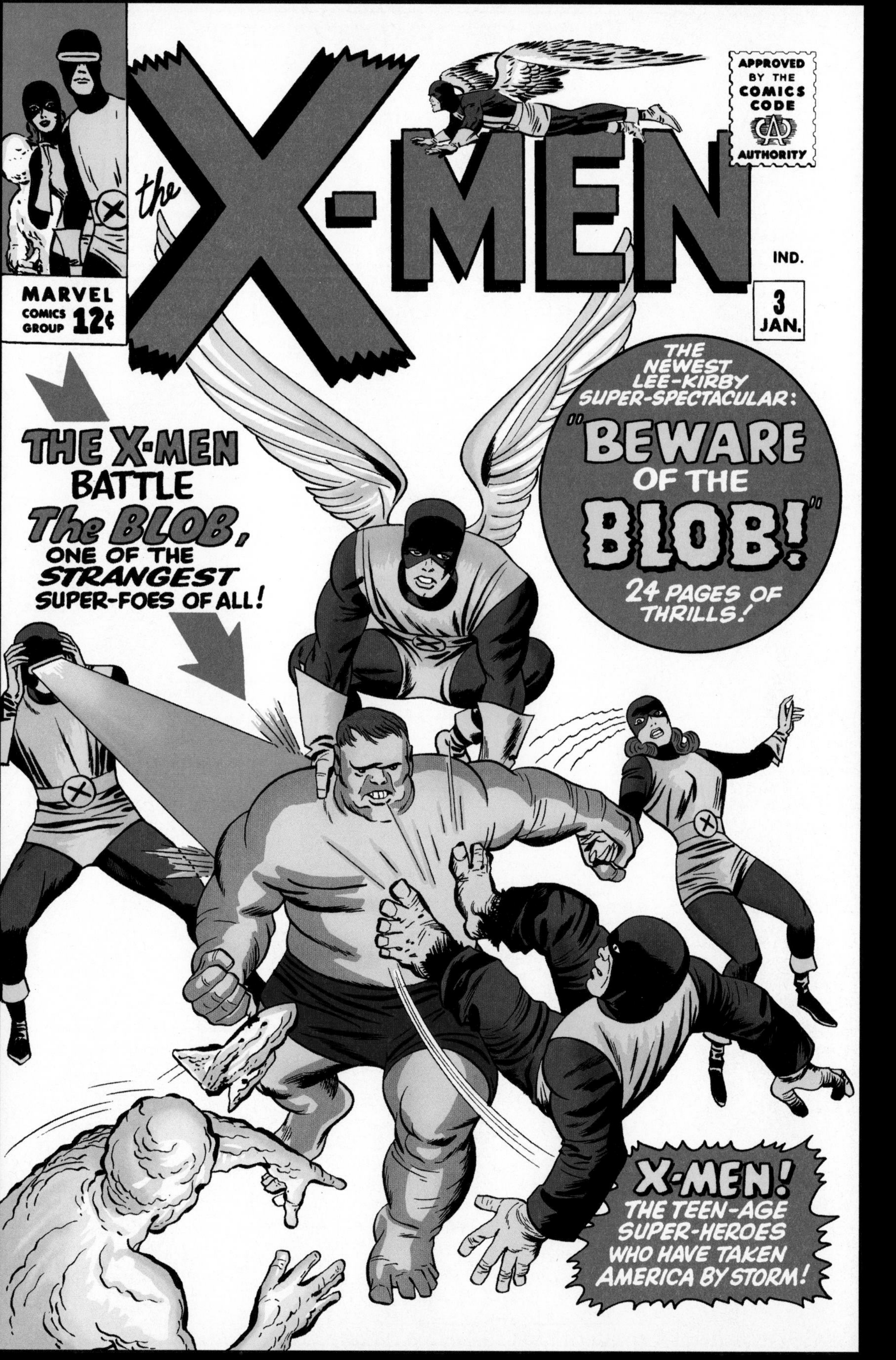
APPROVED BY THE COMICS CODE AUTHORITY
MARVEL COMICS GROUP 12¢
the X-MEN
IND.
3 JAN.
THE NEWEST LEE-KIRBY SUPER-SPECTACULAR:
"BEWARE OF THE BLOB!"
24 PAGES OF THRILLS!
THE X-MEN BATTLE The BLOB, ONE OF THE STRANGEST SUPER-FOES OF ALL!
X-MEN! THE TEEN-AGE SUPER-HEROES WHO HAVE TAKEN AMERICA BY STORM!

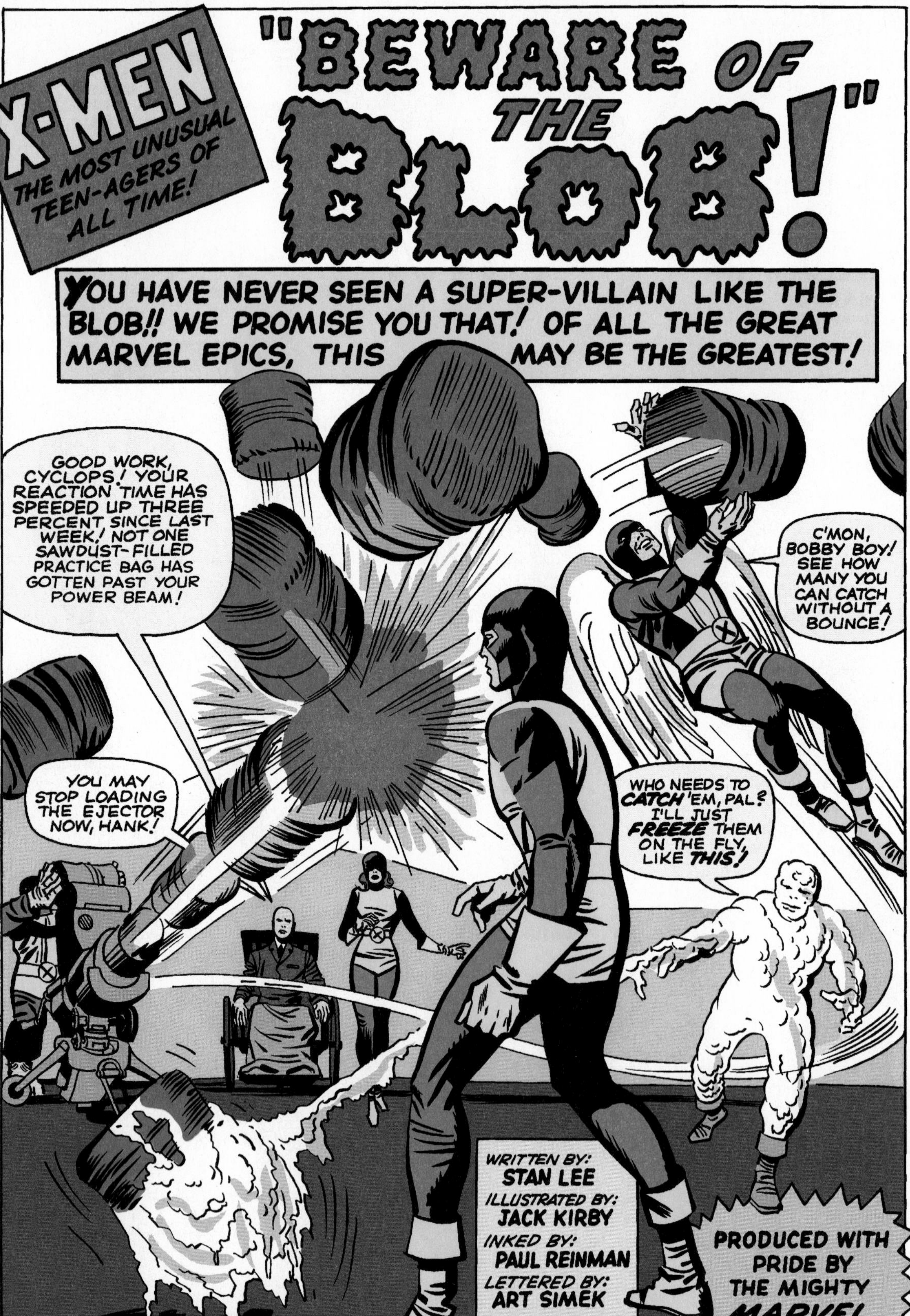
X-MEN
THE MOST UNUSUAL TEEN-AGERS OF ALL TIME!
"BEWARE OF THE BLOB!"
YOU HAVE NEVER SEEN A SUPER-VILLAIN LIKE THE BLOB!! WE PROMISE YOU THAT! OF ALL THE GREAT MARVEL EPICS, THIS MAY BE THE GREATEST!
GOOD WORK, CYCLOPS! YOUR REACTION TIME HAS SPEEDED UP THREE PERCENT SINCE LAST WEEK! NOT ONE SAWDUST-FILLED PRACTICE BAG HAS GOTTEN PAST YOUR POWER BEAM!
C'MON, BOBBY BOY! SEE HOW MANY YOU CAN CATCH WITHOUT A BOUNCE!
YOU MAY STOP LOADING THE EJECTOR NOW, HANK!
WHO NEEDS TO CATCH 'EM, PAL? I'LL JUST FREEZE THEM ON THE FLY, LIKE THIS!
WRITTEN BY: STAN LEE
ILLUSTRATED BY: JACK KIRBY
INKED BY: PAUL REINMAN
LETTERED BY: ART SIMEK
PRODUCED WITH PRIDE BY THE MIGHTY MARVEL COMICS GROUP!
X-554
1

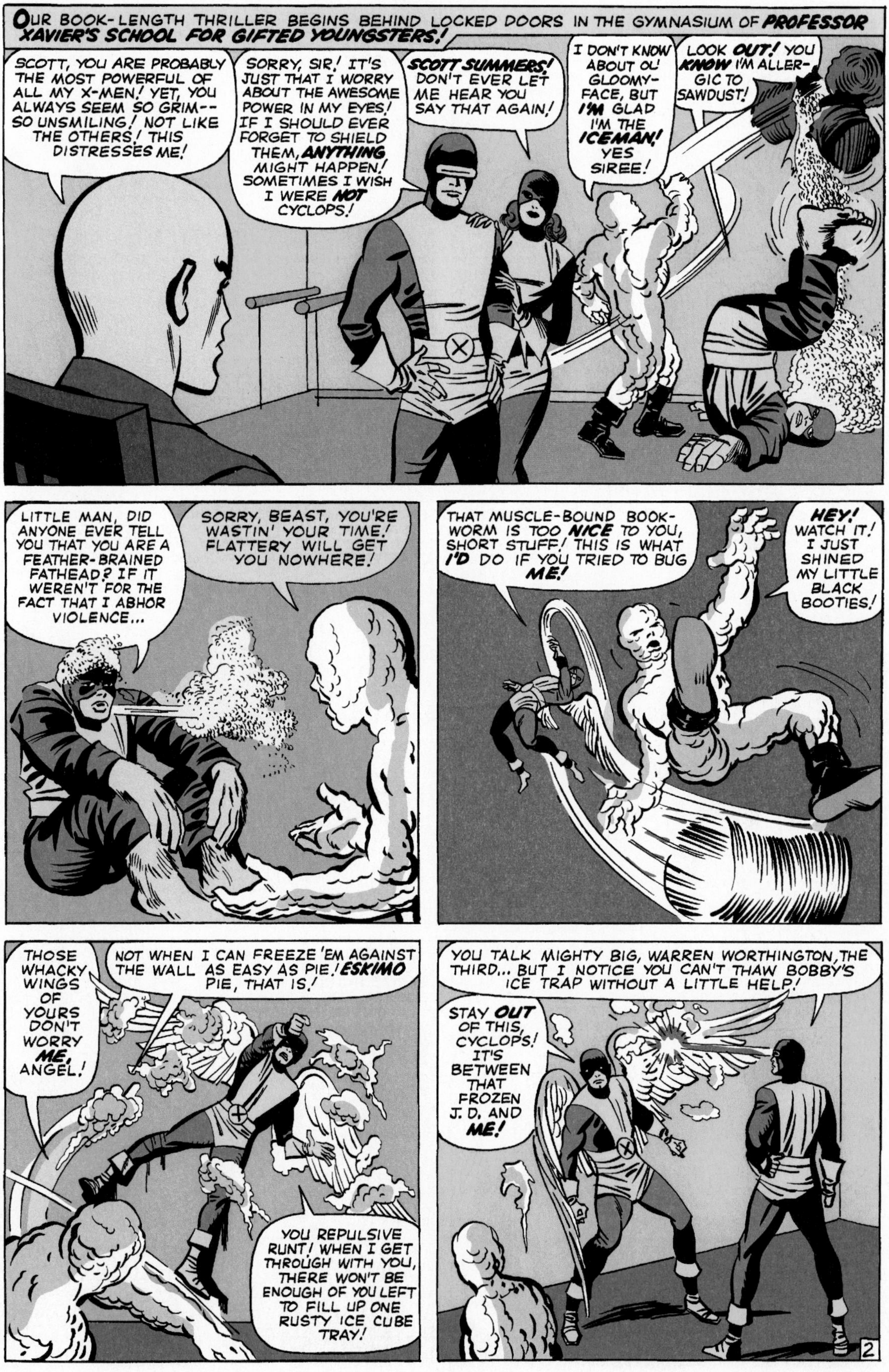
OUR BOOK-LENGTH THRILLER BEGINS BEHIND LOCKED DOORS IN THE GYMNASIUM OF PROFESSOR XAVIER'S SCHOOL FOR GIFTED YOUNGSTERS!
SCOTT, YOU ARE PROBABLY THE MOST POWERFUL OF ALL MY X-MEN! YET, YOU ALWAYS SEEM SO GRIM-- SO UNSMILING! NOT LIKE THE OTHERS! THIS DISTRESSES ME!
SORRY, SIR! IT'S JUST THAT I WORRY ABOUT THE AWESOME POWER IN MY EYES! IF I SHOULD EVER FORGET TO SHIELD THEM, ANYTHING MIGHT HAPPEN! SOMETIMES I WISH I WERE NOT CYCLOPS!
SCOTT SUMMERS! DON'T EVER LET ME HEAR YOU SAY THAT AGAIN!
I DON'T KNOW ABOUT OL' GLOOMY-FACE, BUT I'M GLAD I'M THE ICEMAN! YES SIREE!
LOOK OUT! YOU KNOW I'M ALLERGIC TO SAWDUST!
LITTLE MAN, DID ANYONE EVER TELL YOU THAT YOU ARE A FEATHER-BRAINED FATHEAD? IF IT WEREN'T FOR THE FACT THAT I ABHOR VIOLENCE...
SORRY, BEAST, YOU'RE WASTIN' YOUR TIME! FLATTERY WILL GET YOU NOWHERE!
THAT MUSCLE-BOUND BOOKWORM IS TOO NICE TO YOU, SHORT STUFF! THIS IS WHAT I'D DO IF YOU TRIED TO BUG ME!
HEY! WATCH IT! I JUST SHINED MY LITTLE BLACK BOOTIES!
THOSE WHACKY WINGS OF YOURS DON'T WORRY ME, ANGEL!
NOT WHEN I CAN FREEZE 'EM AGAINST THE WALL AS EASY AS PIE! ESKIMO PIE, THAT IS!
YOU REPULSIVE RUNT! WHEN I GET THROUGH WITH YOU, THERE WON'T BE ENOUGH OF YOU LEFT TO FILL UP ONE RUSTY ICE CUBE TRAY!
YOU TALK MIGHTY BIG, WARREN WORTHINGTON, THE THIRD... BUT I NOTICE YOU CAN'T THAW BOBBY'S ICE TRAP WITHOUT A LITTLE HELP!
STAY OUT OF THIS, CYCLOPS! IT'S BETWEEN THAT FROZEN J. D. AND ME!
2

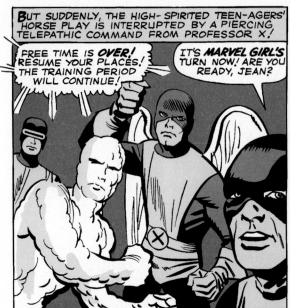

BUT SUDDENLY, THE HIGH-SPIRITED TEEN-AGERS' HORSE PLAY IS INTERRUPTED BY A PIERCING TELEPATHIC COMMAND FROM PROFESSOR X!

FREE TIME IS **OVER!** RESUME YOUR PLACES! THE TRAINING PERIOD WILL CONTINUE!

IT'S **MARVEL GIRL'S** TURN NOW! ARE YOU READY, JEAN?

A MOMENT LATER...

IT IS TIME FOR YOUR **DEXTERITY** TEST, JEAN! HOLD THAT BLOCK OF WOOD MOTIONLESS IN THE AIR! GOOD! GOOD!

AND NOW, SEE HOW QUICKLY YOU CAN FIT IT THROUGH THE VARIOUS FORMS ON THE PRACTICE RACK! **GO!**

ISN'T THIS RATHER **SIMPLE** FOR ONE WITH MY ABILITY, PROFESSOR?

YOU KNOW THE RULES, GIRL! **NO TALKING** DURING TESTING PERIOD!

OH-- SORRY, SIR!

I **KNOW** THE EXTENT OF YOUR TELEKINESIS POWER AS WELL AS YOU, JEAN! BUT IT IS NOT YOUR **POWER** WE ARE TESTING TODAY...

...IT IS HOW SKILLFULLY AND RAPIDLY YOU CAN **USE** IT! **SEVEN SECONDS!** GOOD! A MARKED IMPROVEMENT!

DOES THAT MEAN I'M READY FOR **BIGGER** TASKS NOW, SIR? **PROFESSOR**-- WHAT'S WRONG?

SILENCE! I DETECT THE PRESENCE OF **ANOTHER MUTANT!** CLEAR YOUR MINDS OF ALL THOUGHTS! THERE MUST BE NO INTERFERENCE AS I TRY TO MENTALLY PINPOINT THE LOCATION!

THEN, THERE IN THE SILENT CHAMBER, THE MOST GIFTED OF ALL X-MEN SENDS HIS UNCANNY THOUGHT PROBE OUT OVER THE COUNTRYSIDE, BLANKETING THE AREA WITH INVISIBLE TELEPATHIC EYES!

3

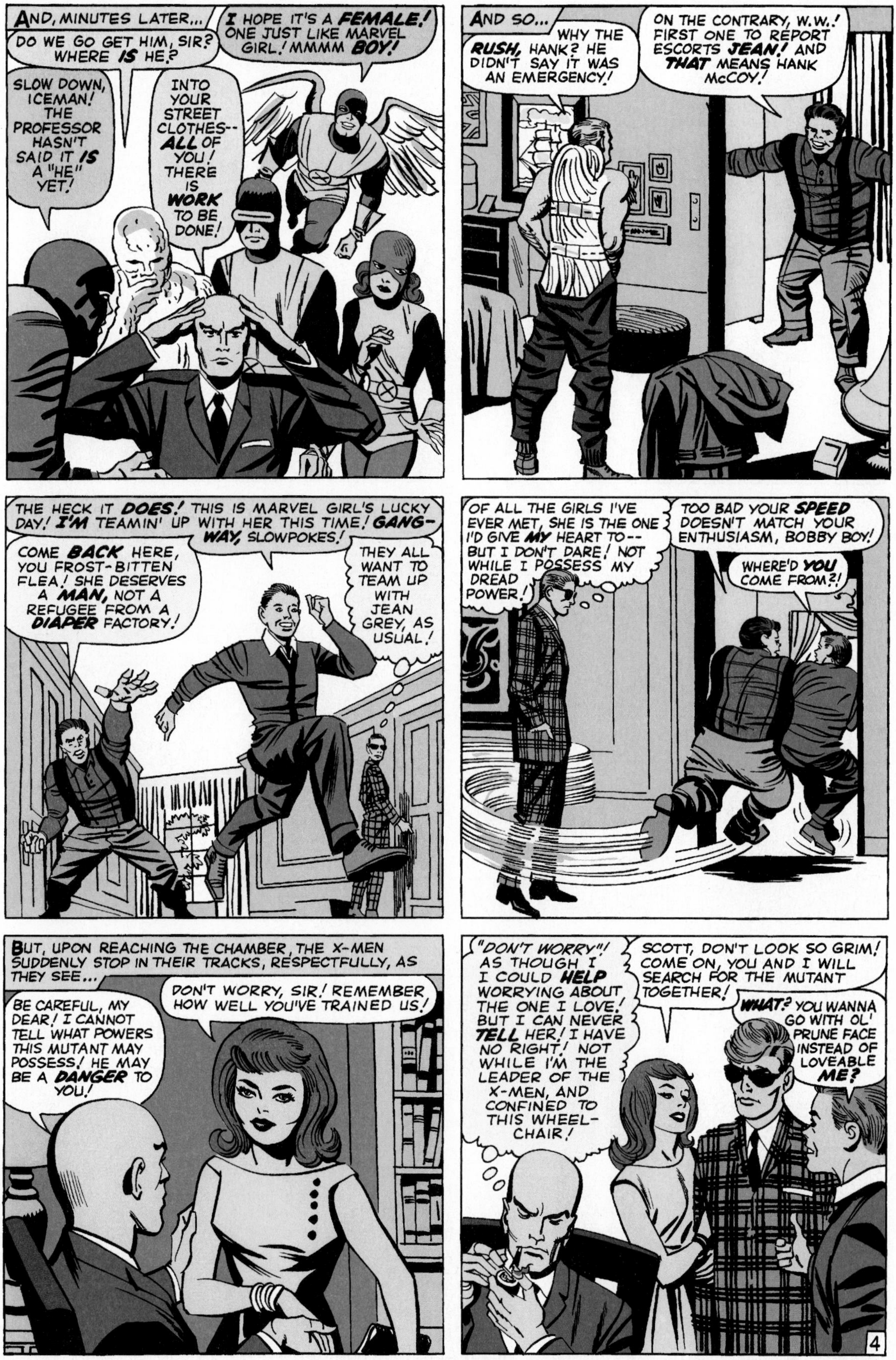
AND, MINUTES LATER...
DO WE GO GET HIM, SIR? WHERE IS HE?
I HOPE IT'S A FEMALE! ONE JUST LIKE MARVEL GIRL! MMMM BOY!
SLOW DOWN, ICEMAN! THE PROFESSOR HASN'T SAID IT IS A "HE" YET!
INTO YOUR STREET CLOTHES--ALL OF YOU! THERE IS WORK TO BE DONE!
AND SO...
WHY THE RUSH, HANK? HE DIDN'T SAY IT WAS AN EMERGENCY!
ON THE CONTRARY, W.W.! FIRST ONE TO REPORT ESCORTS JEAN! AND THAT MEANS HANK McCOY!
THE HECK IT DOES! THIS IS MARVEL GIRL'S LUCKY DAY! I'M TEAMIN' UP WITH HER THIS TIME! GANG-WAY, SLOWPOKES!
COME BACK HERE, YOU FROST-BITTEN FLEA! SHE DESERVES A MAN, NOT A REFUGEE FROM A DIAPER FACTORY!
THEY ALL WANT TO TEAM UP WITH JEAN GREY, AS USUAL!
OF ALL THE GIRLS I'VE EVER MET, SHE IS THE ONE I'D GIVE MY HEART TO--BUT I DON'T DARE! NOT WHILE I POSSESS MY DREAD POWER!
TOO BAD YOUR SPEED DOESN'T MATCH YOUR ENTHUSIASM, BOBBY BOY!
WHERE'D YOU COME FROM?!
BUT, UPON REACHING THE CHAMBER, THE X-MEN SUDDENLY STOP IN THEIR TRACKS, RESPECTFULLY, AS THEY SEE...
BE CAREFUL, MY DEAR! I CANNOT TELL WHAT POWERS THIS MUTANT MAY POSSESS! HE MAY BE A DANGER TO YOU!
DON'T WORRY, SIR! REMEMBER HOW WELL YOU'VE TRAINED US!
"DON'T WORRY"! AS THOUGH I COULD HELP WORRYING ABOUT THE ONE I LOVE! BUT I CAN NEVER TELL HER! I HAVE NO RIGHT! NOT WHILE I'M THE LEADER OF THE X-MEN, AND CONFINED TO THIS WHEEL-CHAIR!
SCOTT, DON'T LOOK SO GRIM! COME ON, YOU AND I WILL SEARCH FOR THE MUTANT TOGETHER!
WHAT? YOU WANNA GO WITH OL' PRUNE FACE INSTEAD OF LOVEABLE ME?
4

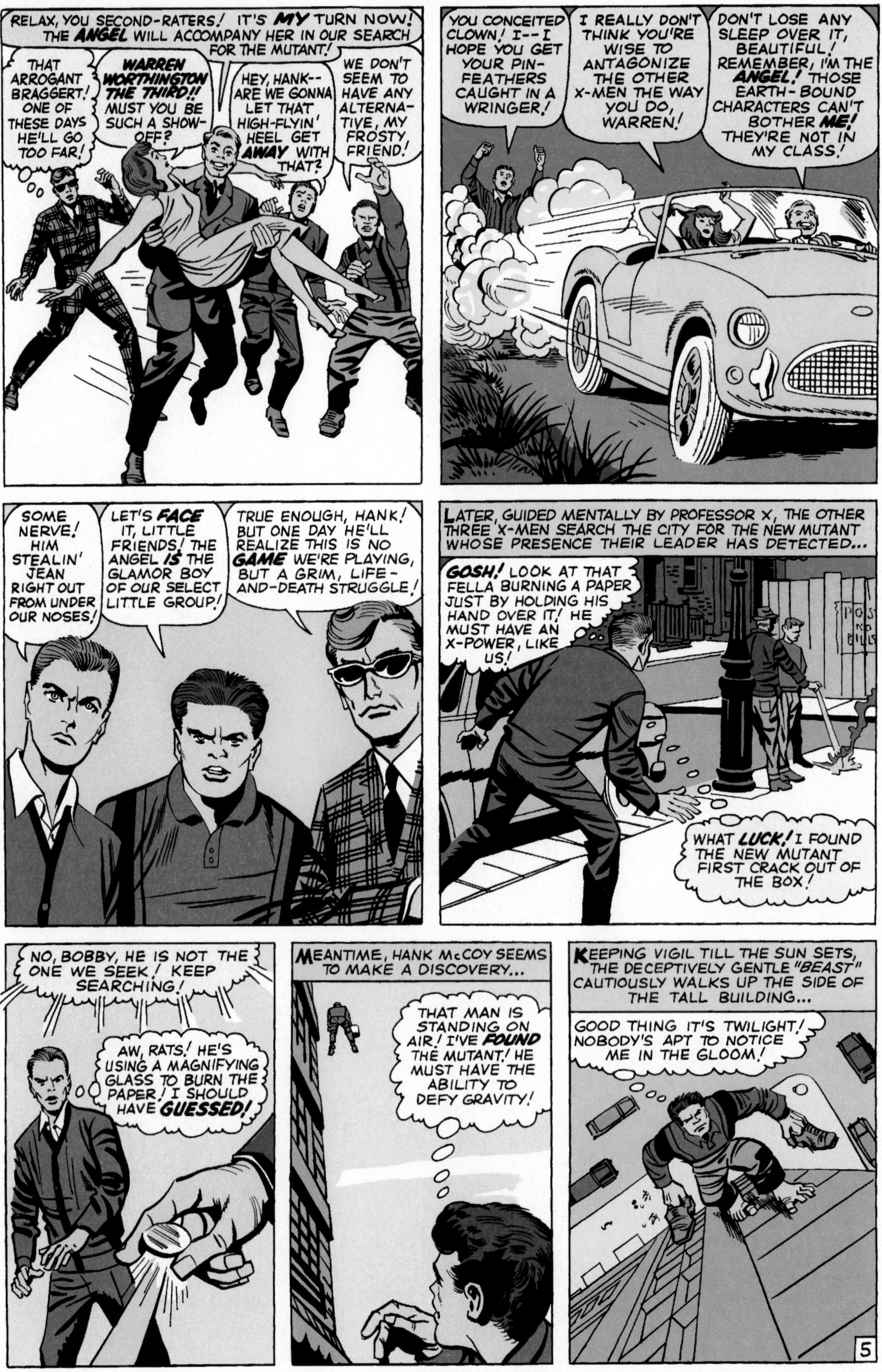
RELAX, YOU SECOND-RATERS! IT'S MY TURN NOW! THE ANGEL WILL ACCOMPANY HER IN OUR SEARCH FOR THE MUTANT!
THAT ARROGANT BRAGGERT! ONE OF THESE DAYS HE'LL GO TOO FAR!
WARREN WORTHINGTON THE THIRD!! MUST YOU BE SUCH A SHOW-OFF?
HEY, HANK-- ARE WE GONNA LET THAT HIGH-FLYIN' HEEL GET AWAY WITH THAT?
WE DON'T SEEM TO HAVE ANY ALTERNATIVE, MY FROSTY FRIEND!
YOU CONCEITED CLOWN! I--I HOPE YOU GET YOUR PIN-FEATHERS CAUGHT IN A WRINGER!
I REALLY DON'T THINK YOU'RE WISE TO ANTAGONIZE THE OTHER X-MEN THE WAY YOU DO, WARREN!
DON'T LOSE ANY SLEEP OVER IT, BEAUTIFUL! REMEMBER, I'M THE ANGEL! THOSE EARTH-BOUND CHARACTERS CAN'T BOTHER ME! THEY'RE NOT IN MY CLASS!
SOME NERVE! HIM STEALIN' JEAN RIGHT OUT FROM UNDER OUR NOSES!
LET'S FACE IT, LITTLE FRIENDS! THE ANGEL IS THE GLAMOR BOY OF OUR SELECT LITTLE GROUP!
TRUE ENOUGH, HANK! BUT ONE DAY HE'LL REALIZE THIS IS NO GAME WE'RE PLAYING, BUT A GRIM, LIFE-AND-DEATH STRUGGLE!
LATER, GUIDED MENTALLY BY PROFESSOR X, THE OTHER THREE X-MEN SEARCH THE CITY FOR THE NEW MUTANT WHOSE PRESENCE THEIR LEADER HAS DETECTED...
GOSH! LOOK AT THAT FELLA BURNING A PAPER JUST BY HOLDING HIS HAND OVER IT! HE MUST HAVE AN X-POWER, LIKE US!
WHAT LUCK! I FOUND THE NEW MUTANT FIRST CRACK OUT OF THE BOX!
NO, BOBBY, HE IS NOT THE ONE WE SEEK! KEEP SEARCHING!
AW, RATS! HE'S USING A MAGNIFYING GLASS TO BURN THE PAPER! I SHOULD HAVE GUESSED!
MEANTIME, HANK McCOY SEEMS TO MAKE A DISCOVERY...
THAT MAN IS STANDING ON AIR! I'VE FOUND THE MUTANT! HE MUST HAVE THE ABILITY TO DEFY GRAVITY!
KEEPING VIGIL TILL THE SUN SETS, THE DECEPTIVELY GENTLE "BEAST" CAUTIOUSLY WALKS UP THE SIDE OF THE TALL BUILDING...
GOOD THING IT'S TWILIGHT! NOBODY'S APT TO NOTICE ME IN THE GLOOM!
5

BUT, UPON REACHING THE FOURTH FLOOR, HANK FINDS...

FALSE ALARM! HE'S MERELY SETTING UP AN ADVERTISING DISPLAY, AND STANDING UPON THE TRANSPARENT GLASS SHIELD WHICH WILL PROTECT THE SIGN!

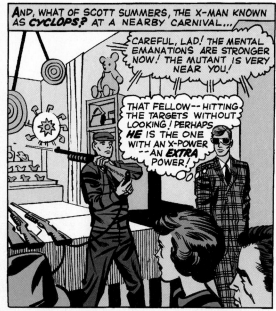

AND, WHAT OF SCOTT SUMMERS, THE X-MAN KNOWN AS CYCLOPS? AT A NEARBY CARNIVAL...

CAREFUL, LAD! THE MENTAL EMANATIONS ARE STRONGER NOW! THE MUTANT IS VERY NEAR YOU!

THAT FELLOW-- HITTING THE TARGETS WITHOUT LOOKING! PERHAPS HE IS THE ONE WITH AN X-POWER --AN EXTRA POWER!

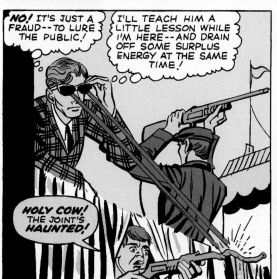

NO! IT'S JUST A FRAUD--TO LURE THE PUBLIC!

I'LL TEACH HIM A LITTLE LESSON WHILE I'M HERE--AND DRAIN OFF SOME SURPLUS ENERGY AT THE SAME TIME!

HOLY COW! THE JOINT'S HAUNTED!

AT THAT MOMENT, CYCLOPS HEARS THE SHRILL SOUND OF A BARKER'S RAUCUS PITCH...

ALL RIGHT, FOLKS, HERE'S OUR MAIN ATTRACTION! WHAT YOU'VE BEEN WAITIN' FOR!

THE ONE, THE ONLY, THE UNBELIEVABLE MARVEL OF THE AGE! FOR ONLY A QUARTER, THE FOURTH PART OF A DOLLAR, YOU CAN STEP INSIDE AND MEET--THE BLOB!

YOU WON'T BELIEVE YOUR EYES WHEN YOU SEE THE FEATS THE BLOB CAN PERFORM! SO HURRY, HURRY, HURRY-- THE SHOW STARTS IN FIVE MINUTES! DON'T PUSH--DON'T CROWD--THERE'S ROOM FOR ALL!!

THE BLOB! PERHAPS-- HE'S THE ONE--??

DON'T BUY A TICKET IF YOU'RE SQUEAMISH! STRONG MEN HAVE BEEN KNOWN TO FAINT WHEN THE BLOB PERFORMS! SO HURRY, HURRY, HURRY--

YES! IT IS HE! THE ONE CALLED THE BLOB!

I'VE FOUND HIM!

6

AND THEN, THE EXHIBITION BEGINS...

I WANT A HALF-DOZEN VOLUNTEERS --BIG, STRONG STRAPPING MEN!

YOU'LL WIN ONE HUNDRED DOLLARS IF YOU CAN MAKE THE BLOB MOVE!

ONE HUNDRED CLAMS!! WOW!

JUST TO MOVE FATSO THERE? IT'LL BE A CINCH!

BUT AFTER TEN EXHAUSTING MINUTES...

IT'S IMPOSSIBLE! WE CAN'T BUDGE HIM!

NO WONDER THEY OFFERED A HUNDRED BUCKS!! NATURE BOY HERE MUST BE NAILED TO THE FLOOR!!

SO HE'S THE MUTANT! HE DOESN'T SEEM SO GREAT TO ME! JUST A BIG, HEAVY GUY!

AND NOW FOR THE SECOND PART OF OUR DEMONSTRATION! THIS IS NOT FOR THE SQUEAMISH!! THE BLOB WILL STOP A RIFLE LOAD OF BULLETS WITH HIS BODY!! READY, TEX?

YES SUH! AH'M READY!

POW POW POW POW POW

SECONDS LATER, AFTER THE SMOKE HAS CLEARED!

FAKE! FAKE! HE WAS PROBABLY SHOOTIN' BLANKS!

WE WANT OUR MONEY BACK!

WAIT!! L-LOOK AT THAT!!

HE REALLY DID STOP THE SHELLS!!

THEY COULDN'T PENETRATE HIS SKIN!

WOW! HE'S TOSSIN' THE SHELLS AWAY JUST BY EXPANDING HIS CHEST!!

NEVER SAW ANYTHING LIKE IT! THE BLOB HAS A BODY LIKE SILLY PUTTY! HE CAN DO ANYTHING!

7

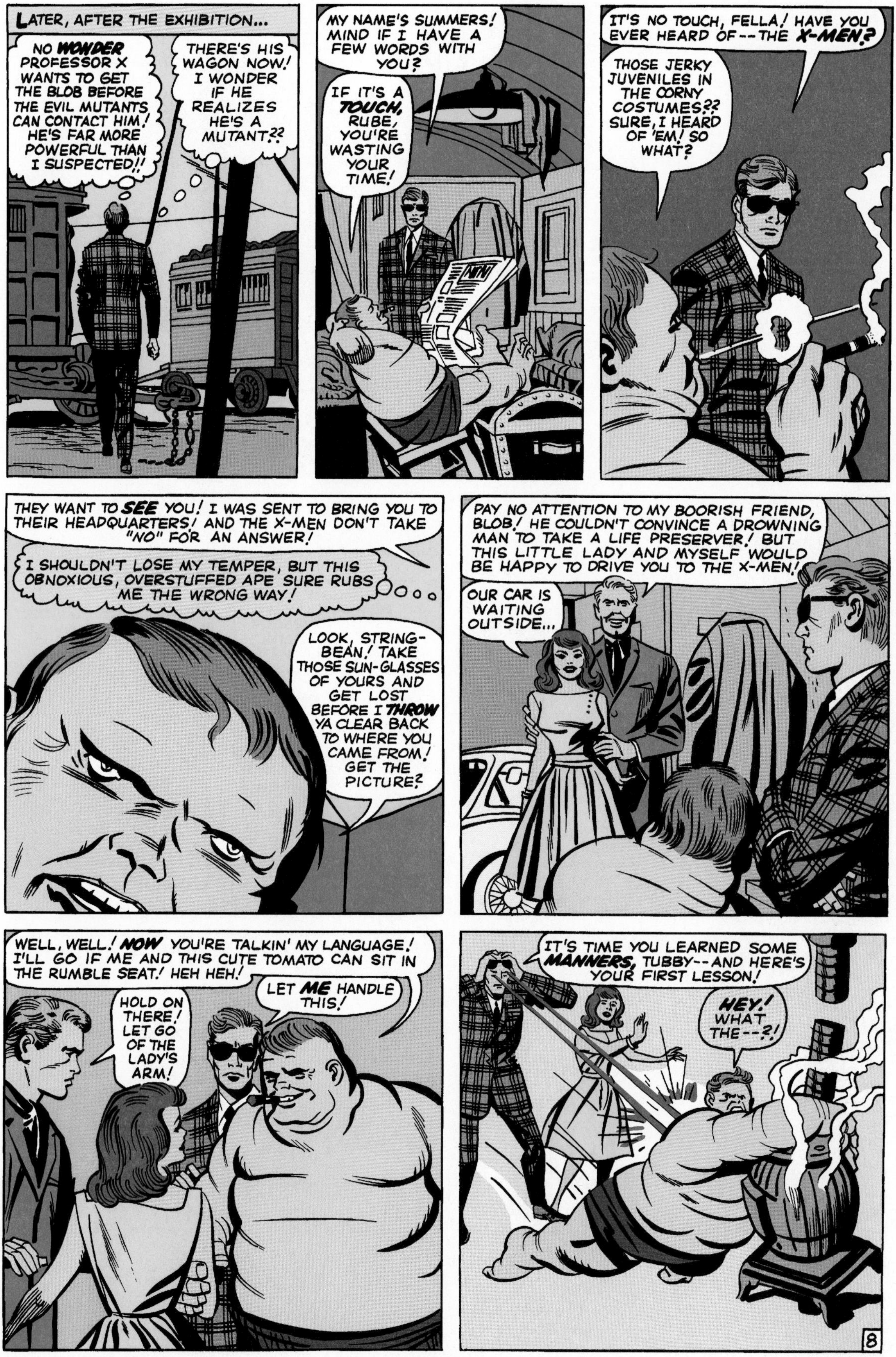

LATER, AFTER THE EXHIBITION...
NO WONDER PROFESSOR X WANTS TO GET THE BLOB BEFORE THE EVIL MUTANTS CAN CONTACT HIM! HE'S FAR MORE POWERFUL THAN I SUSPECTED!!
THERE'S HIS WAGON NOW! I WONDER IF HE REALIZES HE'S A MUTANT??
MY NAME'S SUMMERS! MIND IF I HAVE A FEW WORDS WITH YOU?
IF IT'S A TOUCH, RUBE, YOU'RE WASTING YOUR TIME!
IT'S NO TOUCH, FELLA! HAVE YOU EVER HEARD OF -- THE X-MEN?
THOSE JERKY JUVENILES IN THE CORNY COSTUMES?? SURE, I HEARD OF 'EM! SO WHAT?
THEY WANT TO SEE YOU! I WAS SENT TO BRING YOU TO THEIR HEADQUARTERS! AND THE X-MEN DON'T TAKE "NO" FOR AN ANSWER!
I SHOULDN'T LOSE MY TEMPER, BUT THIS OBNOXIOUS, OVERSTUFFED APE SURE RUBS ME THE WRONG WAY!
LOOK, STRING-BEAN! TAKE THOSE SUN-GLASSES OF YOURS AND GET LOST BEFORE I THROW YA CLEAR BACK TO WHERE YOU CAME FROM! GET THE PICTURE?
PAY NO ATTENTION TO MY BOORISH FRIEND, BLOB! HE COULDN'T CONVINCE A DROWNING MAN TO TAKE A LIFE PRESERVER! BUT THIS LITTLE LADY AND MYSELF WOULD BE HAPPY TO DRIVE YOU TO THE X-MEN!
OUR CAR IS WAITING OUTSIDE...
WELL, WELL! NOW YOU'RE TALKIN' MY LANGUAGE! I'LL GO IF ME AND THIS CUTE TOMATO CAN SIT IN THE RUMBLE SEAT! HEH HEH!
HOLD ON THERE! LET GO OF THE LADY'S ARM!
LET ME HANDLE THIS!
IT'S TIME YOU LEARNED SOME MANNERS, TUBBY--AND HERE'S YOUR FIRST LESSON!
HEY! WHAT THE--?!
8

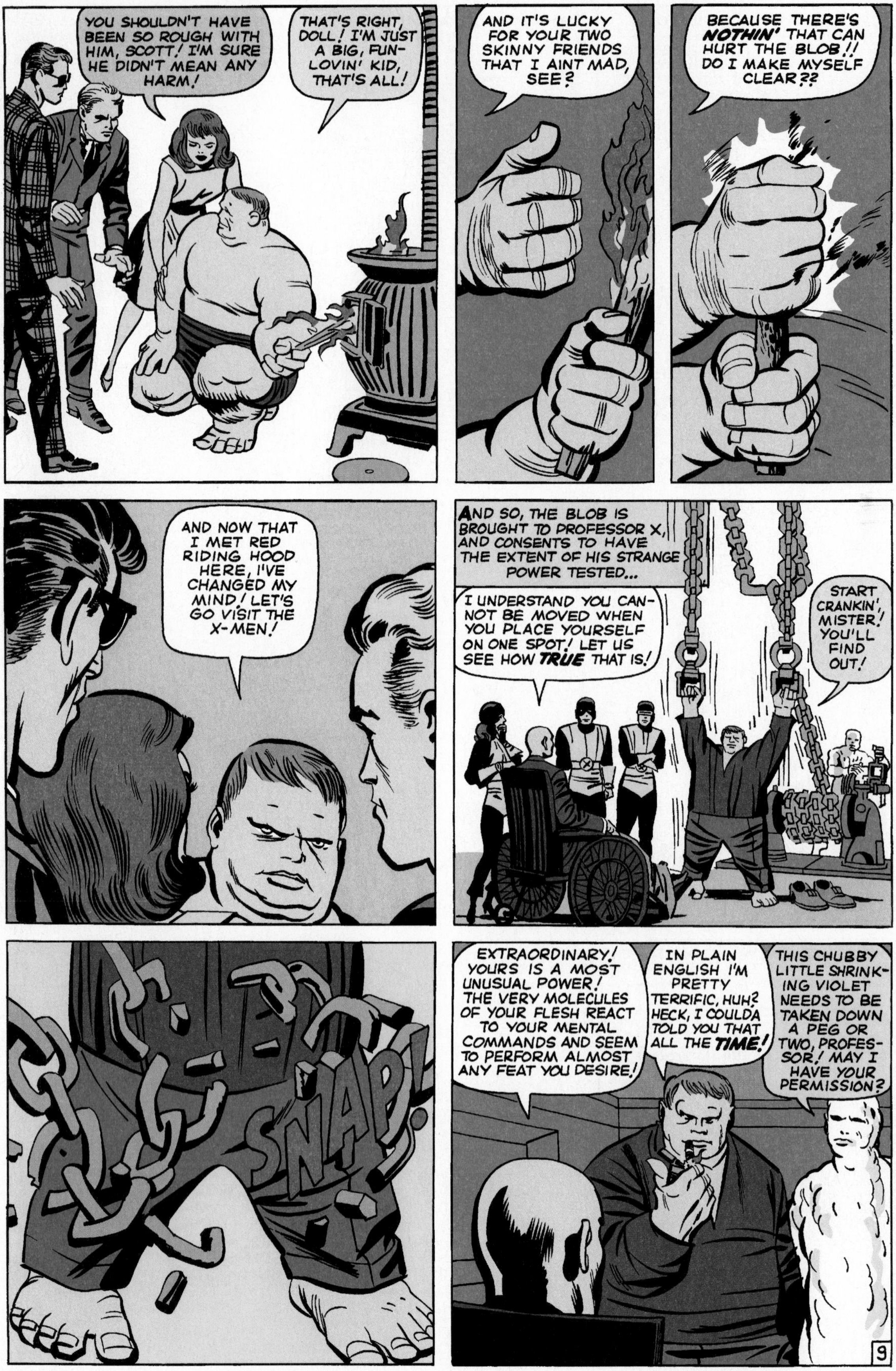

YOU SHOULDN'T HAVE BEEN SO ROUGH WITH HIM, SCOTT! I'M SURE HE DIDN'T MEAN ANY HARM!
THAT'S RIGHT, DOLL! I'M JUST A BIG, FUN-LOVIN' KID, THAT'S ALL!
AND IT'S LUCKY FOR YOUR TWO SKINNY FRIENDS THAT I AINT MAD, SEE?
BECAUSE THERE'S NOTHIN' THAT CAN HURT THE BLOB!! DO I MAKE MYSELF CLEAR??
AND NOW THAT I MET RED RIDING HOOD HERE, I'VE CHANGED MY MIND! LET'S GO VISIT THE X-MEN!
AND SO, THE BLOB IS BROUGHT TO PROFESSOR X, AND CONSENTS TO HAVE THE EXTENT OF HIS STRANGE POWER TESTED...
I UNDERSTAND YOU CAN-NOT BE MOVED WHEN YOU PLACE YOURSELF ON ONE SPOT! LET US SEE HOW TRUE THAT IS!
START CRANKIN', MISTER! YOU'LL FIND OUT!
SNAP!
EXTRAORDINARY! YOURS IS A MOST UNUSUAL POWER! THE VERY MOLECULES OF YOUR FLESH REACT TO YOUR MENTAL COMMANDS AND SEEM TO PERFORM ALMOST ANY FEAT YOU DESIRE!
IN PLAIN ENGLISH I'M PRETTY TERRIFIC, HUH? HECK, I COULDA TOLD YOU THAT ALL THE TIME!
THIS CHUBBY LITTLE SHRINKING VIOLET NEEDS TO BE TAKEN DOWN A PEG OR TWO, PROFESSOR! MAY I HAVE YOUR PERMISSION?
9

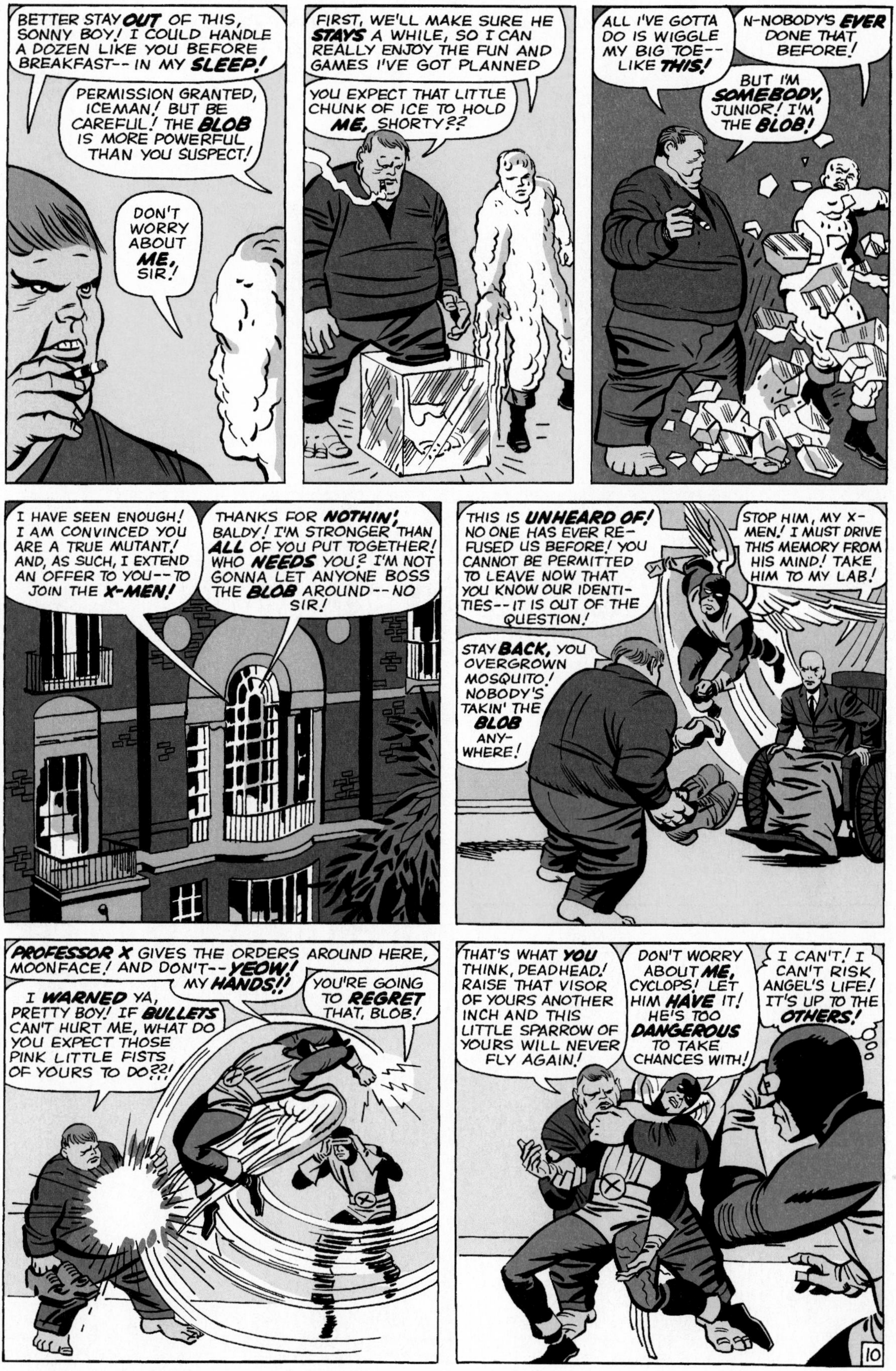
BETTER STAY OUT OF THIS, SONNY BOY! I COULD HANDLE A DOZEN LIKE YOU BEFORE BREAKFAST-- IN MY SLEEP!
PERMISSION GRANTED, ICEMAN! BUT BE CAREFUL! THE BLOB IS MORE POWERFUL THAN YOU SUSPECT!
DON'T WORRY ABOUT ME, SIR!
FIRST, WE'LL MAKE SURE HE STAYS A WHILE, SO I CAN REALLY ENJOY THE FUN AND GAMES I'VE GOT PLANNED
YOU EXPECT THAT LITTLE CHUNK OF ICE TO HOLD ME, SHORTY??
ALL I'VE GOTTA DO IS WIGGLE MY BIG TOE-- LIKE THIS!
N-NOBODY'S EVER DONE THAT BEFORE!
BUT I'M SOMEBODY, JUNIOR! I'M THE BLOB!
I HAVE SEEN ENOUGH! I AM CONVINCED YOU ARE A TRUE MUTANT! AND, AS SUCH, I EXTEND AN OFFER TO YOU--TO JOIN THE X-MEN!
THANKS FOR NOTHIN', BALDY! I'M STRONGER THAN ALL OF YOU PUT TOGETHER! WHO NEEDS YOU? I'M NOT GONNA LET ANYONE BOSS THE BLOB AROUND--NO SIR!
THIS IS UNHEARD OF! NO ONE HAS EVER REFUSED US BEFORE! YOU CANNOT BE PERMITTED TO LEAVE NOW THAT YOU KNOW OUR IDENTITIES--IT IS OUT OF THE QUESTION!
STOP HIM, MY X-MEN! I MUST DRIVE THIS MEMORY FROM HIS MIND! TAKE HIM TO MY LAB!
STAY BACK, YOU OVERGROWN MOSQUITO! NOBODY'S TAKIN' THE BLOB ANYWHERE!
PROFESSOR X GIVES THE ORDERS AROUND HERE, MOONFACE! AND DON'T--YEOW! MY HANDS!!
I WARNED YA, PRETTY BOY! IF BULLETS CAN'T HURT ME, WHAT DO YOU EXPECT THOSE PINK LITTLE FISTS OF YOURS TO DO??!
YOU'RE GOING TO REGRET THAT, BLOB!
THAT'S WHAT YOU THINK, DEADHEAD! RAISE THAT VISOR OF YOURS ANOTHER INCH AND THIS LITTLE SPARROW OF YOURS WILL NEVER FLY AGAIN!
DON'T WORRY ABOUT ME, CYCLOPS! LET HIM HAVE IT! HE'S TOO DANGEROUS TO TAKE CHANCES WITH!
I CAN'T! I CAN'T RISK ANGEL'S LIFE! IT'S UP TO THE OTHERS!
10

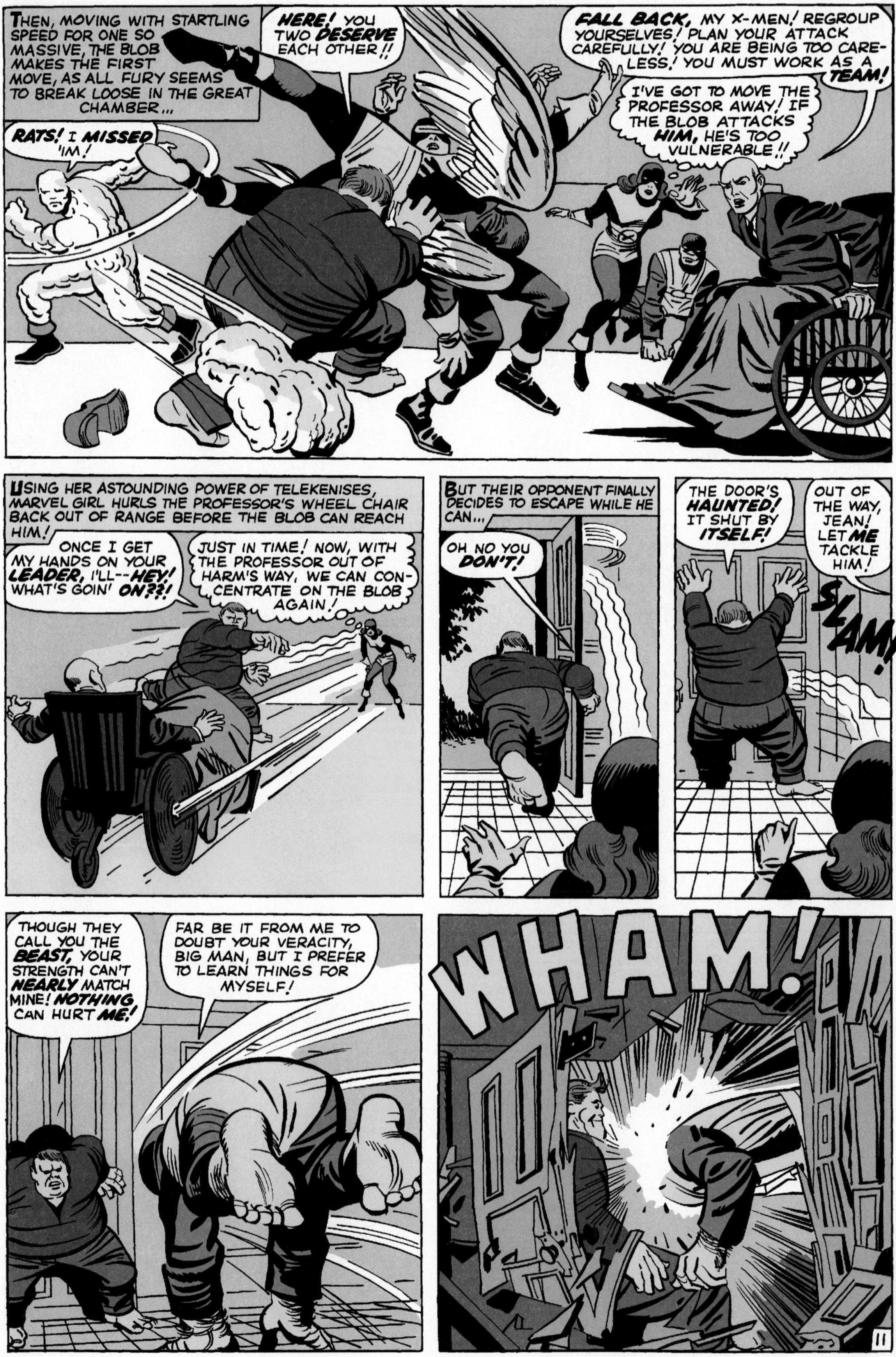
THEN, MOVING WITH STARTLING SPEED FOR ONE SO MASSIVE, THE BLOB MAKES THE FIRST MOVE, AS ALL FURY SEEMS TO BREAK LOOSE IN THE GREAT CHAMBER...
HERE! YOU TWO DESERVE EACH OTHER!!
RATS! I MISSED 'IM!
FALL BACK, MY X-MEN! REGROUP YOURSELVES! PLAN YOUR ATTACK CAREFULLY! YOU ARE BEING TOO CARELESS! YOU MUST WORK AS A TEAM!
I'VE GOT TO MOVE THE PROFESSOR AWAY! IF THE BLOB ATTACKS HIM, HE'S TOO VULNERABLE!!
USING HER ASTOUNDING POWER OF TELEKENISES, MARVEL GIRL HURLS THE PROFESSOR'S WHEEL CHAIR BACK OUT OF RANGE BEFORE THE BLOB CAN REACH HIM!
ONCE I GET MY HANDS ON YOUR LEADER, I'LL--HEY! WHAT'S GOIN' ON??!
JUST IN TIME! NOW, WITH THE PROFESSOR OUT OF HARM'S WAY, WE CAN CONCENTRATE ON THE BLOB AGAIN!
BUT THEIR OPPONENT FINALLY DECIDES TO ESCAPE WHILE HE CAN...
OH NO YOU DON'T!
THE DOOR'S HAUNTED! IT SHUT BY ITSELF!
OUT OF THE WAY, JEAN! LET ME TACKLE HIM!
SLAM!
THOUGH THEY CALL YOU THE BEAST, YOUR STRENGTH CAN'T NEARLY MATCH MINE! NOTHING CAN HURT ME!
FAR BE IT FROM ME TO DOUBT YOUR VERACITY, BIG MAN, BUT I PREFER TO LEARN THINGS FOR MYSELF!
WHAM!
11

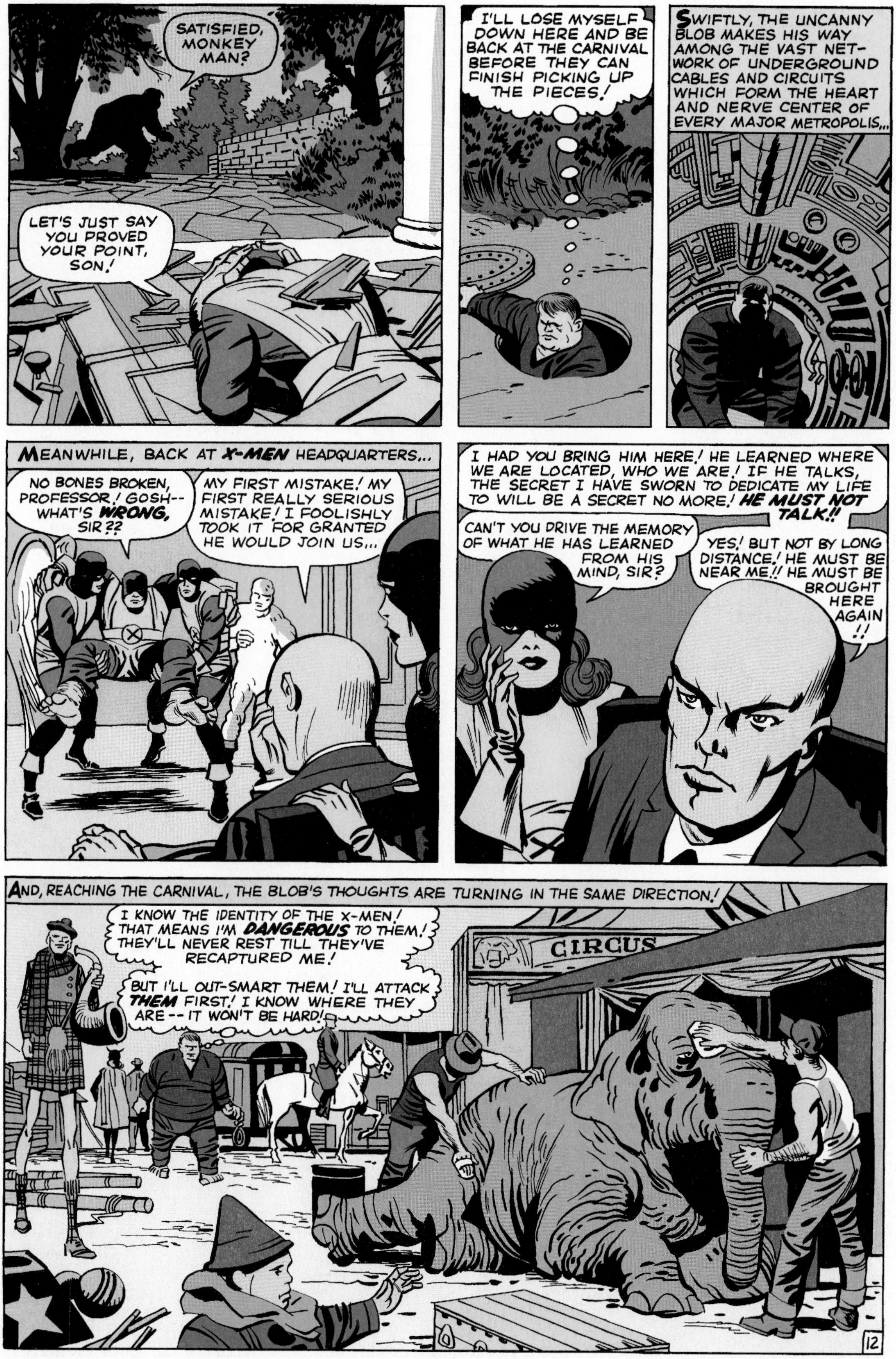
SATISFIED, MONKEY MAN?
LET'S JUST SAY YOU PROVED YOUR POINT, SON!
I'LL LOSE MYSELF DOWN HERE AND BE BACK AT THE CARNIVAL BEFORE THEY CAN FINISH PICKING UP THE PIECES!
SWIFTLY, THE UNCANNY BLOB MAKES HIS WAY AMONG THE VAST NET-WORK OF UNDERGROUND CABLES AND CIRCUITS WHICH FORM THE HEART AND NERVE CENTER OF EVERY MAJOR METROPOLIS...
MEANWHILE, BACK AT X-MEN HEADQUARTERS...
NO BONES BROKEN, PROFESSOR! GOSH-- WHAT'S WRONG, SIR??
MY FIRST MISTAKE! MY FIRST REALLY SERIOUS MISTAKE! I FOOLISHLY TOOK IT FOR GRANTED HE WOULD JOIN US...
I HAD YOU BRING HIM HERE! HE LEARNED WHERE WE ARE LOCATED, WHO WE ARE! IF HE TALKS, THE SECRET I HAVE SWORN TO DEDICATE MY LIFE TO WILL BE A SECRET NO MORE! HE MUST NOT TALK!!
CAN'T YOU DRIVE THE MEMORY OF WHAT HE HAS LEARNED FROM HIS MIND, SIR?
YES! BUT NOT BY LONG DISTANCE! HE MUST BE NEAR ME!! HE MUST BE BROUGHT HERE AGAIN!!
AND, REACHING THE CARNIVAL, THE BLOB'S THOUGHTS ARE TURNING IN THE SAME DIRECTION!
I KNOW THE IDENTITY OF THE X-MEN! THAT MEANS I'M DANGEROUS TO THEM! THEY'LL NEVER REST TILL THEY'VE RECAPTURED ME!
BUT I'LL OUT-SMART THEM! I'LL ATTACK THEM FIRST! I KNOW WHERE THEY ARE -- IT WON'T BE HARD!
CIRCUS
12

THE *BLOB!* WHERE IN SAM HILL HAVE YOU *BEEN,* YOU BRAINLESS LUMMOX?!!

SHUT YOUR MOUTH! AND *STAND UP* WHEN YOU SEE ME! THINGS ARE GONNA BE MIGHTY *DIFFERENT* AROUND HERE NOW!

FOR YEARS I THOUGHT I WAS JUST AN EXTRA-STRONG FREAK! BUT I FOUND OUT WHAT I *REALLY* AM! I'M A *MUTANT!* UNDERSTAND?! I'M ONE OF *HOMO-SUPERIOR!* AND THAT MEANS *I'LL* RUN THIS SHOW FROM NOW ON.!! ANY OBJECTIONS??

N-NO!!

GET EVERYBODY TOGETHER!! ALL THE FREAKS, ACROBATS PERFORMERS--EVERYBODY,!! I WANT THEM HERE IN FIVE MINUTES! NOW HOP TO IT, YOU PUNY HOMO SAPIEN! *MOVE* WHEN I GIVE AN ORDER!!

AND SO...

FROM NOW ON YOU ALL TAKE ORDERS FROM *ME!* AND THOSE WHO *DON'T* WILL WISH THEY *HAD!* I'M GONNA MAKE YOU ALL *FAMOUS!!*

YOU'RE GONNA HELP ME BEAT THE *X-MEN!* I KNOW WHERE THEY'RE HIDDEN! WE'RE ATTACKING THEM!! YOU'VE GOT YOUR WEAPONS, AND YOU'VE GOT *ME!* WE CAN'T LOSE!

HEY, *LOOK!!* THERE'S ONE OF 'EM *NOW!* HE MUST BE *SPYIN'* ON US!! WHAT DO WE DO???

SHOOT HIM *DOWN,* YOU FOOL! *HURRY!*

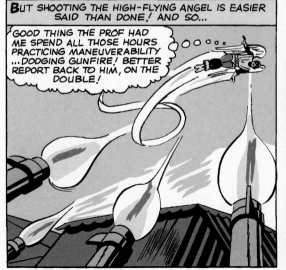

BUT SHOOTING THE HIGH-FLYING ANGEL IS EASIER SAID THAN DONE! AND SO...

GOOD THING THE PROF HAD ME SPEND ALL THOSE HOURS PRACTICING MANEUVERABILITY ...DODGING GUNFIRE! BETTER REPORT BACK TO HIM, ON THE DOUBLE!

MINUTES LATER, BACK AT PROFESSOR X'S PRIVATE LAB,...

GOOD WORK, ANGEL! IT'S AS I FEARED! HE'S PREPARING TO STRIKE AS SOON AS POSSIBLE!

THAT'S WHY I'M RUSHING TO COMPLETE THIS ELECTRONIC MASS INFLUENCER! IT WILL INTENSIFY MY OWN THOUGHT WAVES SO I CAN DRIVE ALL MEMORY OUT OF THE MINDS OF AN ENTIRE CROWD!

13

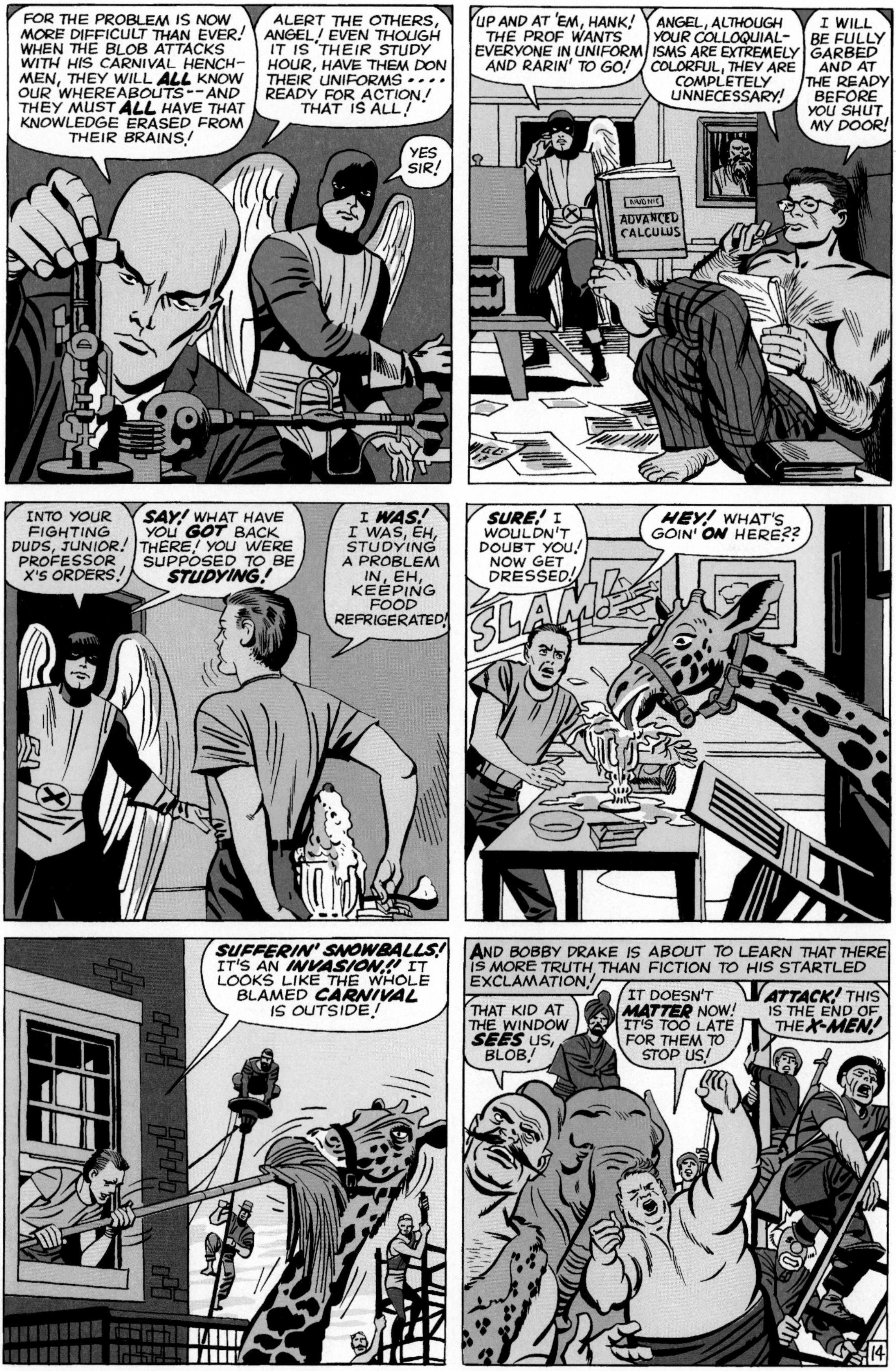
FOR THE PROBLEM IS NOW MORE DIFFICULT THAN EVER! WHEN THE BLOB ATTACKS WITH HIS CARNIVAL HENCHMEN, THEY WILL ALL KNOW OUR WHEREABOUTS--AND THEY MUST ALL HAVE THAT KNOWLEDGE ERASED FROM THEIR BRAINS!
ALERT THE OTHERS, ANGEL! EVEN THOUGH IT IS THEIR STUDY HOUR, HAVE THEM DON THEIR UNIFORMS .... READY FOR ACTION! THAT IS ALL!
YES SIR!
UP AND AT 'EM, HANK! THE PROF WANTS EVERYONE IN UNIFORM AND RARIN' TO GO!
ANGEL, ALTHOUGH YOUR COLLOQUIALISMS ARE EXTREMELY COLORFUL, THEY ARE COMPLETELY UNNECESSARY!
I WILL BE FULLY GARBED AND AT THE READY BEFORE YOU SHUT MY DOOR!
ADVANCED CALCULUS
INTO YOUR FIGHTING DUDS, JUNIOR! PROFESSOR X'S ORDERS!
SAY! WHAT HAVE YOU GOT BACK THERE! YOU WERE SUPPOSED TO BE STUDYING!
I WAS! I WAS, EH, STUDYING A PROBLEM IN, EH, KEEPING FOOD REFRIGERATED!
SURE! I WOULDN'T DOUBT YOU! NOW GET DRESSED!
SLAM!
HEY! WHAT'S GOIN' ON HERE??
SUFFERIN' SNOWBALLS! IT'S AN INVASION!! IT LOOKS LIKE THE WHOLE BLAMED CARNIVAL IS OUTSIDE!
AND BOBBY DRAKE IS ABOUT TO LEARN THAT THERE IS MORE TRUTH THAN FICTION TO HIS STARTLED EXCLAMATION!
THAT KID AT THE WINDOW SEES US, BLOB!
IT DOESN'T MATTER NOW! IT'S TOO LATE FOR THEM TO STOP US!
ATTACK! THIS IS THE END OF THE X-MEN!
14

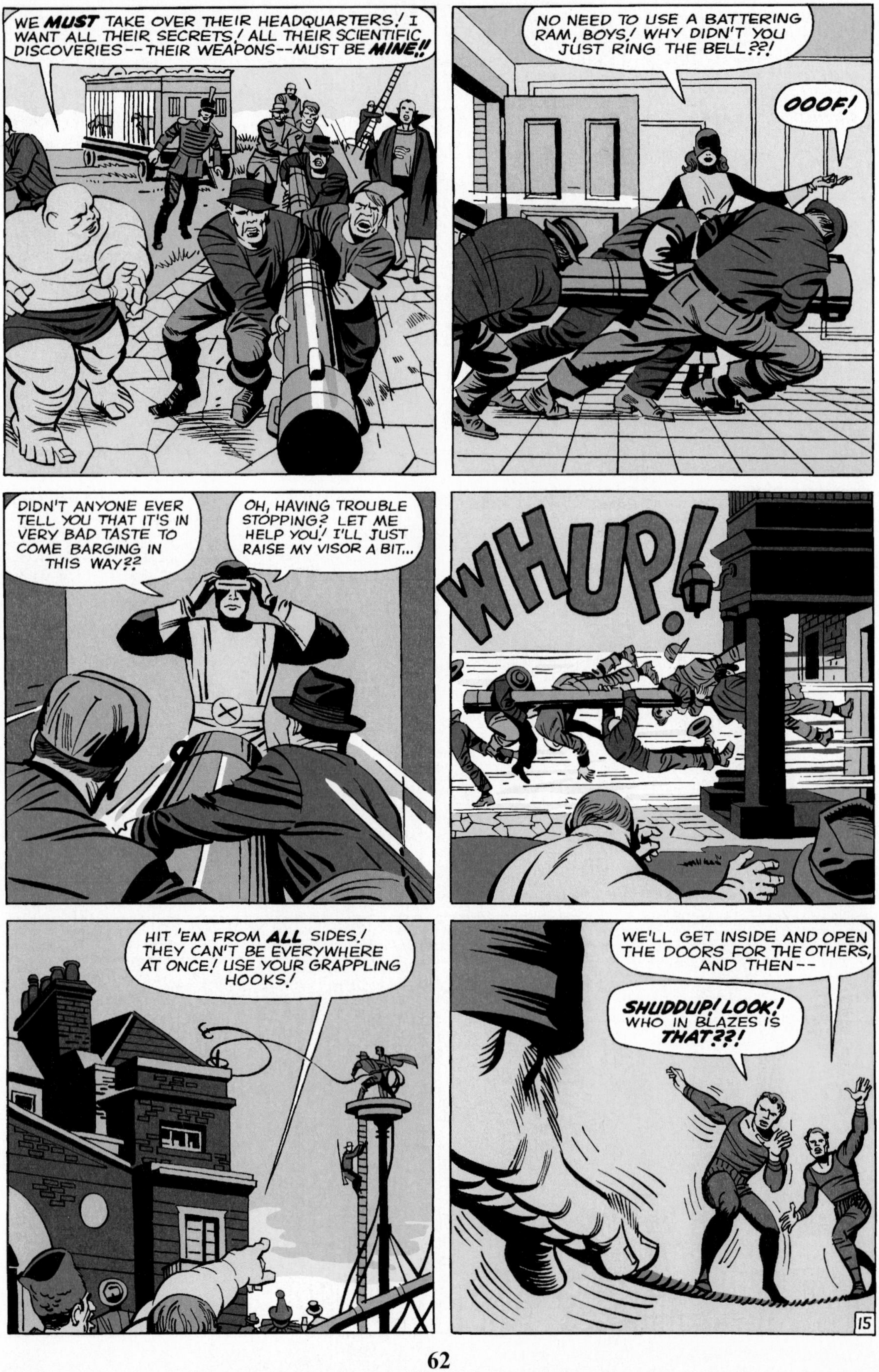
WE MUST TAKE OVER THEIR HEADQUARTERS! I WANT ALL THEIR SECRETS! ALL THEIR SCIENTIFIC DISCOVERIES--THEIR WEAPONS--MUST BE MINE!!
NO NEED TO USE A BATTERING RAM, BOYS! WHY DIDN'T YOU JUST RING THE BELL??!
OOOF!
DIDN'T ANYONE EVER TELL YOU THAT IT'S IN VERY BAD TASTE TO COME BARGING IN THIS WAY??
OH, HAVING TROUBLE STOPPING? LET ME HELP YOU! I'LL JUST RAISE MY VISOR A BIT...
WHUP!
HIT 'EM FROM ALL SIDES! THEY CAN'T BE EVERYWHERE AT ONCE! USE YOUR GRAPPLING HOOKS!
WE'LL GET INSIDE AND OPEN THE DOORS FOR THE OTHERS, AND THEN--
SHUDDUP! LOOK! WHO IN BLAZES IS THAT??!
15

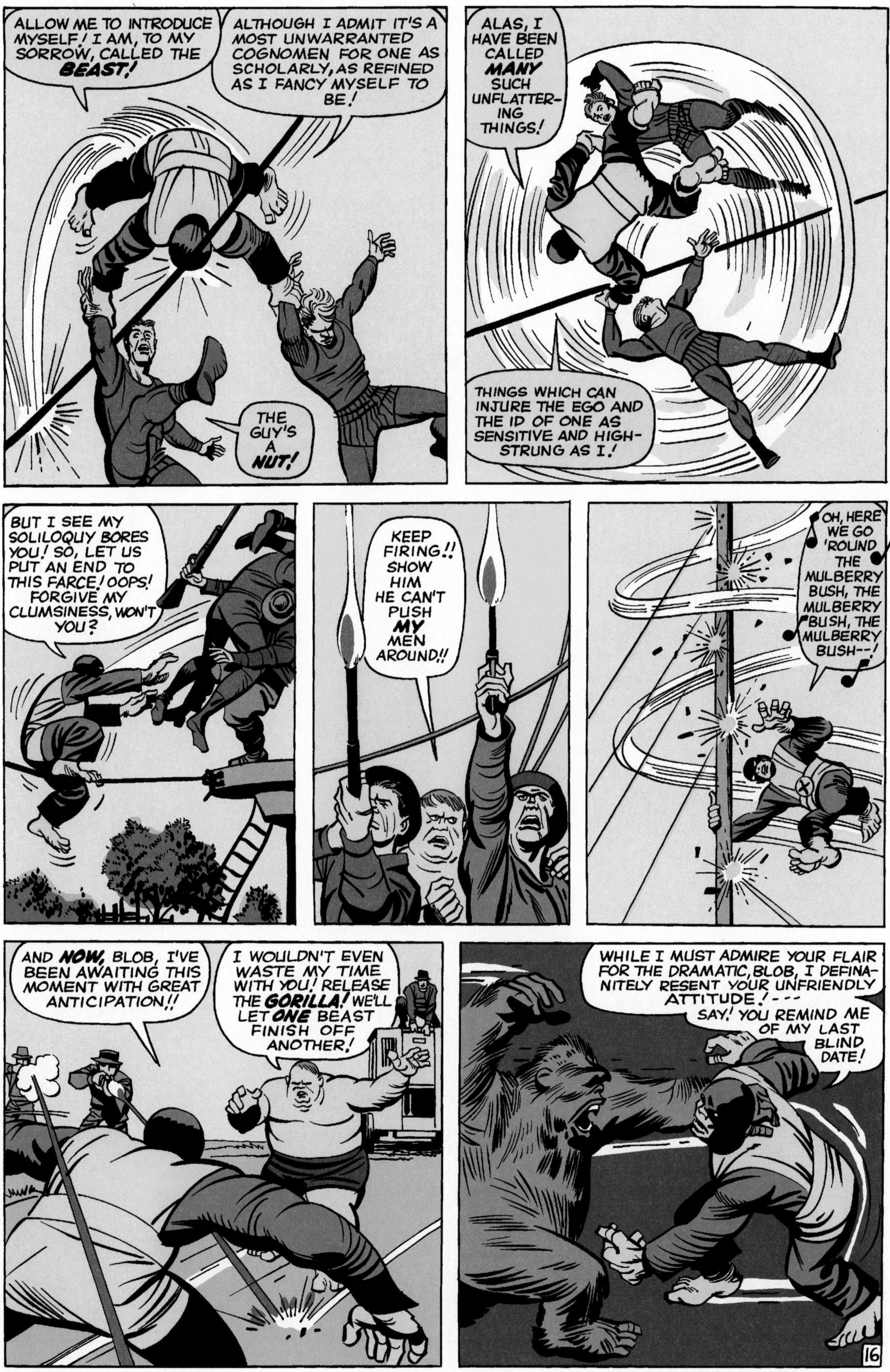
ALLOW ME TO INTRODUCE MYSELF! I AM, TO MY SORROW, CALLED THE BEAST!
ALTHOUGH I ADMIT IT'S A MOST UNWARRANTED COGNOMEN FOR ONE AS SCHOLARLY, AS REFINED AS I FANCY MYSELF TO BE!
THE GUY'S A NUT!
ALAS, I HAVE BEEN CALLED MANY SUCH UNFLATTERING THINGS!
THINGS WHICH CAN INJURE THE EGO AND THE ID OF ONE AS SENSITIVE AND HIGH-STRUNG AS I!
BUT I SEE MY SOLILOQUY BORES YOU! SO, LET US PUT AN END TO THIS FARCE! OOPS! FORGIVE MY CLUMSINESS, WON'T YOU?
KEEP FIRING!! SHOW HIM HE CAN'T PUSH MY MEN AROUND!!
OH, HERE WE GO 'ROUND THE MULBERRY BUSH, THE MULBERRY BUSH, THE MULBERRY BUSH--!
AND NOW, BLOB, I'VE BEEN AWAITING THIS MOMENT WITH GREAT ANTICIPATION!!
I WOULDN'T EVEN WASTE MY TIME WITH YOU! RELEASE THE GORILLA! WE'LL LET ONE BEAST FINISH OFF ANOTHER!
WHILE I MUST ADMIRE YOUR FLAIR FOR THE DRAMATIC, BLOB, I DEFINANITELY RESENT YOUR UNFRIENDLY ATTITUDE! - - -
SAY! YOU REMIND ME OF MY LAST BLIND DATE!
16

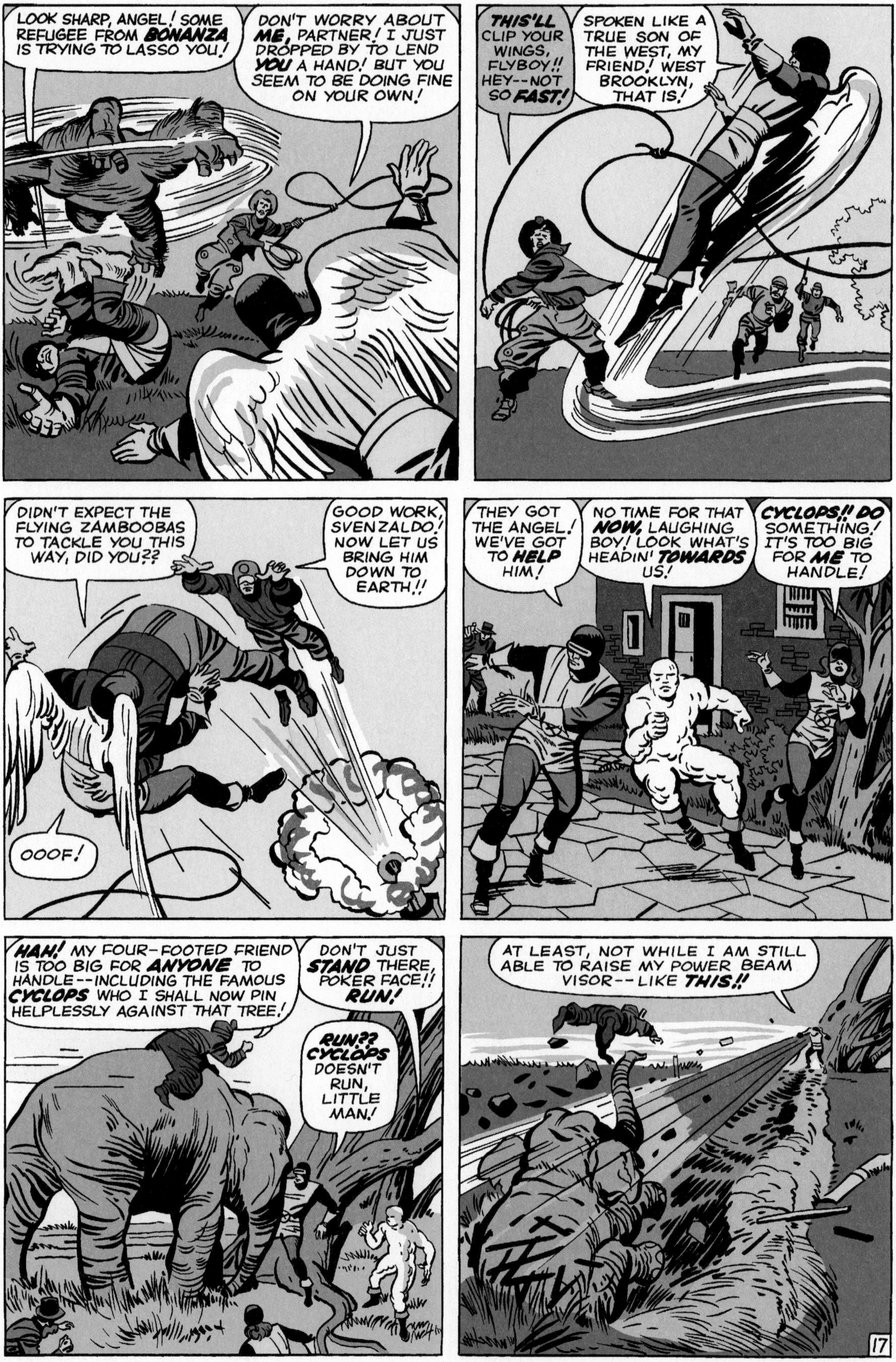
LOOK SHARP, ANGEL! SOME REFUGEE FROM BONANZA IS TRYING TO LASSO YOU!
DON'T WORRY ABOUT ME, PARTNER! I JUST DROPPED BY TO LEND YOU A HAND! BUT YOU SEEM TO BE DOING FINE ON YOUR OWN!
THIS'LL CLIP YOUR WINGS, FLYBOY!! HEY--NOT SO FAST!
SPOKEN LIKE A TRUE SON OF THE WEST, MY FRIEND! WEST BROOKLYN, THAT IS!
DIDN'T EXPECT THE FLYING ZAMBOOBAS TO TACKLE YOU THIS WAY, DID YOU??
GOOD WORK, SVENZALDO! NOW LET US BRING HIM DOWN TO EARTH!!
OOOF!
THEY GOT THE ANGEL! WE'VE GOT TO HELP HIM!
NO TIME FOR THAT NOW, LAUGHING BOY! LOOK WHAT'S HEADIN' TOWARDS US!
CYCLOPS!! DO SOMETHING! IT'S TOO BIG FOR ME TO HANDLE!
HAH! MY FOUR-FOOTED FRIEND IS TOO BIG FOR ANYONE TO HANDLE--INCLUDING THE FAMOUS CYCLOPS WHO I SHALL NOW PIN HELPLESSLY AGAINST THAT TREE!
DON'T JUST STAND THERE, POKER FACE!! RUN!
RUN?? CYCLOPS DOESN'T RUN, LITTLE MAN!
AT LEAST, NOT WHILE I AM STILL ABLE TO RAISE MY POWER BEAM VISOR--LIKE THIS!!
17

BUT THE AMOUNT OF ENERGY REQUIRED FOR SUCH A HIGH-INTENSITY POWER BLAST TEMPORARILY WEAKENS THE POWERFUL CYCLOPS, AND...

NOW'S OUR CHANCE! GRAB HIM!

WITH HIM OUT OF THE WAY, THE OTHERS WILL BE EASY!

BROTHER, ARE YOU LIVIN' IN A FOOLS' PARADISE!!

I'LL JUST TOSS OFF A FEW ICE TORPEDOES AND -- HEY! WHAT THE --??!!

THIS'LL TAKE CARE OF YOU, SMALL FRY!

THE BLOB WAS RIGHT! THESE INSULATED SUITS LET US GET NEAR THIS KID WITHOUT FREEZIN'!

I'VE GOT TO HELP ICEMAN!

BUT MARVEL GIRL SOON FINDS IT IS SHE WHO NEEDS HELP!

SURROUND HER! GOOD! NOW SEIZE HER! SHE CAN'T STOP ALL OF YOU AT ONCE!

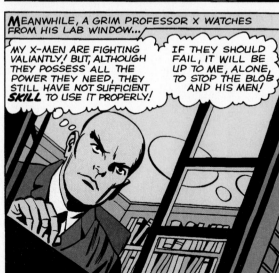

MEANWHILE, A GRIM PROFESSOR X WATCHES FROM HIS LAB WINDOW...

MY X-MEN ARE FIGHTING VALIANTLY! BUT, ALTHOUGH THEY POSSESS ALL THE POWER THEY NEED, THEY STILL HAVE NOT SUFFICIENT SKILL TO USE IT PROPERLY!

IF THEY SHOULD FAIL, IT WILL BE UP TO ME, ALONE, TO STOP THE BLOB AND HIS MEN!

MY LEGS ARE OF NO USE TO ME! I HAVE ONLY THE POWER OF MY BRAIN... AND THE HOPE OF COMPLETING THIS INTENSIFIER IN TIME!

18

65

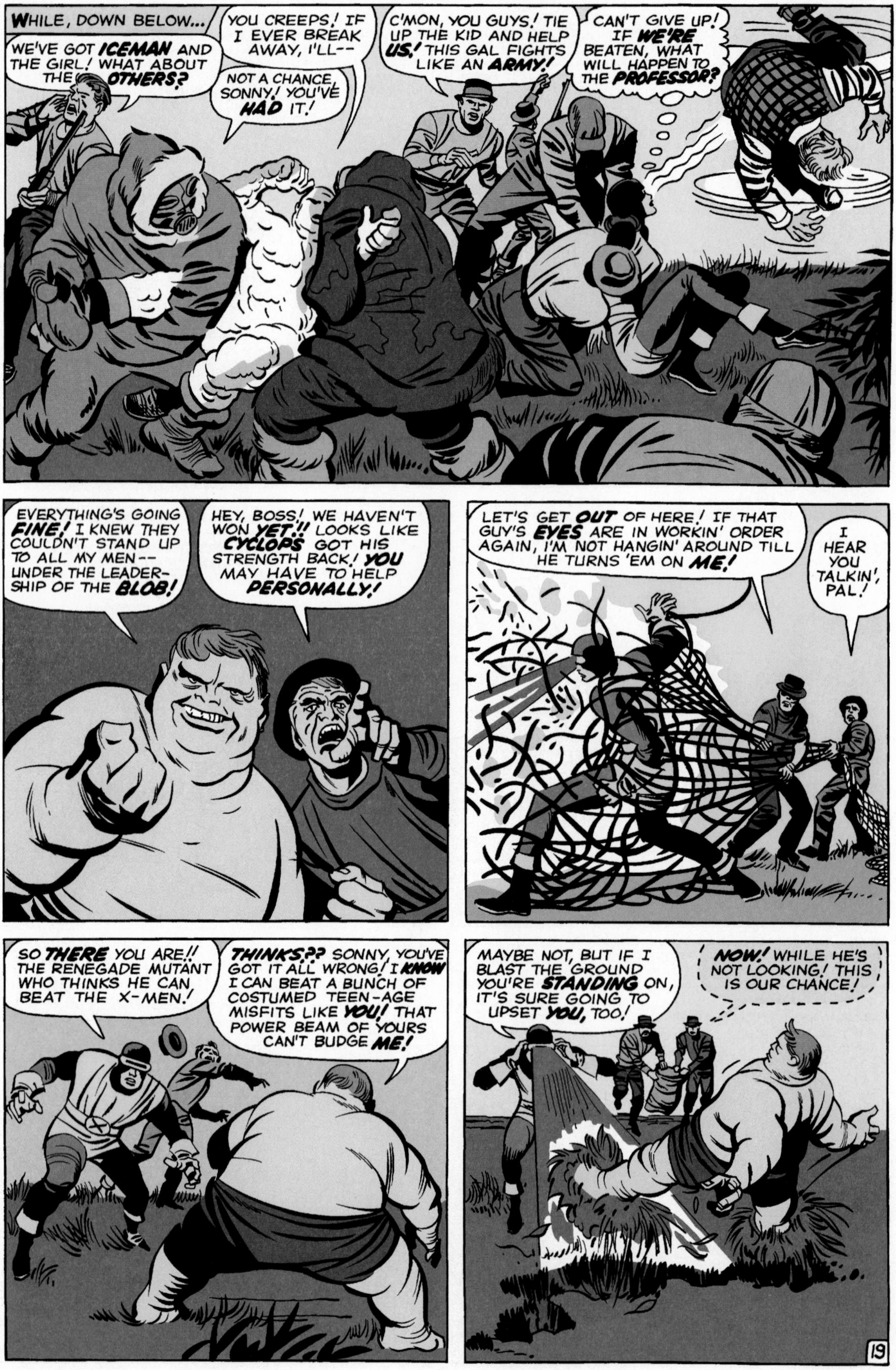
WHILE, DOWN BELOW...
WE'VE GOT ICEMAN AND THE GIRL! WHAT ABOUT THE OTHERS?
YOU CREEPS! IF I EVER BREAK AWAY, I'LL--
NOT A CHANCE, SONNY! YOU'VE HAD IT!
C'MON, YOU GUYS! TIE UP THE KID AND HELP US! THIS GAL FIGHTS LIKE AN ARMY!
CAN'T GIVE UP! IF WE'RE BEATEN, WHAT WILL HAPPEN TO THE PROFESSOR?
EVERYTHING'S GOING FINE! I KNEW THEY COULDN'T STAND UP TO ALL MY MEN-- UNDER THE LEADER-SHIP OF THE BLOB!
HEY, BOSS! WE HAVEN'T WON YET!! LOOKS LIKE CYCLOPS GOT HIS STRENGTH BACK! YOU MAY HAVE TO HELP PERSONALLY!
LET'S GET OUT OF HERE! IF THAT GUY'S EYES ARE IN WORKIN' ORDER AGAIN, I'M NOT HANGIN' AROUND TILL HE TURNS 'EM ON ME!
I HEAR YOU TALKIN', PAL!
SO THERE YOU ARE!! THE RENEGADE MUTANT WHO THINKS HE CAN BEAT THE X-MEN!
THINKS?? SONNY, YOU'VE GOT IT ALL WRONG! I KNOW I CAN BEAT A BUNCH OF COSTUMED TEEN-AGE MISFITS LIKE YOU! THAT POWER BEAM OF YOURS CAN'T BUDGE ME!
MAYBE NOT, BUT IF I BLAST THE GROUND YOU'RE STANDING ON, IT'S SURE GOING TO UPSET YOU, TOO!
NOW! WHILE HE'S NOT LOOKING! THIS IS OUR CHANCE!
19

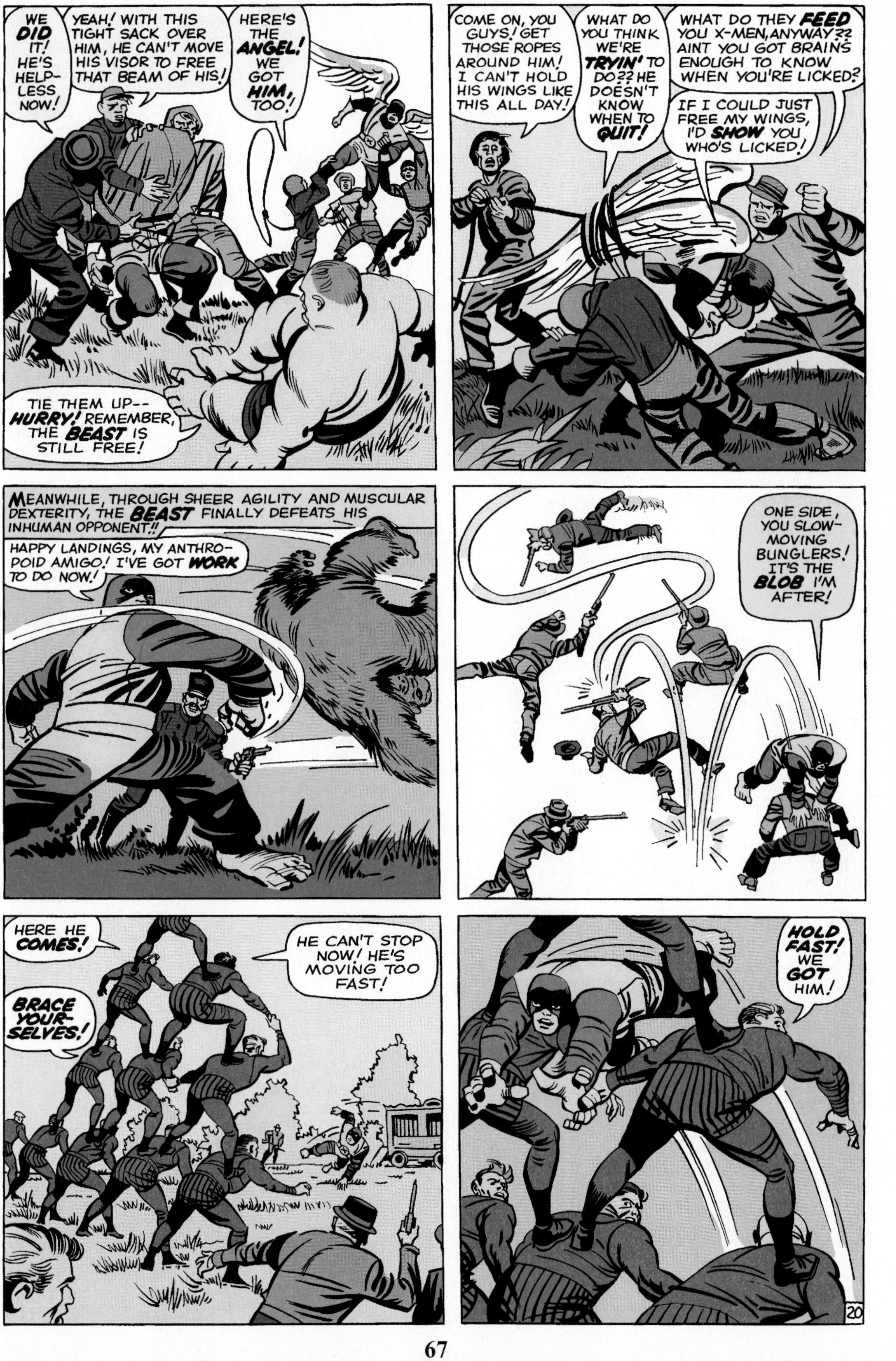
WE DID IT! HE'S HELP-LESS NOW!
YEAH! WITH THIS TIGHT SACK OVER HIM, HE CAN'T MOVE HIS VISOR TO FREE THAT BEAM OF HIS!
HERE'S THE ANGEL! WE GOT HIM, TOO!
TIE THEM UP-- HURRY! REMEMBER, THE BEAST IS STILL FREE!
COME ON, YOU GUYS! GET THOSE ROPES AROUND HIM! I CAN'T HOLD HIS WINGS LIKE THIS ALL DAY!
WHAT DO YOU THINK WE'RE TRYIN' TO DO?? HE DOESN'T KNOW WHEN TO QUIT!
WHAT DO THEY FEED YOU X-MEN, ANYWAY?? AINT YOU GOT BRAINS ENOUGH TO KNOW WHEN YOU'RE LICKED?
IF I COULD JUST FREE MY WINGS, I'D SHOW YOU WHO'S LICKED!
MEANWHILE, THROUGH SHEER AGILITY AND MUSCULAR DEXTERITY, THE BEAST FINALLY DEFEATS HIS INHUMAN OPPONENT!!
HAPPY LANDINGS, MY ANTHROPOID AMIGO! I'VE GOT WORK TO DO NOW!
ONE SIDE, YOU SLOW-MOVING BUNGLERS! IT'S THE BLOB I'M AFTER!
HERE HE COMES!
HE CAN'T STOP NOW! HE'S MOVING TOO FAST!
BRACE YOURSELVES!
HOLD FAST! WE GOT HIM!
20

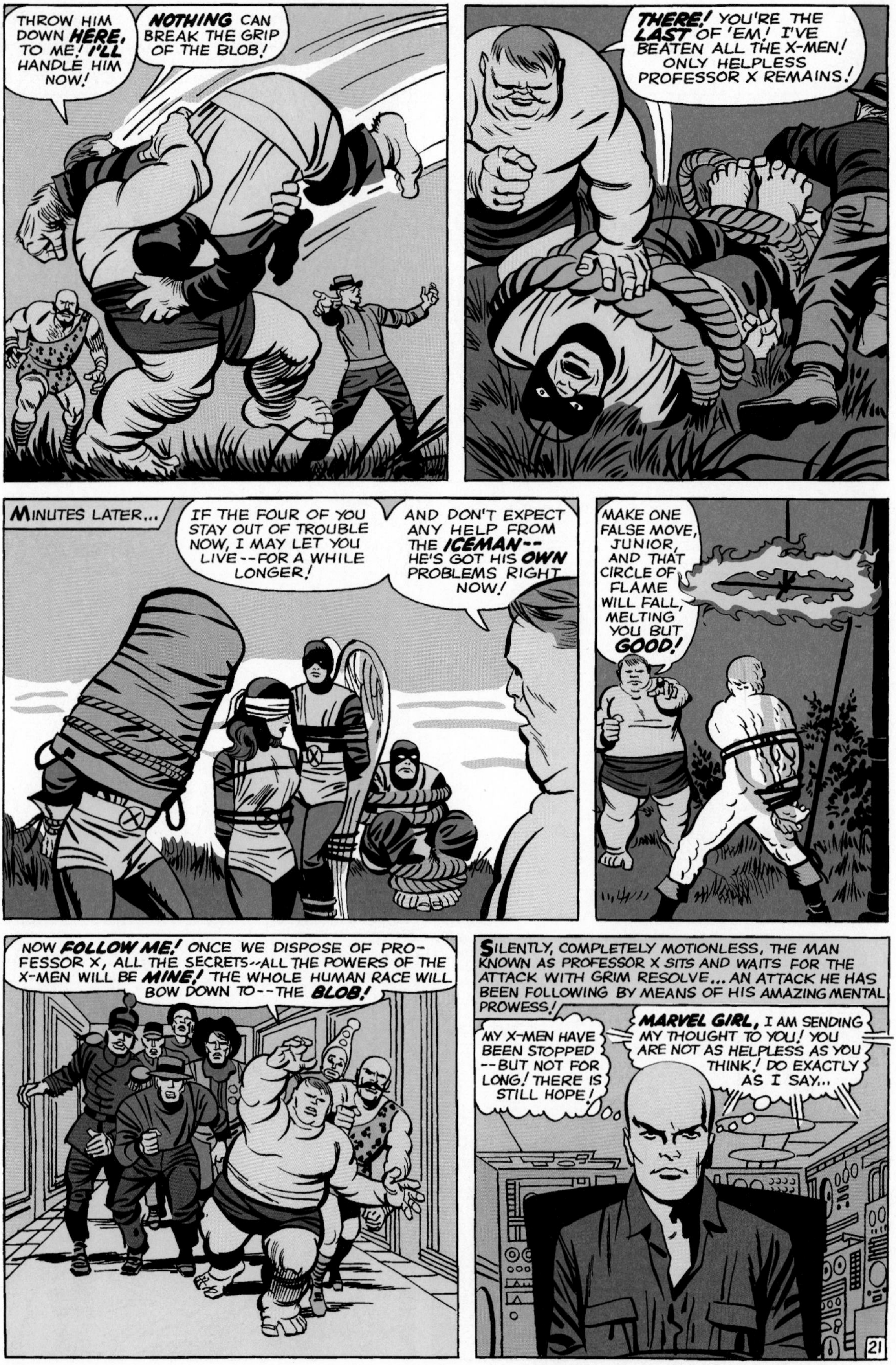
THROW HIM DOWN HERE, TO ME! I'LL HANDLE HIM NOW!
NOTHING CAN BREAK THE GRIP OF THE BLOB!
THERE! YOU'RE THE LAST OF 'EM! I'VE BEATEN ALL THE X-MEN! ONLY HELPLESS PROFESSOR X REMAINS!
MINUTES LATER...
IF THE FOUR OF YOU STAY OUT OF TROUBLE NOW, I MAY LET YOU LIVE--FOR A WHILE LONGER!
AND DON'T EXPECT ANY HELP FROM THE ICEMAN-- HE'S GOT HIS OWN PROBLEMS RIGHT NOW!
MAKE ONE FALSE MOVE, JUNIOR, AND THAT CIRCLE OF FLAME WILL FALL, MELTING YOU BUT GOOD!
NOW FOLLOW ME! ONCE WE DISPOSE OF PROFESSOR X, ALL THE SECRETS--ALL THE POWERS OF THE X-MEN WILL BE MINE! THE WHOLE HUMAN RACE WILL BOW DOWN TO--THE BLOB!
SILENTLY, COMPLETELY MOTIONLESS, THE MAN KNOWN AS PROFESSOR X SITS AND WAITS FOR THE ATTACK WITH GRIM RESOLVE... AN ATTACK HE HAS BEEN FOLLOWING BY MEANS OF HIS AMAZING MENTAL PROWESS!
MY X-MEN HAVE BEEN STOPPED --BUT NOT FOR LONG! THERE IS STILL HOPE!
MARVEL GIRL, I AM SENDING MY THOUGHT TO YOU! YOU ARE NOT AS HELPLESS AS YOU THINK! DO EXACTLY AS I SAY...
21

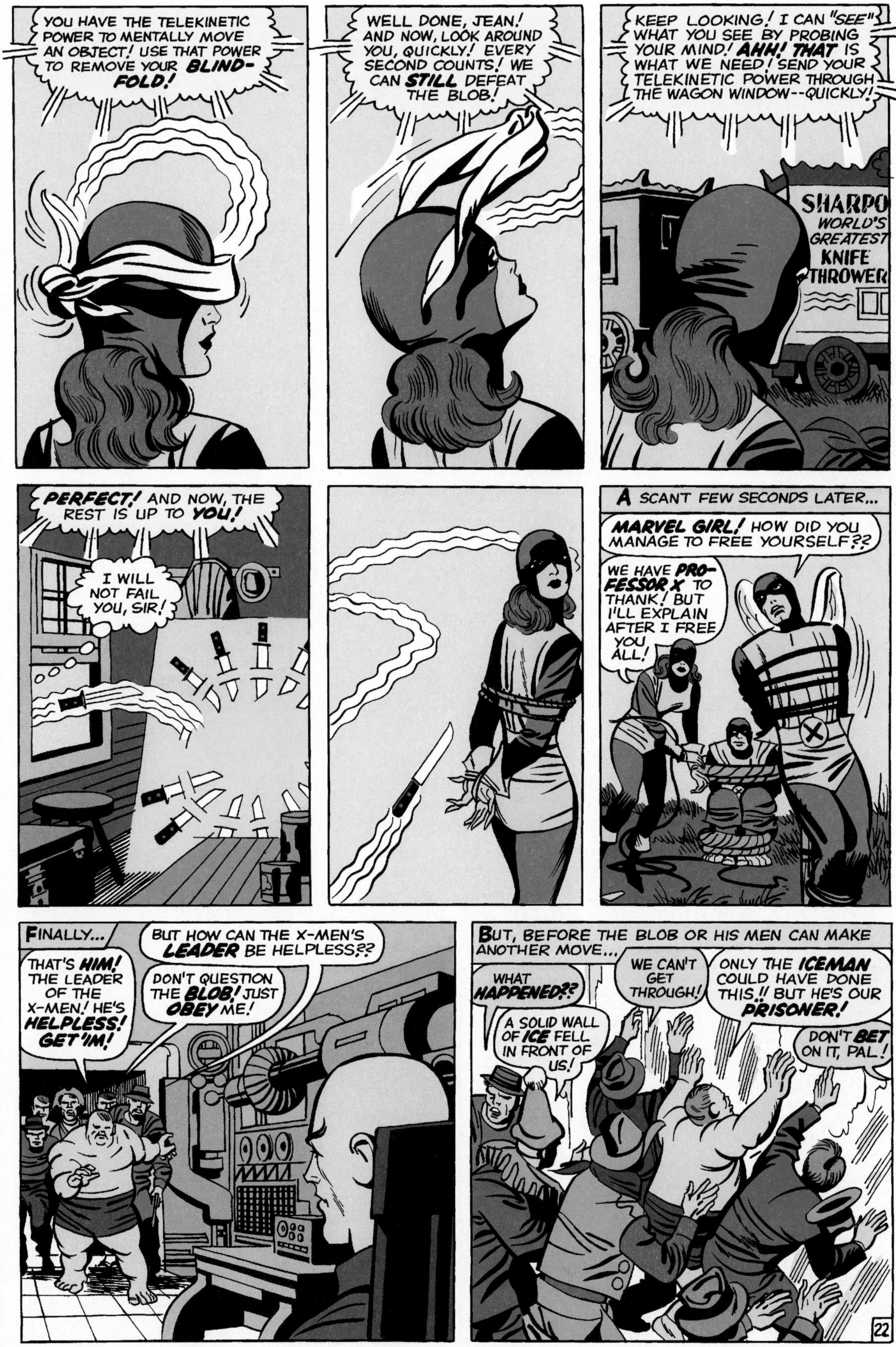

YOU HAVE THE TELEKINETIC POWER TO MENTALLY MOVE AN OBJECT! USE THAT POWER TO REMOVE YOUR BLIND-FOLD!
WELL DONE, JEAN! AND NOW, LOOK AROUND YOU, QUICKLY! EVERY SECOND COUNTS! WE CAN STILL DEFEAT THE BLOB!
KEEP LOOKING! I CAN "SEE" WHAT YOU SEE BY PROBING YOUR MIND! AHH! THAT IS WHAT WE NEED! SEND YOUR TELEKINETIC POWER THROUGH THE WAGON WINDOW--QUICKLY!
SHARPO
WORLD'S GREATEST KNIFE THROWER
PERFECT! AND NOW, THE REST IS UP TO YOU!
I WILL NOT FAIL YOU, SIR!
A SCANT FEW SECONDS LATER...
MARVEL GIRL! HOW DID YOU MANAGE TO FREE YOURSELF??
WE HAVE PRO-FESSOR X TO THANK! BUT I'LL EXPLAIN AFTER I FREE YOU ALL!
FINALLY...
THAT'S HIM! THE LEADER OF THE X-MEN! HE'S HELPLESS! GET 'IM!
BUT HOW CAN THE X-MEN'S LEADER BE HELPLESS??
DON'T QUESTION THE BLOB! JUST OBEY ME!
BUT, BEFORE THE BLOB OR HIS MEN CAN MAKE ANOTHER MOVE...
WHAT HAPPENED??
A SOLID WALL OF ICE FELL IN FRONT OF US!
WE CAN'T GET THROUGH!
ONLY THE ICEMAN COULD HAVE DONE THIS!! BUT HE'S OUR PRISONER!
DON'T BET ON IT, PAL!
22

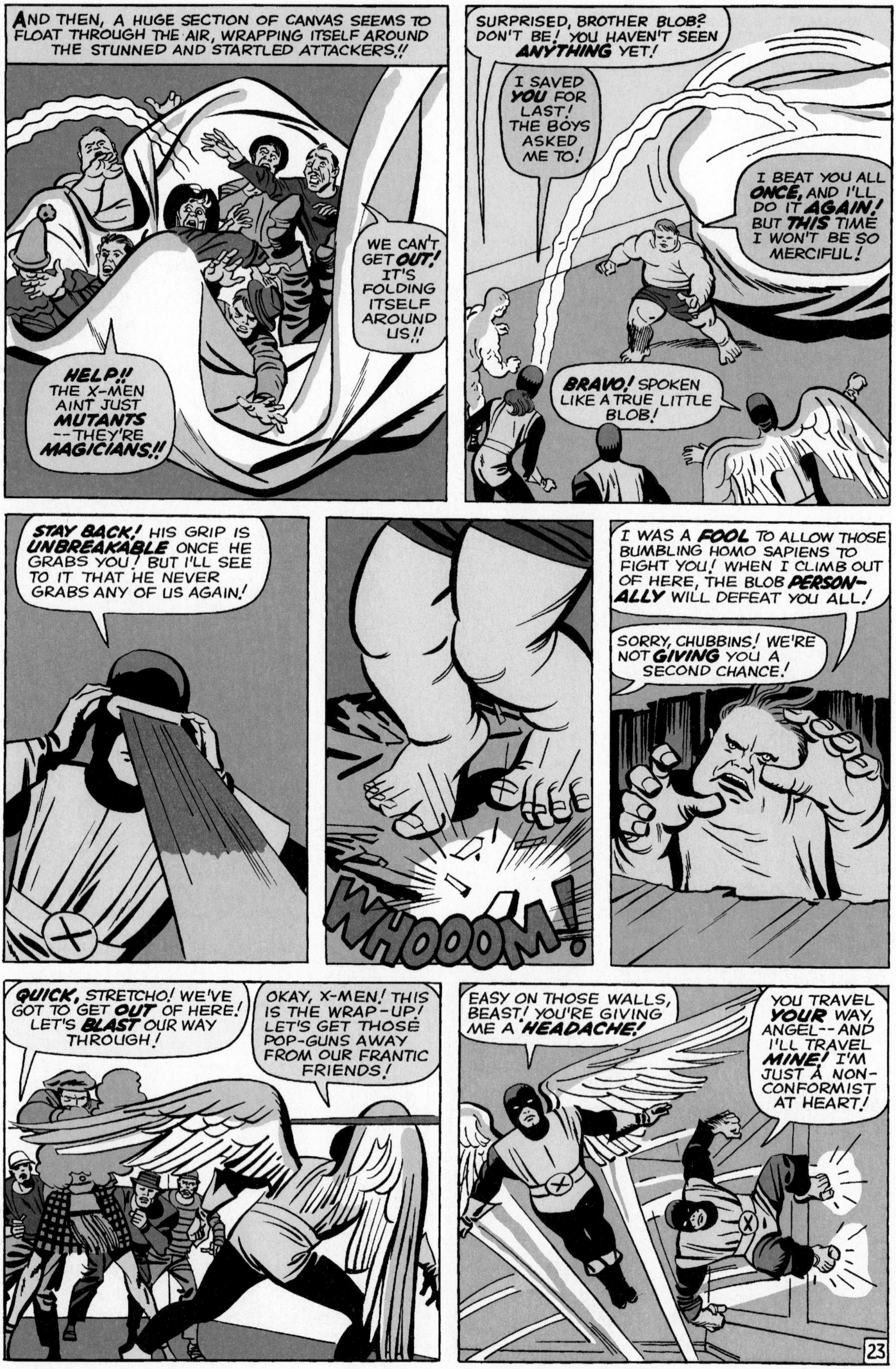
AND THEN, A HUGE SECTION OF CANVAS SEEMS TO FLOAT THROUGH THE AIR, WRAPPING ITSELF AROUND THE STUNNED AND STARTLED ATTACKERS!!
WE CAN'T GET OUT! IT'S FOLDING ITSELF AROUND US!!
HELP!! THE X-MEN AINT JUST MUTANTS --THEY'RE MAGICIANS!!
SURPRISED, BROTHER BLOB? DON'T BE! YOU HAVEN'T SEEN ANYTHING YET!
I SAVED YOU FOR LAST! THE BOYS ASKED ME TO!
I BEAT YOU ALL ONCE, AND I'LL DO IT AGAIN! BUT THIS TIME I WON'T BE SO MERCIFUL!
BRAVO! SPOKEN LIKE A TRUE LITTLE BLOB!
STAY BACK! HIS GRIP IS UNBREAKABLE ONCE HE GRABS YOU! BUT I'LL SEE TO IT THAT HE NEVER GRABS ANY OF US AGAIN!
WHOOOM!
I WAS A FOOL TO ALLOW THOSE BUMBLING HOMO SAPIENS TO FIGHT YOU! WHEN I CLIMB OUT OF HERE, THE BLOB PERSON-ALLY WILL DEFEAT YOU ALL!
SORRY, CHUBBINS! WE'RE NOT GIVING YOU A SECOND CHANCE!
QUICK, STRETCHO! WE'VE GOT TO GET OUT OF HERE! LET'S BLAST OUR WAY THROUGH!
OKAY, X-MEN! THIS IS THE WRAP-UP! LET'S GET THOSE POP-GUNS AWAY FROM OUR FRANTIC FRIENDS!
EASY ON THOSE WALLS, BEAST! YOU'RE GIVING ME A HEADACHE!
YOU TRAVEL YOUR WAY, ANGEL--AND I'LL TRAVEL MINE! I'M JUST A NON-CONFORMIST AT HEART!
23

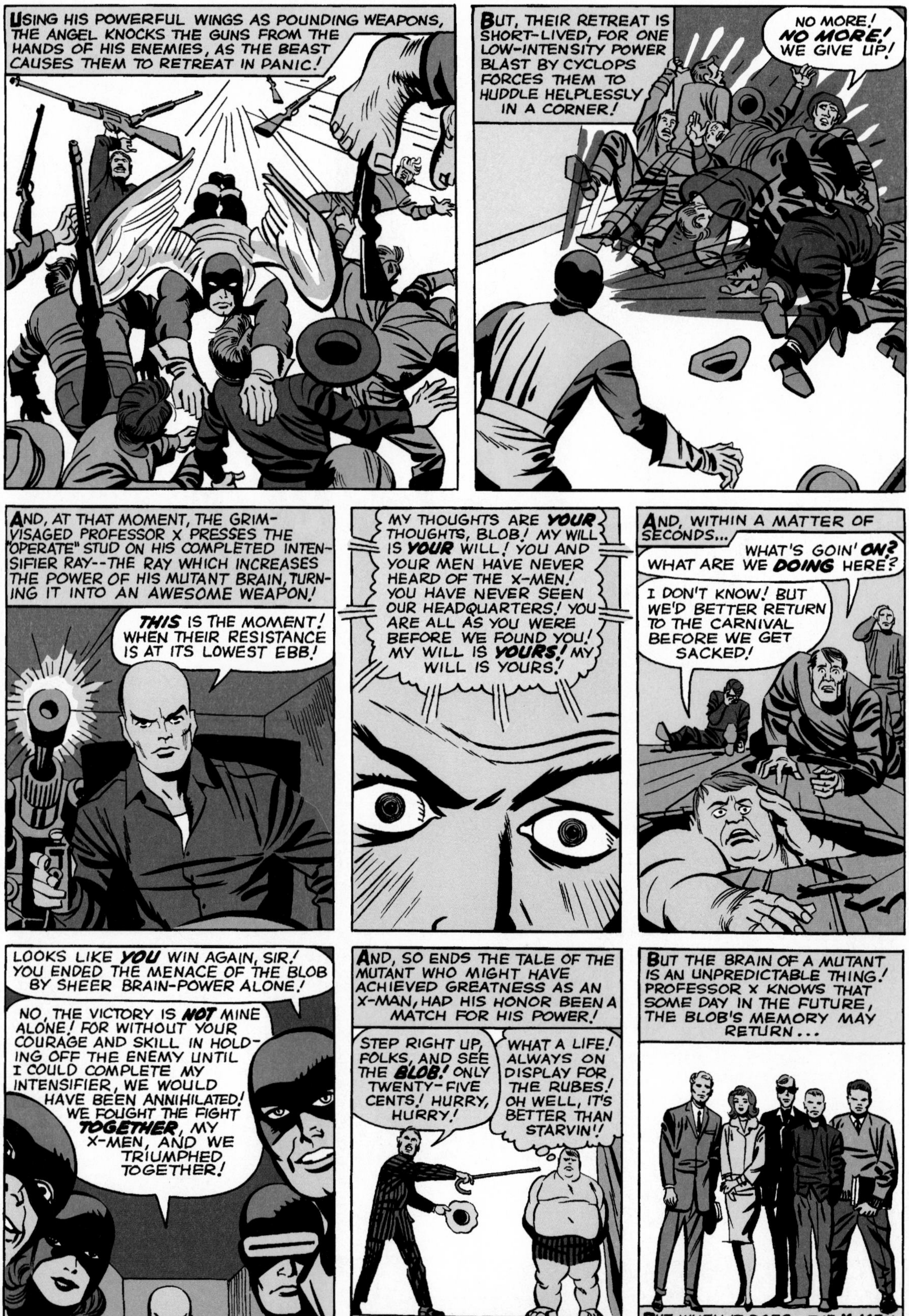
USING HIS POWERFUL WINGS AS POUNDING WEAPONS, THE ANGEL KNOCKS THE GUNS FROM THE HANDS OF HIS ENEMIES, AS THE BEAST CAUSES THEM TO RETREAT IN PANIC!
BUT, THEIR RETREAT IS SHORT-LIVED, FOR ONE LOW-INTENSITY POWER BLAST BY CYCLOPS FORCES THEM TO HUDDLE HELPLESSLY IN A CORNER!
NO MORE! NO MORE! WE GIVE UP!
AND, AT THAT MOMENT, THE GRIM-VISAGED PROFESSOR X PRESSES THE "OPERATE" STUD ON HIS COMPLETED INTENSIFIER RAY--THE RAY WHICH INCREASES THE POWER OF HIS MUTANT BRAIN, TURNING IT INTO AN AWESOME WEAPON!
THIS IS THE MOMENT! WHEN THEIR RESISTANCE IS AT ITS LOWEST EBB!
MY THOUGHTS ARE YOUR THOUGHTS, BLOB! MY WILL IS YOUR WILL! YOU AND YOUR MEN HAVE NEVER HEARD OF THE X-MEN! YOU HAVE NEVER SEEN OUR HEADQUARTERS! YOU ARE ALL AS YOU WERE BEFORE WE FOUND YOU! MY WILL IS YOURS! MY WILL IS YOURS!
AND, WITHIN A MATTER OF SECONDS...
WHAT'S GOIN' ON? WHAT ARE WE DOING HERE?
I DON'T KNOW! BUT WE'D BETTER RETURN TO THE CARNIVAL BEFORE WE GET SACKED!
LOOKS LIKE YOU WIN AGAIN, SIR! YOU ENDED THE MENACE OF THE BLOB BY SHEER BRAIN-POWER ALONE!
NO, THE VICTORY IS NOT MINE ALONE! FOR WITHOUT YOUR COURAGE AND SKILL IN HOLDING OFF THE ENEMY UNTIL I COULD COMPLETE MY INTENSIFIER, WE WOULD HAVE BEEN ANNIHILATED! WE FOUGHT THE FIGHT TOGETHER, MY X-MEN, AND WE TRIUMPHED TOGETHER!
AND, SO ENDS THE TALE OF THE MUTANT WHO MIGHT HAVE ACHIEVED GREATNESS AS AN X-MAN, HAD HIS HONOR BEEN A MATCH FOR HIS POWER!
STEP RIGHT UP, FOLKS, AND SEE THE BLOB! ONLY TWENTY-FIVE CENTS! HURRY, HURRY!
WHAT A LIFE! ALWAYS ON DISPLAY FOR THE RUBES! OH WELL, IT'S BETTER THAN STARVIN'!
BUT THE BRAIN OF A MUTANT IS AN UNPREDICTABLE THING! PROFESSOR X KNOWS THAT SOME DAY IN THE FUTURE, THE BLOB'S MEMORY MAY RETURN...
BUT, WHEN IT DOES... THE X-MEN WILL BE READY! NOW, UNTIL NEXT ISSUE, FROM HOMO SUPERIOR TO HOMO SAPIENS --FAREWELL!
THE END

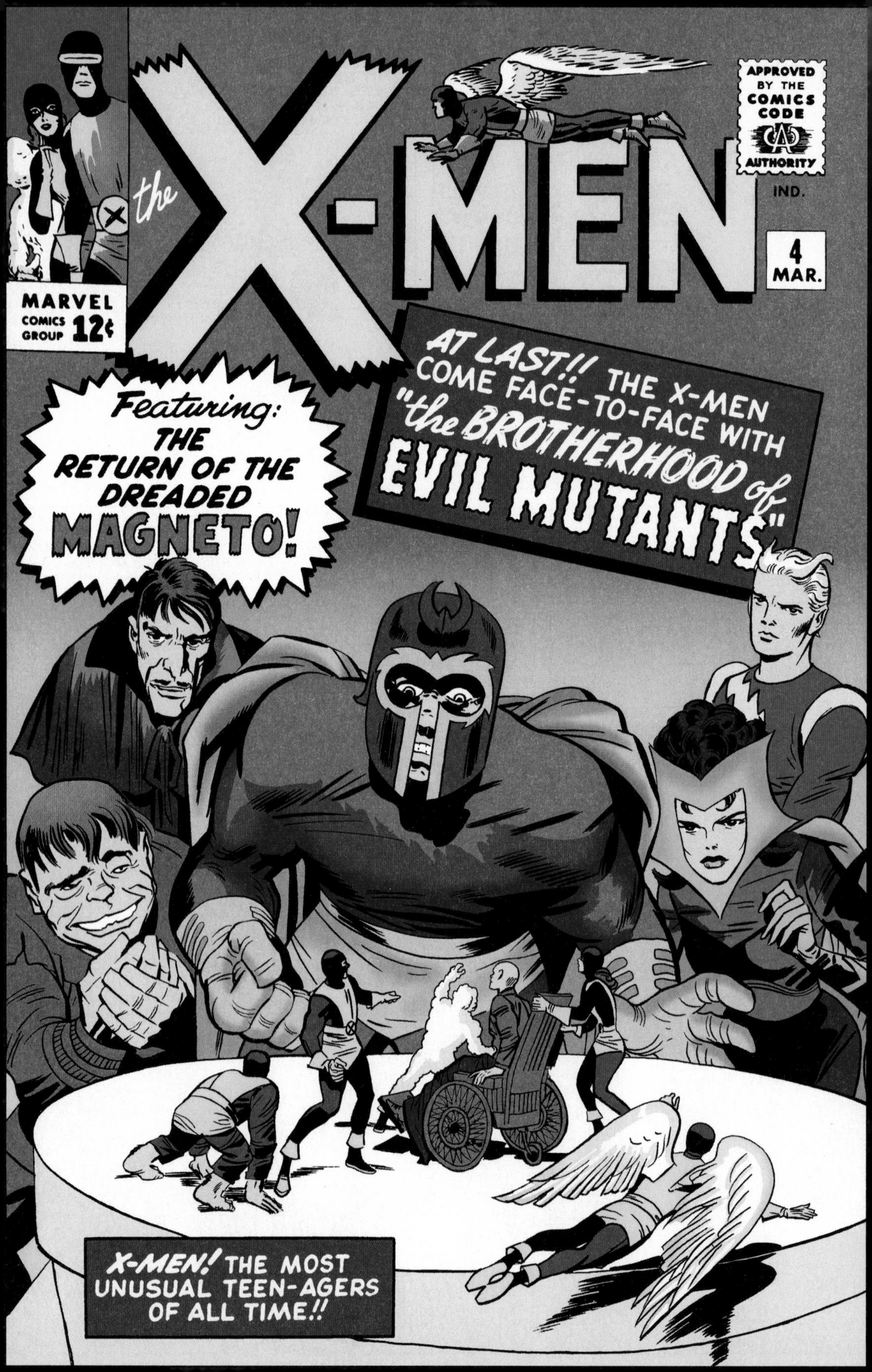

MARVEL COMICS GROUP 12¢
the X-MEN
APPROVED BY THE COMICS CODE AUTHORITY
IND.
4 MAR.
AT LAST!! THE X-MEN COME FACE-TO-FACE WITH "the BROTHERHOOD of EVIL MUTANTS"
Featuring: THE RETURN OF THE DREADED MAGNETO!
X-MEN! THE MOST UNUSUAL TEEN-AGERS OF ALL TIME!!

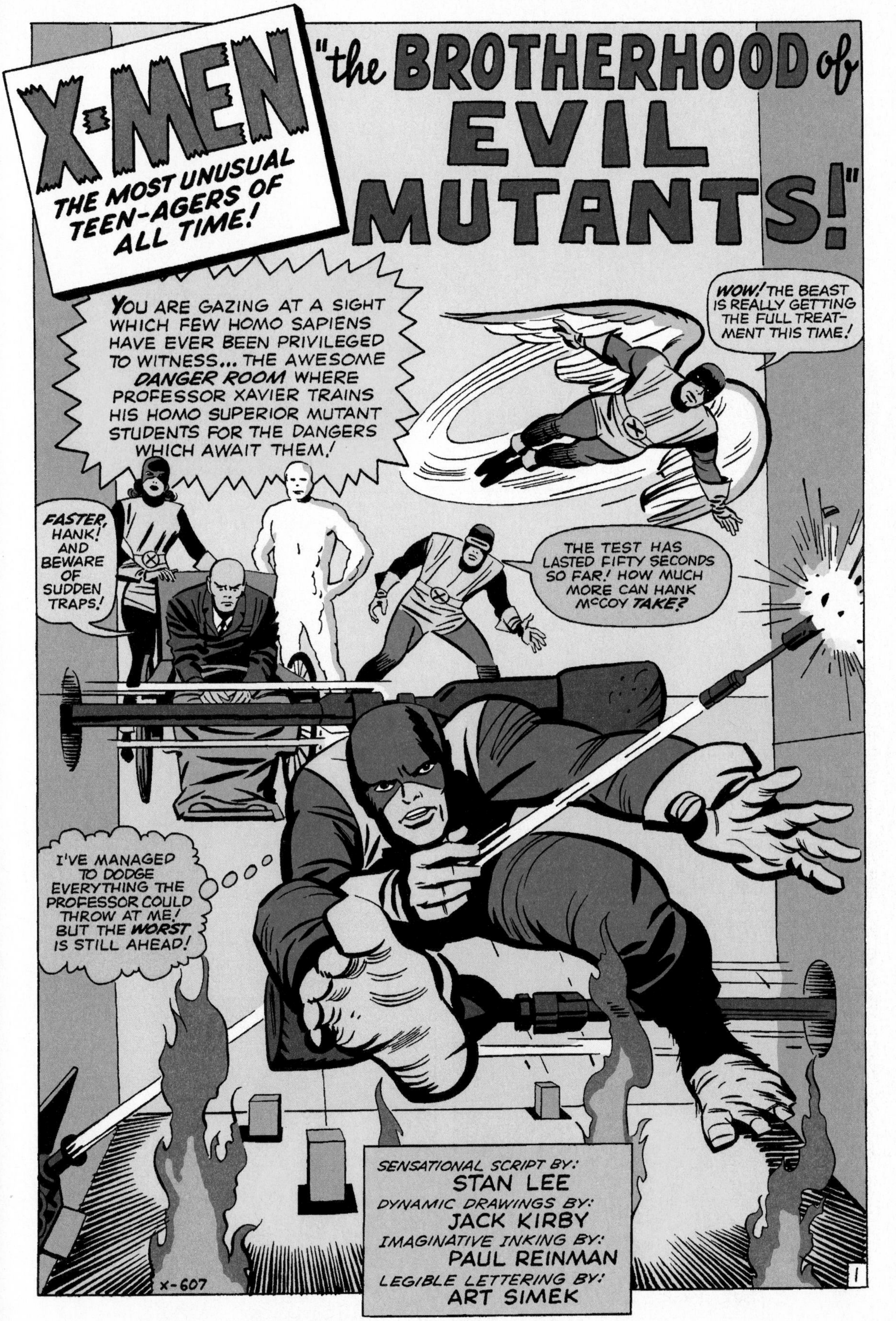
X-MEN
THE MOST UNUSUAL TEEN-AGERS OF ALL TIME!
"the BROTHERHOOD of EVIL MUTANTS!"
YOU ARE GAZING AT A SIGHT WHICH FEW HOMO SAPIENS HAVE EVER BEEN PRIVILEGED TO WITNESS... THE AWESOME DANGER ROOM WHERE PROFESSOR XAVIER TRAINS HIS HOMO SUPERIOR MUTANT STUDENTS FOR THE DANGERS WHICH AWAIT THEM!
WOW! THE BEAST IS REALLY GETTING THE FULL TREAT-MENT THIS TIME!
FASTER, HANK! AND BEWARE OF SUDDEN TRAPS!
THE TEST HAS LASTED FIFTY SECONDS SO FAR! HOW MUCH MORE CAN HANK McCOY TAKE?
I'VE MANAGED TO DODGE EVERYTHING THE PROFESSOR COULD THROW AT ME! BUT THE WORST IS STILL AHEAD!
SENSATIONAL SCRIPT BY: STAN LEE
DYNAMIC DRAWINGS BY: JACK KIRBY
IMAGINATIVE INKING BY: PAUL REINMAN
LEGIBLE LETTERING BY: ART SIMEK
X-607
1

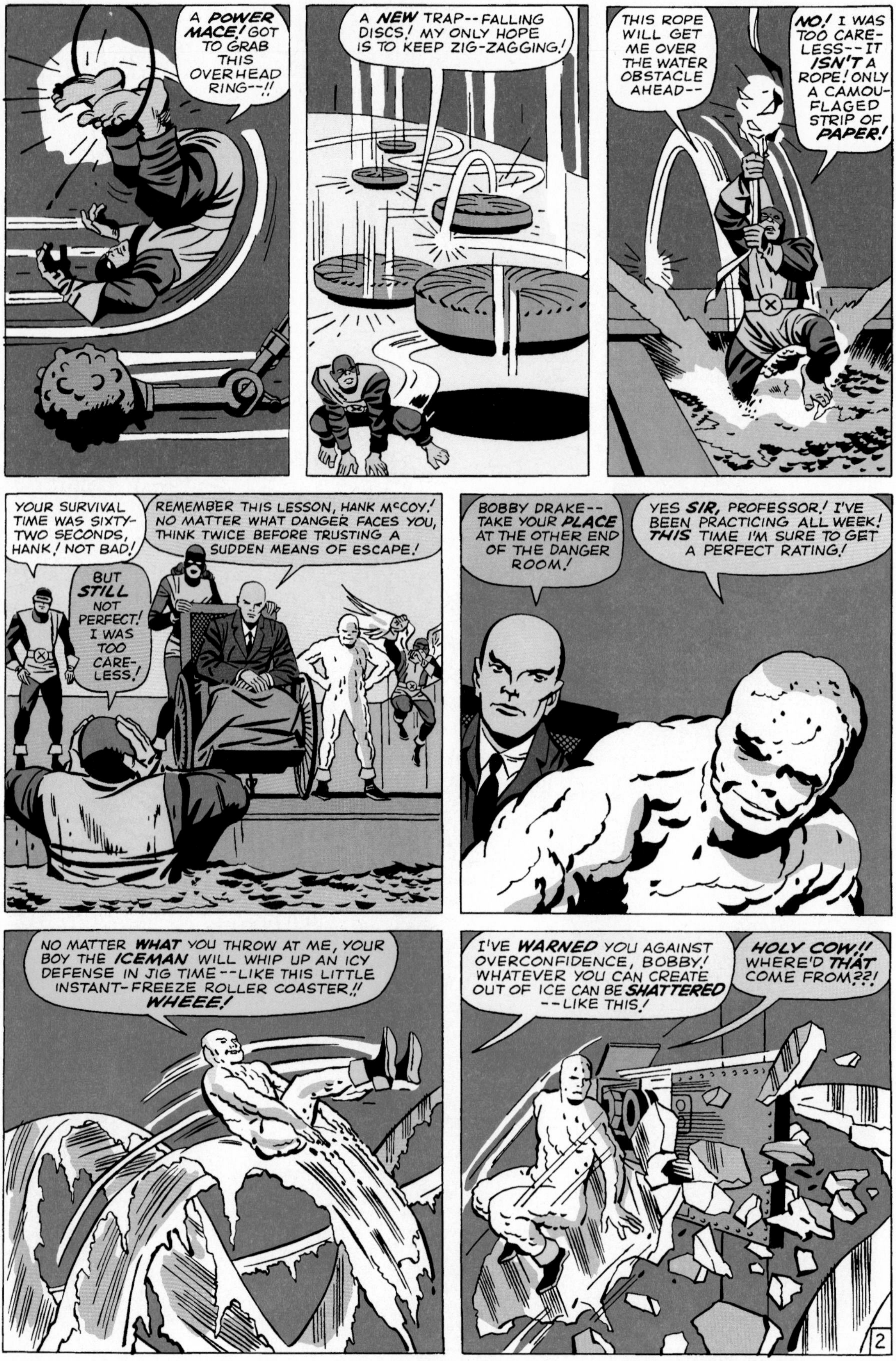
A POWER MACE! GOT TO GRAB THIS OVERHEAD RING--!!
A NEW TRAP--FALLING DISCS! MY ONLY HOPE IS TO KEEP ZIG-ZAGGING!
THIS ROPE WILL GET ME OVER THE WATER OBSTACLE AHEAD--
NO! I WAS TOO CARE-LESS--IT ISN'T A ROPE! ONLY A CAMOU-FLAGED STRIP OF PAPER!
YOUR SURVIVAL TIME WAS SIXTY-TWO SECONDS, HANK! NOT BAD!
BUT STILL NOT PERFECT! I WAS TOO CARE-LESS!
REMEMBER THIS LESSON, HANK McCOY! NO MATTER WHAT DANGER FACES YOU, THINK TWICE BEFORE TRUSTING A SUDDEN MEANS OF ESCAPE!
BOBBY DRAKE--TAKE YOUR PLACE AT THE OTHER END OF THE DANGER ROOM!
YES SIR, PROFESSOR! I'VE BEEN PRACTICING ALL WEEK! THIS TIME I'M SURE TO GET A PERFECT RATING!
NO MATTER WHAT YOU THROW AT ME, YOUR BOY THE ICEMAN WILL WHIP UP AN ICY DEFENSE IN JIG TIME--LIKE THIS LITTLE INSTANT-FREEZE ROLLER COASTER!! WHEEE!
I'VE WARNED YOU AGAINST OVERCONFIDENCE, BOBBY! WHATEVER YOU CAN CREATE OUT OF ICE CAN BE SHATTERED--LIKE THIS!
HOLY COW!! WHERE'D THAT COME FROM??!
2

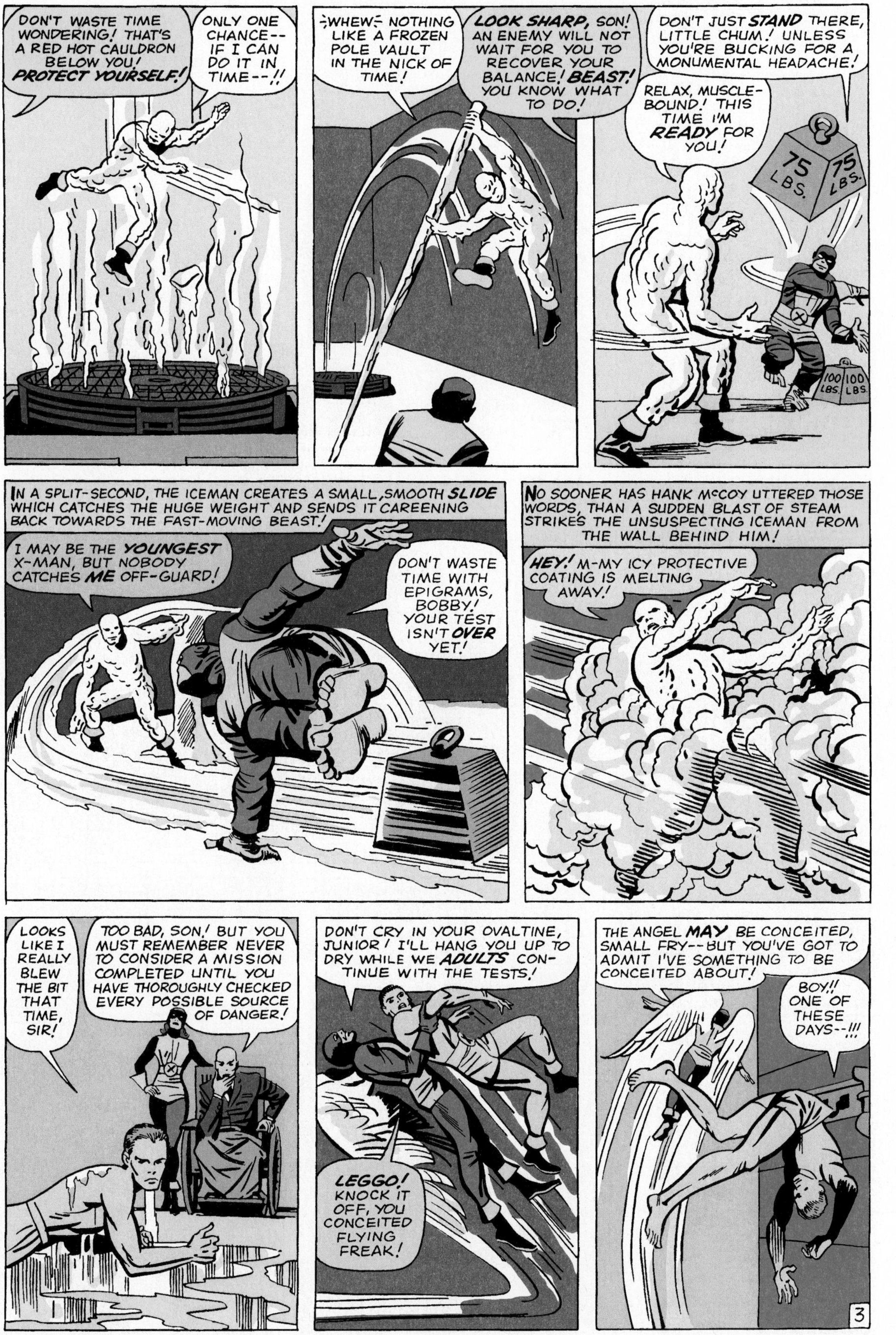

DON'T WASTE TIME WONDERING! THAT'S A RED HOT CAULDRON BELOW YOU! PROTECT YOURSELF!
ONLY ONE CHANCE-- IF I CAN DO IT IN TIME--!!
-WHEW- NOTHING LIKE A FROZEN POLE VAULT IN THE NICK OF TIME!
LOOK SHARP, SON! AN ENEMY WILL NOT WAIT FOR YOU TO RECOVER YOUR BALANCE! BEAST! YOU KNOW WHAT TO DO!
DON'T JUST STAND THERE, LITTLE CHUM! UNLESS YOU'RE BUCKING FOR A MONUMENTAL HEADACHE!
RELAX, MUSCLE-BOUND! THIS TIME I'M READY FOR YOU!
75 LBS.
75 LBS.
100 LBS.
100 LBS.
IN A SPLIT-SECOND, THE ICEMAN CREATES A SMALL, SMOOTH SLIDE WHICH CATCHES THE HUGE WEIGHT AND SENDS IT CAREENING BACK TOWARDS THE FAST-MOVING BEAST!
I MAY BE THE YOUNGEST X-MAN, BUT NOBODY CATCHES ME OFF-GUARD!
DON'T WASTE TIME WITH EPIGRAMS, BOBBY! YOUR TEST ISN'T OVER YET!
NO SOONER HAS HANK McCOY UTTERED THOSE WORDS, THAN A SUDDEN BLAST OF STEAM STRIKES THE UNSUSPECTING ICEMAN FROM THE WALL BEHIND HIM!
HEY! M-MY ICY PROTECTIVE COATING IS MELTING AWAY!
LOOKS LIKE I REALLY BLEW THE BIT THAT TIME, SIR!
TOO BAD, SON! BUT YOU MUST REMEMBER NEVER TO CONSIDER A MISSION COMPLETED UNTIL YOU HAVE THOROUGHLY CHECKED EVERY POSSIBLE SOURCE OF DANGER!
DON'T CRY IN YOUR OVALTINE, JUNIOR! I'LL HANG YOU UP TO DRY WHILE WE ADULTS CONTINUE WITH THE TESTS!
LEGGO! KNOCK IT OFF, YOU CONCEITED FLYING FREAK!
THE ANGEL MAY BE CONCEITED, SMALL FRY--BUT YOU'VE GOT TO ADMIT I'VE SOMETHING TO BE CONCEITED ABOUT!
BOY!! ONE OF THESE DAYS--!!!
3

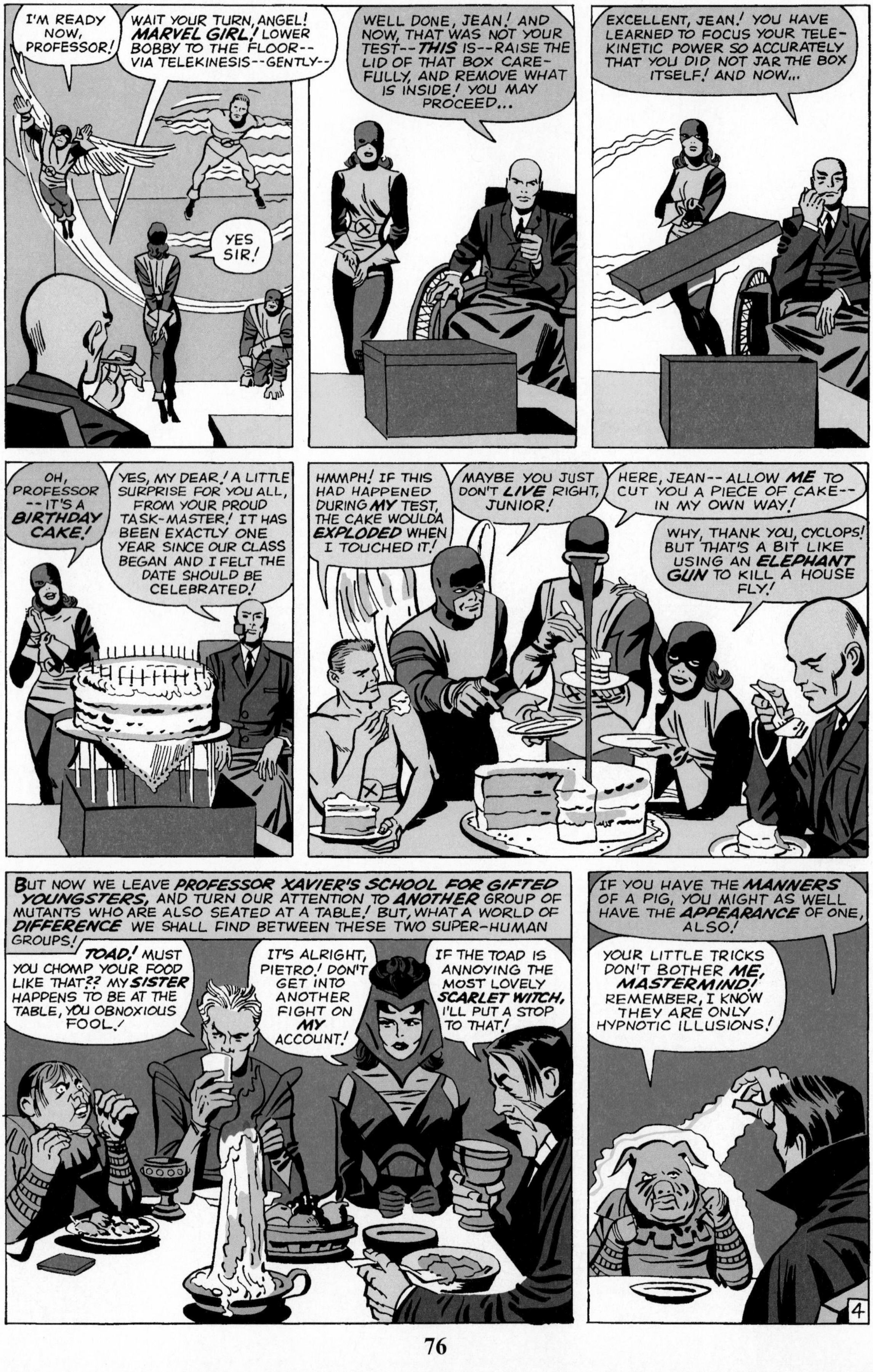
I'M READY NOW, PROFESSOR!
WAIT YOUR TURN, ANGEL! MARVEL GIRL! LOWER BOBBY TO THE FLOOR-- VIA TELEKINESIS--GENTLY--
YES SIR!
WELL DONE, JEAN! AND NOW, THAT WAS NOT YOUR TEST--THIS IS--RAISE THE LID OF THAT BOX CAREFULLY, AND REMOVE WHAT IS INSIDE! YOU MAY PROCEED...
EXCELLENT, JEAN! YOU HAVE LEARNED TO FOCUS YOUR TELEKINETIC POWER SO ACCURATELY THAT YOU DID NOT JAR THE BOX ITSELF! AND NOW...
OH, PROFESSOR --IT'S A BIRTHDAY CAKE!
YES, MY DEAR! A LITTLE SURPRISE FOR YOU ALL, FROM YOUR PROUD TASK-MASTER! IT HAS BEEN EXACTLY ONE YEAR SINCE OUR CLASS BEGAN AND I FELT THE DATE SHOULD BE CELEBRATED!
HMMPH! IF THIS HAD HAPPENED DURING MY TEST, THE CAKE WOULDA EXPLODED WHEN I TOUCHED IT!
MAYBE YOU JUST DON'T LIVE RIGHT, JUNIOR!
HERE, JEAN--ALLOW ME TO CUT YOU A PIECE OF CAKE-- IN MY OWN WAY!
WHY, THANK YOU, CYCLOPS! BUT THAT'S A BIT LIKE USING AN ELEPHANT GUN TO KILL A HOUSE FLY!
BUT NOW WE LEAVE PROFESSOR XAVIER'S SCHOOL FOR GIFTED YOUNGSTERS, AND TURN OUR ATTENTION TO ANOTHER GROUP OF MUTANTS WHO ARE ALSO SEATED AT A TABLE! BUT, WHAT A WORLD OF DIFFERENCE WE SHALL FIND BETWEEN THESE TWO SUPER-HUMAN GROUPS!
TOAD! MUST YOU CHOMP YOUR FOOD LIKE THAT?? MY SISTER HAPPENS TO BE AT THE TABLE, YOU OBNOXIOUS FOOL!
IT'S ALRIGHT, PIETRO! DON'T GET INTO ANOTHER FIGHT ON MY ACCOUNT!
IF THE TOAD IS ANNOYING THE MOST LOVELY SCARLET WITCH, I'LL PUT A STOP TO THAT!
IF YOU HAVE THE MANNERS OF A PIG, YOU MIGHT AS WELL HAVE THE APPEARANCE OF ONE, ALSO!
YOUR LITTLE TRICKS DON'T BOTHER ME, MASTERMIND! REMEMBER, I KNOW THEY ARE ONLY HYPNOTIC ILLUSIONS!
4

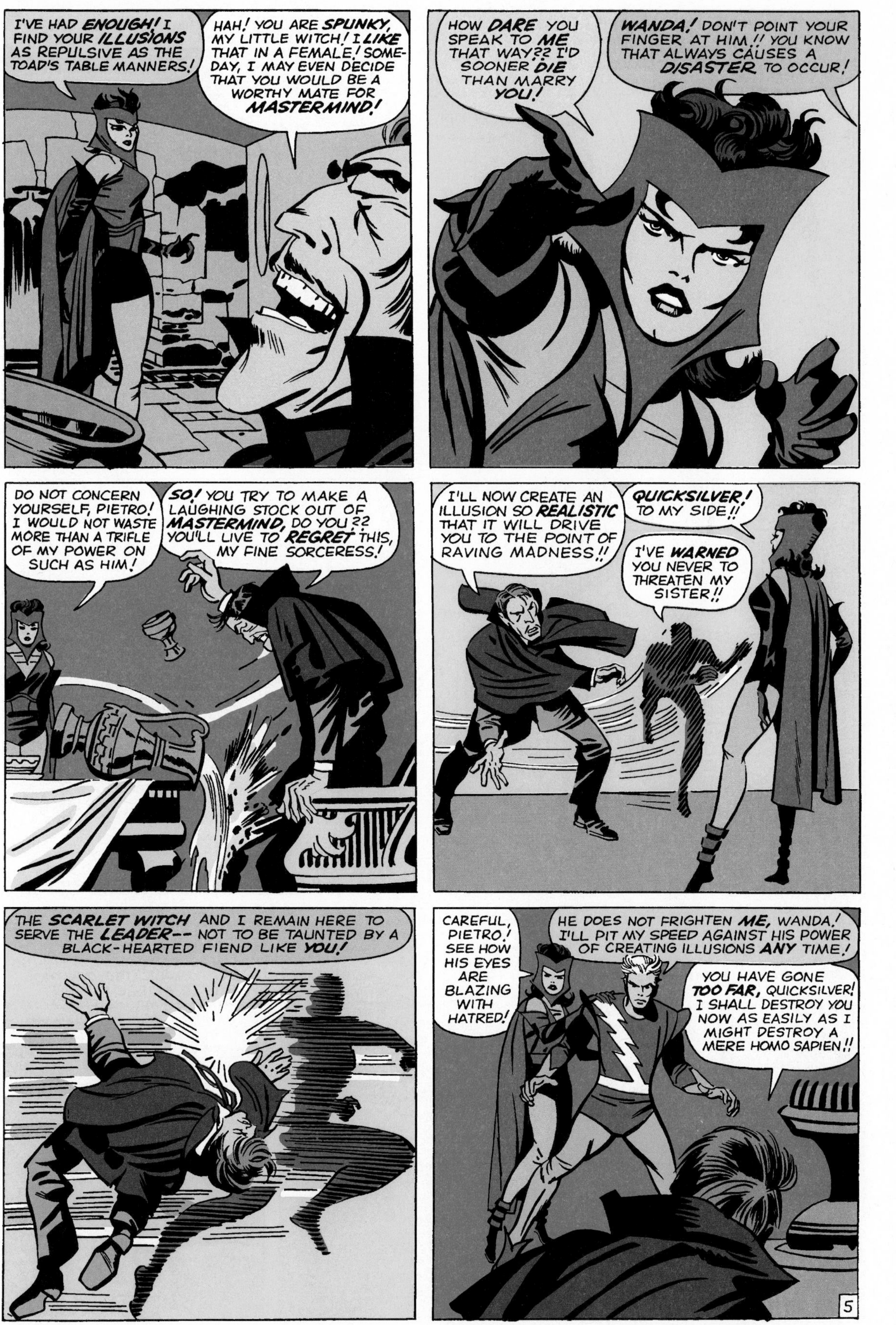
I'VE HAD ENOUGH! I FIND YOUR ILLUSIONS AS REPULSIVE AS THE TOAD'S TABLE MANNERS!
HAH! YOU ARE SPUNKY, MY LITTLE WITCH! I LIKE THAT IN A FEMALE! SOMEDAY, I MAY EVEN DECIDE THAT YOU WOULD BE A WORTHY MATE FOR MASTERMIND!
HOW DARE YOU SPEAK TO ME THAT WAY?? I'D SOONER DIE THAN MARRY YOU!
WANDA! DON'T POINT YOUR FINGER AT HIM!! YOU KNOW THAT ALWAYS CAUSES A DISASTER TO OCCUR!
DO NOT CONCERN YOURSELF, PIETRO! I WOULD NOT WASTE MORE THAN A TRIFLE OF MY POWER ON SUCH AS HIM!
SO! YOU TRY TO MAKE A LAUGHING STOCK OUT OF MASTERMIND, DO YOU?? YOU'LL LIVE TO REGRET THIS, MY FINE SORCERESS!
I'LL NOW CREATE AN ILLUSION SO REALISTIC THAT IT WILL DRIVE YOU TO THE POINT OF RAVING MADNESS!!
QUICKSILVER! TO MY SIDE!!
I'VE WARNED YOU NEVER TO THREATEN MY SISTER!!
THE SCARLET WITCH AND I REMAIN HERE TO SERVE THE LEADER-- NOT TO BE TAUNTED BY A BLACK-HEARTED FIEND LIKE YOU!
CAREFUL, PIETRO! SEE HOW HIS EYES ARE BLAZING WITH HATRED!
HE DOES NOT FRIGHTEN ME, WANDA! I'LL PIT MY SPEED AGAINST HIS POWER OF CREATING ILLUSIONS ANY TIME!
YOU HAVE GONE TOO FAR, QUICKSILVER! I SHALL DESTROY YOU NOW AS EASILY AS I MIGHT DESTROY A MERE HOMO SAPIEN!!
5

DO IT! HA HA HA! **DO IT!** DESTROY EACH OTHER! THEN WHEN THE **LEADER** RETURNS THERE WILL BE ONLY THE TWO OF US! WE WILL RULE THE WORLD **TOGETHER!!**

THE **LEADER!!** I HAD **FORGOTTEN** ABOUT HIM!

DON'T GLOAT SO SOON, TOAD! THE SCARLET WITCH AND I WILL OUTLIVE **ALL** OF YOU! I PROMISE YOU THAT!

YOU ARE IN **LUCK**, QUICKSILVER! I SHALL SPARE YOU THIS TIME, BECAUSE THE LEADER FEELS HE STILL HAS **NEED** OF YOU!

THE **LEADER!** HE'S **ALWAYS** YOUR EXCUSE!

WHERE **IS** OUR GREAT LEADER? WHAT WONDROUS DEED CAN HE BE PERFORMING NOW, TO MAKE HOMO SAPIENS TREMBLE?!!

AS THOUGH IN ANSWER TO THE TOAD'S QUERY, WE ONCE AGAIN CHANGE OUR SCENE--THIS TIME TO THE OFFICE OF A LARGE SHIPPING LINE...

HAVE WE RECEIVED ALL THE BIDS YET FOR THAT OLD EX-CONVOY FREIGHTER WITH THE CANNONS ON HER DECK?

YES SIR! THE BIDS MAY BE OPENED NOW! THEY ARE ALL HERE!

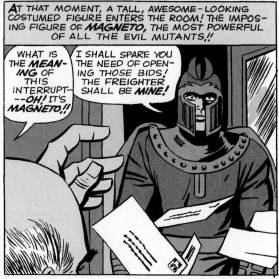

AT THAT MOMENT, A TALL, AWESOME-LOOKING COSTUMED FIGURE ENTERS THE ROOM! THE IMPOSING FIGURE OF **MAGNETO**, THE MOST POWERFUL OF ALL THE EVIL MUTANTS!!

WHAT IS THE **MEANING** OF THIS INTERRUPT---**OH!** IT'S **MAGNETO!!**

I SHALL SPARE YOU THE NEED OF OPENING THOSE BIDS! THE FREIGHTER SHALL BE **MINE!**

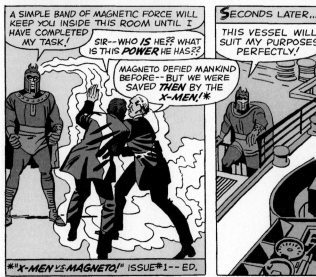

A SIMPLE BAND OF MAGNETIC FORCE WILL KEEP YOU INSIDE THIS ROOM UNTIL I HAVE COMPLETED MY TASK!

SIR--WHO **IS** HE?? WHAT IS THIS **POWER** HE HAS??

MAGNETO DEFIED MANKIND BEFORE-- BUT WE WERE SAVED **THEN** BY THE X-MEN!*

*"X-MEN VS. MAGNETO!" ISSUE #1-- ED.

SECONDS LATER...

THIS VESSEL WILL SUIT MY PURPOSES PERFECTLY!

AND THEN, INCREDIBLE AS IT SEEMS, THE ONE MIGHTY MUTANT, UTILIZING HIS IRRESISTIBLE POWER TO ITS FULLEST, OPERATES EVERY COMPLICATED CONTROL FROM THE BRIDGE OF THE FREIGHTER--MAGNETICALLY--WITH BRILLIANT PRECISION!

CLICK

CLANG

6

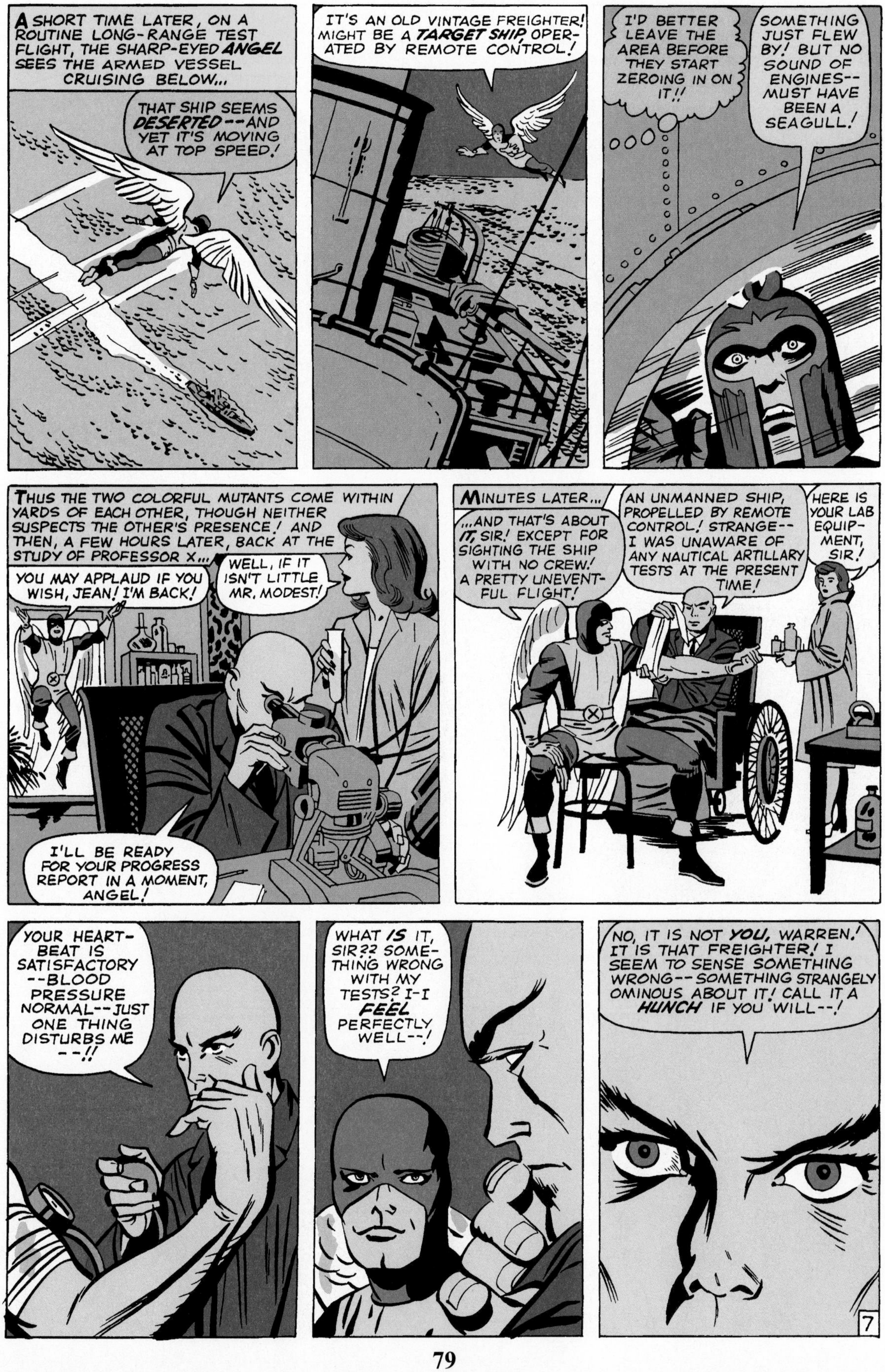
A SHORT TIME LATER, ON A ROUTINE LONG-RANGE TEST FLIGHT, THE SHARP-EYED ANGEL SEES THE ARMED VESSEL CRUISING BELOW...
THAT SHIP SEEMS DESERTED--AND YET IT'S MOVING AT TOP SPEED!
IT'S AN OLD VINTAGE FREIGHTER! MIGHT BE A TARGET SHIP, OPERATED BY REMOTE CONTROL!
I'D BETTER LEAVE THE AREA BEFORE THEY START ZEROING IN ON IT!!
SOMETHING JUST FLEW BY! BUT NO SOUND OF ENGINES--MUST HAVE BEEN A SEAGULL!
THUS THE TWO COLORFUL MUTANTS COME WITHIN YARDS OF EACH OTHER, THOUGH NEITHER SUSPECTS THE OTHER'S PRESENCE! AND THEN, A FEW HOURS LATER, BACK AT THE STUDY OF PROFESSOR X...
YOU MAY APPLAUD IF YOU WISH, JEAN! I'M BACK!
WELL, IF IT ISN'T LITTLE MR. MODEST!
I'LL BE READY FOR YOUR PROGRESS REPORT IN A MOMENT, ANGEL!
MINUTES LATER...
...AND THAT'S ABOUT IT, SIR! EXCEPT FOR SIGHTING THE SHIP WITH NO CREW! A PRETTY UNEVENTFUL FLIGHT!
AN UNMANNED SHIP, PROPELLED BY REMOTE CONTROL! STRANGE--I WAS UNAWARE OF ANY NAUTICAL ARTILLARY TESTS AT THE PRESENT TIME!
HERE IS YOUR LAB EQUIPMENT, SIR!
YOUR HEART-BEAT IS SATISFACTORY--BLOOD PRESSURE NORMAL--JUST ONE THING DISTURBS ME--!!
WHAT IS IT, SIR?? SOMETHING WRONG WITH MY TESTS? I-I FEEL PERFECTLY WELL--!
NO, IT IS NOT YOU, WARREN! IT IS THAT FREIGHTER! I SEEM TO SENSE SOMETHING WRONG--SOMETHING STRANGELY OMINOUS ABOUT IT! CALL IT A HUNCH IF YOU WILL--!
7

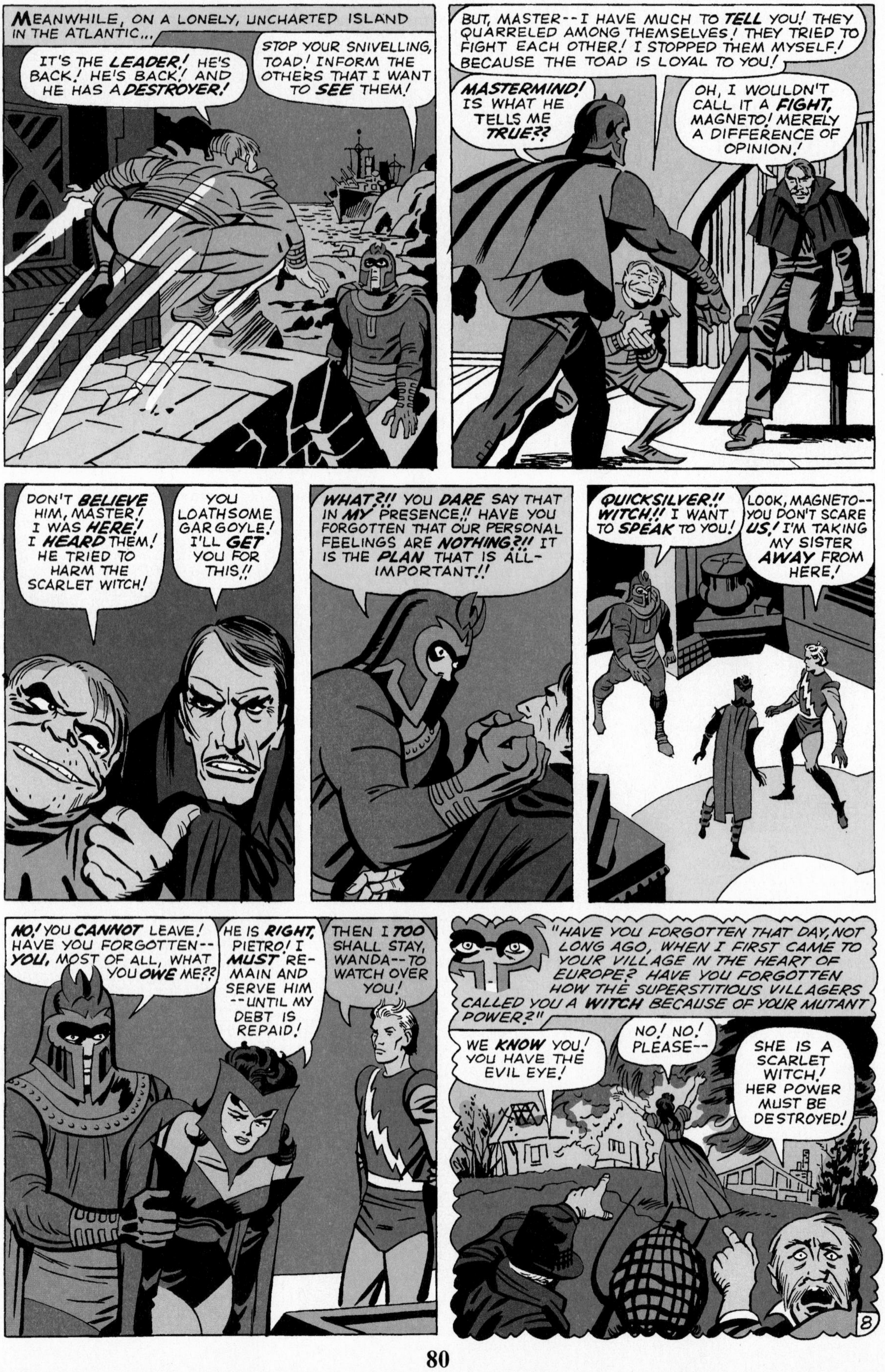

MEANWHILE, ON A LONELY, UNCHARTED ISLAND IN THE ATLANTIC...
IT'S THE LEADER! HE'S BACK! HE'S BACK! AND HE HAS A DESTROYER!
STOP YOUR SNIVELLING, TOAD! INFORM THE OTHERS THAT I WANT TO SEE THEM!
BUT, MASTER--I HAVE MUCH TO TELL YOU! THEY QUARRELED AMONG THEMSELVES! THEY TRIED TO FIGHT EACH OTHER! I STOPPED THEM MYSELF! BECAUSE THE TOAD IS LOYAL TO YOU!
MASTERMIND! IS WHAT HE TELLS ME TRUE??
OH, I WOULDN'T CALL IT A FIGHT, MAGNETO! MERELY A DIFFERENCE OF OPINION!
DON'T BELIEVE HIM, MASTER! I WAS HERE! I HEARD THEM! HE TRIED TO HARM THE SCARLET WITCH!
YOU LOATHSOME GARGOYLE! I'LL GET YOU FOR THIS!!
WHAT?!! YOU DARE SAY THAT IN MY PRESENCE!! HAVE YOU FORGOTTEN THAT OUR PERSONAL FEELINGS ARE NOTHING?!! IT IS THE PLAN THAT IS ALL-IMPORTANT!!
QUICKSILVER!! WITCH!! I WANT TO SPEAK TO YOU!
LOOK, MAGNETO--YOU DON'T SCARE US! I'M TAKING MY SISTER AWAY FROM HERE!
NO! YOU CANNOT LEAVE! HAVE YOU FORGOTTEN--YOU, MOST OF ALL, WHAT YOU OWE ME??
HE IS RIGHT, PIETRO! I MUST REMAIN AND SERVE HIM--UNTIL MY DEBT IS REPAID!
THEN I TOO SHALL STAY, WANDA--TO WATCH OVER YOU!
"HAVE YOU FORGOTTEN THAT DAY, NOT LONG AGO, WHEN I FIRST CAME TO YOUR VILLAGE IN THE HEART OF EUROPE? HAVE YOU FORGOTTEN HOW THE SUPERSTITIOUS VILLAGERS CALLED YOU A WITCH BECAUSE OF YOUR MUTANT POWER?"
WE KNOW YOU! YOU HAVE THE EVIL EYE!
NO! NO! PLEASE--
SHE IS A SCARLET WITCH! HER POWER MUST BE DESTROYED!
8

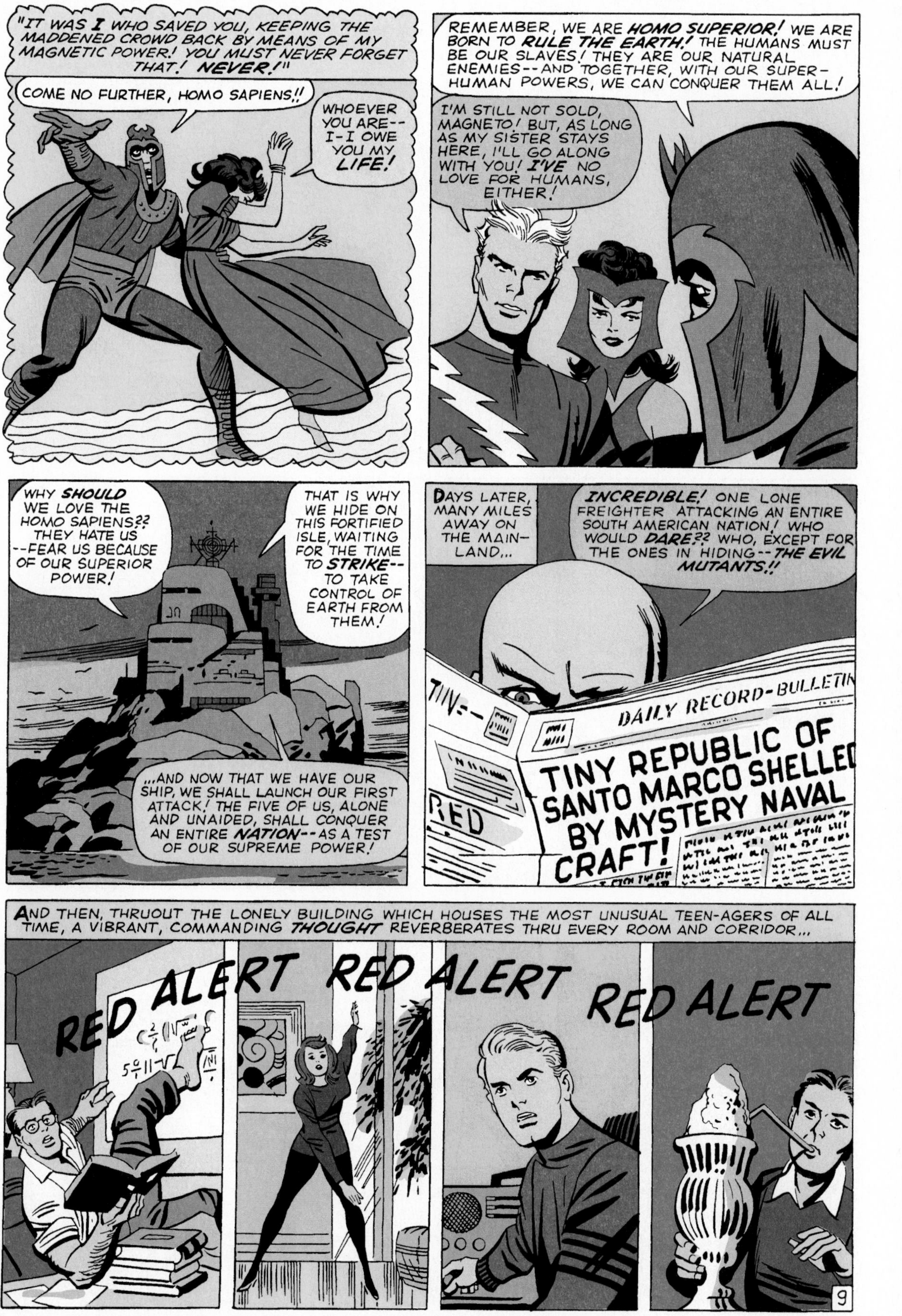
"IT WAS I WHO SAVED YOU, KEEPING THE MADDENED CROWD BACK BY MEANS OF MY MAGNETIC POWER! YOU MUST NEVER FORGET THAT! NEVER!"
COME NO FURTHER, HOMO SAPIENS!!
WHOEVER YOU ARE-- I-I OWE YOU MY LIFE!
REMEMBER, WE ARE HOMO SUPERIOR! WE ARE BORN TO RULE THE EARTH! THE HUMANS MUST BE OUR SLAVES! THEY ARE OUR NATURAL ENEMIES--AND TOGETHER, WITH OUR SUPER-HUMAN POWERS, WE CAN CONQUER THEM ALL!
I'M STILL NOT SOLD, MAGNETO! BUT, AS LONG AS MY SISTER STAYS HERE, I'LL GO ALONG WITH YOU! I'VE NO LOVE FOR HUMANS, EITHER!
WHY SHOULD WE LOVE THE HOMO SAPIENS?? THEY HATE US --FEAR US BECAUSE OF OUR SUPERIOR POWER!
THAT IS WHY WE HIDE ON THIS FORTIFIED ISLE, WAITING FOR THE TIME TO STRIKE-- TO TAKE CONTROL OF EARTH FROM THEM!
...AND NOW THAT WE HAVE OUR SHIP, WE SHALL LAUNCH OUR FIRST ATTACK! THE FIVE OF US, ALONE AND UNAIDED, SHALL CONQUER AN ENTIRE NATION--AS A TEST OF OUR SUPREME POWER!
DAYS LATER, MANY MILES AWAY ON THE MAIN-LAND...
INCREDIBLE! ONE LONE FREIGHTER ATTACKING AN ENTIRE SOUTH AMERICAN NATION! WHO WOULD DARE?? WHO, EXCEPT FOR THE ONES IN HIDING--THE EVIL MUTANTS!!
DAILY RECORD-BULLETIN
TINY REPUBLIC OF SANTO MARCO SHELLED BY MYSTERY NAVAL CRAFT!
AND THEN, THRUOUT THE LONELY BUILDING WHICH HOUSES THE MOST UNUSUAL TEEN-AGERS OF ALL TIME, A VIBRANT, COMMANDING THOUGHT REVERBERATES THRU EVERY ROOM AND CORRIDOR...
RED ALERT RED ALERT RED ALERT
9

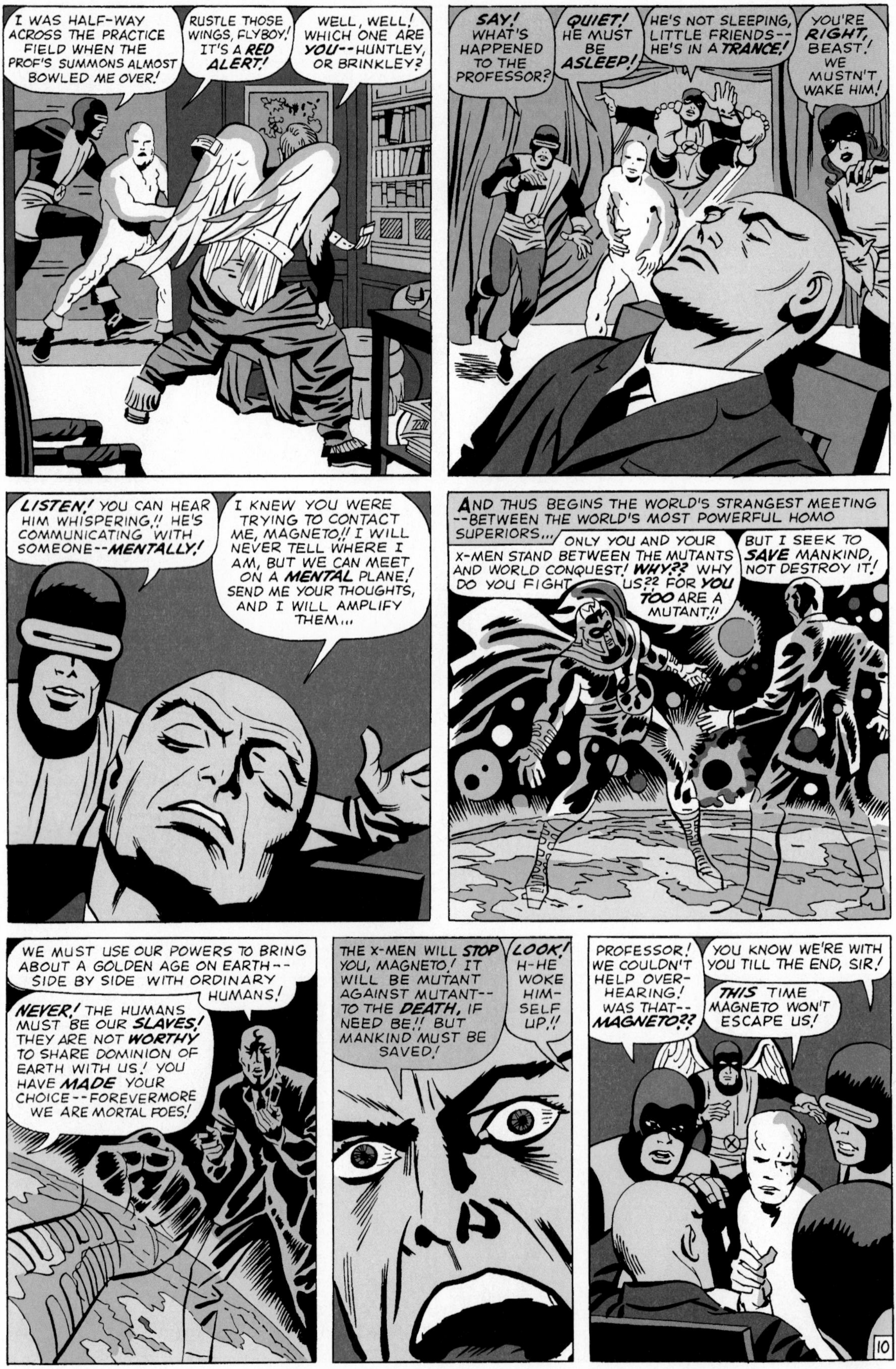

I WAS HALF-WAY ACROSS THE PRACTICE FIELD WHEN THE PROF'S SUMMONS ALMOST BOWLED ME OVER!
RUSTLE THOSE WINGS, FLYBOY! IT'S A RED ALERT!
WELL, WELL! WHICH ONE ARE YOU--HUNTLEY, OR BRINKLEY?
SAY! WHAT'S HAPPENED TO THE PROFESSOR?
QUIET! HE MUST BE ASLEEP!
HE'S NOT SLEEPING, LITTLE FRIENDS-- HE'S IN A TRANCE!
YOU'RE RIGHT, BEAST! WE MUSTN'T WAKE HIM!
LISTEN! YOU CAN HEAR HIM WHISPERING!! HE'S COMMUNICATING WITH SOMEONE--MENTALLY!
I KNEW YOU WERE TRYING TO CONTACT ME, MAGNETO!! I WILL NEVER TELL WHERE I AM, BUT WE CAN MEET ON A MENTAL PLANE! SEND ME YOUR THOUGHTS, AND I WILL AMPLIFY THEM...
AND THUS BEGINS THE WORLD'S STRANGEST MEETING --BETWEEN THE WORLD'S MOST POWERFUL HOMO SUPERIORS...
ONLY YOU AND YOUR X-MEN STAND BETWEEN THE MUTANTS AND WORLD CONQUEST! WHY?? WHY DO YOU FIGHT US?? FOR YOU TOO ARE A MUTANT!!
BUT I SEEK TO SAVE MANKIND, NOT DESTROY IT!
WE MUST USE OUR POWERS TO BRING ABOUT A GOLDEN AGE ON EARTH-- SIDE BY SIDE WITH ORDINARY HUMANS!
NEVER! THE HUMANS MUST BE OUR SLAVES! THEY ARE NOT WORTHY TO SHARE DOMINION OF EARTH WITH US! YOU HAVE MADE YOUR CHOICE--FOREVERMORE WE ARE MORTAL FOES!
THE X-MEN WILL STOP YOU, MAGNETO! IT WILL BE MUTANT AGAINST MUTANT-- TO THE DEATH, IF NEED BE!! BUT MANKIND MUST BE SAVED!
LOOK! H-HE WOKE HIMSELF UP!!
PROFESSOR! WE COULDN'T HELP OVER-HEARING! WAS THAT-- MAGNETO??
YOU KNOW WE'RE WITH YOU TILL THE END, SIR!
THIS TIME MAGNETO WON'T ESCAPE US!
10

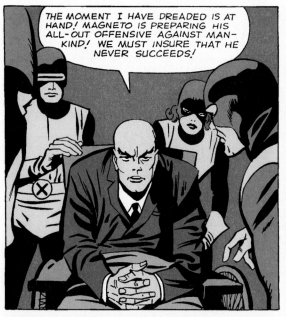

THE MOMENT I HAVE DREADED IS AT HAND! MAGNETO IS PREPARING HIS ALL-OUT OFFENSIVE AGAINST MANKIND! WE MUST INSURE THAT HE NEVER SUCCEEDS!

MEANWHILE, OFF THE COAST OF SANTO MARCO, THE EVIL MUTANTS FINISH THEIR SHELLING OF THE TINY REPUBLIC, FIRING INTO THE HILLS BEHIND THE CITY, TO SHOW THEIR POWER!

SANTO MARCO WILL BE MINE BEFORE NIGHTFALL! THEY HAVE NO FORCE TO OPPOSE US!

NOTHING CAN STOP YOU, MAGNETO! YOU WERE BORN TO RULE!

AT FIRST, THE PROUD PEOPLE OF SANTO MARCO PREPARE TO OFFER STAUNCH RESISTANCE-- UNTIL THEY SEE--

LOOK! MARCHING THRU THE STREETS--!!

IT IS NOT POSSIBLE!

WE CANNOT FIGHT THEM!! WE MUST SURRENDER!

RUN FOR YOUR LIVES!! IT IS AN ENTIRE ENEMY ARMY!

WE ARE LOST! THEY APPEARED AS THOUGH-- BY MAGIC!!

HEE HEE HEE! THEY DO NOT DREAM THAT THE ARMY IS JUST AN ILLUSION!

WELL DONE, MASTER-MIND! CONTINUE THE ILLUSION UNTIL I HAVE THE ENTIRE REPUBLIC UNDER MY CONTROL!

IT'S INCREDIBLE! IF I DIDN'T KNOW BETTER, I TOO WOULD SWEAR I'M GAZING AT A REAL FLESH AND BLOOD ARMY!!

BUT IS IT NECESSARY TO PLANT SUCH FEAR IN THE HEARTS OF THE PEOPLE, MAGNETO?

OF COURSE! HUMANS ARE LIKE SHEEP! THEY RESPOND TO CERTAIN STIMULI-- AND FEAR IS ONE OF THE MOST POTENT!

11

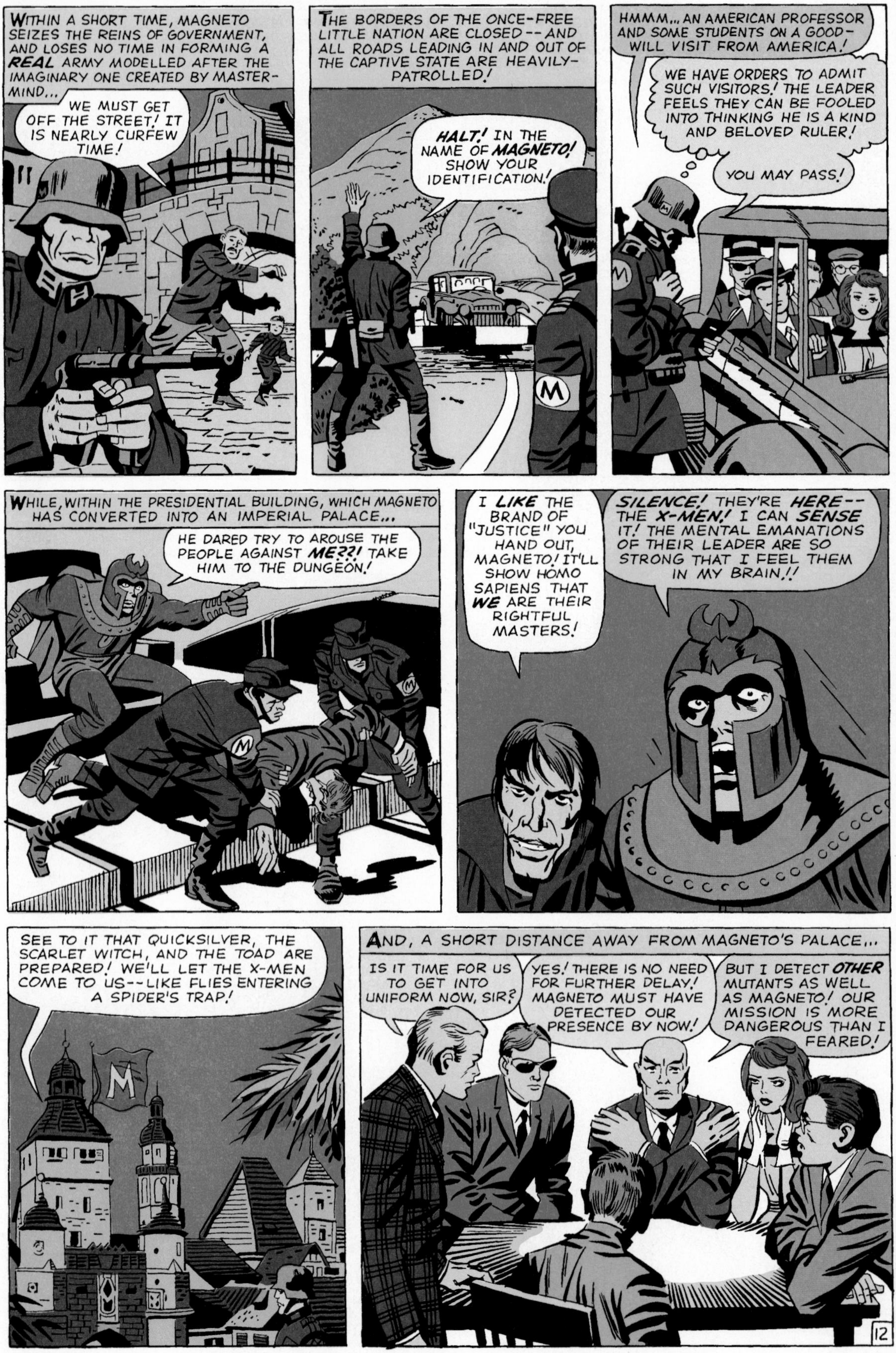
WITHIN A SHORT TIME, MAGNETO SEIZES THE REINS OF GOVERNMENT, AND LOSES NO TIME IN FORMING A REAL ARMY MODELLED AFTER THE IMAGINARY ONE CREATED BY MASTER-MIND...
WE MUST GET OFF THE STREET! IT IS NEARLY CURFEW TIME!
THE BORDERS OF THE ONCE-FREE LITTLE NATION ARE CLOSED -- AND ALL ROADS LEADING IN AND OUT OF THE CAPTIVE STATE ARE HEAVILY-PATROLLED!
HALT! IN THE NAME OF MAGNETO! SHOW YOUR IDENTIFICATION!
HMMM... AN AMERICAN PROFESSOR AND SOME STUDENTS ON A GOOD-WILL VISIT FROM AMERICA!
WE HAVE ORDERS TO ADMIT SUCH VISITORS! THE LEADER FEELS THEY CAN BE FOOLED INTO THINKING HE IS A KIND AND BELOVED RULER!
YOU MAY PASS!
WHILE, WITHIN THE PRESIDENTIAL BUILDING, WHICH MAGNETO HAS CONVERTED INTO AN IMPERIAL PALACE...
HE DARED TRY TO AROUSE THE PEOPLE AGAINST ME??! TAKE HIM TO THE DUNGEON!
I LIKE THE BRAND OF "JUSTICE" YOU HAND OUT, MAGNETO! IT'LL SHOW HOMO SAPIENS THAT WE ARE THEIR RIGHTFUL MASTERS!
SILENCE! THEY'RE HERE -- THE X-MEN! I CAN SENSE IT! THE MENTAL EMANATIONS OF THEIR LEADER ARE SO STRONG THAT I FEEL THEM IN MY BRAIN!!
SEE TO IT THAT QUICKSILVER, THE SCARLET WITCH, AND THE TOAD ARE PREPARED! WE'LL LET THE X-MEN COME TO US -- LIKE FLIES ENTERING A SPIDER'S TRAP!
M
AND, A SHORT DISTANCE AWAY FROM MAGNETO'S PALACE...
IS IT TIME FOR US TO GET INTO UNIFORM NOW, SIR?
YES! THERE IS NO NEED FOR FURTHER DELAY! MAGNETO MUST HAVE DETECTED OUR PRESENCE BY NOW!
BUT I DETECT OTHER MUTANTS AS WELL AS MAGNETO! OUR MISSION IS MORE DANGEROUS THAN I FEARED!
12

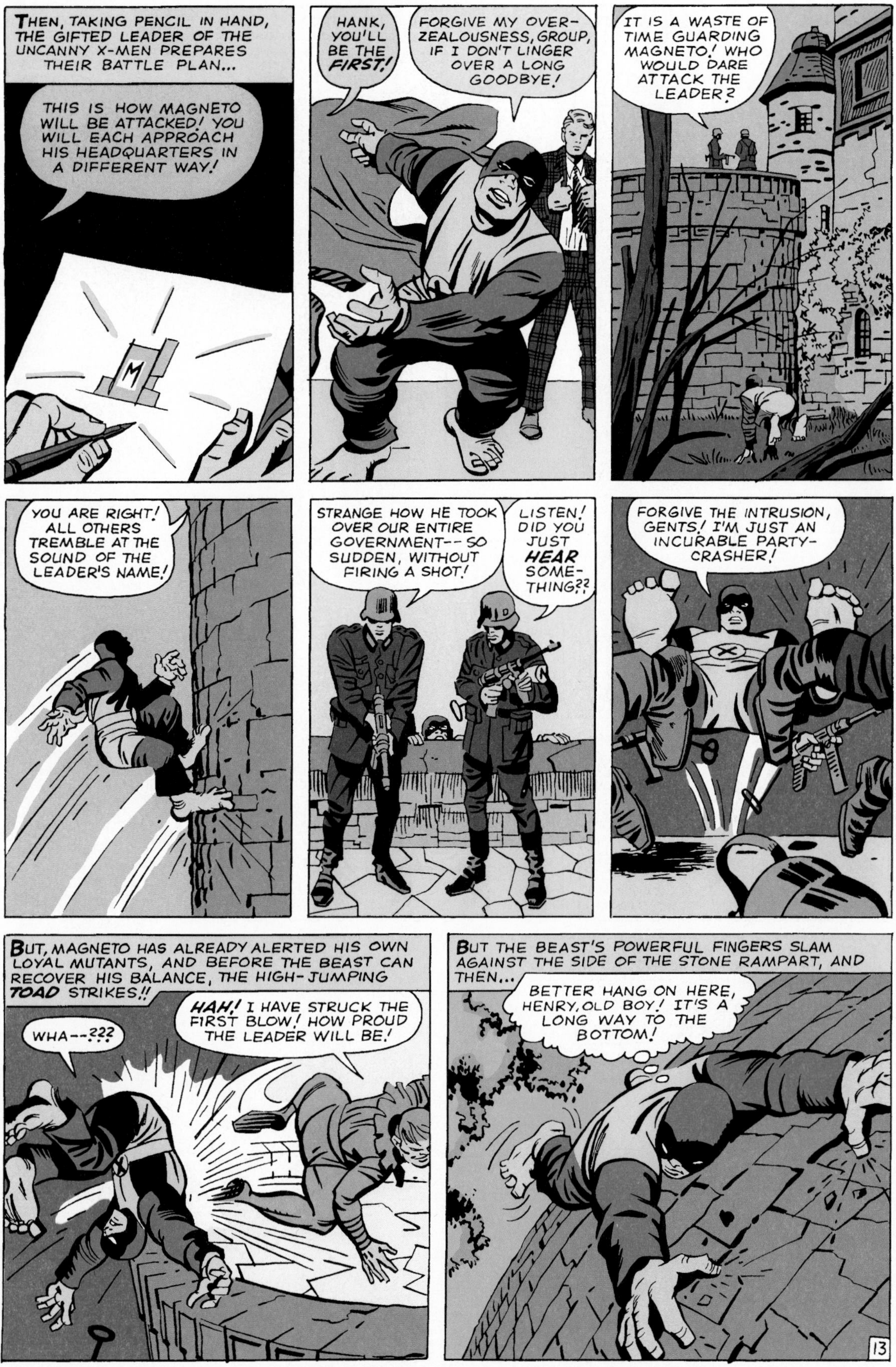
THEN, TAKING PENCIL IN HAND, THE GIFTED LEADER OF THE UNCANNY X-MEN PREPARES THEIR BATTLE PLAN...
THIS IS HOW MAGNETO WILL BE ATTACKED! YOU WILL EACH APPROACH HIS HEADQUARTERS IN A DIFFERENT WAY!
M
HANK, YOU'LL BE THE FIRST!
FORGIVE MY OVER-ZEALOUSNESS, GROUP, IF I DON'T LINGER OVER A LONG GOODBYE!
IT IS A WASTE OF TIME GUARDING MAGNETO! WHO WOULD DARE ATTACK THE LEADER?
YOU ARE RIGHT! ALL OTHERS TREMBLE AT THE SOUND OF THE LEADER'S NAME!
STRANGE HOW HE TOOK OVER OUR ENTIRE GOVERNMENT-- SO SUDDEN, WITHOUT FIRING A SHOT!
LISTEN! DID YOU JUST HEAR SOME-THING??
FORGIVE THE INTRUSION, GENTS! I'M JUST AN INCURABLE PARTY-CRASHER!
BUT, MAGNETO HAS ALREADY ALERTED HIS OWN LOYAL MUTANTS, AND BEFORE THE BEAST CAN RECOVER HIS BALANCE, THE HIGH-JUMPING TOAD STRIKES!!
WHA--???
HAH! I HAVE STRUCK THE FIRST BLOW! HOW PROUD THE LEADER WILL BE!
BUT THE BEAST'S POWERFUL FINGERS SLAM AGAINST THE SIDE OF THE STONE RAMPART, AND THEN...
BETTER HANG ON HERE, HENRY, OLD BOY! IT'S A LONG WAY TO THE BOTTOM!
13

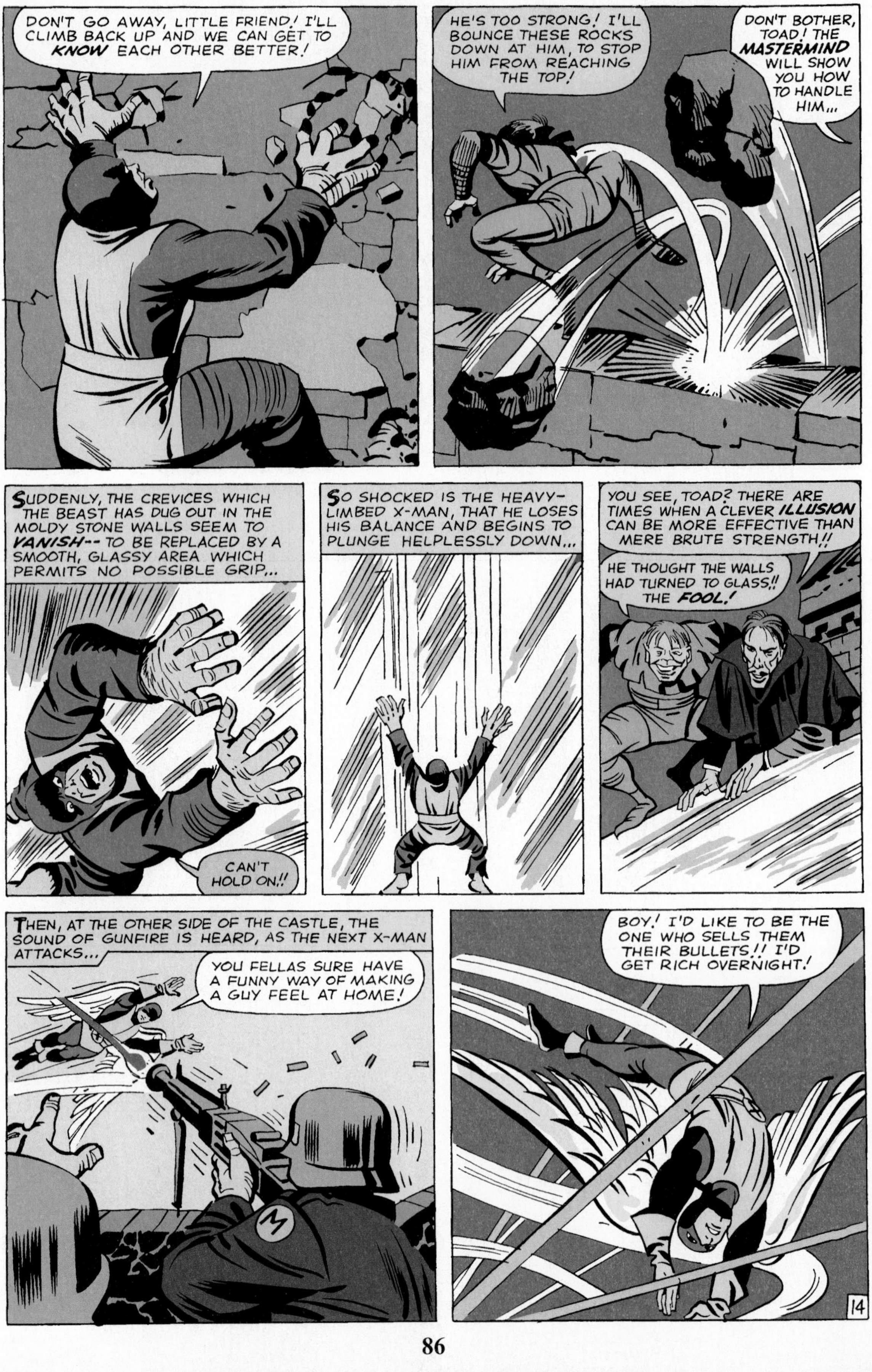
DON'T GO AWAY, LITTLE FRIEND! I'LL CLIMB BACK UP AND WE CAN GET TO KNOW EACH OTHER BETTER!
HE'S TOO STRONG! I'LL BOUNCE THESE ROCKS DOWN AT HIM, TO STOP HIM FROM REACHING THE TOP!
DON'T BOTHER, TOAD! THE MASTERMIND WILL SHOW YOU HOW TO HANDLE HIM...
SUDDENLY, THE CREVICES WHICH THE BEAST HAS DUG OUT IN THE MOLDY STONE WALLS SEEM TO VANISH-- TO BE REPLACED BY A SMOOTH, GLASSY AREA WHICH PERMITS NO POSSIBLE GRIP...
CAN'T HOLD ON!!
SO SHOCKED IS THE HEAVY-LIMBED X-MAN, THAT HE LOSES HIS BALANCE AND BEGINS TO PLUNGE HELPLESSLY DOWN...
YOU SEE, TOAD? THERE ARE TIMES WHEN A CLEVER ILLUSION CAN BE MORE EFFECTIVE THAN MERE BRUTE STRENGTH!!
HE THOUGHT THE WALLS HAD TURNED TO GLASS!! THE FOOL!
THEN, AT THE OTHER SIDE OF THE CASTLE, THE SOUND OF GUNFIRE IS HEARD, AS THE NEXT X-MAN ATTACKS...
YOU FELLAS SURE HAVE A FUNNY WAY OF MAKING A GUY FEEL AT HOME!
BOY! I'D LIKE TO BE THE ONE WHO SELLS THEM THEIR BULLETS!! I'D GET RICH OVERNIGHT!
14

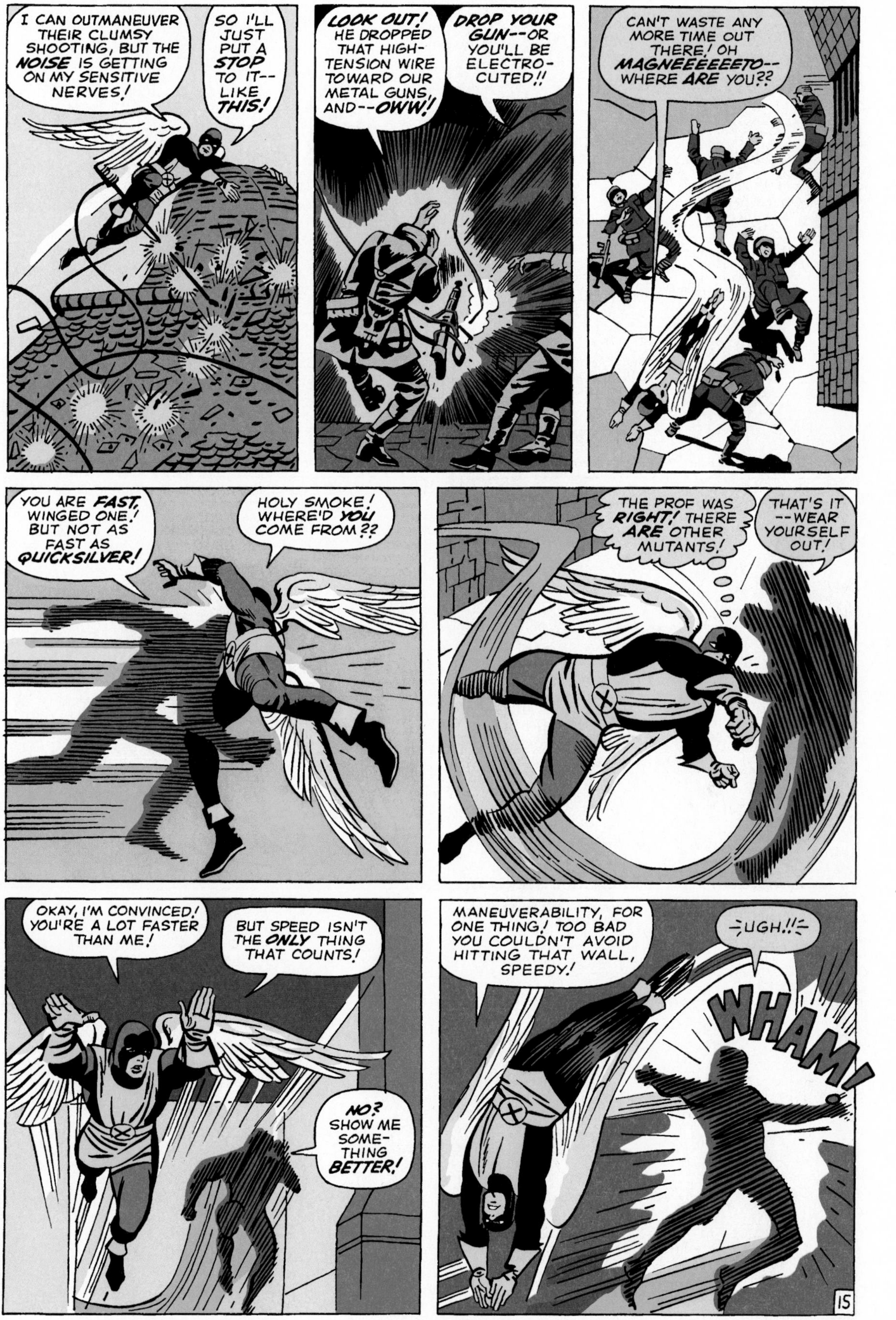
I CAN OUTMANEUVER THEIR CLUMSY SHOOTING, BUT THE NOISE IS GETTING ON MY SENSITIVE NERVES!
SO I'LL JUST PUT A STOP TO IT-- LIKE THIS!
LOOK OUT! HE DROPPED THAT HIGH-TENSION WIRE TOWARD OUR METAL GUNS, AND--OWW!
DROP YOUR GUN--OR YOU'LL BE ELECTROCUTED!!
CAN'T WASTE ANY MORE TIME OUT THERE! OH MAGNEEEEEETO-- WHERE ARE YOU??
YOU ARE FAST, WINGED ONE! BUT NOT AS FAST AS QUICKSILVER!
HOLY SMOKE! WHERE'D YOU COME FROM??
THE PROF WAS RIGHT! THERE ARE OTHER MUTANTS!
THAT'S IT --WEAR YOURSELF OUT!
OKAY, I'M CONVINCED! YOU'RE A LOT FASTER THAN ME!
BUT SPEED ISN'T THE ONLY THING THAT COUNTS!
NO? SHOW ME SOME-THING BETTER!
MANEUVERABILITY, FOR ONE THING! TOO BAD YOU COULDN'T AVOID HITTING THAT WALL, SPEEDY!
UGH!!
WHAM!
15

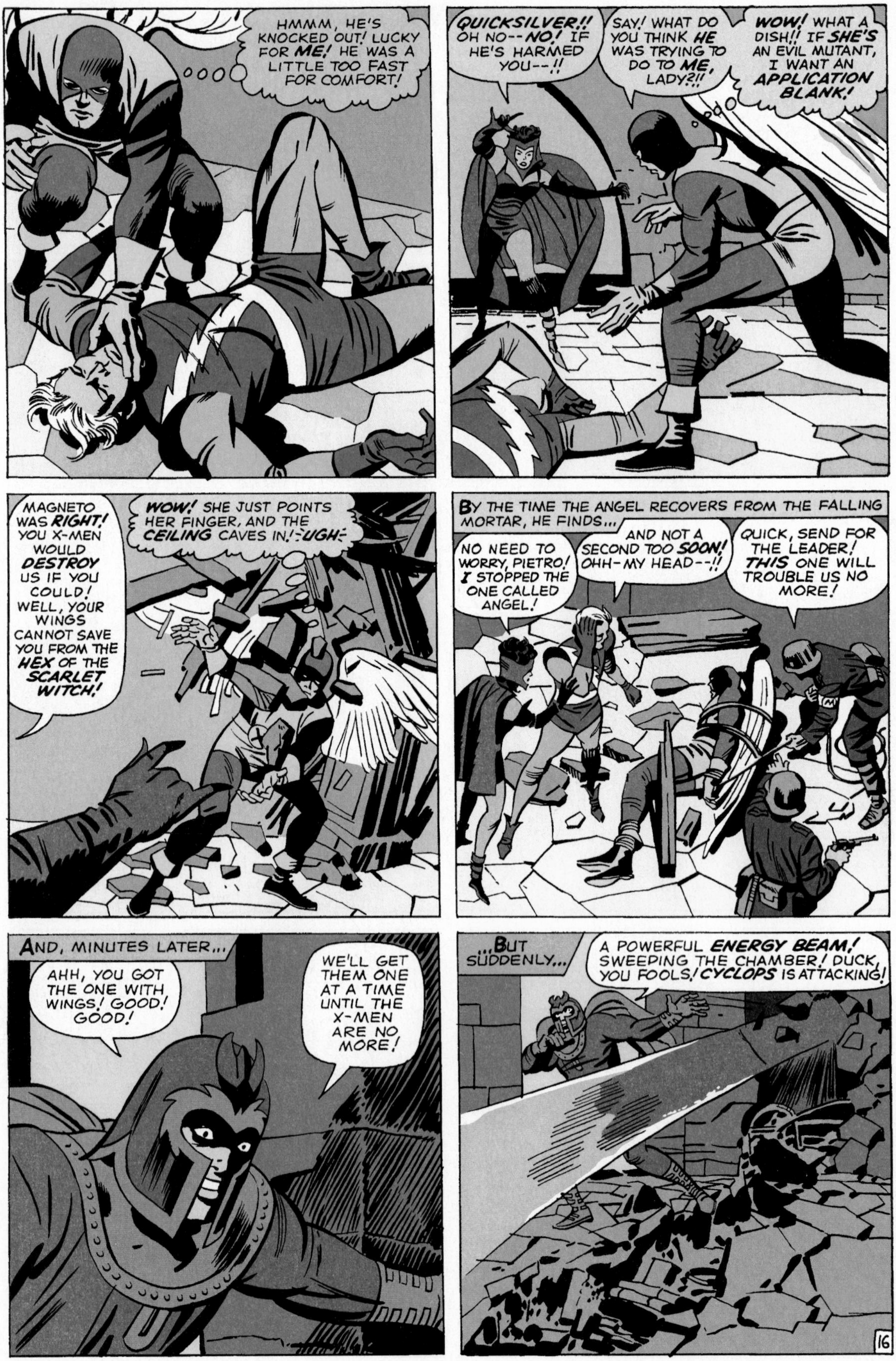

HMMM, HE'S KNOCKED OUT! LUCKY FOR ME! HE WAS A LITTLE TOO FAST FOR COMFORT!
QUICKSILVER!! OH NO--NO! IF HE'S HARMED YOU--!!
SAY! WHAT DO YOU THINK HE WAS TRYING TO DO TO ME, LADY?!!
WOW! WHAT A DISH!! IF SHE'S AN EVIL MUTANT, I WANT AN APPLICATION BLANK!
MAGNETO WAS RIGHT! YOU X-MEN WOULD DESTROY US IF YOU COULD! WELL, YOUR WINGS CANNOT SAVE YOU FROM THE HEX OF THE SCARLET WITCH!
WOW! SHE JUST POINTS HER FINGER, AND THE CEILING CAVES IN! -UGH-
BY THE TIME THE ANGEL RECOVERS FROM THE FALLING MORTAR, HE FINDS...
NO NEED TO WORRY, PIETRO! I STOPPED THE ONE CALLED ANGEL!
AND NOT A SECOND TOO SOON! OHH-MY HEAD--!!
QUICK, SEND FOR THE LEADER! THIS ONE WILL TROUBLE US NO MORE!
AND, MINUTES LATER...
AHH, YOU GOT THE ONE WITH WINGS! GOOD! GOOD!
WE'LL GET THEM ONE AT A TIME UNTIL THE X-MEN ARE NO MORE!
...BUT SUDDENLY...
A POWERFUL ENERGY BEAM! SWEEPING THE CHAMBER! DUCK, YOU FOOLS! CYCLOPS IS ATTACKING!
16

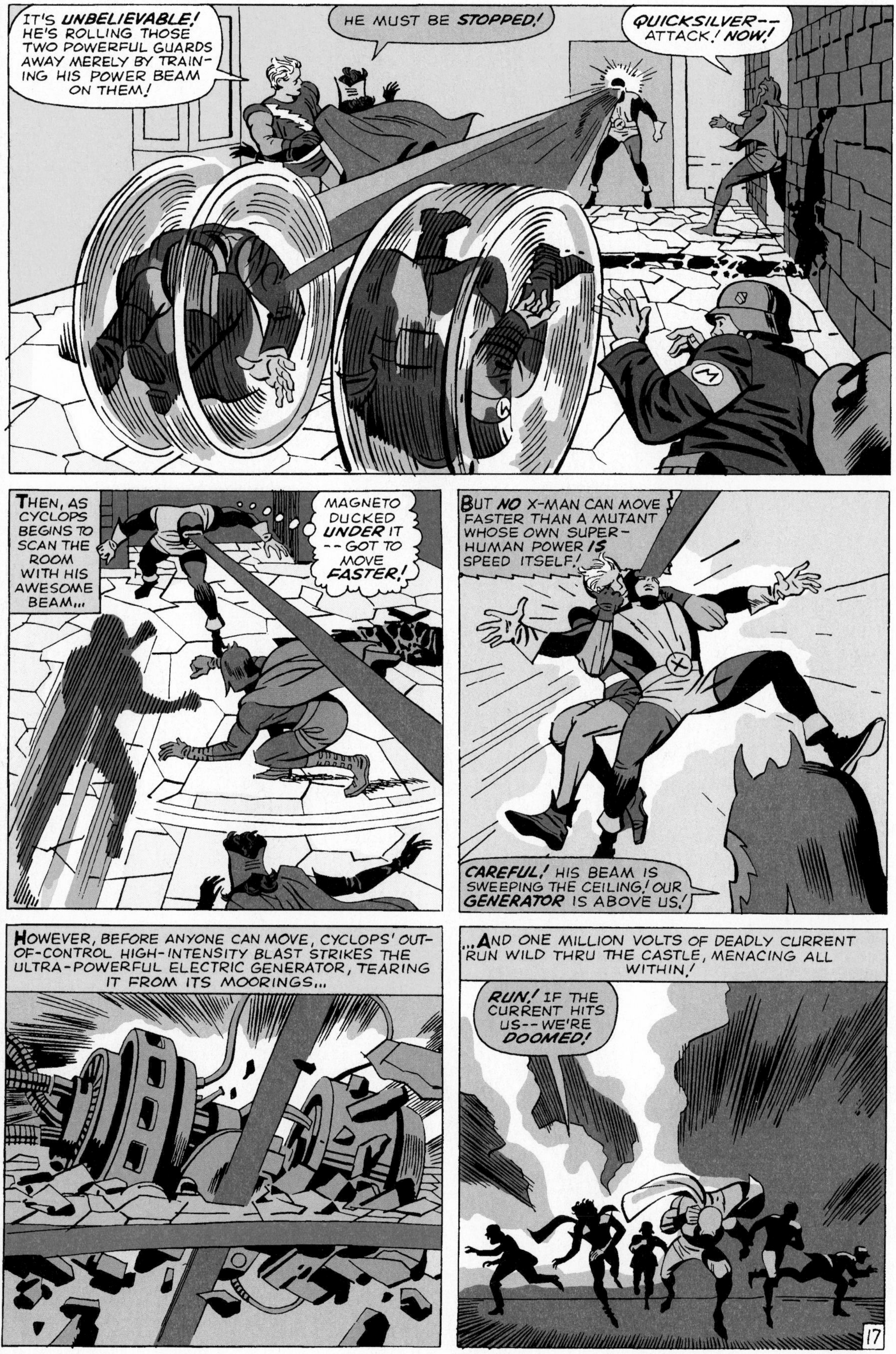
IT'S UNBELIEVABLE! HE'S ROLLING THOSE TWO POWERFUL GUARDS AWAY MERELY BY TRAINING HIS POWER BEAM ON THEM!
HE MUST BE STOPPED!
QUICKSILVER-- ATTACK! NOW!
THEN, AS CYCLOPS BEGINS TO SCAN THE ROOM WITH HIS AWESOME BEAM...
MAGNETO DUCKED UNDER IT --GOT TO MOVE FASTER!
BUT NO X-MAN CAN MOVE FASTER THAN A MUTANT WHOSE OWN SUPER-HUMAN POWER IS SPEED ITSELF!
CAREFUL! HIS BEAM IS SWEEPING THE CEILING! OUR GENERATOR IS ABOVE US!
HOWEVER, BEFORE ANYONE CAN MOVE, CYCLOPS' OUT-OF-CONTROL HIGH-INTENSITY BLAST STRIKES THE ULTRA-POWERFUL ELECTRIC GENERATOR, TEARING IT FROM ITS MOORINGS...
...AND ONE MILLION VOLTS OF DEADLY CURRENT RUN WILD THRU THE CASTLE, MENACING ALL WITHIN!
RUN! IF THE CURRENT HITS US--WE'RE DOOMED!
17

NO TIME TO UNTIE YOU, ANGEL! WE'LL BE *FRIED* IN ANOTHER FEW SECONDS!

SHUT YOUR EYES, *FAST!* I'M GOING TO TRY A DESPERATE GAMBLE!

I'VE GOT TO USE MY FORCE BEAM RIGHT THRU THE WALL--TO GET AT THAT GENERATOR AND *STOP* IT SOMEHOW!

IF THIS DOESN'T WORK-- IT'S CURTAINS FOR US!

WHAM!

CYCLOPS! YOU *DID* IT! YOU BLASTED THE GENERATOR CLEAN THRU THE WALL!

HOLY SMOKE! HE COLLAPSED FROM THE STRAIN! NOW WE'RE *BOTH* HELPLESS! I'M TIED UP, AND HE'S UNCONSCIOUS!

WHILE DIRECTLY OUTSIDE THE CASTLE...

UH OH! IF THAT CONTRAPTION FALLS ON ME, IT'LL BE "GOODBYE ICEMAN!"

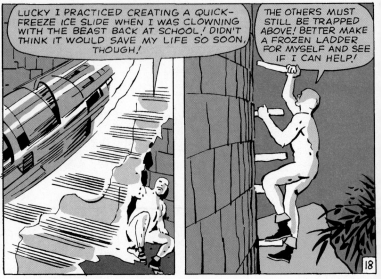

LUCKY I PRACTICED CREATING A QUICK-FREEZE ICE SLIDE WHEN I WAS CLOWNING WITH THE BEAST BACK AT SCHOOL! DIDN'T THINK IT WOULD SAVE MY LIFE SO SOON, THOUGH!

THE OTHERS MUST STILL BE TRAPPED ABOVE! BETTER MAKE A FROZEN LADDER FOR MYSELF AND SEE IF I CAN HELP!

18

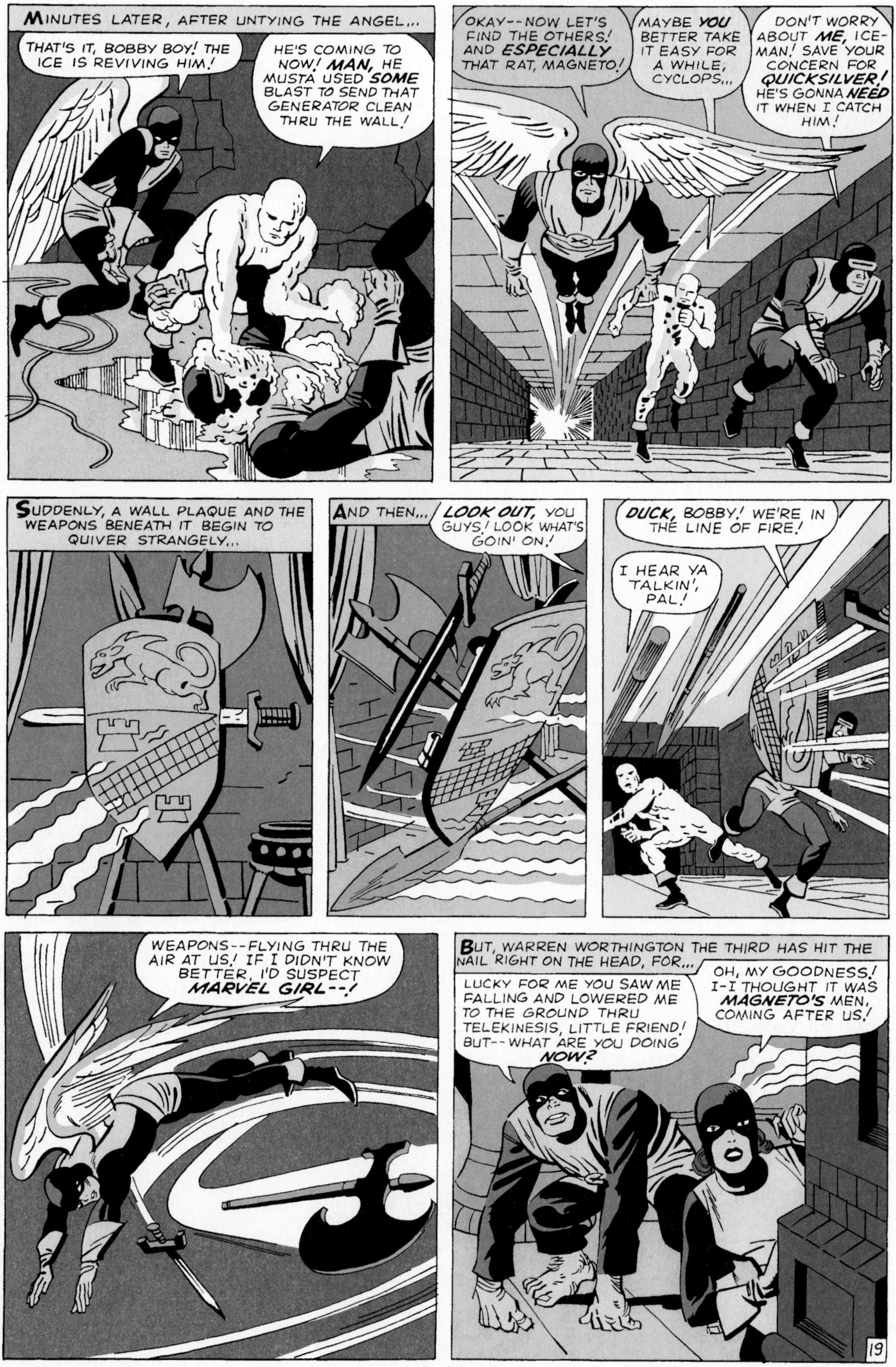
MINUTES LATER, AFTER UNTYING THE ANGEL...
THAT'S IT, BOBBY BOY! THE ICE IS REVIVING HIM!
HE'S COMING TO NOW! MAN, HE MUSTA USED SOME BLAST TO SEND THAT GENERATOR CLEAN THRU THE WALL!
OKAY--NOW LET'S FIND THE OTHERS! AND ESPECIALLY THAT RAT, MAGNETO!
MAYBE YOU BETTER TAKE IT EASY FOR A WHILE, CYCLOPS...
DON'T WORRY ABOUT ME, ICE-MAN! SAVE YOUR CONCERN FOR QUICKSILVER! HE'S GONNA NEED IT WHEN I CATCH HIM!
SUDDENLY, A WALL PLAQUE AND THE WEAPONS BENEATH IT BEGIN TO QUIVER STRANGELY...
AND THEN...
LOOK OUT, YOU GUYS! LOOK WHAT'S GOIN' ON!
DUCK, BOBBY! WE'RE IN THE LINE OF FIRE!
I HEAR YA TALKIN', PAL!
WEAPONS--FLYING THRU THE AIR AT US! IF I DIDN'T KNOW BETTER, I'D SUSPECT MARVEL GIRL--!
BUT, WARREN WORTHINGTON THE THIRD HAS HIT THE NAIL RIGHT ON THE HEAD, FOR...
LUCKY FOR ME YOU SAW ME FALLING AND LOWERED ME TO THE GROUND THRU TELEKINESIS, LITTLE FRIEND! BUT--WHAT ARE YOU DOING NOW?
OH, MY GOODNESS! I-I THOUGHT IT WAS MAGNETO'S MEN, COMING AFTER US!
19

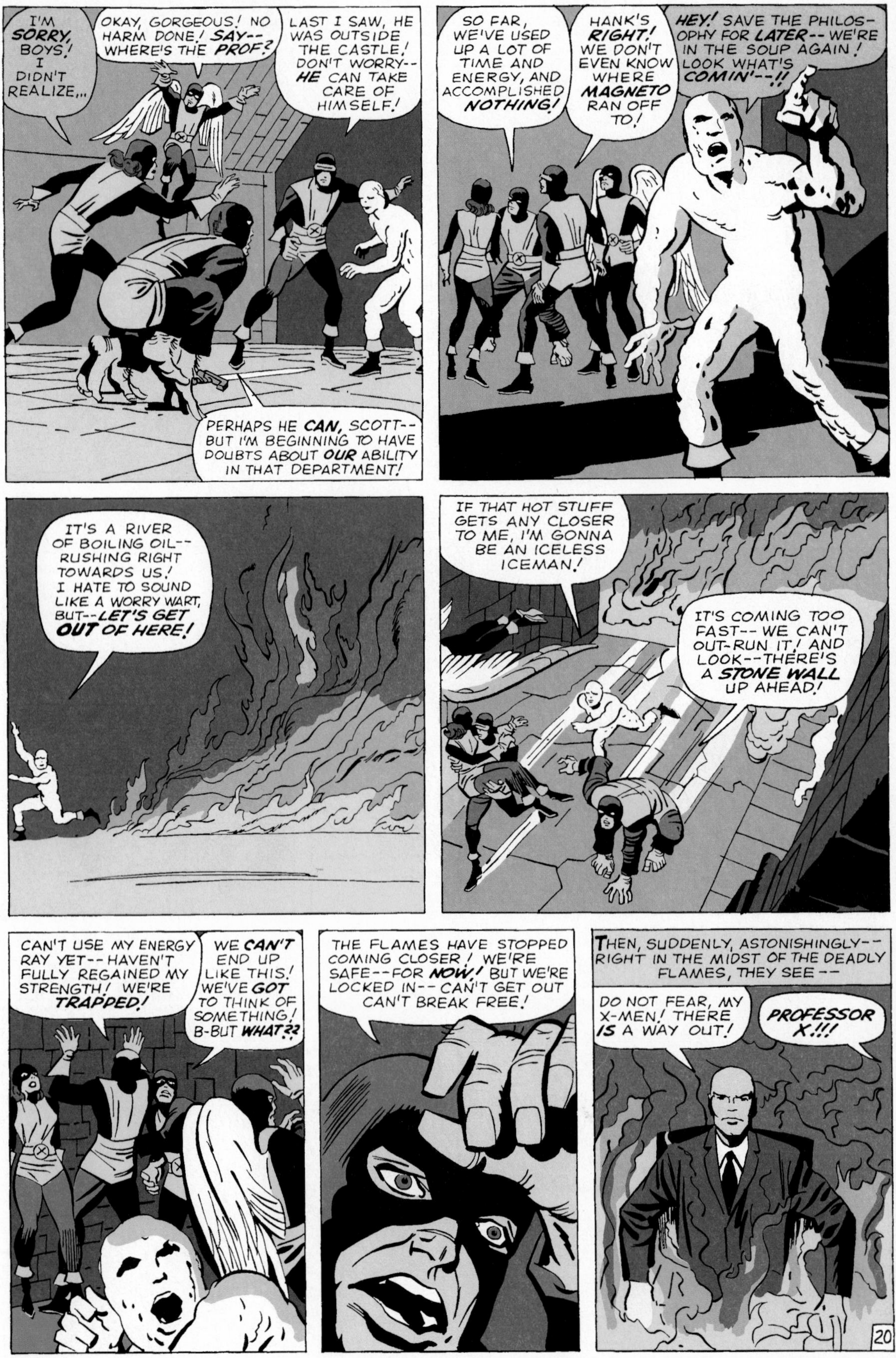

I'M SORRY, BOYS! I DIDN'T REALIZE...
OKAY, GORGEOUS! NO HARM DONE! SAY-- WHERE'S THE PROF?
LAST I SAW, HE WAS OUTSIDE THE CASTLE! DON'T WORRY-- HE CAN TAKE CARE OF HIMSELF!
PERHAPS HE CAN, SCOTT-- BUT I'M BEGINNING TO HAVE DOUBTS ABOUT OUR ABILITY IN THAT DEPARTMENT!
SO FAR, WE'VE USED UP A LOT OF TIME AND ENERGY, AND ACCOMPLISHED NOTHING!
HANK'S RIGHT! WE DON'T EVEN KNOW WHERE MAGNETO RAN OFF TO!
HEY! SAVE THE PHILOSOPHY FOR LATER-- WE'RE IN THE SOUP AGAIN! LOOK WHAT'S COMIN'--!!
IT'S A RIVER OF BOILING OIL-- RUSHING RIGHT TOWARDS US! I HATE TO SOUND LIKE A WORRY WART, BUT--LET'S GET OUT OF HERE!
IF THAT HOT STUFF GETS ANY CLOSER TO ME, I'M GONNA BE AN ICELESS ICEMAN!
IT'S COMING TOO FAST-- WE CAN'T OUT-RUN IT! AND LOOK--THERE'S A STONE WALL UP AHEAD!
CAN'T USE MY ENERGY RAY YET--HAVEN'T FULLY REGAINED MY STRENGTH! WE'RE TRAPPED!
WE CAN'T END UP LIKE THIS! WE'VE GOT TO THINK OF SOMETHING! B-BUT WHAT??
THE FLAMES HAVE STOPPED COMING CLOSER! WE'RE SAFE--FOR NOW! BUT WE'RE LOCKED IN-- CAN'T GET OUT CAN'T BREAK FREE!
THEN, SUDDENLY, ASTONISHINGLY-- RIGHT IN THE MIDST OF THE DEADLY FLAMES, THEY SEE--
DO NOT FEAR, MY X-MEN! THERE IS A WAY OUT!
PROFESSOR X!!!
20

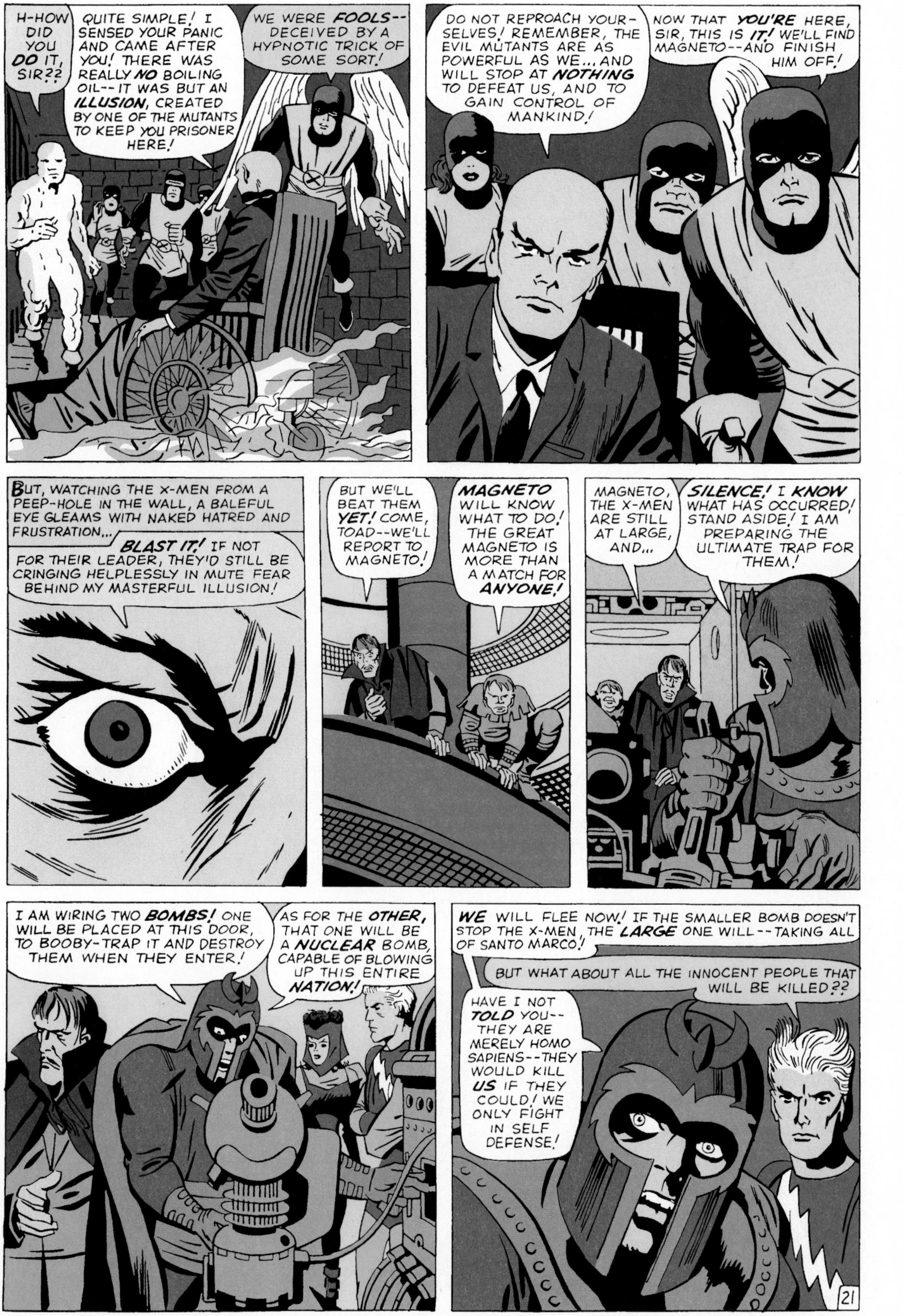
H-HOW DID YOU DO IT, SIR??
QUITE SIMPLE! I SENSED YOUR PANIC AND CAME AFTER YOU! THERE WAS REALLY NO BOILING OIL--IT WAS BUT AN ILLUSION, CREATED BY ONE OF THE MUTANTS TO KEEP YOU PRISONER HERE!
WE WERE FOOLS--DECEIVED BY A HYPNOTIC TRICK OF SOME SORT!
DO NOT REPROACH YOURSELVES! REMEMBER, THE EVIL MUTANTS ARE AS POWERFUL AS WE... AND WILL STOP AT NOTHING TO DEFEAT US, AND TO GAIN CONTROL OF MANKIND!
NOW THAT YOU'RE HERE, SIR, THIS IS IT! WE'LL FIND MAGNETO--AND FINISH HIM OFF!
BUT, WATCHING THE X-MEN FROM A PEEP-HOLE IN THE WALL, A BALEFUL EYE GLEAMS WITH NAKED HATRED AND FRUSTRATION...
BLAST IT! IF NOT FOR THEIR LEADER, THEY'D STILL BE CRINGING HELPLESSLY IN MUTE FEAR BEHIND MY MASTERFUL ILLUSION!
BUT WE'LL BEAT THEM YET! COME, TOAD--WE'LL REPORT TO MAGNETO!
MAGNETO WILL KNOW WHAT TO DO! THE GREAT MAGNETO IS MORE THAN A MATCH FOR ANYONE!
MAGNETO, THE X-MEN ARE STILL AT LARGE, AND...
SILENCE! I KNOW WHAT HAS OCCURRED! STAND ASIDE! I AM PREPARING THE ULTIMATE TRAP FOR THEM!
I AM WIRING TWO BOMBS! ONE WILL BE PLACED AT THIS DOOR, TO BOOBY-TRAP IT AND DESTROY THEM WHEN THEY ENTER!
AS FOR THE OTHER, THAT ONE WILL BE A NUCLEAR BOMB, CAPABLE OF BLOWING UP THIS ENTIRE NATION!
WE WILL FLEE NOW! IF THE SMALLER BOMB DOESN'T STOP THE X-MEN, THE LARGE ONE WILL--TAKING ALL OF SANTO MARCO!
BUT WHAT ABOUT ALL THE INNOCENT PEOPLE THAT WILL BE KILLED??
HAVE I NOT TOLD YOU--THEY ARE MERELY HOMO SAPIENS--THEY WOULD KILL US IF THEY COULD! WE ONLY FIGHT IN SELF DEFENSE!
21

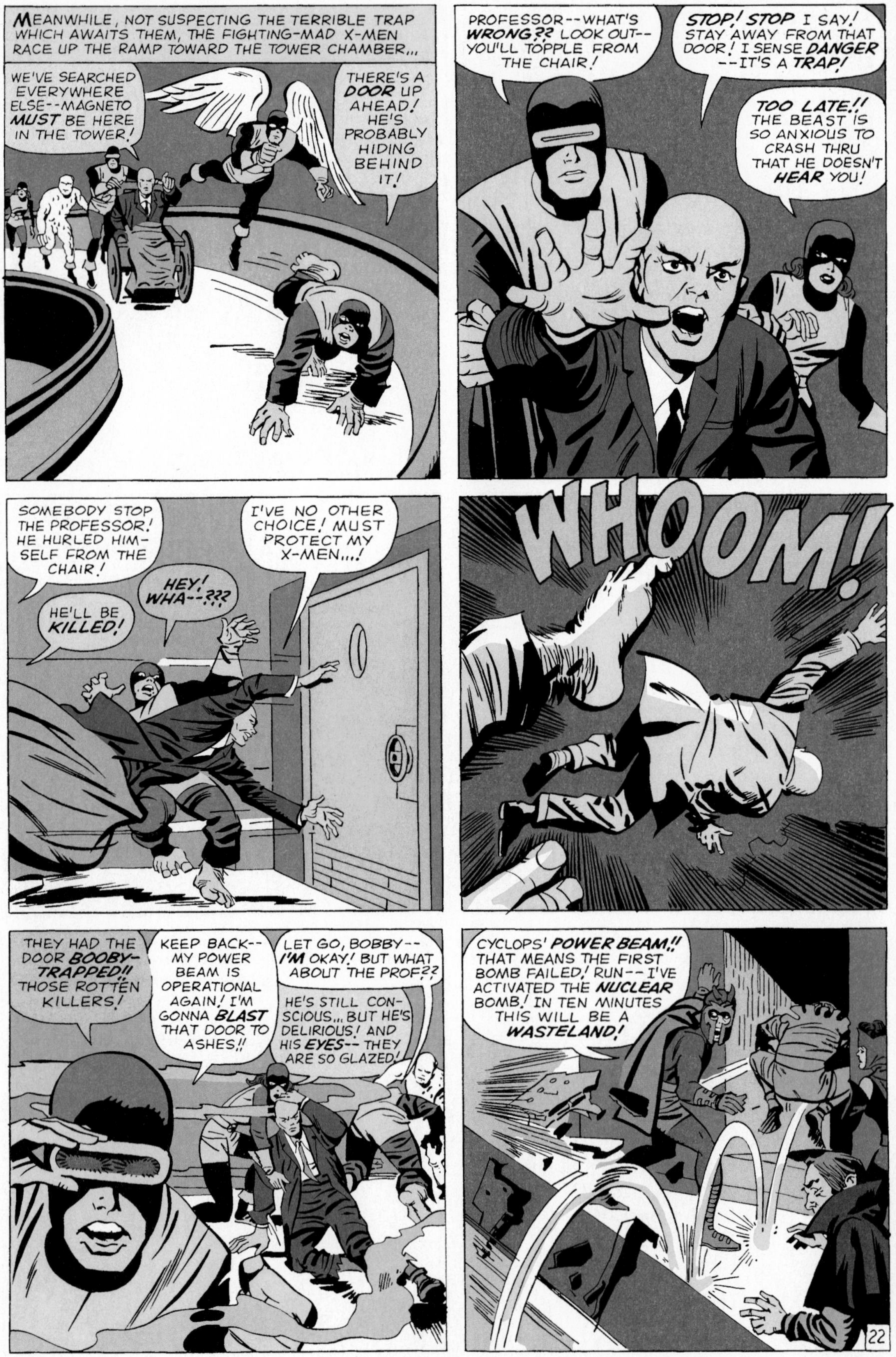
MEANWHILE, NOT SUSPECTING THE TERRIBLE TRAP WHICH AWAITS THEM, THE FIGHTING-MAD X-MEN RACE UP THE RAMP TOWARD THE TOWER CHAMBER...
WE'VE SEARCHED EVERYWHERE ELSE--MAGNETO MUST BE HERE IN THE TOWER!
THERE'S A DOOR UP AHEAD! HE'S PROBABLY HIDING BEHIND IT!
PROFESSOR--WHAT'S WRONG?? LOOK OUT--YOU'LL TOPPLE FROM THE CHAIR!
STOP! STOP I SAY! STAY AWAY FROM THAT DOOR! I SENSE DANGER --IT'S A TRAP!
TOO LATE!! THE BEAST IS SO ANXIOUS TO CRASH THRU THAT HE DOESN'T HEAR YOU!
SOMEBODY STOP THE PROFESSOR! HE HURLED HIMSELF FROM THE CHAIR!
HE'LL BE KILLED!
HEY! WHA--???
I'VE NO OTHER CHOICE! MUST PROTECT MY X-MEN...!
WHOOM!
THEY HAD THE DOOR BOOBY-TRAPPED!! THOSE ROTTEN KILLERS!
KEEP BACK--MY POWER BEAM IS OPERATIONAL AGAIN! I'M GONNA BLAST THAT DOOR TO ASHES!!
LET GO, BOBBY--I'M OKAY! BUT WHAT ABOUT THE PROF??
HE'S STILL CONSCIOUS... BUT HE'S DELIRIOUS! AND HIS EYES-- THEY ARE SO GLAZED!
CYCLOPS' POWER BEAM!! THAT MEANS THE FIRST BOMB FAILED! RUN--I'VE ACTIVATED THE NUCLEAR BOMB! IN TEN MINUTES THIS WILL BE A WASTELAND!
22

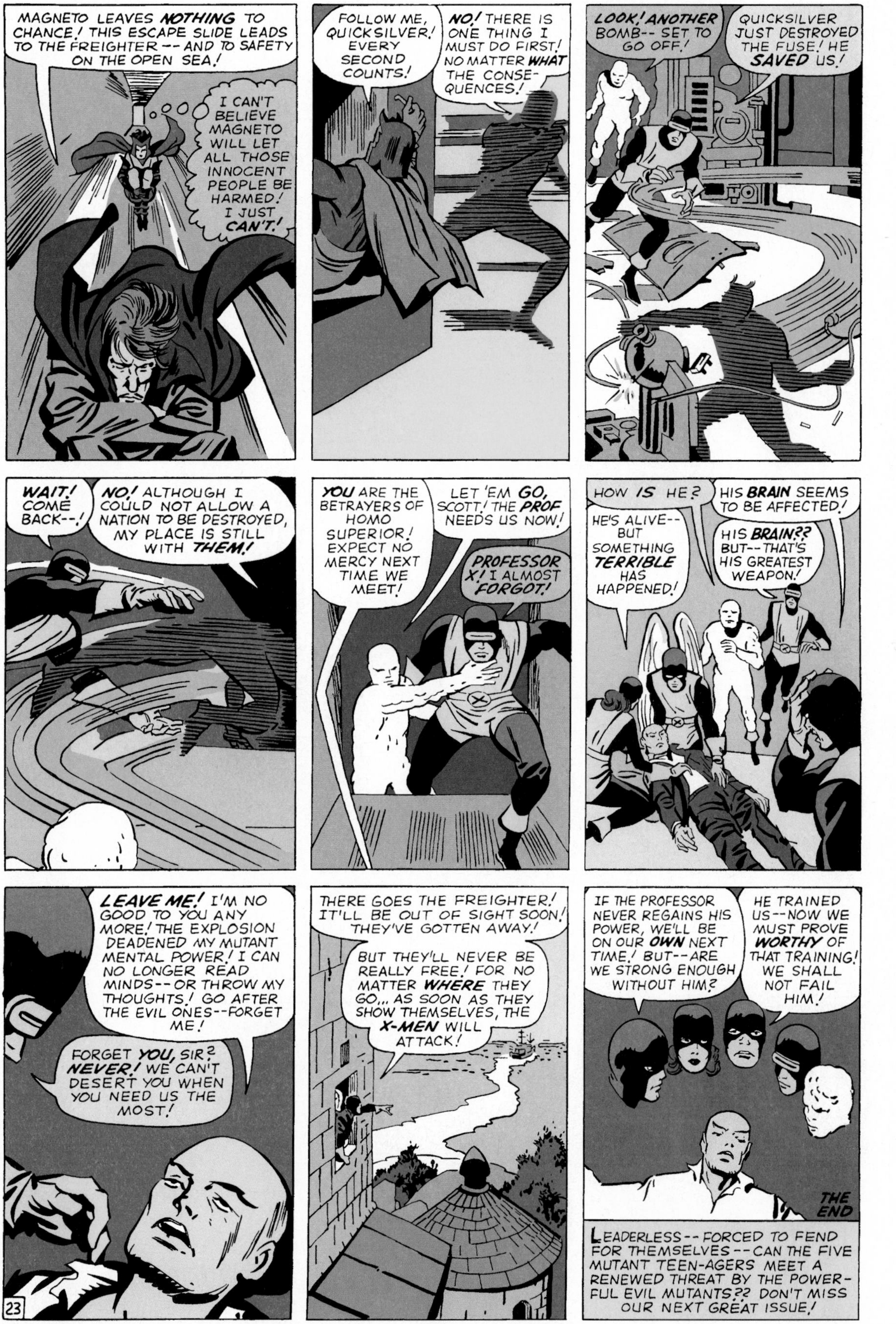
MAGNETO LEAVES NOTHING TO CHANCE! THIS ESCAPE SLIDE LEADS TO THE FREIGHTER -- AND TO SAFETY ON THE OPEN SEA!
I CAN'T BELIEVE MAGNETO WILL LET ALL THOSE INNOCENT PEOPLE BE HARMED! I JUST CAN'T!
FOLLOW ME, QUICKSILVER! EVERY SECOND COUNTS!
NO! THERE IS ONE THING I MUST DO FIRST! NO MATTER WHAT THE CONSEQUENCES!
LOOK! ANOTHER BOMB-- SET TO GO OFF!
QUICKSILVER JUST DESTROYED THE FUSE! HE SAVED US!
WAIT! COME BACK--!
NO! ALTHOUGH I COULD NOT ALLOW A NATION TO BE DESTROYED, MY PLACE IS STILL WITH THEM!
YOU ARE THE BETRAYERS OF HOMO SUPERIOR! EXPECT NO MERCY NEXT TIME WE MEET!
LET 'EM GO, SCOTT! THE PROF NEEDS US NOW!
PROFESSOR X! I ALMOST FORGOT!
HOW IS HE?
HE'S ALIVE-- BUT SOMETHING TERRIBLE HAS HAPPENED!
HIS BRAIN SEEMS TO BE AFFECTED!
HIS BRAIN?? BUT--THAT'S HIS GREATEST WEAPON!
LEAVE ME! I'M NO GOOD TO YOU ANY MORE! THE EXPLOSION DEADENED MY MUTANT MENTAL POWER! I CAN NO LONGER READ MINDS--OR THROW MY THOUGHTS! GO AFTER THE EVIL ONES--FORGET ME!
FORGET YOU, SIR? NEVER! WE CAN'T DESERT YOU WHEN YOU NEED US THE MOST!
23
THERE GOES THE FREIGHTER! IT'LL BE OUT OF SIGHT SOON! THEY'VE GOTTEN AWAY!
BUT THEY'LL NEVER BE REALLY FREE! FOR NO MATTER WHERE THEY GO,.. AS SOON AS THEY SHOW THEMSELVES, THE X-MEN WILL ATTACK!
IF THE PROFESSOR NEVER REGAINS HIS POWER, WE'LL BE ON OUR OWN NEXT TIME! BUT--ARE WE STRONG ENOUGH WITHOUT HIM?
HE TRAINED US--NOW WE MUST PROVE WORTHY OF THAT TRAINING! WE SHALL NOT FAIL HIM!
THE END
LEADERLESS--FORCED TO FEND FOR THEMSELVES--CAN THE FIVE MUTANT TEEN-AGERS MEET A RENEWED THREAT BY THE POWERFUL EVIL MUTANTS?? DON'T MISS OUR NEXT GREAT ISSUE!

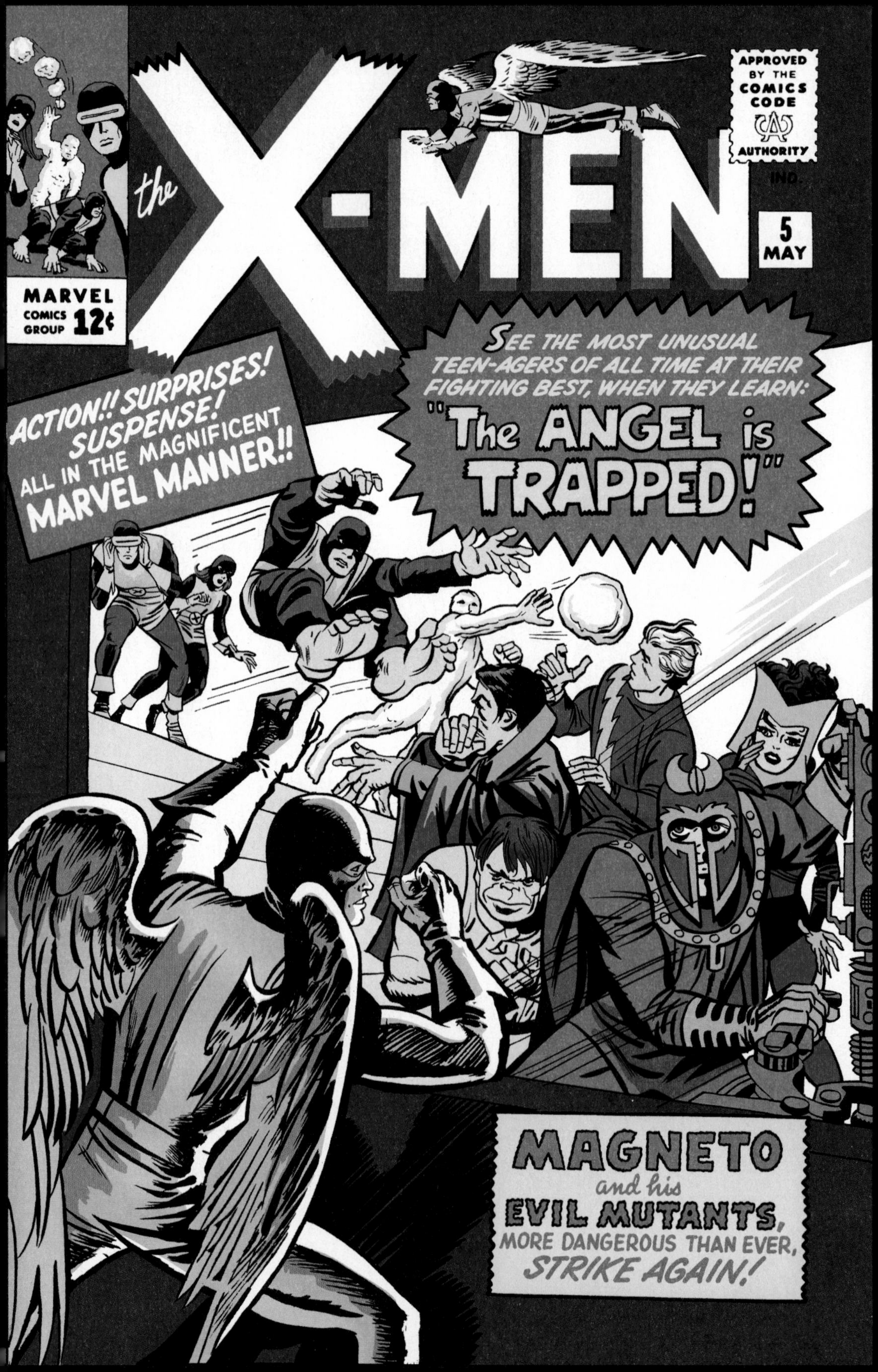

APPROVED BY THE COMICS CODE AUTHORITY
the X-MEN IND.
5 MAY
MARVEL COMICS GROUP 12¢
SEE THE MOST UNUSUAL TEEN-AGERS OF ALL TIME AT THEIR FIGHTING BEST, WHEN THEY LEARN:
"The ANGEL is TRAPPED!"
ACTION!! SURPRISES! SUSPENSE! ALL IN THE MAGNIFICENT MARVEL MANNER!!
MAGNETO and his EVIL MUTANTS, MORE DANGEROUS THAN EVER, STRIKE AGAIN!

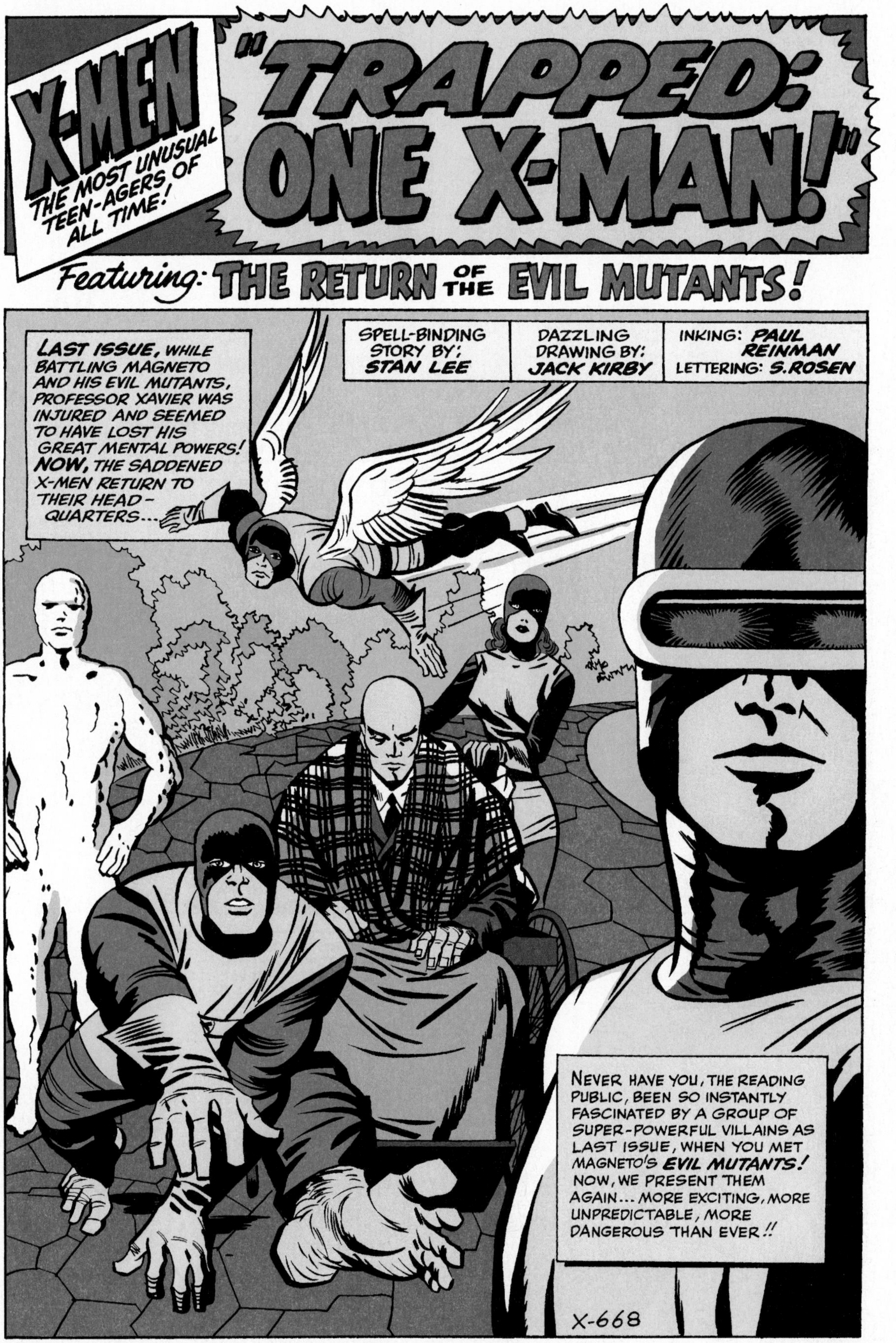
X-MEN
THE MOST UNUSUAL TEEN-AGERS OF ALL TIME!
"TRAPPED: ONE X-MAN!"
Featuring: THE RETURN OF THE EVIL MUTANTS!
LAST ISSUE, WHILE BATTLING MAGNETO AND HIS EVIL MUTANTS, PROFESSOR XAVIER WAS INJURED AND SEEMED TO HAVE LOST HIS GREAT MENTAL POWERS! NOW, THE SADDENED X-MEN RETURN TO THEIR HEAD-QUARTERS...
SPELL-BINDING STORY BY: STAN LEE
DAZZLING DRAWING BY: JACK KIRBY
INKING: PAUL REINMAN
LETTERING: S.ROSEN
NEVER HAVE YOU, THE READING PUBLIC, BEEN SO INSTANTLY FASCINATED BY A GROUP OF SUPER-POWERFUL VILLAINS AS LAST ISSUE, WHEN YOU MET MAGNETO'S EVIL MUTANTS! NOW, WE PRESENT THEM AGAIN... MORE EXCITING, MORE UNPREDICTABLE, MORE DANGEROUS THAN EVER!!
X-668

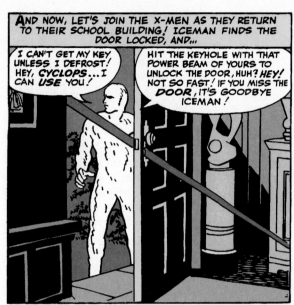

AND NOW, LET'S JOIN THE X-MEN AS THEY RETURN TO THEIR SCHOOL BUILDING! ICEMAN FINDS THE DOOR LOCKED, AND...

I CAN'T GET MY KEY UNLESS I DEFROST! HEY, **CYCLOPS**...I CAN **USE** YOU!

HIT THE KEYHOLE WITH THAT POWER BEAM OF YOURS TO UNLOCK THE DOOR, HUH? **HEY!** NOT SO FAST! IF YOU MISS THE **DOOR**, IT'S GOODBYE ICEMAN!

BOY! IT'S GOOD TO BE BACK AGAIN! IF ONLY THE PROFESSOR WAS OKAY!

I'LL LIFT HIM INTO HIS SITTING ROOM! IT'S THE EASIEST WAY!

SLOWLY, JEAN...YOU'VE ALL THE TIME IN THE WORLD! DON'T JOSTLE HIM!

LET ME REMOVE HIS JACKET BEFORE YOU PUT HIM DOWN! YOU DID AN EXEMPLARY JOB, MARVEL GIRL!

NOW... SET HIM DOWN! GENTLY.. GENTLY...

I'VE CHECKED THE ENTIRE BUILDING! EVERYTHING'S AS WE LEFT IT! WE HAVEN'T BEEN DISCOVERED YET!

IT SURE SEEMS STRANGE TO SEE HIM SLEEPING THAT WAY, JUST LIKE ANY NORMAL HOMO SAPIENS! IT MAKES ME FEEL SO... ALONE...

I KNOW WHAT YOU MEAN, ICEMAN! FROM NOW ON WE **WILL** BE ALONE, FOR THE FIRST TIME!.. WITHOUT THE PROFESSOR TO GUIDE US AND HELP US!

HE'S SPENT COUNTLESS HOURS TRAINING US TO USE OUR POWERS, JEAN! NOW, WE'VE GOT TO PROVE WE WERE **WORTHY** OF THAT TRAINING!

WE'VE GOT TO **CONTINUE** HIS FIGHT AGAINST THE EVIL MUTANTS! BUT WITHOUT HIM TO LEAD US IT'LL BE AN UPHILL JOB, HANK!

WE CAN'T **REMAIN** LEADERLESS! PERHAPS WE SHOULD.. **WAIT!** I HEAR A SOUND IN THE DRIVE-WAY! A **CAR** IS APPROACHING!

2.

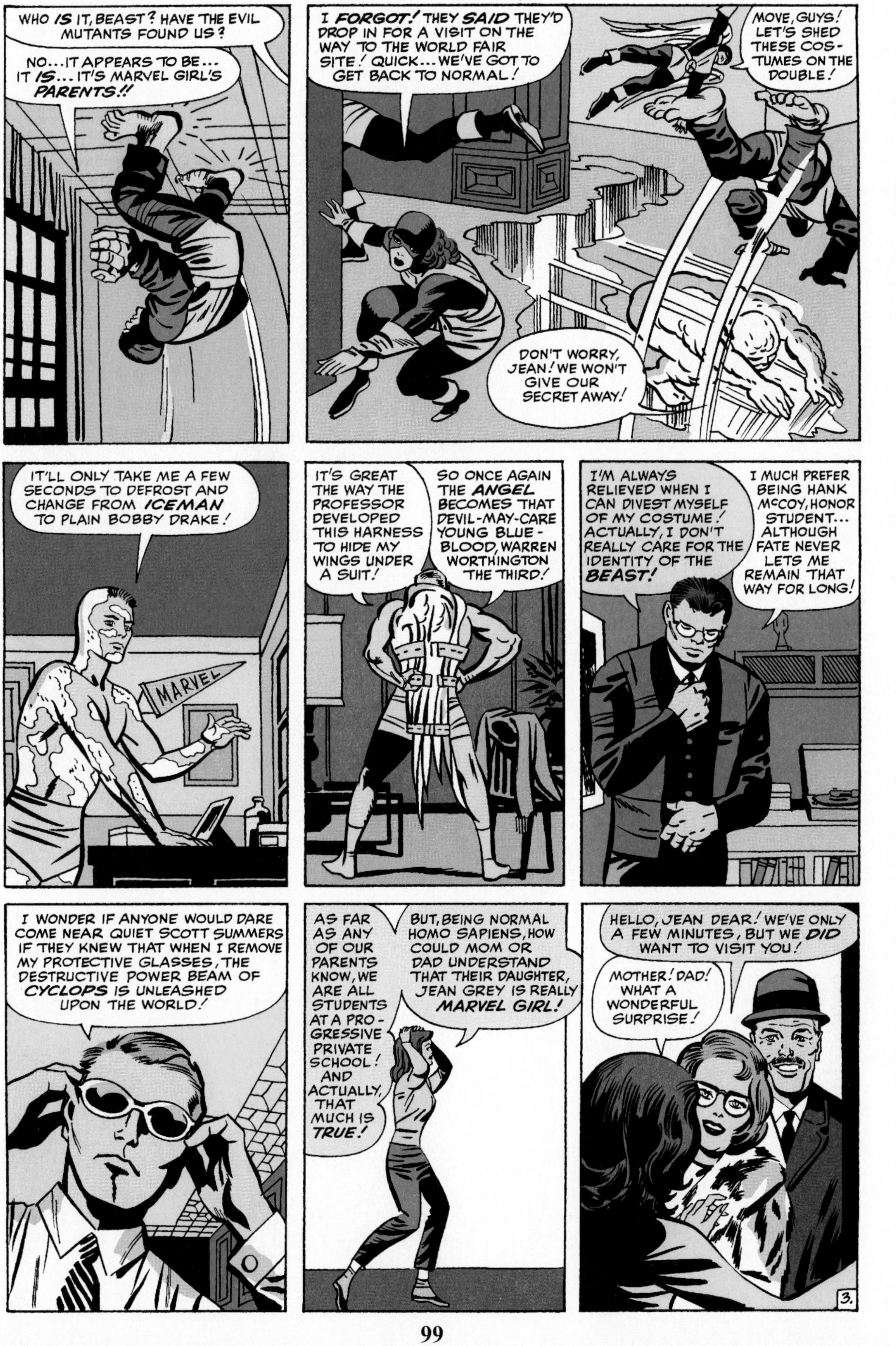
WHO IS IT, BEAST? HAVE THE EVIL MUTANTS FOUND US?
NO... IT APPEARS TO BE... IT IS... IT'S MARVEL GIRL'S PARENTS!!
I FORGOT! THEY SAID THEY'D DROP IN FOR A VISIT ON THE WAY TO THE WORLD FAIR SITE! QUICK... WE'VE GOT TO GET BACK TO NORMAL!
MOVE, GUYS! LET'S SHED THESE COSTUMES ON THE DOUBLE!
DON'T WORRY, JEAN! WE WON'T GIVE OUR SECRET AWAY!
IT'LL ONLY TAKE ME A FEW SECONDS TO DEFROST AND CHANGE FROM ICEMAN TO PLAIN BOBBY DRAKE!
MARVEL
IT'S GREAT THE WAY THE PROFESSOR DEVELOPED THIS HARNESS TO HIDE MY WINGS UNDER A SUIT!
SO ONCE AGAIN THE ANGEL BECOMES THAT DEVIL-MAY-CARE YOUNG BLUE-BLOOD, WARREN WORTHINGTON THE THIRD!
I'M ALWAYS RELIEVED WHEN I CAN DIVEST MYSELF OF MY COSTUME! ACTUALLY, I DON'T REALLY CARE FOR THE IDENTITY OF THE BEAST!
I MUCH PREFER BEING HANK McCOY, HONOR STUDENT... ALTHOUGH FATE NEVER LETS ME REMAIN THAT WAY FOR LONG!
I WONDER IF ANYONE WOULD DARE COME NEAR QUIET SCOTT SUMMERS IF THEY KNEW THAT WHEN I REMOVE MY PROTECTIVE GLASSES, THE DESTRUCTIVE POWER BEAM OF CYCLOPS IS UNLEASHED UPON THE WORLD!
AS FAR AS ANY OF OUR PARENTS KNOW, WE ARE ALL STUDENTS AT A PRO-GRESSIVE PRIVATE SCHOOL! AND ACTUALLY, THAT MUCH IS TRUE!
BUT, BEING NORMAL HOMO SAPIENS, HOW COULD MOM OR DAD UNDERSTAND THAT THEIR DAUGHTER, JEAN GREY IS REALLY MARVEL GIRL!
HELLO, JEAN DEAR! WE'VE ONLY A FEW MINUTES, BUT WE DID WANT TO VISIT YOU!
MOTHER! DAD! WHAT A WONDERFUL SURPRISE!
3.

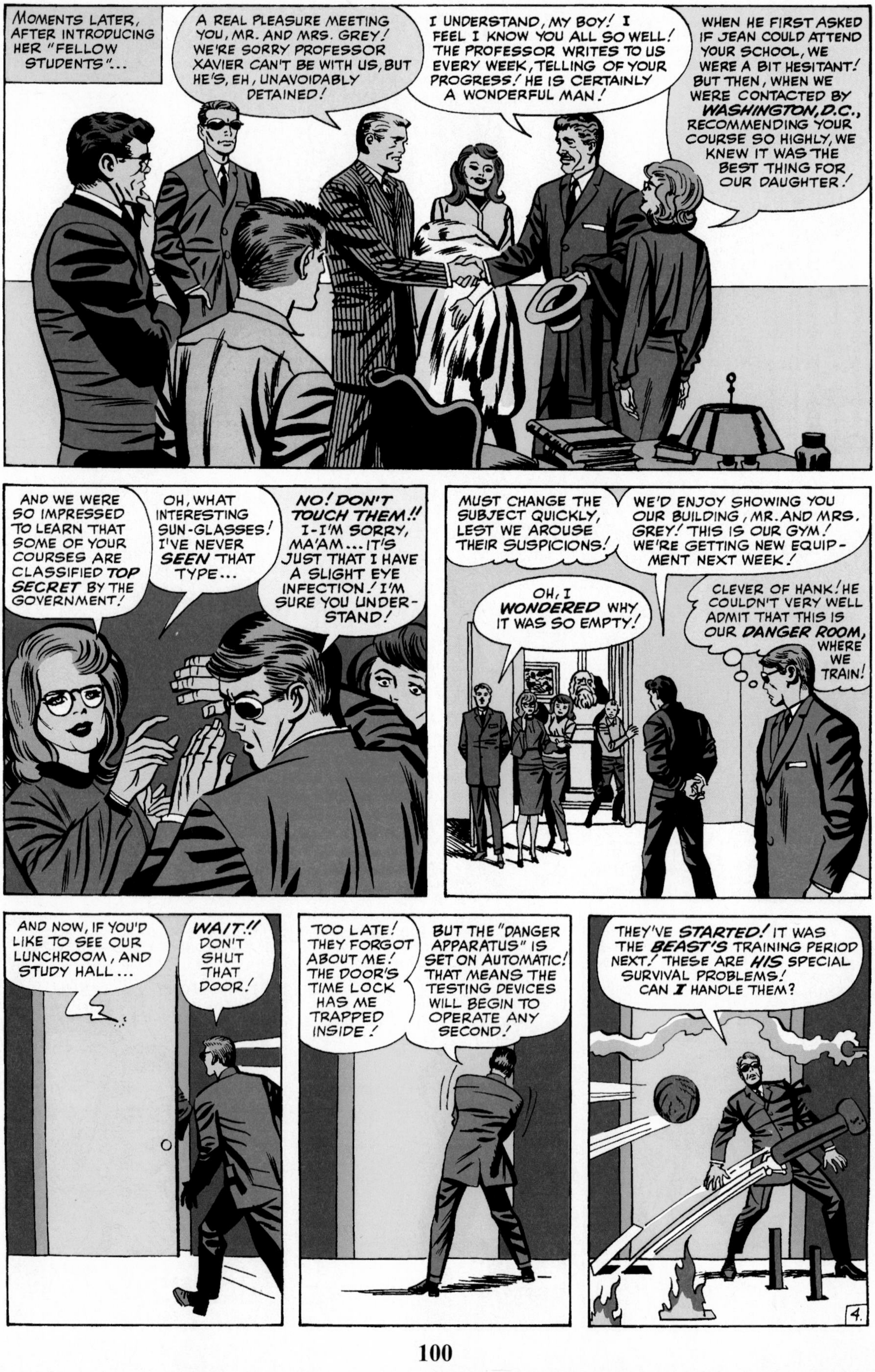
MOMENTS LATER, AFTER INTRODUCING HER "FELLOW STUDENTS"...
A REAL PLEASURE MEETING YOU, MR. AND MRS. GREY! WE'RE SORRY PROFESSOR XAVIER CAN'T BE WITH US, BUT HE'S, EH, UNAVOIDABLY DETAINED!
I UNDERSTAND, MY BOY! I FEEL I KNOW YOU ALL SO WELL! THE PROFESSOR WRITES TO US EVERY WEEK, TELLING OF YOUR PROGRESS! HE IS CERTAINLY A WONDERFUL MAN!
WHEN HE FIRST ASKED IF JEAN COULD ATTEND YOUR SCHOOL, WE WERE A BIT HESITANT! BUT THEN, WHEN WE WERE CONTACTED BY WASHINGTON, D.C., RECOMMENDING YOUR COURSE SO HIGHLY, WE KNEW IT WAS THE BEST THING FOR OUR DAUGHTER!
AND WE WERE SO IMPRESSED TO LEARN THAT SOME OF YOUR COURSES ARE CLASSIFIED TOP SECRET BY THE GOVERNMENT!
OH, WHAT INTERESTING SUN-GLASSES! I'VE NEVER SEEN THAT TYPE...
NO! DON'T TOUCH THEM!! I-I'M SORRY, MA'AM... IT'S JUST THAT I HAVE A SLIGHT EYE INFECTION! I'M SURE YOU UNDERSTAND!
MUST CHANGE THE SUBJECT QUICKLY, LEST WE AROUSE THEIR SUSPICIONS!
WE'D ENJOY SHOWING YOU OUR BUILDING, MR. AND MRS. GREY! THIS IS OUR GYM! WE'RE GETTING NEW EQUIPMENT NEXT WEEK!
OH, I WONDERED WHY IT WAS SO EMPTY!
CLEVER OF HANK! HE COULDN'T VERY WELL ADMIT THAT THIS IS OUR DANGER ROOM, WHERE WE TRAIN!
AND NOW, IF YOU'D LIKE TO SEE OUR LUNCHROOM, AND STUDY HALL...
WAIT!! DON'T SHUT THAT DOOR!
TOO LATE! THEY FORGOT ABOUT ME! THE DOOR'S TIME LOCK HAS ME TRAPPED INSIDE!
BUT THE "DANGER APPARATUS" IS SET ON AUTOMATIC! THAT MEANS THE TESTING DEVICES WILL BEGIN TO OPERATE ANY SECOND!
THEY'VE STARTED! IT WAS THE BEAST'S TRAINING PERIOD NEXT! THESE ARE HIS SPECIAL SURVIVAL PROBLEMS! CAN I HANDLE THEM?
4.

THE **FLOOR** JUST SNAPPED UP...TO TEST THE BEAST'S AGILITY!

GRABBING THIS **TRAPEZE** MAY SAVE ME!

IT WAS THE **WRONG** MOVE! THE TRAPEZE WAS A **DUMMY**...IT SNAPPED! THE BEAST WOULD HAVE **LEAPED** TO THE OTHER SIDE OF THE ROOM! WH..WHAT'S **THIS**??

A GIANT IRON **ROLLER** RUSHING TOWARDS ME! CAN'T DODGE IT THE WAY THE BEAST MIGHT! ONLY TIME FOR ONE THING...

HATE TO DESTROY THAT EXPENSIVE PIECE OF APPARATUS WITH MY POWER BEAM... BUT I HAD NO OTHER CHOICE! **NONE** OF US ARE AS QUICK ON OUR FEET AS THE **BEAST**!

THEN, AS THE REMAINING MINUTES OF THE TEST PERIOD TICK BY...

MY POWER BEAM IS GROWING WEAKER! IF THE TEST DOESN'T END SOON I'LL NEVER HAVE TO WORRY ABOUT MENACING INNOCENT PEOPLE WITH MY EYES AGAIN!

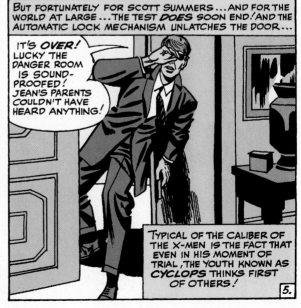

BUT FORTUNATELY FOR SCOTT SUMMERS...AND FOR THE WORLD AT LARGE...THE TEST **DOES** SOON END! AND THE AUTOMATIC LOCK MECHANISM UNLATCHES THE DOOR...

IT'S **OVER!** LUCKY THE DANGER ROOM IS SOUND-PROOFED! JEAN'S PARENTS COULDN'T HAVE HEARD ANYTHING!

TYPICAL OF THE CALIBER OF THE X-MEN IS THE FACT THAT EVEN IN HIS MOMENT OF TRIAL, THE YOUTH KNOWN AS **CYCLOPS** THINKS FIRST OF OTHERS!

5.

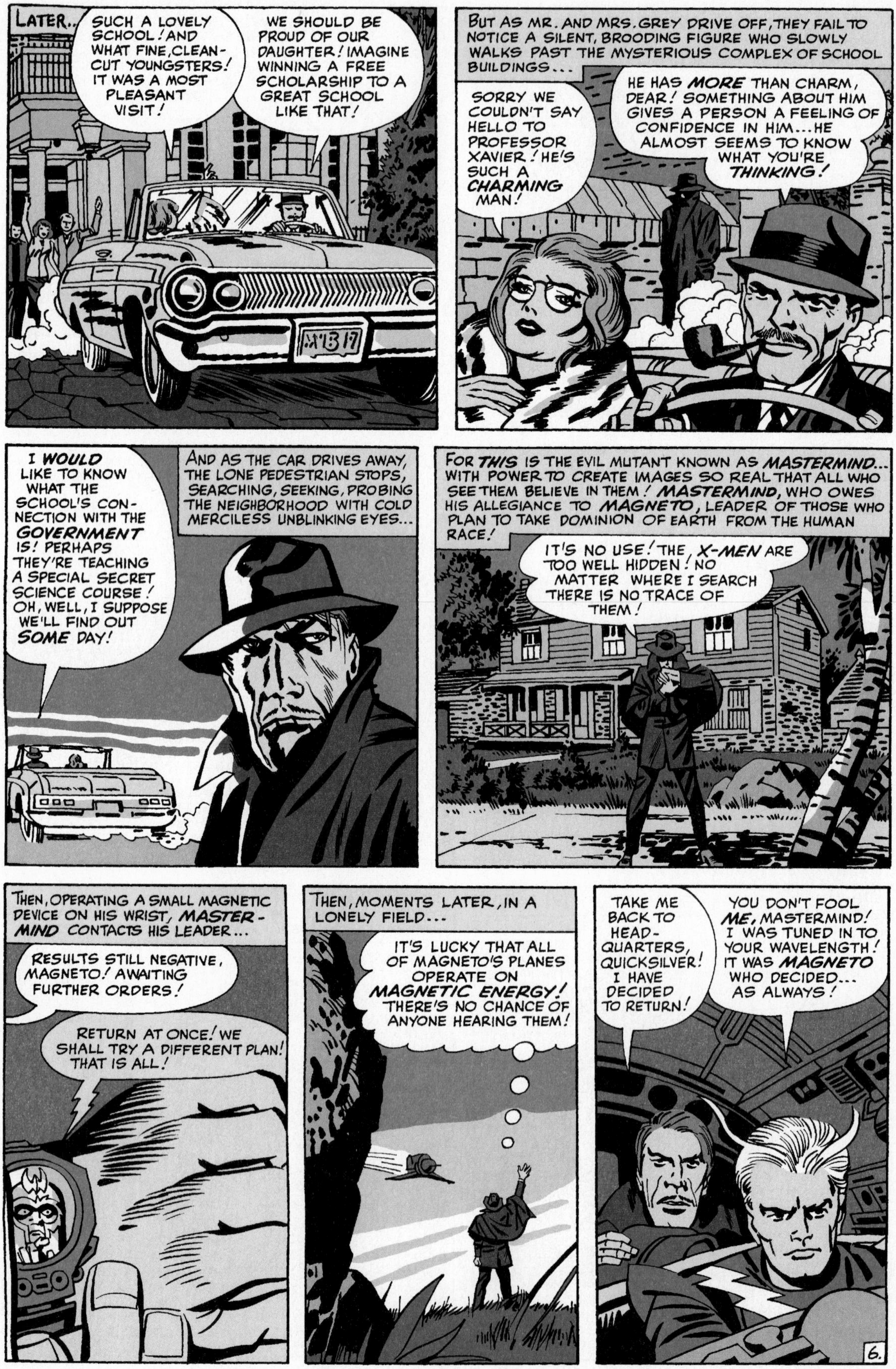
LATER...
SUCH A LOVELY SCHOOL! AND WHAT FINE, CLEAN-CUT YOUNGSTERS! IT WAS A MOST PLEASANT VISIT!
WE SHOULD BE PROUD OF OUR DAUGHTER! IMAGINE WINNING A FREE SCHOLARSHIP TO A GREAT SCHOOL LIKE THAT!
BUT AS MR. AND MRS. GREY DRIVE OFF, THEY FAIL TO NOTICE A SILENT, BROODING FIGURE WHO SLOWLY WALKS PAST THE MYSTERIOUS COMPLEX OF SCHOOL BUILDINGS...
SORRY WE COULDN'T SAY HELLO TO PROFESSOR XAVIER! HE'S SUCH A CHARMING MAN!
HE HAS MORE THAN CHARM, DEAR! SOMETHING ABOUT HIM GIVES A PERSON A FEELING OF CONFIDENCE IN HIM... HE ALMOST SEEMS TO KNOW WHAT YOU'RE THINKING!
I WOULD LIKE TO KNOW WHAT THE SCHOOL'S CONNECTION WITH THE GOVERNMENT IS! PERHAPS THEY'RE TEACHING A SPECIAL SECRET SCIENCE COURSE! OH, WELL, I SUPPOSE WE'LL FIND OUT SOME DAY!
AND AS THE CAR DRIVES AWAY, THE LONE PEDESTRIAN STOPS, SEARCHING, SEEKING, PROBING THE NEIGHBORHOOD WITH COLD MERCILESS UNBLINKING EYES...
FOR THIS IS THE EVIL MUTANT KNOWN AS MASTERMIND... WITH POWER TO CREATE IMAGES SO REAL THAT ALL WHO SEE THEM BELIEVE IN THEM! MASTERMIND, WHO OWES HIS ALLEGIANCE TO MAGNETO, LEADER OF THOSE WHO PLAN TO TAKE DOMINION OF EARTH FROM THE HUMAN RACE!
IT'S NO USE! THE X-MEN ARE TOO WELL HIDDEN! NO MATTER WHERE I SEARCH THERE IS NO TRACE OF THEM!
THEN, OPERATING A SMALL MAGNETIC DEVICE ON HIS WRIST, MASTERMIND CONTACTS HIS LEADER...
RESULTS STILL NEGATIVE, MAGNETO! AWAITING FURTHER ORDERS!
RETURN AT ONCE! WE SHALL TRY A DIFFERENT PLAN! THAT IS ALL!
THEN, MOMENTS LATER, IN A LONELY FIELD...
IT'S LUCKY THAT ALL OF MAGNETO'S PLANES OPERATE ON MAGNETIC ENERGY! THERE'S NO CHANCE OF ANYONE HEARING THEM!
TAKE ME BACK TO HEAD-QUARTERS, QUICKSILVER! I HAVE DECIDED TO RETURN!
YOU DON'T FOOL ME, MASTERMIND! I WAS TUNED IN TO YOUR WAVELENGTH! IT WAS MAGNETO WHO DECIDED... AS ALWAYS!
6.

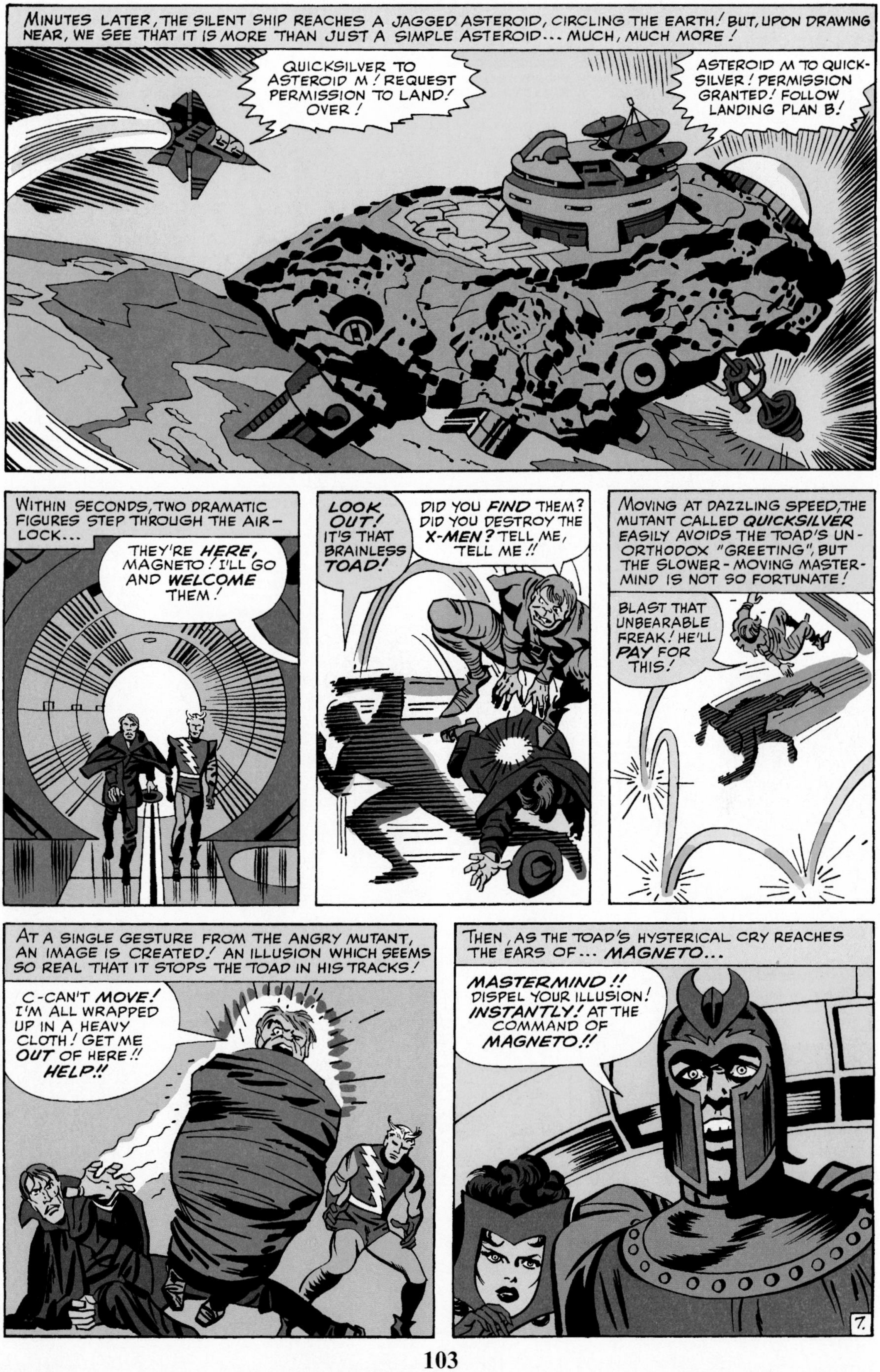
MINUTES LATER, THE SILENT SHIP REACHES A JAGGED ASTEROID, CIRCLING THE EARTH! BUT, UPON DRAWING NEAR, WE SEE THAT IT IS MORE THAN JUST A SIMPLE ASTEROID... MUCH, MUCH MORE!
QUICKSILVER TO ASTEROID M! REQUEST PERMISSION TO LAND! OVER!
ASTEROID M TO QUICK-SILVER! PERMISSION GRANTED! FOLLOW LANDING PLAN B!
WITHIN SECONDS, TWO DRAMATIC FIGURES STEP THROUGH THE AIR-LOCK...
THEY'RE HERE, MAGNETO! I'LL GO AND WELCOME THEM!
LOOK OUT! IT'S THAT BRAINLESS TOAD!
DID YOU FIND THEM? DID YOU DESTROY THE X-MEN? TELL ME, TELL ME!!
MOVING AT DAZZLING SPEED, THE MUTANT CALLED QUICKSILVER EASILY AVOIDS THE TOAD'S UN-ORTHODOX "GREETING", BUT THE SLOWER-MOVING MASTER-MIND IS NOT SO FORTUNATE!
BLAST THAT UNBEARABLE FREAK! HE'LL PAY FOR THIS!
AT A SINGLE GESTURE FROM THE ANGRY MUTANT, AN IMAGE IS CREATED! AN ILLUSION WHICH SEEMS SO REAL THAT IT STOPS THE TOAD IN HIS TRACKS!
C-CAN'T MOVE! I'M ALL WRAPPED UP IN A HEAVY CLOTH! GET ME OUT OF HERE!! HELP!!
THEN, AS THE TOAD'S HYSTERICAL CRY REACHES THE EARS OF... MAGNETO...
MASTERMIND!! DISPEL YOUR ILLUSION! INSTANTLY! AT THE COMMAND OF MAGNETO!!
7.

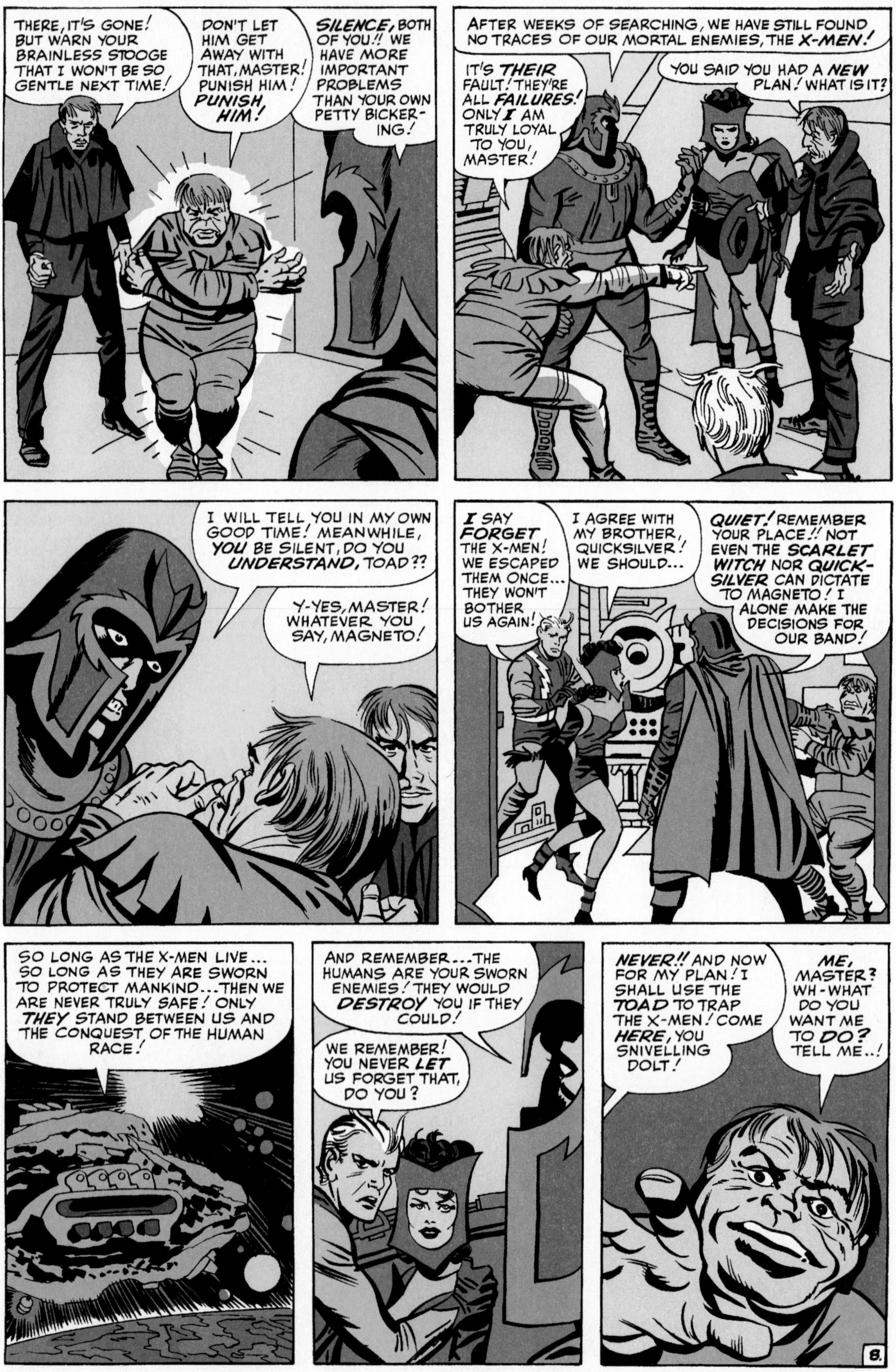
THERE, IT'S GONE! BUT WARN YOUR BRAINLESS STOOGE THAT I WON'T BE SO GENTLE NEXT TIME!
DON'T LET HIM GET AWAY WITH THAT, MASTER! PUNISH HIM! PUNISH HIM!
SILENCE, BOTH OF YOU!! WE HAVE MORE IMPORTANT PROBLEMS THAN YOUR OWN PETTY BICKERING!
AFTER WEEKS OF SEARCHING, WE HAVE STILL FOUND NO TRACES OF OUR MORTAL ENEMIES, THE X-MEN!
IT'S THEIR FAULT! THEY'RE ALL FAILURES! ONLY I AM TRULY LOYAL TO YOU, MASTER!
YOU SAID YOU HAD A NEW PLAN! WHAT IS IT?
I WILL TELL YOU IN MY OWN GOOD TIME! MEANWHILE, YOU BE SILENT, DO YOU UNDERSTAND, TOAD??
Y-YES, MASTER! WHATEVER YOU SAY, MAGNETO!
I SAY FORGET THE X-MEN! WE ESCAPED THEM ONCE... THEY WON'T BOTHER US AGAIN!
I AGREE WITH MY BROTHER, QUICKSILVER! WE SHOULD...
QUIET! REMEMBER YOUR PLACE!! NOT EVEN THE SCARLET WITCH NOR QUICKSILVER CAN DICTATE TO MAGNETO! I ALONE MAKE THE DECISIONS FOR OUR BAND!
SO LONG AS THE X-MEN LIVE... SO LONG AS THEY ARE SWORN TO PROTECT MANKIND...THEN WE ARE NEVER TRULY SAFE! ONLY THEY STAND BETWEEN US AND THE CONQUEST OF THE HUMAN RACE!
AND REMEMBER...THE HUMANS ARE YOUR SWORN ENEMIES! THEY WOULD DESTROY YOU IF THEY COULD!
WE REMEMBER! YOU NEVER LET US FORGET THAT, DO YOU?
NEVER!! AND NOW FOR MY PLAN! I SHALL USE THE TOAD TO TRAP THE X-MEN! COME HERE, YOU SNIVELLING DOLT!
ME, MASTER? WH-WHAT DO YOU WANT ME TO DO? TELL ME..!
8.

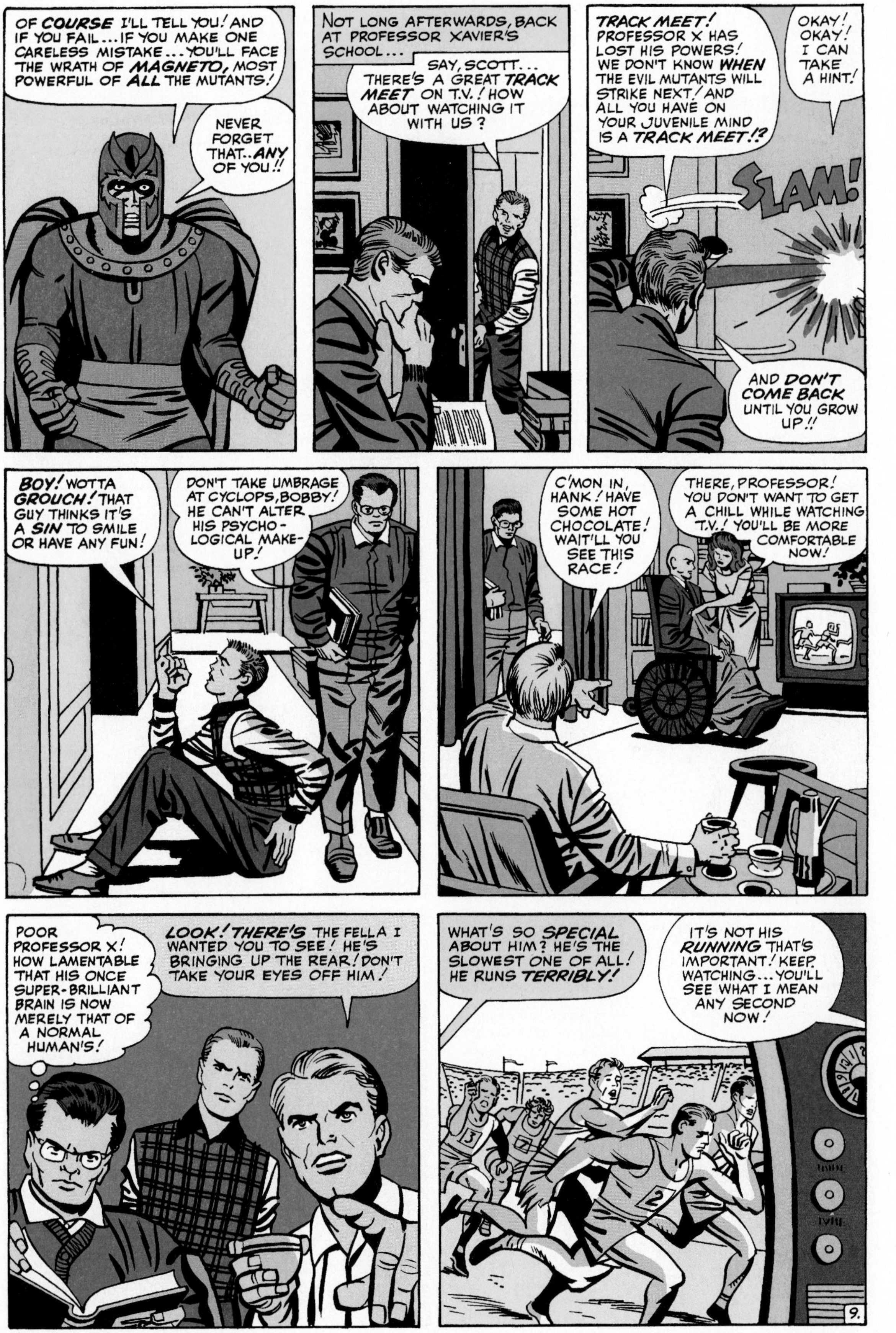

OF COURSE I'LL TELL YOU! AND IF YOU FAIL... IF YOU MAKE ONE CARELESS MISTAKE... YOU'LL FACE THE WRATH OF MAGNETO, MOST POWERFUL OF ALL THE MUTANTS!
NEVER FORGET THAT.. ANY OF YOU!!
NOT LONG AFTERWARDS, BACK AT PROFESSOR XAVIER'S SCHOOL...
SAY, SCOTT... THERE'S A GREAT TRACK MEET ON T.V.! HOW ABOUT WATCHING IT WITH US?
TRACK MEET! PROFESSOR X HAS LOST HIS POWERS! WE DON'T KNOW WHEN THE EVIL MUTANTS WILL STRIKE NEXT! AND ALL YOU HAVE ON YOUR JUVENILE MIND IS A TRACK MEET!?
OKAY! OKAY! I CAN TAKE A HINT!
SLAM!
AND DON'T COME BACK UNTIL YOU GROW UP!!
BOY! WOTTA GROUCH! THAT GUY THINKS IT'S A SIN TO SMILE OR HAVE ANY FUN!
DON'T TAKE UMBRAGE AT CYCLOPS, BOBBY! HE CAN'T ALTER HIS PSYCHO-LOGICAL MAKE-UP!
C'MON IN, HANK! HAVE SOME HOT CHOCOLATE! WAIT'LL YOU SEE THIS RACE!
THERE, PROFESSOR! YOU DON'T WANT TO GET A CHILL WHILE WATCHING T.V.! YOU'LL BE MORE COMFORTABLE NOW!
POOR PROFESSOR X! HOW LAMENTABLE THAT HIS ONCE SUPER-BRILLIANT BRAIN IS NOW MERELY THAT OF A NORMAL HUMAN'S!
LOOK! THERE'S THE FELLA I WANTED YOU TO SEE! HE'S BRINGING UP THE REAR! DON'T TAKE YOUR EYES OFF HIM!
WHAT'S SO SPECIAL ABOUT HIM? HE'S THE SLOWEST ONE OF ALL! HE RUNS TERRIBLY!
IT'S NOT HIS RUNNING THAT'S IMPORTANT! KEEP WATCHING... YOU'LL SEE WHAT I MEAN ANY SECOND NOW!
9.

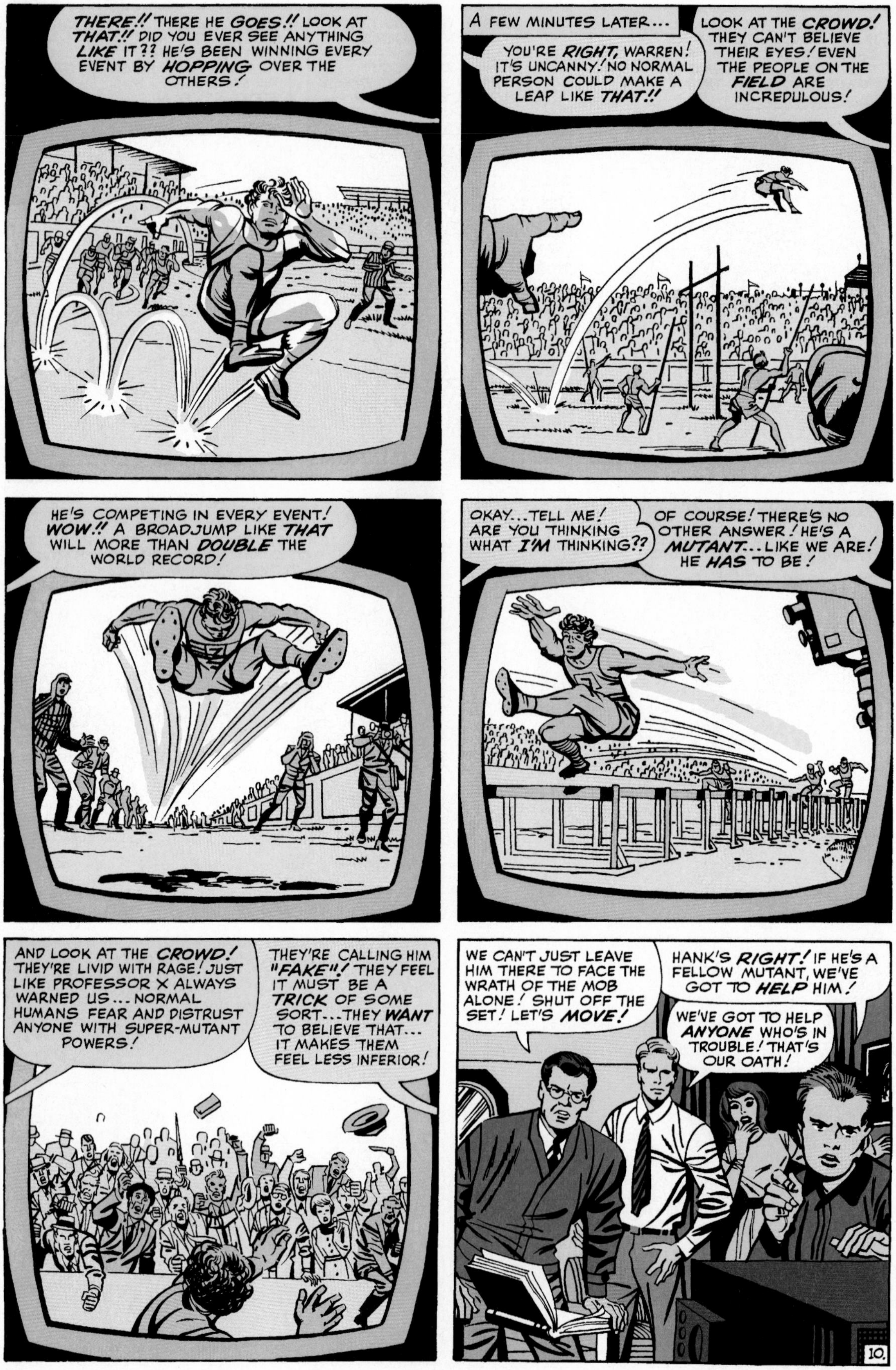
THERE!! THERE HE GOES!! LOOK AT THAT!! DID YOU EVER SEE ANYTHING LIKE IT?? HE'S BEEN WINNING EVERY EVENT BY HOPPING OVER THE OTHERS!
A FEW MINUTES LATER...
YOU'RE RIGHT, WARREN! IT'S UNCANNY! NO NORMAL PERSON COULD MAKE A LEAP LIKE THAT!!
LOOK AT THE CROWD! THEY CAN'T BELIEVE THEIR EYES! EVEN THE PEOPLE ON THE FIELD ARE INCREDULOUS!
HE'S COMPETING IN EVERY EVENT! WOW!! A BROADJUMP LIKE THAT WILL MORE THAN DOUBLE THE WORLD RECORD!
OKAY...TELL ME! ARE YOU THINKING WHAT I'M THINKING??
OF COURSE! THERE'S NO OTHER ANSWER! HE'S A MUTANT...LIKE WE ARE! HE HAS TO BE!
AND LOOK AT THE CROWD! THEY'RE LIVID WITH RAGE! JUST LIKE PROFESSOR X ALWAYS WARNED US...NORMAL HUMANS FEAR AND DISTRUST ANYONE WITH SUPER-MUTANT POWERS!
THEY'RE CALLING HIM "FAKE"! THEY FEEL IT MUST BE A TRICK OF SOME SORT...THEY WANT TO BELIEVE THAT... IT MAKES THEM FEEL LESS INFERIOR!
WE CAN'T JUST LEAVE HIM THERE TO FACE THE WRATH OF THE MOB ALONE! SHUT OFF THE SET! LET'S MOVE!
HANK'S RIGHT! IF HE'S A FELLOW MUTANT, WE'VE GOT TO HELP HIM!
WE'VE GOT TO HELP ANYONE WHO'S IN TROUBLE! THAT'S OUR OATH!
10.

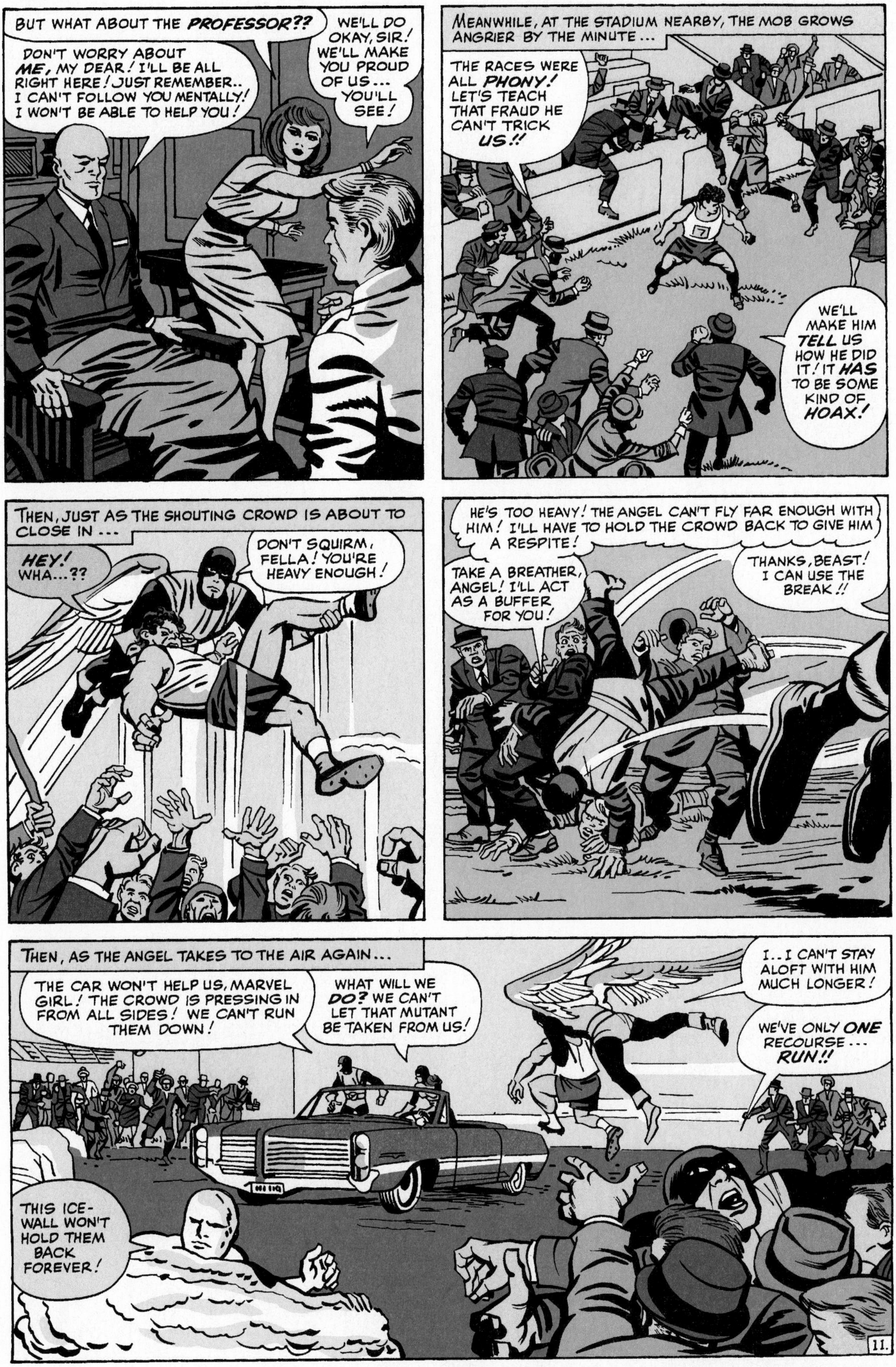
BUT WHAT ABOUT THE PROFESSOR??
DON'T WORRY ABOUT ME, MY DEAR! I'LL BE ALL RIGHT HERE! JUST REMEMBER.. I CAN'T FOLLOW YOU MENTALLY! I WON'T BE ABLE TO HELP YOU!
WE'LL DO OKAY, SIR! WE'LL MAKE YOU PROUD OF US... YOU'LL SEE!
MEANWHILE, AT THE STADIUM NEARBY, THE MOB GROWS ANGRIER BY THE MINUTE...
THE RACES WERE ALL PHONY! LET'S TEACH THAT FRAUD HE CAN'T TRICK US!!
WE'LL MAKE HIM TELL US HOW HE DID IT! IT HAS TO BE SOME KIND OF HOAX!
THEN, JUST AS THE SHOUTING CROWD IS ABOUT TO CLOSE IN...
HEY! WHA...??
DON'T SQUIRM, FELLA! YOU'RE HEAVY ENOUGH!
HE'S TOO HEAVY! THE ANGEL CAN'T FLY FAR ENOUGH WITH HIM! I'LL HAVE TO HOLD THE CROWD BACK TO GIVE HIM A RESPITE!
TAKE A BREATHER, ANGEL! I'LL ACT AS A BUFFER FOR YOU!
THANKS, BEAST! I CAN USE THE BREAK!!
THEN, AS THE ANGEL TAKES TO THE AIR AGAIN...
THE CAR WON'T HELP US, MARVEL GIRL! THE CROWD IS PRESSING IN FROM ALL SIDES! WE CAN'T RUN THEM DOWN!
WHAT WILL WE DO? WE CAN'T LET THAT MUTANT BE TAKEN FROM US!
I.. I CAN'T STAY ALOFT WITH HIM MUCH LONGER!
WE'VE ONLY ONE RECOURSE... RUN!!
THIS ICE-WALL WON'T HOLD THEM BACK FOREVER!
11.

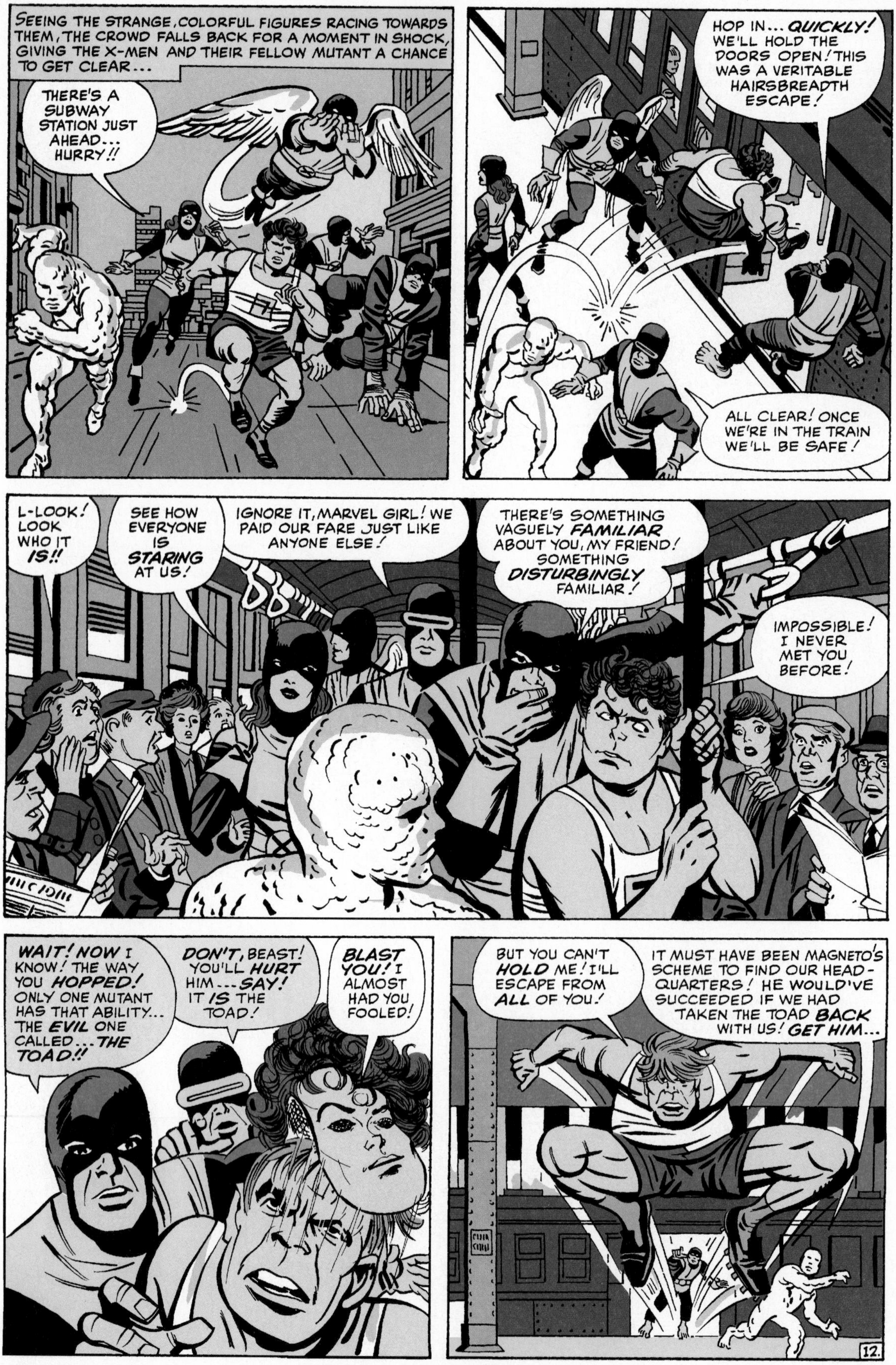
SEEING THE STRANGE, COLORFUL FIGURES RACING TOWARDS THEM, THE CROWD FALLS BACK FOR A MOMENT IN SHOCK, GIVING THE X-MEN AND THEIR FELLOW MUTANT A CHANCE TO GET CLEAR...
THERE'S A SUBWAY STATION JUST AHEAD... HURRY!!
HOP IN... QUICKLY! WE'LL HOLD THE DOORS OPEN! THIS WAS A VERITABLE HAIRSBREADTH ESCAPE!
ALL CLEAR! ONCE WE'RE IN THE TRAIN WE'LL BE SAFE!
L-LOOK! LOOK WHO IT IS!!
SEE HOW EVERYONE IS STARING AT US!
IGNORE IT, MARVEL GIRL! WE PAID OUR FARE JUST LIKE ANYONE ELSE!
THERE'S SOMETHING VAGUELY FAMILIAR ABOUT YOU, MY FRIEND! SOMETHING DISTURBINGLY FAMILIAR!
IMPOSSIBLE! I NEVER MET YOU BEFORE!
WAIT! NOW I KNOW! THE WAY YOU HOPPED! ONLY ONE MUTANT HAS THAT ABILITY... THE EVIL ONE CALLED... THE TOAD!!
DON'T, BEAST! YOU'LL HURT HIM... SAY! IT IS THE TOAD!
BLAST YOU! I ALMOST HAD YOU FOOLED!
BUT YOU CAN'T HOLD ME! I'LL ESCAPE FROM ALL OF YOU!
IT MUST HAVE BEEN MAGNETO'S SCHEME TO FIND OUR HEAD-QUARTERS! HE WOULD'VE SUCCEEDED IF WE HAD TAKEN THE TOAD BACK WITH US! GET HIM...
12.

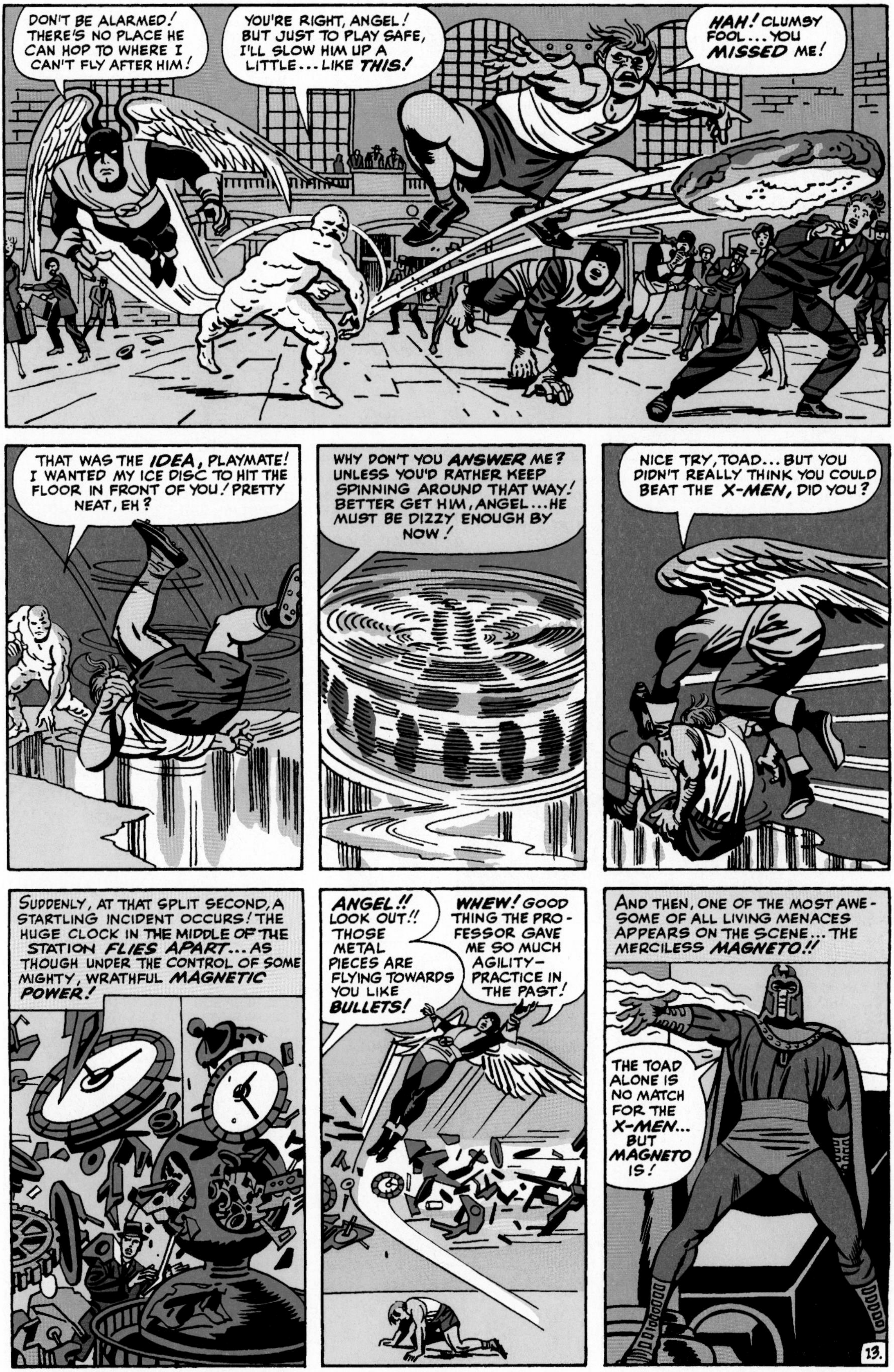
DON'T BE ALARMED! THERE'S NO PLACE HE CAN HOP TO WHERE I CAN'T FLY AFTER HIM!
YOU'RE RIGHT, ANGEL! BUT JUST TO PLAY SAFE, I'LL SLOW HIM UP A LITTLE... LIKE THIS!
HAH! CLUMSY FOOL... YOU MISSED ME!
THAT WAS THE IDEA, PLAYMATE! I WANTED MY ICE DISC TO HIT THE FLOOR IN FRONT OF YOU! PRETTY NEAT, EH?
WHY DON'T YOU ANSWER ME? UNLESS YOU'D RATHER KEEP SPINNING AROUND THAT WAY! BETTER GET HIM, ANGEL... HE MUST BE DIZZY ENOUGH BY NOW!
NICE TRY, TOAD... BUT YOU DIDN'T REALLY THINK YOU COULD BEAT THE X-MEN, DID YOU?
SUDDENLY, AT THAT SPLIT SECOND, A STARTLING INCIDENT OCCURS! THE HUGE CLOCK IN THE MIDDLE OF THE STATION FLIES APART... AS THOUGH UNDER THE CONTROL OF SOME MIGHTY, WRATHFUL MAGNETIC POWER!
ANGEL!! LOOK OUT!! THOSE METAL PIECES ARE FLYING TOWARDS YOU LIKE BULLETS!
WHEW! GOOD THING THE PROFESSOR GAVE ME SO MUCH AGILITY-PRACTICE IN THE PAST!
AND THEN, ONE OF THE MOST AWESOME OF ALL LIVING MENACES APPEARS ON THE SCENE... THE MERCILESS MAGNETO!!
THE TOAD ALONE IS NO MATCH FOR THE X-MEN... BUT MAGNETO IS!
13.

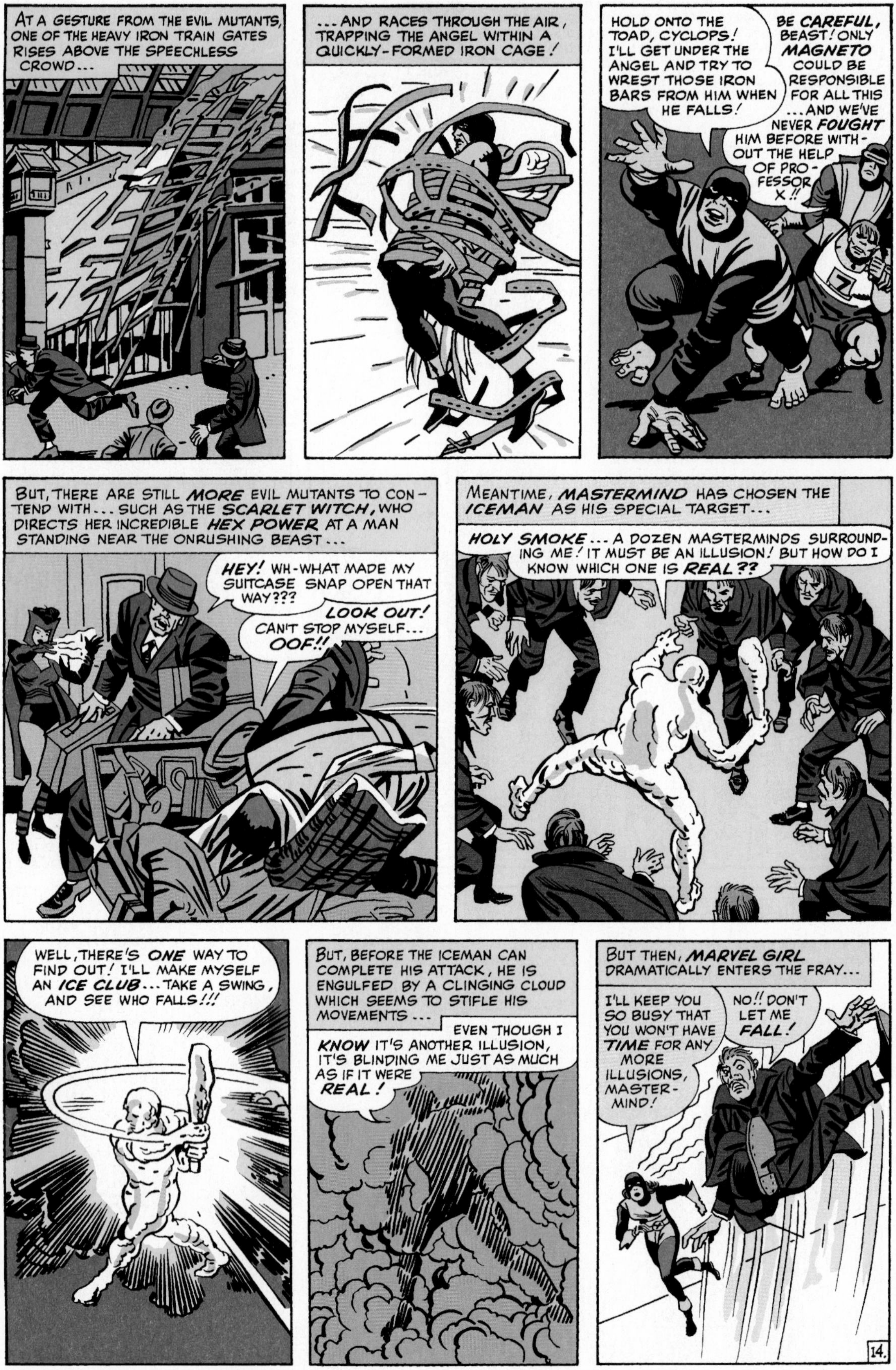
AT A GESTURE FROM THE EVIL MUTANTS, ONE OF THE HEAVY IRON TRAIN GATES RISES ABOVE THE SPEECHLESS CROWD...
...AND RACES THROUGH THE AIR, TRAPPING THE ANGEL WITHIN A QUICKLY-FORMED IRON CAGE!
HOLD ONTO THE TOAD, CYCLOPS! I'LL GET UNDER THE ANGEL AND TRY TO WREST THOSE IRON BARS FROM HIM WHEN HE FALLS!
BE CAREFUL, BEAST! ONLY MAGNETO COULD BE RESPONSIBLE FOR ALL THIS ...AND WE'VE NEVER FOUGHT HIM BEFORE WITHOUT THE HELP OF PROFESSOR X!!
BUT, THERE ARE STILL MORE EVIL MUTANTS TO CONTEND WITH... SUCH AS THE SCARLET WITCH, WHO DIRECTS HER INCREDIBLE HEX POWER AT A MAN STANDING NEAR THE ONRUSHING BEAST...
HEY! WH-WHAT MADE MY SUITCASE SNAP OPEN THAT WAY???
LOOK OUT! CAN'T STOP MYSELF... OOF!!
MEANTIME, MASTERMIND HAS CHOSEN THE ICEMAN AS HIS SPECIAL TARGET...
HOLY SMOKE... A DOZEN MASTERMINDS SURROUNDING ME! IT MUST BE AN ILLUSION! BUT HOW DO I KNOW WHICH ONE IS REAL??
WELL, THERE'S ONE WAY TO FIND OUT! I'LL MAKE MYSELF AN ICE CLUB... TAKE A SWING, AND SEE WHO FALLS!!!
BUT, BEFORE THE ICEMAN CAN COMPLETE HIS ATTACK, HE IS ENGULFED BY A CLINGING CLOUD WHICH SEEMS TO STIFLE HIS MOVEMENTS...
EVEN THOUGH I KNOW IT'S ANOTHER ILLUSION, IT'S BLINDING ME JUST AS MUCH AS IF IT WERE REAL!
BUT THEN, MARVEL GIRL DRAMATICALLY ENTERS THE FRAY...
I'LL KEEP YOU SO BUSY THAT YOU WON'T HAVE TIME FOR ANY MORE ILLUSIONS, MASTERMIND!
NO!! DON'T LET ME FALL!
14.

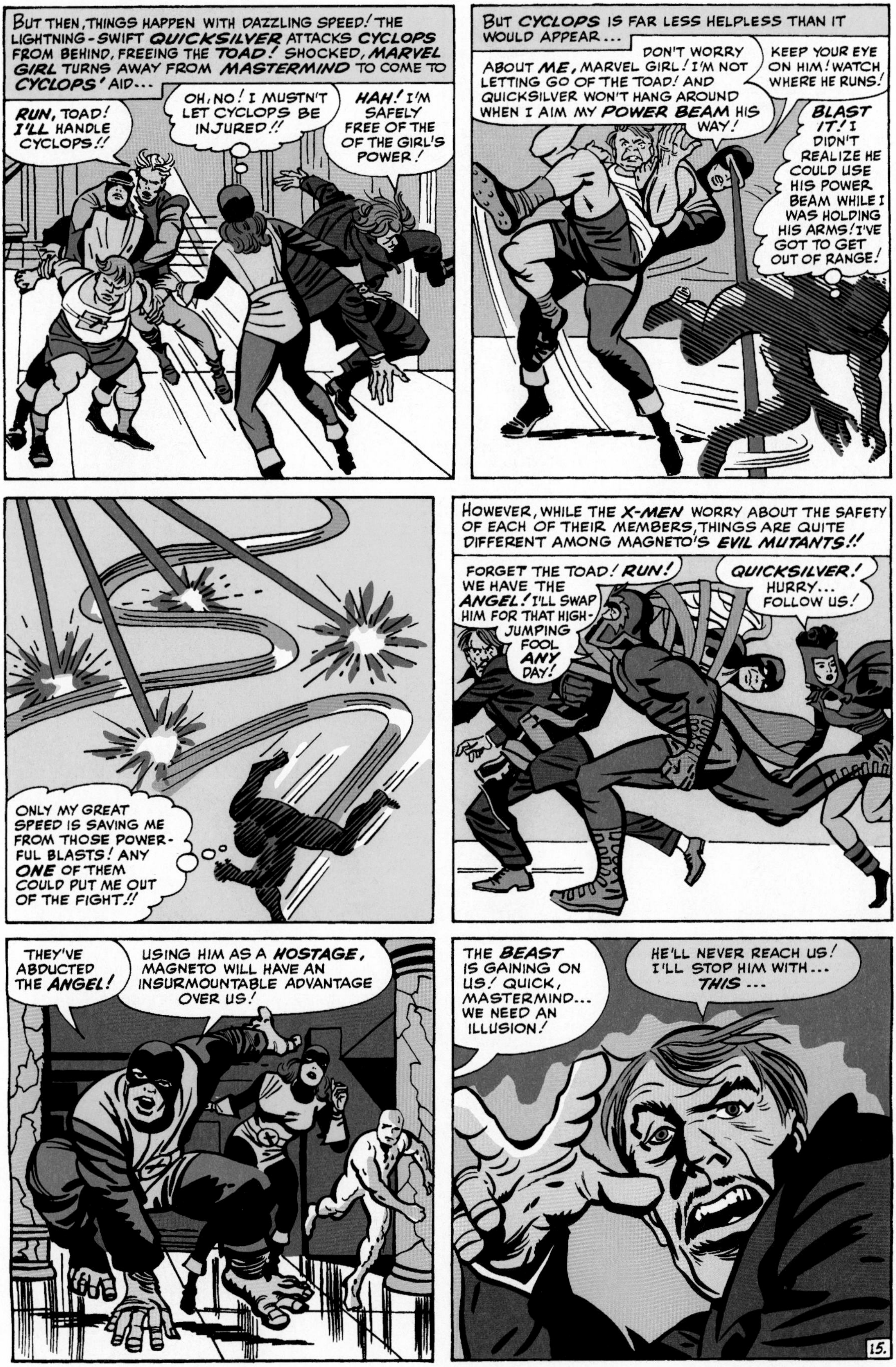

BUT THEN, THINGS HAPPEN WITH DAZZLING SPEED! THE LIGHTNING-SWIFT QUICKSILVER ATTACKS CYCLOPS FROM BEHIND, FREEING THE TOAD! SHOCKED, MARVEL GIRL TURNS AWAY FROM MASTERMIND TO COME TO CYCLOPS' AID...
RUN, TOAD! I'LL HANDLE CYCLOPS!!
OH, NO! I MUSTN'T LET CYCLOPS BE INJURED!!
HAH! I'M SAFELY FREE OF THE OF THE GIRL'S POWER!
BUT CYCLOPS IS FAR LESS HELPLESS THAN IT WOULD APPEAR...
DON'T WORRY ABOUT ME, MARVEL GIRL! I'M NOT LETTING GO OF THE TOAD! AND QUICKSILVER WON'T HANG AROUND WHEN I AIM MY POWER BEAM HIS WAY!
KEEP YOUR EYE ON HIM! WATCH WHERE HE RUNS!
BLAST IT! I DIDN'T REALIZE HE COULD USE HIS POWER BEAM WHILE I WAS HOLDING HIS ARMS! I'VE GOT TO GET OUT OF RANGE!
ONLY MY GREAT SPEED IS SAVING ME FROM THOSE POWER-FUL BLASTS! ANY ONE OF THEM COULD PUT ME OUT OF THE FIGHT!!
HOWEVER, WHILE THE X-MEN WORRY ABOUT THE SAFETY OF EACH OF THEIR MEMBERS, THINGS ARE QUITE DIFFERENT AMONG MAGNETO'S EVIL MUTANTS!!
FORGET THE TOAD! RUN! WE HAVE THE ANGEL! I'LL SWAP HIM FOR THAT HIGH-JUMPING FOOL ANY DAY!
QUICKSILVER! HURRY... FOLLOW US!
THEY'VE ABDUCTED THE ANGEL!
USING HIM AS A HOSTAGE, MAGNETO WILL HAVE AN INSURMOUNTABLE ADVANTAGE OVER US!
THE BEAST IS GAINING ON US! QUICK, MASTERMIND... WE NEED AN ILLUSION!
HE'LL NEVER REACH US! I'LL STOP HIM WITH... THIS...
15.

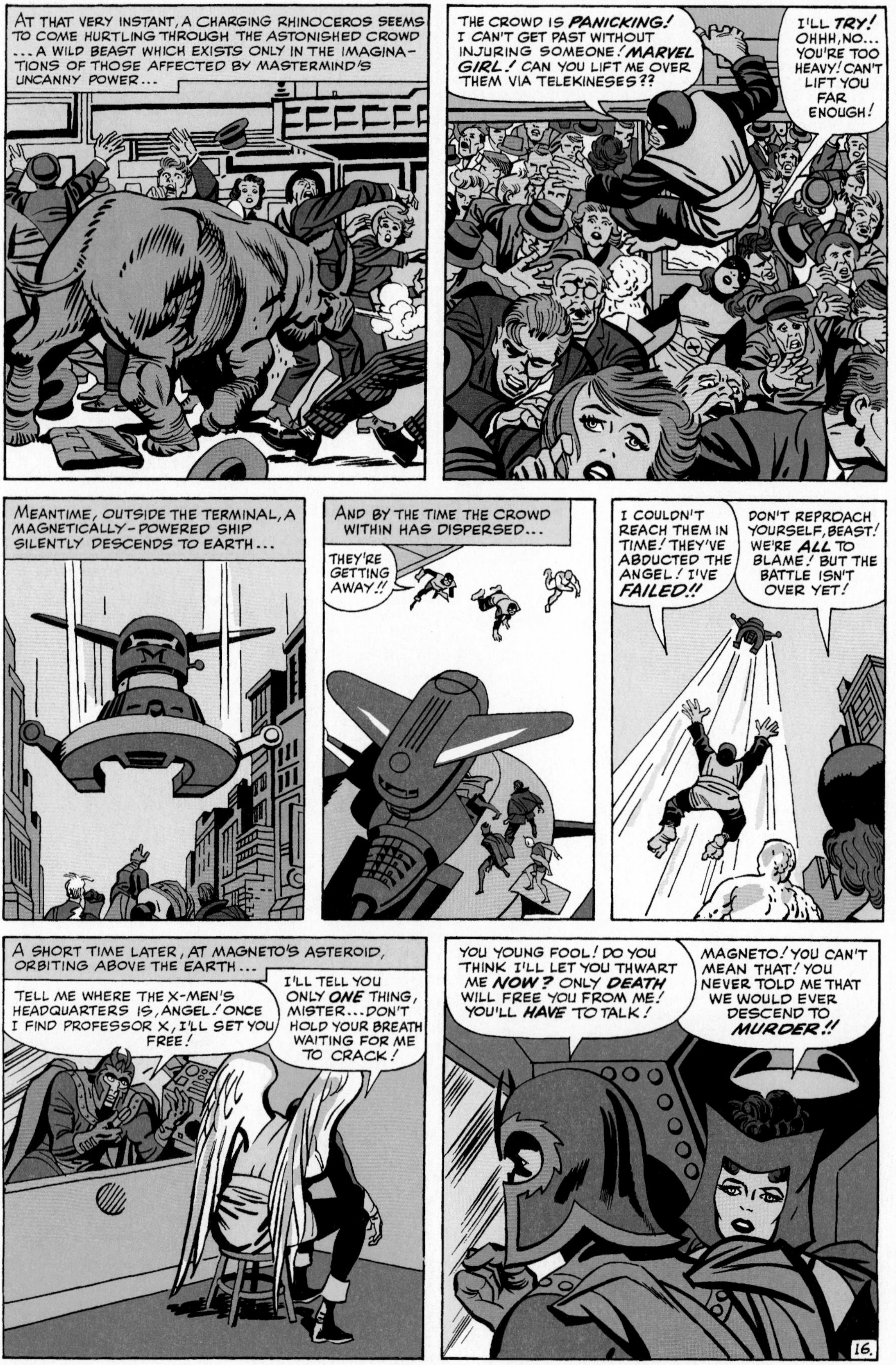
AT THAT VERY INSTANT, A CHARGING RHINOCEROS SEEMS TO COME HURTLING THROUGH THE ASTONISHED CROWD ... A WILD BEAST WHICH EXISTS ONLY IN THE IMAGINATIONS OF THOSE AFFECTED BY MASTERMIND'S UNCANNY POWER...
THE CROWD IS PANICKING! I CAN'T GET PAST WITHOUT INJURING SOMEONE! MARVEL GIRL! CAN YOU LIFT ME OVER THEM VIA TELEKINESES??
I'LL TRY! OHHH, NO... YOU'RE TOO HEAVY! CAN'T LIFT YOU FAR ENOUGH!
MEANTIME, OUTSIDE THE TERMINAL, A MAGNETICALLY-POWERED SHIP SILENTLY DESCENDS TO EARTH...
AND BY THE TIME THE CROWD WITHIN HAS DISPERSED...
THEY'RE GETTING AWAY!!
I COULDN'T REACH THEM IN TIME! THEY'VE ABDUCTED THE ANGEL! I'VE FAILED!!
DON'T REPROACH YOURSELF, BEAST! WE'RE ALL TO BLAME! BUT THE BATTLE ISN'T OVER YET!
A SHORT TIME LATER, AT MAGNETO'S ASTEROID, ORBITING ABOVE THE EARTH...
TELL ME WHERE THE X-MEN'S HEADQUARTERS IS, ANGEL! ONCE I FIND PROFESSOR X, I'LL SET YOU FREE!
I'LL TELL YOU ONLY ONE THING, MISTER... DON'T HOLD YOUR BREATH WAITING FOR ME TO CRACK!
YOU YOUNG FOOL! DO YOU THINK I'LL LET YOU THWART ME NOW? ONLY DEATH WILL FREE YOU FROM ME! YOU'LL HAVE TO TALK!
MAGNETO! YOU CAN'T MEAN THAT! YOU NEVER TOLD ME THAT WE WOULD EVER DESCEND TO MURDER!!
16.

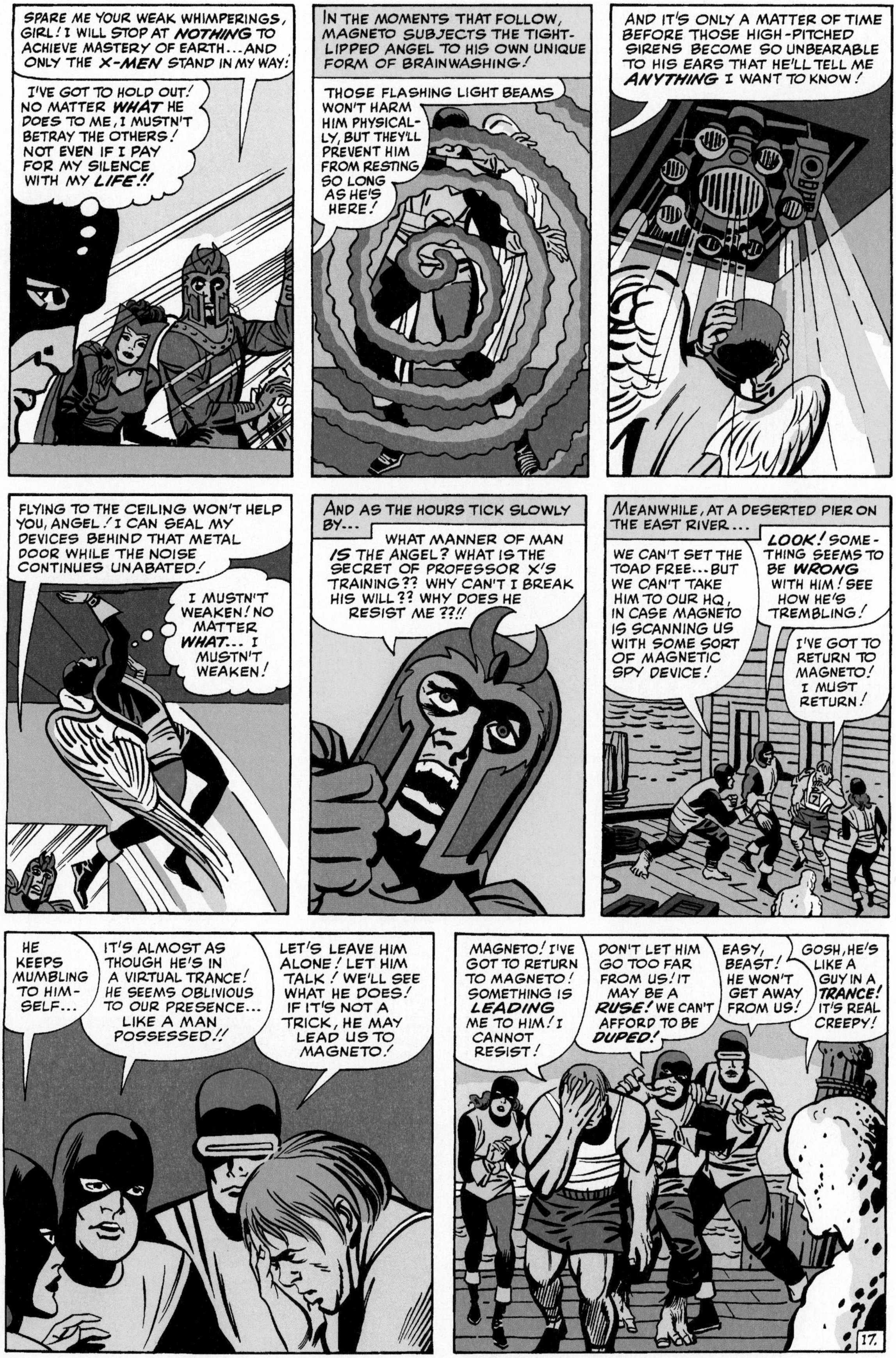
SPARE ME YOUR WEAK WHIMPERINGS, GIRL! I WILL STOP AT NOTHING TO ACHIEVE MASTERY OF EARTH... AND ONLY THE X-MEN STAND IN MY WAY!
I'VE GOT TO HOLD OUT! NO MATTER WHAT HE DOES TO ME, I MUSTN'T BETRAY THE OTHERS! NOT EVEN IF I PAY FOR MY SILENCE WITH MY LIFE!!
IN THE MOMENTS THAT FOLLOW, MAGNETO SUBJECTS THE TIGHT-LIPPED ANGEL TO HIS OWN UNIQUE FORM OF BRAINWASHING!
THOSE FLASHING LIGHT BEAMS WON'T HARM HIM PHYSICALLY, BUT THEY'LL PREVENT HIM FROM RESTING SO LONG AS HE'S HERE!
AND IT'S ONLY A MATTER OF TIME BEFORE THOSE HIGH-PITCHED SIRENS BECOME SO UNBEARABLE TO HIS EARS THAT HE'LL TELL ME ANYTHING I WANT TO KNOW!
FLYING TO THE CEILING WON'T HELP YOU, ANGEL! I CAN SEAL MY DEVICES BEHIND THAT METAL DOOR WHILE THE NOISE CONTINUES UNABATED!
I MUSTN'T WEAKEN! NO MATTER WHAT... I MUSTN'T WEAKEN!
AND AS THE HOURS TICK SLOWLY BY...
WHAT MANNER OF MAN IS THE ANGEL? WHAT IS THE SECRET OF PROFESSOR X'S TRAINING?? WHY CAN'T I BREAK HIS WILL?? WHY DOES HE RESIST ME??!!
MEANWHILE, AT A DESERTED PIER ON THE EAST RIVER...
WE CAN'T SET THE TOAD FREE... BUT WE CAN'T TAKE HIM TO OUR HQ, IN CASE MAGNETO IS SCANNING US WITH SOME SORT OF MAGNETIC SPY DEVICE!
LOOK! SOMETHING SEEMS TO BE WRONG WITH HIM! SEE HOW HE'S TREMBLING!
I'VE GOT TO RETURN TO MAGNETO! I MUST RETURN!
HE KEEPS MUMBLING TO HIMSELF...
IT'S ALMOST AS THOUGH HE'S IN A VIRTUAL TRANCE! HE SEEMS OBLIVIOUS TO OUR PRESENCE... LIKE A MAN POSSESSED!!
LET'S LEAVE HIM ALONE! LET HIM TALK! WE'LL SEE WHAT HE DOES! IF IT'S NOT A TRICK, HE MAY LEAD US TO MAGNETO!
MAGNETO! I'VE GOT TO RETURN TO MAGNETO! SOMETHING IS LEADING ME TO HIM! I CANNOT RESIST!
DON'T LET HIM GO TOO FAR FROM US! IT MAY BE A RUSE! WE CAN'T AFFORD TO BE DUPED!
EASY, BEAST! HE WON'T GET AWAY FROM US!
GOSH, HE'S LIKE A GUY IN A TRANCE! IT'S REAL CREEPY!
17.

LOOK! HE HAD A HIDDEN MAGNETIC *COMMUNICATOR* UNDER HIS SOCK! HE'S CONTACTING MAGNETO WITH IT!!

AND MAGNETO GOT THE MESSAGE!! HERE COMES A DRONE PICK-UP CAPSULE... FROM ABOVE THE CLOUDS!

QUICKLY! WE'VE GOT TO ENTER IT WITH THE TOAD! EVEN IF IT'S A TRAP, WE CAN'T AFFORD TO SHIRK! IT MAY BE OUR ONE CHANCE TO FIND THE ANGEL!

AND WHEN WE *DO* FIND HIM, WE MUST PRAY THAT *OUR* POWER IS MORE THAN A MATCH FOR THE EVIL MUTANTS!

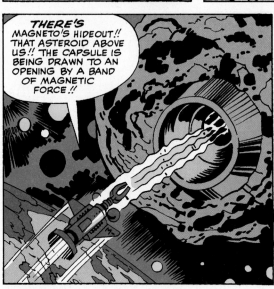

THERE'S MAGNETO'S HIDEOUT!! THAT ASTEROID ABOVE US!! THE CAPSULE IS BEING DRAWN TO AN OPENING BY A BAND OF MAGNETIC FORCE!!

SECONDS LATER...

TOAD!! HOW'D YOU ESCAPE THE X-MEN?? HOW'D YOU *GET* HERE??

I... HAD... TO... COME...

DID YOU *HEAR* THAT?? THEY WEREN'T *EXPECTING* HIM! IT'S *NOT* A TRAP! LET'S *GO!!*

FORGIVE THIS UNSEEMLY INTRUSION, MASTERMIND! BUT BEING WELL-BEHAVED LITTLE X-MEN, WE HATED TO TAKE OUR DEPARTURE WITHOUT SAYING GOOD-BYE!

ATTACK *ME,* WILL YOU?? LET'S SEE HOW WELL YOU FIGHT *NOW!*... WHEN YOU FEEL YOUR LEGS TURNING TO *DOUGH!*

DON'T LET HIM STOP YOU, BEAST! IT'S JUST ANOTHER OF HIS *ILLUSIONS!*

MY *BRAIN* IS AWARE OF THAT... BUT I *STILL* CAN'T MOVE MY *LEGS!*

18.

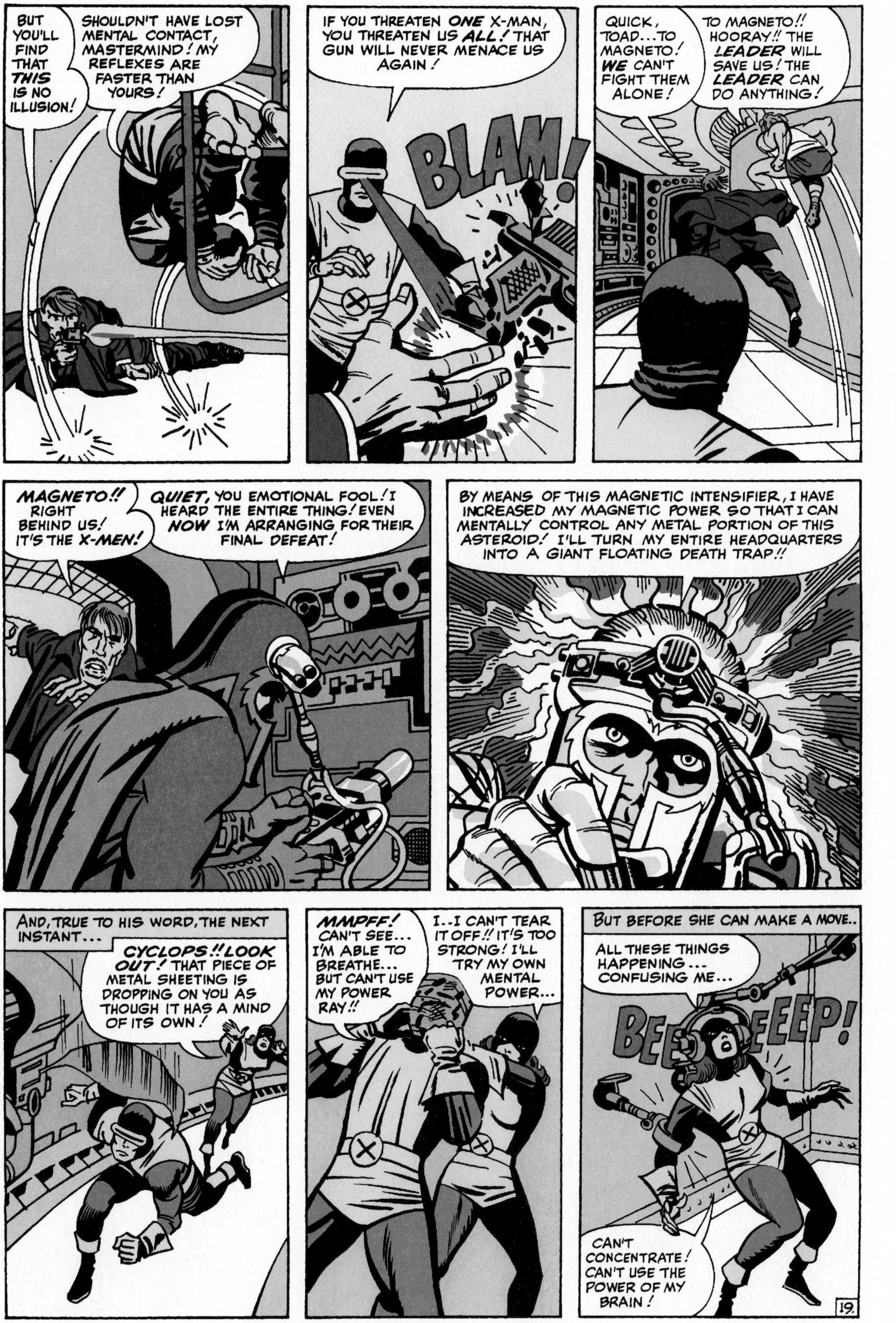
BUT YOU'LL FIND THAT THIS IS NO ILLUSION!
SHOULDN'T HAVE LOST MENTAL CONTACT, MASTERMIND! MY REFLEXES ARE FASTER THAN YOURS!
IF YOU THREATEN ONE X-MAN, YOU THREATEN US ALL! THAT GUN WILL NEVER MENACE US AGAIN!
BLAM!
QUICK, TOAD...TO MAGNETO! WE CAN'T FIGHT THEM ALONE!
TO MAGNETO!! HOORAY!! THE LEADER WILL SAVE US! THE LEADER CAN DO ANYTHING!
MAGNETO!! RIGHT BEHIND US! IT'S THE X-MEN!
QUIET, YOU EMOTIONAL FOOL! I HEARD THE ENTIRE THING! EVEN NOW I'M ARRANGING FOR THEIR FINAL DEFEAT!
BY MEANS OF THIS MAGNETIC INTENSIFIER, I HAVE INCREASED MY MAGNETIC POWER SO THAT I CAN MENTALLY CONTROL ANY METAL PORTION OF THIS ASTEROID! I'LL TURN MY ENTIRE HEADQUARTERS INTO A GIANT FLOATING DEATH TRAP!!
AND, TRUE TO HIS WORD, THE NEXT INSTANT...
CYCLOPS!! LOOK OUT! THAT PIECE OF METAL SHEETING IS DROPPING ON YOU AS THOUGH IT HAS A MIND OF ITS OWN!
MMPFF! CAN'T SEE... I'M ABLE TO BREATHE... BUT CAN'T USE MY POWER RAY!!
I..I CAN'T TEAR IT OFF!! IT'S TOO STRONG! I'LL TRY MY OWN MENTAL POWER...
BUT BEFORE SHE CAN MAKE A MOVE..
ALL THESE THINGS HAPPENING... CONFUSING ME...
BEEEEEEP!
CAN'T CONCENTRATE! CAN'T USE THE POWER OF MY BRAIN!
19.

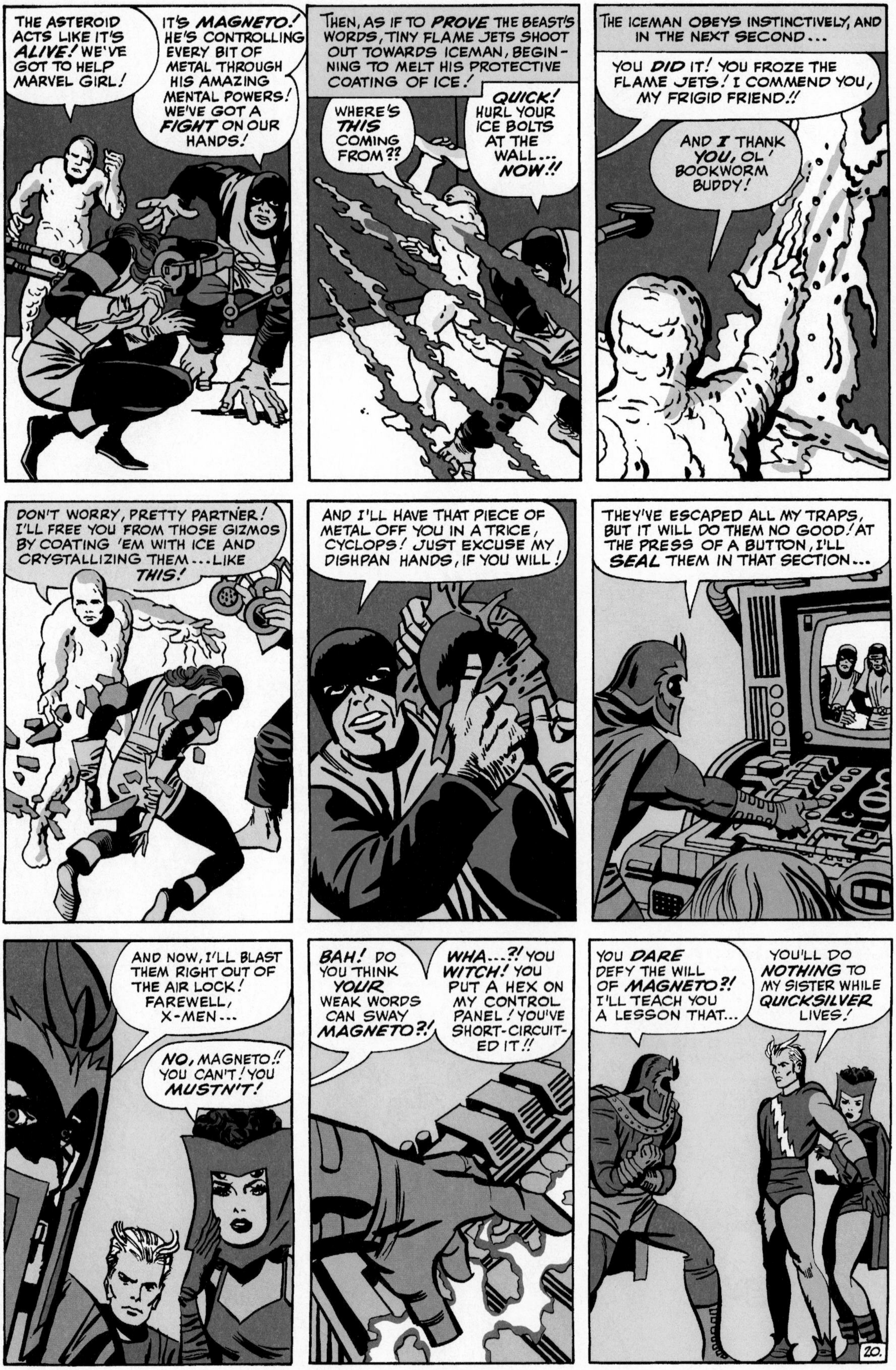
THE ASTEROID ACTS LIKE IT'S ALIVE! WE'VE GOT TO HELP MARVEL GIRL!
IT'S MAGNETO! HE'S CONTROLLING EVERY BIT OF METAL THROUGH HIS AMAZING MENTAL POWERS! WE'VE GOT A FIGHT ON OUR HANDS!
THEN, AS IF TO PROVE THE BEAST'S WORDS, TINY FLAME JETS SHOOT OUT TOWARDS ICEMAN, BEGINNING TO MELT HIS PROTECTIVE COATING OF ICE!
WHERE'S THIS COMING FROM??
QUICK! HURL YOUR ICE BOLTS AT THE WALL... NOW!!
THE ICEMAN OBEYS INSTINCTIVELY, AND IN THE NEXT SECOND...
YOU DID IT! YOU FROZE THE FLAME JETS! I COMMEND YOU, MY FRIGID FRIEND!!
AND I THANK YOU, OL' BOOKWORM BUDDY!
DON'T WORRY, PRETTY PARTNER! I'LL FREE YOU FROM THOSE GIZMOS BY COATING 'EM WITH ICE AND CRYSTALLIZING THEM... LIKE THIS!
AND I'LL HAVE THAT PIECE OF METAL OFF YOU IN A TRICE, CYCLOPS! JUST EXCUSE MY DISHPAN HANDS, IF YOU WILL!
THEY'VE ESCAPED ALL MY TRAPS, BUT IT WILL DO THEM NO GOOD! AT THE PRESS OF A BUTTON, I'LL SEAL THEM IN THAT SECTION...
AND NOW, I'LL BLAST THEM RIGHT OUT OF THE AIR LOCK! FAREWELL, X-MEN...
NO, MAGNETO!! YOU CAN'T! YOU MUSTN'T!
BAH! DO YOU THINK YOUR WEAK WORDS CAN SWAY MAGNETO?!
WHA...?! YOU WITCH! YOU PUT A HEX ON MY CONTROL PANEL! YOU'VE SHORT-CIRCUITED IT!!
YOU DARE DEFY THE WILL OF MAGNETO?! I'LL TEACH YOU A LESSON THAT...
YOU'LL DO NOTHING TO MY SISTER WHILE QUICKSILVER LIVES!
20.

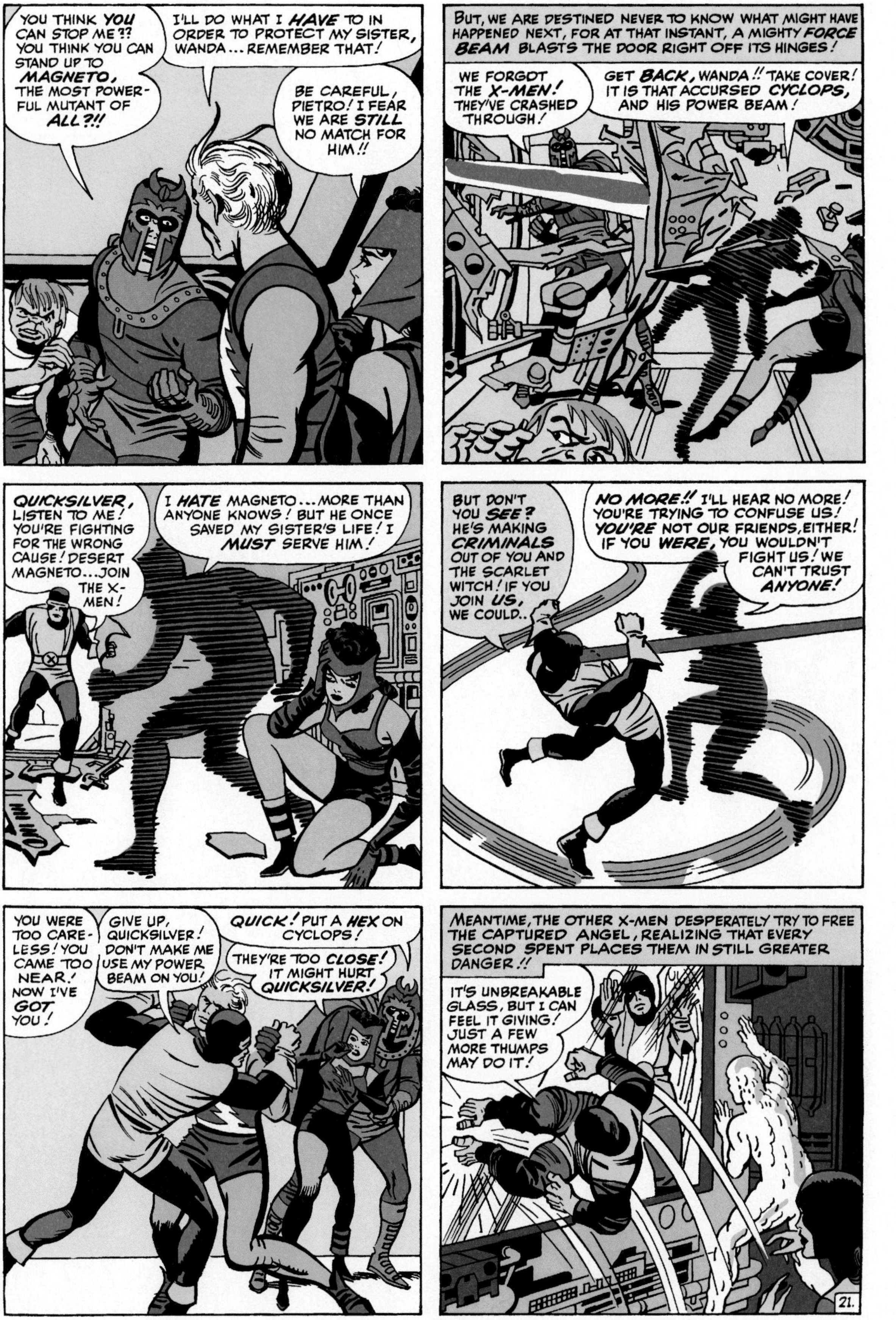
YOU THINK YOU CAN STOP ME?? YOU THINK YOU CAN STAND UP TO MAGNETO, THE MOST POWERFUL MUTANT OF ALL?!!
I'LL DO WHAT I HAVE TO IN ORDER TO PROTECT MY SISTER, WANDA... REMEMBER THAT!
BE CAREFUL, PIETRO! I FEAR WE ARE STILL NO MATCH FOR HIM!!
BUT, WE ARE DESTINED NEVER TO KNOW WHAT MIGHT HAVE HAPPENED NEXT, FOR AT THAT INSTANT, A MIGHTY FORCE BEAM BLASTS THE DOOR RIGHT OFF ITS HINGES!
WE FORGOT THE X-MEN! THEY'VE CRASHED THROUGH!
GET BACK, WANDA!! TAKE COVER! IT IS THAT ACCURSED CYCLOPS, AND HIS POWER BEAM!
QUICKSILVER, LISTEN TO ME! YOU'RE FIGHTING FOR THE WRONG CAUSE! DESERT MAGNETO...JOIN THE X-MEN!
I HATE MAGNETO... MORE THAN ANYONE KNOWS! BUT HE ONCE SAVED MY SISTER'S LIFE! I MUST SERVE HIM!
BUT DON'T YOU SEE? HE'S MAKING CRIMINALS OUT OF YOU AND THE SCARLET WITCH! IF YOU JOIN US, WE COULD..
NO MORE!! I'LL HEAR NO MORE! YOU'RE TRYING TO CONFUSE US! YOU'RE NOT OUR FRIENDS, EITHER! IF YOU WERE, YOU WOULDN'T FIGHT US! WE CAN'T TRUST ANYONE!
YOU WERE TOO CARELESS! YOU CAME TOO NEAR! NOW I'VE GOT YOU!
GIVE UP, QUICKSILVER! DON'T MAKE ME USE MY POWER BEAM ON YOU!
QUICK! PUT A HEX ON CYCLOPS!
THEY'RE TOO CLOSE! IT MIGHT HURT QUICKSILVER!
MEANTIME, THE OTHER X-MEN DESPERATELY TRY TO FREE THE CAPTURED ANGEL, REALIZING THAT EVERY SECOND SPENT PLACES THEM IN STILL GREATER DANGER!!
IT'S UNBREAKABLE GLASS, BUT I CAN FEEL IT GIVING! JUST A FEW MORE THUMPS MAY DO IT!
21.

HOLD IT, HANK! LET ME TRY IT... MY WAY! I CAN MENTALLY HURL ONE OF THESE HEAVY CHEMICAL TANKS AT THE GLASS WITH EVEN GREATER FORCE!!

YOU DID IT! HE CAN EXTRICATE HIMSELF NOW!

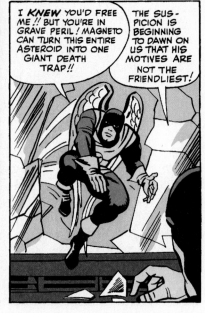

I KNEW YOU'D FREE ME !! BUT YOU'RE IN GRAVE PERIL! MAGNETO CAN TURN THIS ENTIRE ASTEROID INTO ONE GIANT DEATH TRAP!!

THE SUSPICION IS BEGINNING TO DAWN ON US THAT HIS MOTIVES ARE NOT THE FRIENDLIEST!

BUT, PERHAPS WE CAN INSTILL SOME OF THE MILK OF HUMAN KINDNESS IN HIS... SAY! WHAT HAVE WE HERE ??!

DON'T LET IT THROW YOU! IT MUST BE ONE OF MASTERMIND'S IMAGES... WATCH! I'LL PROVE IT!!

AND, NOW, TALL, DARK, AND GRUESOME, WE'VE GOT A LITTLE SETTLING UP TO DO, SO WE MIGHT AS WELL GET STARTED!

HURRY, MASTERMIND... DON'T LET HIM GET YOU! TOO BAD YOU CAN'T HOP AWAY FROM YOUR ENEMIES LIKE THE TOAD!

NO! NO! STAY BACK!

BUT THE SOUNDS OF CONFLICT HAVE REACHED MAGNETO'S EARS, AND SO...

STOP YOUR WHINING, MASTERMIND! MY DART GRENADE WILL SAVE YOU!

X-MEN! LOOK OUT! IT EXPLODED INTO A THOUSAND FLYING DARTS!!

THEY'RE FASTER THAN I THOUGHT! THEY ALL SAVED THEMSELVES BY TAKING COVER! BUT AT LEAST I SLOWED THEIR ATTACK!

WAIT!! THAT RUMBLING SOUND!! CAN IT BE WHAT I THINK??!

22.

118

IT **IS**!! THE ASTEROID IS BREAKING UP!! DURING THE BATTLE SOMEONE MUST HAVE BRUSHED AGAINST SOME OF THE DETONATE BUTTONS!! BUT, I SHALL TURN THIS TO MY ADVANTAGE!

SAVE ME, MAGNETO! I DON'T WANT TO DIE!

SILENCE, TOAD! IT IS THE X-MEN WHO SHOULD BE FEARFUL! **THEY'RE** THE ONES WHO ARE DOOMED!

FIRST, WE MUST GET THEM TOGETHER, ON THE OTHER SIDE OF THE AIR LOCK!

AHH, THERE'S **CYCLOPS!** I'LL START WITH **HIM!**

NOW! BEFORE HE CAN USE HIS POWER BEAM **!!**

FORGIVE ME FOR ATTACKING YOU FROM BEHIND, BUT **WE** DON'T FIGHT BY ANY RULES!

THERE! STAY BEHIND THE AIR CHAMBER WITH YOUR WRETCHED PARTNERS! I LEAVE YOU TO EMPTY SPACE!!

MAGNETO, NO!! YOU'RE MAKING A **MISTAKE!**

IT'S NO USE, TOAD! HE DOESN'T HEAR YOU!

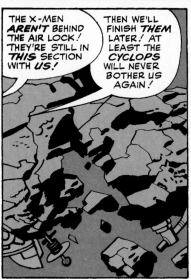

THE X-MEN **AREN'T** BEHIND THE AIR LOCK! THEY'RE STILL IN **THIS** SECTION WITH **US!**

THEN WE'LL FINISH **THEM** LATER! AT LEAST THE **CYCLOPS** WILL NEVER BOTHER US AGAIN!

BUT THE **X-MEN** NEVER DESERT ONE OF THEIR OWN, AND SO...

I'VE GOT TO FLY TO SCOTT BEFORE THAT SECTION CRUMBLES BENEATH HIM AND HE PLUNGES TO EARTH!

WAIT! I'LL **HELP** YOU!

THERE! I FASHIONED A TUBULAR **ICE BRIDGE** FOR YOU...IT'LL PROTECT YOU BOTH FROM THE BITTER COLD OUT THERE!!

23.

SCOTT! SCOTTY BOY! DO YOU *HEAR* ME? I'M COMING, FELLA! HANG ON!

Y-YOU WERE JUST IN TIME, WARREN! THE FRAGMENT WAS CRUMBLING... I COULD JUST BARELY KEEP FROM FALLING!!

YOU'RE OKAY, *NOW*, PARTNER! BUT WE'RE *STILL* NOT IN THE CLEAR! *BOTH* SECTIONS ARE STARTING TO SPLIT APART!

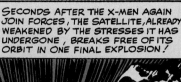

SECONDS AFTER THE X-MEN AGAIN JOIN FORCES, THE SATELLITE, ALREADY WEAKENED BY THE STRESSES IT HAS UNDERGONE, BREAKS FREE OF ITS ORBIT IN ONE FINAL EXPLOSION!

BUT, BEFORE DRIFTING OUT INTO AIR-LESS SPACE, IT LAUNCHES A SILENT, MAGNETICALLY-POWERED ESCAPE SHIP... CONTAINING FIVE WEARY BUT TRIUMPHANT X-MEN!

NOT A SECOND TOO SOON!!

THEN, AS THE TEEN-AGERS REACH SAFETY...

MAGNETO AND HIS MUTANTS MUST STILL BE UP THERE... IT'S RETURN-ING FOR THEM!

IT'S *RISING* AGAIN... BY REMOTE CONTROL!

MAGNETO CAN CONTROL ITS COURSE *MENTALLY!* THERE'S NO TELLING *WHERE* HE'LL LAND!

IF THE EVIL MUTANTS SURVIVED, THIS WAS ONLY THE SECOND ROUND!! THEY'LL BE MORE DANGEROUS THAN *EVER!*

AND SO WILL *WE*, JEAN! WE *PROVED* OUR METTLE TODAY! BY OURSELVES!

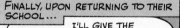

FINALLY, UPON RETURNING TO THEIR SCHOOL...

I'LL GIVE THE PROFESSOR OUR REPORT...

NO *NEED* TO, SCOTT! I WAS WITH YOU ALL THE TIME... LISTENING TO YOUR THOUGHTS!

YOU MEAN... YOU HAVE YOUR MENTAL *POWER* BACK?!

24.

I NEVER *LOST* IT! I ONLY *PRETENDED* TO, AFTER OUR FIRST BATTLE WITH THE EVIL MUTANTS!

BUT... *WHY*, SIR?

REMEMBER, THIS IS A *SCHOOL!* AND YOU CAN'T GRADUATE FROM ANY SCHOOL WITHOUT PASSING YOUR FINAL EXAM! WELL, YOU'VE ALL JUST *TAKEN* YOUR FINAL EXAM... JUST AS I PLANNED IT!

AND I'M PROUD TO SAY THAT YOU'VE ALL *PASSED* WITH FLYING COLORS! YOU'VE PROVEN YOU CAN THINK AND ACT FOR YOURSELVES!! YOUR TRAINING PERIOD IS OVER!! *CONGRATULATIONS*, MY X-MEN!!

EDITOR'S NOTE: NOW THAT THEIR TRAINING IS ENDED, EVEN GREAT-ER DANGERS AWAIT THEM! FOR THE STRANGE SAGA OF THE X-MEN IS JUST *BEGINNING!!* STAN AND JACK HAVE A MILLION SURPRISES IN STORE FOR YOU... SO BE WITH US NEXT ISH! SEE YOU THEN!

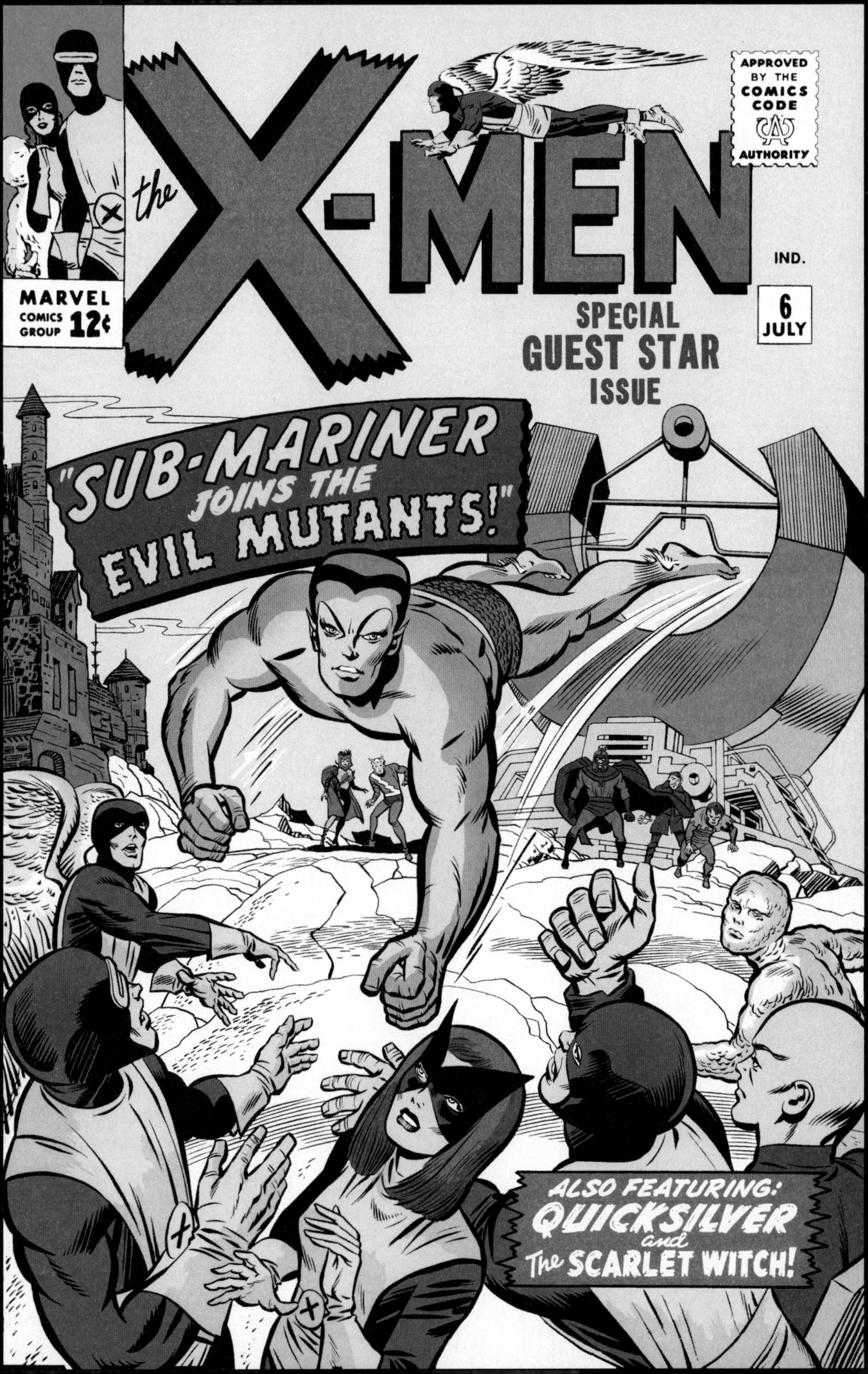
APPROVED BY THE COMICS CODE AUTHORITY
the X-MEN
IND.
MARVEL COMICS GROUP 12¢
6 JULY
SPECIAL GUEST STAR ISSUE
"SUB-MARINER JOINS THE EVIL MUTANTS!"
ALSO FEATURING: QUICKSILVER and The SCARLET WITCH!

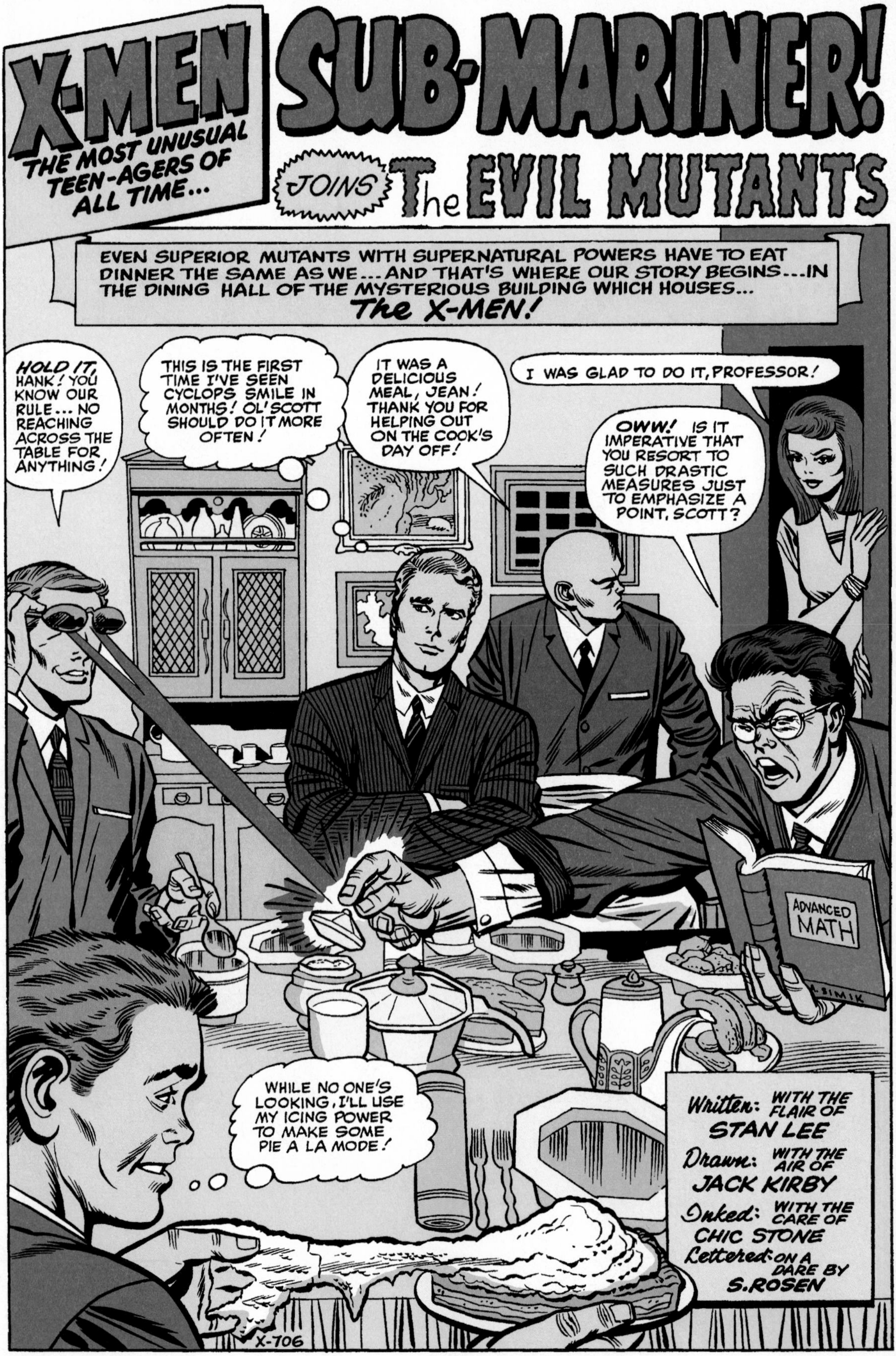
X-MEN
THE MOST UNUSUAL TEEN-AGERS OF ALL TIME...
SUB-MARINER! JOINS The EVIL MUTANTS
EVEN SUPERIOR MUTANTS WITH SUPERNATURAL POWERS HAVE TO EAT DINNER THE SAME AS WE... AND THAT'S WHERE OUR STORY BEGINS...IN THE DINING HALL OF THE MYSTERIOUS BUILDING WHICH HOUSES... The X-MEN!
HOLD IT, HANK! YOU KNOW OUR RULE... NO REACHING ACROSS THE TABLE FOR ANYTHING!
THIS IS THE FIRST TIME I'VE SEEN CYCLOPS SMILE IN MONTHS! OL' SCOTT SHOULD DO IT MORE OFTEN!
IT WAS A DELICIOUS MEAL, JEAN! THANK YOU FOR HELPING OUT ON THE COOK'S DAY OFF!
I WAS GLAD TO DO IT, PROFESSOR!
OWW! IS IT IMPERATIVE THAT YOU RESORT TO SUCH DRASTIC MEASURES JUST TO EMPHASIZE A POINT, SCOTT?
ADVANCED MATH
WHILE NO ONE'S LOOKING, I'LL USE MY ICING POWER TO MAKE SOME PIE A LA MODE!
Written: WITH THE FLAIR OF STAN LEE
Drawn: WITH THE AIR OF JACK KIRBY
Inked: WITH THE CARE OF CHIC STONE
Lettered: ON A DARE BY S. ROSEN
X-706

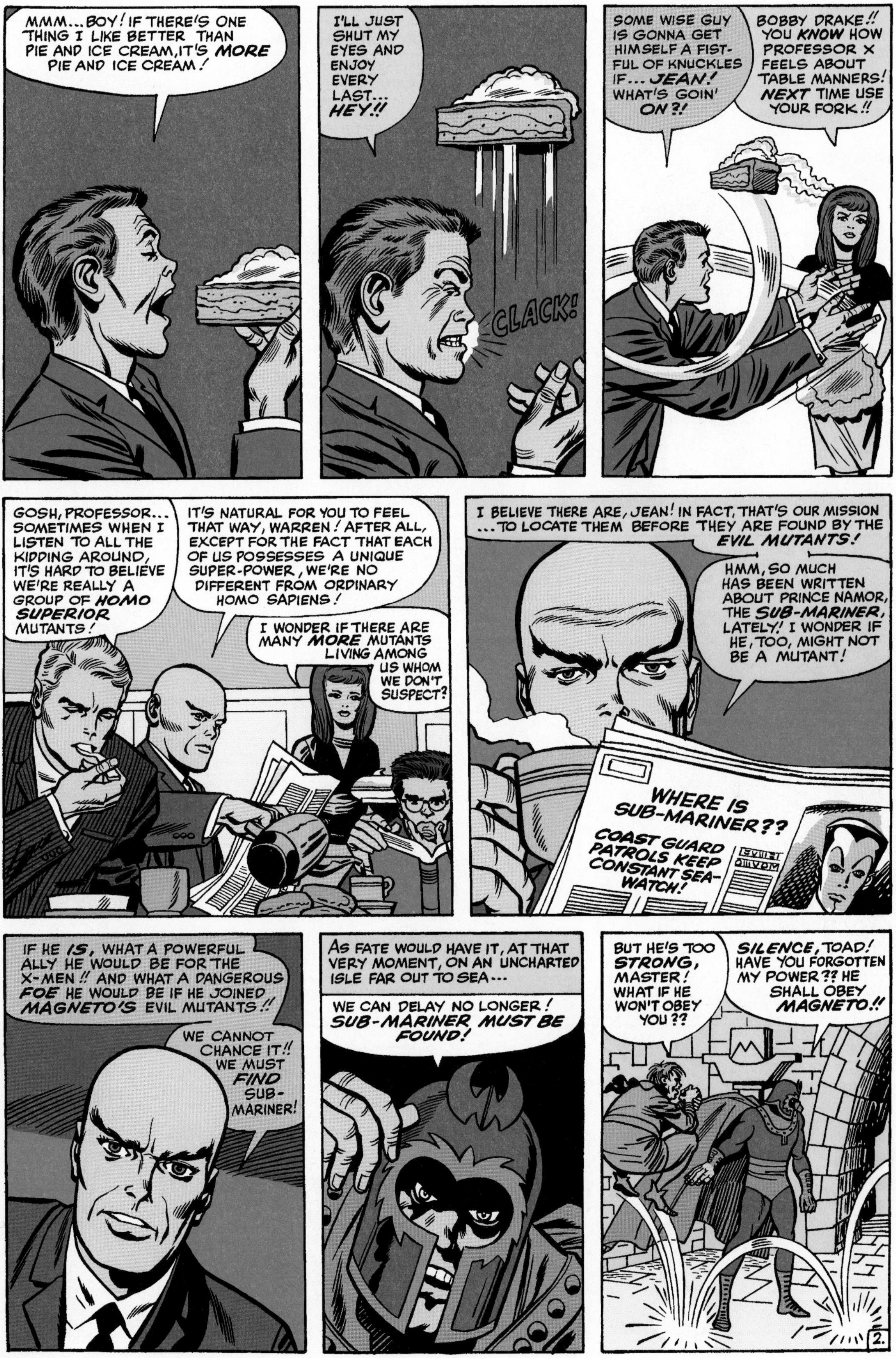
MMM...BOY! IF THERE'S ONE THING I LIKE BETTER THAN PIE AND ICE CREAM, IT'S MORE PIE AND ICE CREAM!
I'LL JUST SHUT MY EYES AND ENJOY EVERY LAST... HEY!!
CLACK!
SOME WISE GUY IS GONNA GET HIMSELF A FISTFUL OF KNUCKLES IF... JEAN! WHAT'S GOIN' ON?!
BOBBY DRAKE!! YOU KNOW HOW PROFESSOR X FEELS ABOUT TABLE MANNERS! NEXT TIME USE YOUR FORK!!
GOSH, PROFESSOR... SOMETIMES WHEN I LISTEN TO ALL THE KIDDING AROUND, IT'S HARD TO BELIEVE WE'RE REALLY A GROUP OF HOMO SUPERIOR MUTANTS!
IT'S NATURAL FOR YOU TO FEEL THAT WAY, WARREN! AFTER ALL, EXCEPT FOR THE FACT THAT EACH OF US POSSESSES A UNIQUE SUPER-POWER, WE'RE NO DIFFERENT FROM ORDINARY HOMO SAPIENS!
I WONDER IF THERE ARE MANY MORE MUTANTS LIVING AMONG US WHOM WE DON'T SUSPECT?
I BELIEVE THERE ARE, JEAN! IN FACT, THAT'S OUR MISSION ...TO LOCATE THEM BEFORE THEY ARE FOUND BY THE EVIL MUTANTS!
HMM, SO MUCH HAS BEEN WRITTEN ABOUT PRINCE NAMOR, THE SUB-MARINER, LATELY! I WONDER IF HE, TOO, MIGHT NOT BE A MUTANT!
WHERE IS SUB-MARINER??
COAST GUARD PATROLS KEEP CONSTANT SEA-WATCH!
IF HE IS, WHAT A POWERFUL ALLY HE WOULD BE FOR THE X-MEN!! AND WHAT A DANGEROUS FOE HE WOULD BE IF HE JOINED MAGNETO'S EVIL MUTANTS!!
WE CANNOT CHANCE IT!! WE MUST FIND SUB-MARINER!
AS FATE WOULD HAVE IT, AT THAT VERY MOMENT, ON AN UNCHARTED ISLE FAR OUT TO SEA...
WE CAN DELAY NO LONGER! SUB-MARINER MUST BE FOUND!
BUT HE'S TOO STRONG, MASTER! WHAT IF HE WON'T OBEY YOU??
SILENCE, TOAD! HAVE YOU FORGOTTEN MY POWER?? HE SHALL OBEY MAGNETO!!
2.

SO FAR THE *X-MEN* HAVE FOILED ME AT EVERY TURN! BUT, WITH THE *SUB-MARINER* SERVING ME, I'LL DEFEAT THEM ONCE AND FOR ALL!

I SHALL CHOOSE MY MOST AWESOME WEAPONS! NAMOR WILL *HAVE* TO YIELD TO ME!

SUDDENLY, INCREDIBLY, ONE OF THE MOST FEARED OF ALL THE *X-MEN* APPEARS IN MAGNETO'S DOORWAY...

IT'S *CYCLOPS*! RUN, MASTER! HE'S RAISING HIS VISOR!!

BAH!! I'LL BLAST HIM TO SMITHEREENS FIRST!

THE RAY WENT RIGHT *THROUGH* HIM! WHAT *NEW* POWER HAS THE ACCURSED TEEN-AGER DEVELOPED?!

WITH NOTHING TO CHECK IT, MAGNETO'S MIGHTY RAY TRAVELS THROUGH THE GREAT HALL, PAST THE MUTANT CALLED *MASTERMIND* WHO RECOILS JUST IN TIME!

BUT ANOTHER OF MAGNETO'S ALLIES, SEEING THE DEADLY RAY, HAS BUT ONE THOUGHT IN MIND... TO MAKE SURE IT DOESN'T STRIKE HIS SISTER! AND SO, THE SUPER-SWIFT *QUICKSILVER* SUDDENLY STREAKS THROUGH THE CASTLE!!

WANDA! I'VE GOT TO REACH WANDA!

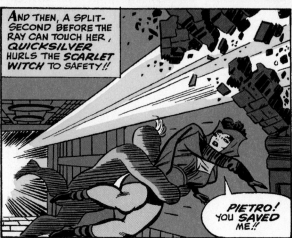

AND THEN, A SPLIT-SECOND BEFORE THE RAY CAN TOUCH HER, *QUICKSILVER* HURLS THE *SCARLET WITCH* TO SAFETY!!

PIETRO! YOU *SAVED* ME!!

WHAT *WAS* IT, PIETRO?? ARE THE *X-MEN* ATTACKING US AGAIN? HOW DID THEY *FIND* US?? WHERE IS *MAGNETO??*

I DO NOT KNOW, WANDA! BUT WHOEVER DARED DO THIS THING WILL *PAY* FOR IT! I HAVE PLEDGED MY LIFE TO GUARD YOU, MY SISTER!

3.

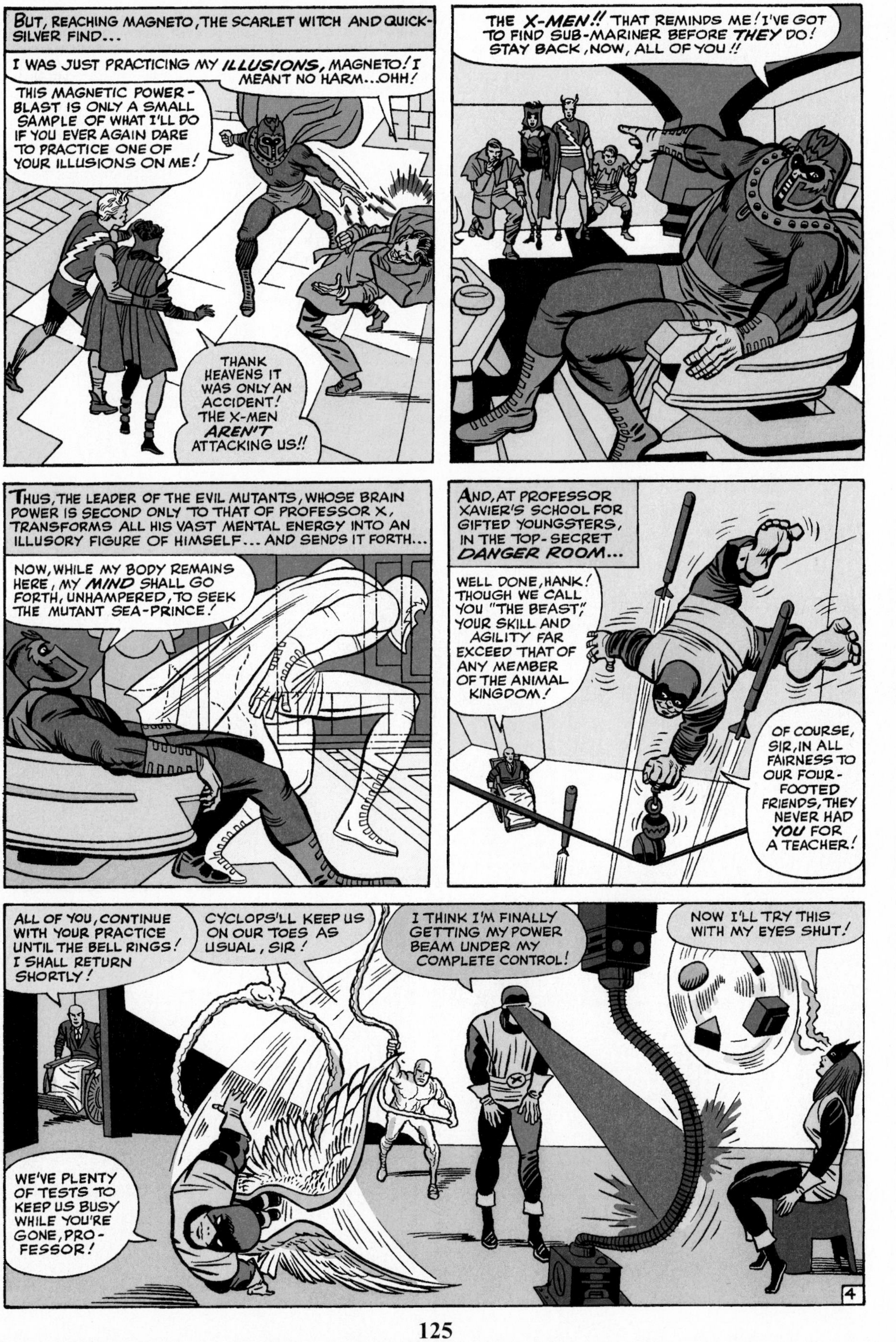

BUT, REACHING MAGNETO, THE SCARLET WITCH AND QUICKSILVER FIND...
I WAS JUST PRACTICING MY ILLUSIONS, MAGNETO! I MEANT NO HARM...OHH!
THIS MAGNETIC POWER-BLAST IS ONLY A SMALL SAMPLE OF WHAT I'LL DO IF YOU EVER AGAIN DARE TO PRACTICE ONE OF YOUR ILLUSIONS ON ME!
THANK HEAVENS IT WAS ONLY AN ACCIDENT! THE X-MEN AREN'T ATTACKING US!!
THE X-MEN!! THAT REMINDS ME! I'VE GOT TO FIND SUB-MARINER BEFORE THEY DO! STAY BACK, NOW, ALL OF YOU!!
THUS, THE LEADER OF THE EVIL MUTANTS, WHOSE BRAIN POWER IS SECOND ONLY TO THAT OF PROFESSOR X, TRANSFORMS ALL HIS VAST MENTAL ENERGY INTO AN ILLUSORY FIGURE OF HIMSELF... AND SENDS IT FORTH...
NOW, WHILE MY BODY REMAINS HERE, MY MIND SHALL GO FORTH, UNHAMPERED, TO SEEK THE MUTANT SEA-PRINCE!
AND, AT PROFESSOR XAVIER'S SCHOOL FOR GIFTED YOUNGSTERS, IN THE TOP-SECRET DANGER ROOM...
WELL DONE, HANK! THOUGH WE CALL YOU "THE BEAST," YOUR SKILL AND AGILITY FAR EXCEED THAT OF ANY MEMBER OF THE ANIMAL KINGDOM!
OF COURSE, SIR, IN ALL FAIRNESS TO OUR FOUR-FOOTED FRIENDS, THEY NEVER HAD YOU FOR A TEACHER!
ALL OF YOU, CONTINUE WITH YOUR PRACTICE UNTIL THE BELL RINGS! I SHALL RETURN SHORTLY!
WE'VE PLENTY OF TESTS TO KEEP US BUSY WHILE YOU'RE GONE, PROFESSOR!
CYCLOPS'LL KEEP US ON OUR TOES AS USUAL, SIR!
I THINK I'M FINALLY GETTING MY POWER BEAM UNDER MY COMPLETE CONTROL!
NOW I'LL TRY THIS WITH MY EYES SHUT!
4

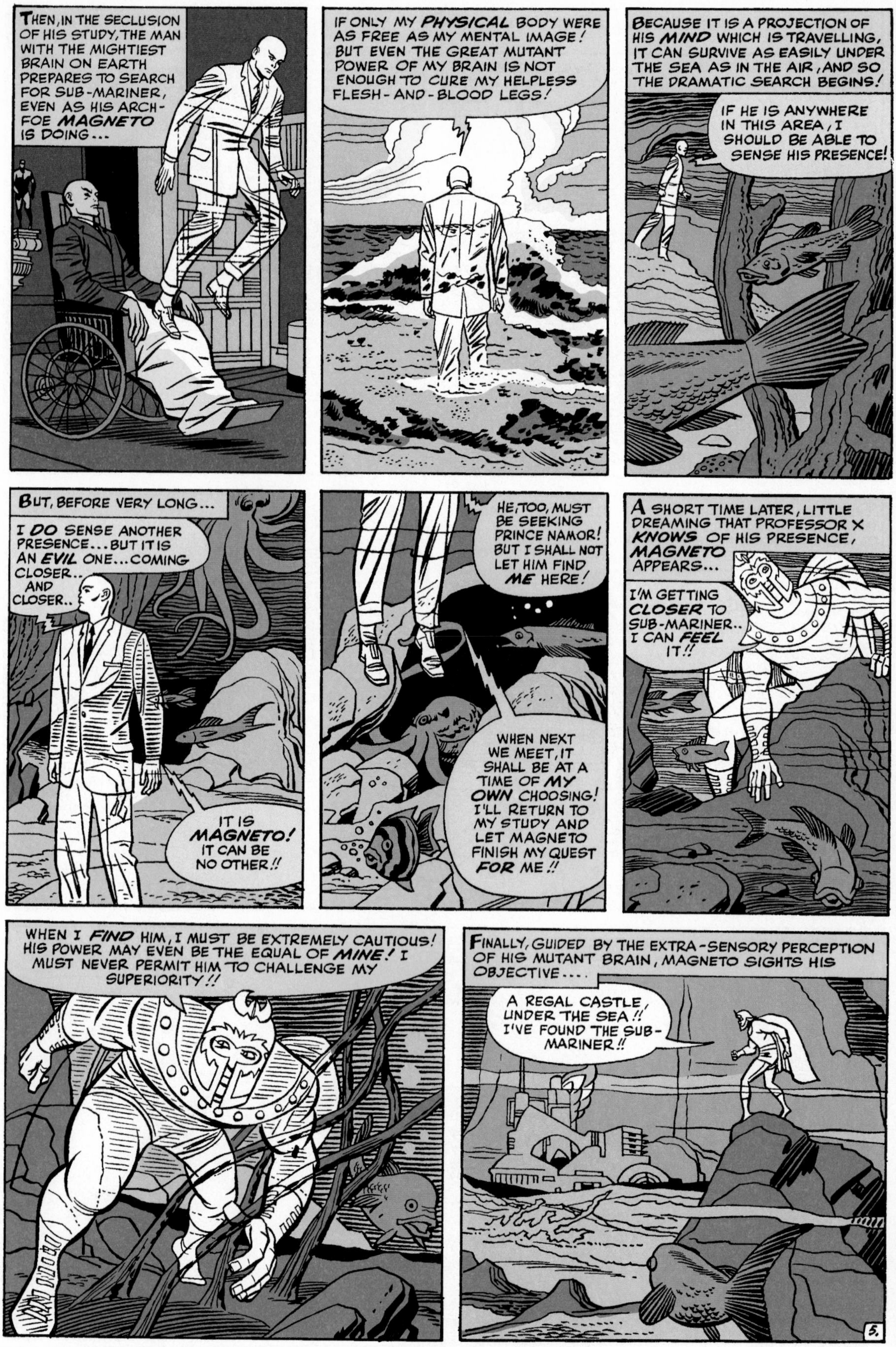
THEN, IN THE SECLUSION OF HIS STUDY, THE MAN WITH THE MIGHTIEST BRAIN ON EARTH PREPARES TO SEARCH FOR SUB-MARINER, EVEN AS HIS ARCH-FOE MAGNETO IS DOING...
IF ONLY MY PHYSICAL BODY WERE AS FREE AS MY MENTAL IMAGE! BUT EVEN THE GREAT MUTANT POWER OF MY BRAIN IS NOT ENOUGH TO CURE MY HELPLESS FLESH-AND-BLOOD LEGS!
BECAUSE IT IS A PROJECTION OF HIS MIND WHICH IS TRAVELLING, IT CAN SURVIVE AS EASILY UNDER THE SEA AS IN THE AIR, AND SO THE DRAMATIC SEARCH BEGINS!
IF HE IS ANYWHERE IN THIS AREA, I SHOULD BE ABLE TO SENSE HIS PRESENCE!
BUT, BEFORE VERY LONG...
I DO SENSE ANOTHER PRESENCE... BUT IT IS AN EVIL ONE... COMING CLOSER.. AND CLOSER..
IT IS MAGNETO! IT CAN BE NO OTHER!!
HE, TOO, MUST BE SEEKING PRINCE NAMOR! BUT I SHALL NOT LET HIM FIND ME HERE!
WHEN NEXT WE MEET, IT SHALL BE AT A TIME OF MY OWN CHOOSING! I'LL RETURN TO MY STUDY AND LET MAGNETO FINISH MY QUEST FOR ME!!
A SHORT TIME LATER, LITTLE DREAMING THAT PROFESSOR X KNOWS OF HIS PRESENCE, MAGNETO APPEARS...
I'M GETTING CLOSER TO SUB-MARINER.. I CAN FEEL IT!!
WHEN I FIND HIM, I MUST BE EXTREMELY CAUTIOUS! HIS POWER MAY EVEN BE THE EQUAL OF MINE! I MUST NEVER PERMIT HIM TO CHALLENGE MY SUPERIORITY!!
FINALLY, GUIDED BY THE EXTRA-SENSORY PERCEPTION OF HIS MUTANT BRAIN, MAGNETO SIGHTS HIS OBJECTIVE....
A REGAL CASTLE, UNDER THE SEA!! I'VE FOUND THE SUB-MARINER!!
5.

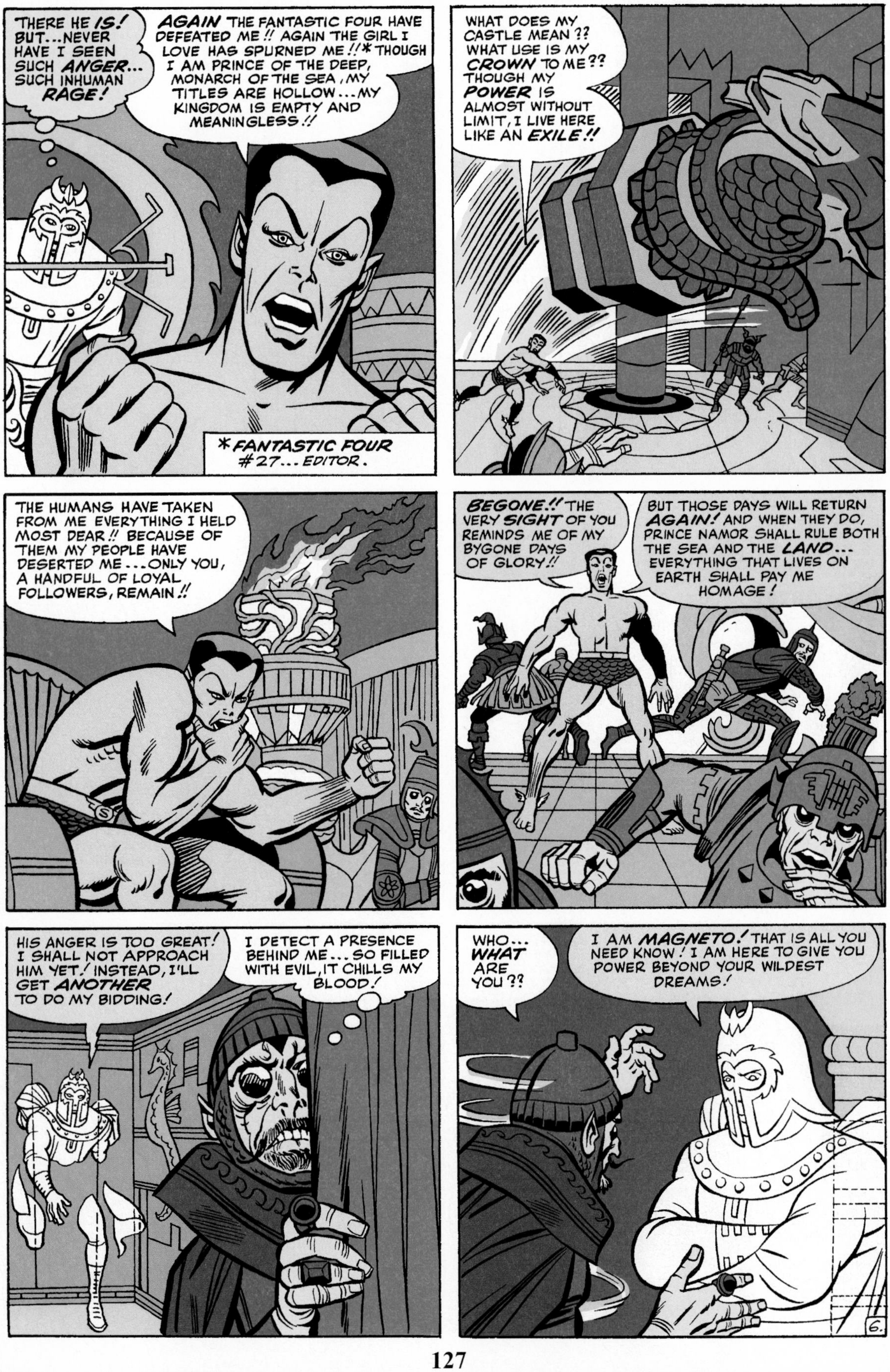

THERE HE IS! BUT...NEVER HAVE I SEEN SUCH ANGER... SUCH INHUMAN RAGE!
AGAIN THE FANTASTIC FOUR HAVE DEFEATED ME!! AGAIN THE GIRL I LOVE HAS SPURNED ME!!* THOUGH I AM PRINCE OF THE DEEP, MONARCH OF THE SEA, MY TITLES ARE HOLLOW...MY KINGDOM IS EMPTY AND MEANINGLESS!!
*FANTASTIC FOUR #27...EDITOR.
WHAT DOES MY CASTLE MEAN?? WHAT USE IS MY CROWN TO ME?? THOUGH MY POWER IS ALMOST WITHOUT LIMIT, I LIVE HERE LIKE AN EXILE!!
THE HUMANS HAVE TAKEN FROM ME EVERYTHING I HELD MOST DEAR!! BECAUSE OF THEM MY PEOPLE HAVE DESERTED ME...ONLY YOU, A HANDFUL OF LOYAL FOLLOWERS, REMAIN!!
BEGONE!! THE VERY SIGHT OF YOU REMINDS ME OF MY BYGONE DAYS OF GLORY!!
BUT THOSE DAYS WILL RETURN AGAIN! AND WHEN THEY DO, PRINCE NAMOR SHALL RULE BOTH THE SEA AND THE LAND... EVERYTHING THAT LIVES ON EARTH SHALL PAY ME HOMAGE!
HIS ANGER IS TOO GREAT! I SHALL NOT APPROACH HIM YET! INSTEAD, I'LL GET ANOTHER TO DO MY BIDDING!
I DETECT A PRESENCE BEHIND ME... SO FILLED WITH EVIL, IT CHILLS MY BLOOD!
WHO... WHAT ARE YOU??
I AM MAGNETO! THAT IS ALL YOU NEED KNOW! I AM HERE TO GIVE YOU POWER BEYOND YOUR WILDEST DREAMS!
6.

I HAVE CHOSEN WELL! I CAN SENSE THE GREED, AND THE ENVY IN THIS MAN'S HEART! HE IS PERFECT!

HOW WOULD YOU LIKE TO REPLACE PRINCE NAMOR AS RULER OF ATLANTIS?!

ME??! HOW??

JUST DO AS I SAY!! GIVE THE SUB-MARINER A *MESSAGE* FROM ME! REPEAT IT EXACTLY AS I TELL YOU TO!

WHY SHOULD I *TRUST* YOU?? WHAT *KIND* OF MESSAGE?

IT IS A MESSAGE THAT WILL MAKE SUB-MARINER *LEAVE* HERE TO JOIN ME... AND WITH HIM GONE... A CLEVER MAN MIGHT EASILY STEAL POWER....!!

HMM!

MEANWHILE, BACK AT HIS HEADQUARTERS, PROFESSOR X COMES OUT OF HIS TRANCE...

GATHER 'ROUND ME, MY X-MEN... WE ARE ABOUT TO BEGIN A NEW MISSION!

OH, BOY! AT *LAST*!!

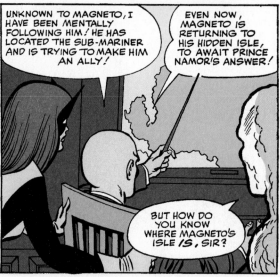

UNKNOWN TO MAGNETO, I HAVE BEEN MENTALLY FOLLOWING HIM! HE HAS LOCATED THE SUB-MARINER AND IS TRYING TO MAKE HIM AN ALLY!

EVEN NOW, MAGNETO IS RETURNING TO HIS HIDDEN ISLE, TO AWAIT PRINCE NAMOR'S ANSWER!

BUT HOW DO YOU KNOW WHERE MAGNETO'S ISLE *IS*, SIR?

"SOME DAYS AGO A FREIGHTER IN THE NORTH ATLANTIC REPORTED THAT ITS COMPASS SEEMED TO HAVE GONE MAD! I INVESTIGATED THE REPORT..!"

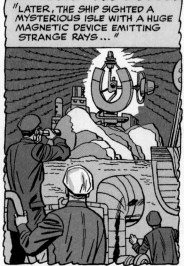

"LATER, THE SHIP SIGHTED A MYSTERIOUS ISLE WITH A HUGE MAGNETIC DEVICE EMITTING STRANGE RAYS ... "

"AND THEN, BEFORE THE CREW COULD BE SURE THEY WEREN'T DREAMING, OR HAVING A MASS HALLUCINATION, THE ENTIRE FREIGHTER SEEMED TO BE LIFTED BY AN IRRESISTIBLE MAGNETIC FORCE, AND WAS FINALLY PUT DOWN FIFTY MILES SOUTH OF BERMUDA!"

7

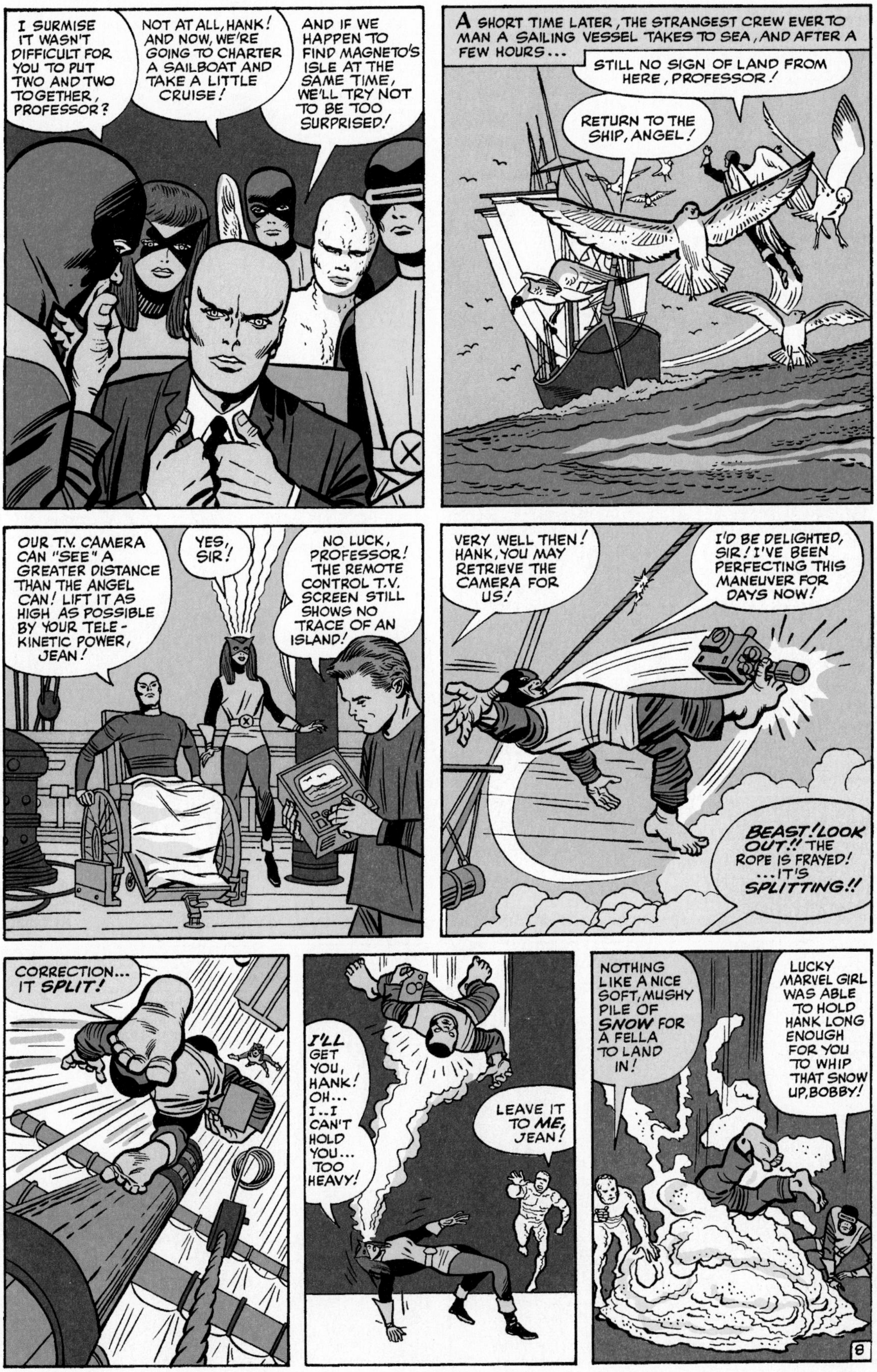
I SURMISE IT WASN'T DIFFICULT FOR YOU TO PUT TWO AND TWO TOGETHER, PROFESSOR?
NOT AT ALL, HANK! AND NOW, WE'RE GOING TO CHARTER A SAILBOAT AND TAKE A LITTLE CRUISE!
AND IF WE HAPPEN TO FIND MAGNETO'S ISLE AT THE SAME TIME, WE'LL TRY NOT TO BE TOO SURPRISED!
A SHORT TIME LATER, THE STRANGEST CREW EVER TO MAN A SAILING VESSEL TAKES TO SEA, AND AFTER A FEW HOURS...
STILL NO SIGN OF LAND FROM HERE, PROFESSOR!
RETURN TO THE SHIP, ANGEL!
OUR T.V. CAMERA CAN "SEE" A GREATER DISTANCE THAN THE ANGEL CAN! LIFT IT AS HIGH AS POSSIBLE BY YOUR TELE-KINETIC POWER, JEAN!
YES, SIR!
NO LUCK, PROFESSOR! THE REMOTE CONTROL T.V. SCREEN STILL SHOWS NO TRACE OF AN ISLAND!
VERY WELL THEN! HANK, YOU MAY RETRIEVE THE CAMERA FOR US!
I'D BE DELIGHTED, SIR! I'VE BEEN PERFECTING THIS MANEUVER FOR DAYS NOW!
BEAST! LOOK OUT!! THE ROPE IS FRAYED! ...IT'S SPLITTING!!
CORRECTION... IT SPLIT!
I'LL GET YOU, HANK! OH... I..I CAN'T HOLD YOU... TOO HEAVY!
LEAVE IT TO ME, JEAN!
NOTHING LIKE A NICE SOFT, MUSHY PILE OF SNOW FOR A FELLA TO LAND IN!
LUCKY MARVEL GIRL WAS ABLE TO HOLD HANK LONG ENOUGH FOR YOU TO WHIP THAT SNOW UP, BOBBY!
8

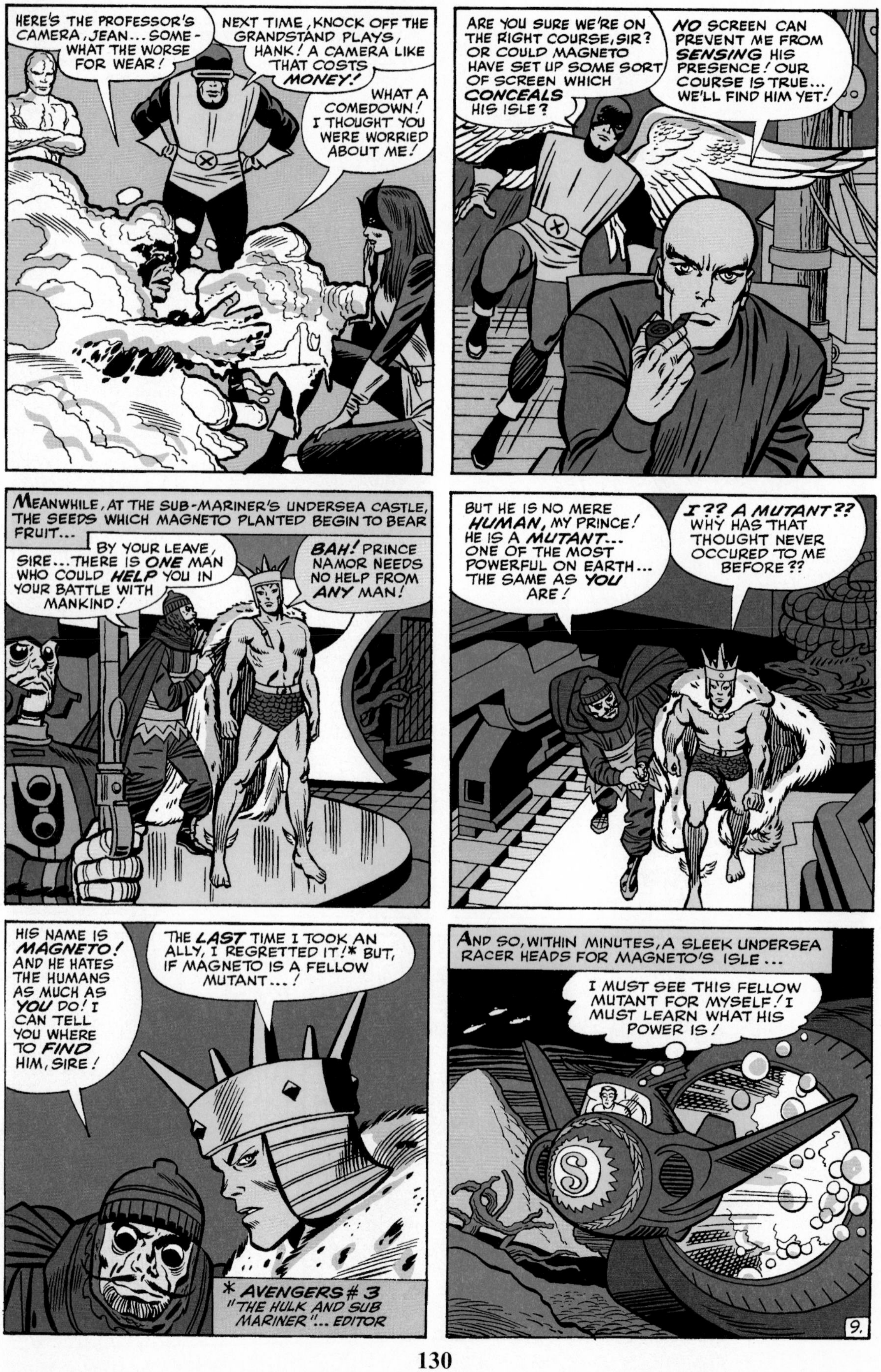
HERE'S THE PROFESSOR'S CAMERA, JEAN... SOME-WHAT THE WORSE FOR WEAR!
NEXT TIME, KNOCK OFF THE GRANDSTAND PLAYS, HANK! A CAMERA LIKE THAT COSTS MONEY!
WHAT A COMEDOWN! I THOUGHT YOU WERE WORRIED ABOUT ME!
ARE YOU SURE WE'RE ON THE RIGHT COURSE, SIR? OR COULD MAGNETO HAVE SET UP SOME SORT OF SCREEN WHICH CONCEALS HIS ISLE?
NO SCREEN CAN PREVENT ME FROM SENSING HIS PRESENCE! OUR COURSE IS TRUE... WE'LL FIND HIM YET!
MEANWHILE, AT THE SUB-MARINER'S UNDERSEA CASTLE, THE SEEDS WHICH MAGNETO PLANTED BEGIN TO BEAR FRUIT...
BY YOUR LEAVE, SIRE... THERE IS ONE MAN WHO COULD HELP YOU IN YOUR BATTLE WITH MANKIND!
BAH! PRINCE NAMOR NEEDS NO HELP FROM ANY MAN!
BUT HE IS NO MERE HUMAN, MY PRINCE! HE IS A MUTANT... ONE OF THE MOST POWERFUL ON EARTH... THE SAME AS YOU ARE!
I?? A MUTANT?? WHY HAS THAT THOUGHT NEVER OCCURED TO ME BEFORE??
HIS NAME IS MAGNETO! AND HE HATES THE HUMANS AS MUCH AS YOU DO! I CAN TELL YOU WHERE TO FIND HIM, SIRE!
THE LAST TIME I TOOK AN ALLY, I REGRETTED IT!* BUT, IF MAGNETO IS A FELLOW MUTANT...!
* AVENGERS #3 "THE HULK AND SUB MARINER"... EDITOR
AND SO, WITHIN MINUTES, A SLEEK UNDERSEA RACER HEADS FOR MAGNETO'S ISLE...
I MUST SEE THIS FELLOW MUTANT FOR MYSELF! I MUST LEARN WHAT HIS POWER IS!
9.

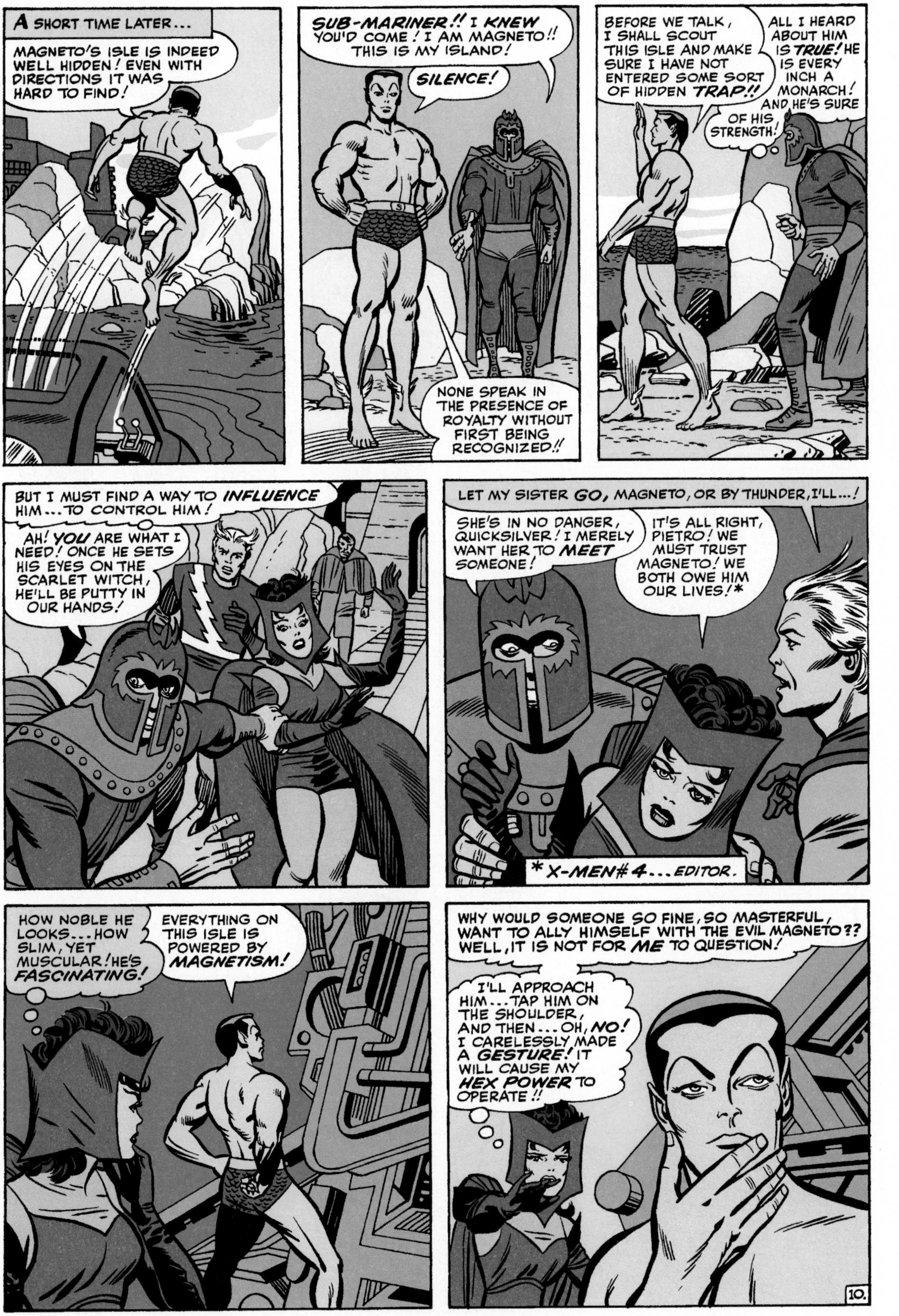
A SHORT TIME LATER...
MAGNETO'S ISLE IS INDEED WELL HIDDEN! EVEN WITH DIRECTIONS IT WAS HARD TO FIND!
SUB-MARINER!! I KNEW YOU'D COME! I AM MAGNETO!! THIS IS MY ISLAND!
SILENCE!
NONE SPEAK IN THE PRESENCE OF ROYALTY WITHOUT FIRST BEING RECOGNIZED!!
BEFORE WE TALK, I SHALL SCOUT THIS ISLE AND MAKE SURE I HAVE NOT ENTERED SOME SORT OF HIDDEN TRAP!!
ALL I HEARD ABOUT HIM IS TRUE! HE IS EVERY INCH A MONARCH! AND HE'S SURE OF HIS STRENGTH!
BUT I MUST FIND A WAY TO INFLUENCE HIM... TO CONTROL HIM!
AH! YOU ARE WHAT I NEED! ONCE HE SETS HIS EYES ON THE SCARLET WITCH, HE'LL BE PUTTY IN OUR HANDS!
LET MY SISTER GO, MAGNETO, OR BY THUNDER, I'LL...!
SHE'S IN NO DANGER, QUICKSILVER! I MERELY WANT HER TO MEET SOMEONE!
IT'S ALL RIGHT, PIETRO! WE MUST TRUST MAGNETO! WE BOTH OWE HIM OUR LIVES!*
*X-MEN#4... EDITOR.
HOW NOBLE HE LOOKS... HOW SLIM, YET MUSCULAR! HE'S FASCINATING!
EVERYTHING ON THIS ISLE IS POWERED BY MAGNETISM!
WHY WOULD SOMEONE SO FINE, SO MASTERFUL, WANT TO ALLY HIMSELF WITH THE EVIL MAGNETO?? WELL, IT IS NOT FOR ME TO QUESTION!
I'LL APPROACH HIM... TAP HIM ON THE SHOULDER, AND THEN... OH, NO! I CARELESSLY MADE A GESTURE! IT WILL CAUSE MY HEX POWER TO OPERATE!!
10.

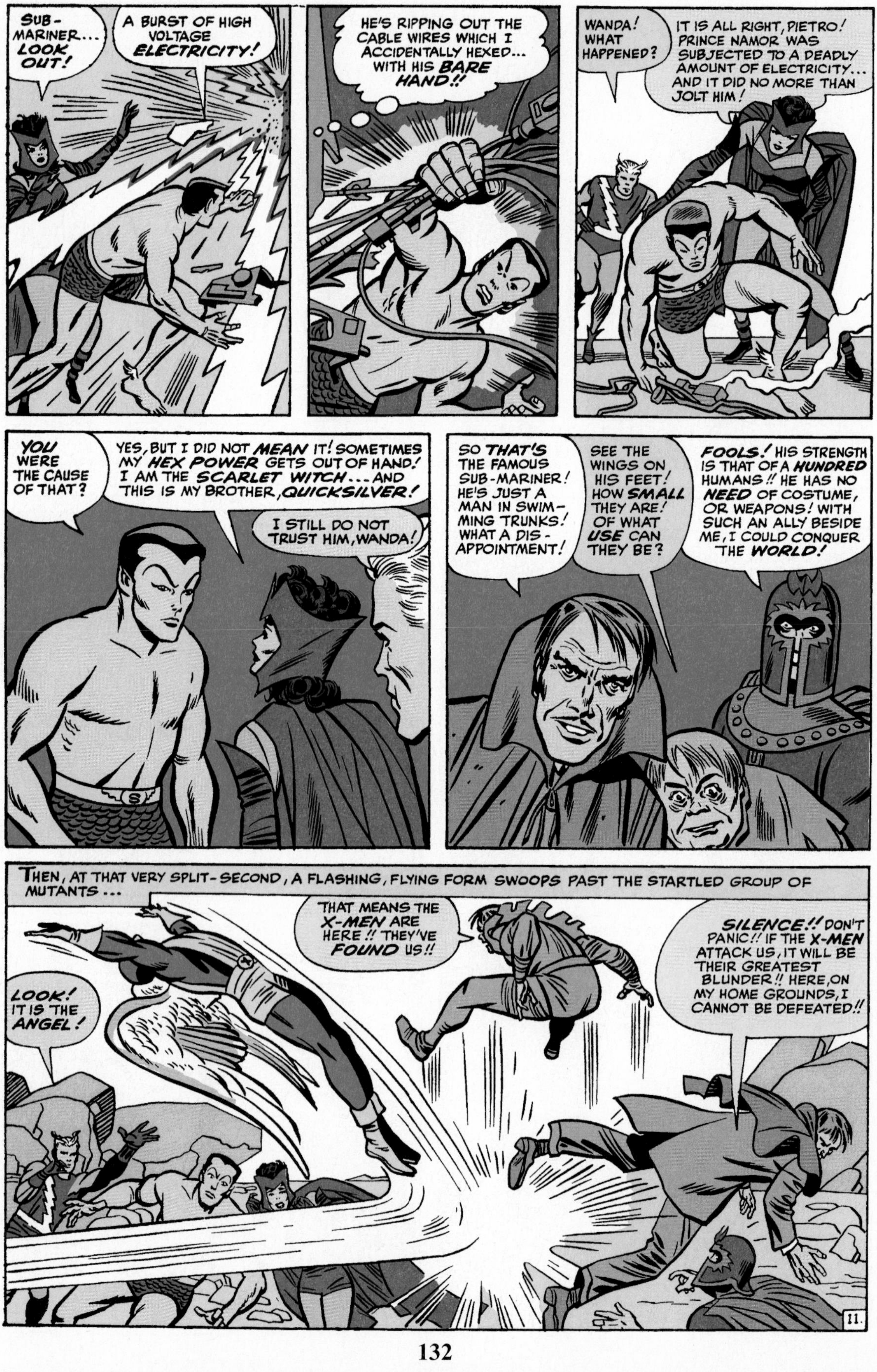
SUB-MARINER... LOOK OUT!
A BURST OF HIGH VOLTAGE ELECTRICITY!
HE'S RIPPING OUT THE CABLE WIRES WHICH I ACCIDENTALLY HEXED... WITH HIS BARE HAND!!
WANDA! WHAT HAPPENED?
IT IS ALL RIGHT, PIETRO! PRINCE NAMOR WAS SUBJECTED TO A DEADLY AMOUNT OF ELECTRICITY... AND IT DID NO MORE THAN JOLT HIM!
YOU WERE THE CAUSE OF THAT?
YES, BUT I DID NOT MEAN IT! SOMETIMES MY HEX POWER GETS OUT OF HAND! I AM THE SCARLET WITCH... AND THIS IS MY BROTHER, QUICKSILVER!
I STILL DO NOT TRUST HIM, WANDA!
SO THAT'S THE FAMOUS SUB-MARINER! HE'S JUST A MAN IN SWIM-MING TRUNKS! WHAT A DIS-APPOINTMENT!
SEE THE WINGS ON HIS FEET! HOW SMALL THEY ARE! OF WHAT USE CAN THEY BE?
FOOLS! HIS STRENGTH IS THAT OF A HUNDRED HUMANS!! HE HAS NO NEED OF COSTUME, OR WEAPONS! WITH SUCH AN ALLY BESIDE ME, I COULD CONQUER THE WORLD!
THEN, AT THAT VERY SPLIT-SECOND, A FLASHING, FLYING FORM SWOOPS PAST THE STARTLED GROUP OF MUTANTS...
LOOK! IT IS THE ANGEL!
THAT MEANS THE X-MEN ARE HERE!! THEY'VE FOUND US!!
SILENCE!! DON'T PANIC!! IF THE X-MEN ATTACK US, IT WILL BE THEIR GREATEST BLUNDER!! HERE, ON MY HOME GROUNDS, I CANNOT BE DEFEATED!!
11.

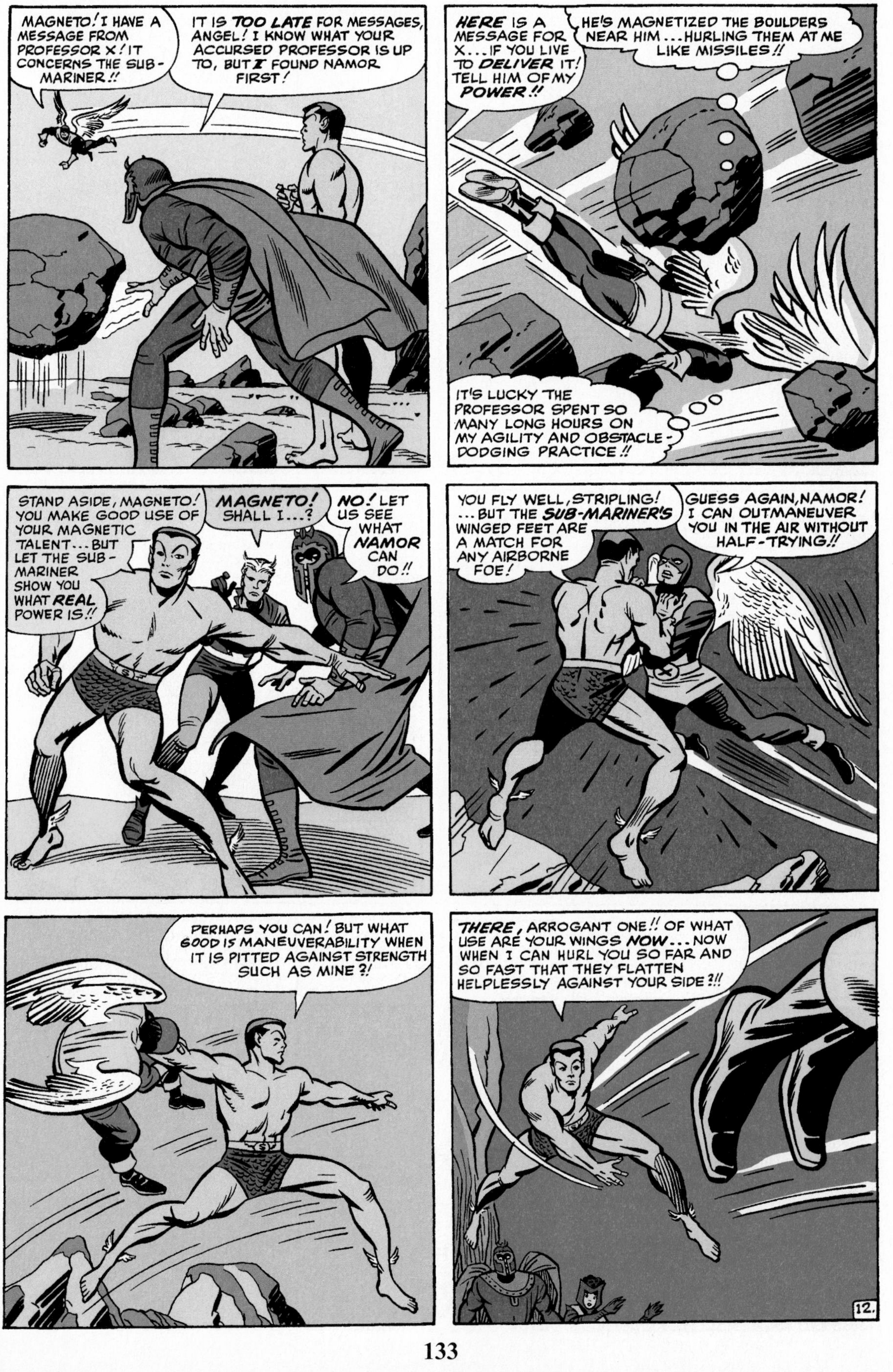
MAGNETO! I HAVE A MESSAGE FROM PROFESSOR X! IT CONCERNS THE SUB-MARINER!!
IT IS TOO LATE FOR MESSAGES, ANGEL! I KNOW WHAT YOUR ACCURSED PROFESSOR IS UP TO, BUT I FOUND NAMOR FIRST!
HERE IS A MESSAGE FOR X... IF YOU LIVE TO DELIVER IT! TELL HIM OF MY POWER!!
HE'S MAGNETIZED THE BOULDERS NEAR HIM... HURLING THEM AT ME LIKE MISSILES!!
IT'S LUCKY THE PROFESSOR SPENT SO MANY LONG HOURS ON MY AGILITY AND OBSTACLE-DODGING PRACTICE!!
STAND ASIDE, MAGNETO! YOU MAKE GOOD USE OF YOUR MAGNETIC TALENT... BUT LET THE SUB-MARINER SHOW YOU WHAT REAL POWER IS!!
MAGNETO! SHALL I...?
NO! LET US SEE WHAT NAMOR CAN DO!!
YOU FLY WELL, STRIPLING! ...BUT THE SUB-MARINER'S WINGED FEET ARE A MATCH FOR ANY AIRBORNE FOE!
GUESS AGAIN, NAMOR! I CAN OUTMANEUVER YOU IN THE AIR WITHOUT HALF-TRYING!!
PERHAPS YOU CAN! BUT WHAT GOOD IS MANEUVERABILITY WHEN IT IS PITTED AGAINST STRENGTH SUCH AS MINE?!
THERE, ARROGANT ONE!! OF WHAT USE ARE YOUR WINGS NOW... NOW WHEN I CAN HURL YOU SO FAR AND SO FAST THAT THEY FLATTEN HELPLESSLY AGAINST YOUR SIDE?!!
12.

A SHORT DISTANCE AWAY, AN ALARM IS SOUNDED...

HANK! ANGEL IS HEADING THIS WAY! HE NEEDS HELP!

HE'S COMING LIKE A **BULLET!** BUT DON'T WORRY...I'LL RETARD HIS PROGRESS!

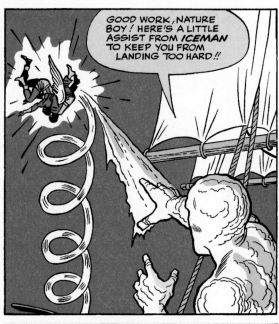

GOOD WORK, NATURE BOY! HERE'S A LITTLE ASSIST FROM **ICEMAN** TO KEEP YOU FROM LANDING TOO HARD!!

FREEZING ON IMPACT, THE SPRAY OF ICE WHICH BOBBY DRAKE HURLED UPWARDS TOWARDS HIS TWO PARTNERS BECOMES A MAKESHIFT **SLIDE,** ENABLING THEM TO REACH THE SHIP SAFELY!

SORRY I DON'T HAVE TIME TO SEND YOU A **SLED,** FELLAS...BUT I GUESS YOU'LL FORGIVE ME!

THAT WAS QUICK-THINKING, HANK! THE PROFESSOR WAS PLEASED!

SPEAKING OF THE PROFESSOR...HE WANTS ANGEL TO REPORT TO HIM AT ONCE!

AND SO...

YOU WERE **RIGHT,** SIR! SUB-MARINER **IS** ON THE ISLE WITH MAGNETO!

THAT'S WHAT I **FEARED!** WE MAY ALREADY BE TOO LATE!

WHAT'S OUR NEXT MOVE, PROFESSOR?

WE CAN'T WASTE A MINUTE! WE'VE GOT TO HIT THEM **FAST..** HIT THEM **HARD!** PREPARE FOR **ACTION,** MY X-MEN!

BUT, KNOWING THE POWER OF THE X-MEN, MAGNETO, **TOO,** PREPARES TO ATTACK, AS THE LARGEST MAGNET ON EARTH IS ZEROED IN ON THE X-MEN'S SHIP!!

13.

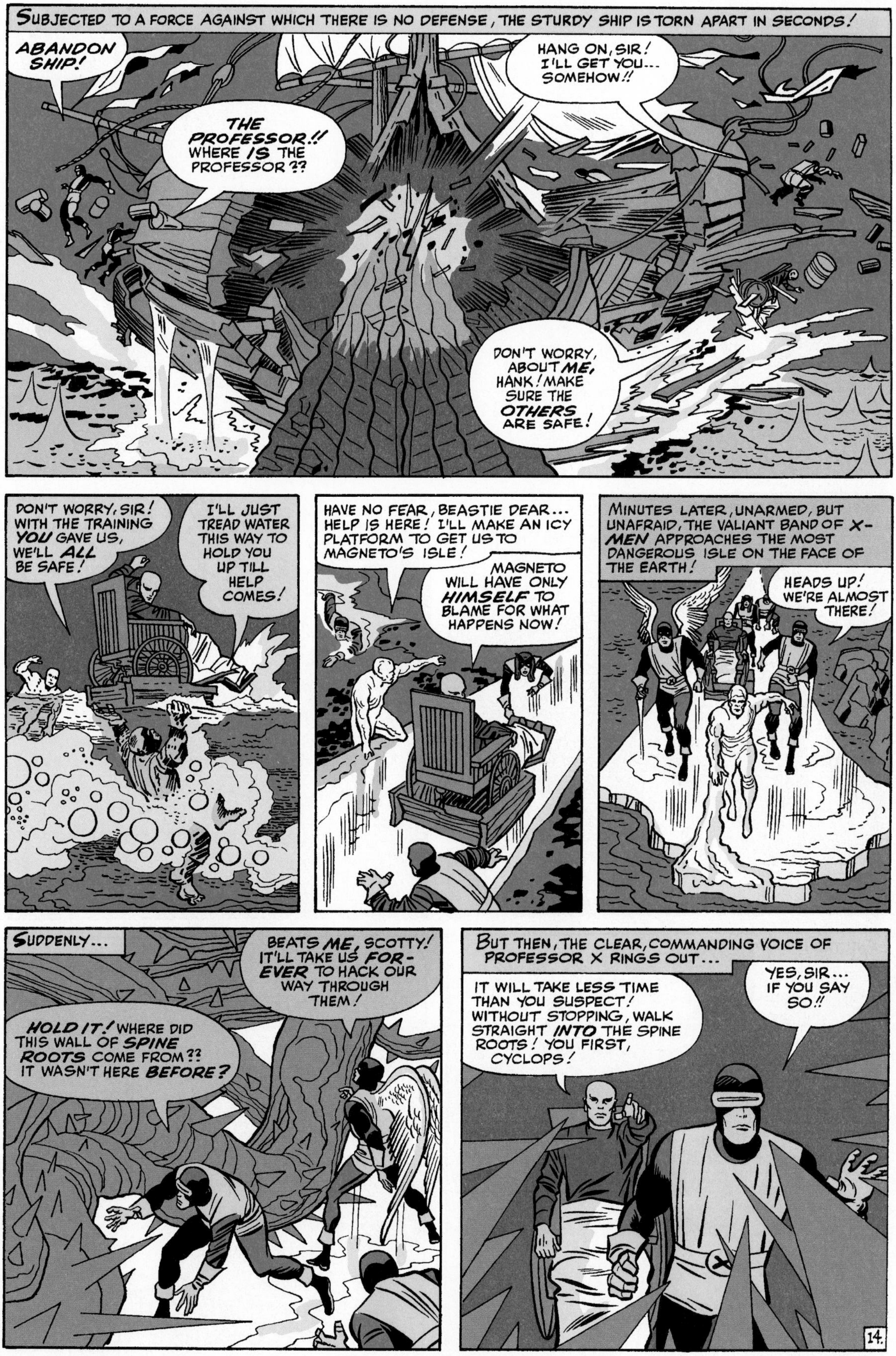
SUBJECTED TO A FORCE AGAINST WHICH THERE IS NO DEFENSE, THE STURDY SHIP IS TORN APART IN SECONDS!
ABANDON SHIP!
THE PROFESSOR!! WHERE IS THE PROFESSOR??
HANG ON, SIR! I'LL GET YOU... SOMEHOW!!
DON'T WORRY, ABOUT ME, HANK! MAKE SURE THE OTHERS ARE SAFE!
DON'T WORRY, SIR! WITH THE TRAINING YOU GAVE US, WE'LL ALL BE SAFE!
I'LL JUST TREAD WATER THIS WAY TO HOLD YOU UP TILL HELP COMES!
HAVE NO FEAR, BEASTIE DEAR... HELP IS HERE! I'LL MAKE AN ICY PLATFORM TO GET US TO MAGNETO'S ISLE!
MAGNETO WILL HAVE ONLY HIMSELF TO BLAME FOR WHAT HAPPENS NOW!
MINUTES LATER, UNARMED, BUT UNAFRAID, THE VALIANT BAND OF X-MEN APPROACHES THE MOST DANGEROUS ISLE ON THE FACE OF THE EARTH!
HEADS UP! WE'RE ALMOST THERE!
SUDDENLY...
HOLD IT! WHERE DID THIS WALL OF SPINE ROOTS COME FROM?? IT WASN'T HERE BEFORE?
BEATS ME, SCOTTY! IT'LL TAKE US FOR-EVER TO HACK OUR WAY THROUGH THEM!
BUT THEN, THE CLEAR, COMMANDING VOICE OF PROFESSOR X RINGS OUT...
IT WILL TAKE LESS TIME THAN YOU SUSPECT! WITHOUT STOPPING, WALK STRAIGHT INTO THE SPINE ROOTS! YOU FIRST, CYCLOPS!
YES, SIR... IF YOU SAY SO!!
14.

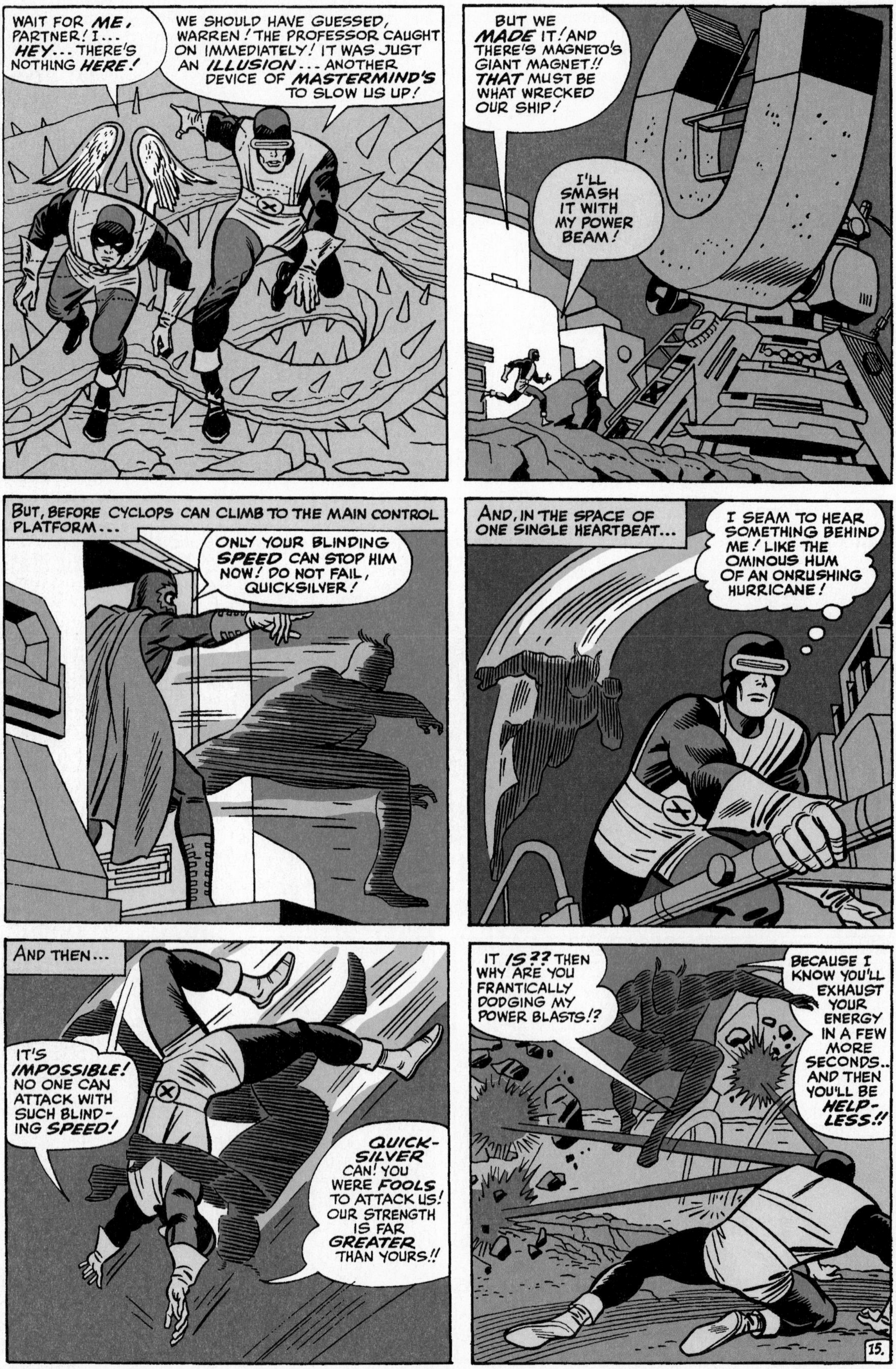

WAIT FOR ME, PARTNER! I... HEY... THERE'S NOTHING HERE!
WE SHOULD HAVE GUESSED, WARREN! THE PROFESSOR CAUGHT ON IMMEDIATELY! IT WAS JUST AN ILLUSION... ANOTHER DEVICE OF MASTERMIND'S TO SLOW US UP!
BUT WE MADE IT! AND THERE'S MAGNETO'S GIANT MAGNET!! THAT MUST BE WHAT WRECKED OUR SHIP!
I'LL SMASH IT WITH MY POWER BEAM!
BUT, BEFORE CYCLOPS CAN CLIMB TO THE MAIN CONTROL PLATFORM...
ONLY YOUR BLINDING SPEED CAN STOP HIM NOW! DO NOT FAIL, QUICKSILVER!
AND, IN THE SPACE OF ONE SINGLE HEARTBEAT...
I SEAM TO HEAR SOMETHING BEHIND ME! LIKE THE OMINOUS HUM OF AN ONRUSHING HURRICANE!
AND THEN...
IT'S IMPOSSIBLE! NO ONE CAN ATTACK WITH SUCH BLINDING SPEED!
QUICKSILVER CAN! YOU WERE FOOLS TO ATTACK US! OUR STRENGTH IS FAR GREATER THAN YOURS!!
IT IS?? THEN WHY ARE YOU FRANTICALLY DODGING MY POWER BLASTS!?
BECAUSE I KNOW YOU'LL EXHAUST YOUR ENERGY IN A FEW MORE SECONDS.. AND THEN YOU'LL BE HELPLESS!!
15.

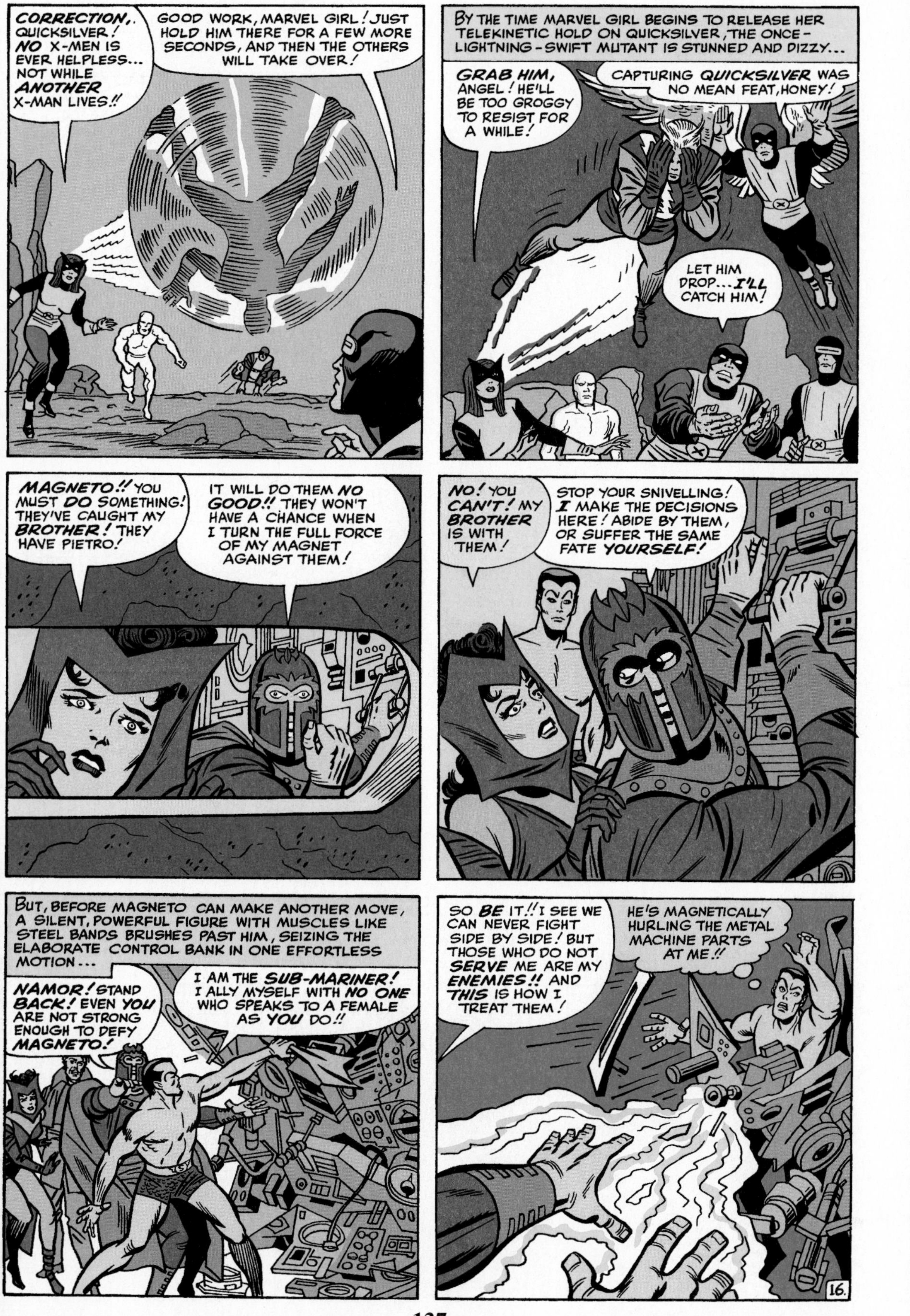
CORRECTION, QUICKSILVER! NO X-MEN IS EVER HELPLESS... NOT WHILE ANOTHER X-MAN LIVES!!
GOOD WORK, MARVEL GIRL! JUST HOLD HIM THERE FOR A FEW MORE SECONDS, AND THEN THE OTHERS WILL TAKE OVER!
BY THE TIME MARVEL GIRL BEGINS TO RELEASE HER TELEKINETIC HOLD ON QUICKSILVER, THE ONCE-LIGHTNING-SWIFT MUTANT IS STUNNED AND DIZZY...
GRAB HIM, ANGEL! HE'LL BE TOO GROGGY TO RESIST FOR A WHILE!
CAPTURING QUICKSILVER WAS NO MEAN FEAT, HONEY!
LET HIM DROP... I'LL CATCH HIM!
MAGNETO!! YOU MUST DO SOMETHING! THEY'VE CAUGHT MY BROTHER! THEY HAVE PIETRO!
IT WILL DO THEM NO GOOD!! THEY WON'T HAVE A CHANCE WHEN I TURN THE FULL FORCE OF MY MAGNET AGAINST THEM!
NO! YOU CAN'T! MY BROTHER IS WITH THEM!
STOP YOUR SNIVELLING! I MAKE THE DECISIONS HERE! ABIDE BY THEM, OR SUFFER THE SAME FATE YOURSELF!
BUT, BEFORE MAGNETO CAN MAKE ANOTHER MOVE, A SILENT, POWERFUL FIGURE WITH MUSCLES LIKE STEEL BANDS BRUSHES PAST HIM, SEIZING THE ELABORATE CONTROL BANK IN ONE EFFORTLESS MOTION...
NAMOR! STAND BACK! EVEN YOU ARE NOT STRONG ENOUGH TO DEFY MAGNETO!
I AM THE SUB-MARINER! I ALLY MYSELF WITH NO ONE WHO SPEAKS TO A FEMALE AS YOU DO!!
SO BE IT!! I SEE WE CAN NEVER FIGHT SIDE BY SIDE! BUT THOSE WHO DO NOT SERVE ME ARE MY ENEMIES!! AND THIS IS HOW I TREAT THEM!
HE'S MAGNETICALLY HURLING THE METAL MACHINE PARTS AT ME!!
16.

I CAN'T SHAKE THESE METAL PIECES OFF ME!! HE'S PRESSING THEM TIGHTER AND TIGHTER... MENTALLY!

I REALIZE NOW THAT I MISJUDGED YOU! ALL YOU POSSESS IS BRUTE STRENGTH! MY POWER IS MUCH GREATER...FOR IT IS THE UNIVERSAL POWER OF MAGNETISM!

BUT, AT THAT MOMENT, A SUDDEN BLAST ROCKS THE CHAMBER, JOLTING MAGNETO AND HIS TWO EVIL HENCHMEN AS THE VERY ISLE SEEMS TO QUIVER WITH THE FORCE OF THE BLAST!

AND THEN, BEFORE THE EVIL MUTANTS REGAIN THEIR BALANCE...

YOU WERE RIGHT ON TARGET, CYCLOPS!

ONE THING ABOUT YOU, SCOTTY...YOU SURE KNOW HOW TO MAKE AN ENTRANCE!

QUICK...RUSH THEM BEFORE THEY RECOVER THEMSELVES!

MAGNETO HAS FLED! WE'RE ALONE! QUICK, MASTERMIND! SAVE US FROM THE X-MEN!

I'VE GOT TO ACT FAST BEFORE HE GETS ME WITH THAT ACCURSED BEAM OF HIS!

GOOD! THE OTHER X-MEN ARE AT HIS SIDE NOW...THIS IS OUR ONLY CHANCE... AN HYPNOTIC ILLUSION WHICH CANNOT FAIL!

WHERE DID THIS SUDDEN FOG COME FROM?

IT WASN'T HERE A SECOND AGO!

IT'S ONE OF MASTERMIND'S ILLUSIONS! IT HAS TO BE!

ILLUSION OR NOT...WE CAN'T SEE!

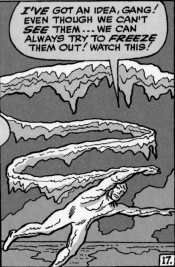

I'VE GOT AN IDEA, GANG! EVEN THOUGH WE CAN'T SEE THEM...WE CAN ALWAYS TRY TO FREEZE THEM OUT! WATCH THIS!

17.

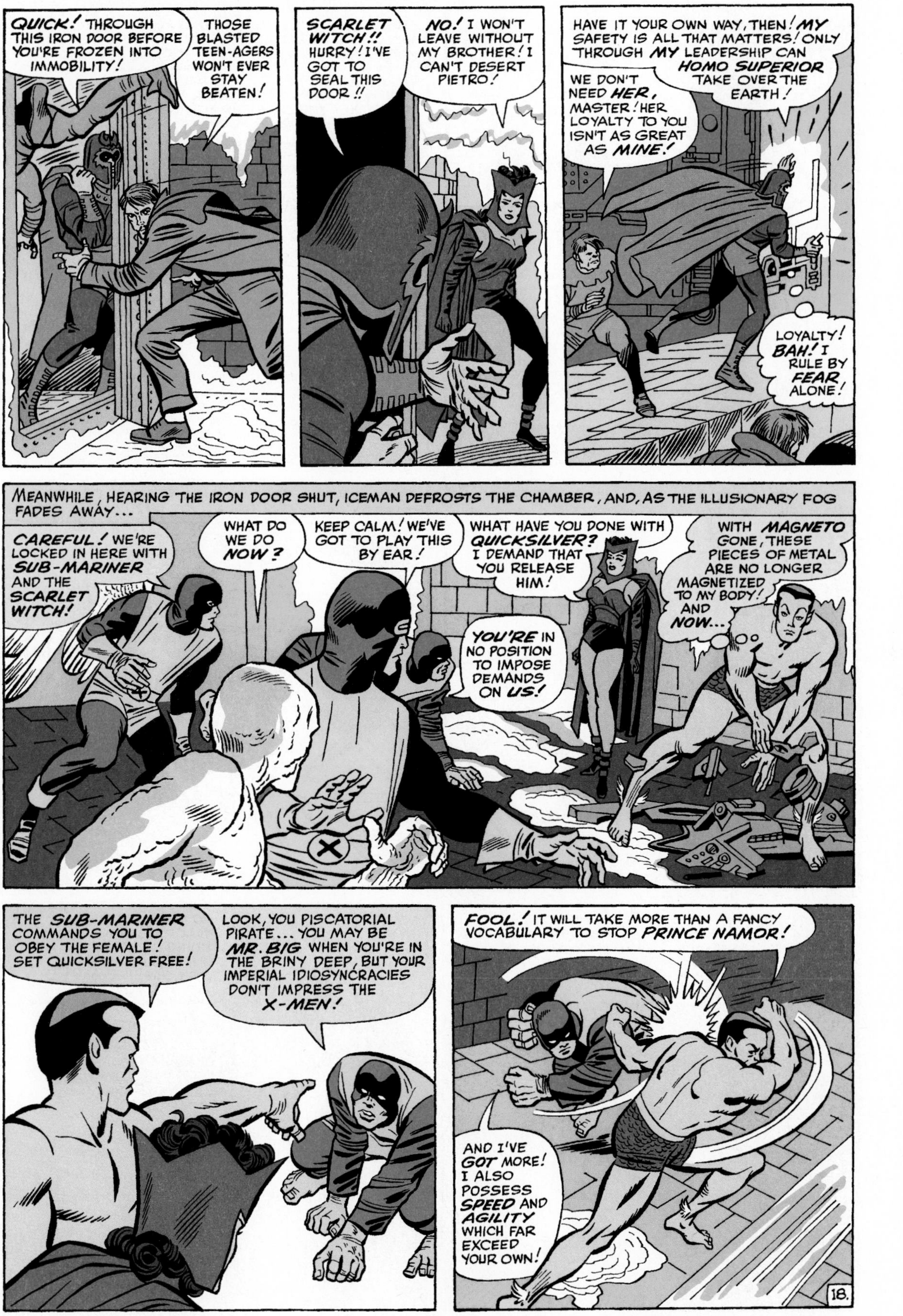

QUICK! THROUGH THIS IRON DOOR BEFORE YOU'RE FROZEN INTO IMMOBILITY!
THOSE BLASTED TEEN-AGERS WON'T EVER STAY BEATEN!
SCARLET WITCH!! HURRY! I'VE GOT TO SEAL THIS DOOR!!
NO! I WON'T LEAVE WITHOUT MY BROTHER! I CAN'T DESERT PIETRO!
HAVE IT YOUR OWN WAY, THEN! MY SAFETY IS ALL THAT MATTERS! ONLY THROUGH MY LEADERSHIP CAN HOMO SUPERIOR TAKE OVER THE EARTH!
WE DON'T NEED HER, MASTER! HER LOYALTY TO YOU ISN'T AS GREAT AS MINE!
LOYALTY! BAH! I RULE BY FEAR ALONE!
MEANWHILE, HEARING THE IRON DOOR SHUT, ICEMAN DEFROSTS THE CHAMBER, AND, AS THE ILLUSIONARY FOG FADES AWAY...
CAREFUL! WE'RE LOCKED IN HERE WITH SUB-MARINER AND THE SCARLET WITCH!
WHAT DO WE DO NOW?
KEEP CALM! WE'VE GOT TO PLAY THIS BY EAR!
WHAT HAVE YOU DONE WITH QUICKSILVER? I DEMAND THAT YOU RELEASE HIM!
YOU'RE IN NO POSITION TO IMPOSE DEMANDS ON US!
WITH MAGNETO GONE, THESE PIECES OF METAL ARE NO LONGER MAGNETIZED TO MY BODY! AND NOW...
THE SUB-MARINER COMMANDS YOU TO OBEY THE FEMALE! SET QUICKSILVER FREE!
LOOK, YOU PISCATORIAL PIRATE... YOU MAY BE MR. BIG WHEN YOU'RE IN THE BRINY DEEP, BUT YOUR IMPERIAL IDIOSYNCRACIES DON'T IMPRESS THE X-MEN!
FOOL! IT WILL TAKE MORE THAN A FANCY VOCABULARY TO STOP PRINCE NAMOR!
AND I'VE GOT MORE! I ALSO POSSESS SPEED AND AGILITY WHICH FAR EXCEED YOUR OWN!
18.

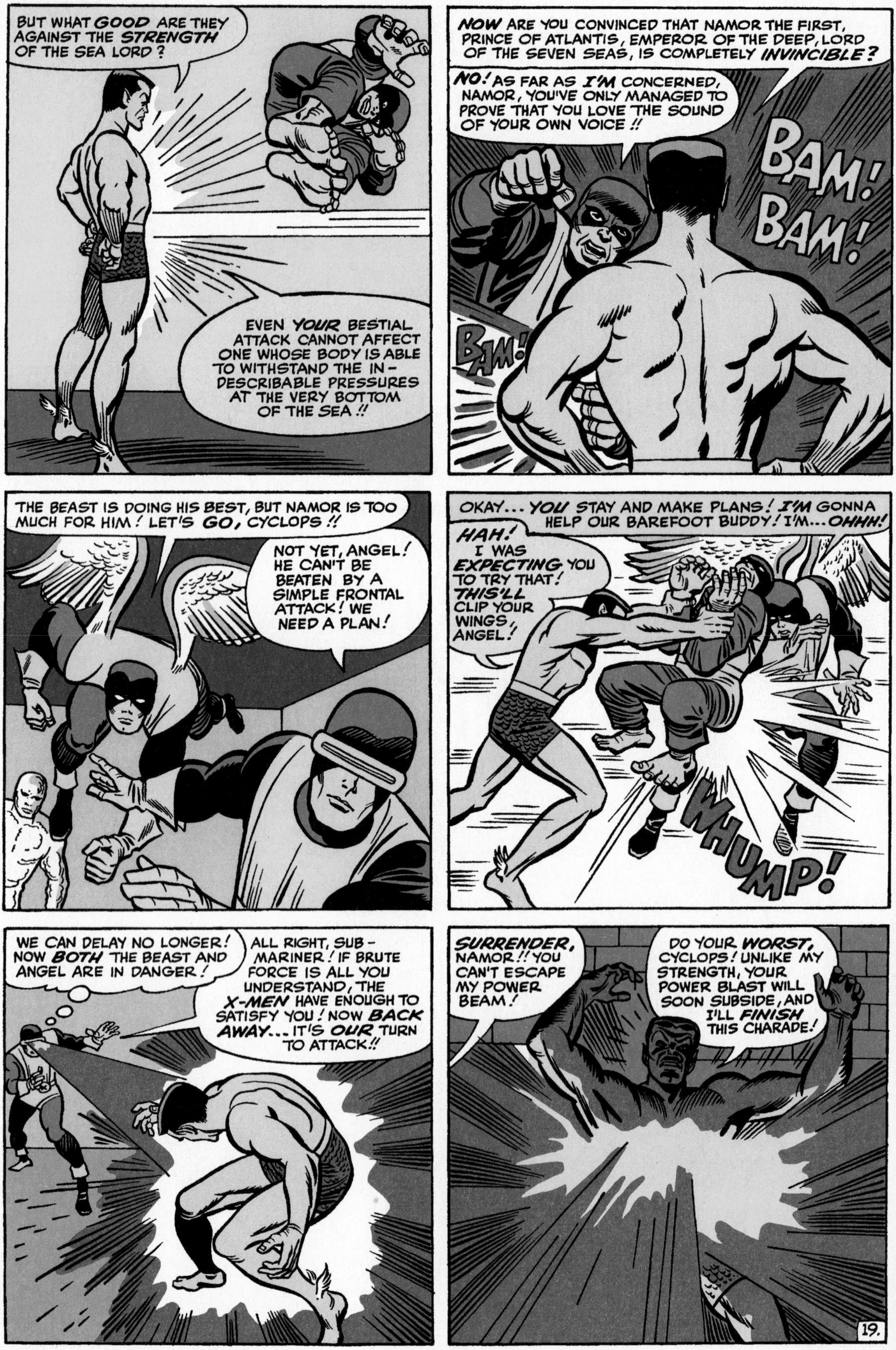
BUT WHAT GOOD ARE THEY AGAINST THE STRENGTH OF THE SEA LORD?
EVEN YOUR BESTIAL ATTACK CANNOT AFFECT ONE WHOSE BODY IS ABLE TO WITHSTAND THE IN-DESCRIBABLE PRESSURES AT THE VERY BOTTOM OF THE SEA!!
NOW ARE YOU CONVINCED THAT NAMOR THE FIRST, PRINCE OF ATLANTIS, EMPEROR OF THE DEEP, LORD OF THE SEVEN SEAS, IS COMPLETELY INVINCIBLE?
NO! AS FAR AS I'M CONCERNED, NAMOR, YOU'VE ONLY MANAGED TO PROVE THAT YOU LOVE THE SOUND OF YOUR OWN VOICE!!
BAM! BAM!
BAM!
THE BEAST IS DOING HIS BEST, BUT NAMOR IS TOO MUCH FOR HIM! LET'S GO, CYCLOPS!!
NOT YET, ANGEL! HE CAN'T BE BEATEN BY A SIMPLE FRONTAL ATTACK! WE NEED A PLAN!
OKAY... YOU STAY AND MAKE PLANS! I'M GONNA HELP OUR BAREFOOT BUDDY! I'M... OHHH!
HAH! I WAS EXPECTING YOU TO TRY THAT! THIS'LL CLIP YOUR WINGS, ANGEL!
WHUMP!
WE CAN DELAY NO LONGER! NOW BOTH THE BEAST AND ANGEL ARE IN DANGER!
ALL RIGHT, SUB-MARINER! IF BRUTE FORCE IS ALL YOU UNDERSTAND, THE X-MEN HAVE ENOUGH TO SATISFY YOU! NOW BACK AWAY... IT'S OUR TURN TO ATTACK!!
SURRENDER, NAMOR!! YOU CAN'T ESCAPE MY POWER BEAM!
DO YOUR WORST, CYCLOPS! UNLIKE MY STRENGTH, YOUR POWER BLAST WILL SOON SUBSIDE, AND I'LL FINISH THIS CHARADE!
19.

DON'T UNDERESTIMATE ME, NAMOR! DON'T MAKE ME USE MY *FULL INTENSITY!* THIS IS YOUR LAST CHANCE.

NAMOR TRIED TO *HELP* ME! I MUST RETURN THE FAVOR! I'LL USE MY *HEX POWER* ON THE FEARLESS X-MAN!

NO SOONER DOES THE *SCARLET WITCH* UNLEASH HER UNCANNY *HEX*, THEN THE VERY STONES SUDDENLY LOOSEN UNDER CYCLOPS' FEET, AND...

WHA...?? I LOST MY BALANCE!!

YOU *HAD* YOUR CHANCE, CYCLOPS! BUT NOW, BEFORE YOU CAN RECOVER YOURSELF, YOU'LL FEEL THE MIGHTY WRATH OF *NAMOR!*

HALT!

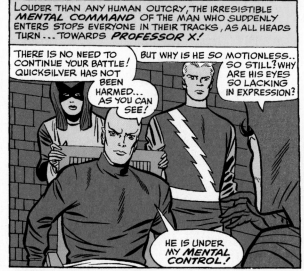

LOUDER THAN ANY HUMAN OUTCRY, THE IRRESISTIBLE *MENTAL COMMAND* OF THE MAN WHO SUDDENLY ENTERS STOPS EVERYONE IN THEIR TRACKS, AS ALL HEADS TURN...TOWARDS *PROFESSOR X!*

THERE IS NO NEED TO CONTINUE YOUR BATTLE! QUICKSILVER HAS NOT BEEN HARMED... AS YOU CAN SEE!

BUT WHY IS HE SO MOTIONLESS.. SO STILL? WHY ARE HIS EYES SO LACKING IN EXPRESSION?

HE IS UNDER MY *MENTAL CONTROL!*

NO! YOU MUST NOT DO THIS DREADFUL THING! *RELEASE HIS BRAIN!* LET HIM BE AS HE WAS!

I SHALL! YOU HAVE NOTHING TO FEAR! MY FIGHT IS NOT WITH YOU...NOR WITH NAMOR! *MAGNETO* IS THE REAL ENEMY! ALL OF YOU ARE BUT *PAWNS!*

PAWNS?!! WHO DARES CALL THE *SUB-MARINER* A PAWN?? *PROTECT YOURSELVES,* X-MEN! WE'LL *SEE* WHICH OF US ARE THE PAWNS!!

NO, NAMOR!! PLEASE..! NOT UNTIL QUICKSILVER IS HIMSELF AGAIN! NOT UNTIL PROFESSOR X RELEASES HIS MENTAL CONTROL!

MARVEL GIRL! PUSH THE PROFESSOR TO SAFETY! *WE'LL* STOP NAMOR!

STAND FAST, MY X-MEN! THE SUB-MARINER IS NO MURDERER! HE WILL NOT STRIKE IF WE DON'T PROVOKE HIM!

TOUCH PROFESSOR X, AND THE OCEAN WON'T BE BIG ENOUGH TO HIDE YOU, NAMOR!

20.

141

AND NOW, I SHALL RELEASE QUICKSILVER! I MUST KEEP MY MIND UNFETTERED, IN READINESS FOR THE BIGGER BATTLE WITH *MAGNETO!*

MAGNETO!! WHAT HAS HAPPENED TO HIM?? WHERE HAS HE GONE? WHAT WILL HE *DO* ABOUT PIETRO AND ME??

I FEEL AS THOUGH I'VE BEEN ASLEEP! MY HEAD FEELS NUMB... DAZED!

BAH! I WAS A FOOL TO HAVE COME HERE! THE *SUB-MARINER* NEEDS NO ALLIANCES! *ALL* SURFACEMEN ARE MY ENEMIES... WHETHER MUTANT OR NOT! I SHALL RETURN TO THE DEEP... WHERE I BELONG!

WHEN NEXT I RETURN, IT SHALL BE TO TAKE MY RIGHTFUL PLACE AS *CONQUEROR* OF THE AIR-BREATHERS, RECLAIMER OF THE SURFACE WORLD FOR THE ANCIENT EMPIRE OF ATLANTIS!!

PROFESSOR!! HE'S *ESCAPING!*

LET HIM GO! SO LONG AS HE DOES NOT JOIN MAGNETO'S MUTANTS, WE HAVE *WON!* HE CAN NEVER TRULY BE ONE OF *US*... HIS ALLEGIANCE IS TO ATLANTIS... *OURS* IS TO THE HUMAN RACE!

NOT SINCE I LOST MY HEART TO SUE STORM HAVE I SEEN SUCH A BEAUTY AS THE *SCARLET WITCH!* BUT I DARE NOT LOVE ANOTHER SURFACE FEMALE... I DARE NOT BE-COME VULNERABLE AGAIN!

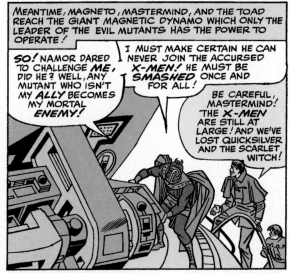

MEANTIME, MAGNETO, MASTERMIND, AND THE TOAD REACH THE GIANT MAGNETIC DYNAMO WHICH ONLY THE LEADER OF THE EVIL MUTANTS HAS THE POWER TO OPERATE!

SO! NAMOR DARED TO CHALLENGE *ME*, DID HE? WELL, ANY MUTANT WHO ISN'T MY *ALLY* BECOMES MY MORTAL *ENEMY!*

I MUST MAKE CERTAIN HE CAN NEVER JOIN THE ACCURSED *X-MEN!* HE MUST BE *SMASHED* ONCE AND FOR ALL!

BE CAREFUL, MASTERMIND! THE *X-MEN* ARE STILL AT LARGE! AND WE'VE LOST QUICKSILVER AND THE SCARLET WITCH!

HOW *LITTLE* YOU KNOW! ONCE *NAMOR* IS DESTROYED, THE *X-MEN* WILL BE NEXT! AND THEN, QUICKSILVER AND HIS SISTER WILL REJOIN US! THERE IS *NO WAY* TO LEAVE MAGNETO'S MUTANTS... EXCEPT BY DEATH!!

NOW BE *SILENT!* I WANT TO ENJOY NAMOR'S DEFEAT!!

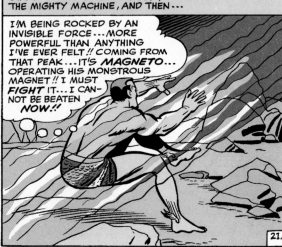

SECONDS LATER, AS THE SEA PRINCE APPEARS ON THE GIANT MAGNET'S VIEWFINDER, MAGNETO ACTIVATES THE MIGHTY MACHINE, AND THEN...

I'M BEING ROCKED BY AN INVISIBLE FORCE... MORE POWERFUL THAN ANYTHING I'VE EVER FELT!! COMING FROM THAT PEAK... IT'S *MAGNETO*... OPERATING HIS MONSTROUS MAGNET!! I MUST *FIGHT* IT... I CAN-NOT BE BEATEN *NOW!!*

21.

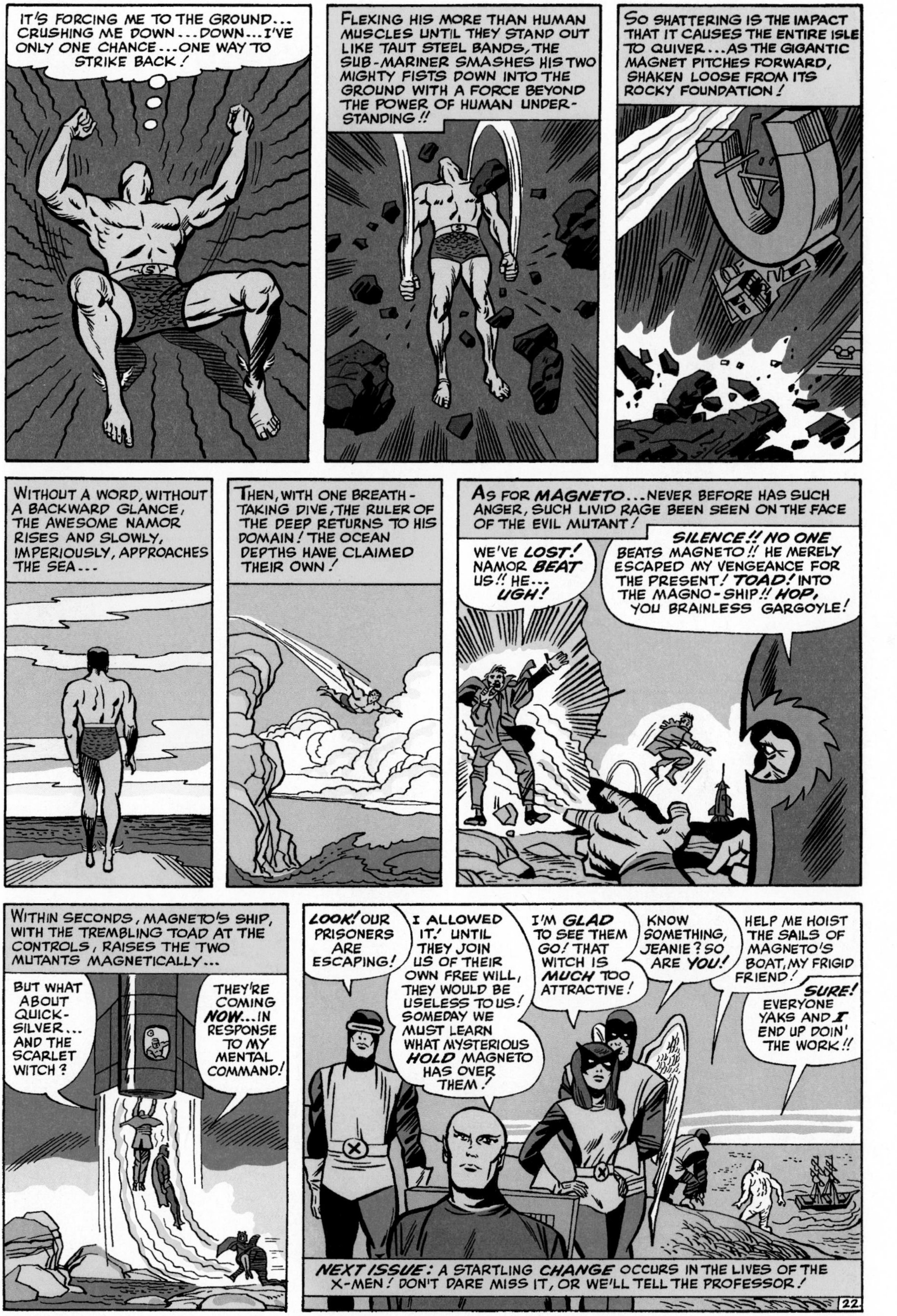
IT'S FORCING ME TO THE GROUND... CRUSHING ME DOWN... DOWN... I'VE ONLY ONE CHANCE... ONE WAY TO STRIKE BACK!
FLEXING HIS MORE THAN HUMAN MUSCLES UNTIL THEY STAND OUT LIKE TAUT STEEL BANDS, THE SUB-MARINER SMASHES HIS TWO MIGHTY FISTS DOWN INTO THE GROUND WITH A FORCE BEYOND THE POWER OF HUMAN UNDER-STANDING!!
SO SHATTERING IS THE IMPACT THAT IT CAUSES THE ENTIRE ISLE TO QUIVER... AS THE GIGANTIC MAGNET PITCHES FORWARD, SHAKEN LOOSE FROM ITS ROCKY FOUNDATION!
WITHOUT A WORD, WITHOUT A BACKWARD GLANCE, THE AWESOME NAMOR RISES AND SLOWLY, IMPERIOUSLY, APPROACHES THE SEA...
THEN, WITH ONE BREATH-TAKING DIVE, THE RULER OF THE DEEP RETURNS TO HIS DOMAIN! THE OCEAN DEPTHS HAVE CLAIMED THEIR OWN!
AS FOR MAGNETO... NEVER BEFORE HAS SUCH ANGER, SUCH LIVID RAGE BEEN SEEN ON THE FACE OF THE EVIL MUTANT!
WE'VE LOST! NAMOR BEAT US!! HE... UGH!
SILENCE!! NO ONE BEATS MAGNETO!! HE MERELY ESCAPED MY VENGEANCE FOR THE PRESENT! TOAD! INTO THE MAGNO-SHIP!! HOP, YOU BRAINLESS GARGOYLE!
WITHIN SECONDS, MAGNETO'S SHIP, WITH THE TREMBLING TOAD AT THE CONTROLS, RAISES THE TWO MUTANTS MAGNETICALLY...
BUT WHAT ABOUT QUICK-SILVER... AND THE SCARLET WITCH?
THEY'RE COMING NOW... IN RESPONSE TO MY MENTAL COMMAND!
LOOK! OUR PRISONERS ARE ESCAPING!
I ALLOWED IT! UNTIL THEY JOIN US OF THEIR OWN FREE WILL, THEY WOULD BE USELESS TO US! SOMEDAY WE MUST LEARN WHAT MYSTERIOUS HOLD MAGNETO HAS OVER THEM!
I'M GLAD TO SEE THEM GO! THAT WITCH IS MUCH TOO ATTRACTIVE!
KNOW SOMETHING, JEANIE? SO ARE YOU!
HELP ME HOIST THE SAILS OF MAGNETO'S BOAT, MY FRIGID FRIEND!
SURE! EVERYONE YAKS AND I END UP DOIN' THE WORK!!
NEXT ISSUE: A STARTLING CHANGE OCCURS IN THE LIVES OF THE X-MEN! DON'T DARE MISS IT, OR WE'LL TELL THE PROFESSOR!
22

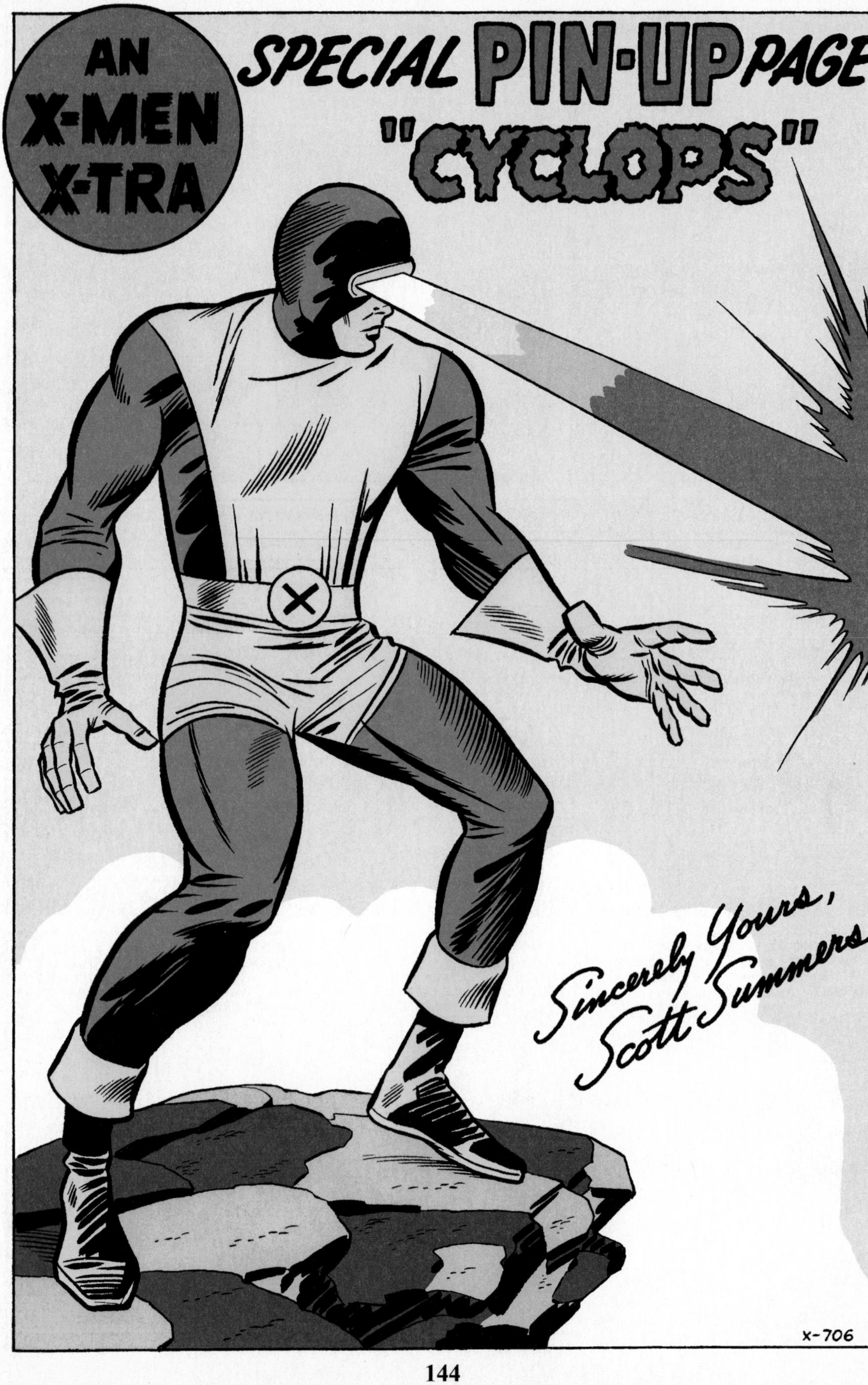
AN X-MEN X-TRA
SPECIAL PIN-UP PAGE
"CYCLOPS"
Sincerely Yours,
Scott Summers
X-706

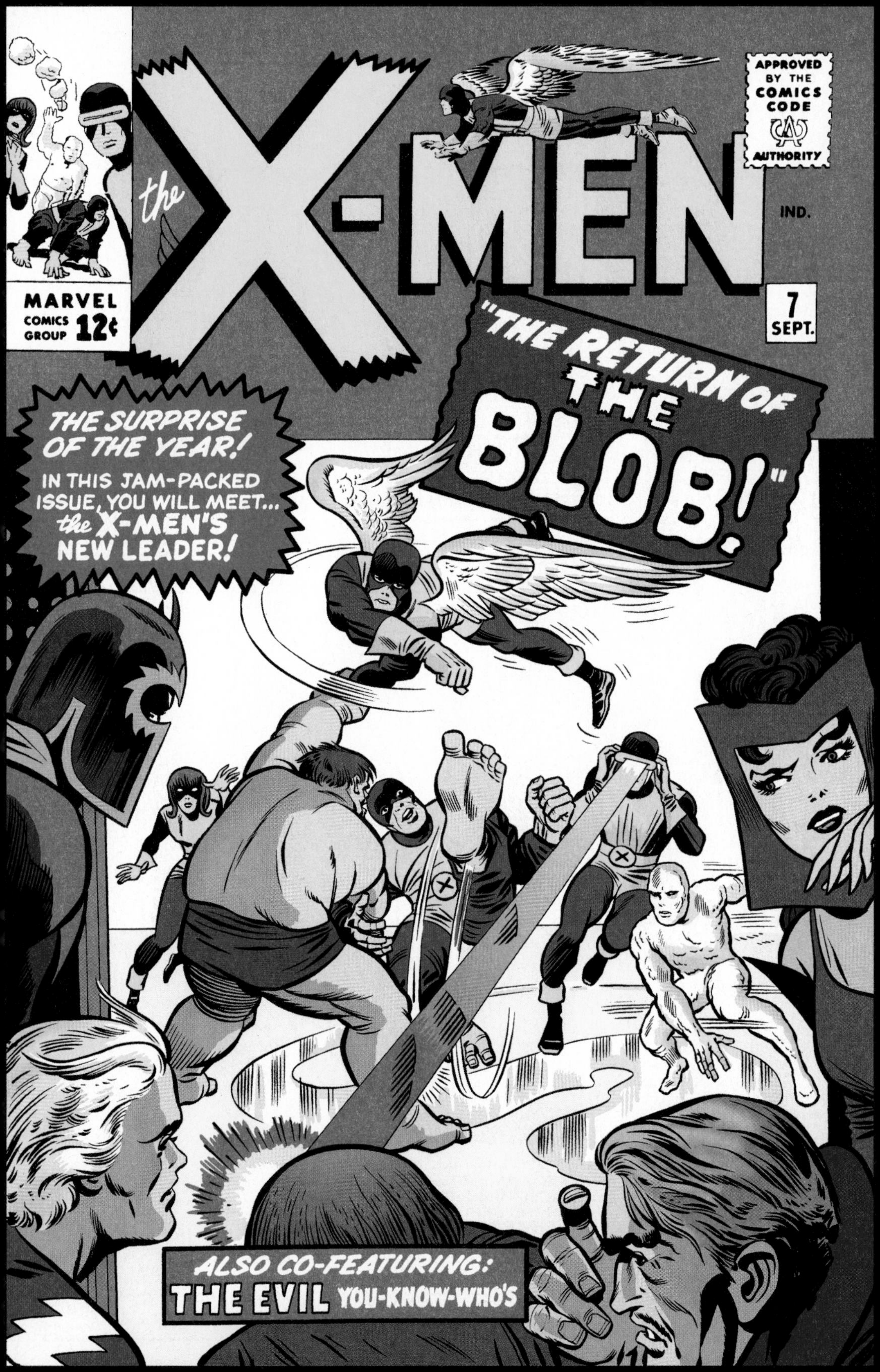

MARVEL COMICS GROUP
12¢
the X-MEN
APPROVED BY THE COMICS CODE AUTHORITY
IND.
7
SEPT.
"THE RETURN OF THE BLOB!"
THE SURPRISE OF THE YEAR!
IN THIS JAM-PACKED ISSUE, YOU WILL MEET... the X-MEN'S NEW LEADER!
ALSO CO-FEATURING:
THE EVIL YOU-KNOW-WHO'S

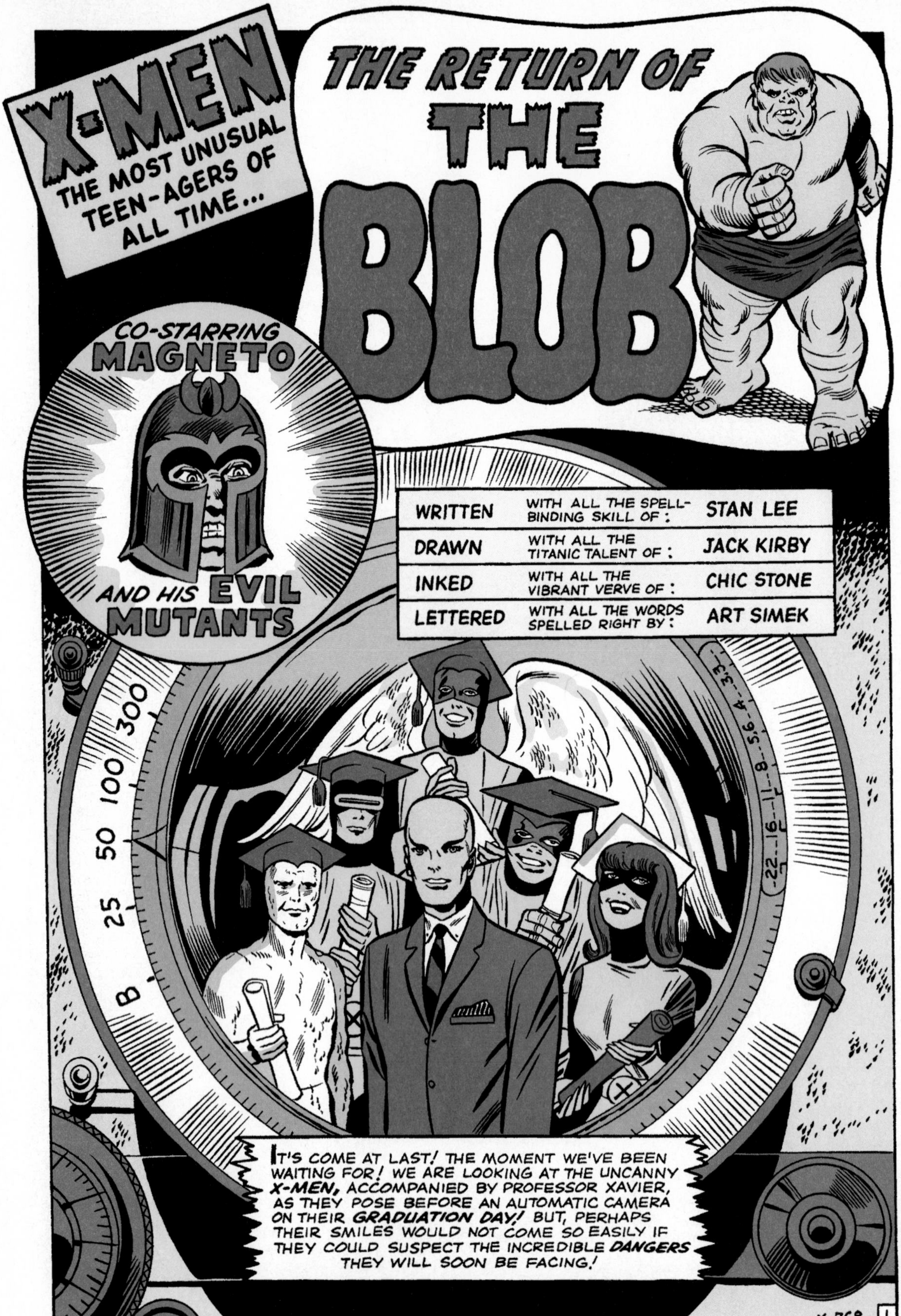
X-MEN
THE MOST UNUSUAL TEEN-AGERS OF ALL TIME...
THE RETURN OF THE BLOB
CO-STARRING MAGNETO AND HIS EVIL MUTANTS
WRITTEN WITH ALL THE SPELL-BINDING SKILL OF: STAN LEE
DRAWN WITH ALL THE TITANIC TALENT OF: JACK KIRBY
INKED WITH ALL THE VIBRANT VERVE OF: CHIC STONE
LETTERED WITH ALL THE WORDS SPELLED RIGHT BY: ART SIMEK
IT'S COME AT LAST! THE MOMENT WE'VE BEEN WAITING FOR! WE ARE LOOKING AT THE UNCANNY X-MEN, ACCOMPANIED BY PROFESSOR XAVIER, AS THEY POSE BEFORE AN AUTOMATIC CAMERA ON THEIR GRADUATION DAY! BUT, PERHAPS THEIR SMILES WOULD NOT COME SO EASILY IF THEY COULD SUSPECT THE INCREDIBLE DANGERS THEY WILL SOON BE FACING!
X-768 1

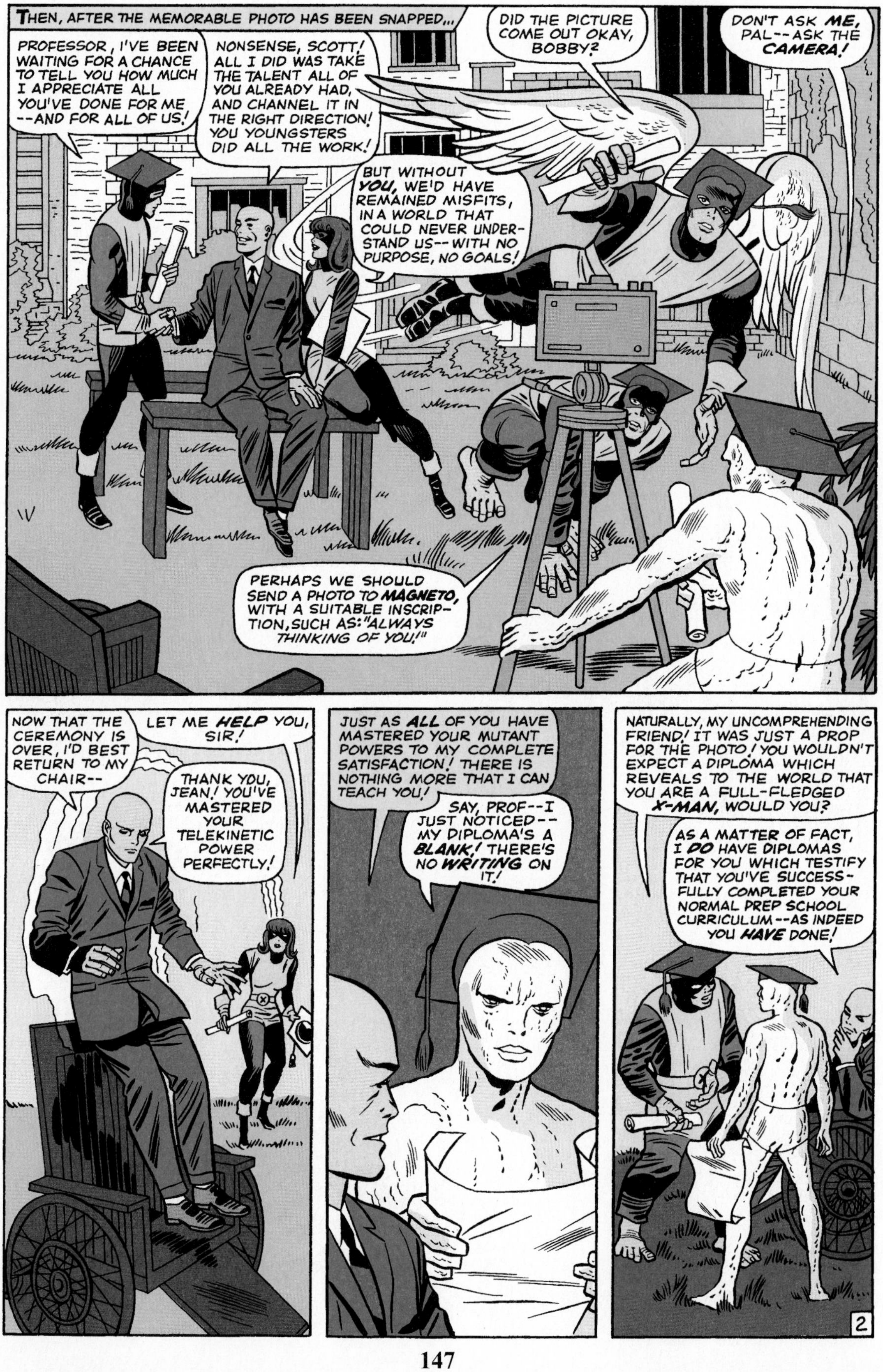
THEN, AFTER THE MEMORABLE PHOTO HAS BEEN SNAPPED...
PROFESSOR, I'VE BEEN WAITING FOR A CHANCE TO TELL YOU HOW MUCH I APPRECIATE ALL YOU'VE DONE FOR ME --AND FOR ALL OF US!
NONSENSE, SCOTT! ALL I DID WAS TAKE THE TALENT ALL OF YOU ALREADY HAD, AND CHANNEL IT IN THE RIGHT DIRECTION! YOU YOUNGSTERS DID ALL THE WORK!
DID THE PICTURE COME OUT OKAY, BOBBY?
DON'T ASK ME, PAL--ASK THE CAMERA!
BUT WITHOUT YOU, WE'D HAVE REMAINED MISFITS, IN A WORLD THAT COULD NEVER UNDERSTAND US--WITH NO PURPOSE, NO GOALS!
PERHAPS WE SHOULD SEND A PHOTO TO MAGNETO, WITH A SUITABLE INSCRIPTION, SUCH AS: "ALWAYS THINKING OF YOU!"
NOW THAT THE CEREMONY IS OVER, I'D BEST RETURN TO MY CHAIR--
LET ME HELP YOU, SIR!
THANK YOU, JEAN! YOU'VE MASTERED YOUR TELEKINETIC POWER PERFECTLY!
JUST AS ALL OF YOU HAVE MASTERED YOUR MUTANT POWERS TO MY COMPLETE SATISFACTION! THERE IS NOTHING MORE THAT I CAN TEACH YOU!
SAY, PROF--I JUST NOTICED--MY DIPLOMA'S A BLANK! THERE'S NO WRITING ON IT!
NATURALLY, MY UNCOMPREHENDING FRIEND! IT WAS JUST A PROP FOR THE PHOTO! YOU WOULDN'T EXPECT A DIPLOMA WHICH REVEALS TO THE WORLD THAT YOU ARE A FULL-FLEDGED X-MAN, WOULD YOU?
AS A MATTER OF FACT, I DO HAVE DIPLOMAS FOR YOU WHICH TESTIFY THAT YOU'VE SUCCESSFULLY COMPLETED YOUR NORMAL PREP SCHOOL CURRICULUM--AS INDEED YOU HAVE DONE!
2

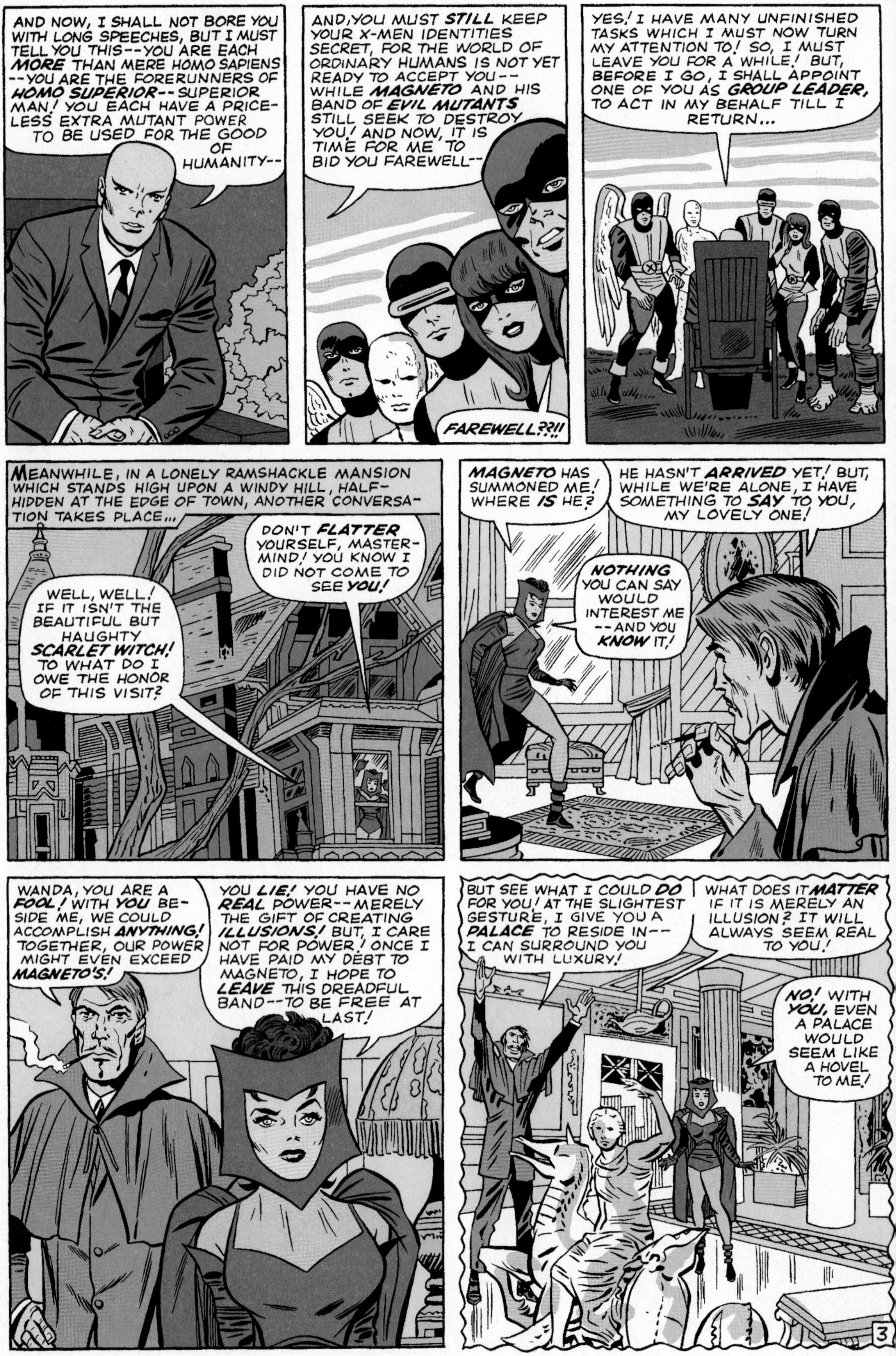
AND NOW, I SHALL NOT BORE YOU WITH LONG SPEECHES, BUT I MUST TELL YOU THIS--YOU ARE EACH MORE THAN MERE HOMO SAPIENS --YOU ARE THE FORERUNNERS OF HOMO SUPERIOR--SUPERIOR MAN! YOU EACH HAVE A PRICELESS EXTRA MUTANT POWER TO BE USED FOR THE GOOD OF HUMANITY--
AND, YOU MUST STILL KEEP YOUR X-MEN IDENTITIES SECRET, FOR THE WORLD OF ORDINARY HUMANS IS NOT YET READY TO ACCEPT YOU--WHILE MAGNETO AND HIS BAND OF EVIL MUTANTS STILL SEEK TO DESTROY YOU! AND NOW, IT IS TIME FOR ME TO BID YOU FAREWELL--
FAREWELL??!!
YES! I HAVE MANY UNFINISHED TASKS WHICH I MUST NOW TURN MY ATTENTION TO! SO, I MUST LEAVE YOU FOR A WHILE! BUT, BEFORE I GO, I SHALL APPOINT ONE OF YOU AS GROUP LEADER, TO ACT IN MY BEHALF TILL I RETURN...
MEANWHILE, IN A LONELY RAMSHACKLE MANSION WHICH STANDS HIGH UPON A WINDY HILL, HALF-HIDDEN AT THE EDGE OF TOWN, ANOTHER CONVERSATION TAKES PLACE...
WELL, WELL! IF IT ISN'T THE BEAUTIFUL BUT HAUGHTY SCARLET WITCH! TO WHAT DO I OWE THE HONOR OF THIS VISIT?
DON'T FLATTER YOURSELF, MASTERMIND! YOU KNOW I DID NOT COME TO SEE YOU!
MAGNETO HAS SUMMONED ME! WHERE IS HE?
HE HASN'T ARRIVED YET! BUT, WHILE WE'RE ALONE, I HAVE SOMETHING TO SAY TO YOU, MY LOVELY ONE!
NOTHING YOU CAN SAY WOULD INTEREST ME --AND YOU KNOW IT!
WANDA, YOU ARE A FOOL! WITH YOU BESIDE ME, WE COULD ACCOMPLISH ANYTHING! TOGETHER, OUR POWER MIGHT EVEN EXCEED MAGNETO'S!
YOU LIE! YOU HAVE NO REAL POWER--MERELY THE GIFT OF CREATING ILLUSIONS! BUT, I CARE NOT FOR POWER! ONCE I HAVE PAID MY DEBT TO MAGNETO, I HOPE TO LEAVE THIS DREADFUL BAND--TO BE FREE AT LAST!
BUT SEE WHAT I COULD DO FOR YOU! AT THE SLIGHTEST GESTURE, I GIVE YOU A PALACE TO RESIDE IN--I CAN SURROUND YOU WITH LUXURY!
WHAT DOES IT MATTER IF IT IS MERELY AN ILLUSION? IT WILL ALWAYS SEEM REAL TO YOU!
NO! WITH YOU, EVEN A PALACE WOULD SEEM LIKE A HOVEL TO ME!
3

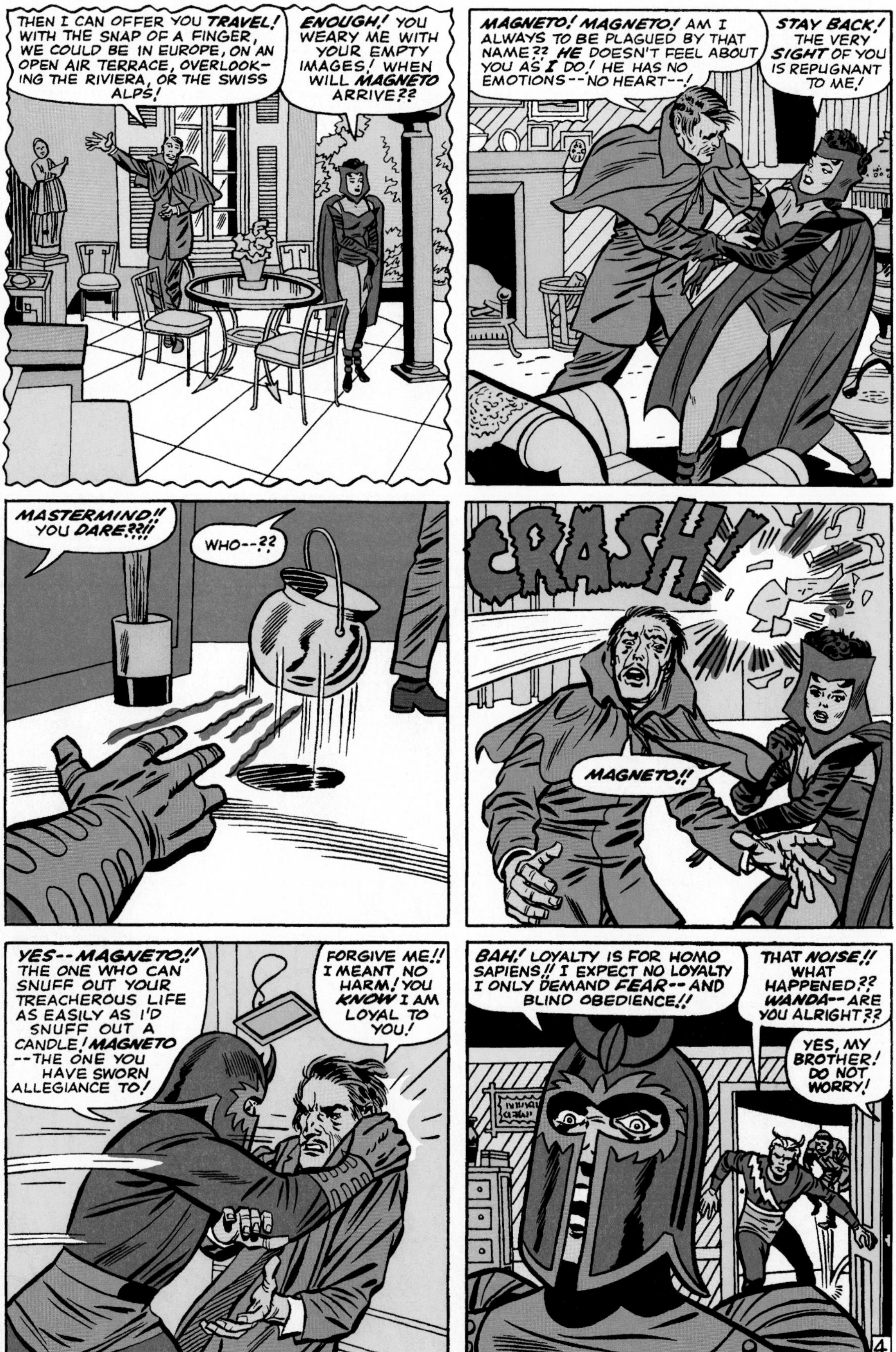
THEN I CAN OFFER YOU TRAVEL! WITH THE SNAP OF A FINGER, WE COULD BE IN EUROPE, ON AN OPEN AIR TERRACE, OVERLOOKING THE RIVIERA, OR THE SWISS ALPS!
ENOUGH! YOU WEARY ME WITH YOUR EMPTY IMAGES! WHEN WILL MAGNETO ARRIVE??
MAGNETO! MAGNETO! AM I ALWAYS TO BE PLAGUED BY THAT NAME?? HE DOESN'T FEEL ABOUT YOU AS I DO! HE HAS NO EMOTIONS--NO HEART--!
STAY BACK! THE VERY SIGHT OF YOU IS REPUGNANT TO ME!
MASTERMIND!! YOU DARE??!!
WHO--??
CRASH!
MAGNETO!!
YES--MAGNETO!! THE ONE WHO CAN SNUFF OUT YOUR TREACHEROUS LIFE AS EASILY AS I'D SNUFF OUT A CANDLE! MAGNETO --THE ONE YOU HAVE SWORN ALLEGIANCE TO!
FORGIVE ME!! I MEANT NO HARM! YOU KNOW I AM LOYAL TO YOU!
BAH! LOYALTY IS FOR HOMO SAPIENS!! I EXPECT NO LOYALTY I ONLY DEMAND FEAR--AND BLIND OBEDIENCE!!
THAT NOISE!! WHAT HAPPENED?? WANDA--ARE YOU ALRIGHT??
YES, MY BROTHER! DO NOT WORRY!
4

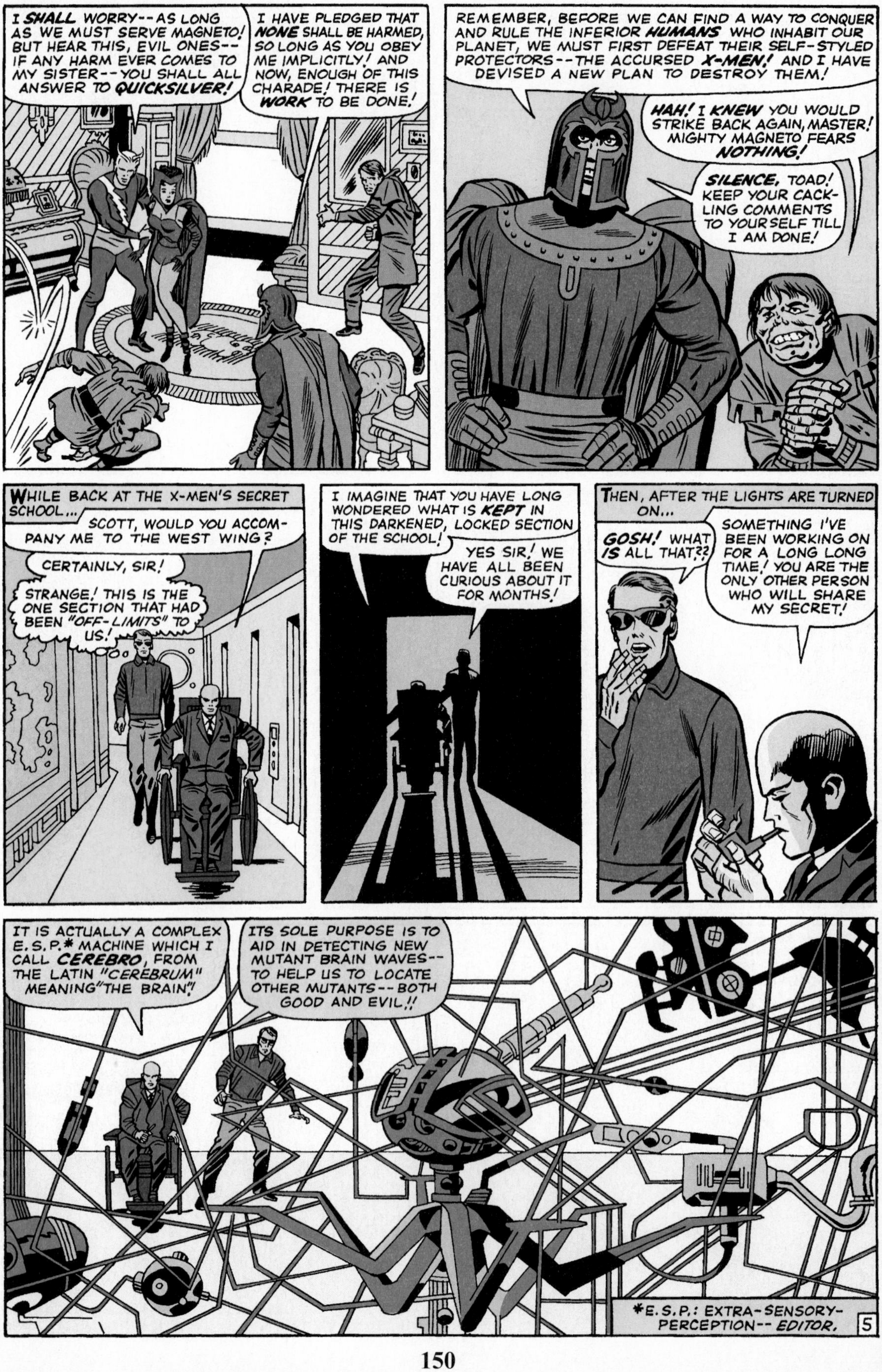
I SHALL WORRY--AS LONG AS WE MUST SERVE MAGNETO! BUT HEAR THIS, EVIL ONES--IF ANY HARM EVER COMES TO MY SISTER--YOU SHALL ALL ANSWER TO QUICKSILVER!
I HAVE PLEDGED THAT NONE SHALL BE HARMED, SO LONG AS YOU OBEY ME IMPLICITLY! AND NOW, ENOUGH OF THIS CHARADE! THERE IS WORK TO BE DONE!
REMEMBER, BEFORE WE CAN FIND A WAY TO CONQUER AND RULE THE INFERIOR HUMANS WHO INHABIT OUR PLANET, WE MUST FIRST DEFEAT THEIR SELF-STYLED PROTECTORS--THE ACCURSED X-MEN! AND I HAVE DEVISED A NEW PLAN TO DESTROY THEM!
HAH! I KNEW YOU WOULD STRIKE BACK AGAIN, MASTER! MIGHTY MAGNETO FEARS NOTHING!
SILENCE, TOAD! KEEP YOUR CACKLING COMMENTS TO YOURSELF TILL I AM DONE!
WHILE BACK AT THE X-MEN'S SECRET SCHOOL...
SCOTT, WOULD YOU ACCOMPANY ME TO THE WEST WING?
CERTAINLY, SIR!
STRANGE! THIS IS THE ONE SECTION THAT HAD BEEN "OFF-LIMITS" TO US!
I IMAGINE THAT YOU HAVE LONG WONDERED WHAT IS KEPT IN THIS DARKENED, LOCKED SECTION OF THE SCHOOL!
YES SIR! WE HAVE ALL BEEN CURIOUS ABOUT IT FOR MONTHS!
THEN, AFTER THE LIGHTS ARE TURNED ON...
GOSH! WHAT IS ALL THAT??
SOMETHING I'VE BEEN WORKING ON FOR A LONG LONG TIME! YOU ARE THE ONLY OTHER PERSON WHO WILL SHARE MY SECRET!
IT IS ACTUALLY A COMPLEX E.S.P.* MACHINE WHICH I CALL CEREBRO, FROM THE LATIN "CEREBRUM" MEANING "THE BRAIN"!
ITS SOLE PURPOSE IS TO AID IN DETECTING NEW MUTANT BRAIN WAVES--TO HELP US TO LOCATE OTHER MUTANTS--BOTH GOOD AND EVIL!!
*E.S.P.: EXTRA-SENSORY PERCEPTION--EDITOR.
5

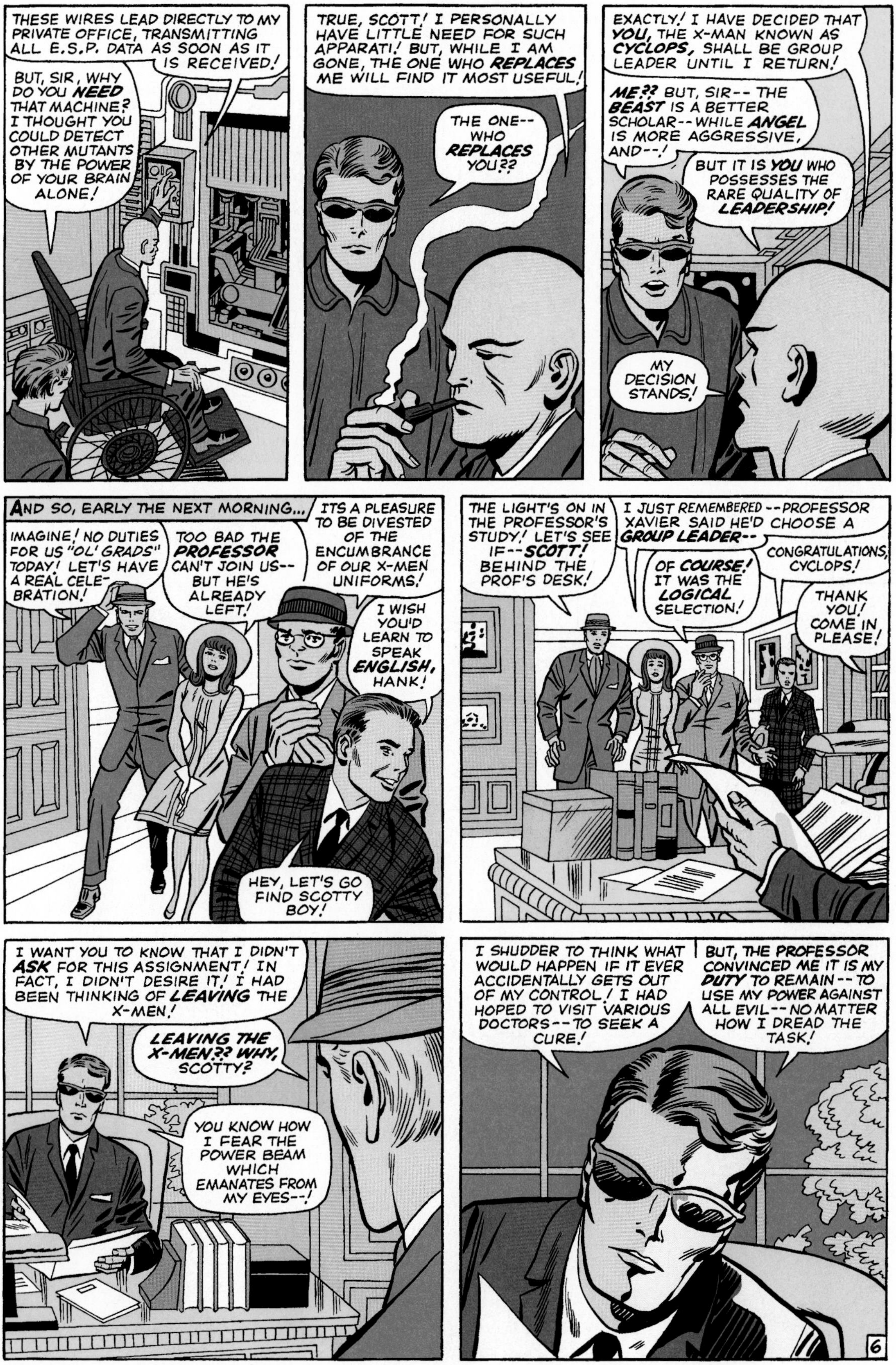
THESE WIRES LEAD DIRECTLY TO MY PRIVATE OFFICE, TRANSMITTING ALL E.S.P. DATA AS SOON AS IT IS RECEIVED!
BUT, SIR, WHY DO YOU NEED THAT MACHINE? I THOUGHT YOU COULD DETECT OTHER MUTANTS BY THE POWER OF YOUR BRAIN ALONE!
TRUE, SCOTT! I PERSONALLY HAVE LITTLE NEED FOR SUCH APPARATI! BUT, WHILE I AM GONE, THE ONE WHO REPLACES ME WILL FIND IT MOST USEFUL!
THE ONE-- WHO REPLACES YOU??
EXACTLY! I HAVE DECIDED THAT YOU, THE X-MAN KNOWN AS CYCLOPS, SHALL BE GROUP LEADER UNTIL I RETURN!
ME?? BUT, SIR-- THE BEAST IS A BETTER SCHOLAR--WHILE ANGEL IS MORE AGGRESSIVE, AND--!
BUT IT IS YOU WHO POSSESSES THE RARE QUALITY OF LEADERSHIP!
MY DECISION STANDS!
AND SO, EARLY THE NEXT MORNING...
IMAGINE! NO DUTIES FOR US "OL' GRADS" TODAY! LET'S HAVE A REAL CELE-BRATION!
TOO BAD THE PROFESSOR CAN'T JOIN US-- BUT HE'S ALREADY LEFT!
ITS A PLEASURE TO BE DIVESTED OF THE ENCUMBRANCE OF OUR X-MEN UNIFORMS!
I WISH YOU'D LEARN TO SPEAK ENGLISH, HANK!
HEY, LET'S GO FIND SCOTTY BOY!
THE LIGHT'S ON IN THE PROFESSOR'S STUDY! LET'S SEE IF--SCOTT! BEHIND THE PROF'S DESK!
I JUST REMEMBERED--PROFESSOR XAVIER SAID HE'D CHOOSE A GROUP LEADER--
OF COURSE! IT WAS THE LOGICAL SELECTION!
CONGRATULATIONS, CYCLOPS!
THANK YOU! COME IN PLEASE!
I WANT YOU TO KNOW THAT I DIDN'T ASK FOR THIS ASSIGNMENT! IN FACT, I DIDN'T DESIRE IT! I HAD BEEN THINKING OF LEAVING THE X-MEN!
LEAVING THE X-MEN?? WHY, SCOTTY?
YOU KNOW HOW I FEAR THE POWER BEAM WHICH EMANATES FROM MY EYES--!
I SHUDDER TO THINK WHAT WOULD HAPPEN IF IT EVER ACCIDENTALLY GETS OUT OF MY CONTROL! I HAD HOPED TO VISIT VARIOUS DOCTORS--TO SEEK A CURE!
BUT, THE PROFESSOR CONVINCED ME IT IS MY DUTY TO REMAIN--TO USE MY POWER AGAINST ALL EVIL--NO MATTER HOW I DREAD THE TASK!
6

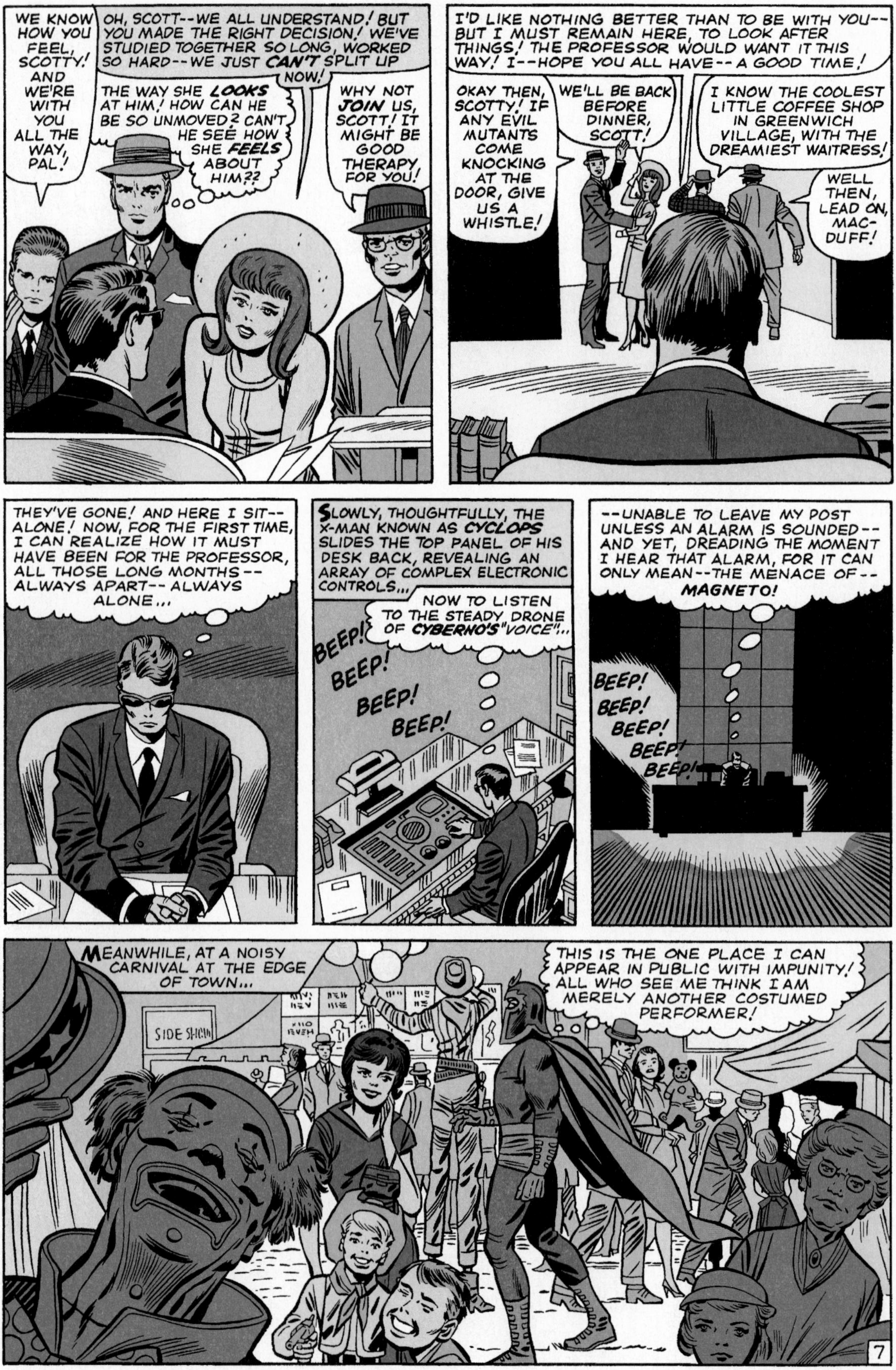
WE KNOW HOW YOU FEEL, SCOTTY! AND WE'RE WITH YOU ALL THE WAY, PAL!
OH, SCOTT--WE ALL UNDERSTAND! BUT YOU MADE THE RIGHT DECISION! WE'VE STUDIED TOGETHER SO LONG, WORKED SO HARD--WE JUST CAN'T SPLIT UP NOW!
THE WAY SHE LOOKS AT HIM! HOW CAN HE BE SO UNMOVED? CAN'T HE SEE HOW SHE FEELS ABOUT HIM??
WHY NOT JOIN US, SCOTT! IT MIGHT BE GOOD THERAPY FOR YOU!
I'D LIKE NOTHING BETTER THAN TO BE WITH YOU--BUT I MUST REMAIN HERE, TO LOOK AFTER THINGS! THE PROFESSOR WOULD WANT IT THIS WAY! I--HOPE YOU ALL HAVE--A GOOD TIME!
OKAY THEN, SCOTTY! IF ANY EVIL MUTANTS COME KNOCKING AT THE DOOR, GIVE US A WHISTLE!
WE'LL BE BACK BEFORE DINNER, SCOTT!
I KNOW THE COOLEST LITTLE COFFEE SHOP IN GREENWICH VILLAGE, WITH THE DREAMIEST WAITRESS!
WELL THEN, LEAD ON, MAC-DUFF!
THEY'VE GONE! AND HERE I SIT--ALONE! NOW, FOR THE FIRST TIME, I CAN REALIZE HOW IT MUST HAVE BEEN FOR THE PROFESSOR, ALL THOSE LONG MONTHS--ALWAYS APART--ALWAYS ALONE...
SLOWLY, THOUGHTFULLY, THE X-MAN KNOWN AS CYCLOPS SLIDES THE TOP PANEL OF HIS DESK BACK, REVEALING AN ARRAY OF COMPLEX ELECTRONIC CONTROLS...
NOW TO LISTEN TO THE STEADY DRONE OF CYBERNO'S "VOICE"!...
BEEP! BEEP! BEEP! BEEP!
--UNABLE TO LEAVE MY POST UNLESS AN ALARM IS SOUNDED--AND YET, DREADING THE MOMENT I HEAR THAT ALARM, FOR IT CAN ONLY MEAN--THE MENACE OF--MAGNETO!
BEEP! BEEP! BEEP! BEEP! BEEP!
MEANWHILE, AT A NOISY CARNIVAL AT THE EDGE OF TOWN...
THIS IS THE ONE PLACE I CAN APPEAR IN PUBLIC WITH IMPUNITY! ALL WHO SEE ME THINK I AM MERELY ANOTHER COSTUMED PERFORMER!
SIDE SHOW
7

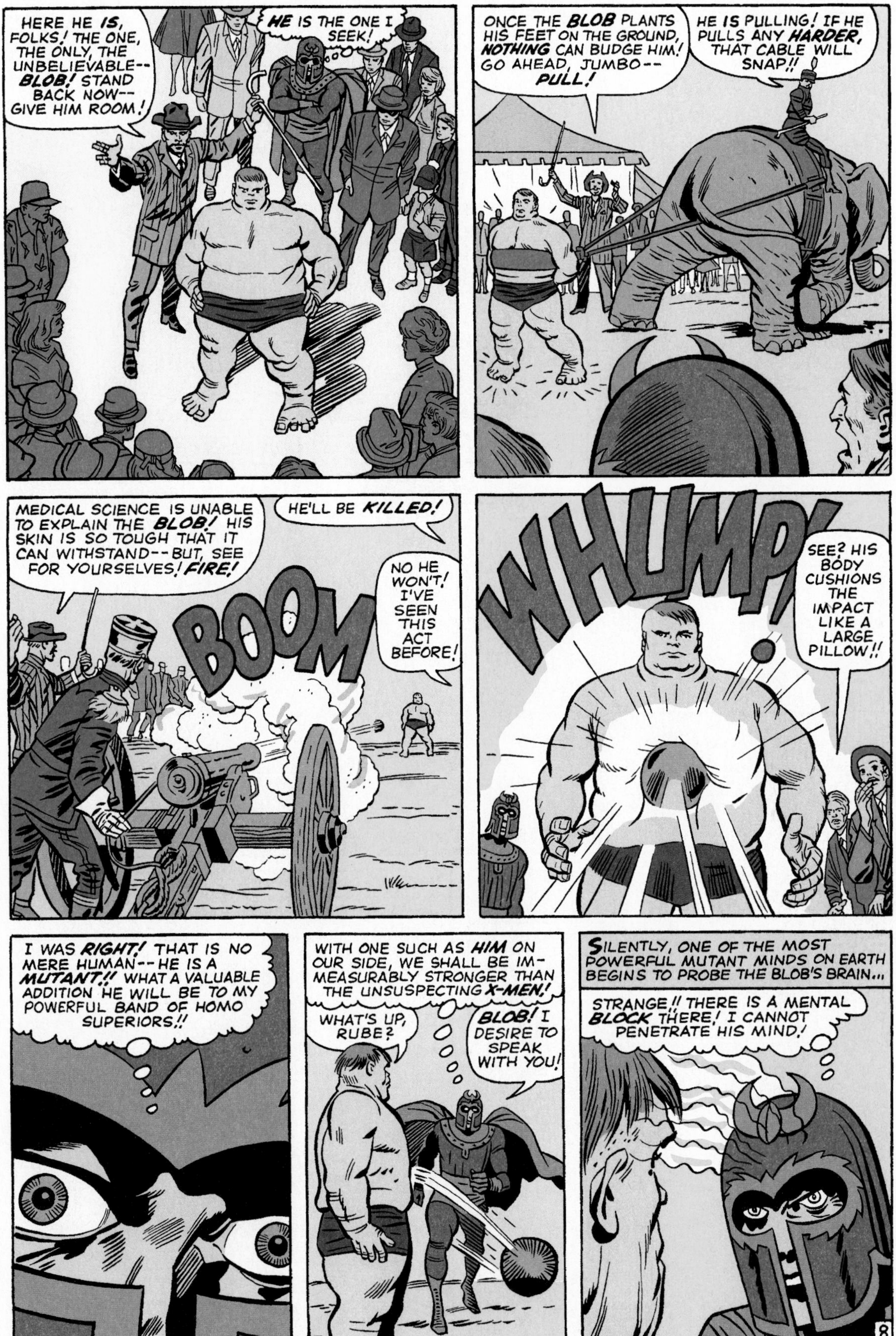
HERE HE IS, FOLKS! THE ONE, THE ONLY, THE UNBELIEVABLE-- BLOB! STAND BACK NOW-- GIVE HIM ROOM!
HE IS THE ONE I SEEK!
ONCE THE BLOB PLANTS HIS FEET ON THE GROUND, NOTHING CAN BUDGE HIM! GO AHEAD, JUMBO-- PULL!
HE IS PULLING! IF HE PULLS ANY HARDER, THAT CABLE WILL SNAP!!
MEDICAL SCIENCE IS UNABLE TO EXPLAIN THE BLOB! HIS SKIN IS SO TOUGH THAT IT CAN WITHSTAND--BUT, SEE FOR YOURSELVES! FIRE!
HE'LL BE KILLED!
NO HE WON'T! I'VE SEEN THIS ACT BEFORE!
BOOM
WHUMP!
SEE? HIS BODY CUSHIONS THE IMPACT LIKE A LARGE PILLOW!!
I WAS RIGHT! THAT IS NO MERE HUMAN--HE IS A MUTANT!! WHAT A VALUABLE ADDITION HE WILL BE TO MY POWERFUL BAND OF HOMO SUPERIORS!!
WITH ONE SUCH AS HIM ON OUR SIDE, WE SHALL BE IMMEASURABLY STRONGER THAN THE UNSUSPECTING X-MEN!
WHAT'S UP, RUBE?
BLOB! I DESIRE TO SPEAK WITH YOU!
SILENTLY, ONE OF THE MOST POWERFUL MUTANT MINDS ON EARTH BEGINS TO PROBE THE BLOB'S BRAIN...
STRANGE!! THERE IS A MENTAL BLOCK THERE! I CANNOT PENETRATE HIS MIND!
8

HEY! WHO IN SAM HILL ARE **YOU**, MAC?? WHAT ARE YOU DOIN' WITH MY PERFORMER??

WHO AM I ??

I AM-- **POWER!!**

BUT **YOU** MAY CALL ME--**MAGNETO!!** MARK THAT NAME WELL, HOMO SAPIEN-- SOON YOU, AND **ALL** YOUR INFERIOR KIND SHALL PAY IT **HOMAGE!!**

I DON'T KNOW WHAT YOUR GAME IS, MAC, BUT IF IT'S A **FIGHT** YOU WANT, YOU CAME TO THE RIGHT PLACE!!

FOOL! YOU **STILL** DO NOT COMPREHEND THE AWESOME FORCE YOU ARE DARING TO CHALLENGE!

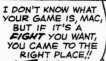

SECONDS LATER, IN ANSWER TO THE TIME-HONORED CARNY BATTLE CRY, A GROUP OF HUSKY ROUSTABOUTS CHARGE THE MIGHTY MUTANT!

LET'S **GET** THAT COSTUMED NUT!!

BUT, BEFORE THEY CAN REACH MAGNETO--

NO ONE MAY TOUCH THE **MASTER!!**

LIKE A HUMAN BOUNCING CANNONBALL, THE INCREDIBLE HIGH-JUMPING **TOAD** LEAPS BACK AND FORTH, UP AND DOWN, SCATTERING THE DAZED ROUSTABOUTS LIKE TENPINS, WITH SPEED AND AGILITY SECOND ONLY TO THAT OF THE **BEAST!**

MAGNETO MUST **NEVER** BE HARMED!!

THEN, BEFORE THE STUNNED CARNY MEN CAN REGROUP THEIR FORCES, A SPEEDING, CAREENING, LIGHTNING-SWIFT FIGURE RACES THRU THEM SO QUICKLY THAT ONLY A HAZY BLUR CAN BE SEEN!!

HEY! WHAT'S GOIN' **ON** HERE!

LOOK OUT! THERE'S **ANOTHER** ONE!

9

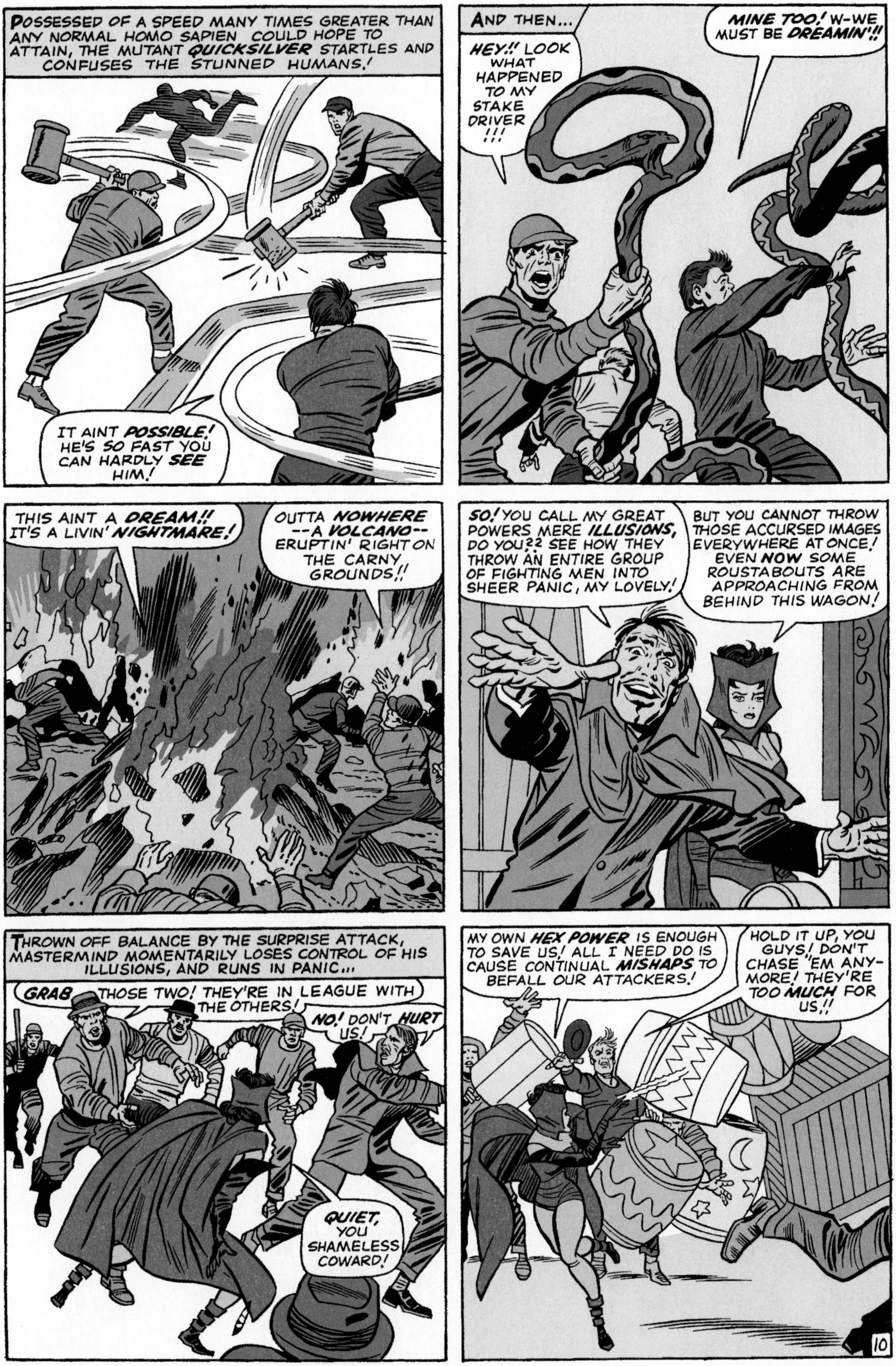
POSSESSED OF A SPEED MANY TIMES GREATER THAN ANY NORMAL HOMO SAPIEN COULD HOPE TO ATTAIN, THE MUTANT QUICKSILVER STARTLES AND CONFUSES THE STUNNED HUMANS!
IT AINT POSSIBLE! HE'S SO FAST YOU CAN HARDLY SEE HIM!
AND THEN...
HEY!! LOOK WHAT HAPPENED TO MY STAKE DRIVER !!!
MINE TOO! W-WE MUST BE DREAMIN'!!
THIS AINT A DREAM!! IT'S A LIVIN' NIGHTMARE!
OUTTA NOWHERE --A VOLCANO-- ERUPTIN' RIGHT ON THE CARNY GROUNDS!!
SO! YOU CALL MY GREAT POWERS MERE ILLUSIONS, DO YOU?? SEE HOW THEY THROW AN ENTIRE GROUP OF FIGHTING MEN INTO SHEER PANIC, MY LOVELY!
BUT YOU CANNOT THROW THOSE ACCURSED IMAGES EVERYWHERE AT ONCE! EVEN NOW SOME ROUSTABOUTS ARE APPROACHING FROM BEHIND THIS WAGON!
THROWN OFF BALANCE BY THE SURPRISE ATTACK, MASTERMIND MOMENTARILY LOSES CONTROL OF HIS ILLUSIONS, AND RUNS IN PANIC...
GRAB THOSE TWO! THEY'RE IN LEAGUE WITH THE OTHERS!
NO! DON'T HURT US!
QUIET, YOU SHAMELESS COWARD!
MY OWN HEX POWER IS ENOUGH TO SAVE US! ALL I NEED DO IS CAUSE CONTINUAL MISHAPS TO BEFALL OUR ATTACKERS!
HOLD IT UP, YOU GUYS! DON'T CHASE 'EM ANY-MORE! THEY'RE TOO MUCH FOR US!!
10

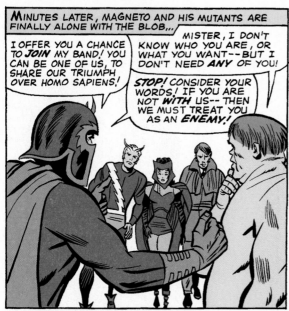

MINUTES LATER, MAGNETO AND HIS MUTANTS ARE FINALLY ALONE WITH THE BLOB...

I OFFER YOU A CHANCE TO *JOIN* MY BAND! YOU CAN BE ONE OF US, TO SHARE OUR TRIUMPH OVER HOMO SAPIENS!

MISTER, I DON'T KNOW WHO YOU ARE, OR WHAT YOU WANT--BUT I DON'T NEED *ANY* OF YOU!

STOP! CONSIDER YOUR WORDS! IF YOU ARE NOT *WITH* US-- THEN WE MUST TREAT YOU AS AN *ENEMY!*

I CANNOT LEAVE YOU HERE, ON THE CHANCE THAT THE *X-MEN* MAY ONE DAY RECRUIT YOU TO JOIN *THEM!* I MUST-- *WHAT??* YOU DARE LAY A HAND ON THE PERSON OF *MAGNETO ??!!*

LOOK, RUBE--I'M GONNA SHOW YOU THAT *NOBODY* SCARES THE *BLOB!* NOT EVEN A BUNCH OF BIG-TALKIN' COSTUMED CLOWNS!

SUDDENLY, AN IRRESISTIBLE MAGNETIC IMPULSE AFFECTS THE UTILITY PIPES DIRECTLY UNDERGROUND, AND THEY SNAP TO THE SURFACE WITH TITANIC FORCE!

FOOL! BE GRATEFUL I HAVE ONLY DEIGNED TO USE ONLY A *FRACTION* OF THE LIMITLESS MAGNETIC POWER WHICH I POSSESS!!

AND THEN, A CAPRICIOUS *FATE* ENTERS THE PICTURE, AS THE FORCE OF IMPACT JARS LOOSE PART OF THE MENTAL BLOCK WHICH *PROFESSOR X* HAD PREVIOUSLY PUT OVER THE BLOB'S MEMORY--!*

I REMEMBER NOW! I'M A *MUTANT!* THE *X-MEN* ARE MY ENEMIES! THEY WERE AFRAID I'D JOIN MAGNETO! BUT I *WILL*-- I *WILL* JOIN HIM!!

*SEE X-MEN #3 "BEWARE THE BLOB!" --EDITOR.

AT THAT VERY INSTANT, AT *X-MEN* HEADQUARTERS, A SIREN BEGINS TO HOWL LIKE A BANSHEE AS THE NAME OF THE *BLOB* LIGHTS UP UNDER THE OTHERS ON A MASTER CONTROL PANEL!

KNOWN HOSTILE MUTANTS

MAGNETO

TOAD

ASTER-MIND

UICK SILVER

ET WITCH

BLOB

UNKNOWN

WHEEÉE!

THE *SIREN!!* THE BLOB'S NAME-- BURSTING INTO LIGHT! IT CAN ONLY MEAN *ONE* THING--!

HIS *MEMORY* HAS RETURNED! HE'S JOINED THE EVIL MUTANTS!

THE PROFESSOR IS GONE! IT'S UP TO *ME* TO TAKE COMMAND! I DARE NOT FAIL!

I'VE GOT TO CONTACT THE OTHERS! I'LL CHECK THEIR DESTINATIONS IN THE SIGN-OUT BOOK! I CAN REACH THE *ANGEL* THRU HIS CAR RADIO--!

11

156

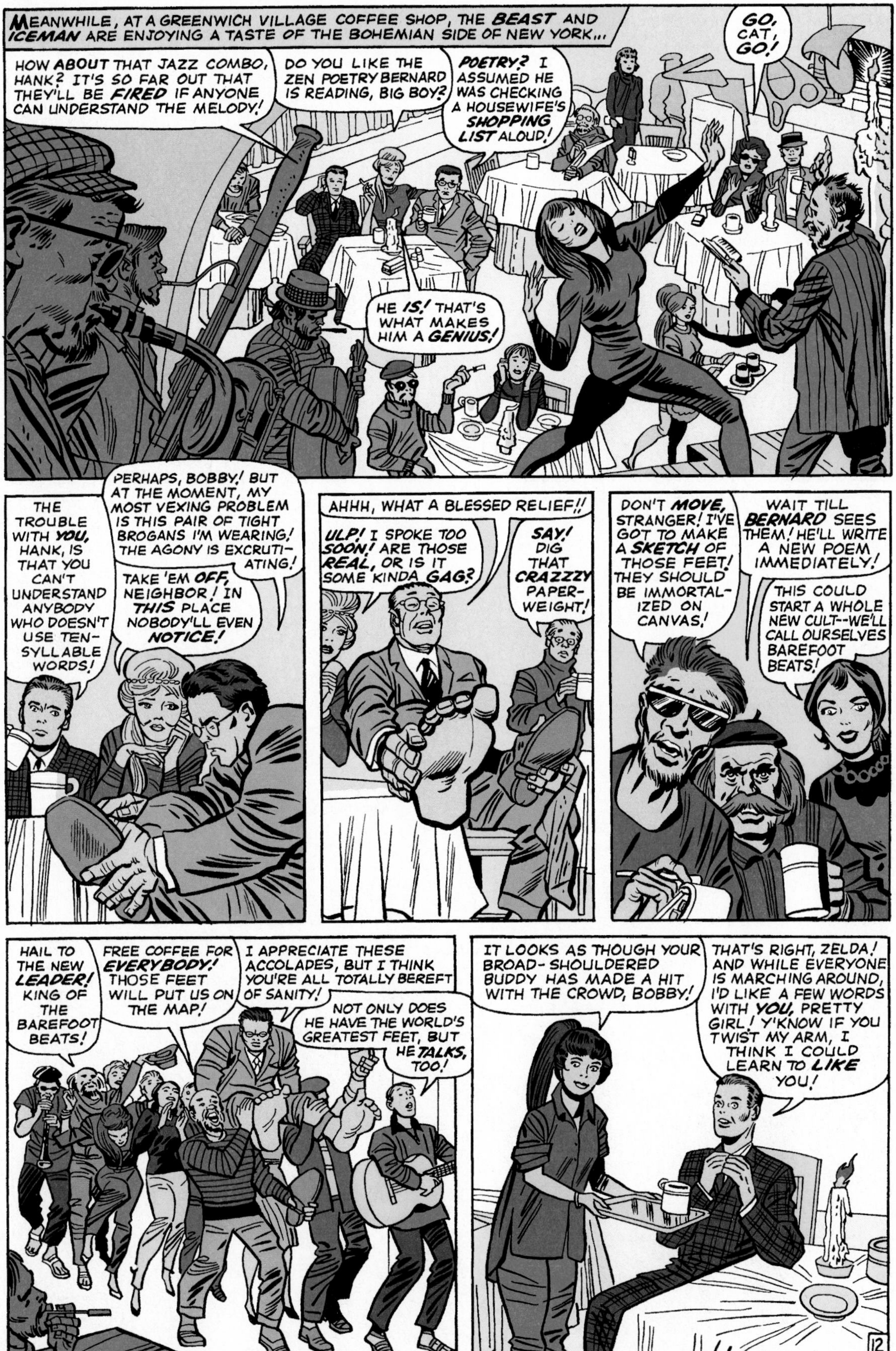

MEANWHILE, AT A GREENWICH VILLAGE COFFEE SHOP, THE BEAST AND ICEMAN ARE ENJOYING A TASTE OF THE BOHEMIAN SIDE OF NEW YORK...
GO, CAT, GO!
HOW ABOUT THAT JAZZ COMBO, HANK? IT'S SO FAR OUT THAT THEY'LL BE FIRED IF ANYONE CAN UNDERSTAND THE MELODY!
DO YOU LIKE THE ZEN POETRY BERNARD IS READING, BIG BOY?
POETRY? I ASSUMED HE WAS CHECKING A HOUSEWIFE'S SHOPPING LIST ALOUD!
HE IS! THAT'S WHAT MAKES HIM A GENIUS!
THE TROUBLE WITH YOU, HANK, IS THAT YOU CAN'T UNDERSTAND ANYBODY WHO DOESN'T USE TEN-SYLLABLE WORDS!
PERHAPS, BOBBY! BUT AT THE MOMENT, MY MOST VEXING PROBLEM IS THIS PAIR OF TIGHT BROGANS I'M WEARING! THE AGONY IS EXCRUTIATING!
TAKE 'EM OFF, NEIGHBOR! IN THIS PLACE NOBODY'LL EVEN NOTICE!
AHHH, WHAT A BLESSED RELIEF!!
ULP! I SPOKE TOO SOON! ARE THOSE REAL, OR IS IT SOME KINDA GAG?
SAY! DIG THAT CRAZZZY PAPER-WEIGHT!
DON'T MOVE, STRANGER! I'VE GOT TO MAKE A SKETCH OF THOSE FEET! THEY SHOULD BE IMMORTALIZED ON CANVAS!
WAIT TILL BERNARD SEES THEM! HE'LL WRITE A NEW POEM IMMEDIATELY!
THIS COULD START A WHOLE NEW CULT--WE'LL CALL OURSELVES BAREFOOT BEATS!
HAIL TO THE NEW LEADER! KING OF THE BAREFOOT BEATS!
FREE COFFEE FOR EVERYBODY! THOSE FEET WILL PUT US ON THE MAP!
I APPRECIATE THESE ACCOLADES, BUT I THINK YOU'RE ALL TOTALLY BEREFT OF SANITY!
NOT ONLY DOES HE HAVE THE WORLD'S GREATEST FEET, BUT HE TALKS, TOO!
IT LOOKS AS THOUGH YOUR BROAD-SHOULDERED BUDDY HAS MADE A HIT WITH THE CROWD, BOBBY!
THAT'S RIGHT, ZELDA! AND WHILE EVERYONE IS MARCHING AROUND, I'D LIKE A FEW WORDS WITH YOU, PRETTY GIRL! Y'KNOW IF YOU TWIST MY ARM, I THINK I COULD LEARN TO LIKE YOU!
12

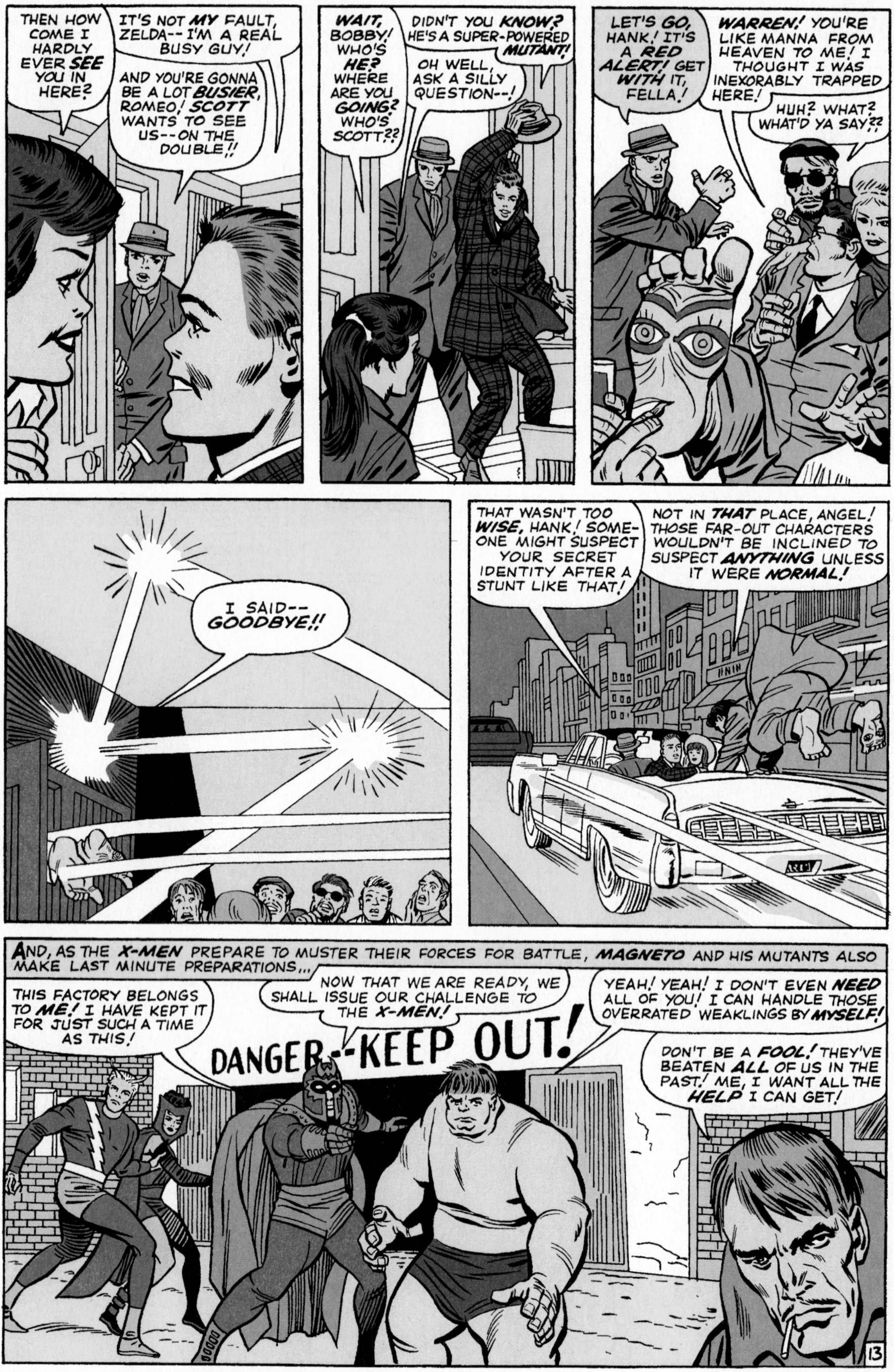

THEN HOW COME I HARDLY EVER SEE YOU IN HERE?
IT'S NOT MY FAULT, ZELDA-- I'M A REAL BUSY GUY!
AND YOU'RE GONNA BE A LOT BUSIER, ROMEO! SCOTT WANTS TO SEE US--ON THE DOUBLE!!
WAIT, BOBBY! WHO'S HE? WHERE ARE YOU GOING? WHO'S SCOTT??
DIDN'T YOU KNOW? HE'S A SUPER-POWERED MUTANT!
OH WELL, ASK A SILLY QUESTION--!
LET'S GO, HANK! IT'S A RED ALERT! GET WITH IT, FELLA!
WARREN! YOU'RE LIKE MANNA FROM HEAVEN TO ME! I THOUGHT I WAS INEXORABLY TRAPPED HERE!
HUH? WHAT? WHAT'D YA SAY??
I SAID-- GOODBYE!!
THAT WASN'T TOO WISE, HANK! SOMEONE MIGHT SUSPECT YOUR SECRET IDENTITY AFTER A STUNT LIKE THAT!
NOT IN THAT PLACE, ANGEL! THOSE FAR-OUT CHARACTERS WOULDN'T BE INCLINED TO SUSPECT ANYTHING UNLESS IT WERE NORMAL!
AND, AS THE X-MEN PREPARE TO MUSTER THEIR FORCES FOR BATTLE, MAGNETO AND HIS MUTANTS ALSO MAKE LAST MINUTE PREPARATIONS...
THIS FACTORY BELONGS TO ME! I HAVE KEPT IT FOR JUST SUCH A TIME AS THIS!
NOW THAT WE ARE READY, WE SHALL ISSUE OUR CHALLENGE TO THE X-MEN!
YEAH! YEAH! I DON'T EVEN NEED ALL OF YOU! I CAN HANDLE THOSE OVERRATED WEAKLINGS BY MYSELF!
DON'T BE A FOOL! THEY'VE BEATEN ALL OF US IN THE PAST! ME, I WANT ALL THE HELP I CAN GET!
DANGER--KEEP OUT!
13

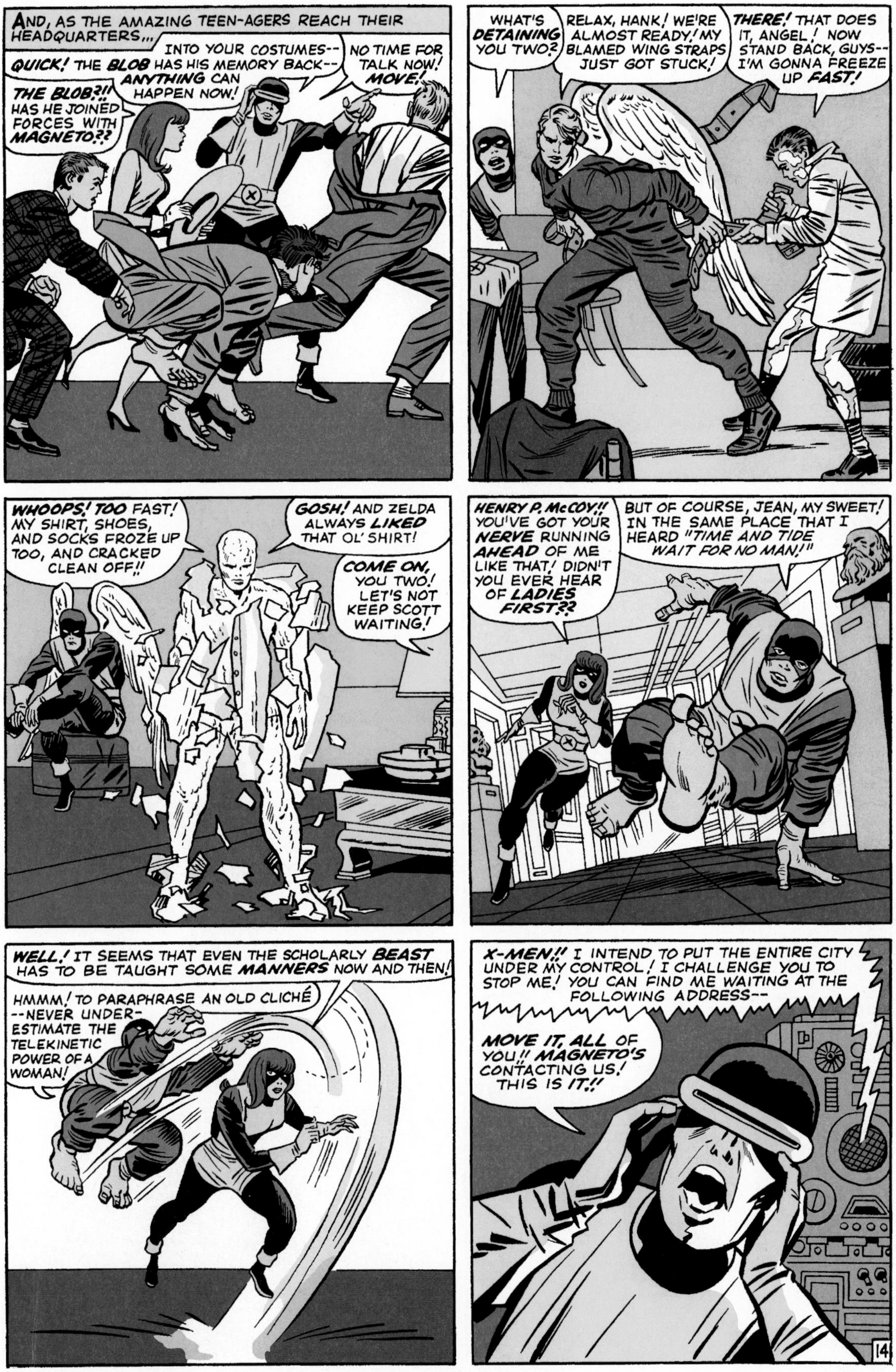
AND, AS THE AMAZING TEEN-AGERS REACH THEIR HEADQUARTERS...
INTO YOUR COSTUMES-- QUICK! THE BLOB HAS HIS MEMORY BACK-- ANYTHING CAN HAPPEN NOW!
NO TIME FOR TALK NOW! MOVE!
THE BLOB?!! HAS HE JOINED FORCES WITH MAGNETO??
WHAT'S DETAINING YOU TWO?
RELAX, HANK! WE'RE ALMOST READY! MY BLAMED WING STRAPS JUST GOT STUCK!
THERE! THAT DOES IT, ANGEL! NOW STAND BACK, GUYS-- I'M GONNA FREEZE UP FAST!
WHOOPS! TOO FAST! MY SHIRT, SHOES, AND SOCKS FROZE UP TOO, AND CRACKED CLEAN OFF!!
GOSH! AND ZELDA ALWAYS LIKED THAT OL' SHIRT!
COME ON, YOU TWO! LET'S NOT KEEP SCOTT WAITING!
HENRY P. McCOY!! YOU'VE GOT YOUR NERVE RUNNING AHEAD OF ME LIKE THAT! DIDN'T YOU EVER HEAR OF LADIES FIRST??
BUT OF COURSE, JEAN, MY SWEET! IN THE SAME PLACE THAT I HEARD "TIME AND TIDE WAIT FOR NO MAN!"
WELL! IT SEEMS THAT EVEN THE SCHOLARLY BEAST HAS TO BE TAUGHT SOME MANNERS NOW AND THEN!
HMMM! TO PARAPHRASE AN OLD CLICHÉ --NEVER UNDER-ESTIMATE THE TELEKINETIC POWER OF A WOMAN!
X-MEN!! I INTEND TO PUT THE ENTIRE CITY UNDER MY CONTROL! I CHALLENGE YOU TO STOP ME! YOU CAN FIND ME WAITING AT THE FOLLOWING ADDRESS--
MOVE IT, ALL OF YOU!! MAGNETO'S CONTACTING US! THIS IS IT!!
14

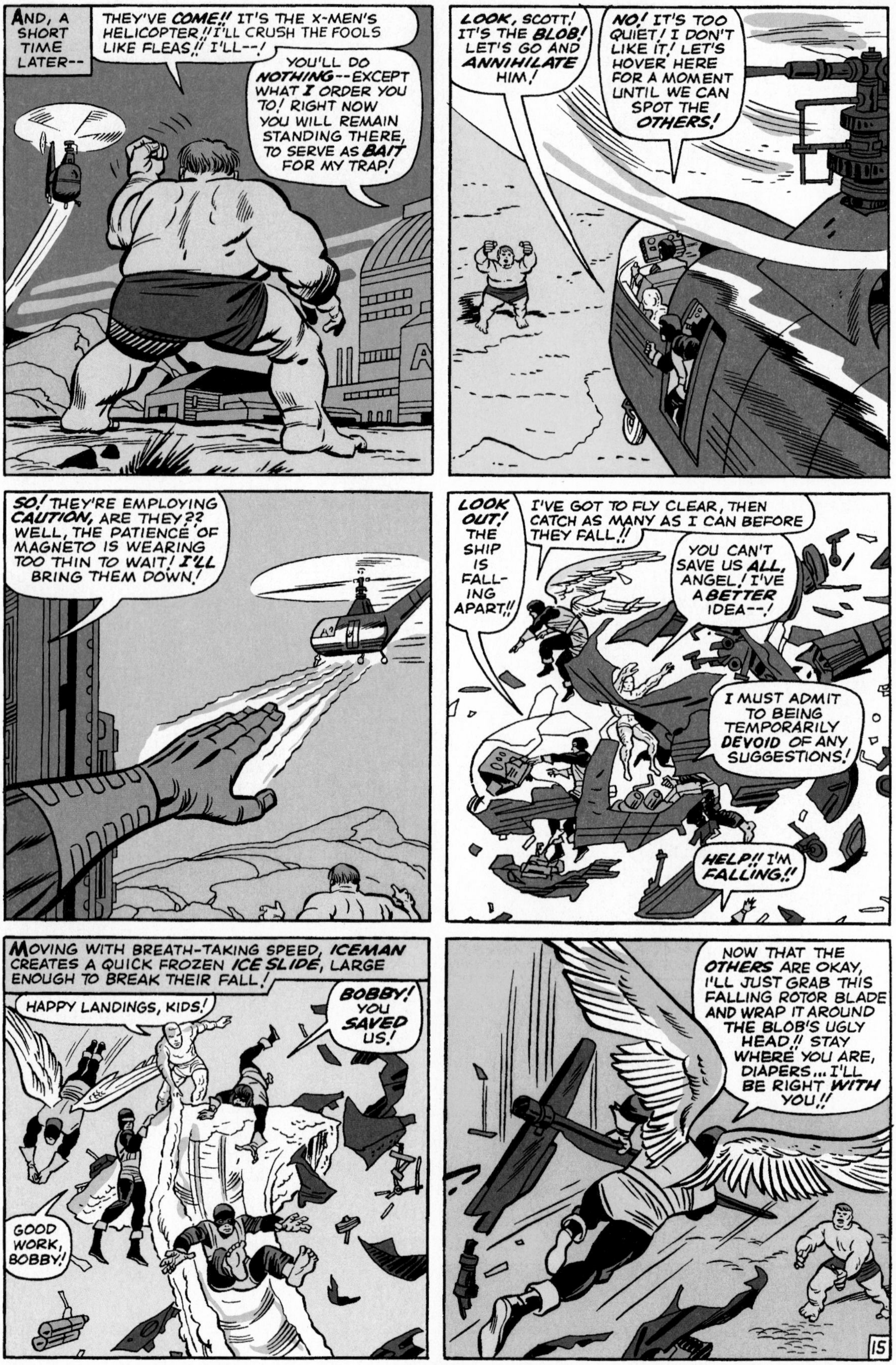

AND, A SHORT TIME LATER--
THEY'VE COME!! IT'S THE X-MEN'S HELICOPTER!! I'LL CRUSH THE FOOLS LIKE FLEAS!! I'LL--!
YOU'LL DO NOTHING--EXCEPT WHAT I ORDER YOU TO! RIGHT NOW YOU WILL REMAIN STANDING THERE, TO SERVE AS BAIT FOR MY TRAP!
LOOK, SCOTT! IT'S THE BLOB! LET'S GO AND ANNIHILATE HIM!
NO! IT'S TOO QUIET! I DON'T LIKE IT! LET'S HOVER HERE FOR A MOMENT UNTIL WE CAN SPOT THE OTHERS!
SO! THEY'RE EMPLOYING CAUTION, ARE THEY?? WELL, THE PATIENCE OF MAGNETO IS WEARING TOO THIN TO WAIT! I'LL BRING THEM DOWN!
LOOK OUT! THE SHIP IS FALL-ING APART!!
I'VE GOT TO FLY CLEAR, THEN CATCH AS MANY AS I CAN BEFORE THEY FALL!!
YOU CAN'T SAVE US ALL, ANGEL! I'VE A BETTER IDEA--!
I MUST ADMIT TO BEING TEMPORARILY DEVOID OF ANY SUGGESTIONS!
HELP!! I'M FALLING!!
MOVING WITH BREATH-TAKING SPEED, ICEMAN CREATES A QUICK FROZEN ICE SLIDE, LARGE ENOUGH TO BREAK THEIR FALL!
HAPPY LANDINGS, KIDS!
BOBBY! YOU SAVED US!
GOOD WORK, BOBBY!
NOW THAT THE OTHERS ARE OKAY, I'LL JUST GRAB THIS FALLING ROTOR BLADE AND WRAP IT AROUND THE BLOB'S UGLY HEAD!! STAY WHERE YOU ARE, DIAPERS... I'LL BE RIGHT WITH YOU!!
15

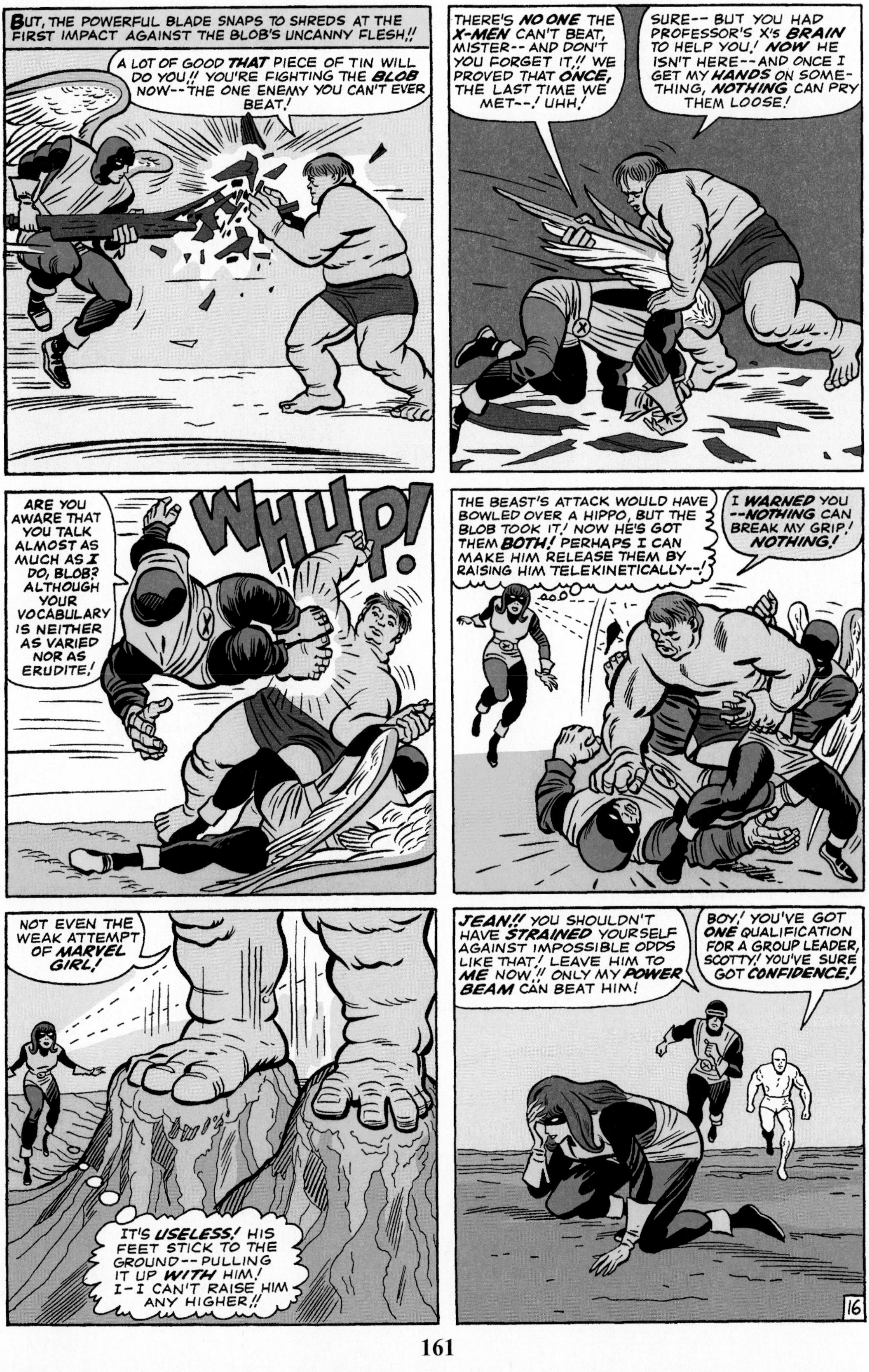
BUT, THE POWERFUL BLADE SNAPS TO SHREDS AT THE FIRST IMPACT AGAINST THE BLOB'S UNCANNY FLESH!!
A LOT OF GOOD THAT PIECE OF TIN WILL DO YOU!! YOU'RE FIGHTING THE BLOB NOW--THE ONE ENEMY YOU CAN'T EVER BEAT!
THERE'S NO ONE THE X-MEN CAN'T BEAT, MISTER-- AND DON'T YOU FORGET IT!! WE PROVED THAT ONCE, THE LAST TIME WE MET--! UHH!
SURE-- BUT YOU HAD PROFESSOR'S X'S BRAIN TO HELP YOU! NOW HE ISN'T HERE--AND ONCE I GET MY HANDS ON SOMETHING, NOTHING CAN PRY THEM LOOSE!
ARE YOU AWARE THAT YOU TALK ALMOST AS MUCH AS I DO, BLOB? ALTHOUGH YOUR VOCABULARY IS NEITHER AS VARIED NOR AS ERUDITE!
WHUP!
THE BEAST'S ATTACK WOULD HAVE BOWLED OVER A HIPPO, BUT THE BLOB TOOK IT! NOW HE'S GOT THEM BOTH! PERHAPS I CAN MAKE HIM RELEASE THEM BY RAISING HIM TELEKINETICALLY--!
I WARNED YOU --NOTHING CAN BREAK MY GRIP! NOTHING!
NOT EVEN THE WEAK ATTEMPT OF MARVEL GIRL!
IT'S USELESS! HIS FEET STICK TO THE GROUND--PULLING IT UP WITH HIM! I-I CAN'T RAISE HIM ANY HIGHER!!
JEAN!! YOU SHOULDN'T HAVE STRAINED YOURSELF AGAINST IMPOSSIBLE ODDS LIKE THAT! LEAVE HIM TO ME NOW!! ONLY MY POWER BEAM CAN BEAT HIM!
BOY! YOU'VE GOT ONE QUALIFICATION FOR A GROUP LEADER, SCOTTY! YOU'VE SURE GOT CONFIDENCE!
16

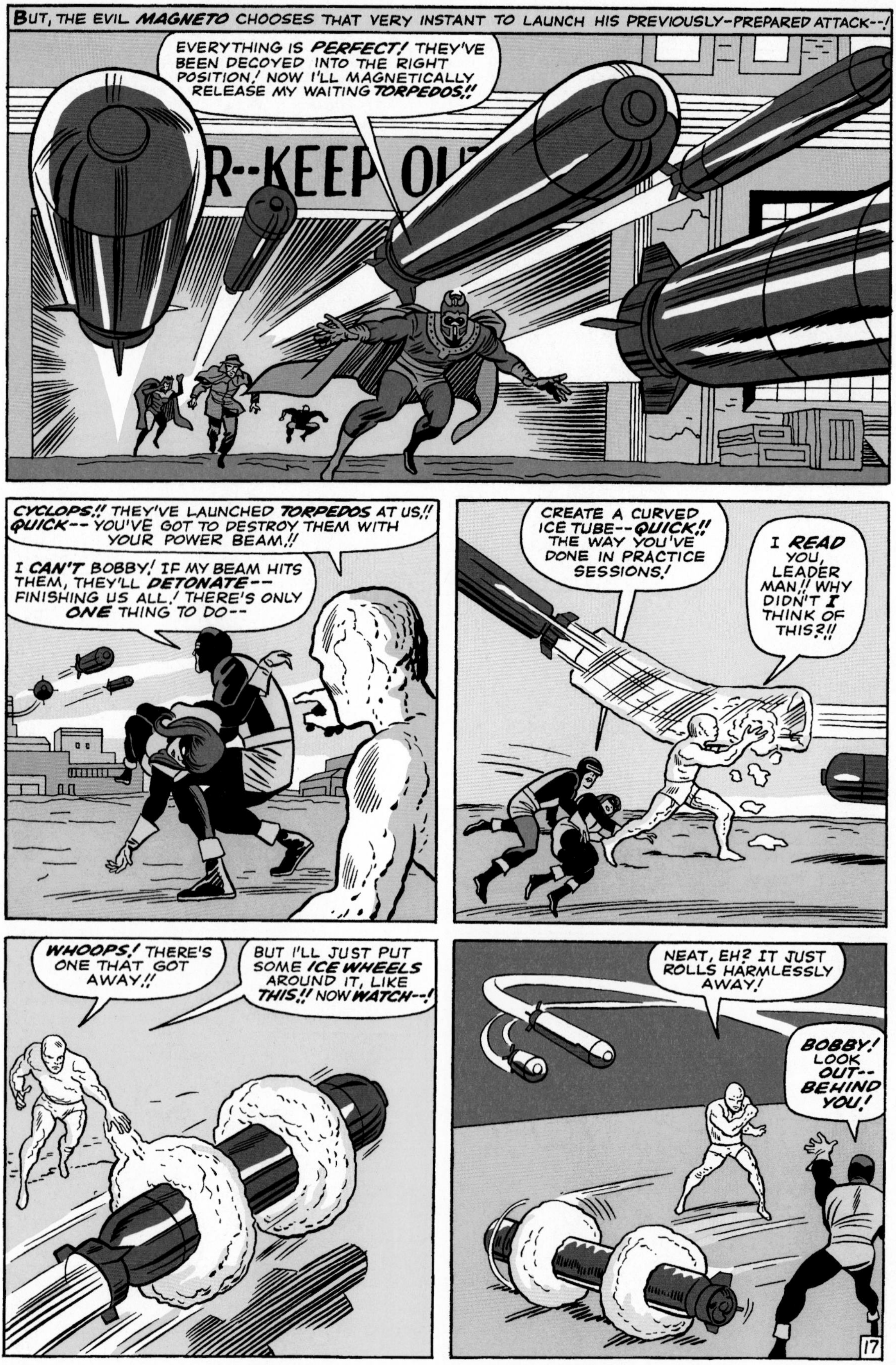
BUT, THE EVIL MAGNETO CHOOSES THAT VERY INSTANT TO LAUNCH HIS PREVIOUSLY-PREPARED ATTACK--!
EVERYTHING IS PERFECT! THEY'VE BEEN DECOYED INTO THE RIGHT POSITION! NOW I'LL MAGNETICALLY RELEASE MY WAITING TORPEDOS!!
R--KEEP OU
CYCLOPS!! THEY'VE LAUNCHED TORPEDOS AT US!! QUICK-- YOU'VE GOT TO DESTROY THEM WITH YOUR POWER BEAM!!
I CAN'T BOBBY! IF MY BEAM HITS THEM, THEY'LL DETONATE-- FINISHING US ALL! THERE'S ONLY ONE THING TO DO--
CREATE A CURVED ICE TUBE--QUICK!! THE WAY YOU'VE DONE IN PRACTICE SESSIONS!
I READ YOU, LEADER MAN!! WHY DIDN'T I THINK OF THIS?!!
WHOOPS! THERE'S ONE THAT GOT AWAY!!
BUT I'LL JUST PUT SOME ICE WHEELS AROUND IT, LIKE THIS!! NOW WATCH--!
NEAT, EH? IT JUST ROLLS HARMLESSLY AWAY!
BOBBY! LOOK OUT-- BEHIND YOU!
17

MOVING WITH THE SPEED OF THOUGHT, THE DYNAMIC **CYCLOPS** BLASTS A HOLE UNDER ICE-MAN'S FEET, DEEP ENOUGH FOR BOBBY TO DROP BELOW THE PATH OF THE DEADLY MISSILES!!

OWW WAH!!

DUCK, KID-- DUCK!

THEY'RE TOO FAST-- TOO CLEVER FOR MY TORPEDOS! BUT, IF I CAN GET THEM WITHIN REACH OF *YOU*, BLOB--!

I *TOLD* YOU I COULD HANDLE THEM! JUST GET THEM OVER TO ME-- LET ME GET MY HANDS ON *ALL* OF THEM !!

BUT, UNLIKE THE *BLOB*, THE QUICK-THINKING *BEAST* HAS HIS *WITS* TO RELY ON, AS WELL AS HIS STRENGTH--!

I'LL CONCEDE YOUR SUPERIORITY IN AN ARM-WRESTLING MATCH-- BUT LET'S SEE HOW YOU COPE WITH SOME SUDDEN *MUD* IN YOUR EYE!

TAKEN UNAWARES, THE SLOWER-WITTED BLOB RELEASES HIS UNBREAKABLE GRIP AS HE FOLLOWS THE NATURAL IMPULSE TO RUB HIS EYES!

WHA--?? CAN'T *SEE*!! GOT TO GET THE MUD OUT OF MY EYES,!!

BUT, INSTEAD OF RACING OUT OF REACH OF THE BLOB, THE BEAST ONCE MORE MAKES AN UNEX-PECTED MOVE, WHILE HIS GARGANTUAN OPPONENT IS STILL OFF-BALANCE--!

EUREKA! I THOUGHT THIS MANEUVER WOULD SUCCEED!

EVEN *YOU* CAN'T MAIN-TAIN YOUR STANCE WHEN DEALT A BLOW WHICH YOU HAVEN'T PREPARED YOURSELF FOR!

WUP!

BLAST THE LUCK! THOSE X-MEN NEVER SEEM TO KNOW WHEN THEY'RE BEATEN! I'LL SHIELD MYSELF FROM THE *ANGEL* WITH A FLYING TORPEDO BARRIER!

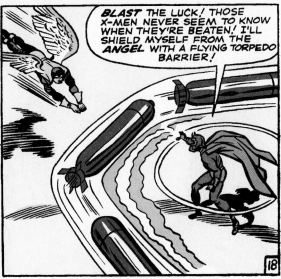

18

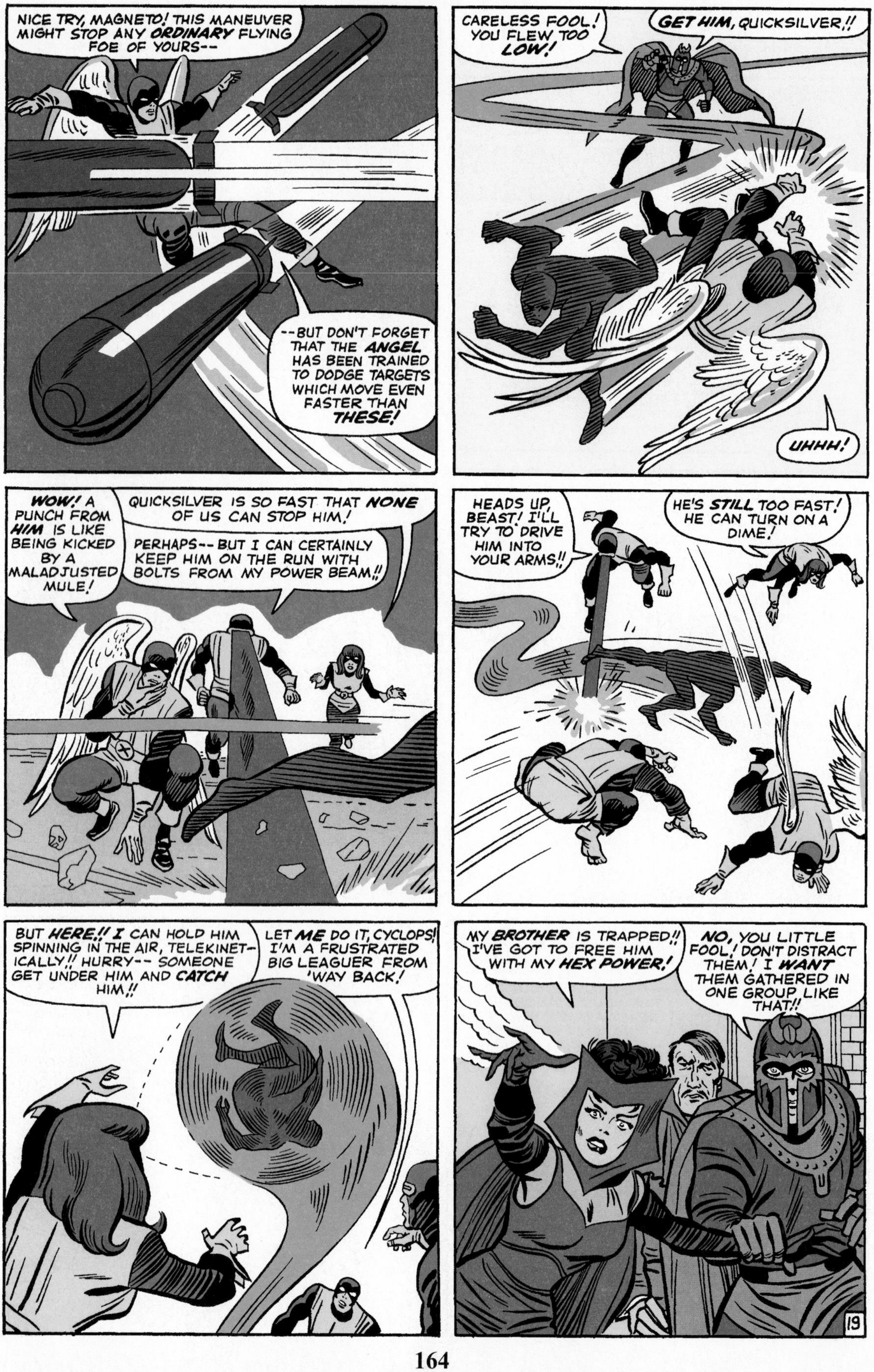
NICE TRY, MAGNETO! THIS MANEUVER MIGHT STOP ANY ORDINARY FLYING FOE OF YOURS--
--BUT DON'T FORGET THAT THE ANGEL HAS BEEN TRAINED TO DODGE TARGETS WHICH MOVE EVEN FASTER THAN THESE!
CARELESS FOOL! YOU FLEW TOO LOW!
GET HIM, QUICKSILVER!!
UHHH!
WOW! A PUNCH FROM HIM IS LIKE BEING KICKED BY A MALADJUSTED MULE!
QUICKSILVER IS SO FAST THAT NONE OF US CAN STOP HIM!
PERHAPS-- BUT I CAN CERTAINLY KEEP HIM ON THE RUN WITH BOLTS FROM MY POWER BEAM!!
HEADS UP, BEAST! I'LL TRY TO DRIVE HIM INTO YOUR ARMS!!
HE'S STILL TOO FAST! HE CAN TURN ON A DIME!
BUT HERE!! I CAN HOLD HIM SPINNING IN THE AIR, TELEKINETICALLY!! HURRY-- SOMEONE GET UNDER HIM AND CATCH HIM!!
LET ME DO IT, CYCLOPS! I'M A FRUSTRATED BIG LEAGUER FROM 'WAY BACK!
MY BROTHER IS TRAPPED!! I'VE GOT TO FREE HIM WITH MY HEX POWER!
NO, YOU LITTLE FOOL! DON'T DISTRACT THEM! I WANT THEM GATHERED IN ONE GROUP LIKE THAT!!
19

BUT MAGNETO'S COMMAND COMES TOO LATE! HIT WITH THE *SCARLET WITCH'S* HEX POWER, THE BEAST AND CYCLOPS CANNOT STOP THEMSELVES FROM COLLIDING INTO EACH OTHER!

THUMP!

OHHH!

I'M *FREE!* NOTHING WILL EVER CATCH ME *NOW!*

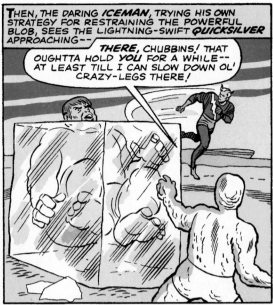

THEN, THE DARING *ICEMAN,* TRYING HIS OWN STRATEGY FOR RESTRAINING THE POWERFUL BLOB, SEES THE LIGHTNING-SWIFT *QUICKSILVER* APPROACHING--

THERE, CHUBBINS! THAT OUGHTTA HOLD *YOU* FOR A WHILE-- AT LEAST TILL I CAN SLOW DOWN OL' CRAZY-LEGS THERE!

BUT, SO UNIMAGINABLY SWIFT IS QUICKSILVER, THAT EVEN THE COMBINED EFFORTS OF *ALL* THE X-MEN ARE NOT ENOUGH TO CAPTURE THE SPEEDING MUTANT!

WELL DONE, PIETRO!! I *KNEW* THEY COULD NOT CATCH YOU, MY BELOVED BROTHER!

FALL IN BEHIND ME NOW! THE BATTLE LINE IS DRAWN--WE'RE ALL TOGETHER IN A BODY--JUST AS *MAGNETO'S* MUTANTS ARE--THIS IS *IT--* THE FINAL ATTACK!

JUST SAY THE WORD, CYCLOPS! WE'LL MAKE THEM THINK *WATERLOO* WAS A SOCIAL TEA PARTY!

HEY! STOP FLAPPIN' THOSE WINGS OF YOURS, ANGEL! YOU'RE TICKLIN' MY EARS!

BUT, BEFORE ANOTHER MOVE CAN BE MADE, THE GARGANTUAN *BLOB* EXPANDS HIS ENORMOUS BULK UNTIL THE BLOCK OF ICE WHICH CONFINED HIM SHATTERS WITH A DEAFENING ROAR!

BAROOM!

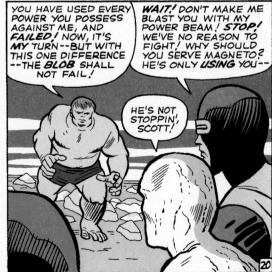

YOU HAVE USED EVERY POWER YOU POSSESS AGAINST ME, AND *FAILED!* NOW, IT'S *MY* TURN--BUT WITH THIS ONE DIFFERENCE --THE *BLOB* SHALL NOT FAIL!

WAIT! DON'T MAKE ME BLAST YOU WITH MY POWER BEAM! *STOP!* WE'VE NO REASON TO FIGHT! WHY SHOULD YOU SERVE MAGNETO? HE'S ONLY *USING* YOU--

HE'S NOT STOPPIN', SCOTT!

20

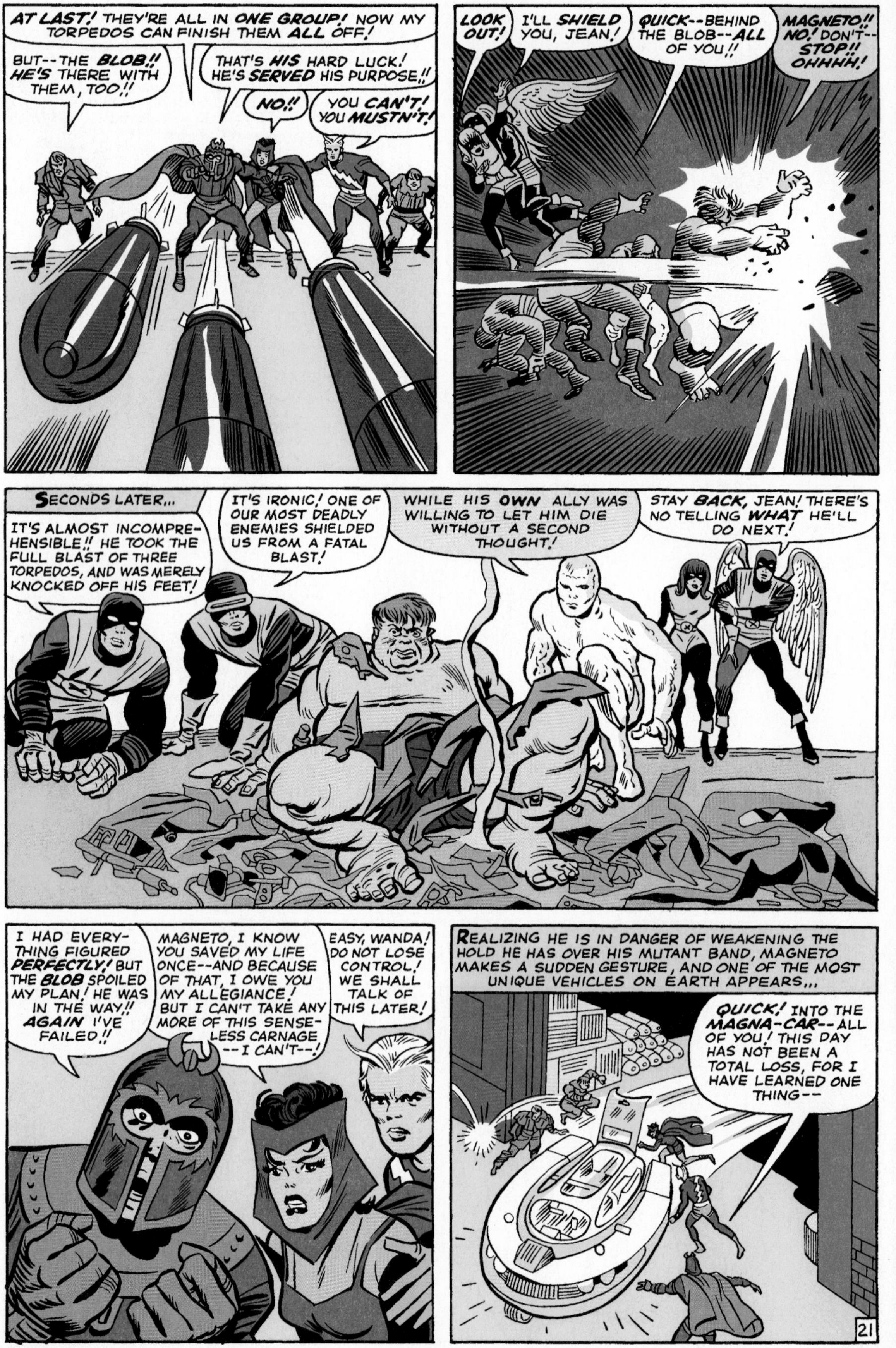
AT LAST! THEY'RE ALL IN ONE GROUP! NOW MY TORPEDOS CAN FINISH THEM ALL OFF!
BUT--THE BLOB!! HE'S THERE WITH THEM, TOO!!
THAT'S HIS HARD LUCK! HE'S SERVED HIS PURPOSE!!
NO!!
YOU CAN'T! YOU MUSTN'T!
LOOK OUT!
I'LL SHIELD YOU, JEAN!
QUICK--BEHIND THE BLOB--ALL OF YOU!!
MAGNETO!! NO! DON'T-- STOP!! OHHHH!
SECONDS LATER...
IT'S ALMOST INCOMPRE-HENSIBLE!! HE TOOK THE FULL BLAST OF THREE TORPEDOS, AND WAS MERELY KNOCKED OFF HIS FEET!
IT'S IRONIC! ONE OF OUR MOST DEADLY ENEMIES SHIELDED US FROM A FATAL BLAST!
WHILE HIS OWN ALLY WAS WILLING TO LET HIM DIE WITHOUT A SECOND THOUGHT!
STAY BACK, JEAN! THERE'S NO TELLING WHAT HE'LL DO NEXT!
I HAD EVERY-THING FIGURED PERFECTLY! BUT THE BLOB SPOILED MY PLAN! HE WAS IN THE WAY!! AGAIN I'VE FAILED!!
MAGNETO, I KNOW YOU SAVED MY LIFE ONCE--AND BECAUSE OF THAT, I OWE YOU MY ALLEGIANCE! BUT I CAN'T TAKE ANY MORE OF THIS SENSE-LESS CARNAGE --I CAN'T--!
EASY, WANDA! DO NOT LOSE CONTROL! WE SHALL TALK OF THIS LATER!
REALIZING HE IS IN DANGER OF WEAKENING THE HOLD HE HAS OVER HIS MUTANT BAND, MAGNETO MAKES A SUDDEN GESTURE, AND ONE OF THE MOST UNIQUE VEHICLES ON EARTH APPEARS...
QUICK! INTO THE MAGNA-CAR--ALL OF YOU! THIS DAY HAS NOT BEEN A TOTAL LOSS, FOR I HAVE LEARNED ONE THING--
21

PROFESSOR X WAS NOT WITH THEM TODAY-- NOT EVEN *MENTALLY*, ELSE I WOULD HAVE SENSED HIS BRAIN WAVES! THAT MEANS THE X-MEN FIGHT *ALONE* NOW! THEREFORE, I SHALL PLAN MY STRATEGY *DIFFERENTLY* FOR OUR NEXT BATTLE!

CYCLOPS! THEY'RE GETTING *AWAY!*

NOT *THIS* TIME! I'LL *BLAST* THEM TO THE GROUND!

WAIT! THE *SCARLET WITCH*-- SHE'S ABOARD ALSO!

YOU'RE *RIGHT!* AND HER BROTHER, *QUICKSILVER!* SOMEHOW, I CAN'T BRING MYSELF TO BELIEVE THAT THEY ARE AS *EVIL* AS THE OTHERS!

WELL, PUDGY-- IT LOOKS AS IF YOUR PALS RAN OUT ON YOU, EH?

PALS?? THE BLOB *HAS* NO PALS!! I REALIZE THAT NOW!

WHY DON'T YOU JOIN *US??* WE'VE NO NEED TO BE ENEMIES!

YOU COULD RECEIVE *X-MAN* TRAINING! AND PERHAPS, IN TIME, IF YOU *QUALIFY*--

NO! I'M THRU WITH MUTANTS-- THRU WITH FIGHTING *OTHER* PEOPLE'S FIGHTS! I'LL NEVER TRUST ANYONE AGAIN!

I SEEM TO REMEMBER SOMETHING THE PROFESSOR ONCE SAID-- LONG AGO--

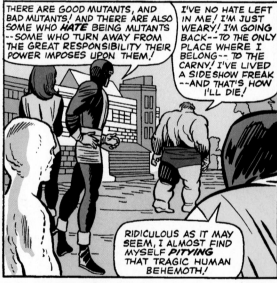

THERE ARE GOOD MUTANTS, AND BAD MUTANTS! AND THERE ARE ALSO SOME WHO *HATE* BEING MUTANTS-- SOME WHO TURN AWAY FROM THE GREAT RESPONSIBILITY THEIR POWER IMPOSES UPON THEM!

I'VE NO HATE LEFT IN ME! I'M JUST *WEARY!* I'M GOING BACK-- TO THE ONLY PLACE WHERE I BELONG-- TO THE *CARNY!* I'VE LIVED A SIDESHOW FREAK --AND THAT'S *HOW* I'LL DIE!

RIDICULOUS AS IT MAY SEEM, I ALMOST FIND MYSELF *PITYING* THAT TRAGIC HUMAN BEHEMOTH!

I SURE HOPE HE NEVER CHANGES HIS MIND! I WOULDN'T WANNA HAVE TO FIGHT *HIM* AGAIN!

SCRATCH ONE WHIRLY-BIRD, X-MEN! THIS WRECKAGE IS BEYOND REPAIR!

WELL, I GUESS WE'LL HAVE TO PHONE FOR A *TAXI!* UH OH-- I HAVEN'T ANY CHANGE IN MY POCKETS-- IN FACT-- *NO POCKETS!*

KNOW SOME-THIN'? WE'RE GONNA FEEL LIKE *NUTS* WALKING HOME THRU THE STREETS LIKE THIS!

HAVE NO FEAR-- *ANGEL'S* HERE! I'LL FLY AHEAD AND HAIL A TAXI FOR US!

WHILE YOU'RE AT IT, BORROW THE FARE! YOUR "GROUP LEADER'S" *BROKE!*

- THE END

AND SO ANOTHER X-MAN ADVENTURE BECOMES HISTORY! BUT, WILL WE SEE *MORE* OF MAGNETO'S EVIL MUTANTS? WILL WE SEE *NEW* DANGER AND SURPRISES? *WILL* WE?? ARE YOU *KIDDIN'??!* NOW, TO ALL YOU HAPPY HOMO SAPIENS-- *SO LONG... TILL NEXT ISH!*

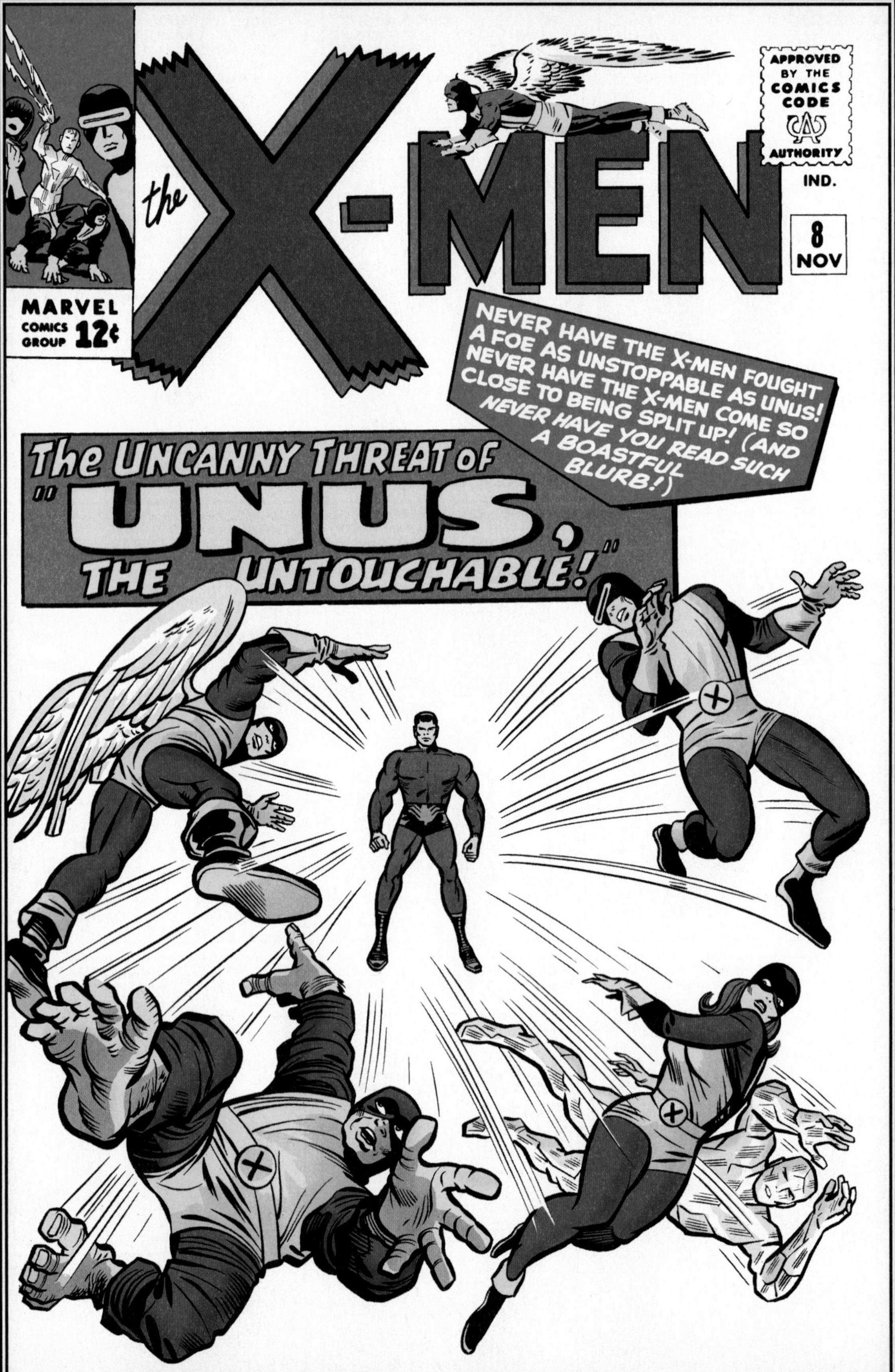
APPROVED BY THE COMICS CODE CA AUTHORITY
IND.
the X-MEN
8 NOV
MARVEL COMICS GROUP 12¢
NEVER HAVE THE X-MEN FOUGHT A FOE AS UNSTOPPABLE AS UNUS! NEVER HAVE THE X-MEN COME SO CLOSE TO BEING SPLIT UP! (AND NEVER HAVE YOU READ SUCH A BOASTFUL BLURB!)
The UNCANNY THREAT of "UNUS, THE UNTOUCHABLE!"

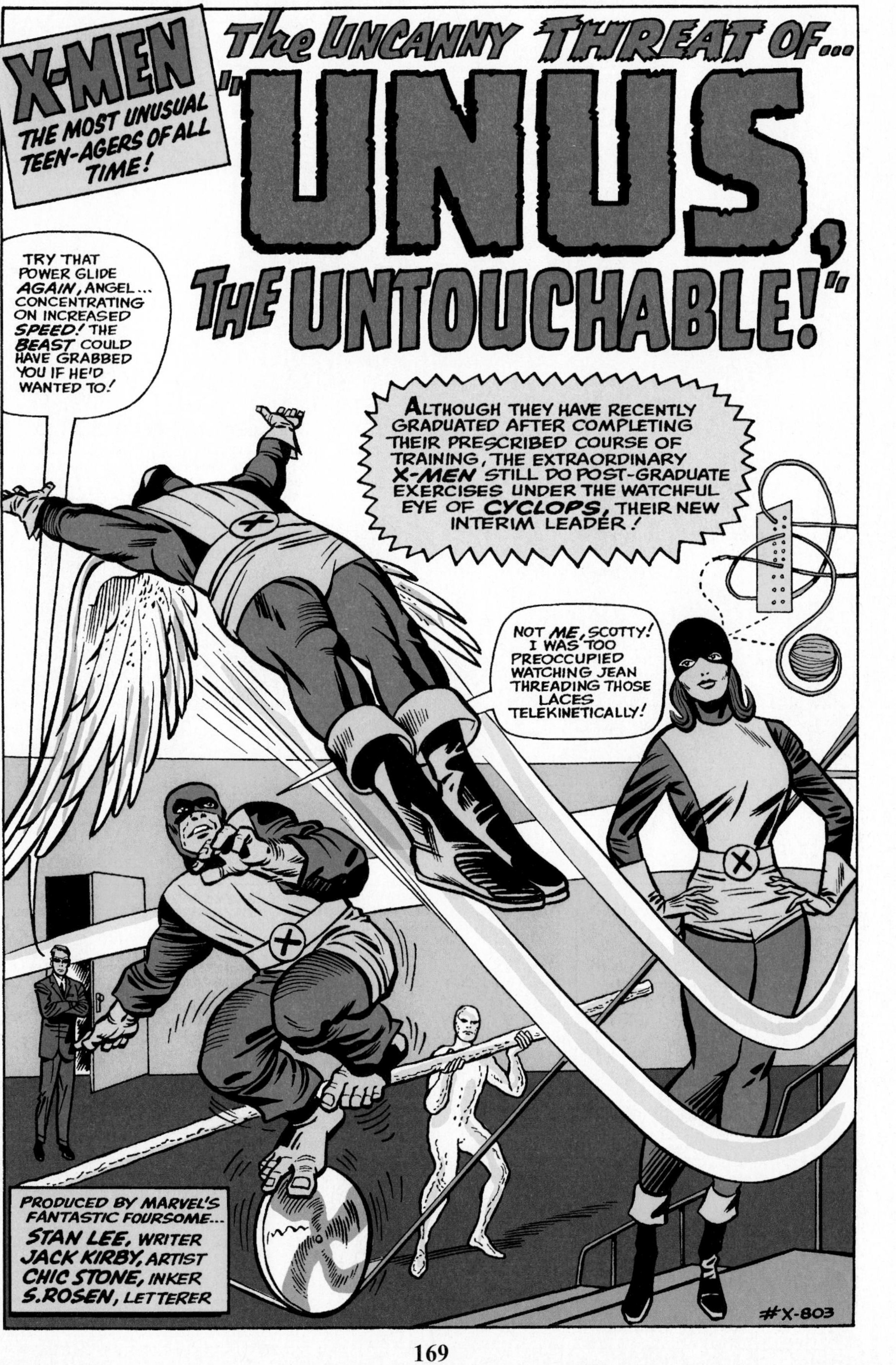
X-MEN
THE MOST UNUSUAL TEEN-AGERS OF ALL TIME!
The UNCANNY THREAT OF... "UNUS, THE UNTOUCHABLE!"
TRY THAT POWER GLIDE AGAIN, ANGEL... CONCENTRATING ON INCREASED SPEED! THE BEAST COULD HAVE GRABBED YOU IF HE'D WANTED TO!
ALTHOUGH THEY HAVE RECENTLY GRADUATED AFTER COMPLETING THEIR PRESCRIBED COURSE OF TRAINING, THE EXTRAORDINARY X-MEN STILL DO POST-GRADUATE EXERCISES UNDER THE WATCHFUL EYE OF CYCLOPS, THEIR NEW INTERIM LEADER!
NOT ME, SCOTTY! I WAS TOO PREOCCUPIED WATCHING JEAN THREADING THOSE LACES TELEKINETICALLY!
PRODUCED BY MARVEL'S FANTASTIC FOURSOME... STAN LEE, WRITER JACK KIRBY, ARTIST CHIC STONE, INKER S.ROSEN, LETTERER
#X-803

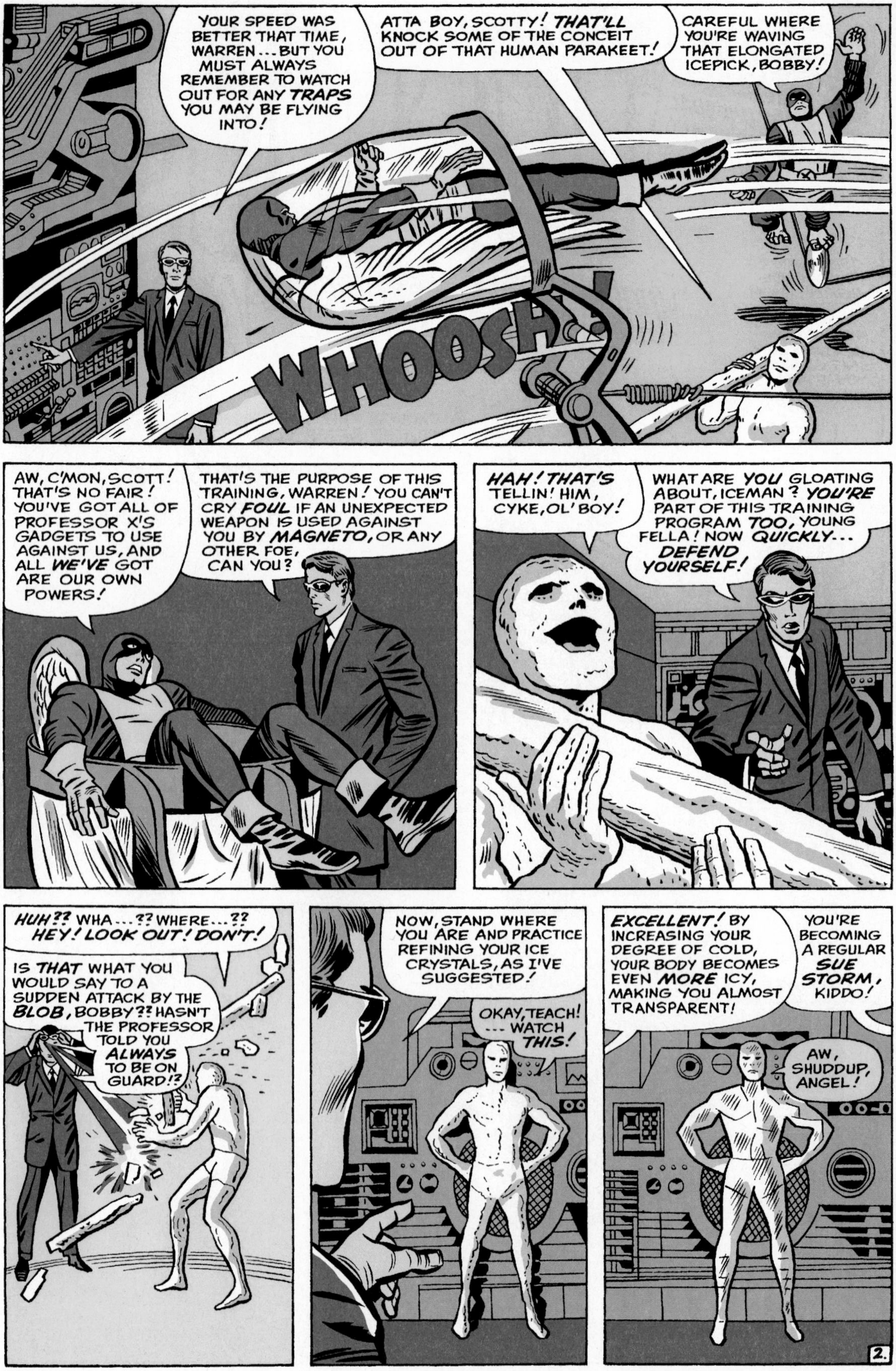

YOUR SPEED WAS BETTER THAT TIME, WARREN... BUT YOU MUST ALWAYS REMEMBER TO WATCH OUT FOR ANY TRAPS YOU MAY BE FLYING INTO!
ATTA BOY, SCOTTY! THAT'LL KNOCK SOME OF THE CONCEIT OUT OF THAT HUMAN PARAKEET!
CAREFUL WHERE YOU'RE WAVING THAT ELONGATED ICEPICK, BOBBY!
WHOOSH!
AW, C'MON, SCOTT! THAT'S NO FAIR! YOU'VE GOT ALL OF PROFESSOR X'S GADGETS TO USE AGAINST US, AND ALL WE'VE GOT ARE OUR OWN POWERS!
THAT'S THE PURPOSE OF THIS TRAINING, WARREN! YOU CAN'T CRY FOUL IF AN UNEXPECTED WEAPON IS USED AGAINST YOU BY MAGNETO, OR ANY OTHER FOE, CAN YOU?
HAH! THAT'S TELLIN' HIM, CYKE, OL' BOY!
WHAT ARE YOU GLOATING ABOUT, ICEMAN? YOU'RE PART OF THIS TRAINING PROGRAM TOO, YOUNG FELLA! NOW QUICKLY... DEFEND YOURSELF!
HUH?? WHA...?? WHERE...?? HEY! LOOK OUT! DON'T!
IS THAT WHAT YOU WOULD SAY TO A SUDDEN ATTACK BY THE BLOB, BOBBY?? HASN'T THE PROFESSOR TOLD YOU ALWAYS TO BE ON GUARD!?
NOW, STAND WHERE YOU ARE AND PRACTICE REFINING YOUR ICE CRYSTALS, AS I'VE SUGGESTED!
OKAY, TEACH! --- WATCH THIS!
EXCELLENT! BY INCREASING YOUR DEGREE OF COLD, YOUR BODY BECOMES EVEN MORE ICY, MAKING YOU ALMOST TRANSPARENT!
YOU'RE BECOMING A REGULAR SUE STORM, KIDDO!
AW, SHUDDUP, ANGEL!
2.

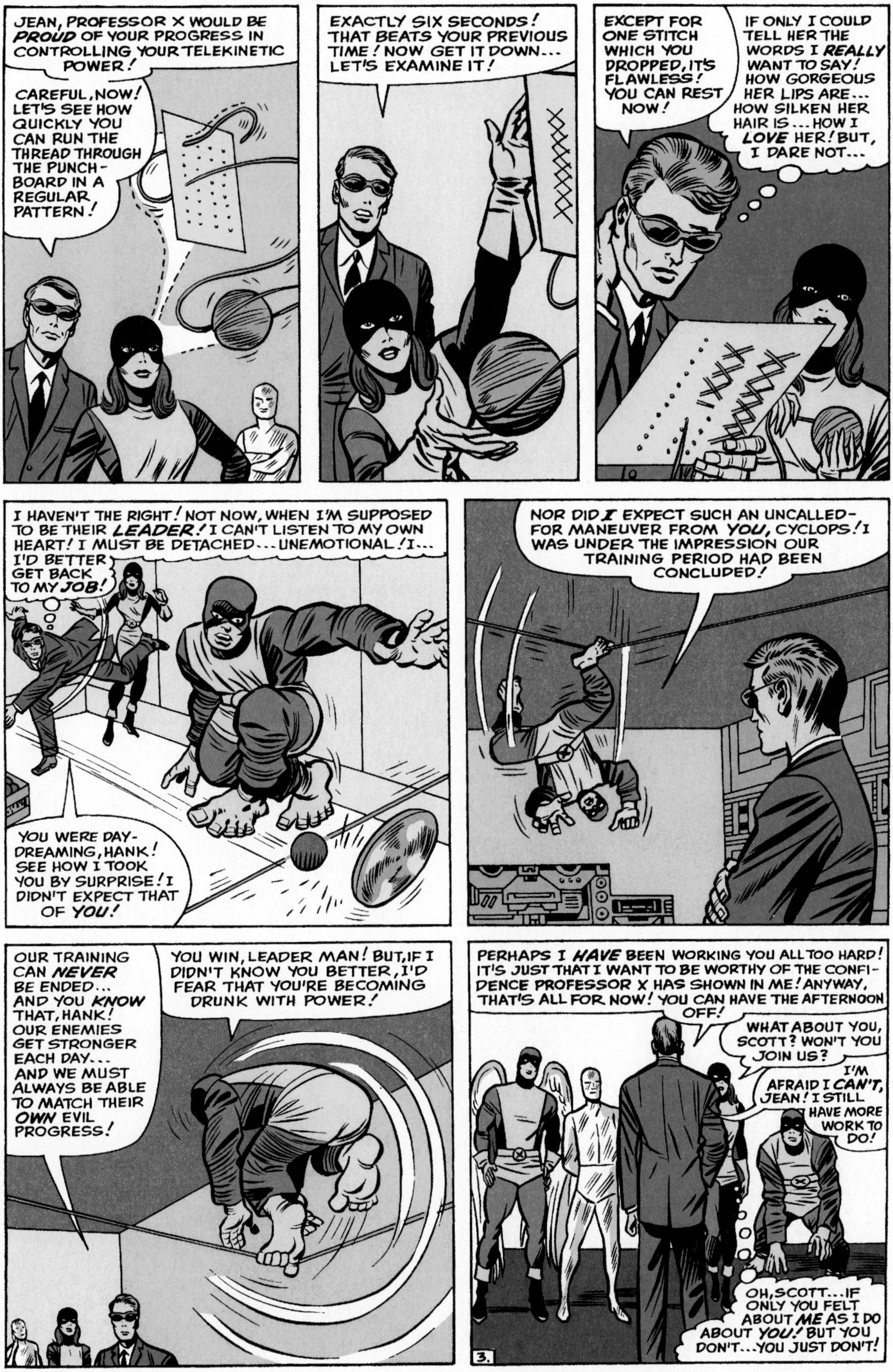
JEAN, PROFESSOR X WOULD BE PROUD OF YOUR PROGRESS IN CONTROLLING YOUR TELEKINETIC POWER!
CAREFUL, NOW! LET'S SEE HOW QUICKLY YOU CAN RUN THE THREAD THROUGH THE PUNCH-BOARD IN A REGULAR PATTERN!
EXACTLY SIX SECONDS! THAT BEATS YOUR PREVIOUS TIME! NOW GET IT DOWN... LET'S EXAMINE IT!
EXCEPT FOR ONE STITCH WHICH YOU DROPPED, IT'S FLAWLESS! YOU CAN REST NOW!
IF ONLY I COULD TELL HER THE WORDS I REALLY WANT TO SAY! HOW GORGEOUS HER LIPS ARE... HOW SILKEN HER HAIR IS... HOW I LOVE HER! BUT, I DARE NOT...
I HAVEN'T THE RIGHT! NOT NOW, WHEN I'M SUPPOSED TO BE THEIR LEADER! I CAN'T LISTEN TO MY OWN HEART! I MUST BE DETACHED... UNEMOTIONAL! I...
I'D BETTER GET BACK TO MY JOB!
YOU WERE DAY-DREAMING, HANK! SEE HOW I TOOK YOU BY SURPRISE! I DIDN'T EXPECT THAT OF YOU!
NOR DID I EXPECT SUCH AN UNCALLED-FOR MANEUVER FROM YOU, CYCLOPS! I WAS UNDER THE IMPRESSION OUR TRAINING PERIOD HAD BEEN CONCLUDED!
OUR TRAINING CAN NEVER BE ENDED... AND YOU KNOW THAT, HANK! OUR ENEMIES GET STRONGER EACH DAY... AND WE MUST ALWAYS BE ABLE TO MATCH THEIR OWN EVIL PROGRESS!
YOU WIN, LEADER MAN! BUT, IF I DIDN'T KNOW YOU BETTER, I'D FEAR THAT YOU'RE BECOMING DRUNK WITH POWER!
PERHAPS I HAVE BEEN WORKING YOU ALL TOO HARD! IT'S JUST THAT I WANT TO BE WORTHY OF THE CONFI-DENCE PROFESSOR X HAS SHOWN IN ME! ANYWAY, THAT'S ALL FOR NOW! YOU CAN HAVE THE AFTERNOON OFF!
WHAT ABOUT YOU, SCOTT? WON'T YOU JOIN US?
I'M AFRAID I CAN'T, JEAN! I STILL HAVE MORE WORK TO DO!
OH, SCOTT... IF ONLY YOU FELT ABOUT ME AS I DO ABOUT YOU! BUT YOU DON'T... YOU JUST DON'T!
3.

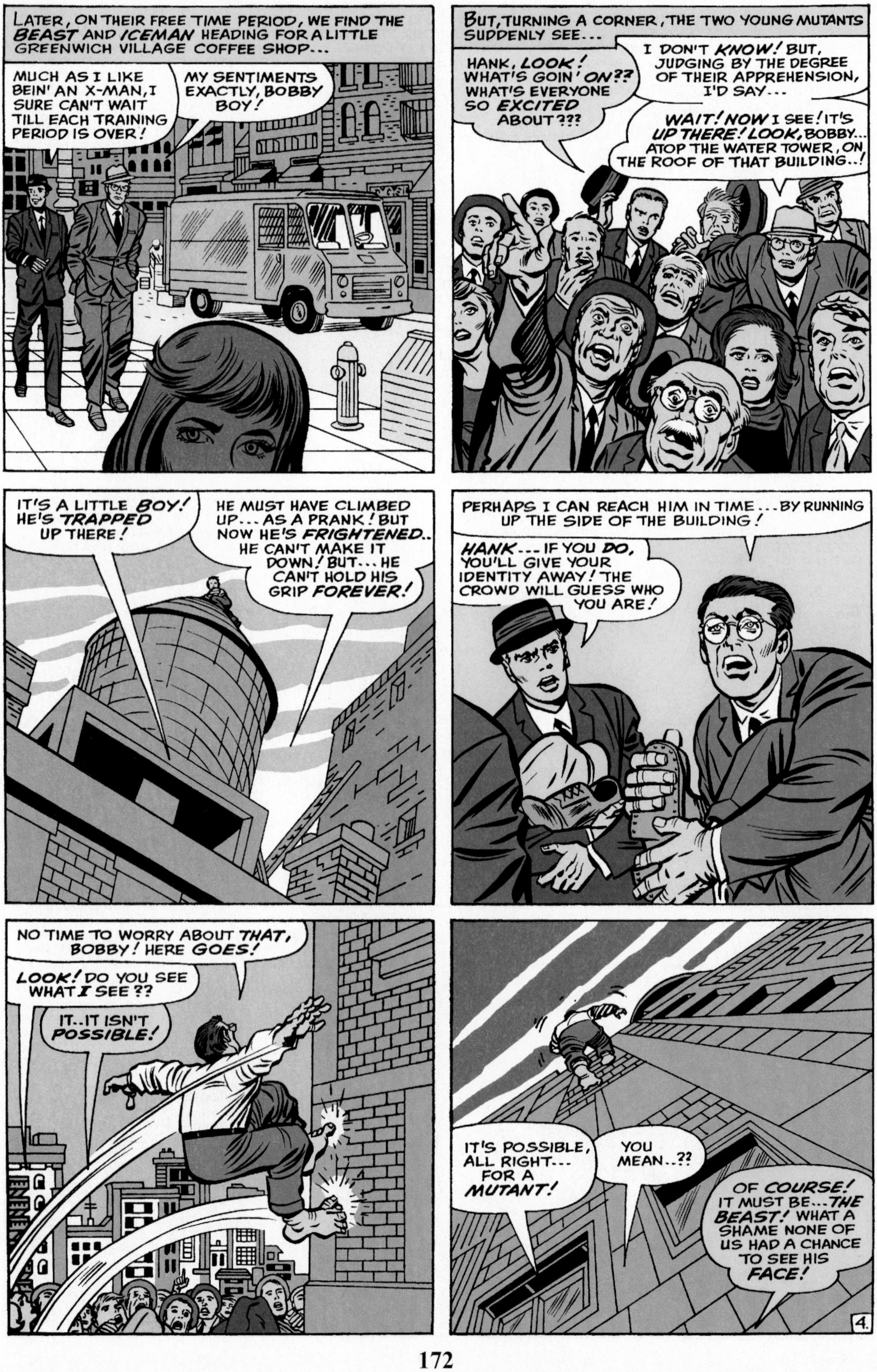
LATER, ON THEIR FREE TIME PERIOD, WE FIND THE BEAST AND ICEMAN HEADING FOR A LITTLE GREENWICH VILLAGE COFFEE SHOP...
MUCH AS I LIKE BEIN' AN X-MAN, I SURE CAN'T WAIT TILL EACH TRAINING PERIOD IS OVER!
MY SENTIMENTS EXACTLY, BOBBY BOY!
BUT, TURNING A CORNER, THE TWO YOUNG MUTANTS SUDDENLY SEE...
HANK, LOOK! WHAT'S GOIN' ON?? WHAT'S EVERYONE SO EXCITED ABOUT???
I DON'T KNOW! BUT, JUDGING BY THE DEGREE OF THEIR APPREHENSION, I'D SAY...
WAIT! NOW I SEE! IT'S UP THERE! LOOK, BOBBY... ATOP THE WATER TOWER, ON THE ROOF OF THAT BUILDING..!
IT'S A LITTLE BOY! HE'S TRAPPED UP THERE!
HE MUST HAVE CLIMBED UP... AS A PRANK! BUT NOW HE'S FRIGHTENED.. HE CAN'T MAKE IT DOWN! BUT... HE CAN'T HOLD HIS GRIP FOREVER!
PERHAPS I CAN REACH HIM IN TIME... BY RUNNING UP THE SIDE OF THE BUILDING!
HANK... IF YOU DO, YOU'LL GIVE YOUR IDENTITY AWAY! THE CROWD WILL GUESS WHO YOU ARE!
NO TIME TO WORRY ABOUT THAT, BOBBY! HERE GOES!
LOOK! DO YOU SEE WHAT I SEE??
IT..IT ISN'T POSSIBLE!
IT'S POSSIBLE, ALL RIGHT... FOR A MUTANT!
YOU MEAN..??
OF COURSE! IT MUST BE... THE BEAST! WHAT A SHAME NONE OF US HAD A CHANCE TO SEE HIS FACE!
4.

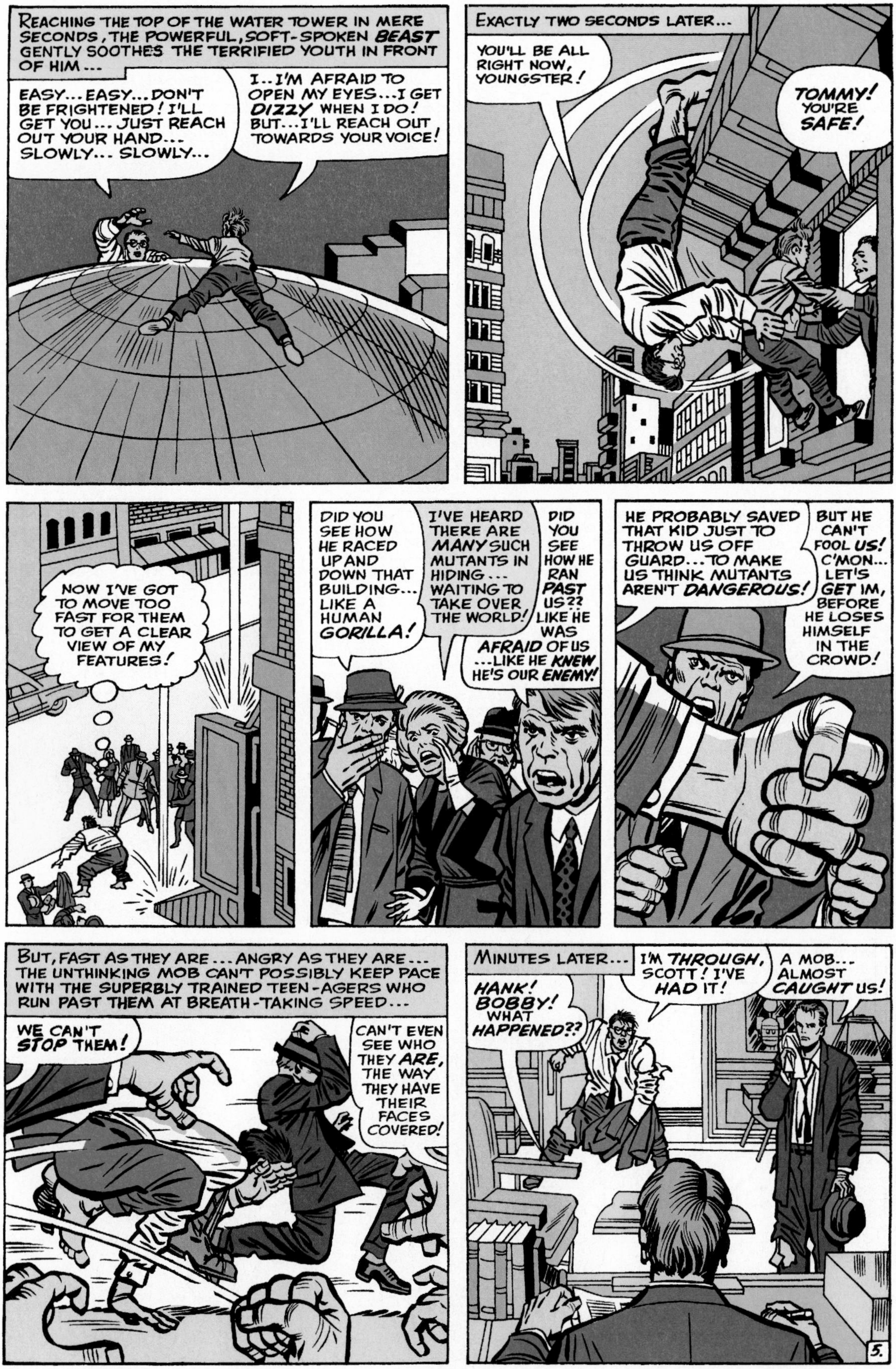
REACHING THE TOP OF THE WATER TOWER IN MERE SECONDS, THE POWERFUL, SOFT-SPOKEN BEAST GENTLY SOOTHES THE TERRIFIED YOUTH IN FRONT OF HIM...
EASY... EASY... DON'T BE FRIGHTENED! I'LL GET YOU... JUST REACH OUT YOUR HAND... SLOWLY... SLOWLY...
I.. I'M AFRAID TO OPEN MY EYES... I GET DIZZY WHEN I DO! BUT... I'LL REACH OUT TOWARDS YOUR VOICE!
EXACTLY TWO SECONDS LATER...
YOU'LL BE ALL RIGHT NOW, YOUNGSTER!
TOMMY! YOU'RE SAFE!
NOW I'VE GOT TO MOVE TOO FAST FOR THEM TO GET A CLEAR VIEW OF MY FEATURES!
DID YOU SEE HOW HE RACED UP AND DOWN THAT BUILDING... LIKE A HUMAN GORILLA!
I'VE HEARD THERE ARE MANY SUCH MUTANTS IN HIDING... WAITING TO TAKE OVER THE WORLD!
DID YOU SEE HOW HE RAN PAST US?? LIKE HE WAS AFRAID OF US ...LIKE HE KNEW HE'S OUR ENEMY!
HE PROBABLY SAVED THAT KID JUST TO THROW US OFF GUARD... TO MAKE US THINK MUTANTS AREN'T DANGEROUS!
BUT HE CAN'T FOOL US! C'MON... LET'S GET IM, BEFORE HE LOSES HIMSELF IN THE CROWD!
BUT, FAST AS THEY ARE... ANGRY AS THEY ARE... THE UNTHINKING MOB CAN'T POSSIBLY KEEP PACE WITH THE SUPERBLY TRAINED TEEN-AGERS WHO RUN PAST THEM AT BREATH-TAKING SPEED...
WE CAN'T STOP THEM!
CAN'T EVEN SEE WHO THEY ARE, THE WAY THEY HAVE THEIR FACES COVERED!
MINUTES LATER...
HANK! BOBBY! WHAT HAPPENED??
I'M THROUGH, SCOTT! I'VE HAD IT!
A MOB... ALMOST CAUGHT US!
5.

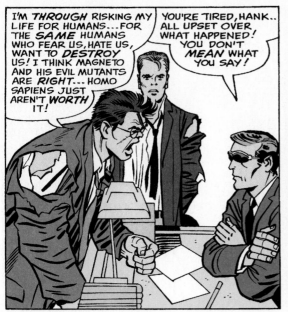

I'M *THROUGH* RISKING MY LIFE FOR HUMANS...FOR THE *SAME* HUMANS WHO FEAR US, HATE US, WANT TO *DESTROY* US! I THINK MAGNETO AND HIS EVIL MUTANTS ARE *RIGHT*...HOMO SAPIENS JUST AREN'T *WORTH* IT!

YOU'RE TIRED, HANK.. ALL UPSET OVER WHAT HAPPENED! YOU DON'T *MEAN* WHAT YOU SAY!

I'M IN FULL POSSESSION OF MY FACULTIES, SCOTT! I MEAN EVERY WORD! I'M *RESIGNING* FROM THE X-MEN!

BUT, HANK.. ALL YOUR TRAINING... YOUR WORK.. YOU CAN'T JUST TOSS IT ALL ASIDE!

CAN'T I? JUST *WATCH* ME! FROM NOW ON I'LL USE MY POWERS TO HELP JUST *ONE* PERSON...HENRY McCOY...YOURS TRULY! THE HUMAN RACE CAN GO FLY A KITE!

BUT WHERE WILL YOU *GO*? WHAT WILL YOU *DO*??

DON'T WORRY ABOUT *ME*, FELLA! I'LL GET ALONG! IF THE HUMAN RACE IS GONNA BE MY ENEMY-FINE! BUT *I'LL* MAKE THE RULES FOR MY NEXT FIGHT!

HANK..KEEP IN TOUCH WITH US! CALL IF YOU NEED ME! TAKE *CARE* OF YOURSELF, YOU BIG, BAD-TEMPERED LUG!

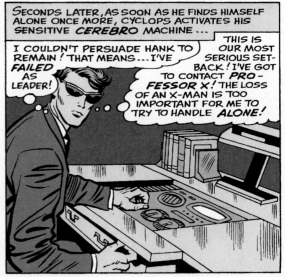

Seconds later, as soon as he finds himself alone once more, Cyclops activates his sensitive CEREBRO machine...

I COULDN'T PERSUADE HANK TO REMAIN! THAT MEANS...I'VE *FAILED* AS LEADER!

THIS IS OUR MOST SERIOUS SET-BACK! I'VE GOT TO CONTACT *PRO-FESSOR X*! THE LOSS OF AN X-MAN IS TOO IMPORTANT FOR ME TO TRY TO HANDLE *ALONE*!

Slowly, the thought image of Professor Xavier is con-verted into a VISUAL image on the glowing screen, and then...

I'VE MADE *CONTACT*!

PROFESSOR, THIS IS CYCLOPS! WHERE *ARE* YOU, SIR?

I AM IN THE HEART OF THE BALKANS, IN EUROPE... DESCENDING INTO AN ALMOST BOTTOMLESS CAVE!

Then, after Cyclops has related the situation, through mental transmission...

WHAT DO I DO, *NOW*, SIR?

NOTHING! HE WILL *NOT* JOIN MAGNETO'S EVIL MUTANTS! YOU DID ALL YOU COULD!

6.

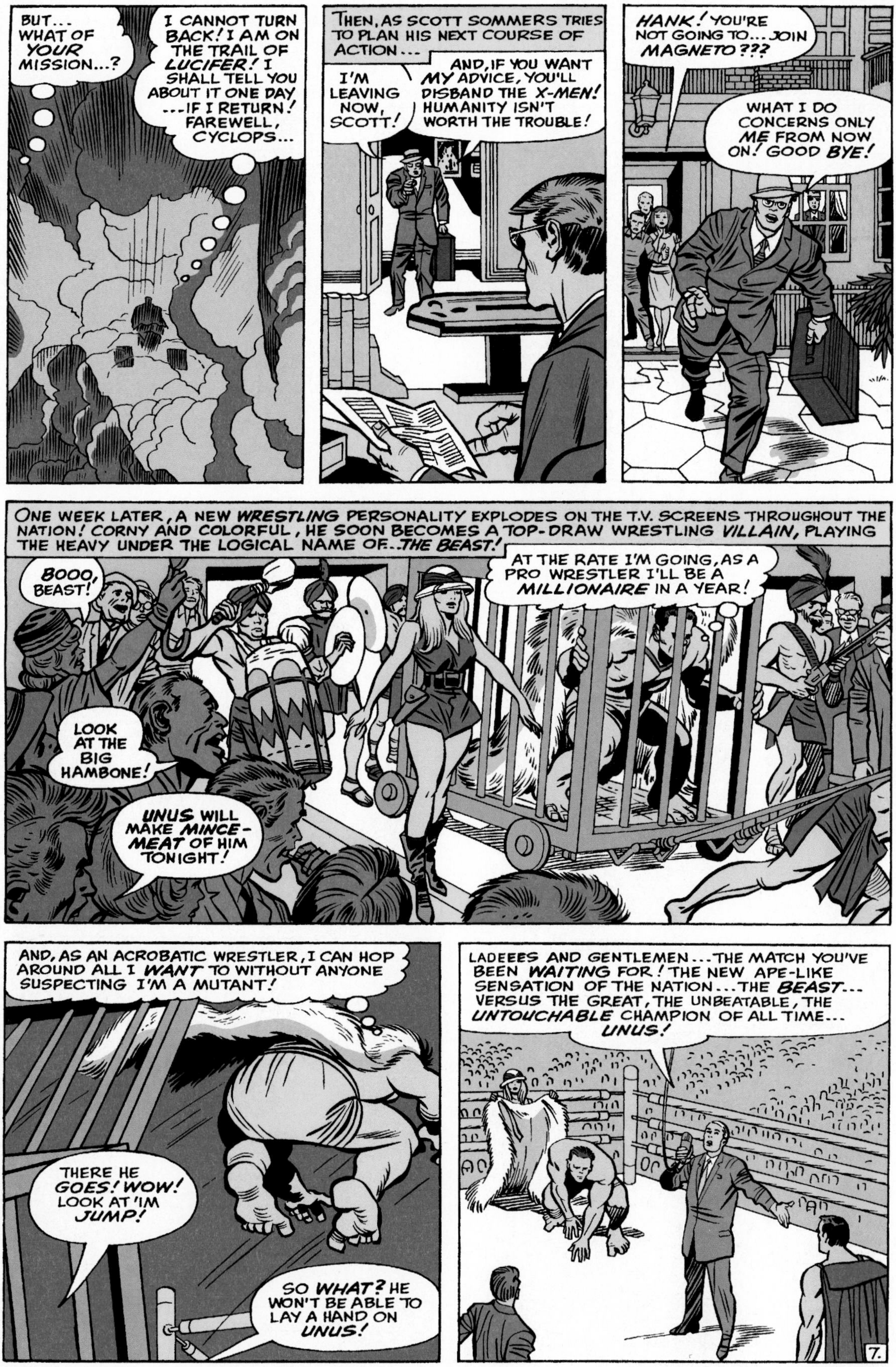
BUT... WHAT OF YOUR MISSION...?
I CANNOT TURN BACK! I AM ON THE TRAIL OF LUCIFER! I SHALL TELL YOU ABOUT IT ONE DAY ...IF I RETURN! FAREWELL, CYCLOPS...
THEN, AS SCOTT SOMMERS TRIES TO PLAN HIS NEXT COURSE OF ACTION...
I'M LEAVING NOW, SCOTT!
AND, IF YOU WANT MY ADVICE, YOU'LL DISBAND THE X-MEN! HUMANITY ISN'T WORTH THE TROUBLE!
HANK! YOU'RE NOT GOING TO... JOIN MAGNETO???
WHAT I DO CONCERNS ONLY ME FROM NOW ON! GOOD BYE!
ONE WEEK LATER, A NEW WRESTLING PERSONALITY EXPLODES ON THE T.V. SCREENS THROUGHOUT THE NATION! CORNY AND COLORFUL, HE SOON BECOMES A TOP-DRAW WRESTLING VILLAIN, PLAYING THE HEAVY UNDER THE LOGICAL NAME OF..THE BEAST!
BOOO, BEAST!
AT THE RATE I'M GOING, AS A PRO WRESTLER I'LL BE A MILLIONAIRE IN A YEAR!
LOOK AT THE BIG HAMBONE!
UNUS WILL MAKE MINCE-MEAT OF HIM TONIGHT!
AND, AS AN ACROBATIC WRESTLER, I CAN HOP AROUND ALL I WANT TO WITHOUT ANYONE SUSPECTING I'M A MUTANT!
THERE HE GOES! WOW! LOOK AT 'IM JUMP!
SO WHAT? HE WON'T BE ABLE TO LAY A HAND ON UNUS!
LADEEES AND GENTLEMEN...THE MATCH YOU'VE BEEN WAITING FOR! THE NEW APE-LIKE SENSATION OF THE NATION...THE BEAST... VERSUS THE GREAT, THE UNBEATABLE, THE UNTOUCHABLE CHAMPION OF ALL TIME... UNUS!
7.

SO *THAT'S* UNUS, EH? HE LOOKS LIKE A FORMIDABLE FOE... BUT *I'M* NO PUSHOVER MYSELF!

I'LL RUSH HIM QUICKLY, AND GET IT OVER WITH FAST SO THAT HE DOESN'T GET HURT!

BUT, AS THE BEAST MAKES ONE OF HIS POWERHOUSE CHARGES...

YOU THINK A MERE CLUMSY RUSH CAN AFFECT *ME* ??!

I DIDN'T SEE HIM *MOVE!* AND YET... I'M BEING HURLED BACK LIKE A PING PONG BALL!

IT'S INCOMPREHENSIBLE! NO MATTER HOW HARD I SWING, I CAN'T MAKE CONTACT WITH HIM !!

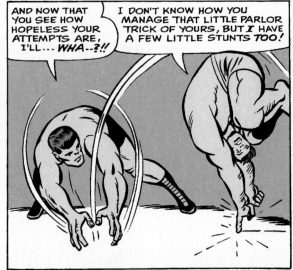

AND NOW THAT YOU SEE HOW HOPELESS YOUR ATTEMPTS ARE, I'LL... *WHA--?!!*

I DON'T KNOW HOW YOU MANAGE THAT LITTLE PARLOR TRICK OF YOURS, BUT *I* HAVE A FEW LITTLE STUNTS *TOO!*

I'LL KEEP SPRINGING UP TO GAIN MAXIMUM MOMENTUM, THEN I'LL DIVE DOWN AT HIM WHEN HE LEAST EXPECTS IT!

NOW!

176

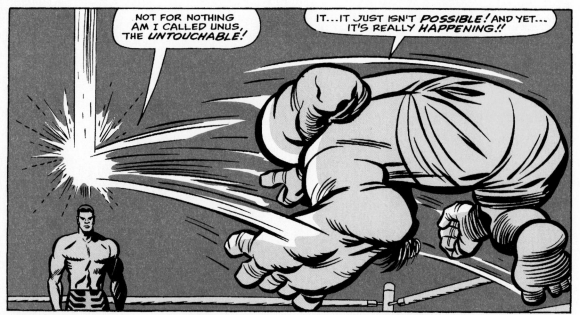

NOT FOR NOTHING AM I CALLED UNUS, THE *UNTOUCHABLE!*

IT...IT JUST ISN'T *POSSIBLE!* AND YET... IT'S REALLY *HAPPENING!!*

GOWAN BACK WHERE YOU *CAME* FROM, BEAST!

WHY DON'TCHA GIVE UP, YA BUM?!!

NOBODY CAN BEAT UNUS! YOU HAVEN'T GOT A CHANCE!

THERE'S *MORE* TO UNUS THAN THESE HYSTERICAL FANS *SUSPECT!* HE POSSESSES SOME SORT OF AWE-SOME *POWER!*

BOOO! WHERE'D *YOU* EVER LEARN TO RASSLE??

IT'S TAKING YA SO LONG TO CLIMB BACK IN THE RING THAT THE REF'S COUNTING YOU *OUT!* UNUS WILL WIN *AGAIN!*

THAT FACE IN THE AUDIENCE! IT *IS*...IT *HAS* TO BE...*MASTER-MIND!!* ONE OF *MAGNETO'S EVIL MUTANTS!*

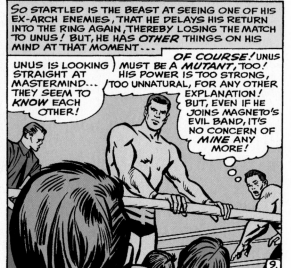

So STARTLED is the BEAST at seeing one of his EX-ARCH ENEMIES, that he DELAYS his return into the ring again, thereby LOSING the match to UNUS! But, he has *OTHER* things on his mind at that moment---

UNUS IS LOOKING STRAIGHT AT MASTERMIND... THEY SEEM TO *KNOW* EACH OTHER!

OF COURSE! UNUS MUST BE A *MUTANT,* TOO! HIS POWER IS TOO STRONG, TOO UNNATURAL, FOR ANY OTHER EXPLANATION! BUT, EVEN IF HE JOINS MAGNETO'S EVIL BAND, IT'S *NO* CONCERN OF *MINE* ANY MORE!

9.

177

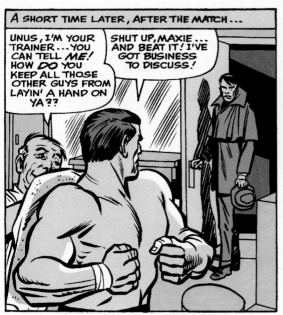

A SHORT TIME LATER, AFTER THE MATCH...

UNUS, I'M YOUR TRAINER...YOU CAN TELL *ME!* HOW *DO* YOU KEEP ALL THOSE OTHER GUYS FROM LAYIN' A HAND ON YA??

SHUT UP, MAXIE... AND BEAT IT! I'VE GOT BUSINESS TO DISCUSS!

WELL, MASTERMIND? WHAT'S MAGNETO'S VERDICT? CAN I JOIN YOUR GROUP OF MUTANTS?

NOT SO FAST, UNUS! MAGNETO HAS BEEN *DISAPPOINTED* BEFORE! * HE WANTS TO MAKE SURE HE CAN *TRUST* YOU!

* SEE X-MEN #7 "RETURN OF THE BLOB!"...STAN

HE'S CONVINCED THAT YOU'RE A REAL MUTANT... AND HE FEELS YOU'VE GOT PLENTY ON THE BALL...BUT HE WANTS YOU TO *PROVE* YOURSELF!

HOW? WHAT CAN I *DO?*

WELL, IF YOU WERE TO FIND THE *X-MEN* FOR US, FOR EXAMPLE... OR EVEN TO *BEAT* ONE OF THEM...!

LATER, AS UNUS THOUGHTFULLY WALKS THROUGH THE STREET...

OF *COURSE* I COULD BEAT ONE OF THE X-MEN... OR *ALL* OF THEM! *NOTHING* CAN DEFEAT ME! BUT WHERE DO I *FIND* THEM? I'VE NEVER EVEN *SEEN* ONE IN PERSON!

MC 2417

AT THAT POINT, *FATE* HERSELF STEPS IN! FOR UNUS ACCIDENTALLY STUMBLES ONTO A BIG BANK ROBBERY WHICH IS IN PROGRESS AROUND THE CORNER...

GUNMEN! ROBBING THE BANK! COME TO THINK OF IT, *I* CAN PUT THAT MONEY TO BETTER USE THAN *THEY* CAN!

MOVE...BEFORE THE PLACE IS SWARMIN' WITH COPS!!

ALL WE HAVETA DO IS MAKE IT TO THE GETAWAY CAR ACROSS THE STREET!

BANK

10.

178

BUT, THE STARTLED CRIMINALS ARE NEVER DESTINED TO *REACH* THAT WAITING CAR! AT LEAST, NOT WITH ANY STOLEN MONEY!

I'LL TAKE THAT MONEY BAG!

IF MAGNETO *DOESN'T* ALLOW ME TO JOIN HIS BROTHERHOOD, AT LEAST THIS MONEY WILL HELP LAUNCH ME ON MY *OWN* CAREER OF CONQUEST!

HEY, *LOOK,* CHARLIE! MY BULLETS DON'T EVEN *TOUCH* 'IM! THEY JUST GO FLYIN' AWAY!

DON'T YA KNOW WHO THAT *IS?* IT'S *UNUS,* THE *UNTOUCHABLE!*

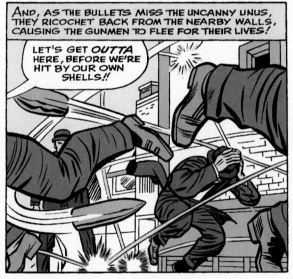

AND, AS THE BULLETS MISS THE UNCANNY UNUS, THEY RICOCHET BACK FROM THE NEARBY WALLS, CAUSING THE GUNMEN TO FLEE FOR THEIR LIVES!

LET'S GET *OUTTA* HERE, BEFORE WE'RE HIT BY OUR OWN SHELLS!!

MEANWHILE, A POWERFUL, PRIVATELY-OWNED HELICOPTER IS RAPIDLY APPROACHING THAT SAME AREA...

WHAT MAKES YOU THINK THERE'S A NEW MUTANT AT LARGE, CYCLOPS?

PROFESSOR X'S *CEREBRO* MACHINE DETECTED HIS PRESENCE ...AND THE READINGS SEEMED TO INDICATE THIS NEIGHBORHOOD!

IT JUST DOESN'T SEEM THE SAME TO BE HEADING INTO A NEW ADVENTURE WITHOUT THE *BEAST!*

WE *ALL* FEEL THE SAME WAY, WARREN ...BUT LET'S CON-CENTRATE ON THE JOB AT HAND NOW!

LOOK! SOMETHING'S GOING *ON* DOWN THERE!

THE *BANK'S* BEEN ROBBED! YOU LAND THE CHOPPER...I'LL GLIDE DOWN UNDER MY OWN POWER AND LOOK AROUND!

11.

179

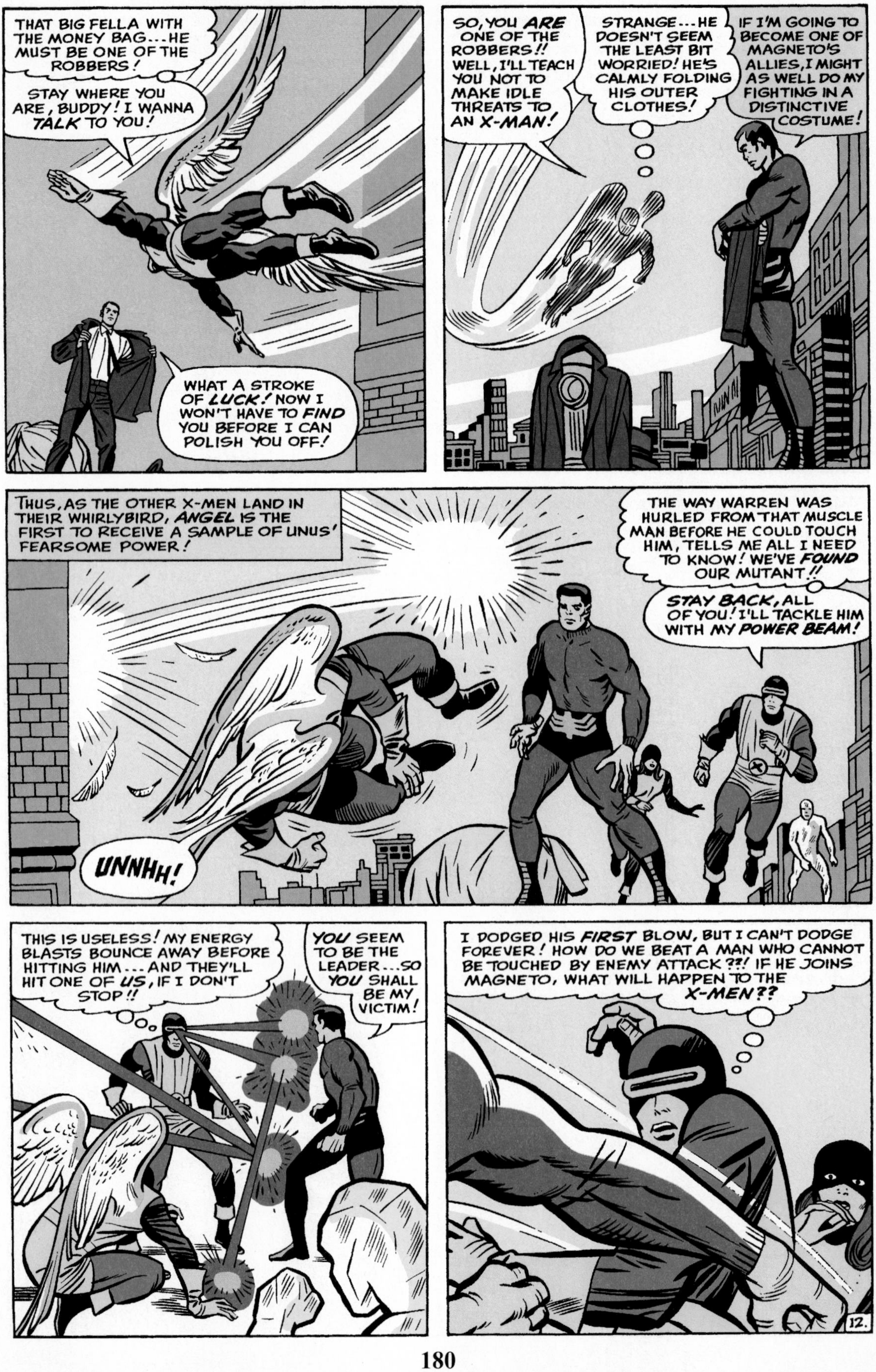
THAT BIG FELLA WITH THE MONEY BAG... HE MUST BE ONE OF THE ROBBERS!
STAY WHERE YOU ARE, BUDDY! I WANNA TALK TO YOU!
WHAT A STROKE OF LUCK! NOW I WON'T HAVE TO FIND YOU BEFORE I CAN POLISH YOU OFF!
SO, YOU ARE ONE OF THE ROBBERS!! WELL, I'LL TEACH YOU NOT TO MAKE IDLE THREATS TO AN X-MAN!
STRANGE... HE DOESN'T SEEM THE LEAST BIT WORRIED! HE'S CALMLY FOLDING HIS OUTER CLOTHES!
IF I'M GOING TO BECOME ONE OF MAGNETO'S ALLIES, I MIGHT AS WELL DO MY FIGHTING IN A DISTINCTIVE COSTUME!
THUS, AS THE OTHER X-MEN LAND IN THEIR WHIRLYBIRD, ANGEL IS THE FIRST TO RECEIVE A SAMPLE OF UNUS' FEARSOME POWER!
THE WAY WARREN WAS HURLED FROM THAT MUSCLE MAN BEFORE HE COULD TOUCH HIM, TELLS ME ALL I NEED TO KNOW! WE'VE FOUND OUR MUTANT!!
STAY BACK, ALL OF YOU! I'LL TACKLE HIM WITH MY POWER BEAM!
UNNHH!
THIS IS USELESS! MY ENERGY BLASTS BOUNCE AWAY BEFORE HITTING HIM... AND THEY'LL HIT ONE OF US, IF I DON'T STOP!!
YOU SEEM TO BE THE LEADER... SO YOU SHALL BE MY VICTIM!
I DODGED HIS FIRST BLOW, BUT I CAN'T DODGE FOREVER! HOW DO WE BEAT A MAN WHO CANNOT BE TOUCHED BY ENEMY ATTACK??! IF HE JOINS MAGNETO, WHAT WILL HAPPEN TO THE X-MEN??
12.

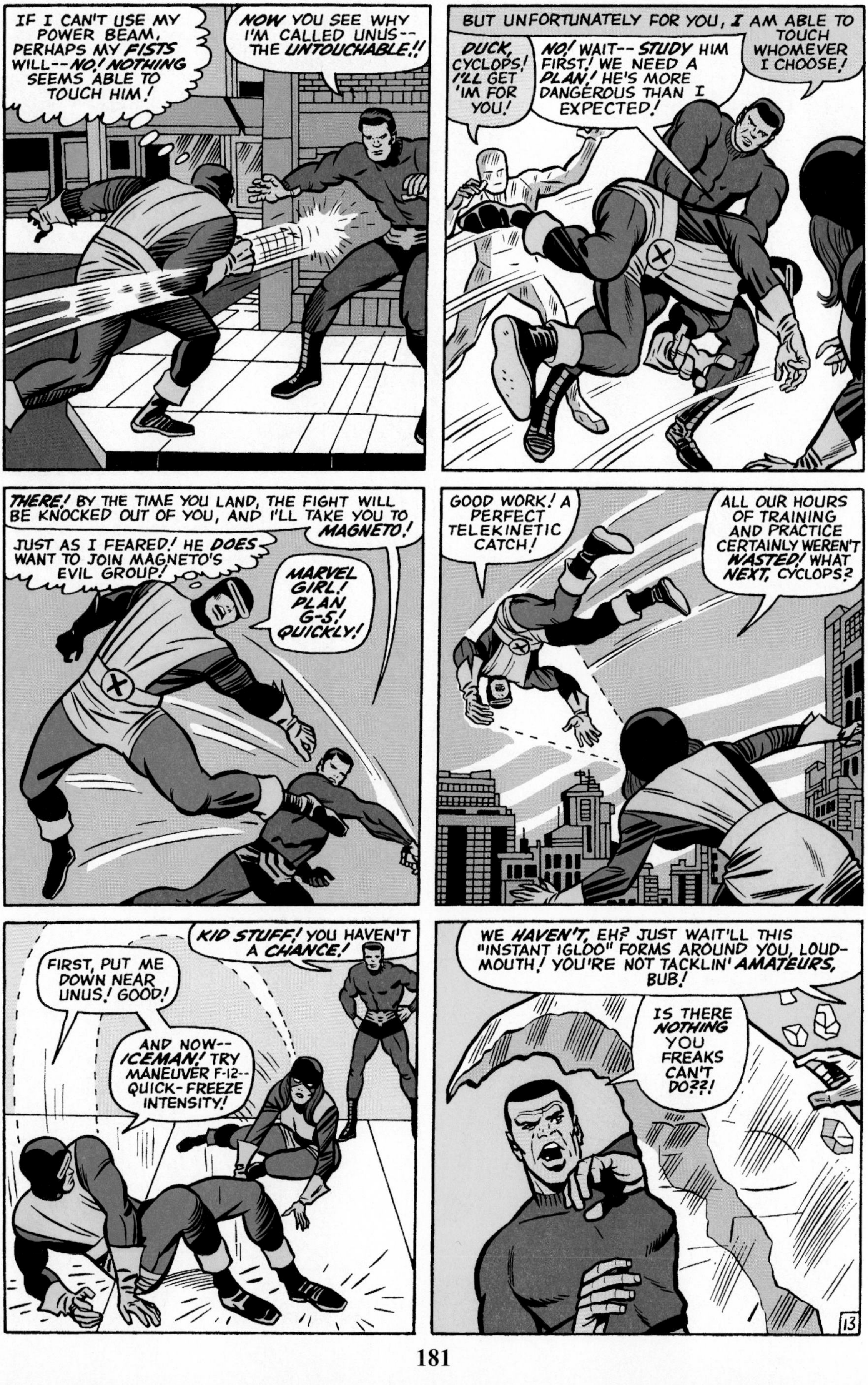
IF I CAN'T USE MY POWER BEAM, PERHAPS MY FISTS WILL--NO! NOTHING SEEMS ABLE TO TOUCH HIM!
NOW YOU SEE WHY I'M CALLED UNUS-- THE UNTOUCHABLE!!
BUT UNFORTUNATELY FOR YOU, I AM ABLE TO TOUCH WHOMEVER I CHOOSE!
DUCK, CYCLOPS! I'LL GET 'IM FOR YOU!
NO! WAIT-- STUDY HIM FIRST! WE NEED A PLAN! HE'S MORE DANGEROUS THAN I EXPECTED!
THERE! BY THE TIME YOU LAND, THE FIGHT WILL BE KNOCKED OUT OF YOU, AND I'LL TAKE YOU TO MAGNETO!
JUST AS I FEARED! HE DOES WANT TO JOIN MAGNETO'S EVIL GROUP!
MARVEL GIRL! PLAN G-5! QUICKLY!
GOOD WORK! A PERFECT TELEKINETIC CATCH!
ALL OUR HOURS OF TRAINING AND PRACTICE CERTAINLY WEREN'T WASTED! WHAT NEXT, CYCLOPS?
KID STUFF! YOU HAVEN'T A CHANCE!
FIRST, PUT ME DOWN NEAR UNUS! GOOD!
AND NOW-- ICEMAN! TRY MANEUVER F-12-- QUICK-FREEZE INTENSITY!
WE HAVEN'T, EH? JUST WAIT'LL THIS "INSTANT IGLOO" FORMS AROUND YOU, LOUD-MOUTH! YOU'RE NOT TACKLIN' AMATEURS, BUB!
IS THERE NOTHING YOU FREAKS CAN'T DO??!
13

WHEN YOU TACKLE *ONE* X-MAN, YOU TACKLE *ALL* OF US! AND DON'T YOU *FORGET* IT!

NO TEEN-AGE BRAT OF A MUTANT CAN TALK TO *UNUS* THAT WAY! IT'LL TAKE MORE THAN AN *ICY* CAGE TO HOLD *ME*!!

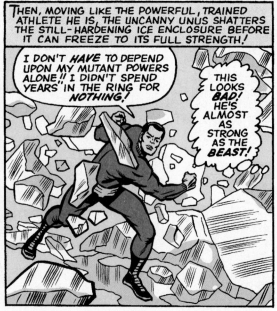

THEN, MOVING LIKE THE POWERFUL, TRAINED ATHLETE HE IS, THE UNCANNY UNUS SHATTERS THE STILL-HARDENING ICE ENCLOSURE BEFORE IT CAN FREEZE TO ITS FULL STRENGTH!

I DON'T *HAVE* TO DEPEND UPON MY MUTANT POWERS ALONE!! I DIDN'T SPEND YEARS" IN THE RING FOR *NOTHING*!

THIS LOOKS *BAD*! HE'S ALMOST AS STRONG AS THE *BEAST*!

THEN, BEFORE THE STARTLED ICEMAN CAN REGATHER HIS ENERGY FOR ANOTHER ATTACK...

AND *NOW*-- I'LL SHATTER YOU LIKE A PANE OF WINDOW GLASS--!!

WHAT *ODDS* WILL YOU GIVE, MUSCLE-BOUND ??

ANOTHER ONE, EH? IT DOESN'T MATTER TO ME-- ANY *ONE* OF YOU WILL DO!

YOUR ONLY POWER IS IN YOUR *WINGS*--AND THEY CAN'T DO YOU ANY GOOD AGAINST A BREAK-PROOF *WRESTLING HOLD*!

CAN'T LAND A *BLOW*! HAVE TO TRY SOMETHING *ELSE*!

SUDDENLY, THE GREAT BEATING *WINGS* SPREAD OUT, AND BOTH MUTANTS SOAR INTO THE SKY ABOVE...!

ANYONE CAN RASSLE, UNUS! BUT HERE'S A LITTLE *FLYING LESSON* FOR YOU!

YOU CAN'T HANG ON FOREVER!

WE'LL SEE HOW MUCH GOOD YOUR POWER DOES YOU--WHEN YOU *FALL*!

YOU CAN'T BLUFF ME! YOU'RE NOT MURDERERS-- AND I *KNOW* IT!

14

I WAS *AFRAID* OUR PLEDGE NEVER TO CAUSE HARM WITH OUR POWER WOULD ONE DAY WORK AGAINST US!

OKAY! MAYBE I *CAN'T* LET YOU BE HARMED... BUT I'LL SURE STOP *YOU* FROM HURTING ANYONE *ELSE!*

YOU CAN STAY UP *THERE* FOR A WHILE TO COOL OFF! AND I MAY NOT BE SO CHARITABLE *NEXT* TIME!

NICE GOING, WARREN!

WE STOPPED HIM FOR *NOW!* BUT WHAT HAPPENS IF HE MENACES US *AGAIN?*

NEXT TIME HE'LL BE TOO SMART TO TRY TO GRAB *YOU*, ANGEL!

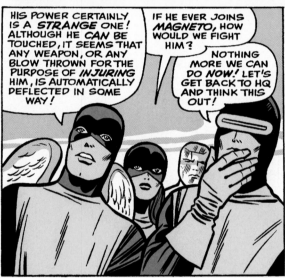

HIS POWER CERTAINLY IS A *STRANGE* ONE! ALTHOUGH HE *CAN* BE TOUCHED, IT SEEMS THAT ANY WEAPON, OR ANY BLOW THROWN FOR THE PURPOSE OF *INJURING* HIM, IS AUTOMATICALLY DEFLECTED IN SOME WAY!

IF HE EVER JOINS *MAGNETO*, HOW WOULD WE FIGHT HIM?

NOTHING MORE WE CAN DO *NOW!* LET'S GET BACK TO HQ AND THINK THIS OUT!

AND SO...

EVEN IF THE *BEAST* HADN'T QUIT, HIS STRENGTH COULDN'T HELP US! HE'D BE UNABLE TO LAND A BLOW!

HOLD IT! THERE'S SOMEONE IN THE *LAB!!*

IT'S... THE *BEAST!*

HANK! WHAT ARE YOU DOING *BACK* HERE? DOES THIS MEAN...?

IT PROBABLY MEANS I'M A KING-SIZED, ADDLE-PATED GLUTTON FOR PUNISHMENT!!

BUT, SINCE I'M APPARENTLY THE ONLY ONE WITH THE TECHNICAL SKILL AND INTELLECTUAL CAPACITY TO DEVISE A COUNTER-WEAPON TO UNUS' POWER, IT BEHOOVES ME TO SAVE YOU FROM A POSSIBLE IGNOMINIOUS DEFEAT!

WHAT *TYPE* OF WEAPON *IS* THAT?

15.

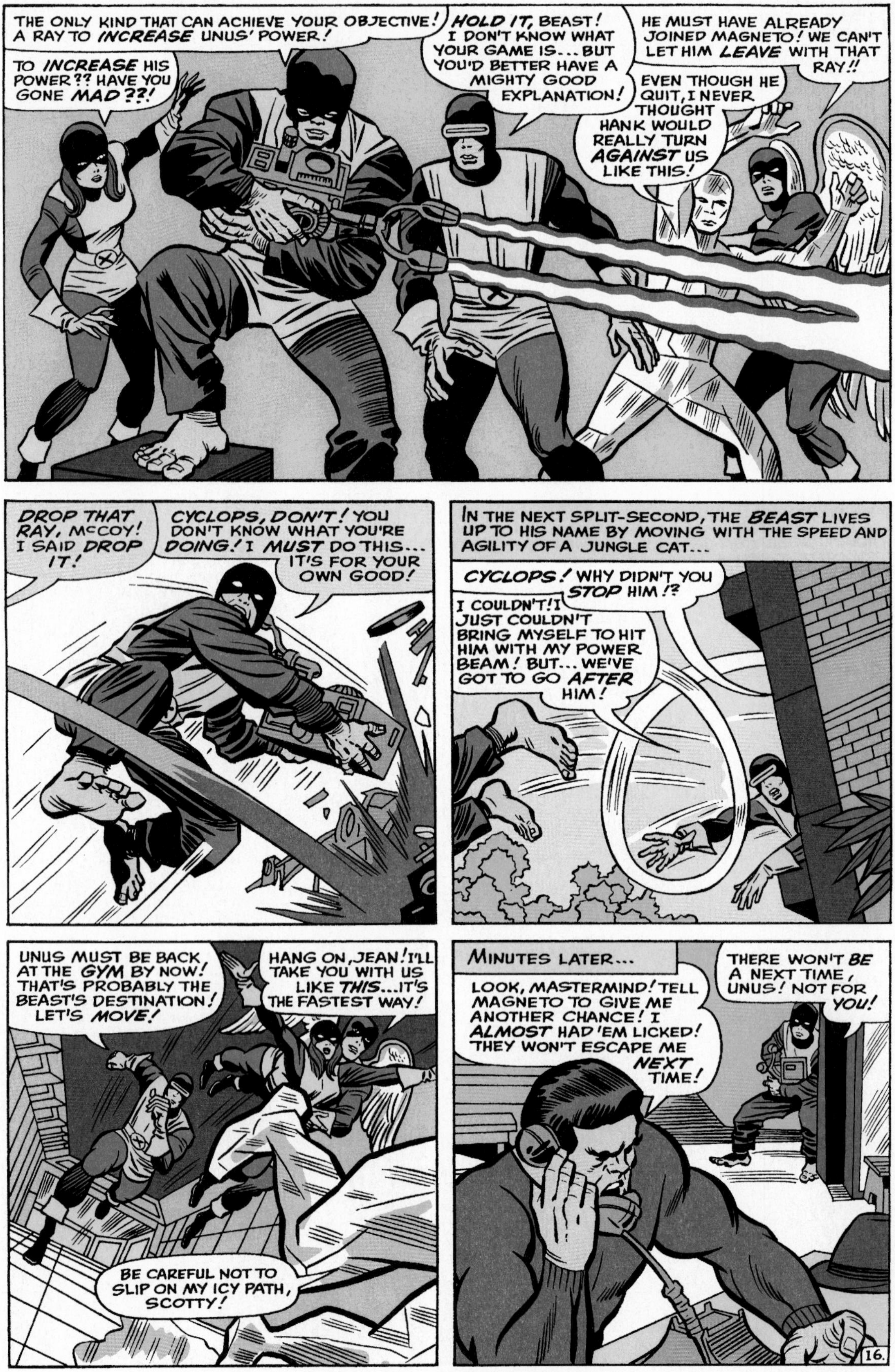
THE ONLY KIND THAT CAN ACHIEVE YOUR OBJECTIVE! A RAY TO INCREASE UNUS' POWER!
TO INCREASE HIS POWER?? HAVE YOU GONE MAD??!
HOLD IT, BEAST! I DON'T KNOW WHAT YOUR GAME IS... BUT YOU'D BETTER HAVE A MIGHTY GOOD EXPLANATION!
HE MUST HAVE ALREADY JOINED MAGNETO! WE CAN'T LET HIM LEAVE WITH THAT RAY!!
EVEN THOUGH HE QUIT, I NEVER THOUGHT HANK WOULD REALLY TURN AGAINST US LIKE THIS!
DROP THAT RAY, McCOY! I SAID DROP IT!
CYCLOPS, DON'T! YOU DON'T KNOW WHAT YOU'RE DOING! I MUST DO THIS... IT'S FOR YOUR OWN GOOD!
IN THE NEXT SPLIT-SECOND, THE BEAST LIVES UP TO HIS NAME BY MOVING WITH THE SPEED AND AGILITY OF A JUNGLE CAT...
CYCLOPS! WHY DIDN'T YOU STOP HIM!?
I COULDN'T! I JUST COULDN'T BRING MYSELF TO HIT HIM WITH MY POWER BEAM! BUT... WE'VE GOT TO GO AFTER HIM!
UNUS MUST BE BACK AT THE GYM BY NOW! THAT'S PROBABLY THE BEAST'S DESTINATION! LET'S MOVE!
HANG ON, JEAN! I'LL TAKE YOU WITH US LIKE THIS... IT'S THE FASTEST WAY!
BE CAREFUL NOT TO SLIP ON MY ICY PATH, SCOTTY!
MINUTES LATER...
LOOK, MASTERMIND! TELL MAGNETO TO GIVE ME ANOTHER CHANCE! I ALMOST HAD 'EM LICKED! THEY WON'T ESCAPE ME NEXT TIME!
THERE WON'T BE A NEXT TIME, UNUS! NOT FOR YOU!
16.

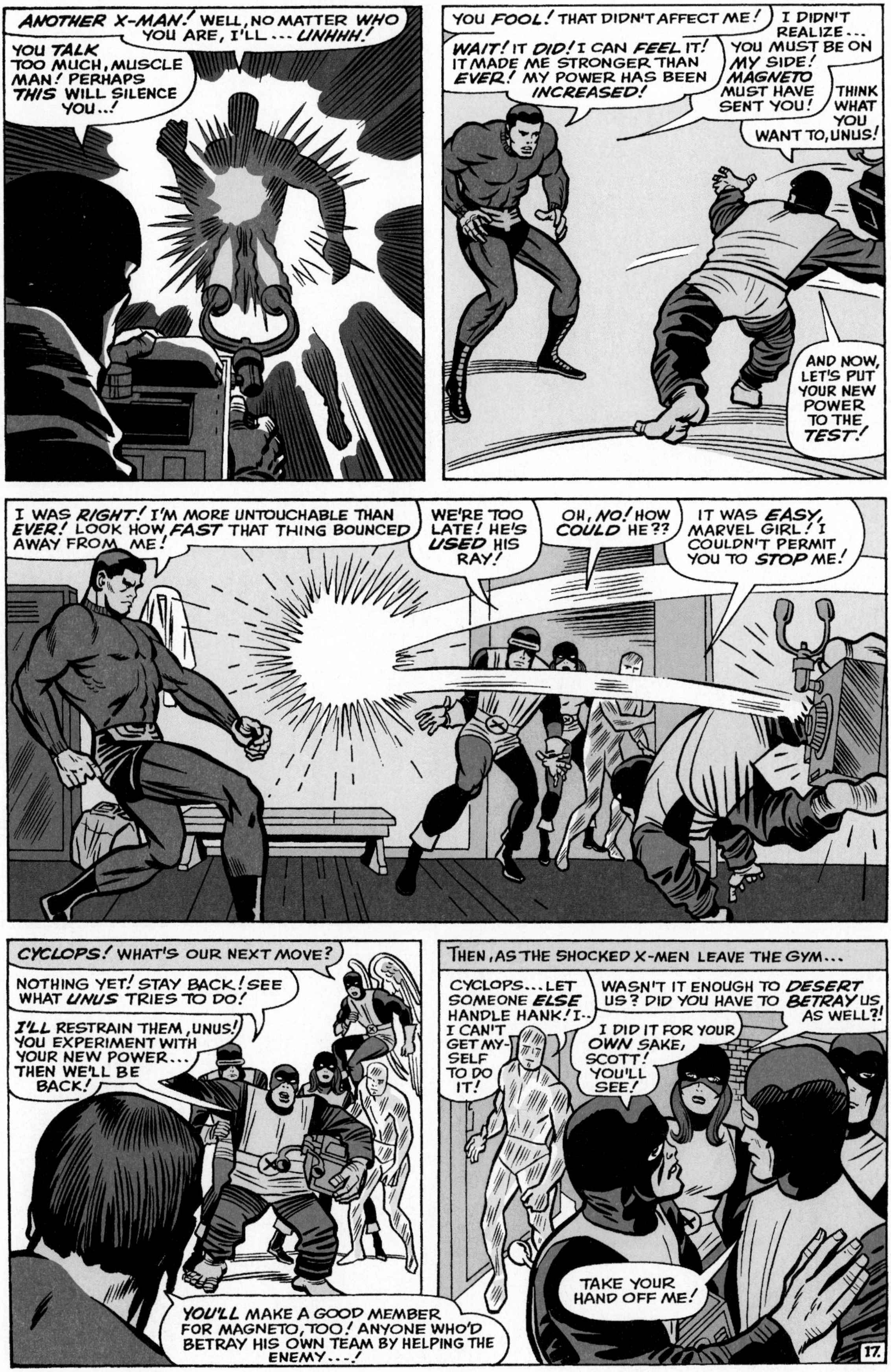
ANOTHER X-MAN! WELL, NO MATTER WHO YOU ARE, I'LL --- UNHHH!
YOU TALK TOO MUCH, MUSCLE MAN! PERHAPS THIS WILL SILENCE YOU...!
YOU FOOL! THAT DIDN'T AFFECT ME!
WAIT! IT DID! I CAN FEEL IT! IT MADE ME STRONGER THAN EVER! MY POWER HAS BEEN INCREASED!
I DIDN'T REALIZE... YOU MUST BE ON MY SIDE! MAGNETO MUST HAVE SENT YOU!
THINK WHAT YOU WANT TO, UNUS!
AND NOW, LET'S PUT YOUR NEW POWER TO THE TEST!
I WAS RIGHT! I'M MORE UNTOUCHABLE THAN EVER! LOOK HOW FAST THAT THING BOUNCED AWAY FROM ME!
WE'RE TOO LATE! HE'S USED HIS RAY!
OH, NO! HOW COULD HE??
IT WAS EASY, MARVEL GIRL! I COULDN'T PERMIT YOU TO STOP ME!
CYCLOPS! WHAT'S OUR NEXT MOVE?
NOTHING YET! STAY BACK! SEE WHAT UNUS TRIES TO DO!
I'LL RESTRAIN THEM, UNUS! YOU EXPERIMENT WITH YOUR NEW POWER... THEN WE'LL BE BACK!
YOU'LL MAKE A GOOD MEMBER FOR MAGNETO, TOO! ANYONE WHO'D BETRAY HIS OWN TEAM BY HELPING THE ENEMY---!
THEN, AS THE SHOCKED X-MEN LEAVE THE GYM...
CYCLOPS... LET SOMEONE ELSE HANDLE HANK! I-- I CAN'T GET MY-SELF TO DO IT!
WASN'T IT ENOUGH TO DESERT US? DID YOU HAVE TO BETRAY US AS WELL?!
I DID IT FOR YOUR OWN SAKE, SCOTT! YOU'LL SEE!
TAKE YOUR HAND OFF ME!
17.

LATER, BACK INSIDE THE GYM, UNUS CROWS IN TRIUMPH...!

HEARS THAT ONE OF THE X-MEN WAS SO FRIGHTENED OF ME THAT HE *INCREASED* MY POWER IN ORDER TO BECOME MY ALLY!

WAIT'LL MAGNETO HEARS THAT ONE OF THE X-MEN

HE'LL *HAVE* TO LET ME JOIN HIS MUTANT BAND AFTER THAT!

NOW, NOT ONLY ARE MENACING BLOWS AND WEAPONS UNABLE TO TOUCH ME, BUT I CAN MAKE *ANYTHING* SPIN AWAY FROM ME BY MERELY GETTING NEAR IT!

I'M *COMPLETELY* UNTOUCHABLE! I'M THE MOST INVULNER- ABLE MAN ALIVE! *NOTHING* CAN TOUCH ME... THEREFORE NOTHING CAN *HARM* ME!

I'LL GRAB A CIGARETTE WHILE I CALL MASTERMIND AND TELL HIM WHAT HAP... *HEY!!*

I CAN'T *TOUCH* THE BLAMED THING! IT KEEPS MOVING *AWAY* FROM ME!

BLAST IT! NO BLAMED CIGARETTE IS GONNA STOP *ME* FROM SMOKIN' IT!

I'LL THROW MYSELF ON TOP OF THE TABLE AND GRAB IT BEFORE IT CAN... *WAIT!!*

MISSED IT AGAIN!

THIS IS *CRAZY!* NOW EVEN THE *TABLE* IS SHOVIN' ITSELF AWAY FROM ME!

WHAT'S GOIN' *ON* HERE?? WHAT'S *HAPPENING* TO ME?? WHAT *GOOD* IS MY NEW POWER IF I CAN'T *CONTROL* IT??

18.

186

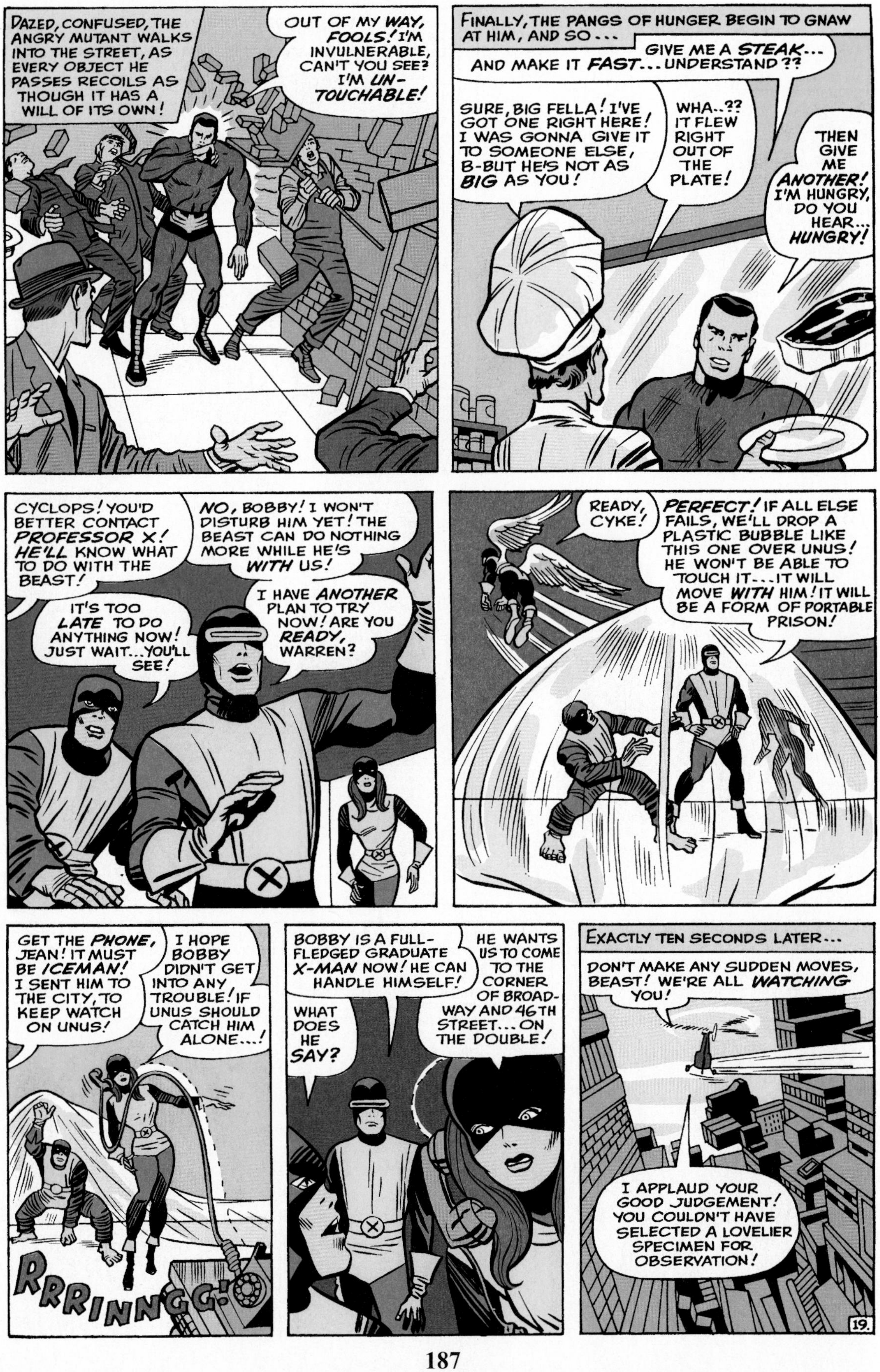
DAZED, CONFUSED, THE ANGRY MUTANT WALKS INTO THE STREET, AS EVERY OBJECT HE PASSES RECOILS AS THOUGH IT HAS A WILL OF ITS OWN!
OUT OF MY WAY, FOOLS! I'M INVULNERABLE, CAN'T YOU SEE? I'M UN-TOUCHABLE!
FINALLY, THE PANGS OF HUNGER BEGIN TO GNAW AT HIM, AND SO...
GIVE ME A STEAK... AND MAKE IT FAST... UNDERSTAND??
SURE, BIG FELLA! I'VE GOT ONE RIGHT HERE! I WAS GONNA GIVE IT TO SOMEONE ELSE, B-BUT HE'S NOT AS BIG AS YOU!
WHA..?? IT FLEW RIGHT OUT OF THE PLATE!
THEN GIVE ME ANOTHER! I'M HUNGRY, DO YOU HEAR... HUNGRY!
CYCLOPS! YOU'D BETTER CONTACT PROFESSOR X! HE'LL KNOW WHAT TO DO WITH THE BEAST!
NO, BOBBY! I WON'T DISTURB HIM YET! THE BEAST CAN DO NOTHING MORE WHILE HE'S WITH US!
IT'S TOO LATE TO DO ANYTHING NOW! JUST WAIT... YOU'LL SEE!
I HAVE ANOTHER PLAN TO TRY NOW! ARE YOU READY, WARREN?
READY, CYKE!
PERFECT! IF ALL ELSE FAILS, WE'LL DROP A PLASTIC BUBBLE LIKE THIS ONE OVER UNUS! HE WON'T BE ABLE TO TOUCH IT... IT WILL MOVE WITH HIM! IT WILL BE A FORM OF PORTABLE PRISON!
GET THE PHONE, JEAN! IT MUST BE ICEMAN! I SENT HIM TO THE CITY, TO KEEP WATCH ON UNUS!
I HOPE BOBBY DIDN'T GET INTO ANY TROUBLE! IF UNUS SHOULD CATCH HIM ALONE...!
RRRINNNGG!
BOBBY IS A FULL-FLEDGED GRADUATE X-MAN NOW! HE CAN HANDLE HIMSELF!
WHAT DOES HE SAY?
HE WANTS US TO COME TO THE CORNER OF BROAD-WAY AND 46TH STREET... ON THE DOUBLE!
EXACTLY TEN SECONDS LATER...
DON'T MAKE ANY SUDDEN MOVES, BEAST! WE'RE ALL WATCHING YOU!
I APPLAUD YOUR GOOD JUDGEMENT! YOU COULDN'T HAVE SELECTED A LOVELIER SPECIMEN FOR OBSERVATION!
19.

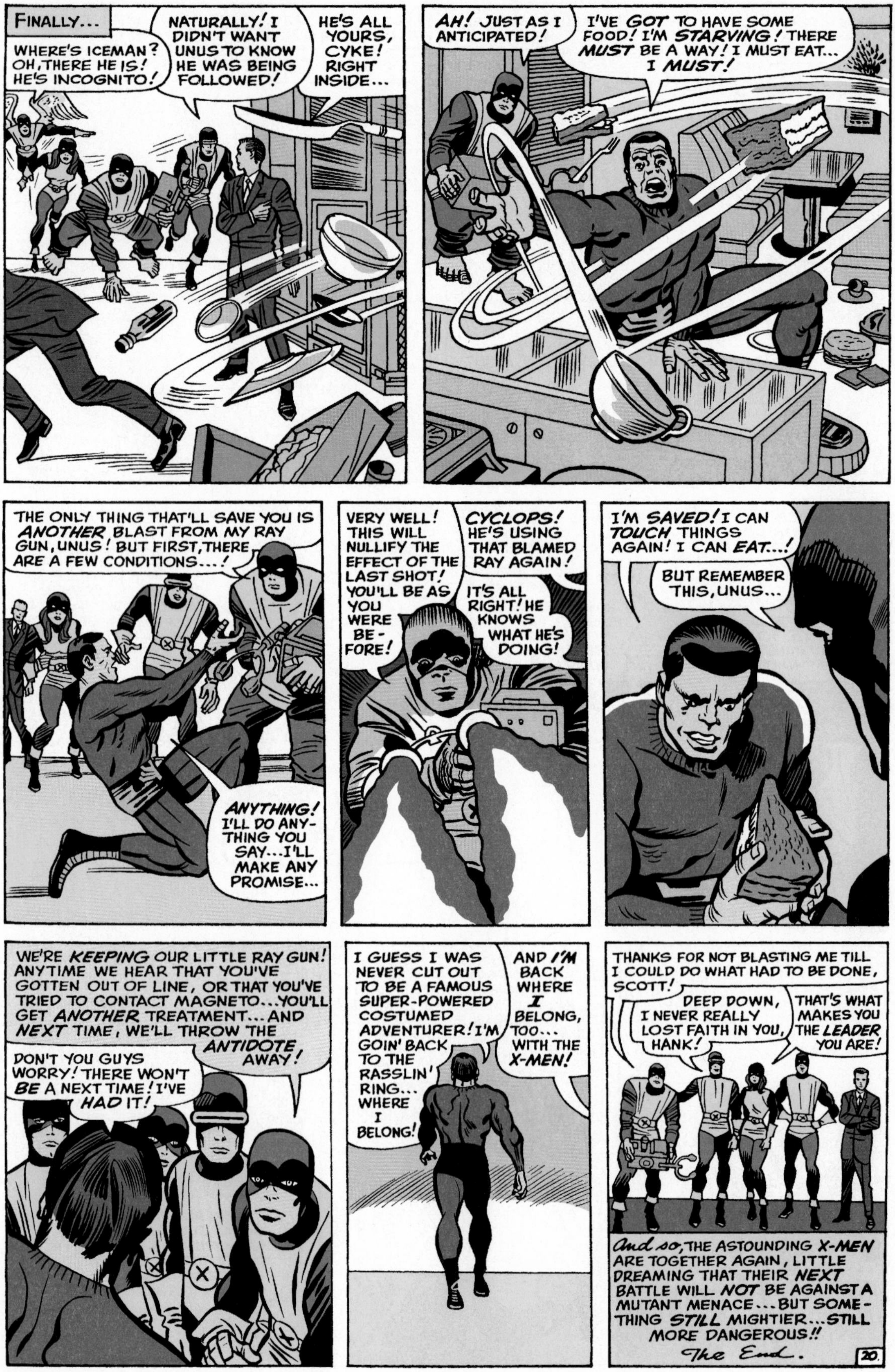
FINALLY...
WHERE'S ICEMAN? OH, THERE HE IS! HE'S INCOGNITO!
NATURALLY! I DIDN'T WANT UNUS TO KNOW HE WAS BEING FOLLOWED!
HE'S ALL YOURS, CYKE! RIGHT INSIDE...
AH! JUST AS I ANTICIPATED!
I'VE GOT TO HAVE SOME FOOD! I'M STARVING! THERE MUST BE A WAY! I MUST EAT... I MUST!
THE ONLY THING THAT'LL SAVE YOU IS ANOTHER BLAST FROM MY RAY GUN, UNUS! BUT FIRST, THERE ARE A FEW CONDITIONS...!
ANYTHING! I'LL DO ANYTHING YOU SAY...I'LL MAKE ANY PROMISE...
VERY WELL! THIS WILL NULLIFY THE EFFECT OF THE LAST SHOT! YOU'LL BE AS YOU WERE BEFORE!
CYCLOPS! HE'S USING THAT BLAMED RAY AGAIN!
IT'S ALL RIGHT! HE KNOWS WHAT HE'S DOING!
I'M SAVED! I CAN TOUCH THINGS AGAIN! I CAN EAT...!
BUT REMEMBER THIS, UNUS...
WE'RE KEEPING OUR LITTLE RAY GUN! ANYTIME WE HEAR THAT YOU'VE GOTTEN OUT OF LINE, OR THAT YOU'VE TRIED TO CONTACT MAGNETO...YOU'LL GET ANOTHER TREATMENT...AND NEXT TIME, WE'LL THROW THE ANTIDOTE AWAY!
DON'T YOU GUYS WORRY! THERE WON'T BE A NEXT TIME! I'VE HAD IT!
I GUESS I WAS NEVER CUT OUT TO BE A FAMOUS SUPER-POWERED COSTUMED ADVENTURER! I'M GOIN' BACK TO THE RASSLIN' RING... WHERE I BELONG!
AND I'M BACK WHERE I BELONG, TOO... WITH THE X-MEN!
THANKS FOR NOT BLASTING ME TILL I COULD DO WHAT HAD TO BE DONE, SCOTT!
DEEP DOWN, I NEVER REALLY LOST FAITH IN YOU, HANK!
THAT'S WHAT MAKES YOU THE LEADER YOU ARE!
And so, THE ASTOUNDING X-MEN ARE TOGETHER AGAIN, LITTLE DREAMING THAT THEIR NEXT BATTLE WILL NOT BE AGAINST A MUTANT MENACE...BUT SOMETHING STILL MIGHTIER...STILL MORE DANGEROUS!!
The End.
20.

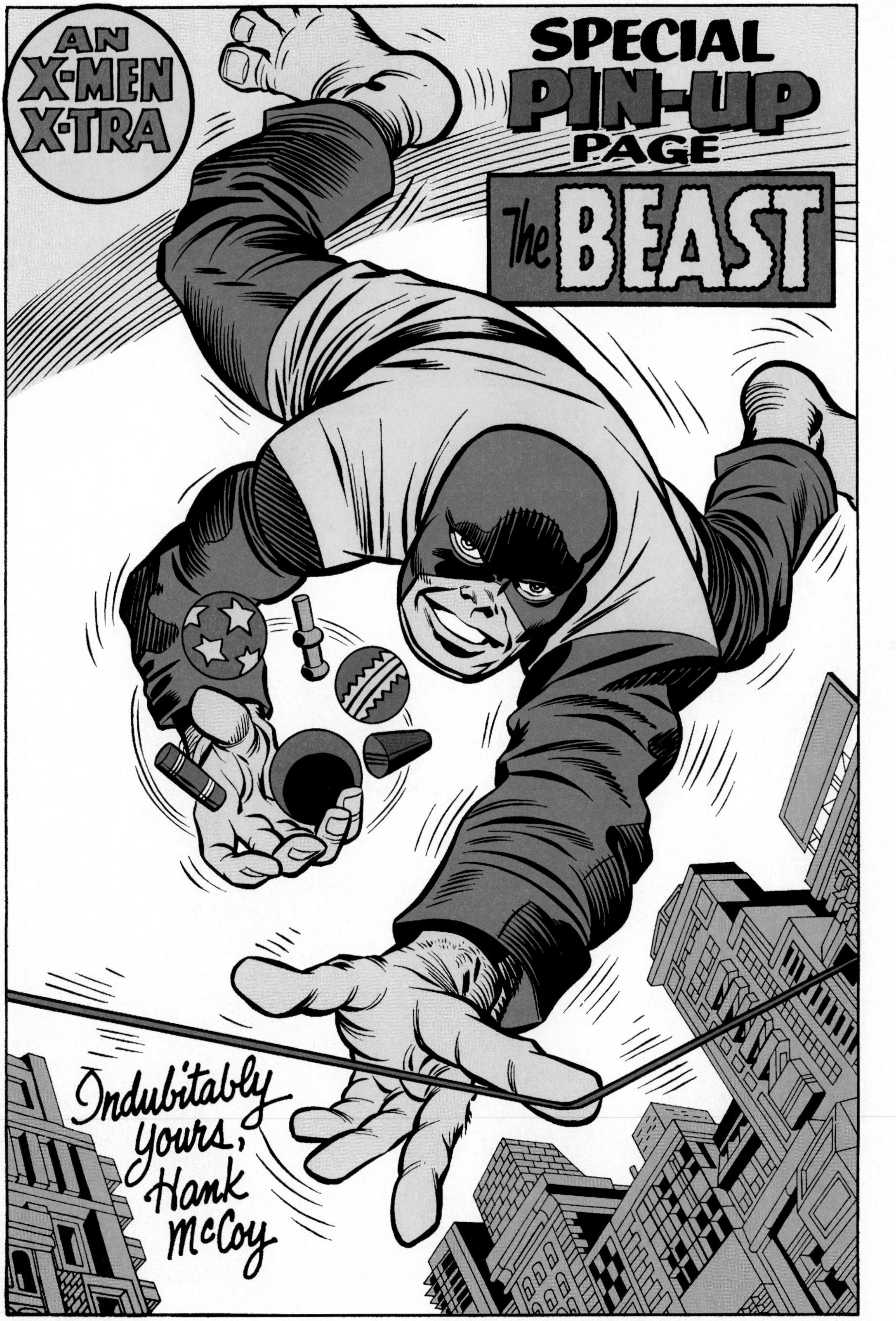
AN X-MEN X-TRA
SPECIAL PIN-UP PAGE
The BEAST
Indubitably yours, Hank McCoy

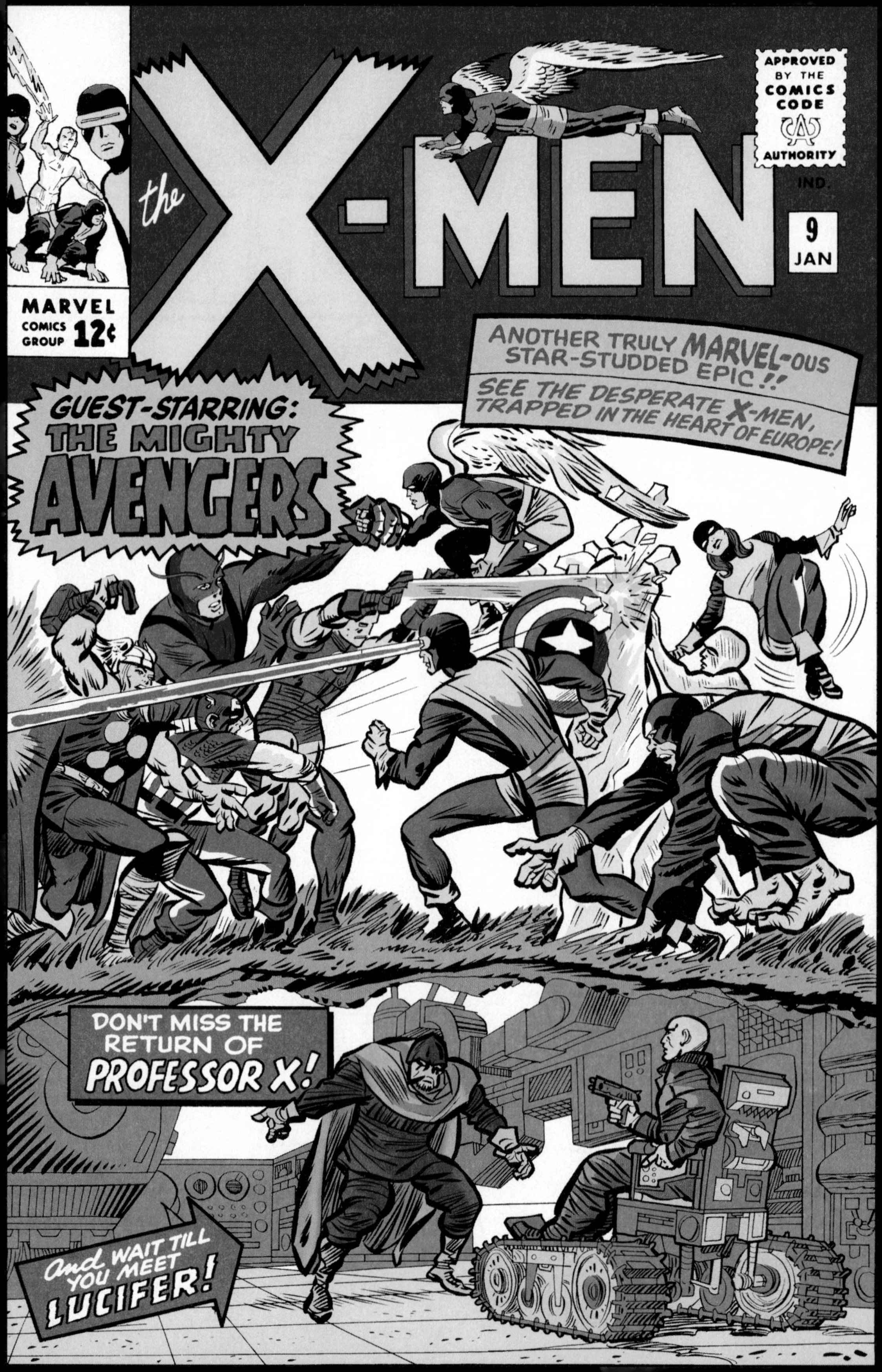
MARVEL COMICS GROUP 12¢
the X-MEN
APPROVED BY THE COMICS CODE AUTHORITY
IND.
9 JAN
ANOTHER TRULY MARVEL-OUS STAR-STUDDED EPIC!!
SEE THE DESPERATE X-MEN, TRAPPED IN THE HEART OF EUROPE!
GUEST-STARRING: THE MIGHTY AVENGERS
DON'T MISS THE RETURN OF PROFESSOR X!
and WAIT TILL YOU MEET LUCIFER!

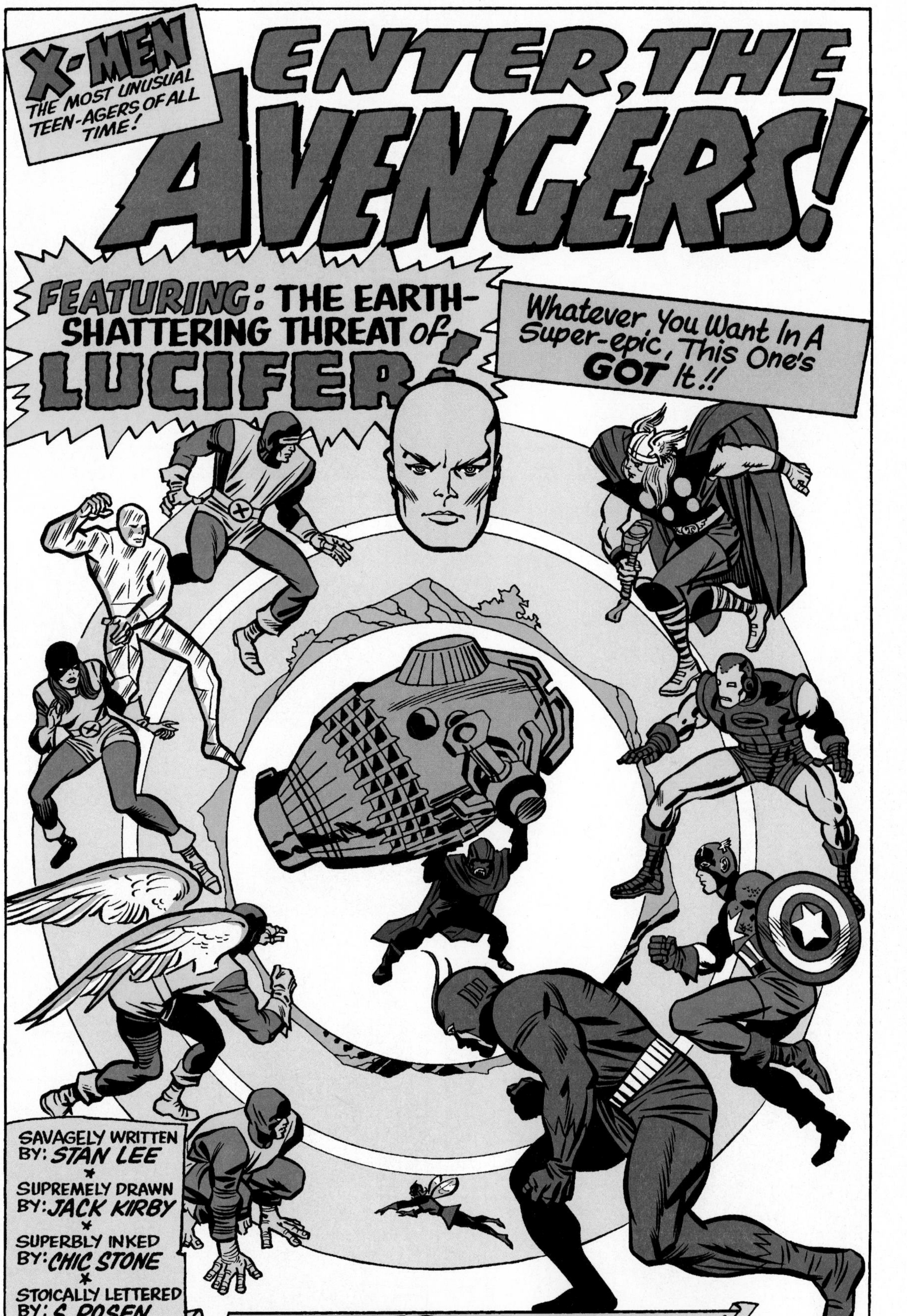
X-MEN
THE MOST UNUSUAL TEEN-AGERS OF ALL TIME!
ENTER, THE AVENGERS!
FEATURING: THE EARTH-SHATTERING THREAT of LUCIFER!
Whatever You Want In A Super-epic, This One's GOT It!!
SAVAGELY WRITTEN BY: STAN LEE
SUPREMELY DRAWN BY: JACK KIRBY
SUPERBLY INKED BY: CHIC STONE
STOICALLY LETTERED BY: S. ROSEN
MIGHTY MARVEL DOES IT AGAIN!

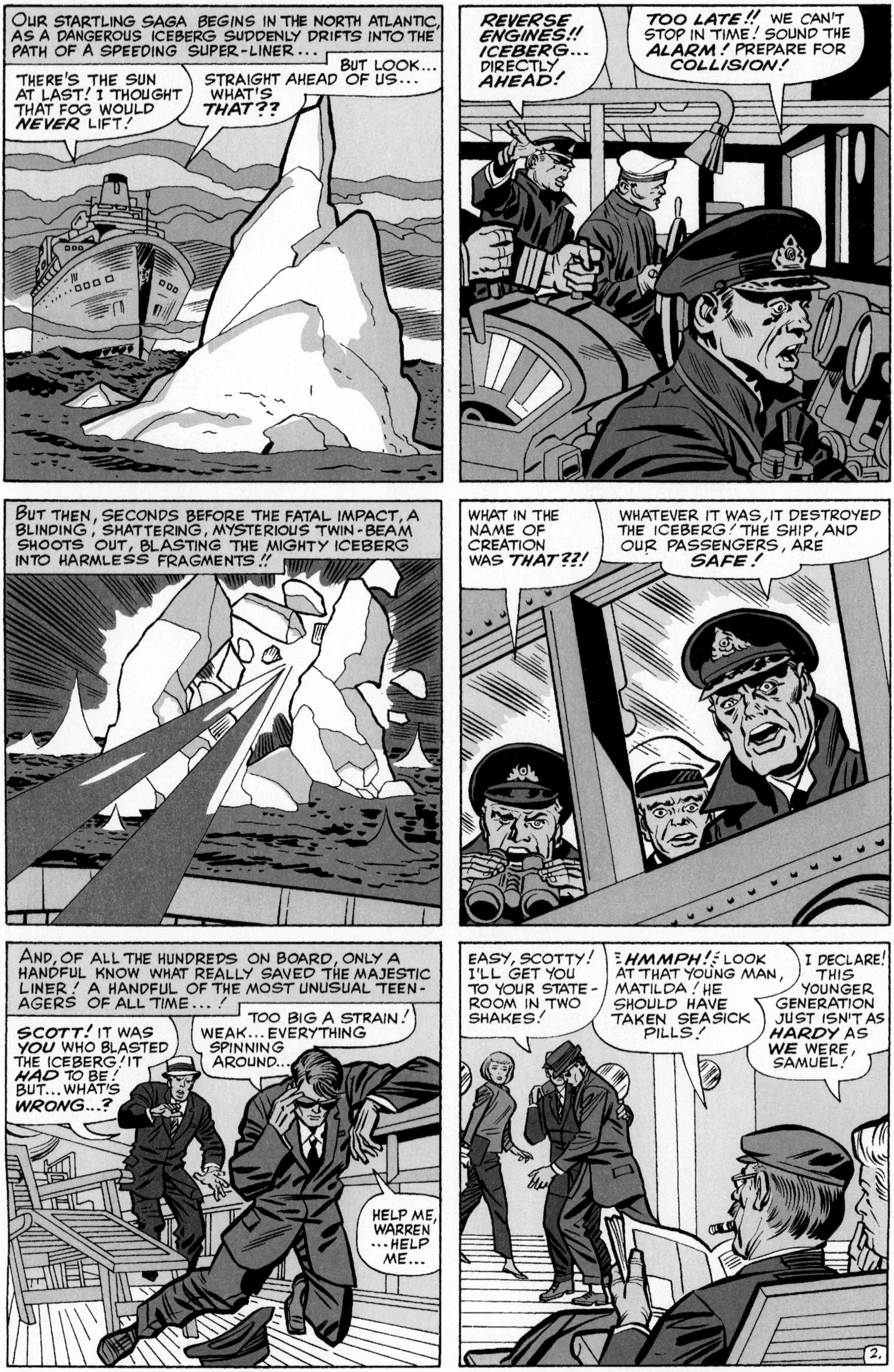
OUR STARTLING SAGA BEGINS IN THE NORTH ATLANTIC, AS A DANGEROUS ICEBERG SUDDENLY DRIFTS INTO THE PATH OF A SPEEDING SUPER-LINER...
THERE'S THE SUN AT LAST! I THOUGHT THAT FOG WOULD NEVER LIFT!
BUT LOOK... STRAIGHT AHEAD OF US... WHAT'S THAT??
REVERSE ENGINES!! ICEBERG... DIRECTLY AHEAD!
TOO LATE!! WE CAN'T STOP IN TIME! SOUND THE ALARM! PREPARE FOR COLLISION!
BUT THEN, SECONDS BEFORE THE FATAL IMPACT, A BLINDING, SHATTERING, MYSTERIOUS TWIN-BEAM SHOOTS OUT, BLASTING THE MIGHTY ICEBERG INTO HARMLESS FRAGMENTS!!
WHAT IN THE NAME OF CREATION WAS THAT??!
WHATEVER IT WAS, IT DESTROYED THE ICEBERG! THE SHIP, AND OUR PASSENGERS, ARE SAFE!
AND, OF ALL THE HUNDREDS ON BOARD, ONLY A HANDFUL KNOW WHAT REALLY SAVED THE MAJESTIC LINER! A HANDFUL OF THE MOST UNUSUAL TEEN-AGERS OF ALL TIME...!
SCOTT! IT WAS YOU WHO BLASTED THE ICEBERG! IT HAD TO BE! BUT... WHAT'S WRONG...?
TOO BIG A STRAIN! WEAK... EVERYTHING SPINNING AROUND...
HELP ME, WARREN ...HELP ME...
EASY, SCOTTY! I'LL GET YOU TO YOUR STATE-ROOM IN TWO SHAKES!
HMMPH! LOOK AT THAT YOUNG MAN, MATILDA! HE SHOULD HAVE TAKEN SEASICK PILLS!
I DECLARE! THIS YOUNGER GENERATION JUST ISN'T AS HARDY AS WE WERE, SAMUEL!
2.

MOMENTS LATER...

IT'S LUCKY FOR ME THAT EVERYONE WAS AT THE RAILING, LOOKING OUT TO SEA! SO THEY DIDN'T NOTICE *WHO* TRANSMITTED THE POWER BEAM, BOBBY!

YOU'RE RIGHT, SCOTTY! THERE'D BE A *PANIC* ON BOARD IF FOLKS KNEW THE *X-MEN* WERE AMONG THEM! HERE, I'LL WHIP UP SOME ICE CUBES FOR YOU, LEADER MAN!

DON'T BOTHER GETTING AN ICE-PACK, BOBBY! I'LL COOL SCOTT'S BROW WITH THEM *TELEKINETICALLY!*

THANKS, JEAN! THAT'S JUST WHAT I NEEDED!

OH, SCOTT! MY HEART JUST BREAKS WHEN I SEE YOU SO PALE, SO SHAKEN! IF ONLY I COULD COMFORT YOU WITH MY ARMS... MY LIPS... BUT I KNOW I MUSTN'T! AS OUR ACTING LEADER, YOU'VE NO TIME FOR THOUGHTS OF... ROMANCE!

IF ONLY WE WERE ORDINARY HUMANS... FREE TO FOLLOW THE URGINGS OF OUR HEARTS! BUT, I MUSTN'T ALLOW MYSELF SUCH HOPELESS DREAMS...!

WE'LL BE DOCKING IN EUROPE SOON, SCOTTY! FEEL WELL ENOUGH TO GET INTO UNIFORM?

SURE! I'LL BE FINE, ANGEL! I JUST WANT TO REST FOR A FEW MINUTES MORE!

USING A FULL-INTENSITY POWER BLAST REALLY KNOCKS ME OUT! MY MOUTH IS DRY AS A BLOTTER!

I'LL REMEDY *THAT*, BROTHER CYCLOPS! ONE *ICED TEA* COMING UP!

THANKS, HANK! AND NOW, I KNOW YOU'RE WONDERING WHY I ORDERED THIS TRIP...

PROFESSOR X CONTACTED ME LAST WEEK! HE SAID THERE WAS A MISSION FOR US IN EUROPE! IN FACT, I EXPECT FURTHER DETAILS FROM HIM ANY MINUTE!

I HAD A *FEELING* WE'D HEAR FROM THE PROF SOONER OR LATER!

ONE ICED TEA... COMPLIMENTS OF THE BENEVOLENT BEAST!

DON'T YOU EVER QUIT GRAND-STANDING, HANK?

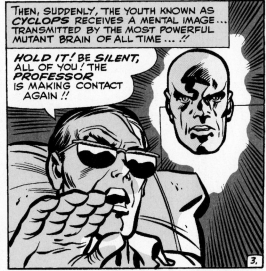

THEN, SUDDENLY, THE YOUTH KNOWN AS *CYCLOPS* RECEIVES A MENTAL IMAGE... TRANSMITTED BY THE MOST POWERFUL MUTANT BRAIN OF ALL TIME...!!

HOLD IT! BE SILENT, ALL OF YOU! THE *PROFESSOR* IS MAKING CONTACT AGAIN!!

3.

I HAVE FINALLY LOCATED THE HIDDEN CAVE OF *LUCIFER!* NOW HERE, IN THE HEART OF THE BALKANS, I FACE MY MOST CRUCIAL BATTLE!

IT WAS *LUCIFER* WHO LOST ME THE USE OF MY LEGS.... YEARS AGO! SOMEDAY I SHALL TELL YOU THE WHOLE STORY... IF I SURVIVE THE NEXT FEW HOURS! BUT NOW, CYCLOPS... THESE ARE YOUR INSTRUCTIONS...!

IF I SHOULD BE DEFEATED, THEN YOU, MY X-MEN, MUST CARRY ON! *LUCIFER* MUST NEVER MENACE MANKIND AGAIN! I HAVE TRANSMITTED MY LOCATION TO YOU! I CAN DO NO MORE!

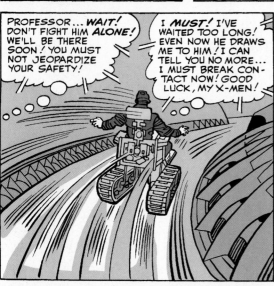

PROFESSOR... *WAIT!* DON'T FIGHT HIM *ALONE!* WE'LL BE THERE SOON! YOU MUST NOT JEOPARDIZE YOUR SAFETY!

I *MUST!* I'VE WAITED TOO LONG! EVEN NOW HE DRAWS ME TO HIM! I CAN TELL YOU NO MORE... I MUST BREAK CONTACT NOW! GOOD LUCK, MY X-MEN!

THE GROUND FELL AWAY BENEATH MY TREADS! *LUCIFER* TRIED TO *TRAP* ME!

BUT I *EXPECTED* SOMETHING OF THIS SORT! MY HYDRAULIC EXTENDO-ARMS CAN HOLD ME SAFELY!

AND, A SHORT DISTANCE AWAY, A PAIR OF COLD, UNBLINKING EYES SURVEYS THE SCENE WITH NAKED HATRED!!

HE IS AS ALERT AS EVER! BUT *THIS* TIME NOT EVEN HIS BRILLIANT BRAIN CAN SAVE HIM!

EVEN *HE* CANNOT OVERCOME THE POWER OF AN ARTIFICIAL *DUST DEVIL!*

4.

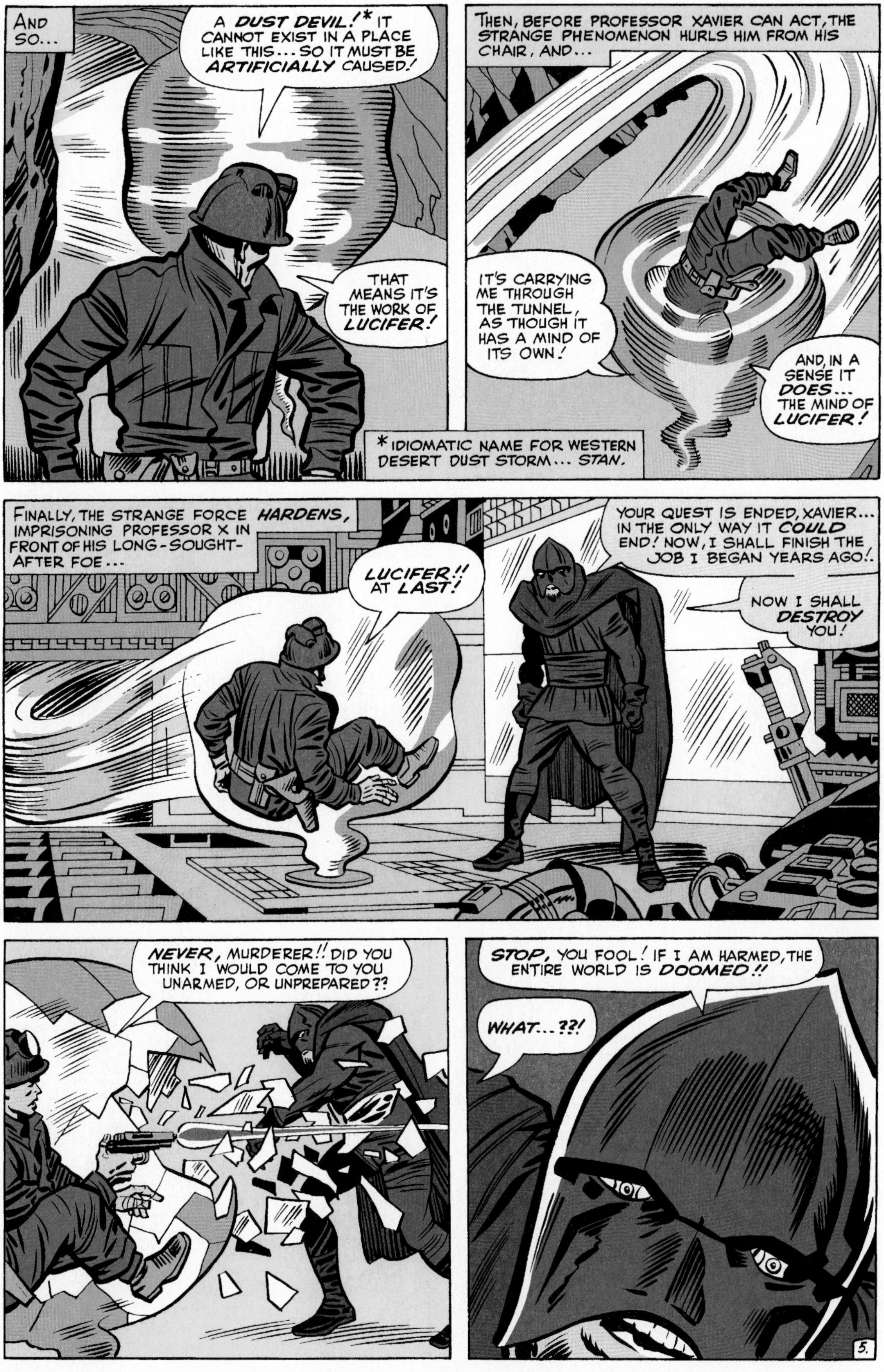
AND SO...
A DUST DEVIL!* IT CANNOT EXIST IN A PLACE LIKE THIS... SO IT MUST BE ARTIFICIALLY CAUSED!
THAT MEANS IT'S THE WORK OF LUCIFER!
THEN, BEFORE PROFESSOR XAVIER CAN ACT, THE STRANGE PHENOMENON HURLS HIM FROM HIS CHAIR, AND...
IT'S CARRYING ME THROUGH THE TUNNEL, AS THOUGH IT HAS A MIND OF ITS OWN!
AND, IN A SENSE IT DOES... THE MIND OF LUCIFER!
*IDIOMATIC NAME FOR WESTERN DESERT DUST STORM... STAN.
FINALLY, THE STRANGE FORCE HARDENS, IMPRISONING PROFESSOR X IN FRONT OF HIS LONG-SOUGHT-AFTER FOE...
LUCIFER!! AT LAST!
YOUR QUEST IS ENDED, XAVIER... IN THE ONLY WAY IT COULD END! NOW, I SHALL FINISH THE JOB I BEGAN YEARS AGO!.
NOW I SHALL DESTROY YOU!
NEVER, MURDERER!! DID YOU THINK I WOULD COME TO YOU UNARMED, OR UNPREPARED??
STOP, YOU FOOL! IF I AM HARMED, THE ENTIRE WORLD IS DOOMED!!
WHAT...??!
5.

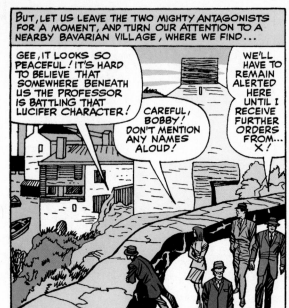

BUT, LET US LEAVE THE TWO MIGHTY ANTAGONISTS FOR A MOMENT, AND TURN OUR ATTENTION TO A NEARBY BAVARIAN VILLAGE, WHERE WE FIND...

GEE, IT LOOKS SO PEACEFUL! IT'S HARD TO BELIEVE THAT SOMEWHERE BENEATH US THE PROFESSOR IS BATTLING THAT LUCIFER CHARACTER!

CAREFUL, BOBBY! DON'T MENTION ANY NAMES ALOUD!

WE'LL HAVE TO REMAIN ALERTED HERE UNTIL I RECEIVE FURTHER ORDERS FROM... X!

SUDDENLY, A POWERFUL, DRAMATIC FIGURE PLUMMETS DOWN FROM THE SKY, BEHIND THE X-MEN...

AT LAST! I SEEM TO BE NEARING THE END OF OUR SEARCH!

WHAT IS IT, THOR? WHY DID YOU STOP?

WE HAVE FOLLOWED THESE STRANGE IMPULSES ALL THE WAY FROM AMERICA... BUT NOW...

... MY HAMMER BEGINS TO QUIVER! OUR GOAL IS NEAR AT HAND!

WELL, IT'S ABOUT TIME!

I HOPE THAT SO-CALLED ENCHANTED HAMMER OF YOURS HASN'T LED US ON A WILD GOOSE CHASE, PARTNER!

IMPOSSIBLE! THE IMPULSES WHICH IT DETECTED ARE SO STRONG... THAT THEY MUST BE FOUND!

HOLD IT, AVENGERS! IT LOOKS AS THOUGH WE HAVE COMPANY! BUT, JUDGING BY THE CAR, IT'S JUST A TOURIST!

I SEEM TO HAVE LOST MY WAY! COULD YOU DIRECT ME TO... TO... ≡ULP!≡

I SUGGEST YOU JUST KEEP GOING, FRIEND! THIS NEIGHBORHOOD MAY BECOME DANGEROUS BEFORE LONG!

6.

BUT...I DON'T UNDERSTAND..

WE DO NOT MEAN TO FRIGHTEN YOU, BUT A STRANGE *MENACE* LURKS NEARBY!

WE CAN'T EXPLAIN ANY MORE THAN THAT, BUT WE SUGGEST YOU LEAVE THE AREA AS SOON AS POSSIBLE!

FOR GOODNESS SAKE!! DO YOU NEED A *HOUSE* TO FALL ON YOU? CAN'T YOU TAKE A *HINT*? NOW GO ON... SCAT!!

AND, WITH THAT, THE STARTLED TOURIST "GETS THE MESSAGE"!!

V-O-O-M

WELL! HE *COULD* HAVE SAID GOODBYE!

THEN, JUST A FEW BRIEF MINUTES LATER...

HEY! WHAT'S GOIN' ON HERE??

NORMAL PEOPLE AT *LAST*!! THANK GOODNESS!

SCREECH!

LOOK OUT!

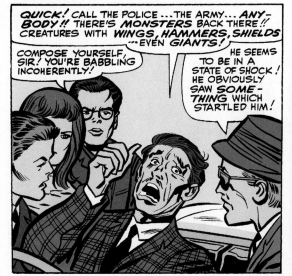

QUICK! CALL THE POLICE ...THE ARMY... *ANY-BODY*!! THERE'S *MONSTERS* BACK THERE!! CREATURES WITH *WINGS, HAMMERS, SHIELDS* ...EVEN *GIANTS*!

COMPOSE YOURSELF, SIR! YOU'RE BABBLING INCOHERENTLY!

HE SEEMS TO BE IN A STATE OF SHOCK! HE OBVIOUSLY SAW *SOME-THING* WHICH STARTLED HIM!

IT MAY BE CONNECTED WITH *LUCIFER*! YOU'D BETTER SCOUT THE AREA, *ANGEL*!

BE CAREFUL, WARREN!

DON'T WORRY, *JEAN*! MY BLUE CROSS IS ALL PAID UP!

7.

197

I WON'T TAKE THE TIME TO DON MY UNIFORM! NOBODY *HERE* IS APT TO RECOGNIZE ME AS WARREN WORTHINGTON, THE THIRD! BESIDES, EVERY SECOND MAY COUNT!

FLIGHT! WHAT A *GLORIOUS* FEELING! *THIS* IS WHAT I WAS BORN FOR!

OH, *NO!* WHA...WHAT HAVE I GOTTEN *INTO?*

NEXT, I'LL BE SEEING *PINK ELEPHANTS* AND GREMLINS! *GANGWAY!!* I'M TAKING THE NEXT PLANE BACK TO OHIO!

WAIT! WE DIDN'T MEAN TO *FRIGHTEN* YOU...!

NO! LET HIM *GO,* JEAN! IT'S BETTER THIS WAY! THIS ENTIRE AREA MAY BE UNSAFE FOR *ANY* NORMAL HUMANS AS FAR AS WE KNOW!

WHILE, HUNDREDS OF YARDS BELOW, IN THE CAVE OF *LUCIFER...*

TALK!! WHY IS THE WORLD IN DANGER IF YOU SHOULD BE HARMED??

BECAUSE I HAVE *OUT-SMARTED* YOU, XAVIER!

TURN YOUR HEAD...SEE WHAT I HAVE CREATED IN THE NEXT CHAMBER...

A GIANT *THERMAL BOMB!!* LARGE ENOUGH TO BLOW UP A *CONTINENT!*

EXACTLY!! NOW STUDY THE WIRING PATTERN! WITH YOUR INTELLECT, YOU'LL NOTICE THE TRUTH IN SECONDS!

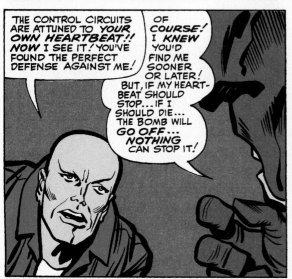

THE CONTROL CIRCUITS ARE ATTUNED TO *YOUR OWN HEARTBEAT!! NOW* I SEE IT! YOU'VE FOUND THE PERFECT DEFENSE AGAINST ME!

OF *COURSE!* I *KNEW* YOU'D FIND ME SOONER OR LATER! BUT, IF MY HEART-BEAT SHOULD STOP...IF I SHOULD DIE... THE BOMB WILL GO OFF... *NOTHING* CAN STOP IT!

NOW YOU SEE WHY YOU'RE *HELPLESS* AGAINST ME! AND *YOU* ARE THE ONLY ONE I FEAR! NO OTHER CAN MATCH MY BRILLIANCE!

AND SO, I AM FREE TO CONTINUE MY MASTER PLAN FOR POWER! I SHALL BEGIN BY ATTACKING YOUR PUNY X-MEN WHO WAIT ABOVE, SO INNOCENTLY... SO UNSUSPECTING!

8.

USING A MENTAL DIRECTIONAL IMPULSE, I SHALL HURL A DESTRUCTIVE IONIC RAY AT THEM!!

I HAVE WAITED FOR *YEARS* TO BEGIN MY ATTACK UPON HUMANITY! AND, WHAT A DRAMATIC BEGINNING THIS SHALL BE! MY FIRST VICTIMS... THE *X-MEN* THEMSELVES!!

BUT, THE MOST POWERFUL BRAIN ON EARTH IS NOT WITHOUT ITS *OWN* RESOURCES! IN THAT SAME SPLIT-SECOND, PROFESSOR X HURLS A MENTAL ILLUSORY FIGURE OF HIMSELF TOWARDS THE SURFACE....!!

I MUST HARNESS EVERY OUNCE OF MENTAL ENERGY I POSSESS!! THE VERY LIVES OF MY X-MEN ARE *ALL* AT STAKE!

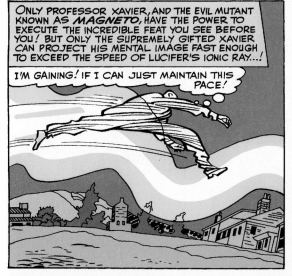

ONLY PROFESSOR XAVIER, AND THE EVIL MUTANT KNOWN AS *MAGNETO*, HAVE THE POWER TO EXECUTE THE INCREDIBLE FEAT YOU SEE BEFORE YOU! BUT ONLY THE SUPREMELY GIFTED XAVIER CAN PROJECT HIS MENTAL IMAGE FAST ENOUGH TO EXCEED THE SPEED OF LUCIFER'S IONIC RAY...!

I'M GAINING! IF I CAN JUST MAINTAIN THIS PACE!

AND THEN, THE PROFESSOR SENDS A WARNING THOUGHT SPEEDING AHEAD OF HIS OWN IMAGE...!

DANGER, MY X-MEN!! *SCATTER! DISPERSE!!*

IT'S THE PROFESSOR! *RUN!!*

YOU *HEARD* THE MAN!!

LEAPING INTO ACTION WITHOUT HESITATION... JUSTIFYING THEIR LONG, HARD MONTHS OF INTENSIVE TRAINING... THE X-MEN ESCAPE THE DREADED IONIC RAY BY MERE SECONDS!!

ZZZZT!

9.

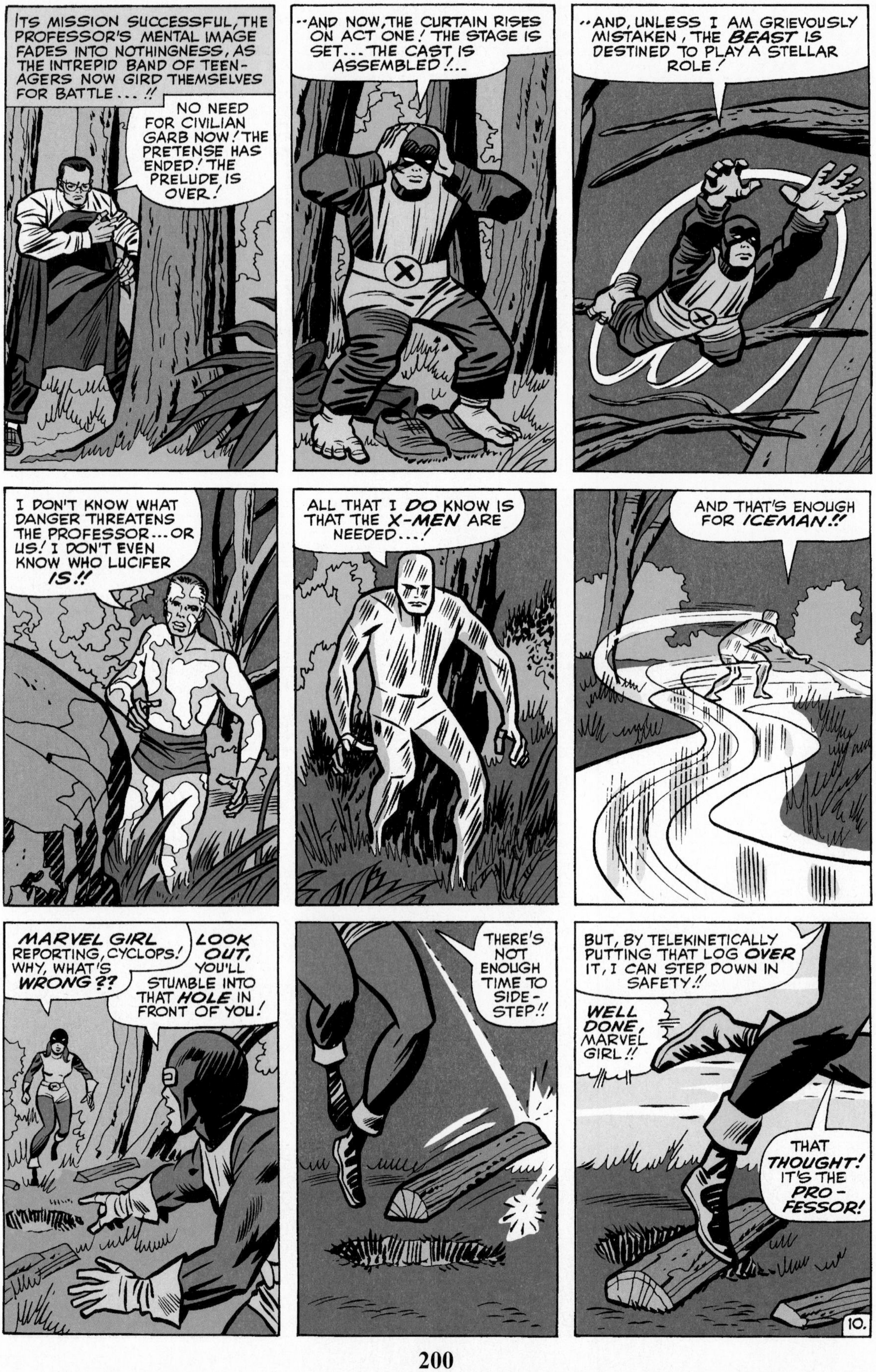

ITS MISSION SUCCESSFUL, THE PROFESSOR'S MENTAL IMAGE FADES INTO NOTHINGNESS, AS THE INTREPID BAND OF TEEN-AGERS NOW GIRD THEMSELVES FOR BATTLE...!!
NO NEED FOR CIVILIAN GARB NOW! THE PRETENSE HAS ENDED! THE PRELUDE IS OVER!
..AND NOW, THE CURTAIN RISES ON ACT ONE! THE STAGE IS SET... THE CAST IS ASSEMBLED!...
..AND, UNLESS I AM GRIEVOUSLY MISTAKEN, THE BEAST IS DESTINED TO PLAY A STELLAR ROLE!
I DON'T KNOW WHAT DANGER THREATENS THE PROFESSOR... OR US! I DON'T EVEN KNOW WHO LUCIFER IS!!
ALL THAT I DO KNOW IS THAT THE X-MEN ARE NEEDED...!
AND THAT'S ENOUGH FOR ICEMAN!!
MARVEL GIRL REPORTING, CYCLOPS! WHY, WHAT'S WRONG??
LOOK OUT, YOU'LL STUMBLE INTO THAT HOLE IN FRONT OF YOU!
THERE'S NOT ENOUGH TIME TO SIDE-STEP!!
BUT, BY TELEKINETICALLY PUTTING THAT LOG OVER IT, I CAN STEP DOWN IN SAFETY!!
WELL DONE, MARVEL GIRL!!
THAT THOUGHT! IT'S THE PRO-FESSOR!
10.

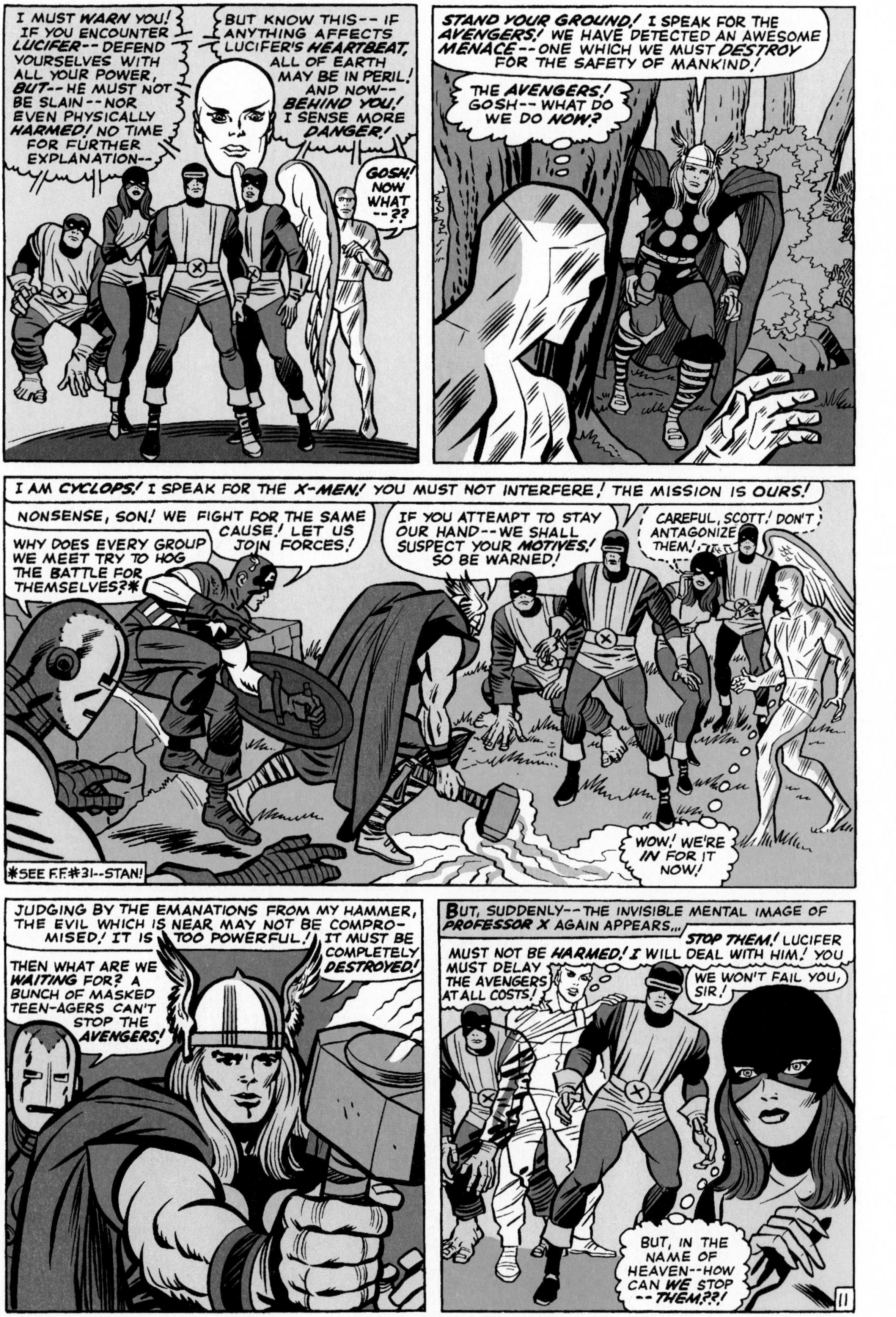
I MUST WARN YOU! IF YOU ENCOUNTER LUCIFER-- DEFEND YOURSELVES WITH ALL YOUR POWER, BUT-- HE MUST NOT BE SLAIN--NOR EVEN PHYSICALLY HARMED! NO TIME FOR FURTHER EXPLANATION--
BUT KNOW THIS-- IF ANYTHING AFFECTS LUCIFER'S HEARTBEAT, ALL OF EARTH MAY BE IN PERIL! AND NOW-- BEHIND YOU! I SENSE MORE DANGER!
GOSH! NOW WHAT --??
STAND YOUR GROUND! I SPEAK FOR THE AVENGERS! WE HAVE DETECTED AN AWESOME MENACE--ONE WHICH WE MUST DESTROY FOR THE SAFETY OF MANKIND!
THE AVENGERS! GOSH--WHAT DO WE DO NOW?
I AM CYCLOPS! I SPEAK FOR THE X-MEN! YOU MUST NOT INTERFERE! THE MISSION IS OURS!
NONSENSE, SON! WE FIGHT FOR THE SAME CAUSE! LET US JOIN FORCES!
WHY DOES EVERY GROUP WE MEET TRY TO HOG THE BATTLE FOR THEMSELVES?*
IF YOU ATTEMPT TO STAY OUR HAND--WE SHALL SUSPECT YOUR MOTIVES! SO BE WARNED!
CAREFUL, SCOTT! DON'T ANTAGONIZE THEM!
WOW! WE'RE IN FOR IT NOW!
*SEE F.F.#31--STAN!
JUDGING BY THE EMANATIONS FROM MY HAMMER, THE EVIL WHICH IS NEAR MAY NOT BE COMPROMISED! IT IS TOO POWERFUL! IT MUST BE COMPLETELY DESTROYED!
THEN WHAT ARE WE WAITING FOR? A BUNCH OF MASKED TEEN-AGERS CAN'T STOP THE AVENGERS!
BUT, SUDDENLY--THE INVISIBLE MENTAL IMAGE OF PROFESSOR X AGAIN APPEARS...
STOP THEM! LUCIFER MUST NOT BE HARMED! I WILL DEAL WITH HIM! YOU MUST DELAY THE AVENGERS AT ALL COSTS!
WE WON'T FAIL YOU, SIR!
BUT, IN THE NAME OF HEAVEN--HOW CAN WE STOP --THEM??!
11

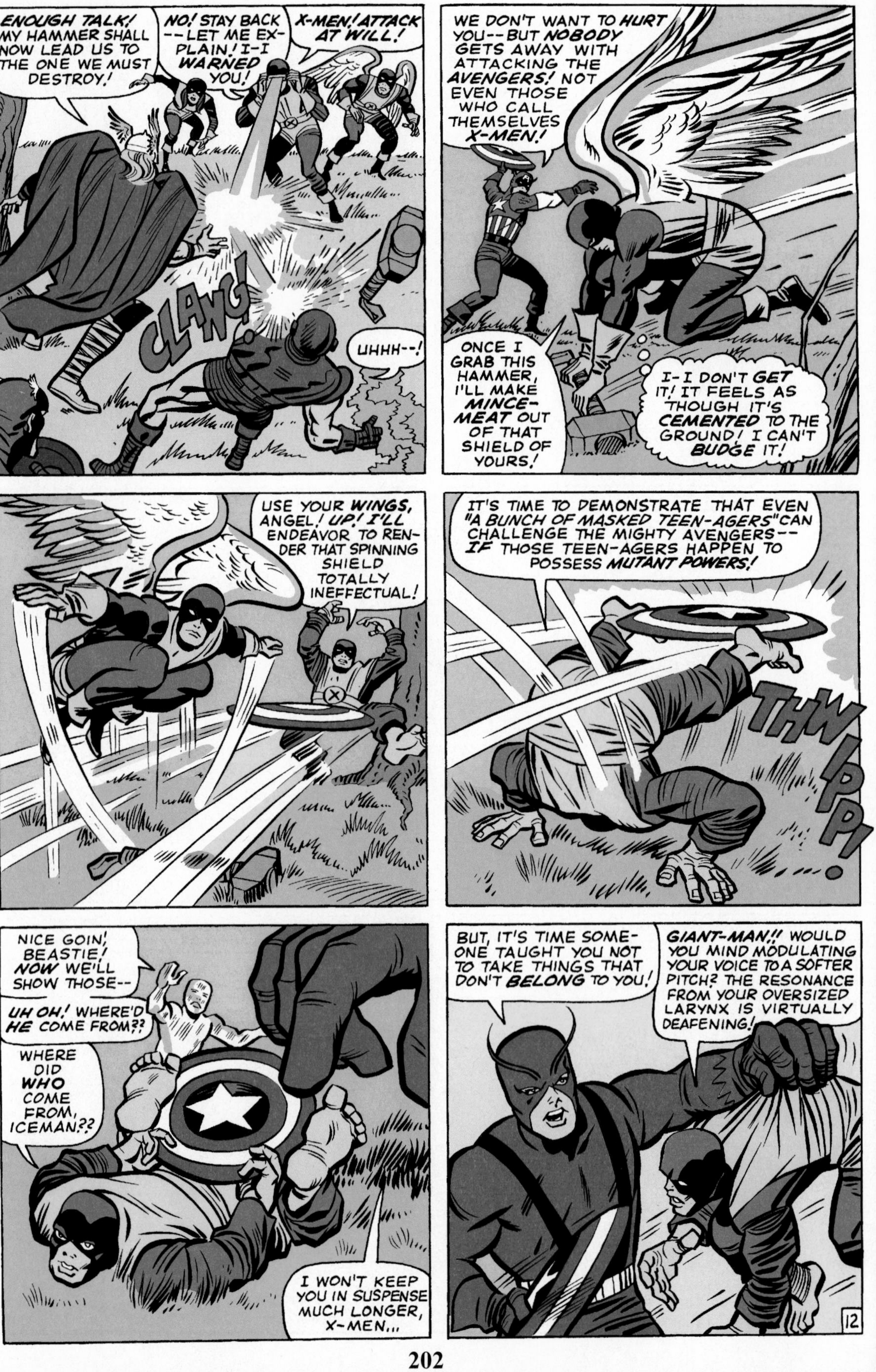

ENOUGH TALK! MY HAMMER SHALL NOW LEAD US TO THE ONE WE MUST DESTROY!
NO! STAY BACK --LET ME EXPLAIN! I-I WARNED YOU!
X-MEN! ATTACK AT WILL!
CLANG!
UHHH--!
WE DON'T WANT TO HURT YOU--BUT NOBODY GETS AWAY WITH ATTACKING THE AVENGERS! NOT EVEN THOSE WHO CALL THEMSELVES X-MEN!
ONCE I GRAB THIS HAMMER, I'LL MAKE MINCE-MEAT OUT OF THAT SHIELD OF YOURS!
I-I DON'T GET IT! IT FEELS AS THOUGH IT'S CEMENTED TO THE GROUND! I CAN'T BUDGE IT!
USE YOUR WINGS, ANGEL! UP! I'LL ENDEAVOR TO RENDER THAT SPINNING SHIELD TOTALLY INEFFECTUAL!
IT'S TIME TO DEMONSTRATE THAT EVEN "A BUNCH OF MASKED TEEN-AGERS" CAN CHALLENGE THE MIGHTY AVENGERS-- IF THOSE TEEN-AGERS HAPPEN TO POSSESS MUTANT POWERS!
THWIPP!
NICE GOIN', BEASTIE! NOW WE'LL SHOW THOSE--
UH OH! WHERE'D HE COME FROM??
WHERE DID WHO COME FROM, ICEMAN??
I WON'T KEEP YOU IN SUSPENSE MUCH LONGER, X-MEN...
BUT, IT'S TIME SOMEONE TAUGHT YOU NOT TO TAKE THINGS THAT DON'T BELONG TO YOU!
GIANT-MAN!! WOULD YOU MIND MODULATING YOUR VOICE TO A SOFTER PITCH? THE RESONANCE FROM YOUR OVERSIZED LARYNX IS VIRTUALLY DEAFENING!
12

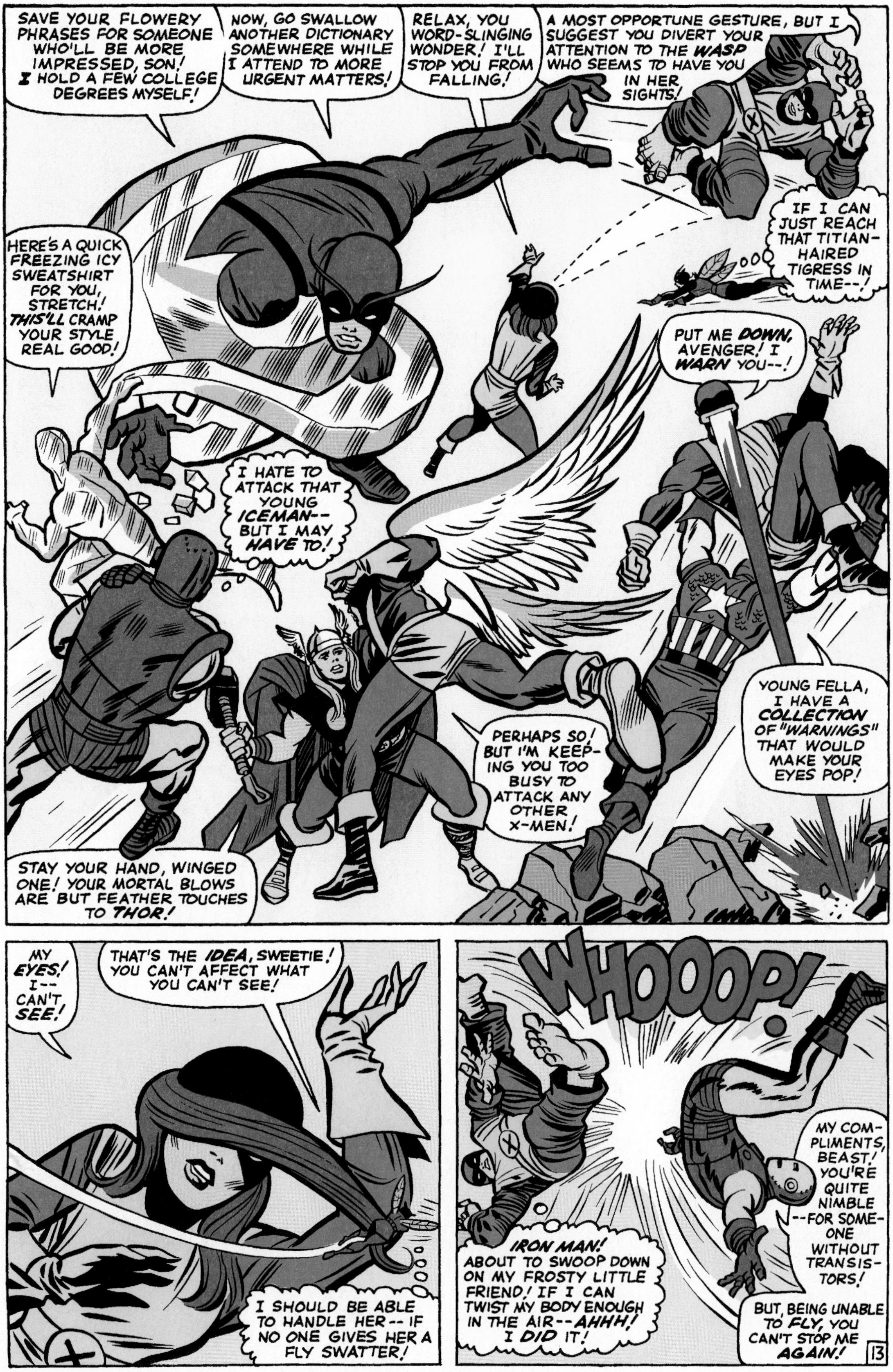

SAVE YOUR FLOWERY PHRASES FOR SOMEONE WHO'LL BE MORE IMPRESSED, SON! I HOLD A FEW COLLEGE DEGREES MYSELF!
NOW, GO SWALLOW ANOTHER DICTIONARY SOMEWHERE WHILE I ATTEND TO MORE URGENT MATTERS!
RELAX, YOU WORD-SLINGING WONDER! I'LL STOP YOU FROM FALLING!
A MOST OPPORTUNE GESTURE, BUT I SUGGEST YOU DIVERT YOUR ATTENTION TO THE WASP WHO SEEMS TO HAVE YOU IN HER SIGHTS!
IF I CAN JUST REACH THAT TITIAN-HAIRED TIGRESS IN TIME--!
HERE'S A QUICK FREEZING ICY SWEATSHIRT FOR YOU, STRETCH! THIS'LL CRAMP YOUR STYLE REAL GOOD!
PUT ME DOWN, AVENGER! I WARN YOU--!
I HATE TO ATTACK THAT YOUNG ICEMAN-- BUT I MAY HAVE TO!
YOUNG FELLA, I HAVE A COLLECTION OF "WARNINGS" THAT WOULD MAKE YOUR EYES POP!
PERHAPS SO! BUT I'M KEEPING YOU TOO BUSY TO ATTACK ANY OTHER X-MEN!
STAY YOUR HAND, WINGED ONE! YOUR MORTAL BLOWS ARE BUT FEATHER TOUCHES TO THOR!
MY EYES! I-- CAN'T SEE!
THAT'S THE IDEA, SWEETIE! YOU CAN'T AFFECT WHAT YOU CAN'T SEE!
I SHOULD BE ABLE TO HANDLE HER -- IF NO ONE GIVES HER A FLY SWATTER!
WHOOOP!
IRON MAN! ABOUT TO SWOOP DOWN ON MY FROSTY LITTLE FRIEND! IF I CAN TWIST MY BODY ENOUGH IN THE AIR--AHHH! I DID IT!
MY COMPLIMENTS, BEAST! YOU'RE QUITE NIMBLE --FOR SOMEONE WITHOUT TRANSISTORS!
BUT, BEING UNABLE TO FLY, YOU CAN'T STOP ME AGAIN!
13

MEANTIME, HAVING DONE ALL HE CAN ON THE SURFACE, PROFESSOR X ONCE AGAIN TURNS HIS FULL ATTENTION TO THE DEADLY FOE WHO STANDS BEFORE A WIRELESS VIDEO-VIEWER...

YOUR *X-MEN* ARE KEEPING THE *AVENGERS* FROM ME! A VERY WISE MOVE ON THEIR PART!

AND NOW THAT I HAVE YOU CRINGING HELPLESSLY BEFORE ME, I SHALL WIN MY GREATEST VICTORY! YOUR TIME HAS COME, XAVIER!

THERE IS NO PHYSICAL FORCE I CAN USE-- OR WOULD *DARE* TO USE AGAINST HIM....!

BUT, MY GREATEST POWER HAS EVER BEEN THE POWER OF --MY *BRAIN*!

AND *THIS* WILL BE MY MOST DIFFICULT TASK!

I MUST NARROW A MENTAL SHOCK WAVE ENOUGH TO *STUN* HIM WITHOUT INJURING HIM IN ANY WAY!

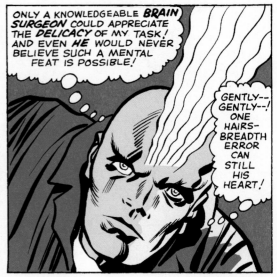

ONLY A KNOWLEDGEABLE *BRAIN SURGEON* COULD APPRECIATE THE *DELICACY* OF MY TASK! AND EVEN *HE* WOULD NEVER BELIEVE SUCH A MENTAL FEAT IS POSSIBLE!

GENTLY-- GENTLY--! ONE HAIRS- BREADTH ERROR CAN STILL HIS HEART!

IN MY MIND'S EYE, I SEE HIS BRAIN AS CLEARLY AS A TRAVELLER READS A ROAD MAP! I MUST CIRCUMVENT THE PORTION OF THE MEDULLA OBLONGATA NEAREST THE SPINAL COLUMN AS I PENETRATE THE MOST SENSITIVE AREA OF HIS CEREBELLUM...

WHAT IS *HAPPENING* TO ME?? WHY HAVE MY MOVEMENTS BECOME SO STIFF...?

NO MATTER! IT WILL TAKE BUT *ONE* SHOT TO-- TO--

--MY BRAIN IS CLOUDED--CAN'T THINK! CAN'T REMEMBER--EVERY- THING GOING BLANK --BLANK--!

14

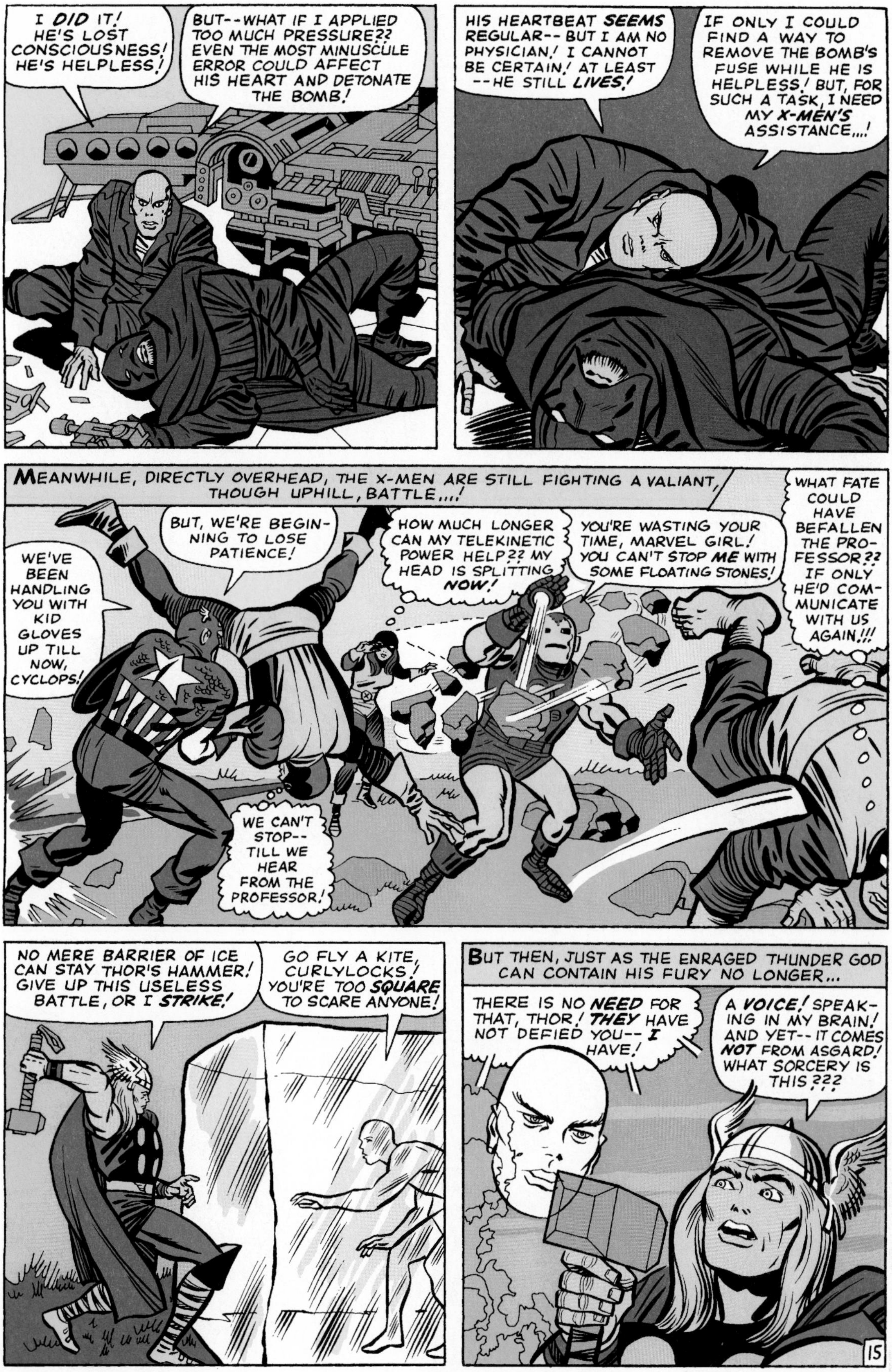
I DID IT! HE'S LOST CONSCIOUSNESS! HE'S HELPLESS!
BUT--WHAT IF I APPLIED TOO MUCH PRESSURE?? EVEN THE MOST MINUSCULE ERROR COULD AFFECT HIS HEART AND DETONATE THE BOMB!
HIS HEARTBEAT SEEMS REGULAR-- BUT I AM NO PHYSICIAN! I CANNOT BE CERTAIN! AT LEAST --HE STILL LIVES!
IF ONLY I COULD FIND A WAY TO REMOVE THE BOMB'S FUSE WHILE HE IS HELPLESS! BUT, FOR SUCH A TASK, I NEED MY X-MEN'S ASSISTANCE...!
MEANWHILE, DIRECTLY OVERHEAD, THE X-MEN ARE STILL FIGHTING A VALIANT, THOUGH UPHILL, BATTLE...!
WE'VE BEEN HANDLING YOU WITH KID GLOVES UP TILL NOW, CYCLOPS!
BUT, WE'RE BEGINNING TO LOSE PATIENCE!
WE CAN'T STOP-- TILL WE HEAR FROM THE PROFESSOR!
HOW MUCH LONGER CAN MY TELEKINETIC POWER HELP?? MY HEAD IS SPLITTING NOW!
YOU'RE WASTING YOUR TIME, MARVEL GIRL! YOU CAN'T STOP ME WITH SOME FLOATING STONES!
WHAT FATE COULD HAVE BEFALLEN THE PROFESSOR?? IF ONLY HE'D COMMUNICATE WITH US AGAIN!!!
NO MERE BARRIER OF ICE CAN STAY THOR'S HAMMER! GIVE UP THIS USELESS BATTLE, OR I STRIKE!
GO FLY A KITE, CURLYLOCKS! YOU'RE TOO SQUARE TO SCARE ANYONE!
BUT THEN, JUST AS THE ENRAGED THUNDER GOD CAN CONTAIN HIS FURY NO LONGER...
THERE IS NO NEED FOR THAT, THOR! THEY HAVE NOT DEFIED YOU-- I HAVE!
A VOICE! SPEAKING IN MY BRAIN! AND YET-- IT COMES NOT FROM ASGARD! WHAT SORCERY IS THIS???
15

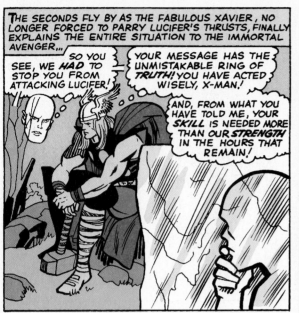

THE SECONDS FLY BY AS THE FABULOUS XAVIER, NO LONGER FORCED TO PARRY LUCIFER'S THRUSTS, FINALLY EXPLAINS THE ENTIRE SITUATION TO THE IMMORTAL AVENGER...

SO YOU SEE, WE *HAD* TO STOP YOU FROM ATTACKING LUCIFER!

YOUR MESSAGE HAS THE UNMISTAKABLE RING OF *TRUTH!* YOU HAVE ACTED WISELY, X-MAN!

AND, FROM WHAT YOU HAVE TOLD ME, YOUR *SKILL* IS NEEDED MORE THAN OUR *STRENGTH* IN THE HOURS THAT REMAIN!

THE FIGHT IS ENDED, ICEMAN! YOU WILL HAVE NO FURTHER NEED TO SHIELD YOURSELF FROM THOR!

≶WHEW≶ LUCKY FOR *ME!* HE SMASHED MY INTENSIFIED ICE AS THOUGH IT'S A THIN PANE OF WINDOW GLASS!

AND SO, THE UNWARRANTED BATTLE COMES TO AN INCONCLUSIVE END!

AVENGERS --ASSEMBLE!

HIS ARMS ARE OUTSTRETCHED! THAT'S OUR SIGNAL TO END HOSTILITIES!

HMMM-- SOUNDS IMPORTANT!

IT TAKES THE THUNDER GOD BUT A MOMENT TO CUE THE OTHERS IN, AND THEN...

I VOTE WE ALLOW THE *X-MEN* TO DEAL WITH THEIR FOE IN THEIR OWN MANNER! ALL IN FAVOR SIGNIFY *AYE!*

I STAND WITH THOR-- BUT I VOTE WE MAKE IT *UNANIMOUS!*

SO BE IT!

AYE!

WELL, LITTLE ONES, IT SEEMS WE'VE TRAVELED CLEAR ACROSS THE ATLANTIC ONLY TO BLUNDER INTO SOMEONE ELSE'S FIGHT!

BETTER FALL IN BEHIND *CAP,* THOR! YOUR TIME HAS EXPIRED! IT'S *HIS* TURN TO BE GROUP CHAIRMAN FOR THE WEEK!

THEY MAKE ME REALIZE THAT HUMANITY IS *WORTH* DEFENDING!

IT WASN'T *ALL* A WASTE! I *DID* GET TO MEET THAT DREAMY *ANGEL!*

AWW, I'M WASTING MY MY TIME -- AS USUAL! HANK IS TOO SMART TO ACT JEALOUS!

TOO BAD GOLDILOCKS BROKE IT UP SO SOON! I WAS JUST GETTIN' *WARMED UP!*

DREAM ON, BOBBY! BY NEXT WEEK, YOU'LL HAVE YOURSELF CONVINCED THEY WERE ALL BEGGING FOR MERCY JUST BEFORE THE FIGHT ENDED!

LET'S DISPENSE WITH THE POST MORTEMS, COLLEAGUES! *CYCLOPS* IS CALLING US!

16

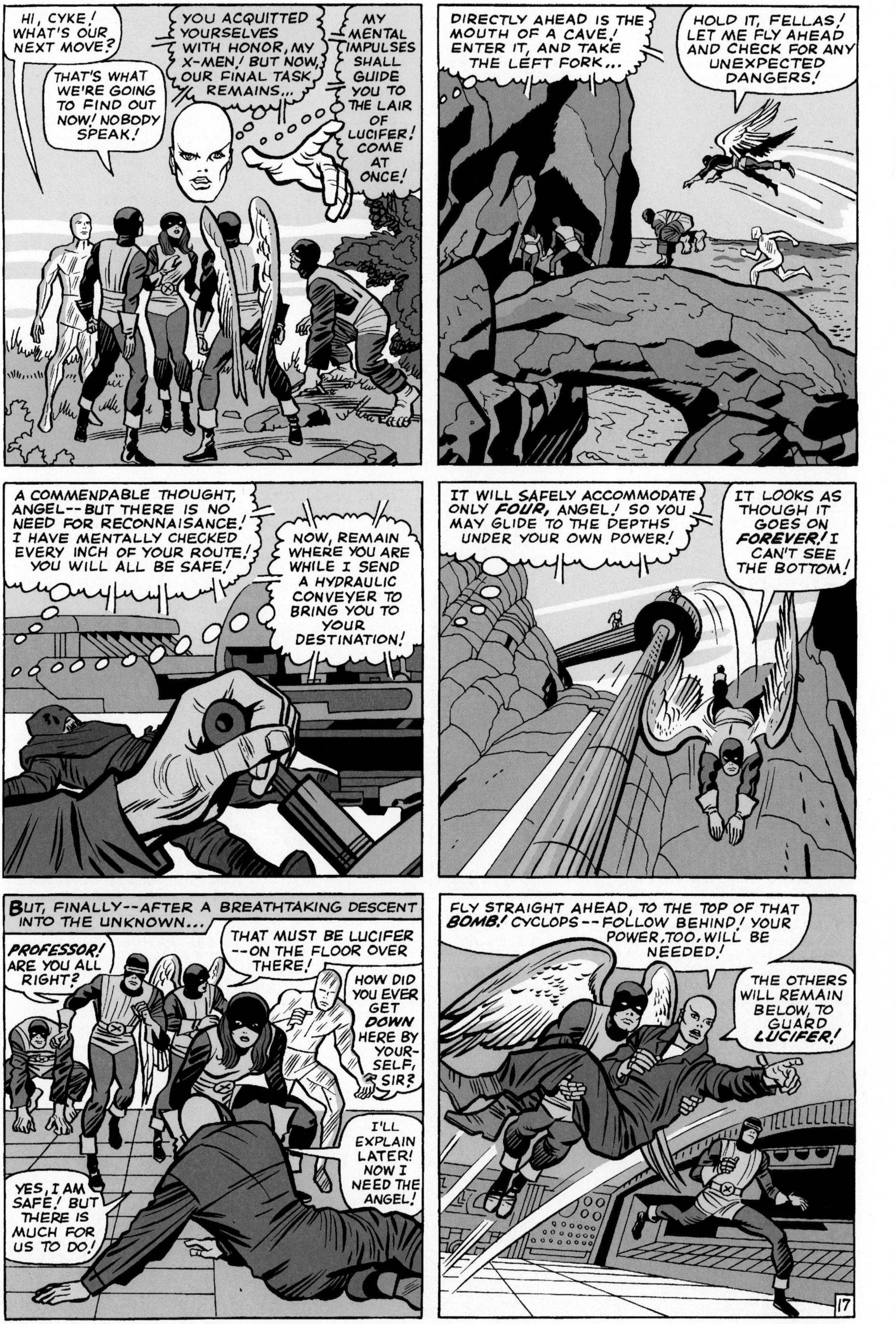
HI, CYKE! WHAT'S OUR NEXT MOVE?
THAT'S WHAT WE'RE GOING TO FIND OUT NOW! NOBODY SPEAK!
YOU ACQUITTED YOURSELVES WITH HONOR, MY X-MEN! BUT NOW, OUR FINAL TASK REMAINS...
MY MENTAL IMPULSES SHALL GUIDE YOU TO THE LAIR OF LUCIFER! COME AT ONCE!
DIRECTLY AHEAD IS THE MOUTH OF A CAVE! ENTER IT, AND TAKE THE LEFT FORK...
HOLD IT, FELLAS! LET ME FLY AHEAD AND CHECK FOR ANY UNEXPECTED DANGERS!
A COMMENDABLE THOUGHT, ANGEL--BUT THERE IS NO NEED FOR RECONNAISANCE! I HAVE MENTALLY CHECKED EVERY INCH OF YOUR ROUTE! YOU WILL ALL BE SAFE!
NOW, REMAIN WHERE YOU ARE WHILE I SEND A HYDRAULIC CONVEYER TO BRING YOU TO YOUR DESTINATION!
IT WILL SAFELY ACCOMMODATE ONLY FOUR, ANGEL! SO YOU MAY GLIDE TO THE DEPTHS UNDER YOUR OWN POWER!
IT LOOKS AS THOUGH IT GOES ON FOREVER! I CAN'T SEE THE BOTTOM!
BUT, FINALLY--AFTER A BREATHTAKING DESCENT INTO THE UNKNOWN...
PROFESSOR! ARE YOU ALL RIGHT?
THAT MUST BE LUCIFER --ON THE FLOOR OVER THERE!
HOW DID YOU EVER GET DOWN HERE BY YOURSELF, SIR?
I'LL EXPLAIN LATER! NOW I NEED THE ANGEL!
YES, I AM SAFE! BUT THERE IS MUCH FOR US TO DO!
FLY STRAIGHT AHEAD, TO THE TOP OF THAT BOMB! CYCLOPS--FOLLOW BEHIND! YOUR POWER, TOO, WILL BE NEEDED!
THE OTHERS WILL REMAIN BELOW, TO GUARD LUCIFER!
17

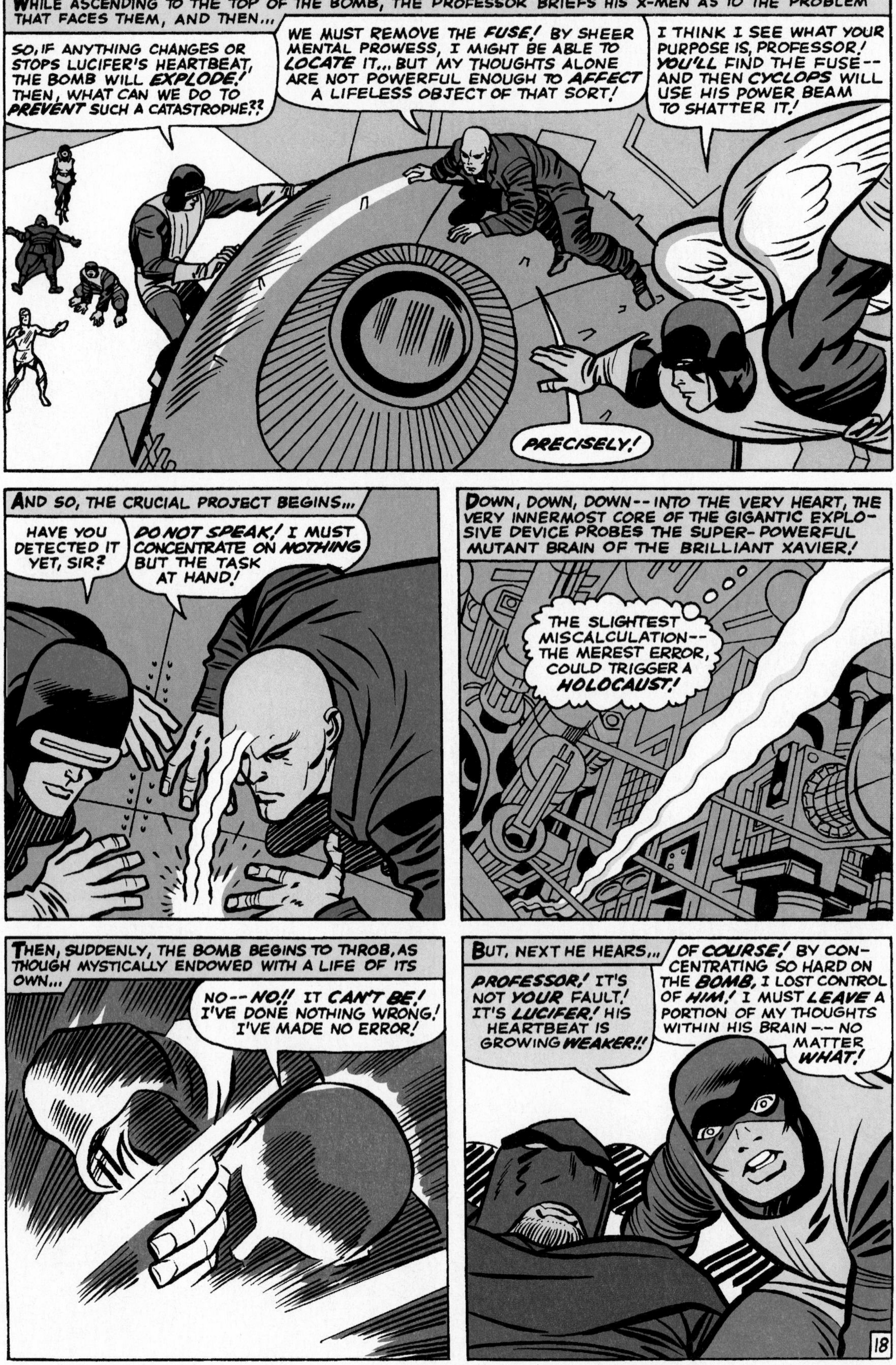

WHILE ASCENDING TO THE TOP OF THE BOMB, THE PROFESSOR BRIEFS HIS X-MEN AS TO THE PROBLEM THAT FACES THEM, AND THEN...
SO, IF ANYTHING CHANGES OR STOPS LUCIFER'S HEARTBEAT, THE BOMB WILL EXPLODE! THEN, WHAT CAN WE DO TO PREVENT SUCH A CATASTROPHE??
WE MUST REMOVE THE FUSE! BY SHEER MENTAL PROWESS, I MIGHT BE ABLE TO LOCATE IT... BUT MY THOUGHTS ALONE ARE NOT POWERFUL ENOUGH TO AFFECT A LIFELESS OBJECT OF THAT SORT!
I THINK I SEE WHAT YOUR PURPOSE IS, PROFESSOR! YOU'LL FIND THE FUSE-- AND THEN CYCLOPS WILL USE HIS POWER BEAM TO SHATTER IT!
PRECISELY!
AND SO, THE CRUCIAL PROJECT BEGINS...
HAVE YOU DETECTED IT YET, SIR?
DO NOT SPEAK! I MUST CONCENTRATE ON NOTHING BUT THE TASK AT HAND!
DOWN, DOWN, DOWN-- INTO THE VERY HEART, THE VERY INNERMOST CORE OF THE GIGANTIC EXPLOSIVE DEVICE PROBES THE SUPER-POWERFUL MUTANT BRAIN OF THE BRILLIANT XAVIER!
THE SLIGHTEST MISCALCULATION-- THE MEREST ERROR, COULD TRIGGER A HOLOCAUST!
THEN, SUDDENLY, THE BOMB BEGINS TO THROB, AS THOUGH MYSTICALLY ENDOWED WITH A LIFE OF ITS OWN...
NO-- NO!! IT CAN'T BE! I'VE DONE NOTHING WRONG! I'VE MADE NO ERROR!
BUT, NEXT HE HEARS...
PROFESSOR! IT'S NOT YOUR FAULT! IT'S LUCIFER! HIS HEARTBEAT IS GROWING WEAKER!!
OF COURSE! BY CONCENTRATING SO HARD ON THE BOMB, I LOST CONTROL OF HIM! I MUST LEAVE A PORTION OF MY THOUGHTS WITHIN HIS BRAIN -- NO MATTER WHAT!
18

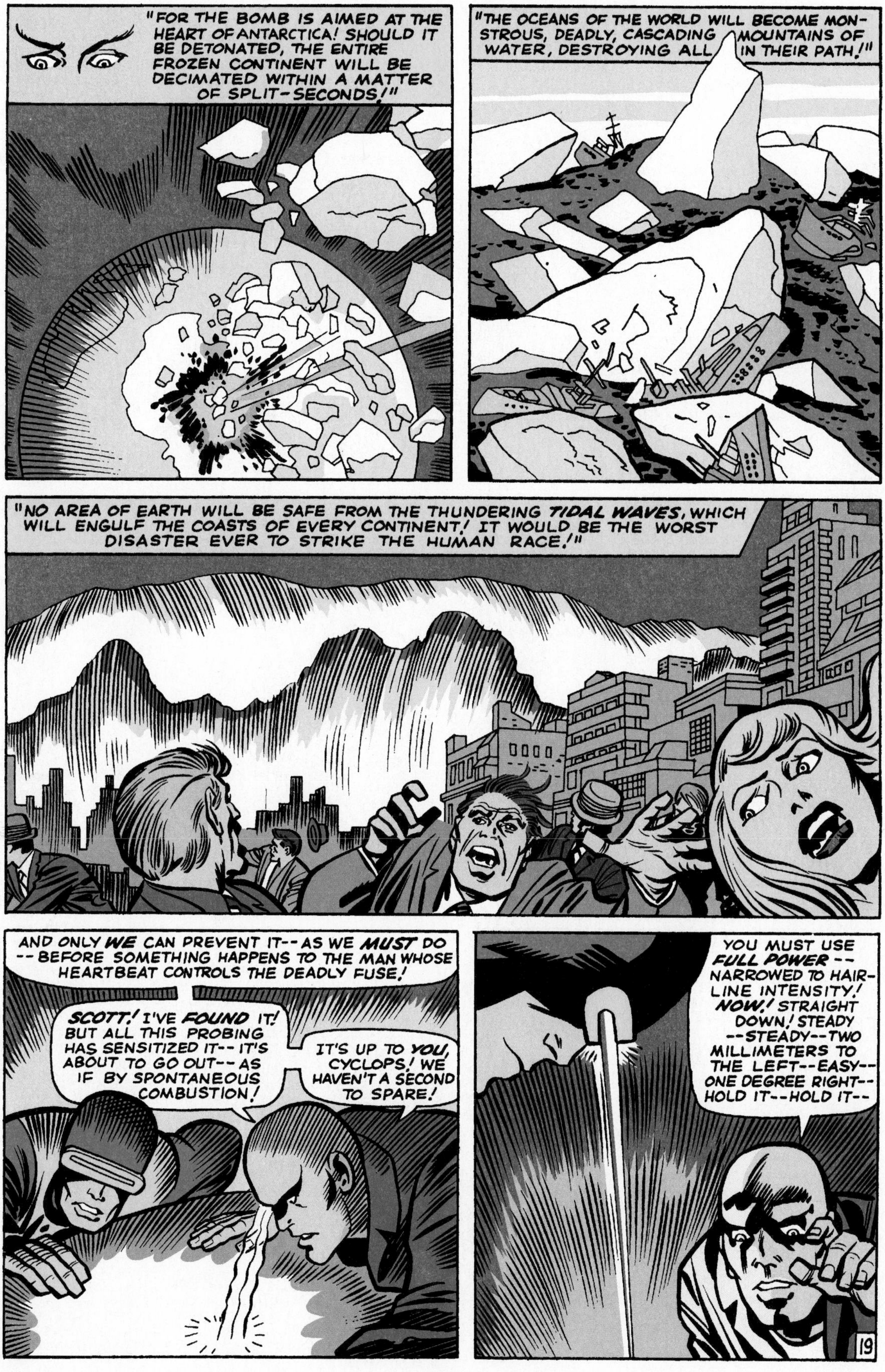
"FOR THE BOMB IS AIMED AT THE HEART OF ANTARCTICA! SHOULD IT BE DETONATED, THE ENTIRE FROZEN CONTINENT WILL BE DECIMATED WITHIN A MATTER OF SPLIT-SECONDS!"
"THE OCEANS OF THE WORLD WILL BECOME MONSTROUS, DEADLY, CASCADING MOUNTAINS OF WATER, DESTROYING ALL IN THEIR PATH!"
"NO AREA OF EARTH WILL BE SAFE FROM THE THUNDERING TIDAL WAVES, WHICH WILL ENGULF THE COASTS OF EVERY CONTINENT! IT WOULD BE THE WORST DISASTER EVER TO STRIKE THE HUMAN RACE!"
AND ONLY WE CAN PREVENT IT-- AS WE MUST DO -- BEFORE SOMETHING HAPPENS TO THE MAN WHOSE HEARTBEAT CONTROLS THE DEADLY FUSE!
SCOTT! I'VE FOUND IT! BUT ALL THIS PROBING HAS SENSITIZED IT-- IT'S ABOUT TO GO OUT-- AS IF BY SPONTANEOUS COMBUSTION!
IT'S UP TO YOU, CYCLOPS! WE HAVEN'T A SECOND TO SPARE!
YOU MUST USE FULL POWER -- NARROWED TO HAIR-LINE INTENSITY! NOW! STRAIGHT DOWN! STEADY --STEADY--TWO MILLIMETERS TO THE LEFT--EASY-- ONE DEGREE RIGHT-- HOLD IT--HOLD IT--
19

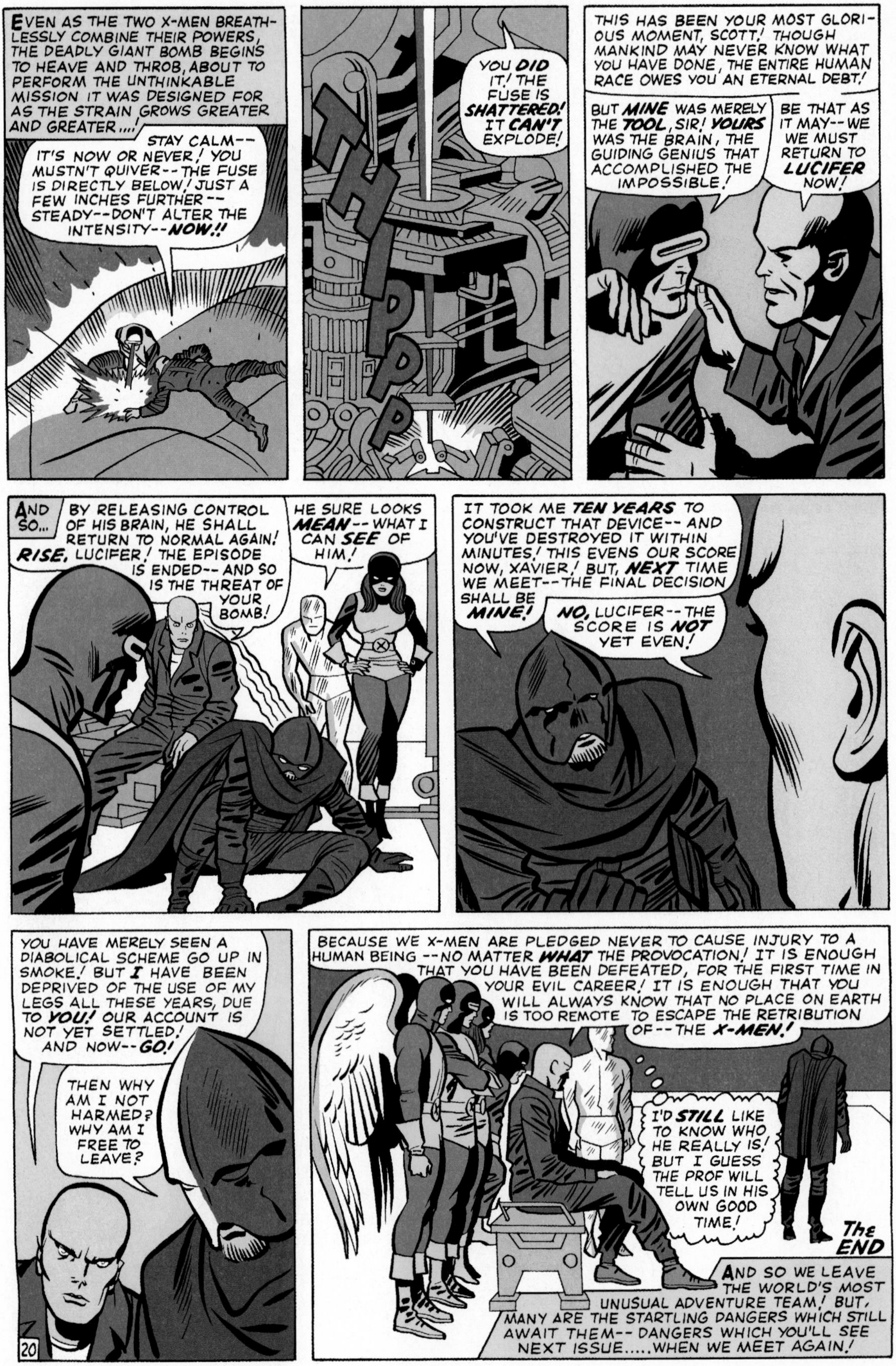
EVEN AS THE TWO X-MEN BREATHLESSLY COMBINE THEIR POWERS, THE DEADLY GIANT BOMB BEGINS TO HEAVE AND THROB, ABOUT TO PERFORM THE UNTHINKABLE MISSION IT WAS DESIGNED FOR AS THE STRAIN GROWS GREATER AND GREATER....!
STAY CALM-- IT'S NOW OR NEVER! YOU MUSTN'T QUIVER-- THE FUSE IS DIRECTLY BELOW! JUST A FEW INCHES FURTHER-- STEADY--DON'T ALTER THE INTENSITY--NOW!!
THIPPP
YOU DID IT! THE FUSE IS SHATTERED! IT CAN'T EXPLODE!
THIS HAS BEEN YOUR MOST GLORIOUS MOMENT, SCOTT! THOUGH MANKIND MAY NEVER KNOW WHAT YOU HAVE DONE, THE ENTIRE HUMAN RACE OWES YOU AN ETERNAL DEBT!
BUT MINE WAS MERELY THE TOOL, SIR! YOURS WAS THE BRAIN, THE GUIDING GENIUS THAT ACCOMPLISHED THE IMPOSSIBLE!
BE THAT AS IT MAY-- WE MUST RETURN TO LUCIFER NOW!
AND SO...
BY RELEASING CONTROL OF HIS BRAIN, HE SHALL RETURN TO NORMAL AGAIN! RISE, LUCIFER! THE EPISODE IS ENDED-- AND SO IS THE THREAT OF YOUR BOMB!
HE SURE LOOKS MEAN-- WHAT I CAN SEE OF HIM!
IT TOOK ME TEN YEARS TO CONSTRUCT THAT DEVICE-- AND YOU'VE DESTROYED IT WITHIN MINUTES! THIS EVENS OUR SCORE NOW, XAVIER! BUT, NEXT TIME WE MEET--THE FINAL DECISION SHALL BE MINE!
NO, LUCIFER-- THE SCORE IS NOT YET EVEN!
YOU HAVE MERELY SEEN A DIABOLICAL SCHEME GO UP IN SMOKE! BUT I HAVE BEEN DEPRIVED OF THE USE OF MY LEGS ALL THESE YEARS, DUE TO YOU! OUR ACCOUNT IS NOT YET SETTLED! AND NOW--GO!
THEN WHY AM I NOT HARMED? WHY AM I FREE TO LEAVE?
20
BECAUSE WE X-MEN ARE PLEDGED NEVER TO CAUSE INJURY TO A HUMAN BEING --NO MATTER WHAT THE PROVOCATION! IT IS ENOUGH THAT YOU HAVE BEEN DEFEATED, FOR THE FIRST TIME IN YOUR EVIL CAREER! IT IS ENOUGH THAT YOU WILL ALWAYS KNOW THAT NO PLACE ON EARTH IS TOO REMOTE TO ESCAPE THE RETRIBUTION OF--THE X-MEN!
I'D STILL LIKE TO KNOW WHO HE REALLY IS! BUT I GUESS THE PROF WILL TELL US IN HIS OWN GOOD TIME!
THE END
AND SO WE LEAVE THE WORLD'S MOST UNUSUAL ADVENTURE TEAM! BUT, MANY ARE THE STARTLING DANGERS WHICH STILL AWAIT THEM-- DANGERS WHICH YOU'LL SEE NEXT ISSUE.....WHEN WE MEET AGAIN!

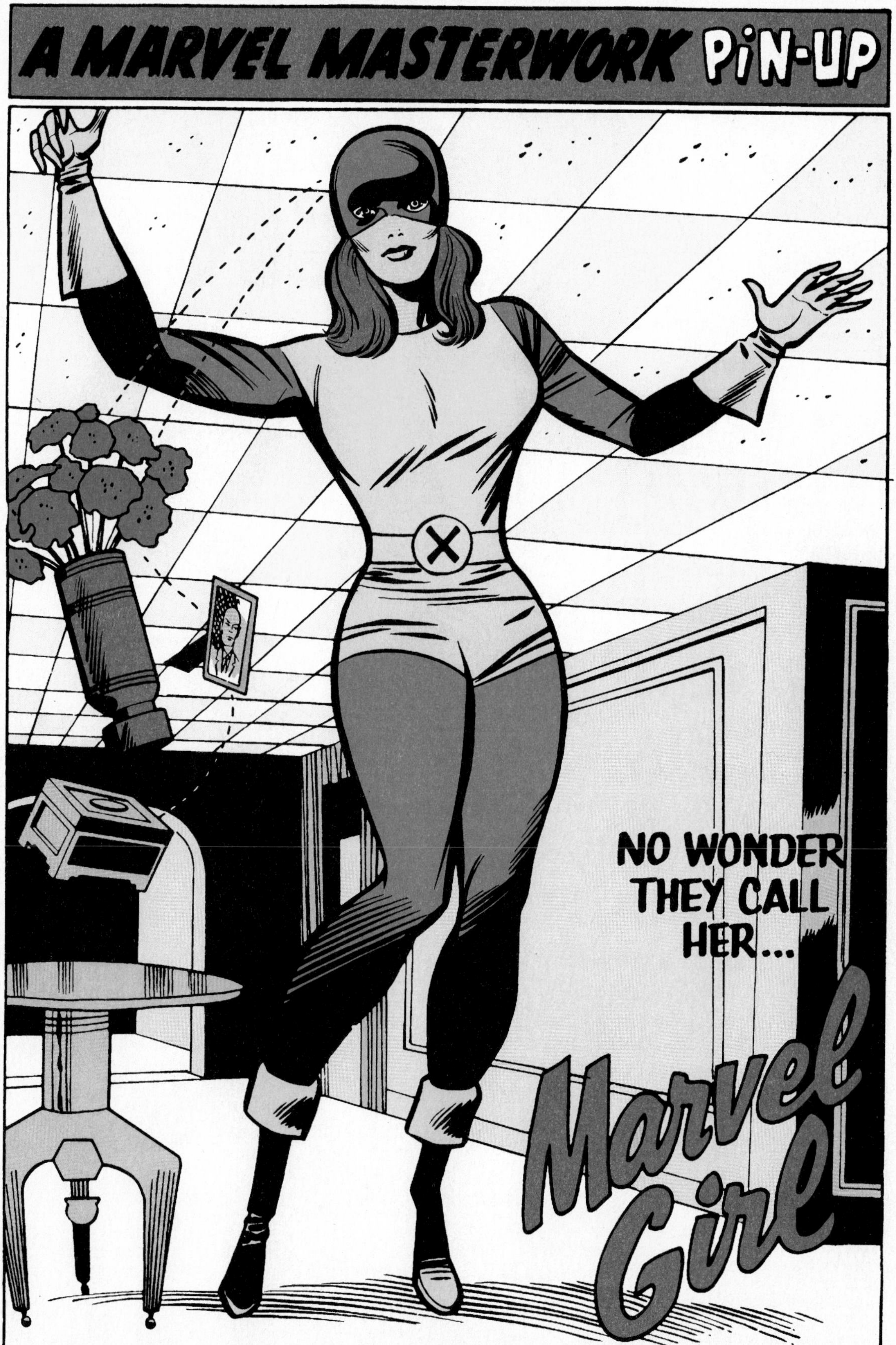
A MARVEL MASTERWORK PiN-UP
NO WONDER THEY CALL HER...
Marvel Girl

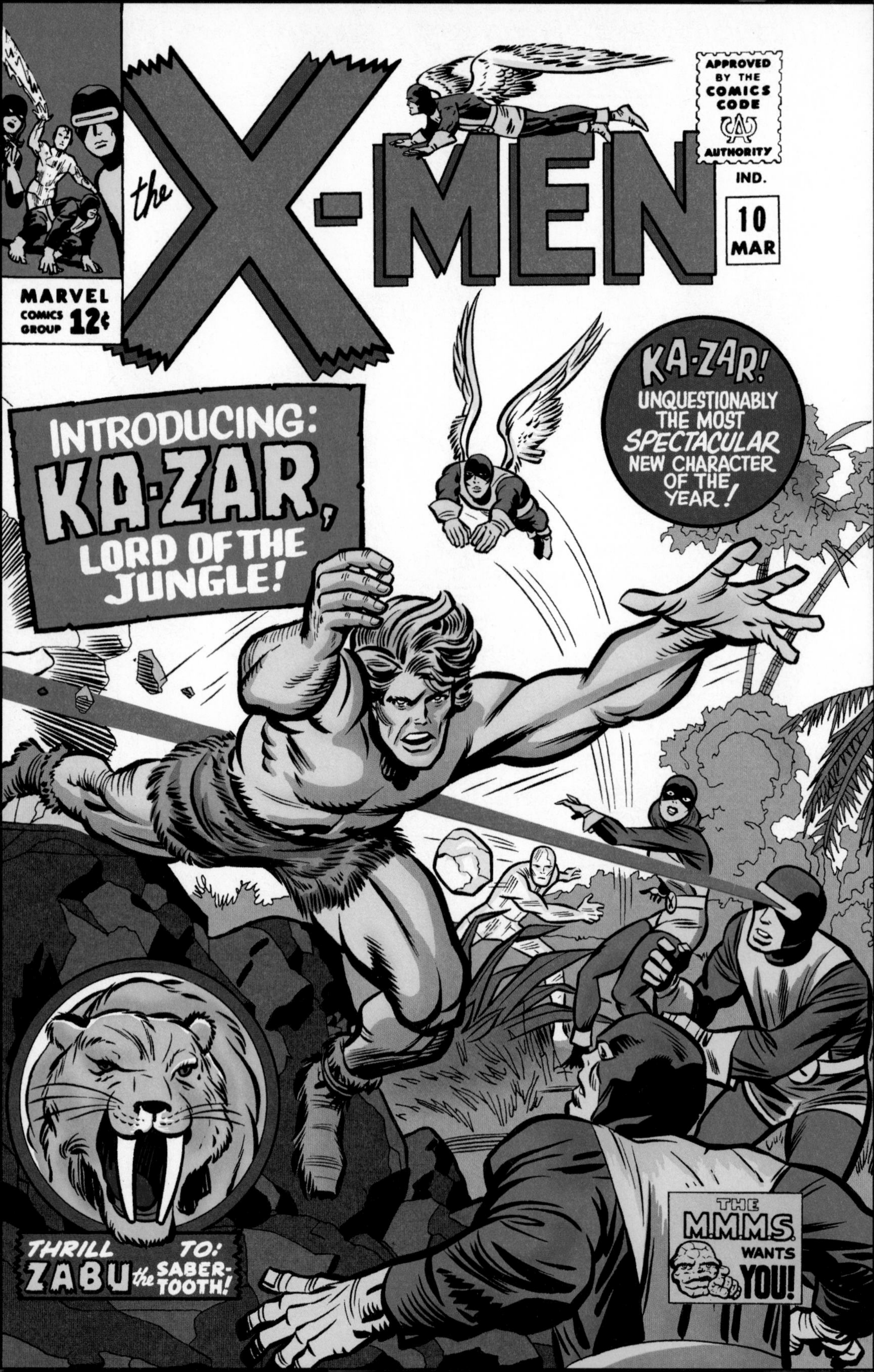
MARVEL COMICS GROUP 12¢
the X-MEN
APPROVED BY THE COMICS CODE AUTHORITY
IND.
10 MAR
INTRODUCING: KA-ZAR, LORD OF THE JUNGLE!
KA-ZAR! UNQUESTIONABLY THE MOST SPECTACULAR NEW CHARACTER OF THE YEAR!
THRILL TO: ZABU the SABER-TOOTH!
THE M.M.M.S. WANTS YOU!

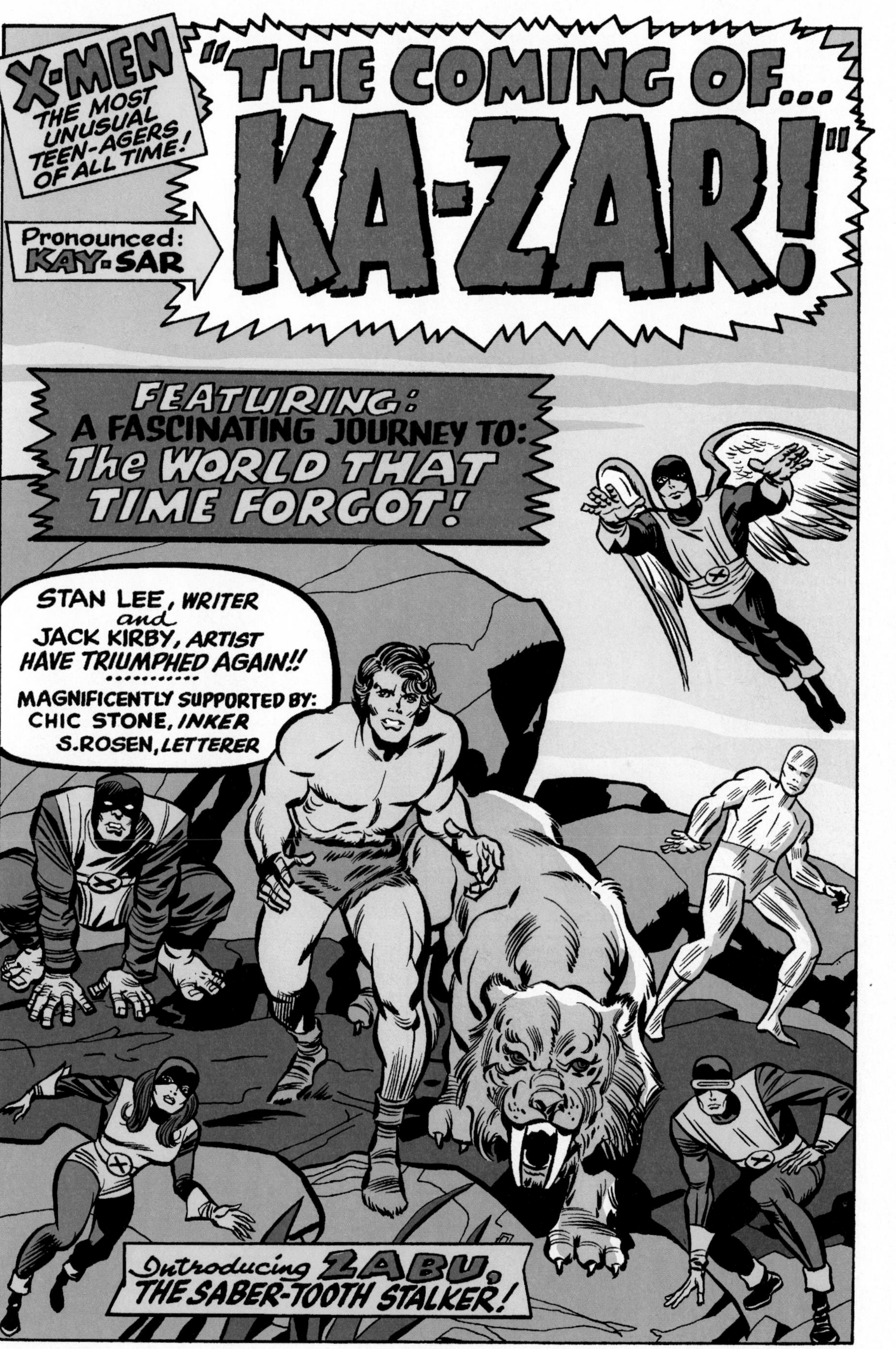
X-MEN THE MOST UNUSUAL TEEN-AGERS OF ALL TIME!
"THE COMING OF... KA-ZAR!"
Pronounced: KAY-SAR
FEATURING: A FASCINATING JOURNEY TO: The WORLD THAT TIME FORGOT!
STAN LEE, WRITER and JACK KIRBY, ARTIST HAVE TRIUMPHED AGAIN!! MAGNIFICENTLY SUPPORTED BY: CHIC STONE, INKER S.ROSEN, LETTERER
Introducing ZABU, THE SABER-TOOTH STALKER!

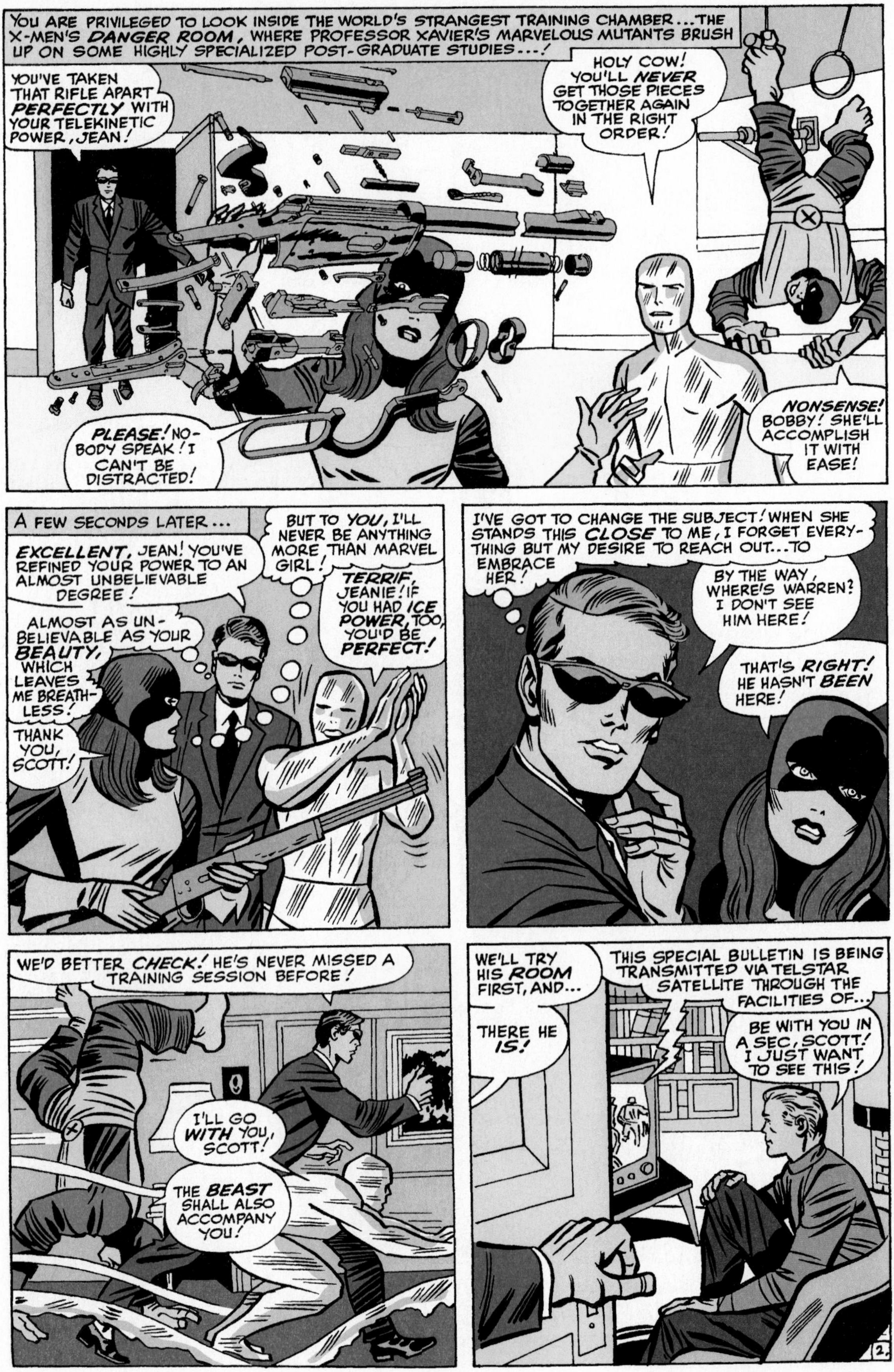
YOU ARE PRIVILEGED TO LOOK INSIDE THE WORLD'S STRANGEST TRAINING CHAMBER... THE X-MEN'S DANGER ROOM, WHERE PROFESSOR XAVIER'S MARVELOUS MUTANTS BRUSH UP ON SOME HIGHLY SPECIALIZED POST-GRADUATE STUDIES...!
YOU'VE TAKEN THAT RIFLE APART PERFECTLY WITH YOUR TELEKINETIC POWER, JEAN!
HOLY COW! YOU'LL NEVER GET THOSE PIECES TOGETHER AGAIN IN THE RIGHT ORDER!
PLEASE! NOBODY SPEAK! I CAN'T BE DISTRACTED!
NONSENSE! BOBBY! SHE'LL ACCOMPLISH IT WITH EASE!
A FEW SECONDS LATER...
EXCELLENT, JEAN! YOU'VE REFINED YOUR POWER TO AN ALMOST UNBELIEVABLE DEGREE!
BUT TO YOU, I'LL NEVER BE ANYTHING MORE THAN MARVEL GIRL!
ALMOST AS UNBELIEVABLE AS YOUR BEAUTY, WHICH LEAVES ME BREATHLESS!
TERRIF, JEANIE! IF YOU HAD ICE POWER, TOO, YOU'D BE PERFECT!
THANK YOU, SCOTT!
I'VE GOT TO CHANGE THE SUBJECT! WHEN SHE STANDS THIS CLOSE TO ME, I FORGET EVERYTHING BUT MY DESIRE TO REACH OUT... TO EMBRACE HER!
BY THE WAY, WHERE'S WARREN? I DON'T SEE HIM HERE!
THAT'S RIGHT! HE HASN'T BEEN HERE!
WE'D BETTER CHECK! HE'S NEVER MISSED A TRAINING SESSION BEFORE!
I'LL GO WITH YOU, SCOTT!
THE BEAST SHALL ALSO ACCOMPANY YOU!
WE'LL TRY HIS ROOM FIRST, AND...
THIS SPECIAL BULLETIN IS BEING TRANSMITTED VIA TELSTAR SATELLITE THROUGH THE FACILITIES OF...
THERE HE IS!
BE WITH YOU IN A SEC, SCOTT! I JUST WANT TO SEE THIS!
2.

MR. WORTHINGTON! MAY I REMIND YOU THAT *NO ONE* IS EXCUSED FROM POST-GRADUATE WORK WITHOUT EXPRESS PERMISSION OF *PROFESSOR X* HIMSELF?!!

I *KNOW*, SCOTTY! BUT THIS MAY CONCERN *ALL* OF US! *WATCH!*

SAY! WHAT'S GOIN' *ON* THERE, ANY-WAY?

IT'S A VIDEOTAPE BROADCAST OF SOMETHING THAT HAPPENED YESTERDAY AT ANTARCTICA...

...ONE OF THE EXPLORATION PARTY HAD BEEN MISSING AND CONSIDERED LOST, UNTIL HE WAS CARRIED TO THE CAMP BY A FANTASTIC FIGURE CLAD ONLY IN A LOIN CLOTH!

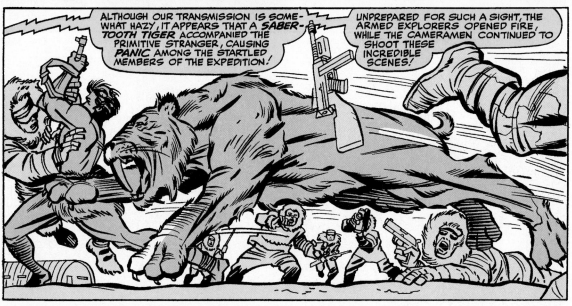

ALTHOUGH OUR TRANSMISSION IS SOME-WHAT HAZY, IT APPEARS THAT A *SABER-TOOTH TIGER* ACCOMPANIED THE PRIMITIVE STRANGER, CAUSING *PANIC* AMONG THE STARTLED MEMBERS OF THE EXPEDITION!

UNPREPARED FOR SUCH A SIGHT, THE ARMED EXPLORERS OPENED FIRE, WHILE THE CAMERAMEN CONTINUED TO SHOOT THESE INCREDIBLE SCENES!

ONLY A MIRACLE PREVENTED ANY FATALITIES, AND THE SAVAGE MAN AND BEAST SOON FADED INTO THE NIGHT AFTER RUNNING AMOK THROUGH THE CAMP!

IT'S *IMPOSSIBLE!* SABER-TOOTH TIGERS HAVE BEEN *EXTINCT* FOR AGES! AND YET... WE *SAW* IT!

HOW *ABOUT* THAT?!

THAT WILD MAN...LIKE A LATTER DAY TARZAN... IN THAT FRIGID CLIMATE WITHOUT PROTECTIVE CLOTHES! COULD HE BE...??

..HE *MUST* BE!! A *MUTANT!!*

3.

215

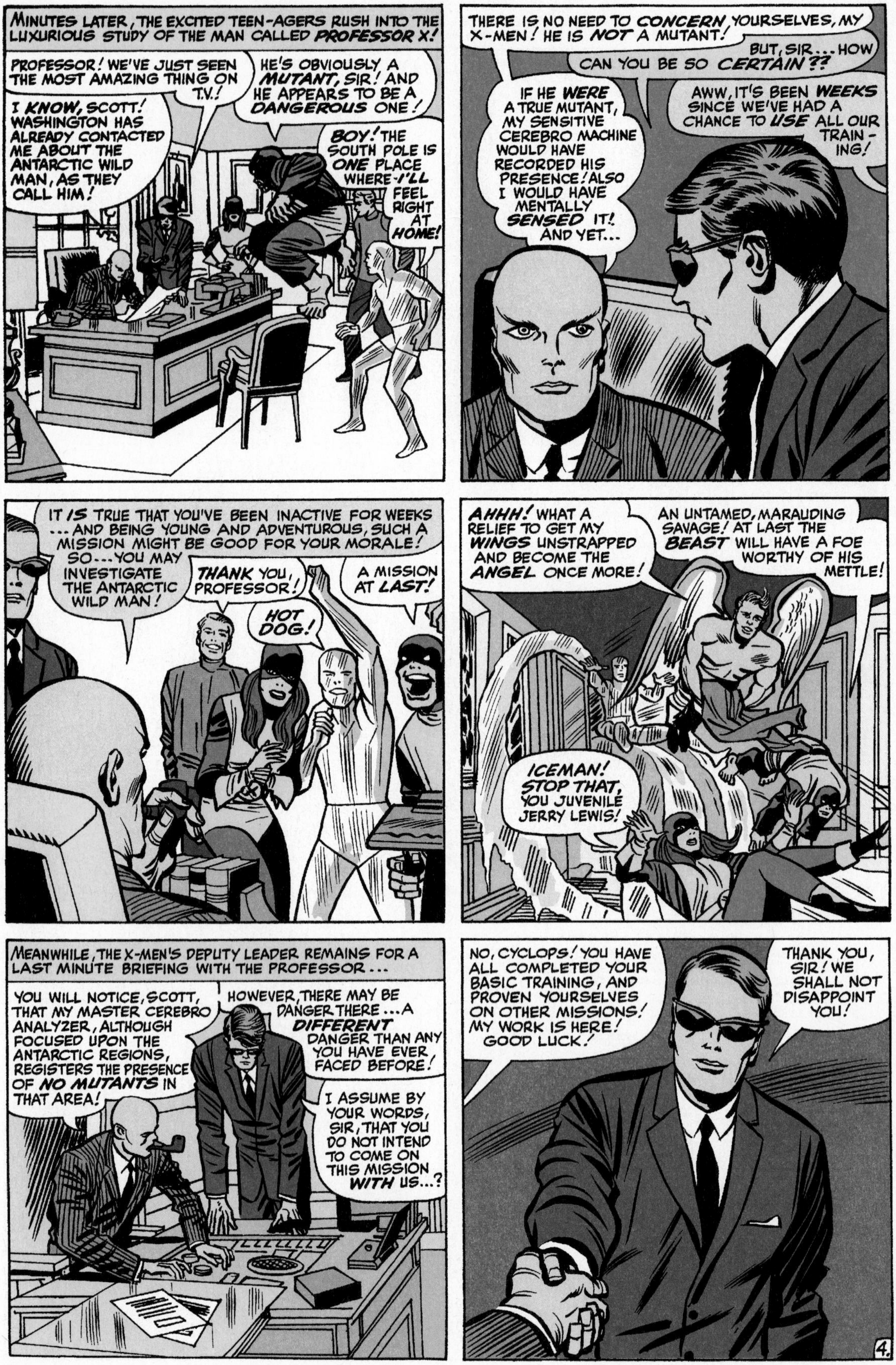
MINUTES LATER, THE EXCITED TEEN-AGERS RUSH INTO THE LUXURIOUS STUDY OF THE MAN CALLED PROFESSOR X!
PROFESSOR! WE'VE JUST SEEN THE MOST AMAZING THING ON T.V.!
HE'S OBVIOUSLY A MUTANT, SIR! AND HE APPEARS TO BE A DANGEROUS ONE!
I KNOW, SCOTT! WASHINGTON HAS ALREADY CONTACTED ME ABOUT THE ANTARCTIC WILD MAN, AS THEY CALL HIM!
BOY! THE SOUTH POLE IS ONE PLACE WHERE I'LL FEEL RIGHT AT HOME!
THERE IS NO NEED TO CONCERN YOURSELVES, MY X-MEN! HE IS NOT A MUTANT!
BUT, SIR... HOW CAN YOU BE SO CERTAIN??
IF HE WERE A TRUE MUTANT, MY SENSITIVE CEREBRO MACHINE WOULD HAVE RECORDED HIS PRESENCE! ALSO I WOULD HAVE MENTALLY SENSED IT! AND YET...
AWW, IT'S BEEN WEEKS SINCE WE'VE HAD A CHANCE TO USE ALL OUR TRAINING!
IT IS TRUE THAT YOU'VE BEEN INACTIVE FOR WEEKS ... AND BEING YOUNG AND ADVENTUROUS, SUCH A MISSION MIGHT BE GOOD FOR YOUR MORALE! SO... YOU MAY INVESTIGATE THE ANTARCTIC WILD MAN!
THANK YOU, PROFESSOR!
A MISSION AT LAST!
HOT DOG!
AHHH! WHAT A RELIEF TO GET MY WINGS UNSTRAPPED AND BECOME THE ANGEL ONCE MORE!
AN UNTAMED, MARAUDING SAVAGE! AT LAST THE BEAST WILL HAVE A FOE WORTHY OF HIS METTLE!
ICEMAN! STOP THAT, YOU JUVENILE JERRY LEWIS!
MEANWHILE, THE X-MEN'S DEPUTY LEADER REMAINS FOR A LAST MINUTE BRIEFING WITH THE PROFESSOR...
YOU WILL NOTICE, SCOTT, THAT MY MASTER CEREBRO ANALYZER, ALTHOUGH FOCUSED UPON THE ANTARCTIC REGIONS, REGISTERS THE PRESENCE OF NO MUTANTS IN THAT AREA!
HOWEVER, THERE MAY BE DANGER THERE ... A DIFFERENT DANGER THAN ANY YOU HAVE EVER FACED BEFORE!
I ASSUME BY YOUR WORDS, SIR, THAT YOU DO NOT INTEND TO COME ON THIS MISSION WITH US...?
NO, CYCLOPS! YOU HAVE ALL COMPLETED YOUR BASIC TRAINING, AND PROVEN YOURSELVES ON OTHER MISSIONS! MY WORK IS HERE! GOOD LUCK!
THANK YOU, SIR! WE SHALL NOT DISAPPOINT YOU!
4.

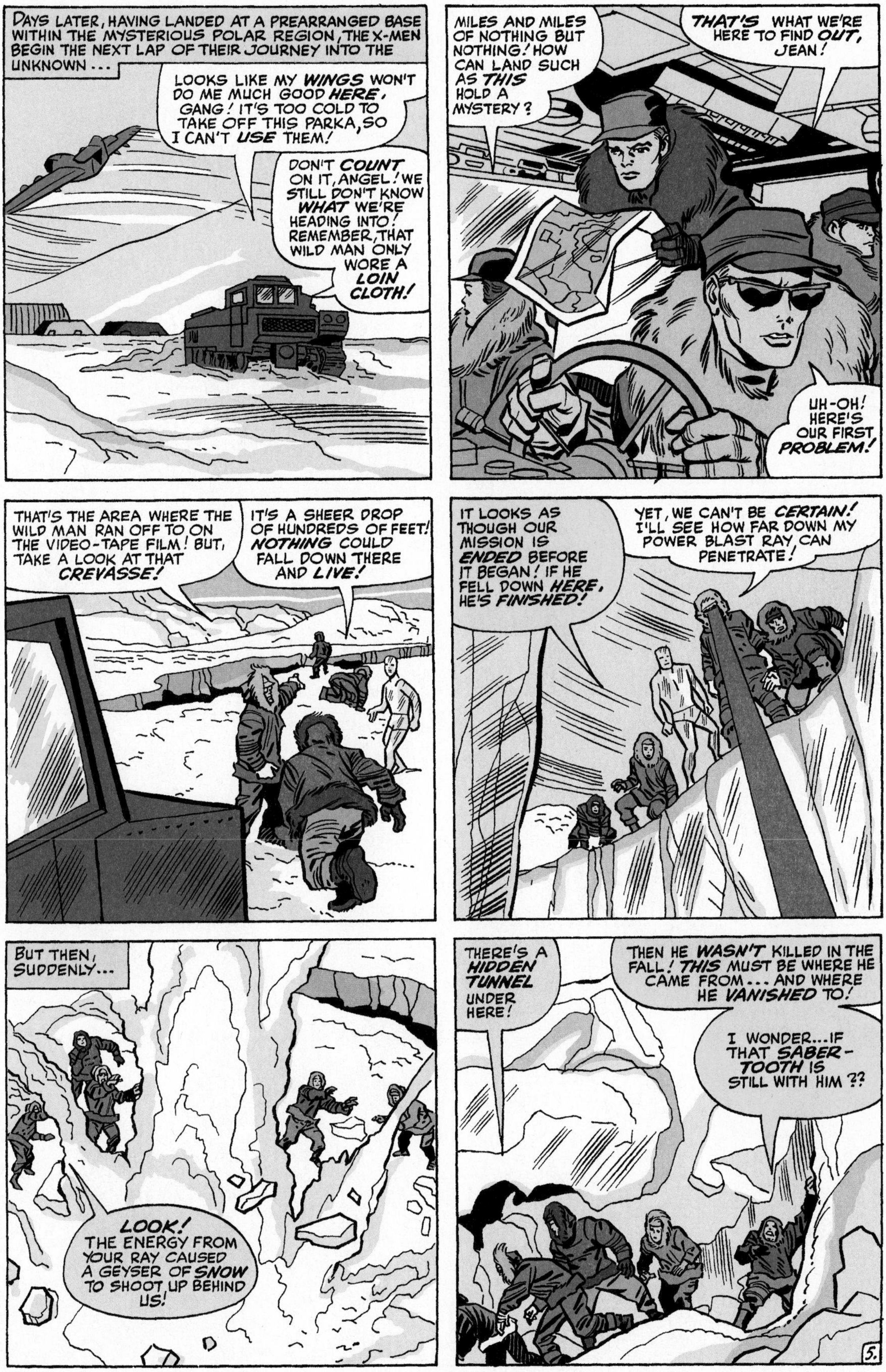
DAYS LATER, HAVING LANDED AT A PREARRANGED BASE WITHIN THE MYSTERIOUS POLAR REGION, THE X-MEN BEGIN THE NEXT LAP OF THEIR JOURNEY INTO THE UNKNOWN...
LOOKS LIKE MY WINGS WON'T DO ME MUCH GOOD HERE, GANG! IT'S TOO COLD TO TAKE OFF THIS PARKA, SO I CAN'T USE THEM!
DON'T COUNT ON IT, ANGEL! WE STILL DON'T KNOW WHAT WE'RE HEADING INTO! REMEMBER, THAT WILD MAN ONLY WORE A LOIN CLOTH!
MILES AND MILES OF NOTHING BUT NOTHING! HOW CAN LAND SUCH AS THIS HOLD A MYSTERY?
THAT'S WHAT WE'RE HERE TO FIND OUT, JEAN!
UH-OH! HERE'S OUR FIRST PROBLEM!
THAT'S THE AREA WHERE THE WILD MAN RAN OFF TO ON THE VIDEO-TAPE FILM! BUT, TAKE A LOOK AT THAT CREVASSE!
IT'S A SHEER DROP OF HUNDREDS OF FEET! NOTHING COULD FALL DOWN THERE AND LIVE!
IT LOOKS AS THOUGH OUR MISSION IS ENDED BEFORE IT BEGAN! IF HE FELL DOWN HERE, HE'S FINISHED!
YET, WE CAN'T BE CERTAIN! I'LL SEE HOW FAR DOWN MY POWER BLAST RAY CAN PENETRATE!
BUT THEN, SUDDENLY...
LOOK! THE ENERGY FROM YOUR RAY CAUSED A GEYSER OF SNOW TO SHOOT UP BEHIND US!
THERE'S A HIDDEN TUNNEL UNDER HERE!
THEN HE WASN'T KILLED IN THE FALL! THIS MUST BE WHERE HE CAME FROM... AND WHERE HE VANISHED TO!
I WONDER... IF THAT SABER-TOOTH IS STILL WITH HIM??
5.

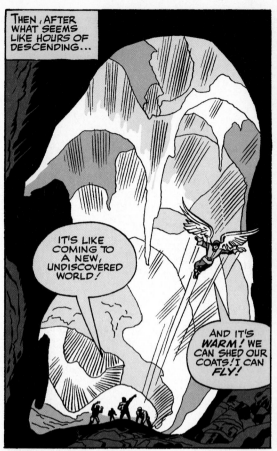

THEN, AFTER WHAT SEEMS LIKE HOURS OF DESCENDING...

IT'S LIKE COMING TO A NEW, UNDISCOVERED WORLD!

AND IT'S WARM! WE CAN SHED OUR COATS! I CAN FLY!

SCOUTING AHEAD, THE AWE-STRICKEN ANGEL SOON SEES...

IT'S LIKE A VAST ANIMAL BURIAL GROUND! BUT THE BONES...THEY'RE THE WRONG SIZE! THEY'RE THE SKELETONS OF... MONSTERS!

THEN, EMERGING FROM THE GIGANTIC CAVE, ANGEL HEARS A BLOOD-CURDLING SCREECH ABOVE, AND TURNS AROUND TO FIND...

PTERODACTYLS!! BIRDS FROM THE DINOSAUR ERA! H-HOW CAN IT BE??

BUT, THE WINGED MUTANT HAS NO TIME FOR IDLE SPECULATION... AS THE FLYING KILLERS ATTACK...!

CLACK!

WOW! THAT WAS TOO CLOSE FOR COMFORT!

6.

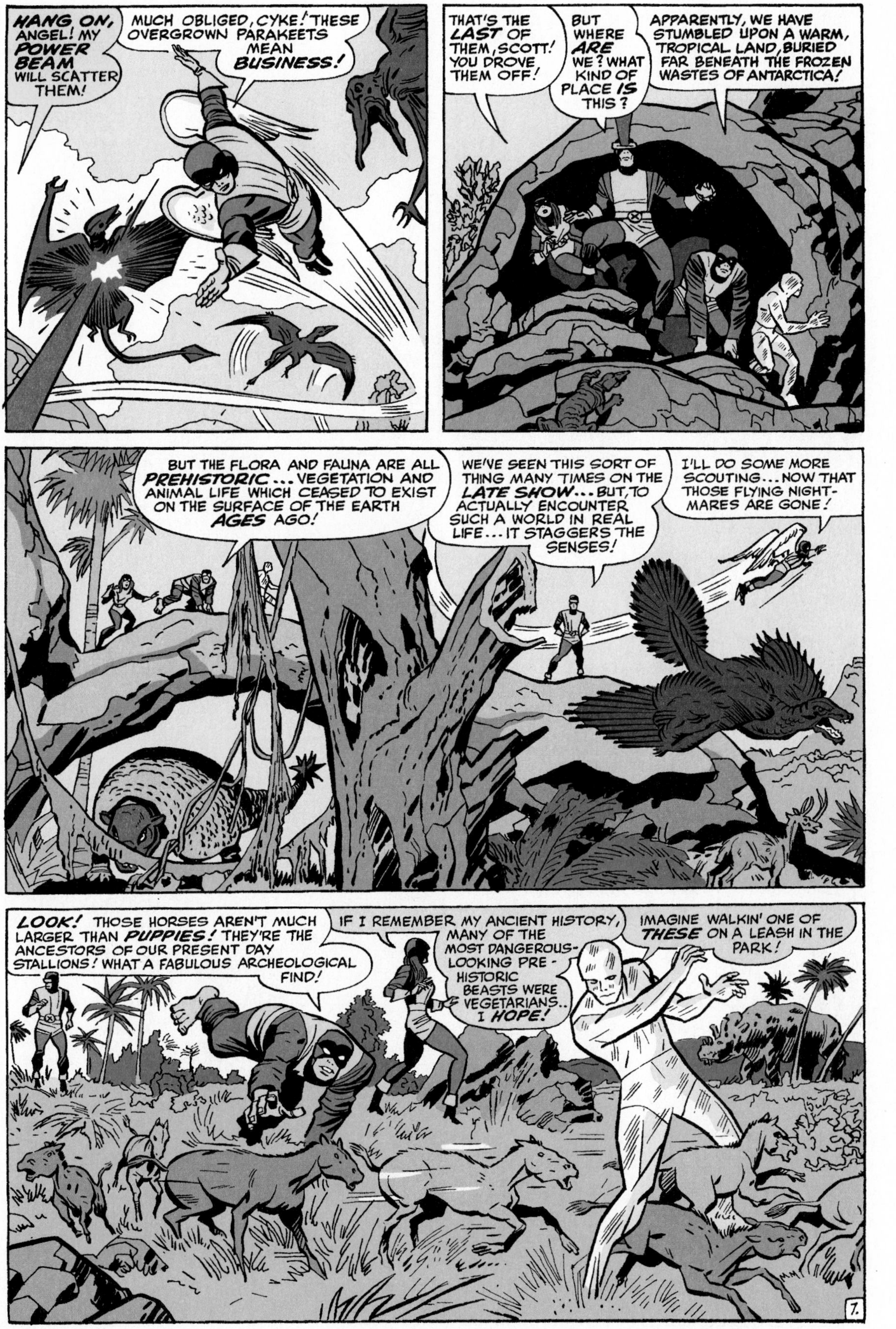
HANG ON, ANGEL! MY POWER BEAM WILL SCATTER THEM!
MUCH OBLIGED, CYKE! THESE OVERGROWN PARAKEETS MEAN BUSINESS!
THAT'S THE LAST OF THEM, SCOTT! YOU DROVE THEM OFF!
BUT WHERE ARE WE? WHAT KIND OF PLACE IS THIS?
APPARENTLY, WE HAVE STUMBLED UPON A WARM, TROPICAL LAND, BURIED FAR BENEATH THE FROZEN WASTES OF ANTARCTICA!
BUT THE FLORA AND FAUNA ARE ALL PREHISTORIC... VEGETATION AND ANIMAL LIFE WHICH CEASED TO EXIST ON THE SURFACE OF THE EARTH AGES AGO!
WE'VE SEEN THIS SORT OF THING MANY TIMES ON THE LATE SHOW... BUT, TO ACTUALLY ENCOUNTER SUCH A WORLD IN REAL LIFE... IT STAGGERS THE SENSES!
I'LL DO SOME MORE SCOUTING... NOW THAT THOSE FLYING NIGHT-MARES ARE GONE!
LOOK! THOSE HORSES AREN'T MUCH LARGER THAN PUPPIES! THEY'RE THE ANCESTORS OF OUR PRESENT DAY STALLIONS! WHAT A FABULOUS ARCHEOLOGICAL FIND!
IF I REMEMBER MY ANCIENT HISTORY, MANY OF THE MOST DANGEROUS-LOOKING PRE-HISTORIC BEASTS WERE VEGETARIANS.. I HOPE!
IMAGINE WALKIN' ONE OF THESE ON A LEASH IN THE PARK!
7.

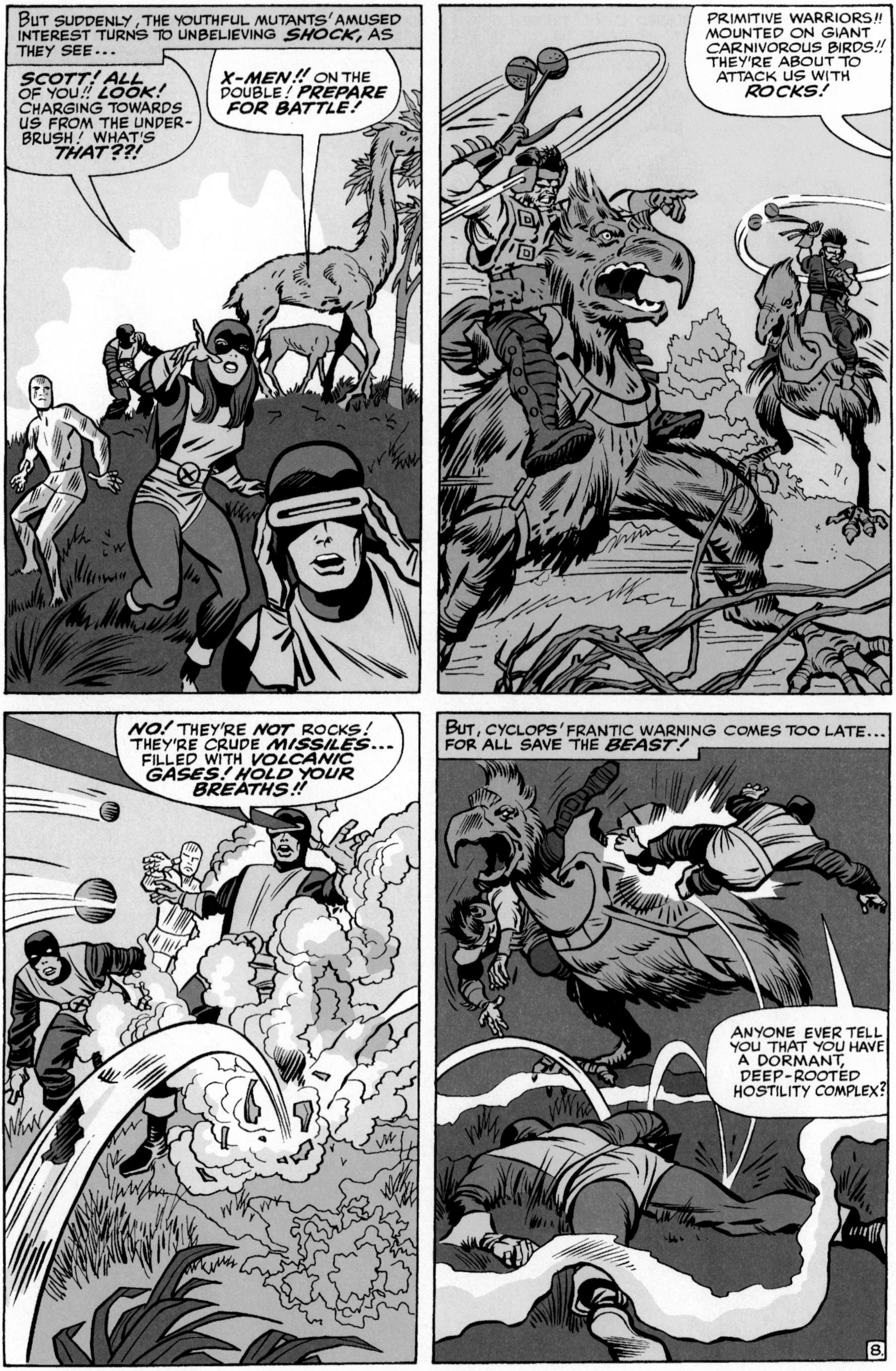
BUT SUDDENLY, THE YOUTHFUL MUTANTS' AMUSED INTEREST TURNS TO UNBELIEVING SHOCK, AS THEY SEE...
SCOTT! ALL OF YOU!! LOOK! CHARGING TOWARDS US FROM THE UNDER-BRUSH! WHAT'S THAT??!
X-MEN!! ON THE DOUBLE! PREPARE FOR BATTLE!
PRIMITIVE WARRIORS!! MOUNTED ON GIANT CARNIVOROUS BIRDS!! THEY'RE ABOUT TO ATTACK US WITH ROCKS!
NO! THEY'RE NOT ROCKS! THEY'RE CRUDE MISSILES... FILLED WITH VOLCANIC GASES! HOLD YOUR BREATHS!!
BUT, CYCLOPS' FRANTIC WARNING COMES TOO LATE... FOR ALL SAVE THE BEAST!
ANYONE EVER TELL YOU THAT YOU HAVE A DORMANT, DEEP-ROOTED HOSTILITY COMPLEX?
8.

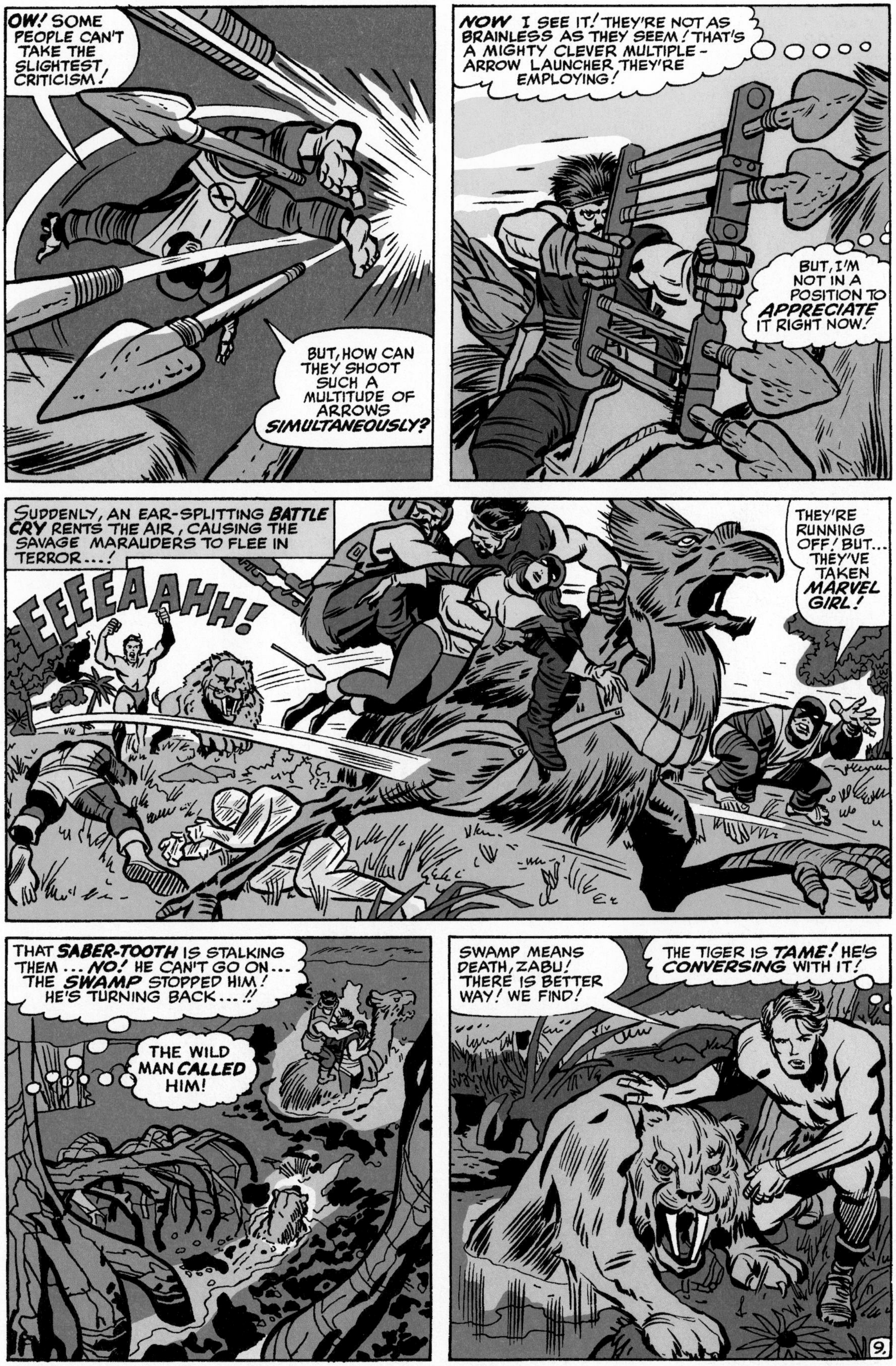
OW! SOME PEOPLE CAN'T TAKE THE SLIGHTEST CRITICISM!
BUT, HOW CAN THEY SHOOT SUCH A MULTITUDE OF ARROWS SIMULTANEOUSLY?
NOW I SEE IT! THEY'RE NOT AS BRAINLESS AS THEY SEEM! THAT'S A MIGHTY CLEVER MULTIPLE-ARROW LAUNCHER THEY'RE EMPLOYING!
BUT, I'M NOT IN A POSITION TO APPRECIATE IT RIGHT NOW!
SUDDENLY, AN EAR-SPLITTING BATTLE CRY RENTS THE AIR, CAUSING THE SAVAGE MARAUDERS TO FLEE IN TERROR...!
EEEEAAHH!
THEY'RE RUNNING OFF! BUT... THEY'VE TAKEN MARVEL GIRL!
THAT SABER-TOOTH IS STALKING THEM... NO! HE CAN'T GO ON... THE SWAMP STOPPED HIM! HE'S TURNING BACK...!!
THE WILD MAN CALLED HIM!
SWAMP MEANS DEATH, ZABU! THERE IS BETTER WAY! WE FIND!
THE TIGER IS TAME! HE'S CONVERSING WITH IT!
9.

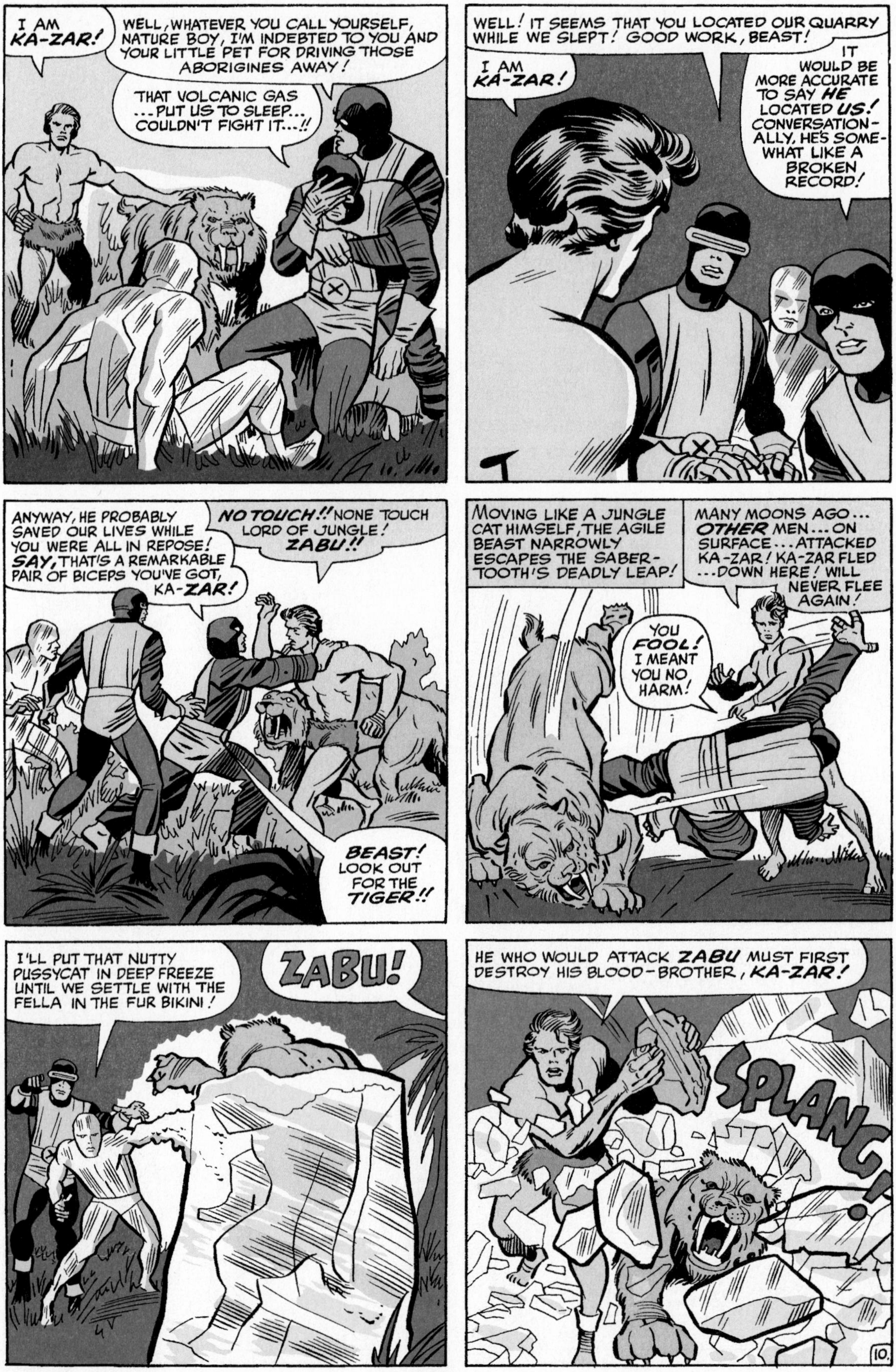
I AM KA-ZAR!
WELL, WHATEVER YOU CALL YOURSELF, NATURE BOY, I'M INDEBTED TO YOU AND YOUR LITTLE PET FOR DRIVING THOSE ABORIGINES AWAY!
THAT VOLCANIC GAS ...PUT US TO SLEEP... COULDN'T FIGHT IT...!!
WELL! IT SEEMS THAT YOU LOCATED OUR QUARRY WHILE WE SLEPT! GOOD WORK, BEAST!
I AM KA-ZAR!
IT WOULD BE MORE ACCURATE TO SAY HE LOCATED US! CONVERSATION-ALLY, HE'S SOME-WHAT LIKE A BROKEN RECORD!
ANYWAY, HE PROBABLY SAVED OUR LIVES WHILE YOU WERE ALL IN REPOSE! SAY, THAT'S A REMARKABLE PAIR OF BICEPS YOU'VE GOT, KA-ZAR!
NO TOUCH!! NONE TOUCH LORD OF JUNGLE! ZABU!!
BEAST! LOOK OUT FOR THE TIGER!!
MOVING LIKE A JUNGLE CAT HIMSELF, THE AGILE BEAST NARROWLY ESCAPES THE SABER-TOOTH'S DEADLY LEAP!
MANY MOONS AGO... OTHER MEN... ON SURFACE... ATTACKED KA-ZAR! KA-ZAR FLED ...DOWN HERE! WILL NEVER FLEE AGAIN!
YOU FOOL! I MEANT YOU NO HARM!
I'LL PUT THAT NUTTY PUSSYCAT IN DEEP FREEZE UNTIL WE SETTLE WITH THE FELLA IN THE FUR BIKINI!
ZABU!
HE WHO WOULD ATTACK ZABU MUST FIRST DESTROY HIS BLOOD-BROTHER, KA-ZAR!
SPLANG!
10.

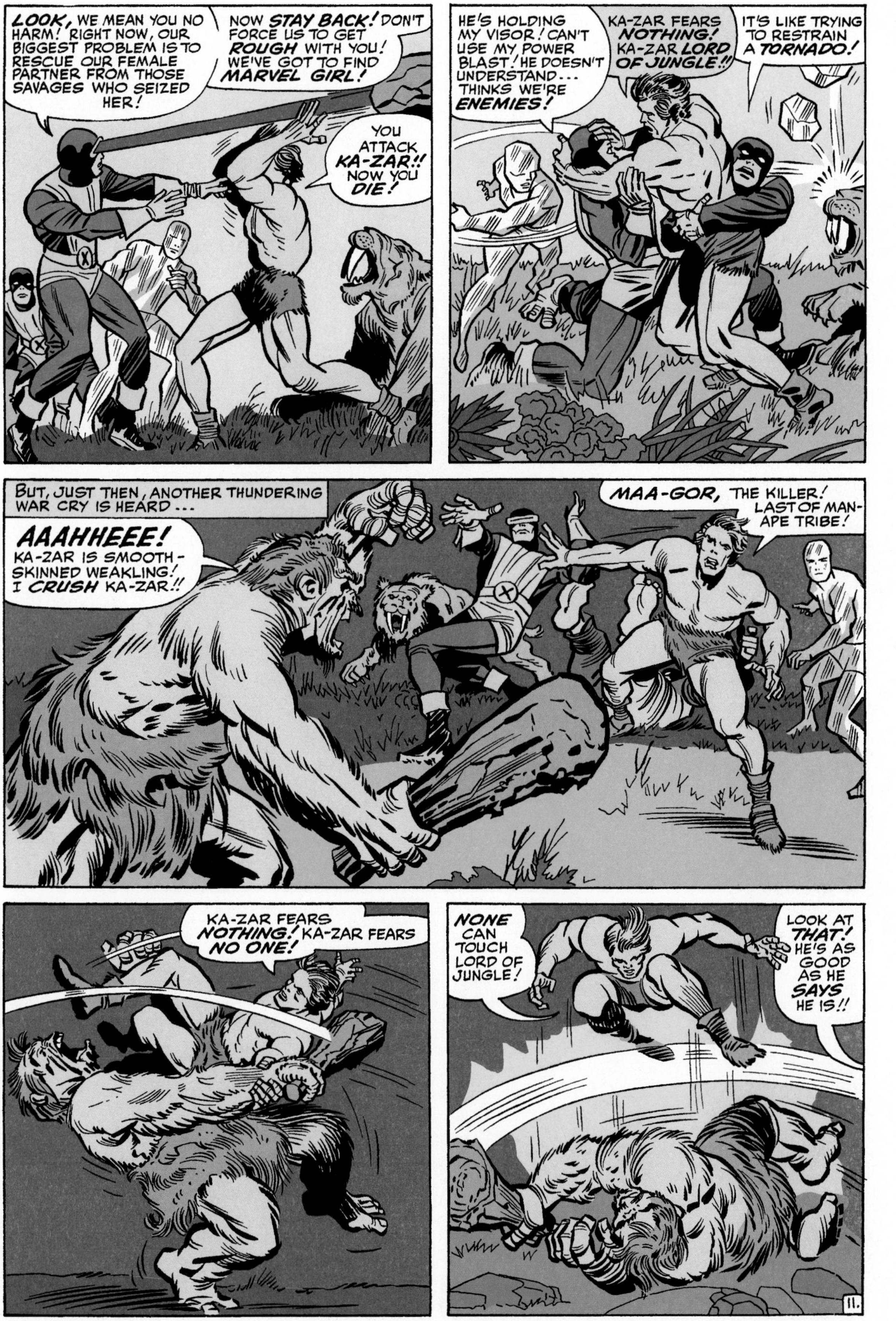
LOOK, WE MEAN YOU NO HARM! RIGHT NOW, OUR BIGGEST PROBLEM IS TO RESCUE OUR FEMALE PARTNER FROM THOSE SAVAGES WHO SEIZED HER!
NOW STAY BACK! DON'T FORCE US TO GET ROUGH WITH YOU! WE'VE GOT TO FIND MARVEL GIRL!
YOU ATTACK KA-ZAR!! NOW YOU DIE!
HE'S HOLDING MY VISOR! CAN'T USE MY POWER BLAST! HE DOESN'T UNDERSTAND... THINKS WE'RE ENEMIES!
KA-ZAR FEARS NOTHING! KA-ZAR LORD OF JUNGLE!!
IT'S LIKE TRYING TO RESTRAIN A TORNADO!
BUT, JUST THEN, ANOTHER THUNDERING WAR CRY IS HEARD...
AAAHHEEE! KA-ZAR IS SMOOTH-SKINNED WEAKLING! I CRUSH KA-ZAR!!
MAA-GOR, THE KILLER! LAST OF MAN-APE TRIBE!
KA-ZAR FEARS NOTHING! KA-ZAR FEARS NO ONE!
NONE CAN TOUCH LORD OF JUNGLE!
LOOK AT THAT! HE'S AS GOOD AS HE SAYS HE IS!!
11.

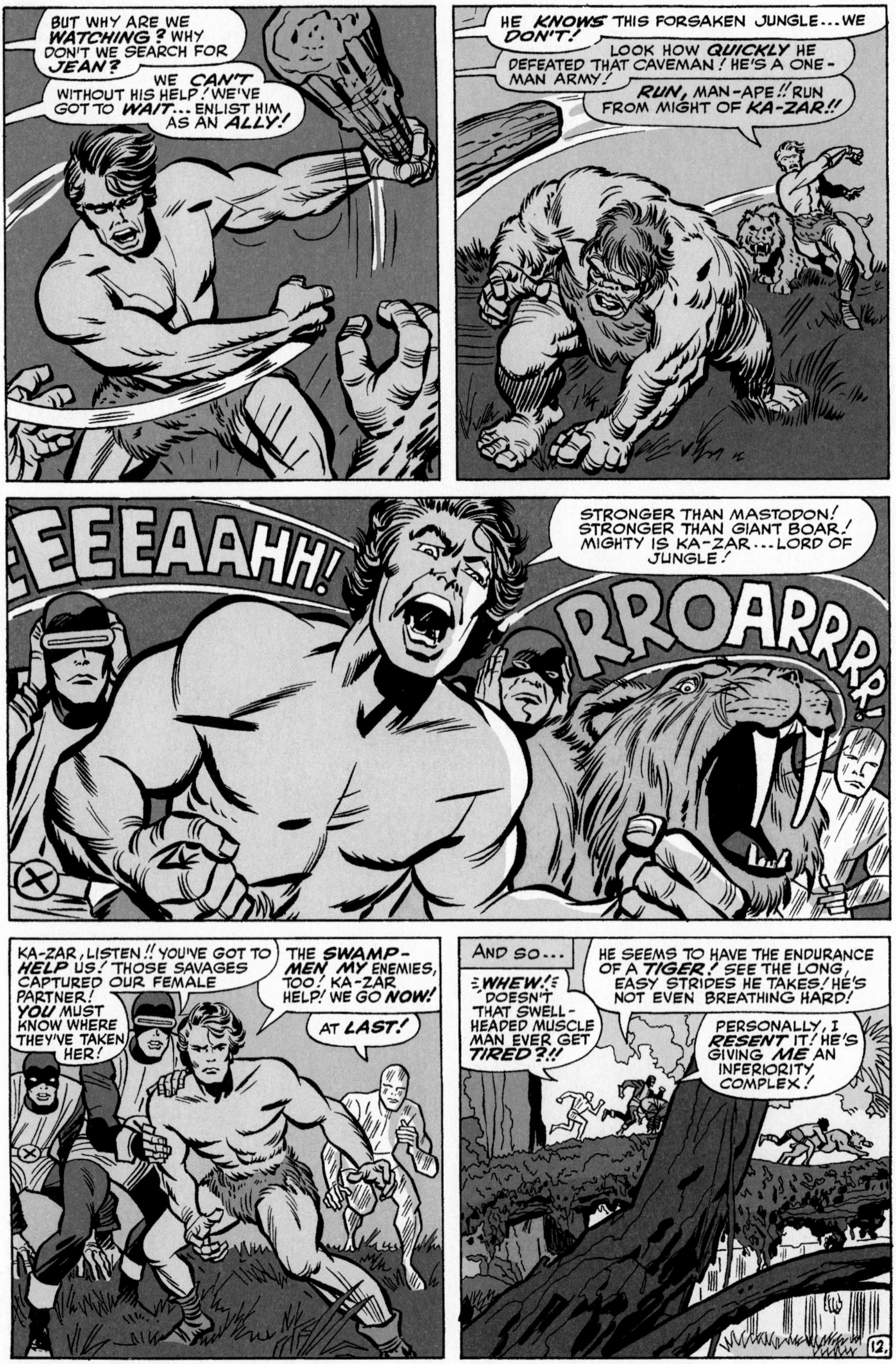

BUT WHY ARE WE WATCHING? WHY DON'T WE SEARCH FOR JEAN?
WE CAN'T WITHOUT HIS HELP! WE'VE GOT TO WAIT... ENLIST HIM AS AN ALLY!
HE KNOWS THIS FORSAKEN JUNGLE... WE DON'T!
LOOK HOW QUICKLY HE DEFEATED THAT CAVEMAN! HE'S A ONE-MAN ARMY!
RUN, MAN-APE!! RUN FROM MIGHT OF KA-ZAR!!
EEEAAHH!
STRONGER THAN MASTODON! STRONGER THAN GIANT BOAR! MIGHTY IS KA-ZAR... LORD OF JUNGLE!
RROARRRR!
KA-ZAR, LISTEN!! YOU'VE GOT TO HELP US! THOSE SAVAGES CAPTURED OUR FEMALE PARTNER! YOU MUST KNOW WHERE THEY'VE TAKEN HER!
THE SWAMP-MEN MY ENEMIES, TOO! KA-ZAR HELP! WE GO NOW!
AT LAST!
AND SO...
WHEW! DOESN'T THAT SWELL-HEADED MUSCLE MAN EVER GET TIRED?!!
HE SEEMS TO HAVE THE ENDURANCE OF A TIGER! SEE THE LONG, EASY STRIDES HE TAKES! HE'S NOT EVEN BREATHING HARD!
PERSONALLY, I RESENT IT! HE'S GIVING ME AN INFERIORITY COMPLEX!
12.

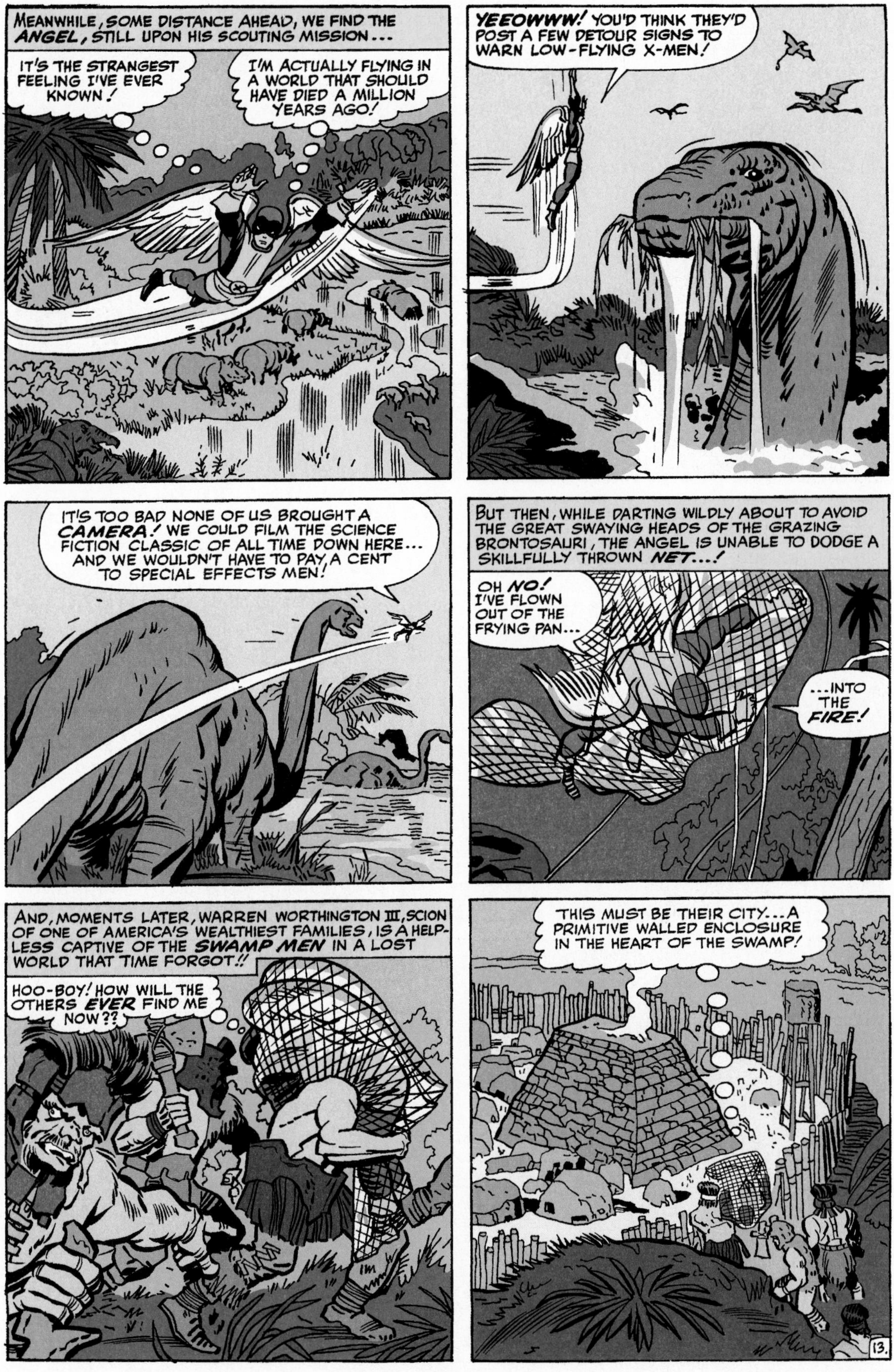
MEANWHILE, SOME DISTANCE AHEAD, WE FIND THE ANGEL, STILL UPON HIS SCOUTING MISSION...
IT'S THE STRANGEST FEELING I'VE EVER KNOWN!
I'M ACTUALLY FLYING IN A WORLD THAT SHOULD HAVE DIED A MILLION YEARS AGO!
YEEOWWW! YOU'D THINK THEY'D POST A FEW DETOUR SIGNS TO WARN LOW-FLYING X-MEN!
IT'S TOO BAD NONE OF US BROUGHT A CAMERA! WE COULD FILM THE SCIENCE FICTION CLASSIC OF ALL TIME DOWN HERE... AND WE WOULDN'T HAVE TO PAY A CENT TO SPECIAL EFFECTS MEN!
BUT THEN, WHILE DARTING WILDLY ABOUT TO AVOID THE GREAT SWAYING HEADS OF THE GRAZING BRONTOSAURI, THE ANGEL IS UNABLE TO DODGE A SKILLFULLY THROWN NET...!
OH NO! I'VE FLOWN OUT OF THE FRYING PAN...
...INTO THE FIRE!
AND, MOMENTS LATER, WARREN WORTHINGTON III, SCION OF ONE OF AMERICA'S WEALTHIEST FAMILIES, IS A HELPLESS CAPTIVE OF THE SWAMP MEN IN A LOST WORLD THAT TIME FORGOT!!
HOO-BOY! HOW WILL THE OTHERS EVER FIND ME NOW??
THIS MUST BE THEIR CITY... A PRIMITIVE WALLED ENCLOSURE IN THE HEART OF THE SWAMP!
13.

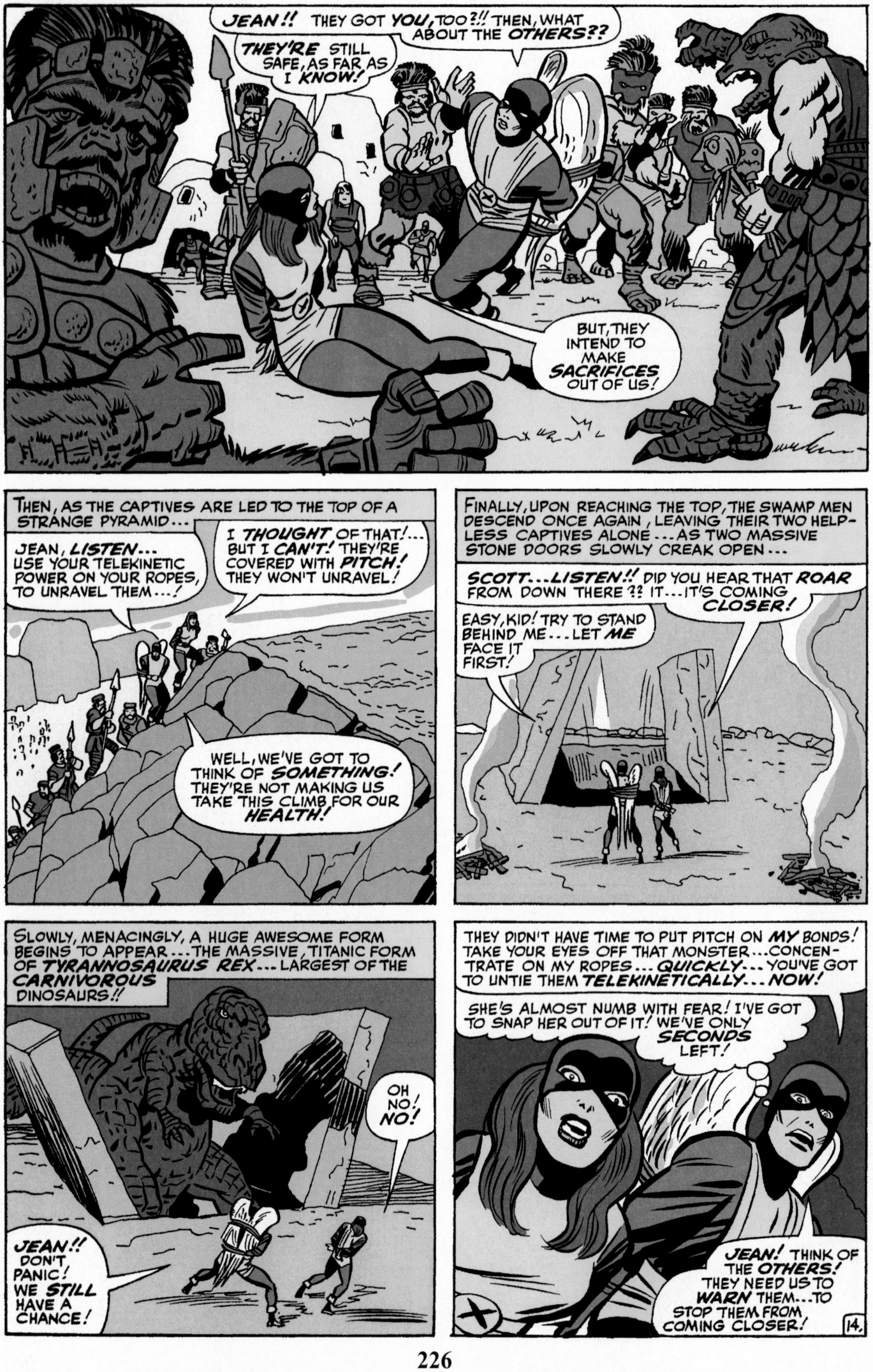
JEAN!! THEY GOT YOU, TOO?!! THEN, WHAT ABOUT THE OTHERS??
THEY'RE STILL SAFE, AS FAR AS I KNOW!
BUT, THEY INTEND TO MAKE SACRIFICES OUT OF US!
THEN, AS THE CAPTIVES ARE LED TO THE TOP OF A STRANGE PYRAMID...
JEAN, LISTEN... USE YOUR TELEKINETIC POWER ON YOUR ROPES, TO UNRAVEL THEM...!
I THOUGHT OF THAT!... BUT I CAN'T! THEY'RE COVERED WITH PITCH! THEY WON'T UNRAVEL!
WELL, WE'VE GOT TO THINK OF SOMETHING! THEY'RE NOT MAKING US TAKE THIS CLIMB FOR OUR HEALTH!
FINALLY, UPON REACHING THE TOP, THE SWAMP MEN DESCEND ONCE AGAIN, LEAVING THEIR TWO HELPLESS CAPTIVES ALONE... AS TWO MASSIVE STONE DOORS SLOWLY CREAK OPEN...
SCOTT... LISTEN!! DID YOU HEAR THAT ROAR FROM DOWN THERE ?? IT... IT'S COMING CLOSER!
EASY, KID! TRY TO STAND BEHIND ME... LET ME FACE IT FIRST!
SLOWLY, MENACINGLY, A HUGE AWESOME FORM BEGINS TO APPEAR... THE MASSIVE, TITANIC FORM OF TYRANNOSAURUS REX... LARGEST OF THE CARNIVOROUS DINOSAURS!!
OH NO! NO!
JEAN!! DON'T PANIC! WE STILL HAVE A CHANCE!
THEY DIDN'T HAVE TIME TO PUT PITCH ON MY BONDS! TAKE YOUR EYES OFF THAT MONSTER... CONCENTRATE ON MY ROPES... QUICKLY... YOU'VE GOT TO UNTIE THEM TELEKINETICALLY... NOW!
SHE'S ALMOST NUMB WITH FEAR! I'VE GOT TO SNAP HER OUT OF IT! WE'VE ONLY SECONDS LEFT!
JEAN! THINK OF THE OTHERS! THEY NEED US TO WARN THEM... TO STOP THEM FROM COMING CLOSER!
14.

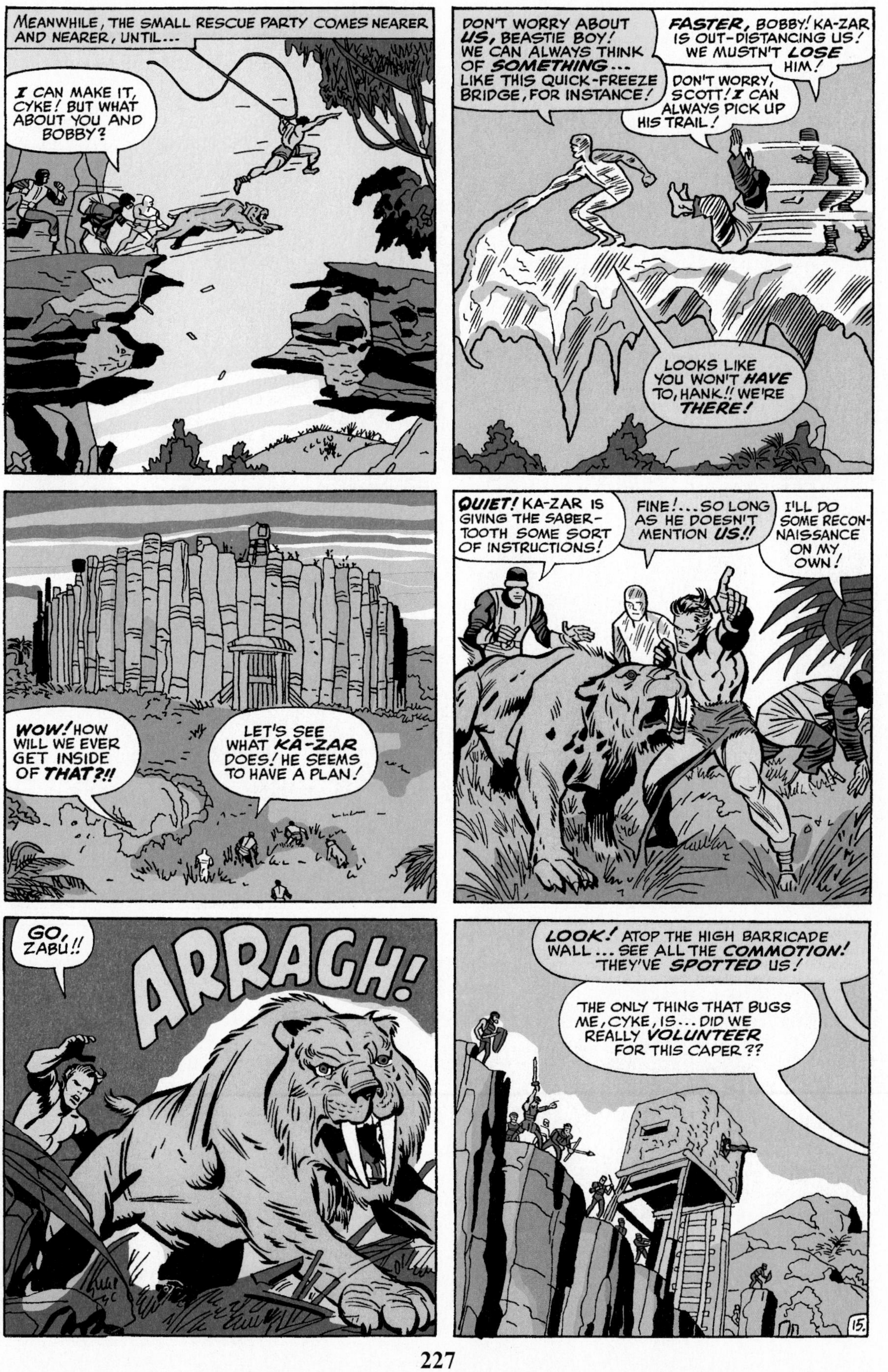
MEANWHILE, THE SMALL RESCUE PARTY COMES NEARER AND NEARER, UNTIL...
I CAN MAKE IT, CYKE! BUT WHAT ABOUT YOU AND BOBBY?
DON'T WORRY ABOUT US, BEASTIE BOY! WE CAN ALWAYS THINK OF SOMETHING... LIKE THIS QUICK-FREEZE BRIDGE, FOR INSTANCE!
FASTER, BOBBY! KA-ZAR IS OUT-DISTANCING US! WE MUSTN'T LOSE HIM!
DON'T WORRY, SCOTT! I CAN ALWAYS PICK UP HIS TRAIL!
LOOKS LIKE YOU WON'T HAVE TO, HANK!! WE'RE THERE!
WOW! HOW WILL WE EVER GET INSIDE OF THAT?!!
LET'S SEE WHAT KA-ZAR DOES! HE SEEMS TO HAVE A PLAN!
QUIET! KA-ZAR IS GIVING THE SABER-TOOTH SOME SORT OF INSTRUCTIONS!
FINE!... SO LONG AS HE DOESN'T MENTION US!!
I'LL DO SOME RECON-NAISSANCE ON MY OWN!
GO, ZABU!!
ARRAGH!
LOOK! ATOP THE HIGH BARRICADE WALL... SEE ALL THE COMMOTION! THEY'VE SPOTTED US!
THE ONLY THING THAT BUGS ME, CYKE, IS... DID WE REALLY VOLUNTEER FOR THIS CAPER??
15.

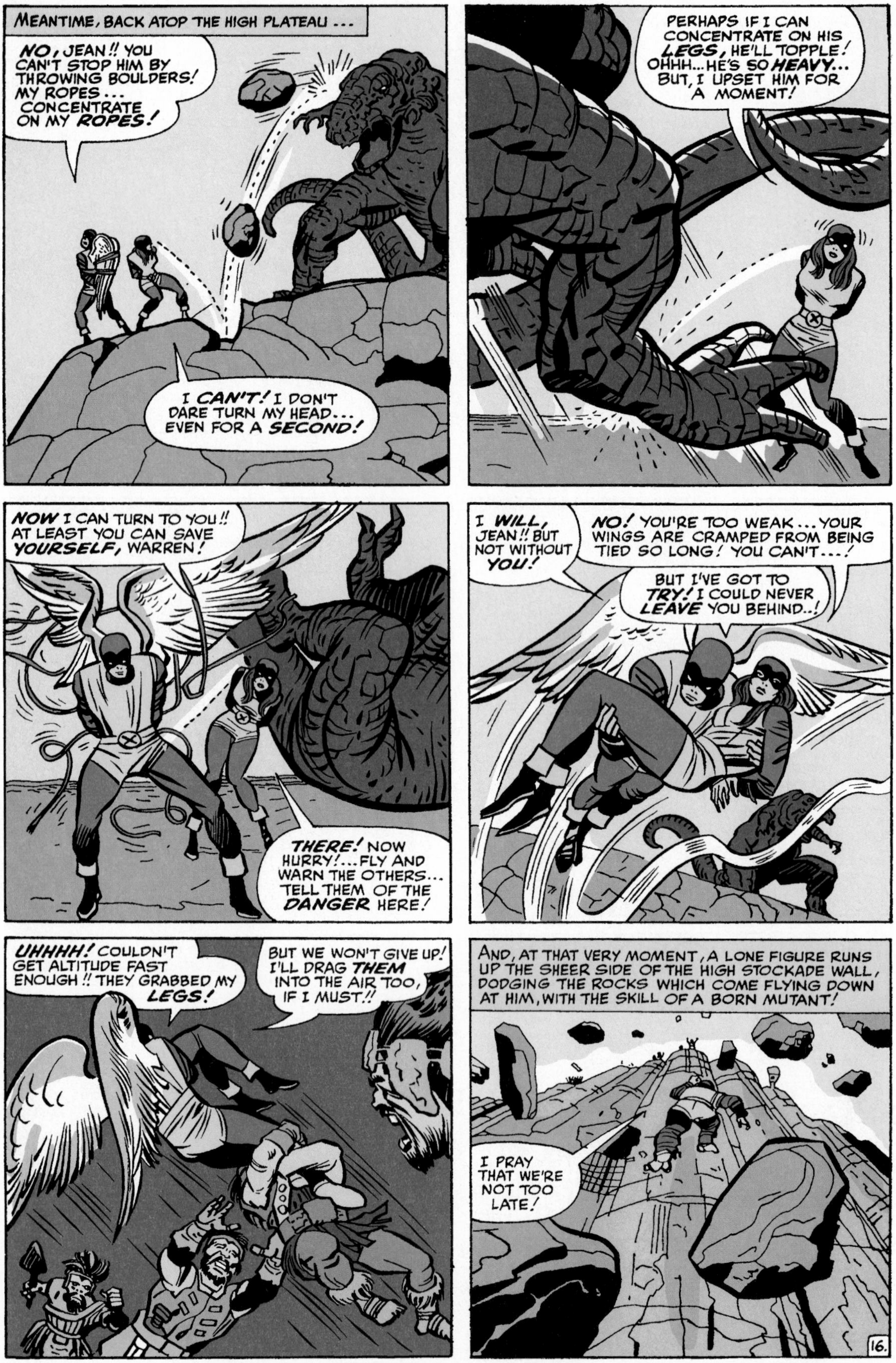
MEANTIME, BACK ATOP THE HIGH PLATEAU ...
NO, JEAN!! YOU CAN'T STOP HIM BY THROWING BOULDERS! MY ROPES... CONCENTRATE ON MY ROPES!
I CAN'T! I DON'T DARE TURN MY HEAD... EVEN FOR A SECOND!
PERHAPS IF I CAN CONCENTRATE ON HIS LEGS, HE'LL TOPPLE! OHHH... HE'S SO HEAVY... BUT, I UPSET HIM FOR A MOMENT!
NOW I CAN TURN TO YOU!! AT LEAST YOU CAN SAVE YOURSELF, WARREN!
THERE! NOW HURRY!... FLY AND WARN THE OTHERS... TELL THEM OF THE DANGER HERE!
I WILL, JEAN!! BUT NOT WITHOUT YOU!
NO! YOU'RE TOO WEAK... YOUR WINGS ARE CRAMPED FROM BEING TIED SO LONG! YOU CAN'T...!
BUT I'VE GOT TO TRY! I COULD NEVER LEAVE YOU BEHIND..!
UHHHH! COULDN'T GET ALTITUDE FAST ENOUGH!! THEY GRABBED MY LEGS!
BUT WE WON'T GIVE UP! I'LL DRAG THEM INTO THE AIR TOO, IF I MUST!!
AND, AT THAT VERY MOMENT, A LONE FIGURE RUNS UP THE SHEER SIDE OF THE HIGH STOCKADE WALL, DODGING THE ROCKS WHICH COME FLYING DOWN AT HIM, WITH THE SKILL OF A BORN MUTANT!
I PRAY THAT WE'RE NOT TOO LATE!
16.

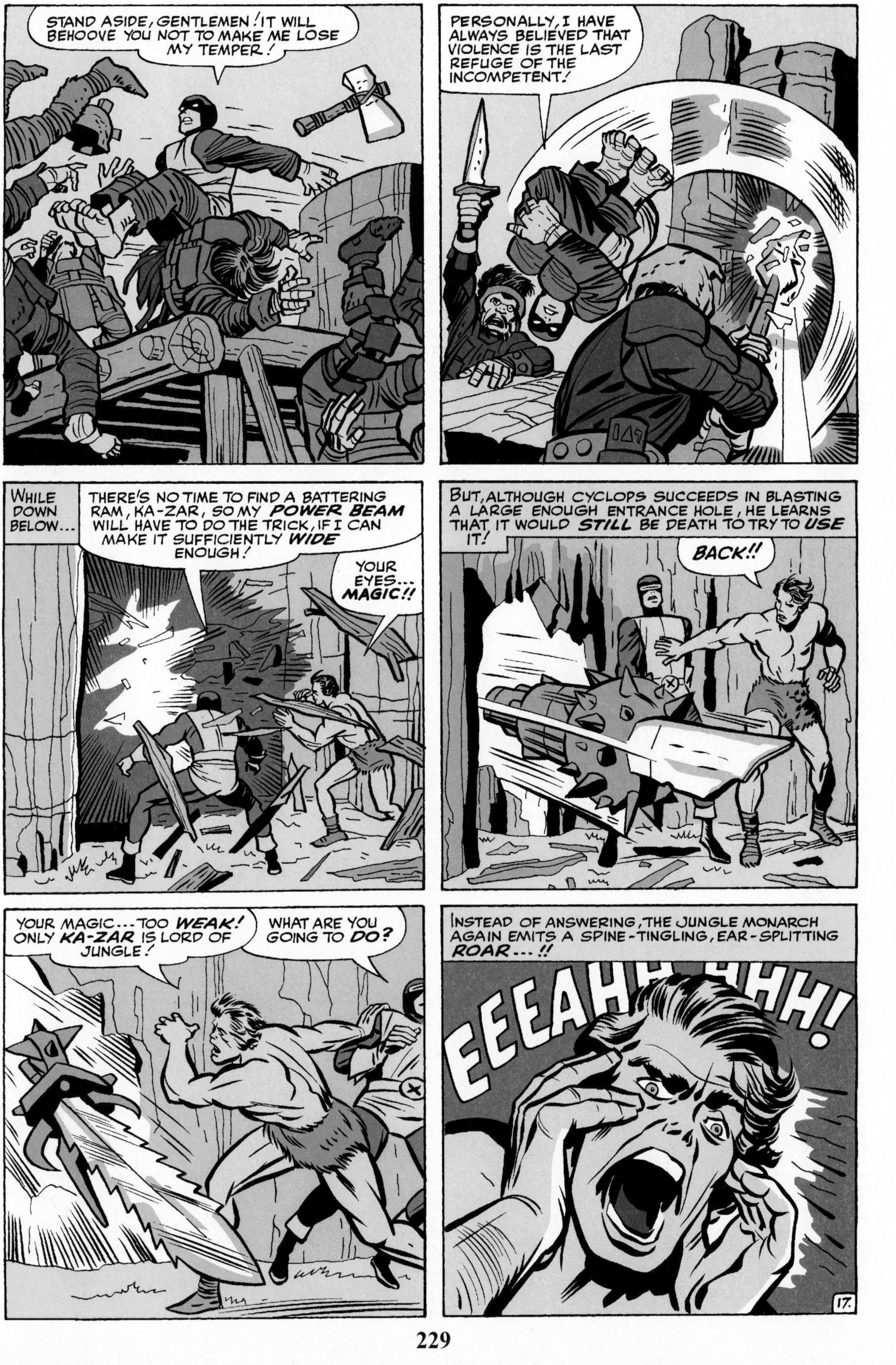
STAND ASIDE, GENTLEMEN! IT WILL BEHOOVE YOU NOT TO MAKE ME LOSE MY TEMPER!
PERSONALLY, I HAVE ALWAYS BELIEVED THAT VIOLENCE IS THE LAST REFUGE OF THE INCOMPETENT!
WHILE DOWN BELOW...
THERE'S NO TIME TO FIND A BATTERING RAM, KA-ZAR, SO MY POWER BEAM WILL HAVE TO DO THE TRICK, IF I CAN MAKE IT SUFFICIENTLY WIDE ENOUGH!
YOUR EYES... MAGIC!!
BUT, ALTHOUGH CYCLOPS SUCCEEDS IN BLASTING A LARGE ENOUGH ENTRANCE HOLE, HE LEARNS THAT IT WOULD STILL BE DEATH TO TRY TO USE IT!
BACK!!
YOUR MAGIC... TOO WEAK! ONLY KA-ZAR IS LORD OF JUNGLE!
WHAT ARE YOU GOING TO DO?
INSTEAD OF ANSWERING, THE JUNGLE MONARCH AGAIN EMITS A SPINE-TINGLING, EAR-SPLITTING ROAR...!!
EEEAHH AHHH!
17.

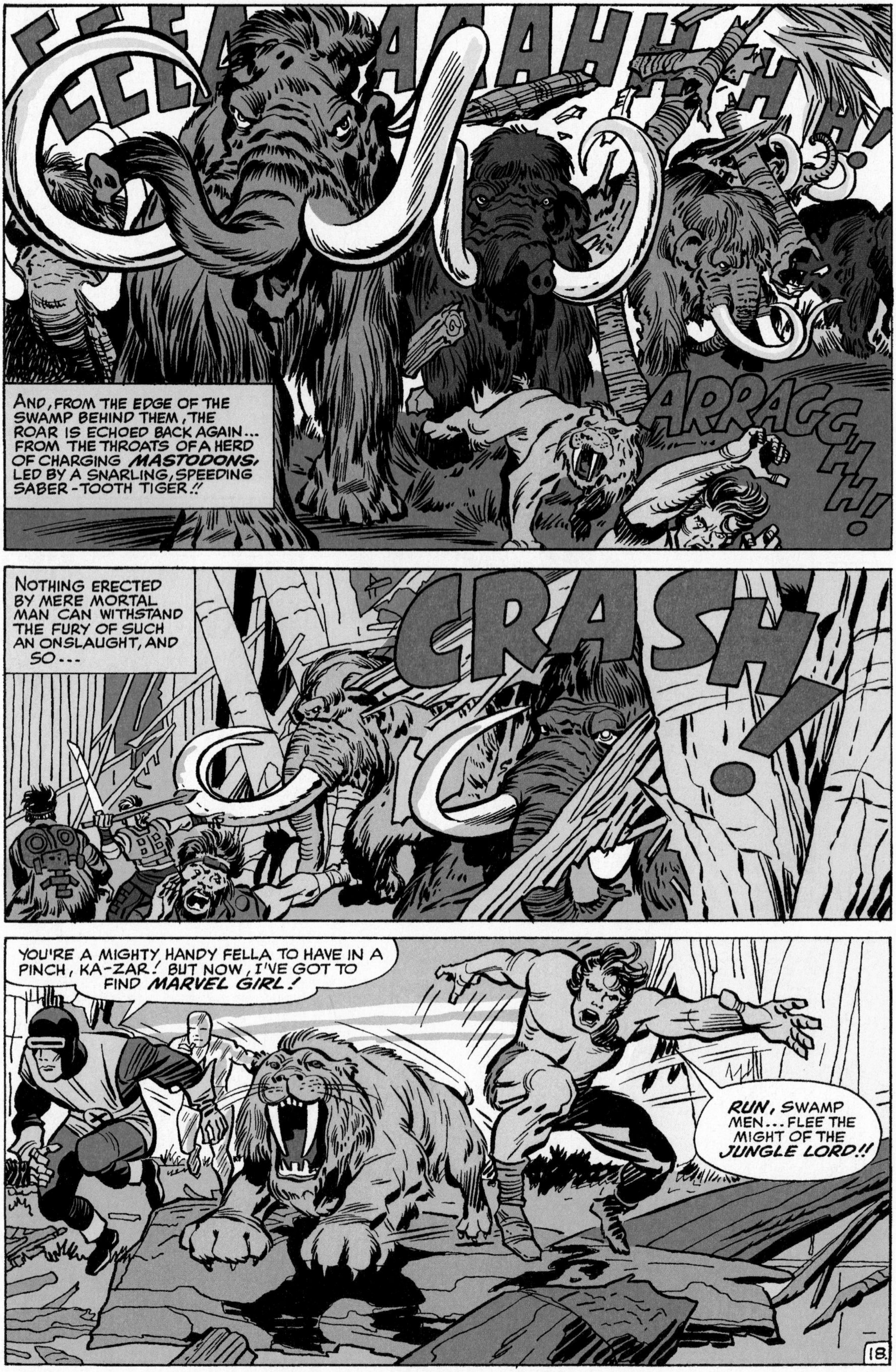
EEEEAAAAAHHHHH!
AND, FROM THE EDGE OF THE SWAMP BEHIND THEM, THE ROAR IS ECHOED BACK AGAIN... FROM THE THROATS OF A HERD OF CHARGING MASTODONS, LED BY A SNARLING, SPEEDING SABER-TOOTH TIGER!!
ARRAGGHHH!
NOTHING ERECTED BY MERE MORTAL MAN CAN WITHSTAND THE FURY OF SUCH AN ONSLAUGHT, AND SO---
CRASH!
YOU'RE A MIGHTY HANDY FELLA TO HAVE IN A PINCH, KA-ZAR! BUT NOW, I'VE GOT TO FIND MARVEL GIRL!
RUN, SWAMP MEN... FLEE THE MIGHT OF THE JUNGLE LORD!!
18.

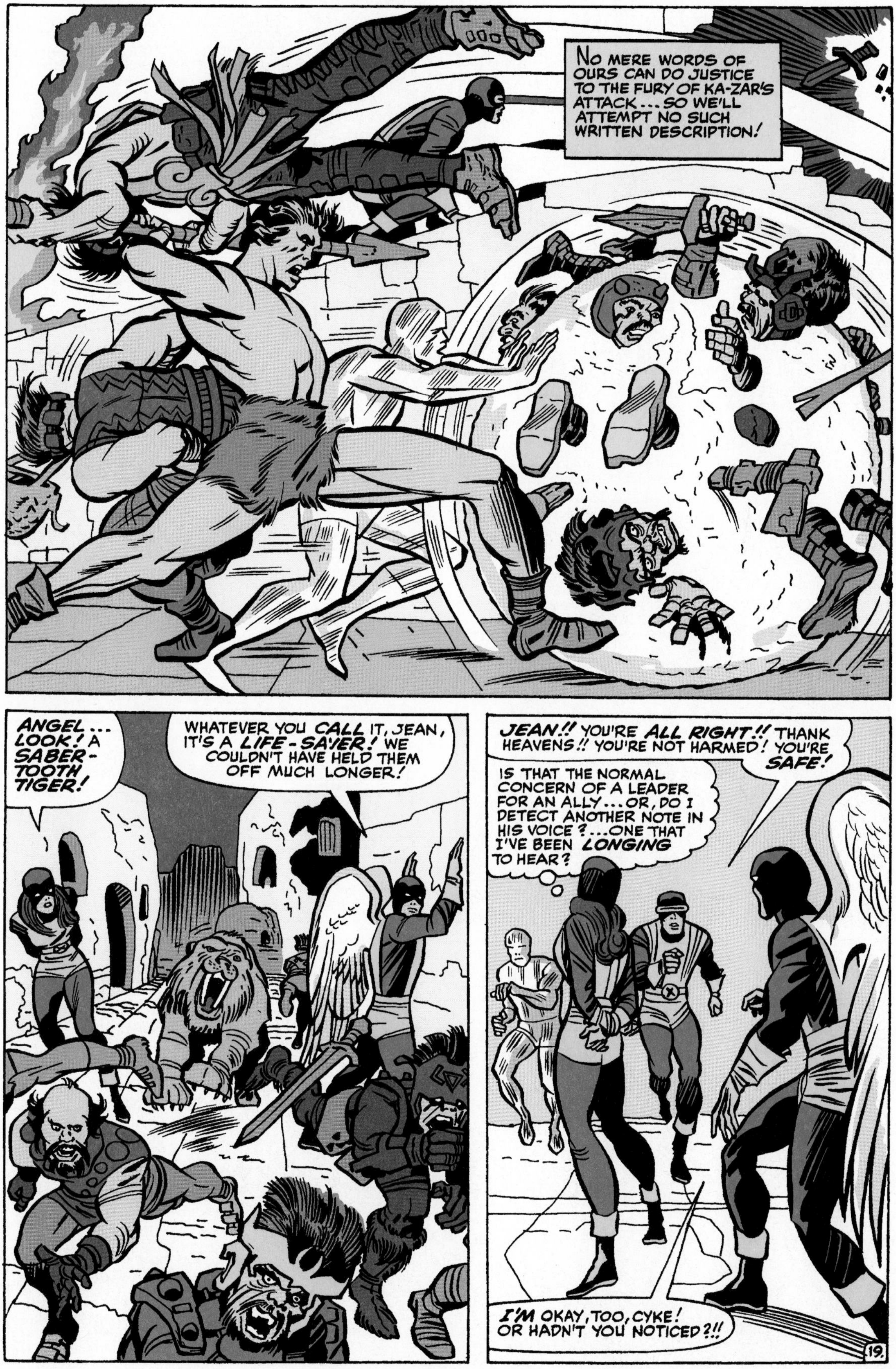
No mere words of ours can do justice to the fury of Ka-Zar's attack... so we'll attempt no such written description!
ANGEL... LOOK! A SABER-TOOTH TIGER!
WHATEVER YOU CALL IT, JEAN, IT'S A LIFE-SAVER! WE COULDN'T HAVE HELD THEM OFF MUCH LONGER!
JEAN!! YOU'RE ALL RIGHT!! THANK HEAVENS!! YOU'RE NOT HARMED! YOU'RE SAFE!
IS THAT THE NORMAL CONCERN OF A LEADER FOR AN ALLY... OR, DO I DETECT ANOTHER NOTE IN HIS VOICE?... ONE THAT I'VE BEEN LONGING TO HEAR?
I'M OKAY, TOO, CYKE! OR HADN'T YOU NOTICED?!!
19

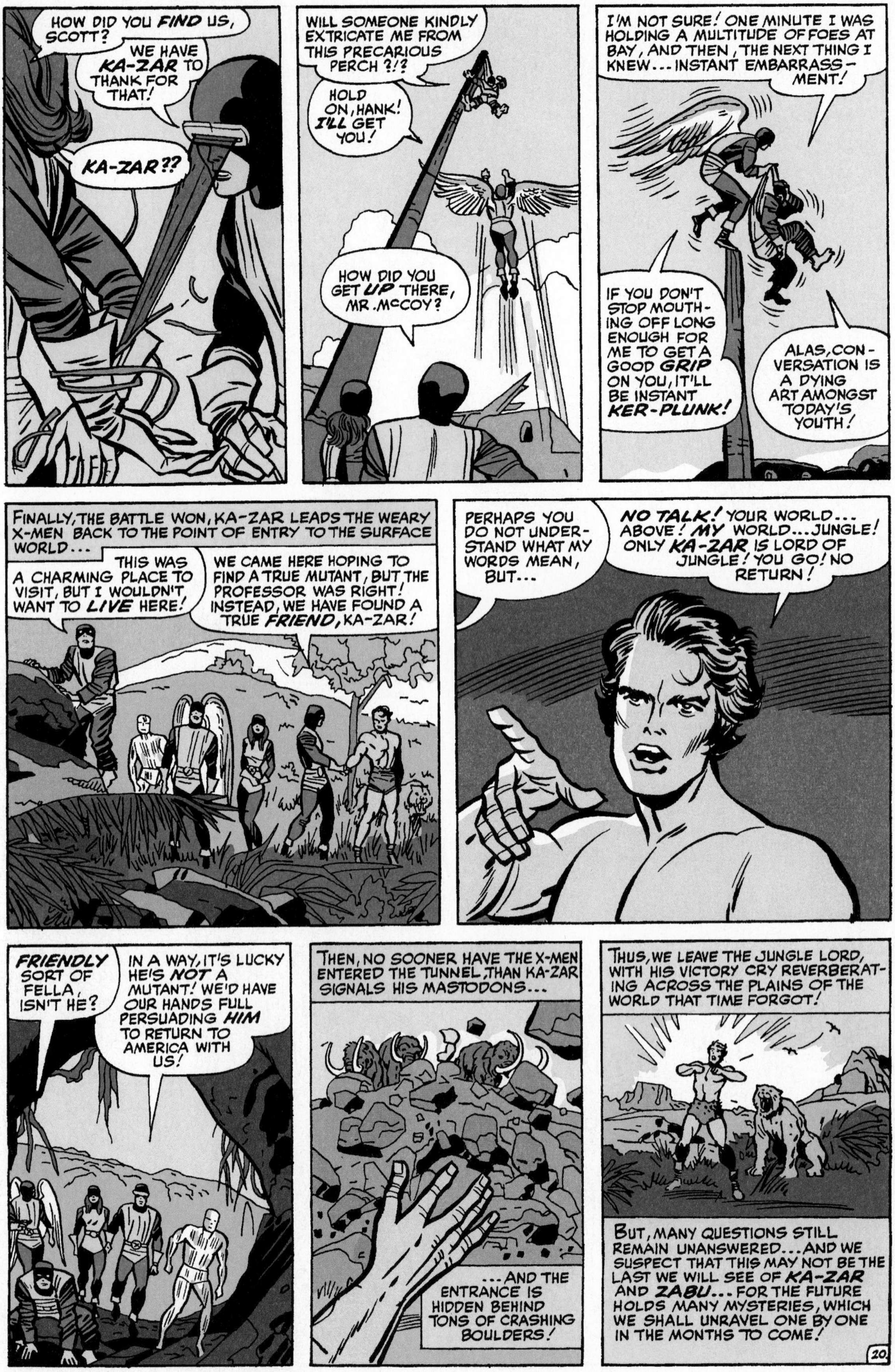
HOW DID YOU FIND US, SCOTT?
WE HAVE KA-ZAR TO THANK FOR THAT!
KA-ZAR??
WILL SOMEONE KINDLY EXTRICATE ME FROM THIS PRECARIOUS PERCH ?!?
HOLD ON, HANK! I'LL GET YOU!
HOW DID YOU GET UP THERE, MR. McCOY?
I'M NOT SURE! ONE MINUTE I WAS HOLDING A MULTITUDE OF FOES AT BAY, AND THEN, THE NEXT THING I KNEW... INSTANT EMBARRASS-MENT!
IF YOU DON'T STOP MOUTHING OFF LONG ENOUGH FOR ME TO GET A GOOD GRIP ON YOU, IT'LL BE INSTANT KER-PLUNK!
ALAS, CONVERSATION IS A DYING ART AMONGST TODAY'S YOUTH!
FINALLY, THE BATTLE WON, KA-ZAR LEADS THE WEARY X-MEN BACK TO THE POINT OF ENTRY TO THE SURFACE WORLD...
THIS WAS A CHARMING PLACE TO VISIT, BUT I WOULDN'T WANT TO LIVE HERE!
WE CAME HERE HOPING TO FIND A TRUE MUTANT, BUT THE PROFESSOR WAS RIGHT! INSTEAD, WE HAVE FOUND A TRUE FRIEND, KA-ZAR!
PERHAPS YOU DO NOT UNDERSTAND WHAT MY WORDS MEAN, BUT...
NO TALK! YOUR WORLD... ABOVE! MY WORLD... JUNGLE! ONLY KA-ZAR IS LORD OF JUNGLE! YOU GO! NO RETURN!
FRIENDLY SORT OF FELLA, ISN'T HE?
IN A WAY, IT'S LUCKY HE'S NOT A MUTANT! WE'D HAVE OUR HANDS FULL PERSUADING HIM TO RETURN TO AMERICA WITH US!
THEN, NO SOONER HAVE THE X-MEN ENTERED THE TUNNEL, THAN KA-ZAR SIGNALS HIS MASTODONS...
...AND THE ENTRANCE IS HIDDEN BEHIND TONS OF CRASHING BOULDERS!
THUS, WE LEAVE THE JUNGLE LORD, WITH HIS VICTORY CRY REVERBERATING ACROSS THE PLAINS OF THE WORLD THAT TIME FORGOT!
BUT, MANY QUESTIONS STILL REMAIN UNANSWERED... AND WE SUSPECT THAT THIS MAY NOT BE THE LAST WE WILL SEE OF KA-ZAR AND ZABU... FOR THE FUTURE HOLDS MANY MYSTERIES, WHICH WE SHALL UNRAVEL ONE BY ONE IN THE MONTHS TO COME!
20

The X-Men #10 unused cover art
by Jack Kirby & Chic Stone

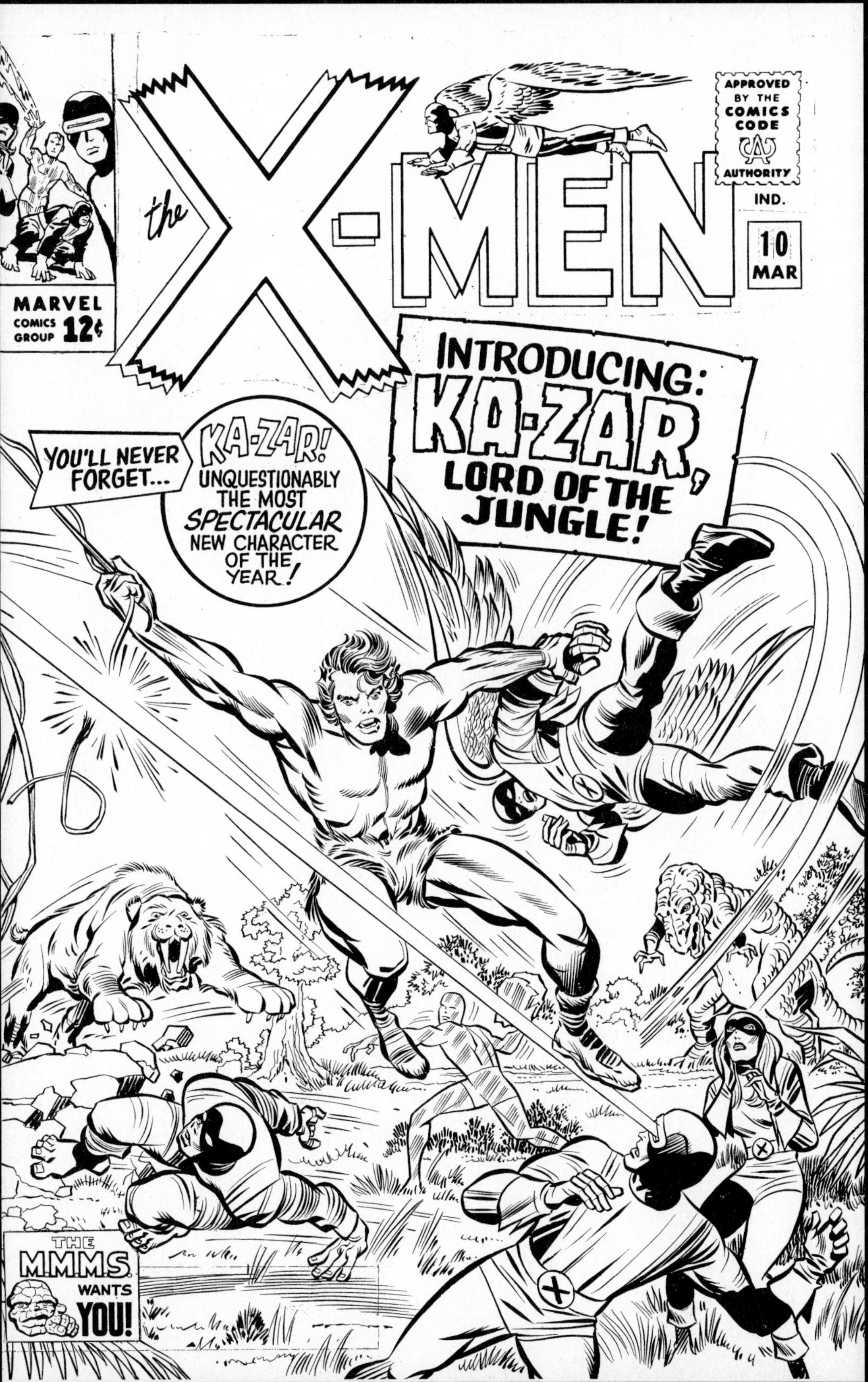
MARVEL COMICS GROUP 12¢
the X-MEN
APPROVED BY THE COMICS CODE AUTHORITY
IND.
10 MAR
INTRODUCING: KA-ZAR, LORD OF THE JUNGLE!
YOU'LL NEVER FORGET...
KA-ZAR! UNQUESTIONABLY THE MOST SPECTACULAR NEW CHARACTER OF THE YEAR!
THE M.M.M.S. WANTS YOU!

X-MEN. 1 - P. 6

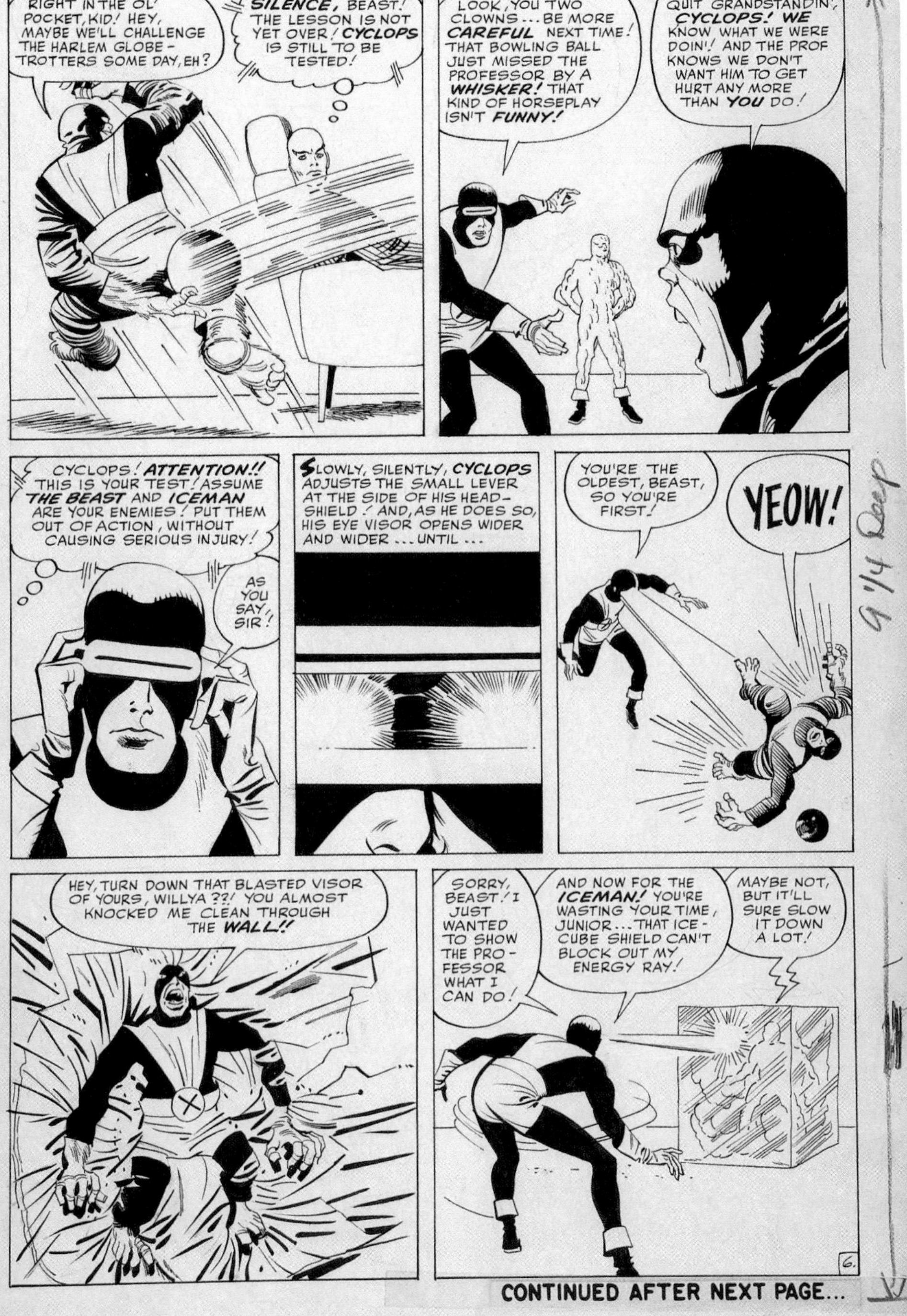

RIGHT IN THE OL' POCKET, KID! HEY, MAYBE WE'LL CHALLENGE THE HARLEM GLOBE-TROTTERS SOME DAY, EH?
SILENCE, BEAST! THE LESSON IS NOT YET OVER! CYCLOPS IS STILL TO BE TESTED!
LOOK, YOU TWO CLOWNS... BE MORE CAREFUL NEXT TIME! THAT BOWLING BALL JUST MISSED THE PROFESSOR BY A WHISKER! THAT KIND OF HORSEPLAY ISN'T FUNNY!
QUIT GRANDSTANDIN', CYCLOPS! WE KNOW WHAT WE WERE DOIN'! AND THE PROF KNOWS WE DON'T WANT HIM TO GET HURT ANY MORE THAN YOU DO!
CYCLOPS! ATTENTION!! THIS IS YOUR TEST! ASSUME THE BEAST AND ICEMAN ARE YOUR ENEMIES! PUT THEM OUT OF ACTION, WITHOUT CAUSING SERIOUS INJURY!
AS YOU SAY, SIR!
SLOWLY, SILENTLY, CYCLOPS ADJUSTS THE SMALL LEVER AT THE SIDE OF HIS HEAD-SHIELD! AND, AS HE DOES SO, HIS EYE VISOR OPENS WIDER AND WIDER... UNTIL...
YOU'RE THE OLDEST, BEAST, SO YOU'RE FIRST!
YEOW!
HEY, TURN DOWN THAT BLASTED VISOR OF YOURS, WILLYA??! YOU ALMOST KNOCKED ME CLEAN THROUGH THE WALL!!
SORRY, BEAST! I JUST WANTED TO SHOW THE PRO-FESSOR WHAT I CAN DO!
AND NOW FOR THE ICEMAN! YOU'RE WASTING YOUR TIME, JUNIOR... THAT ICE-CUBE SHIELD CAN'T BLOCK OUT MY ENERGY RAY!
MAYBE NOT, BUT IT'LL SURE SLOW IT DOWN A LOT!
6.
9 1/4 Deep
CONTINUED AFTER NEXT PAGE...

6.

The X-Men #1, page 11 original art
by Jack Kirby & Paul Reinman

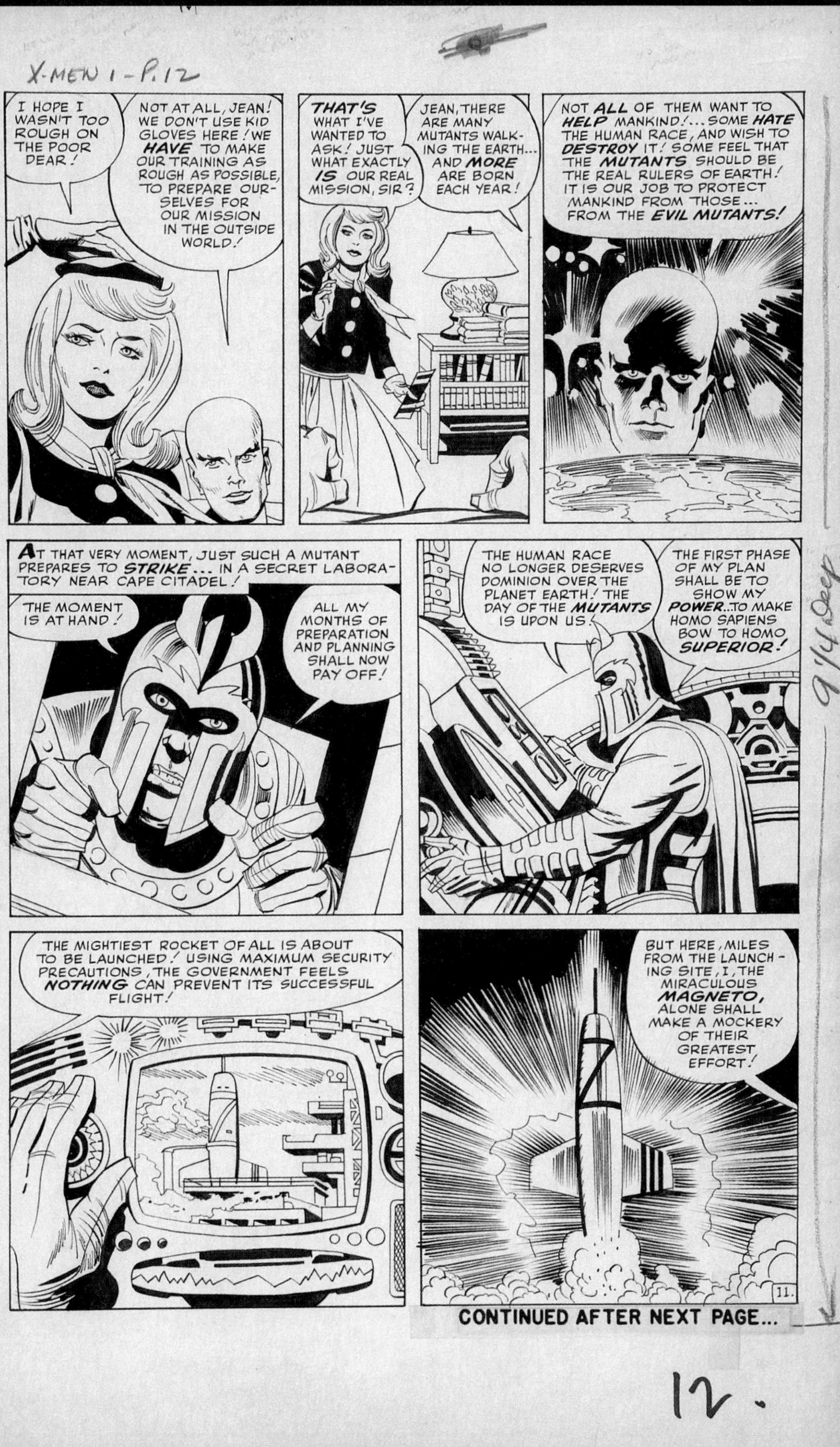
X-MEN 1 - P. 12
I HOPE I WASN'T TOO ROUGH ON THE POOR DEAR!
NOT AT ALL, JEAN! WE DON'T USE KID GLOVES HERE! WE HAVE TO MAKE OUR TRAINING AS ROUGH AS POSSIBLE, TO PREPARE OURSELVES FOR OUR MISSION IN THE OUTSIDE WORLD!
THAT'S WHAT I'VE WANTED TO ASK! JUST WHAT EXACTLY IS OUR REAL MISSION, SIR?
JEAN, THERE ARE MANY MUTANTS WALKING THE EARTH... AND MORE ARE BORN EACH YEAR!
NOT ALL OF THEM WANT TO HELP MANKIND!... SOME HATE THE HUMAN RACE, AND WISH TO DESTROY IT! SOME FEEL THAT THE MUTANTS SHOULD BE THE REAL RULERS OF EARTH! IT IS OUR JOB TO PROTECT MANKIND FROM THOSE... FROM THE EVIL MUTANTS!
AT THAT VERY MOMENT, JUST SUCH A MUTANT PREPARES TO STRIKE... IN A SECRET LABORATORY NEAR CAPE CITADEL!
THE MOMENT IS AT HAND!
ALL MY MONTHS OF PREPARATION AND PLANNING SHALL NOW PAY OFF!
THE HUMAN RACE NO LONGER DESERVES DOMINION OVER THE PLANET EARTH! THE DAY OF THE MUTANTS IS UPON US!
THE FIRST PHASE OF MY PLAN SHALL BE TO SHOW MY POWER...TO MAKE HOMO SAPIENS BOW TO HOMO SUPERIOR!
THE MIGHTIEST ROCKET OF ALL IS ABOUT TO BE LAUNCHED! USING MAXIMUM SECURITY PRECAUTIONS, THE GOVERNMENT FEELS NOTHING CAN PREVENT ITS SUCCESSFUL FLIGHT!
BUT HERE, MILES FROM THE LAUNCHING SITE, I, THE MIRACULOUS MAGNETO, ALONE SHALL MAKE A MOCKERY OF THEIR GREATEST EFFORT!
11.
CONTINUED AFTER NEXT PAGE...
9/14 Dep
12.

May 1963 house ad for the release of *The X-Men* #1

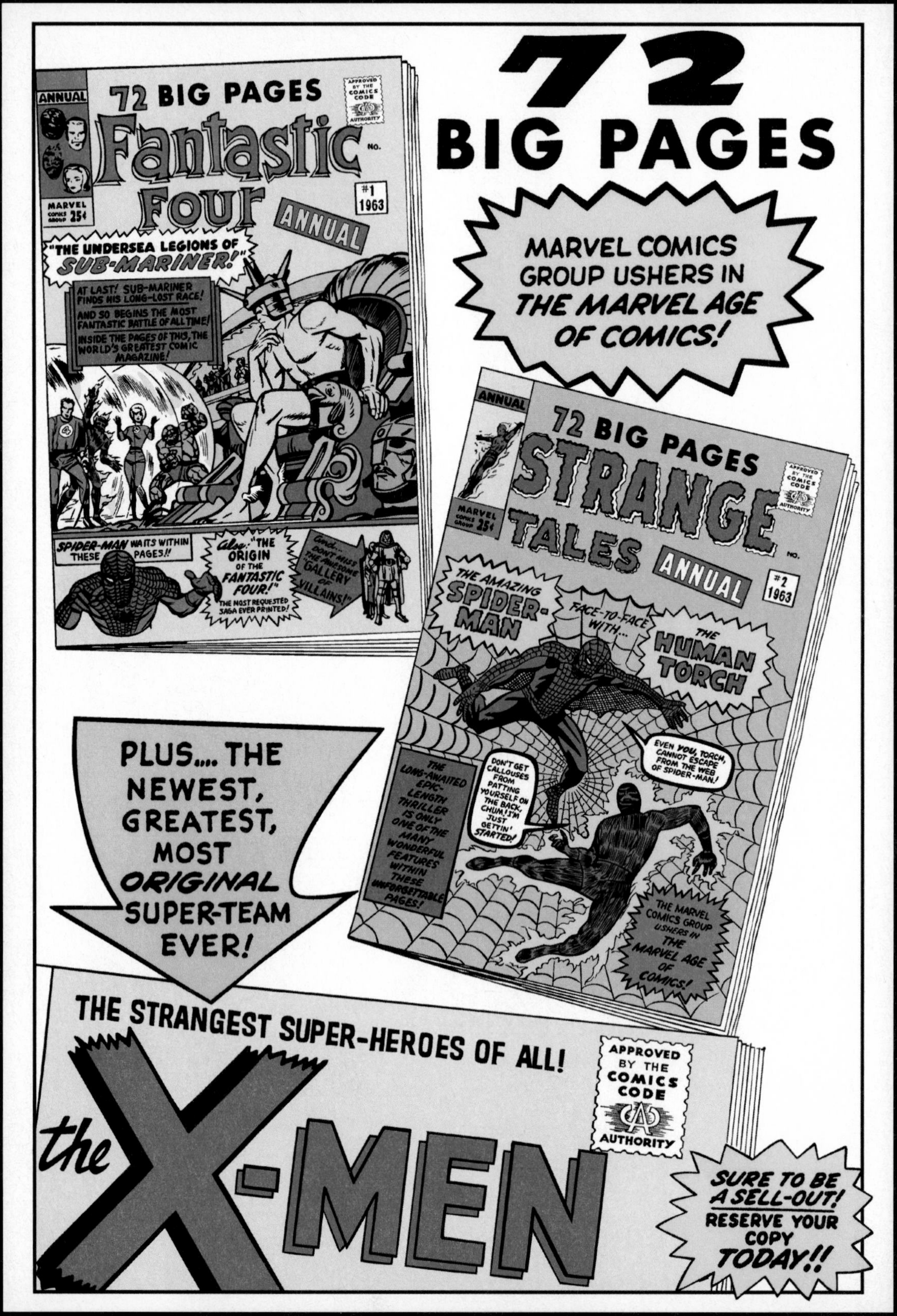
72 BIG PAGES
MARVEL COMICS GROUP USHERS IN THE MARVEL AGE OF COMICS!
ANNUAL
72 BIG PAGES
APPROVED BY THE COMICS CODE AUTHORITY
Fantastic Four
NO.
#1 1963
MARVEL COMICS GROUP 25¢
ANNUAL
"THE UNDERSEA LEGIONS OF SUB-MARINER!"
AT LAST! SUB-MARINER FINDS HIS LONG-LOST RACE!
AND SO BEGINS THE MOST FANTASTIC BATTLE OF ALL TIME!
INSIDE THE PAGES OF THIS, THE WORLD'S GREATEST COMIC MAGAZINE!
SPIDER-MAN WAITS WITHIN THESE PAGES!!
Also: "THE ORIGIN OF THE FANTASTIC FOUR!" THE MOST REQUESTED SAGA EVER PRINTED!
And... DON'T MISS THE AWESOME GALLERY OF VILLAINS!
ANNUAL
72 BIG PAGES
STRANGE TALES
MARVEL COMICS GROUP 25¢
APPROVED BY THE COMICS CODE AUTHORITY
ANNUAL
NO.
#2 1963
THE AMAZING SPIDER-MAN
FACE-TO-FACE WITH...
THE HUMAN TORCH
EVEN YOU, TORCH, CANNOT ESCAPE FROM THE WEB OF SPIDER-MAN!
DON'T GET CALLOUSES FROM PATTING YOURSELF ON THE BACK, CHUM! I'M JUST GETTIN' STARTED!
THE LONG-AWAITED EPIC-LENGTH THRILLER IS ONLY ONE OF THE MANY WONDERFUL FEATURES WITHIN THESE UNFORGETTABLE PAGES!
THE MARVEL COMICS GROUP USHERS IN THE MARVEL AGE OF COMICS!
PLUS.... THE NEWEST, GREATEST, MOST ORIGINAL SUPER-TEAM EVER!
THE STRANGEST SUPER-HEROES OF ALL!
APPROVED BY THE COMICS CODE AUTHORITY
the X-MEN
SURE TO BE A SELL-OUT! RESERVE YOUR COPY TODAY!!

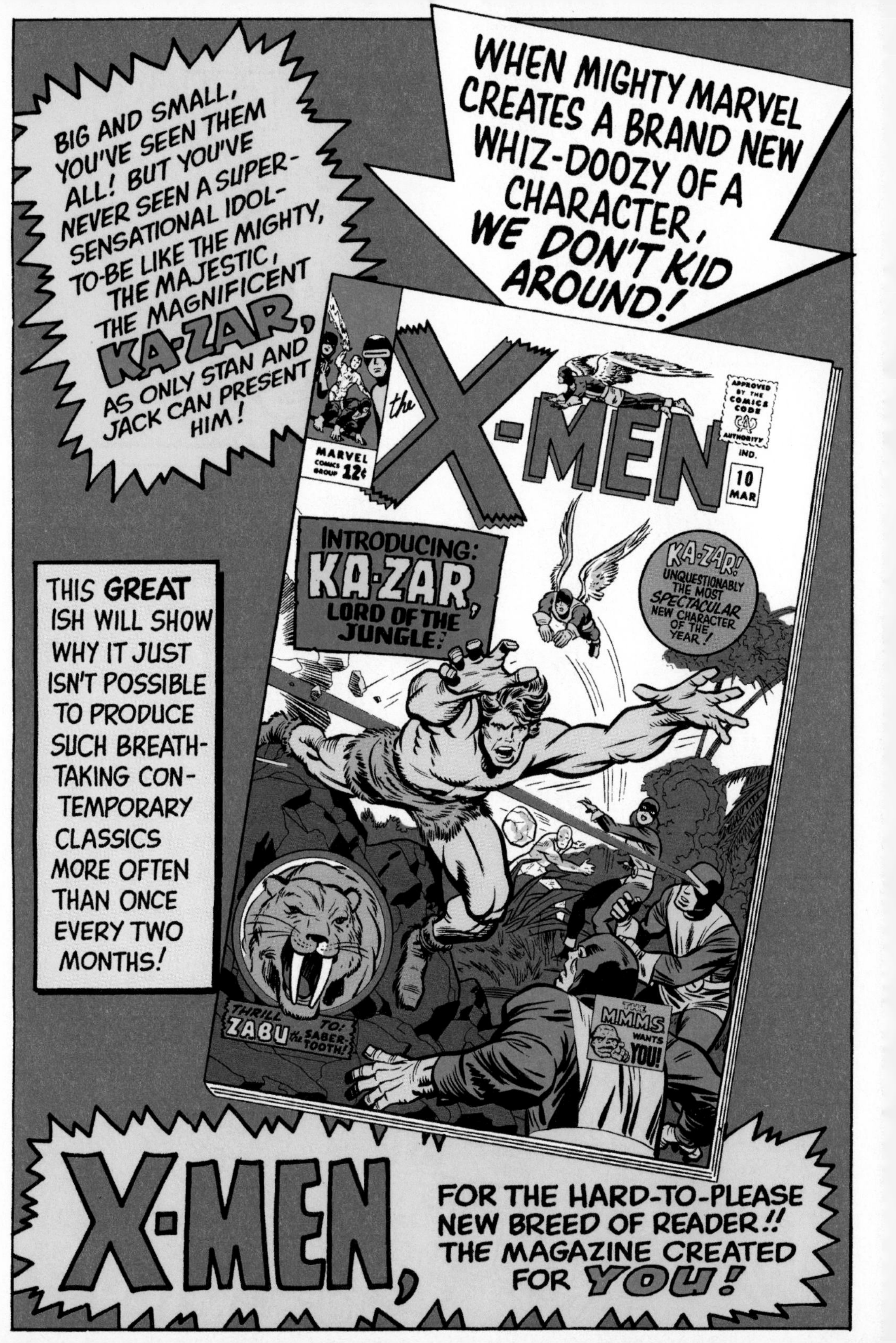
BIG AND SMALL, YOU'VE SEEN THEM ALL! BUT YOU'VE NEVER SEEN A SUPER-SENSATIONAL IDOL-TO-BE LIKE THE MIGHTY, THE MAJESTIC, THE MAGNIFICENT KA-ZAR, AS ONLY STAN AND JACK CAN PRESENT HIM!
WHEN MIGHTY MARVEL CREATES A BRAND NEW WHIZ-DOOZY OF A CHARACTER, WE DON'T KID AROUND!
the X-MEN
MARVEL COMICS GROUP 12¢
APPROVED BY THE COMICS CODE AUTHORITY
IND.
10 MAR
INTRODUCING: KA-ZAR, LORD OF THE JUNGLE!
KA-ZAR! UNQUESTIONABLY THE MOST SPECTACULAR NEW CHARACTER OF THE YEAR!
THRILL TO: ZABU the SABER-TOOTH!
THE M.M.M.S. WANTS YOU!
THIS GREAT ISH WILL SHOW WHY IT JUST ISN'T POSSIBLE TO PRODUCE SUCH BREATH-TAKING CON-TEMPORARY CLASSICS MORE OFTEN THAN ONCE EVERY TWO MONTHS!
X-MEN,
FOR THE HARD-TO-PLEASE NEW BREED OF READER!! THE MAGAZINE CREATED FOR YOU!

WHO SAYS THIS ISN'T THE MARVEL AGE OF COMICS?!

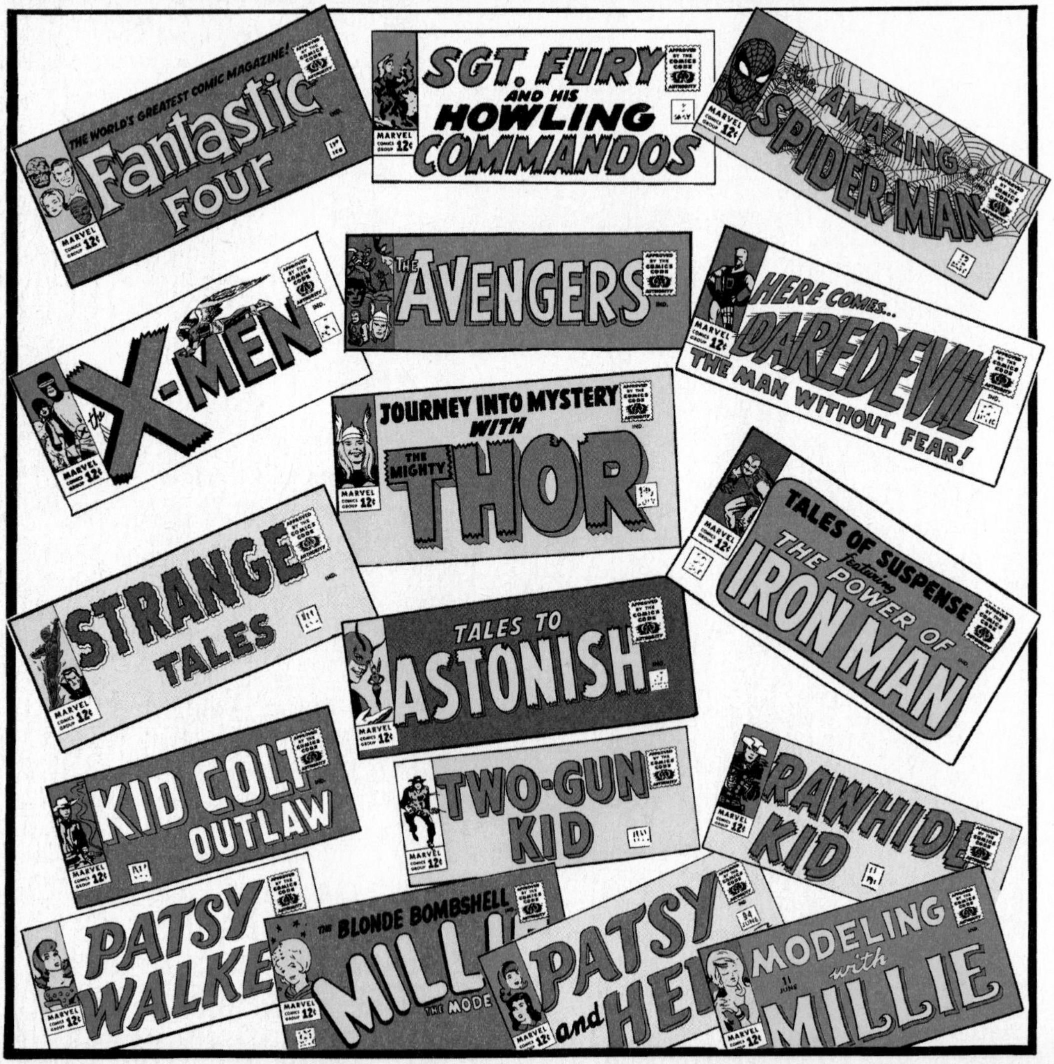
THE WORLD'S GREATEST COMIC MAGAZINE!
Fantastic Four
SGT. FURY AND HIS HOWLING COMMANDOS
THE AMAZING SPIDER-MAN
THE X-MEN
THE AVENGERS
HERE COMES... DAREDEVIL THE MAN WITHOUT FEAR!
JOURNEY INTO MYSTERY WITH THE MIGHTY THOR
TALES OF SUSPENSE featuring THE POWER OF IRON MAN
STRANGE TALES
TALES TO ASTONISH
KID COLT OUTLAW
TWO-GUN KID
RAWHIDE KID
PATSY WALKE
THE BLONDE BOMBSHELL MILL
PATSY and HE
MODELING with MILLIE